DOROTHY DANDRIDGE

Also by Donald Bogle

Toms, Coons, Mulattoes, Mammies, and Bucks:
An Interpretative History of Blacks in American Films

Brown Sugar: Eighty Years of America's Black
Female Superstars

Blacks in American Films and Television: An
Illustrated Encyclopedia

Black Arts Annual, 1987/1988, editor
Black Arts Annual, 1988/1989, ed.
Black Arts Annual, 1989/1990, ed.

DOROTHY DANDRIDGE

A Biography by

DONALD BOGLE

Amistad

New York, New York

Amistad Press, Inc.
1271 Avenue of the Americas
New York, New York 10020

Distributed by:
St. Martin's Press c/oVHPS
175 Fifth Avenue
New York, New York 10010

Designed by Gilbert D. Fletcher

1 2 3 4 5 6 7 8 9 10

Library of Congress Cataloging-in-Publication Data

Bogle, Donald.
        Dorothy Dandridge: a biography / by Donald Bogle.
                p. cm.
        Includes bibliographical references and index.
        ISBN 1-56743-034-1
        1. Dandridge, Dorothy. 1924-1965. 2. Motion picture
        actors and actresses--United States--Biography. 3. Afro-
        American motion picture actors and actresses--United States-
        -Biography. I. Title.
        PN2287.D256864 1997
        791.43'028'092--dc21   97-16478
        [B]   CIP

For my mother Roslyn

Alcia Woods Williams
Carolyn Woods Daughtry

In memory of
Catherine Bogle Garcia, my beloved Kate

And great friends:

Geri Branton, who shared so much of Dottie's
life with me

Phil Bertelsen, who literally opened the doors
of Dottie's homes for me

and finally,
Charlotte, who once said there's always a reason
to go on,
well, almost always

CONTENTS

Preface   XVIII
Prologue   XXXIII

PART I

1. Cleveland   1
2. A Hollywood Girlhood   29
3. The Dandridge Sisters   54
4. Career, Courtship, and Marriage   79
5. Lynn   113

PART II

6. Career Thrust   151
7. Rising   193
8. The Saloons   224
9. Making *Carmen*   253
10. Stardom   296
11. Peaking   344

PART III

12. Making *Porgy*   394
13. Hoping   424
14. Collapse   467
15. Lonely Days, Long Nights, Last Rites   506

Acknowledgments   555
Book Notes   561
Bibliography   581
The Films of Dorothy Dandridge   585
Index   590

How many heartfuls of sorrow shall balance a
bushel of wheat?
... And all this life and love and strife and failure—
is it the twilight of nightfall or the flush of some
faint-dawning day?

W. E. B. DuBois

Only those who are being burned know what fire is like.

Ethel Waters

PREFACE

$\mathcal{L}$ike many other African Americans kids of the late fifties and sixties, I grew up hearing about Dorothy Dandridge. My parents mentioned the name often. My father was the Vice-President and Advertising Director of *The Philadelphia Tribune*, one of America's oldest Black newspapers, and during breakfast and dinner conversations, both he and my mother often discussed those Black Americans who were breaking new ground and emerging as symbols or signs of racial/social progress. My parents spoke of Dandridge much as they did Jackie Robinson: as someone distinct and pioneering; someone who was altering mainstream conceptions what Black Americans could or could not do. From what I gathered, Dandridge was an altogether unique and unprecedented cultural phenomenon: a successful Black dramatic actress in Hollywood and perhaps Black America's first bonafide movie star, already a glowing figure of legend and glamour.

I remember how I felt when I first saw a photograph of her. Leafing through stacks of old *Ebony* magazines lying around the house, I stumbled across an article about her screen test for *Carmen Jones* with actor James Edwards. "So here she is!" I said to myself. Needless to say, I had a crush on her.

Once I actually saw her perform in *Carmen Jones*, I fully understood what all the fuss was about. I sat in the theater intoxicated by her beauty, her energy, her sexiness, and her dazzling ability to float through the movie's world at her own rhythm and from her own perspective. Dandridge's image on screen affected me a great deal as it had countless other Black Americans—and many white Americans as well—male and female. Few goddesses in movie history had ever seemed so confident and so in control. Few had been so beautiful with such a high-flung sense of drama. No woman anywhere seemed at all like her. Even as a kid, I understood that Dorothy Dandridge called a lie to the assumption that the movie goddess could only be some fair-haired white beauty. She had proved that Black women could be cast as something other than giggling maids or hefty nurturers without lives of their own.

Consequently, it was all the more disturbing and shocking when I learned how short her life was. Not long after I'd discovered her, she was found dead of an overdose of pills at the age of 42. It was 1965 and the news ran on the front pages of Black newspapers (and some White ones) throughout the country. But it affected the African American community in an intensely personal way. Soon the expected questions were asked. How it happened that the dreamgirl who seemed so new and modern, so daring and independent, could end up in such a way? Had Hollywood destroyed her? Or had a set of personal demons made her life such a living hell that she had decided to end it?

The possibility that Dorothy Dandridge had committed suicide made her story seem truly tragic and even more disturbing. Some drew the seemingly inevitable comparisons between Dandridge and Marilyn Monroe. In the popular imagination, both appeared to be sensitive fragile women in a cutthroat film industry controlled by men. Yet their lives—and the pressures they had to live with—were often vastly different. Dandridge's personal and professional tragedy had an unusual kind of power because it seemed to say something not only about Hollywood in general but about African Americans and the shifting dynamics of race and gender in the film capital and across the landscape of popular culture itself. As Harry Belafonte once said, she had been the right person in the right place at the wrong time. She was left languishing in Hollywood.

Still, it was telling to see the responses to Dandridge and Monroe, which was an indication of the two different perspectives of White and Black America. Though Monroe, while alive, was sometimes considered a sexy "joke"—even she must have felt that some of her most famous characters were brilliant parodies rather than flesh and blood women—Monroe was eventually embraced by the critical establishment and accorded her place as a major twentieth century icon. Dorothy Dandridge, however, was forgotten by the cultural mainstream. Film histories overlooked her contributions, and in all those gilded studies of movie stardom, she was ignored and became the invisible woman. Some might argue that because she had only one major film, she wasn't entitled her to join the ranks of great stars. But James Dean only had three films, and Louise Brooks, arguably only one major film role. Yet they became film legends while Dandridge was consigned to the ashheap. Generations of White Americans grew up knowing nothing about her. It was almost as if she had never existed.

Black America, however, refused to forget her. Dorothy Dandridge had been a great and powerful enough presence to survive in its consciousness whether the official culture gave any stamp of approval or not. She remained an enduring cultural icon for Black America and the most haunting of movieland figures. Despite her "acceptable" look—the keen features and the lighter color—she had reached the movie capital's upper echelons without, as her searing performance as Carmen demonstrated, losing her ethnic beat and rhythm. From the sound of her voice, with its warm honey tones, to her movements, and, of course, her *attitude*, her Carmen always seemed to be speaking directly to her Black audiences, saying, "The picture may not be real, but I am." Moreover, off-screen her haughty elegance and worldly sophistication heralded a new era when African Americans would confidently integrate American society, infusing it with their particular sense of style and energy.

For years after, Dorothy Dandridge's name was kept alive via the potent memories of her generation. In this respect, her story is similar to Billie Holiday in the late Sixties when she was known mainly by jazz critics and aficionados. It took the 1972 movie *Lady Sings the Blues* to bring awareness of her life and work to the mainstream. Within Black America though, Dandridge, like the early Holiday, had become a part of popular mythology. But still Dorothy Dandridge was not in the film history books, and that troubled me.

My interest was not just in Dorothy Dandridge, the actress and symbol, but Dandridge, the woman. I always intuitively felt that behind the sparkling eyes and the inviting smile there was a fascinating and compelling woman. For years, while a student and then later, as I began to professionally write about African Americans in film, I remained intrigued by her. From the first time I saw her photograph, I probably unconsciously started compiling information on her, tucking all sorts of stories I heard in the back of my head. I yearned to know more about her: the way she viewed the world; the forces that shaped her and those that later destroyed her.

Some of those questions were answered in the seventies when I talked to director Otto Preminger. Between studies, I had been fortunate enough to land a job working for Preminger as a story editor. I read scripts, stories, treatments, and novels in search of projects he might want to adapt for the screen.

Preminger was at the end of his legendary career. The big movies —like *The Man with the Golden Arm* and *Anatomy of a Murder*— had long since been gone; the glory days were behind him. But he remained a charismatic, larger-than-life-figure, who could inspire awe and terror. At the close of my first day on the job when he inquired if I had any questions, I naively asked, "Can you tell me something about Dorothy Dandridge?" He seemed surprised by the question, but he answered thoughtfully and tersely. The first thing he said—and he was emphatic—was that he was convinced she had taken her own life. Then he spoke of her talent. Preminger believed that by all rights, she should have become a major star. He didn't want to accept the fact that race—racism—had aborted a promising career.

I remembered his comments, and returned to talk to him in a more formal way. By this time, I was doing research for what became my first book, a history of African Americans in American films and hoped he might elaborate on some of the questions I had casually posed in the past. He recounted an incident that had occurred during the filming of *Porgy and Bess*. He also spoke again of her marriage to Jack Denison, who seemed to be beneath Preminger's contempt. It appeared that Preminger was still stung by that marriage, which he felt contributed greatly to her decline. Sitting in his large office in the old Columbia Pictures building on New York's Fifth Avenue, Preminger was gracious and informative, but there was much he didn't say. I suspected that he was troubled by the memory of Dandridge. He never did tell me, what I already knew, that he had been her lover.

I was too shy at the time to bluntly ask him about their affair. I'm not sure if he would have answered me anyway. Years later though, I realized that much of what Preminger told me had to be decoded. There was another layer, another story, a subtext beneath everything he said. He was always dropping hints about this and that. He was clear though, that afternoon, when he suggested that I speak to Vivian, Dorothy's sister, who was then living in New York.

When I first contacted Vivian Dandridge, she was hesitant about giving me an interview. It was only after she had spoken to Preminger that she agreed to see me. I realize now that when Otto Preminger arranged the introduction to Vivian Dandridge, he was giving me a gift. For that, I will always be grateful. He was a shrewd man, and I've often wondered if he felt she might tell me some of the things he didn't feel comfortable discussing; things, however, that he felt it important that I know.

It was with intense anticipation that I found myself one afternoon—with tape recorder in hand—entering Vivian Dandridge's apartment on New York's Upper West Side. Unaware of what to expect, I only knew I would now be as close to Dorothy Dandridge as I could hope to get.

I was struck by her resemblance to her sister. Contrary to all the stories I had heard that her looks paled in comparison to Dorothy's, Vivian Dandridge was, in my eyes, a striking woman. Not as lush and perfect, certainly not as delicate as her sister, but attractive and charismatic nonetheless. Her hair was pulled back from her forehead and tied in the back in a neat bun. Her skin was smooth and clear; her eyes, dark and lively; her mouth, large and sensual with a very dramatic jaw line and chin and a slender long neck.

Upon closer examination, I could see a thin layer of makeup that highlighted her rich color and cheekbones, that deepened the red of her lips, and of course, outlined the dark eyes. Everything about Vivian's look seemed selected for dramatic effects. So was the seemingly simple way that she was dressed. Dark tight slacks, similar to the Capri pants that women wore in the Fifties. And a large loose white blouse that looked as if it was actually a man's shirt. She was a real knockout that day and she knew it. As a veteran performer who had prepared herself countless times for the gaze of an inquisitive eye, she no doubt felt that *visually* she was up to the occasion. True to reports, she was very sexy. I soon discovered that she also had a wicked sense of humor and down to earth naturalness. It was impossible not to like her.

As she invited me in, I saw that the apartment was small and crowded with furniture, scattered memorabilia (personal items rather than professional ones), and books and magazines here and there. Oddly, though, I don't recall seeing one photograph of either Dorothy or their mother Ruby or Vivian's son. (In fact, years later when Vivian wanted a picture of Dorothy, she had to ask me for one.)

I had the feeling that Vivian believed she was living in reduced circumstances. Yet her living situation—rich in character and color— was filled with her own essence, and aura. Vivian Dandridge carried within her a set of rich experiences and memories, some glorious and others painful.

Her confidence showed. So did that flicker of suspicion (similar to Otto's) in her eyes. Immediately, she looked me over in that kind of instinctual *quick read* way that seasoned performers—especially those who are survivors—do. Later she admitted that I was completely different from what she had expected. Why I was like a kid, she said, young enough to be her son. That helped her drop some defenses and make surprisingly frank comments. She later told me, she had originally planned to talk to me for only a half hour. By the time the day ended, we had spent about eight hours together.

I asked her point blank if she thought Dorothy had committed suicide. She answered, "My sister was a very unhappy person." She went on to describe Dorothy as a precocious child who, during the years when she and Vivian performed as The Wonder Children and then as The Dandridge Sisters, loved entertaining but felt exploited. She spoke of Dorothy's first marriage to the great dancer Harold Nicholas and their brain-damaged daughter Lynn, whose condition caused Dorothy unending guilt and unhappiness.

Vivian said a little about Otto Preminger that day. Amusingly, what she did say was expressed in little grunts, groans, and sighs. She did confess that she had warned Dorothy that Otto would never marry her.

She had a lot to say, in searing detail about Dorothy's heady years of stardom in the fifties and of its effect on those around her. Vivian discussed the fact that she had left Los Angeles after having a terrible disagreement with Dorothy. Ten years later, she picked up a newspaper and learned that her sister was dead. "I felt guilty for a long time," said Vivian. At that moment, I saw glimmers of the long complicated family history that would be so much a part of the story I would unearth.

Vivian also revealed the most striking and surprising aspect of Dorothy's personality. She described this woman who most assumed from *Carmen Jones* to be an assured, take-charge, relentlessly social creature, as a "shy sensitive introvert." Dorothy, said Vivian, seemed to be afraid of people and felt most comfortable when she could shut the door and withdraw from them. That didn't mean she was a hermit. She had a few close friends. And there were times when she enjoyed the parties, receptions, and openings. But at heart, Dorothy Dandridge felt alone.

A reclusive movie star was not what I had expected to find. But

Preminger had hinted at the same aspect too when he told me the reason for the failure of the restaurant that Dorothy's second husband opened. He had depended on Dorothy to draw in patrons, when in essence Dorothy did not have the outgoing personality needed to do so and keep up business in such an establishment.

I found Vivian intelligent, perceptive, witty, and funny. Often hers was a self-deprecating humor. But she also used humor to puncture the pretensions and shams of others. That, I knew, had sustained and saved her. Much that she said that day stuck with me, and was useful when I wrote about Dorothy in my first books. But I didn't use everything I learned. Some things remained locked away somewhere in the back of my head for years to come.

Not long after our first meeting, Vivian Dandridge left New York. She eventually returned to Los Angeles and then moved to Seattle. We exchanged letters and talked on the phone, and through her, I met others who knew Dorothy: Etta Jones, who had performed as one of The Dandridge Sisters; and Juliette Ball, a childhood friend of the sisters. Later when I did my PBS series *Brown Sugar*, I did a long pre-interview and then a formal taped interview with her for the program. As far as I know, I'm the only writer she ever formally talked to.

By then, I had decided to do a biography on Dorothy, and at one point, Vivian and I talked of collaborating on a book. But as the talks became more serious and as I asked more personal questions, Vivian backed off. Eventually, she decided to do a memoir of her own. Afterwards as I began work on the book, she was helpful and answered questions whenever I needed some information verified. Though we continued to discuss Dorothy whenever we talked by phone, she never sat down again for another formal interview. Finally, when it looked as if she might allow me to fly to Seattle to talk to her again, she suddenly died.

I later realized that, despite Vivian's warmth and general openness, she subscribed to an old Hollywood custom: she preferred to keep some matters secrets. In some ways, both she and Otto appeared to be respecting Dorothy's privacy. Yet, also like Preminger, she recounted incidents with an underlying subtext.

Later when I reviewed my old Vivian Dandridge interviews I came across things I'd forgotten about and what I found most interesting about our first conversation was the fact that she hadn't discussed her mother, Ruby Dandridge, in any detail. (I also recalled that Preminger had asked me if I knew anything about Ruby Dandridge.) In time, Vivian passingly made a number of comments about Ruby. Rarely did she ever pass judgment on her mother, but it was clear that she disagreed with her on some important issues, especially concerning Dorothy's marriage to Jack Denison. One of my most moving memories of Vivian came after Ruby Dandridge died. She sent me a copy of Ruby's will, which had left nothing to Vivian, her only surviving child. I think it saddened her that now there would always be unresolved matters between Ruby and herself.

At that point it became clear that Dorothy Dandridge's story was three-fold. Foremost, it was a personal story about a gifted, complex woman. Then, it was something of a family drama, a web of tangled relationships. And, of course, finally it was a look at the movie industry and the Black Hollywood that existed within the larger filmland culture. Of course, the views of Vivian Dandridge and Otto Preminger didn't tell the entire story. Through the years, I was fortunate enough to meet many of the other major players in Dorothy's life: her first husband, Harold Nicholas; her lively, outgoing, one-time brother-in-law, Fayard Nicholas; the intellectual arranger/composer Phil Moore; her agent Harold Jovien; and her various directors, friends, and associates. Amusingly, most of the men in her life seemed to refuse to believe that Dorothy ever was interested in any man other than himself. Most spoke of her with regret and remorse. They seemed to feel they had failed her in some way. She had not dimmed in their memories in the thirty years since her death.

But the most important person to shift Dorothy into another perspective was her closest friend, Geri Branton. Clear-eyed, intelligent, perceptive, balanced, and sane in a show business environment where most are openly a bit crazed, Branton saw Dorothy up close from the time Dorothy was nineteen to the end of her life. She had been her confidante and understood, far better than most, the changes that overcame her—and her need to withdraw into a world of personal fantasies. Geri provided key details in Dorothy's life and also put her relationships with both Vivian and Preminger, as well as her mother Ruby and others, in a different context. When many had turned their backs on Dorothy in her final desperate years Branton didn't. Her presence was a stabilizing factor in an otherwise turbulent life. She spoke of her friend with the greatest affection and warmth but also with an intelligent objectivity.

Throughout the writing of this biography, I kept a framed picture of Dorothy Dandridge—her 1954 *Life* magazine cover—on my desk. It faced me every hour, day, week, month, year that I sat before my computer. It seemed to speak to me of mysteries, intrigues, dreams, fears, tensions, and loves that were mine alone to comprehend, to rectify, to set straight. Always I knew it was important not only to see Dorothy as others had viewed her but, if possible, to see Dorothy as she saw herself.

As I pieced together her story, I often felt like the beleaguered hero from a Preminger movie, the 1944 film *Laura*. In *Laura*, a detective investigates the death—a murder—of a beautiful young woman. Roaming through her apartment, eyeing her objects, and meeting her friends and associates who loved or were envious of her--the detective understands that each is telling a story about her from his or her own perspective—and that each is aware that Laura was at the center of pivotal events in his/her life. Slowly, the detective finds himself seductively drawn into Laura's life—her drives, motivations, and emotional rhythms. In her apartment, he stares at her portrait—haughty, glamorous, beautiful, narcissistic. In time, he arrives at his own seemingly objective yet passionate analysis of the woman. Though he doesn't quite realize it, Laura has invaded his unconscious, altering his dreams and hopes, moving and romancing him from the grave. He doesn't want to admit it, but he's fallen in love with a dead woman. One day the detective, having fallen asleep in Laura's apartment with her portrait looking down on him, awakens to discover that the real Laura is standing before him. Laura hasn't been murdered at all. She's alive. And now he's free to *really* fall in love with her. Only in the movies!

No such luck for me. But putting together the pieces of Dandridge's life has been an extraordinary experience.

Perhaps the best reward any author can hope for is to come to love his or her subject, warts and all. And, frankly, I can't think of anyone better to fall in love with than Dorothy Dandridge.

PROLOGUE

*O*scar night is always magical, but when Dorothy Dandridge stepped out of a limousine in front of New York's Century Theatre on Oscar night, March 30, 1955, she represented nothing less than a breakthrough in motion picture history.

The crowds behind the police barricades went wild; screaming and shouting out her name. Photographers and reporters rushed toward her, snapping pictures and asking her for a comment, as she smiled and waved. The fans scrambled to get a closer look. She was a dazzling sight. Dark eyes, sensuous mouth, and the color— usually described in the press as *café au lait*—that set her apart from all of Hollywood's other beauties. She was every inch the movie star.

Moving amid the crush of bodies, Dorothy's sister, Vivian, followed. They had grown up working together in an act called The Wonder Children; raised and groomed for show business careers by their mother, Ruby, an actress and comedienne who also had stars in her eyes. They had become veterans in the entertainment world as family but this evening Dorothy stood apart. This was her moment and she glowed in the thought that this was the peak thus far of her solo career.

She had taken time out of her career to marry dancer Harold Nicholas, and to give birth to their daughter Lynn. But when the marriage—to the younger half of the renowned Nicholas Brothers— failed, she returned to show business, becoming famous in nightclubs for her hot/cool style—the sexy voice, the sensual, dramatic dance-like movements, the intelligent, ironic interpretation of the lyrics—

that drove patrons mad. There was no woman like her on the American nightclub scene.

But club stardom was not her goal. Against the odds, she aspired to the silver screen and ultimately won the role coveted by every Black actress in Hollywood: the fiery Carmen in Otto Preminger's all-star Black musical *Carmen Jones*. Dorothy transformed an old hack conception—the reckless, sexually charged woman who destroys her men and therefore must herself be destroyed—into something all her own. Her Carmen came to represent a compelling modern Black woman: confident, determined to live life on her terms, and fearless in a man's world. This promising actress had surprised and startled everyone, including director Preminger, who by now was in love with her.

But, most important, her celebrated performance had also, as this night proved, made history. Dorothy Dandridge had become the first Black woman to be nominated for an Academy Award as Best Leading Actress of the Year. For a Black performer in Fifties Hollywood, being nominated for the Oscar was tantamount to actually winning the award.

In an age that celebrated Marilyn and Liz and Grace and Audrey, Dorothy Dandridge had brought the Black actress in films from behind the shadows and had emerged as Hollywood's first authentic movie goddess of color. She had reconfigured the very definition of what a movie star was supposed to be. During these dawning years of the Civil Rights Movement, she was not only a glamorous, popular icon but a symbol of a new day in America. Dorothy Dandridge looked as if she would integrate mainstream cinema—appearing in a lineup of powerful dramatic films—in the same way that Jackie Robinson had changed the face of American sports.

As Dorothy took her seat at the Century Theatre, her eyes looked especially bright, but her emotions were mixed. She was a fatalist whose life had never turned out as she'd hoped, and despite all outward appearances, she had doubts about the future. Yet, she was also a romantic and still wanted a happy ending. So maybe, she thought, everything would work out. As Otto Preminger had predicted, Oscar night was just the beginning. . . .

PART I

ONE

CLEVELAND

*E*ven before she was born, Dorothy Dandridge was at the center of a domestic storm. Her mother Ruby—strong-willed and outspoken—left her husband Cyril Dandridge when she was five months pregnant with Dorothy. It was the summer of 1922. The couple had been married for almost three years and was living in Cleveland. Their first-born child—a daughter named Vivian—was only a little over a year old. But while Cyril Dandridge considered himself a lucky man, Ruby was restless and fed up with him and her life, and she didn't care who knew it. Nor did she care that women in the early 1920s, especially African American women, weren't supposed to walk out on their husbands.

Ruby Dandridge, however, was no ordinary woman. She had already separated from Cyril once before, but she had come back. A few years before that, she moved to Cleveland from Wichita, perhaps hoping the new city would give her a chance to express the ambition and aspiration that burned within her. But Cleveland and Cyril both had failed her, and Ruby, despite being pregnant, was willing to risk everything to live as she wanted. Cyril, however, wasn't about to let Ruby just run off with his firstborn daughter and with the unborn child. He set out to find her. And she set out to flee him again.

And so Dorothy Dandridge—the little girl who would grow up to be one of her era's most beautiful women and its most famous African American actress—came into the world at the heart of a heated domestic discord that, in its own quiet, unstated way, would trouble and haunt her for the next forty years. Throughout her life, she would

1

struggle to understand her parents, but mainly to piece together the puzzle of her own identity; to discover and define herself first as a daughter, then as a sister, a wife, a mother, a singer, an actress, and finally as the most unexpected and elusive of personages, a Black film star in a Hollywood that worshiped her, yet at the same time, clearly made no place for her.

As a woman always searching for answers, Dorothy would often wonder how differently it all might have turned out had she grownup with the father whom she had never really known. And she may well have wondered too what direction her life might have taken had her mother Ruby never ventured to Cleveland and stayed instead on the wide plains of Kansas.

Wichita, Kansas was a quiet, sleepy city in the early years of the century. For most of Wichita's citizens, life moved along at a leisurely pace with everything done one day at a time. Boys were to be strong and in charge. Girls were to be domesticated and sweet. No matter whether the girls were Colored or White, the same rules usually applied, except that the Colored girls were supposed to be even more mindful of their place, of abiding by the laws of both race and gender. For Ruby Jean Butler, born in Wichita, Kansas on March 1, 1899, the rules were carefully proscribed and locked in place. All she had to do was learn to live by them, which was something that always proved hard for Ruby.

She was the daughter of George Butler and his wife, née Nellie Simmons. Both George, born in 1860, and Nellie, born in 1870, had migrated to Kansas from North Carolina. The Butlers had four children, three of whom were sons. Ruby, their only daughter, was the youngest. For a time the family resided at 625 North Main Street.

Ruby Dandridge, who liked to concoct her own version of the events of her life, passed on to her daughter Dorothy a genealogy that was dubious but held some elements of truth. Ruby's scenario made no mention of George Butler or Nellie ever having lived in North Carolina. Instead her version of the story was that her father, sometimes called George Frank, was a Jamaican who immigrated as a child to the United States in the late 19th century and later married a young Mexican woman. Ruby also liked to boast that George was an entertainer who travelled about and performed for Colored and White audiences, then settled in Wichita, where he ran a local grocery and a Negro school.

Ruby's embellishments aside, it seems unlikely that her mother Nellie Simmons was Mexican. Her father George Butler, however, may have done all the things Ruby spoke of, but he also held other jobs in Wichita. He worked as a janitor at the Union National Bank for a spell. He was also a minister with a church that stood prominently on a street corner, recalled photographer Vera Jackson, who as a little girl lived near the Butlers in Wichita. Well-known and well-liked, Reverend Butler was outgoing and friendly, both traits that were passed on to daughter Ruby.

Butler apparently also passed on to his young daughter the tricks of the trade of show business: he taught her to sing, dance, and perform acrobatics. An apt pupil, little Ruby learned to do all those things well. From her father, Ruby probably also inherited a love for a life of illusion—and a sense for the dramatic.

In Wichita, Ruby grew to be a big-boned, plump, brown-skinned girl with an attractive face, smooth skin, a large bright smile, and lively eyes. As a young woman, she would weigh almost two hundred pounds and even more as the years moved on. Everyone who met her agreed that Ruby was lively, funny, and blessed with the gift of gab. People kidded that she could talk a mile a minute. And sometimes she did. Making friends came easily to her. Few who met her ever forgot her.

"I was only five or six," said Vera Jackson, recalling her first impressions of Ruby. "But I remember Ruby, who was older. We were all close there in Wichita. She was very close to my aunt Alta Johnson. We lived on Sherwood Avenue and I think [at one time] she did too because she and my aunt were always together. So we saw a lot of Ruby Dandridge. We liked her very much."

"She joked a lot. Laughed a lot," said Dorothy Hughes McConnell, who as a little girl later met Ruby in Cleveland.

What struck everyone most about Ruby was her girlish high-pitched voice which rose even higher when she was excited. Or when she feigned excitement. That voice later served her well as an actress in movies, radio, and television. Usually playing comic, befuddled maids, all Ruby had to do was open her mouth and let that squeaky voice come forth, and audiences would break into hysterics.

In private quarters, though, Ruby's baby-like voice could be tiresome, even strident; its boundless rush of enthusiasm and energy could seem forced and phoney, almost a caricature of an optimistic, happy-go-lucky soul. If anything, Ruby's voice made her seem flighty, giggly, and scatterbrained. Could anyone be *that* peppy, people wondered?

Could anybody dismiss problems so readily with such a sigh or laughter? Later, behind her back, Ruby's Hollywood friends and associates sometimes imitated and mocked her. And the first thing they did was mimic her high-pitched voice. Outward appearances masked another side of Ruby: when it suited her, Ruby Jean Butler was anything but flighty or absent-minded. Rather she was a born strategist and survivor, possessing a sharp, calculating mind; a woman who could quickly *read* a person or situation and then manipulate almost anyone or anything to her advantage. If necessary, she was able to cut her losses and walk away from a situation without regret or remorse. It was never a problem for her to ignore the pain suffered by others, especially pain she inflicted. Ruby never had any difficulty seeing what was right in front of her. But more often than not, Ruby simply refused to see. Or she chose to see through the prism of her own interests.

"Ruby could be a cruel person," said actress Avanelle Harris, who as a little girl studied dance with Ruby's daughters Vivian and Dorothy. To actor Mel Bryant, Ruby was a phoney, who, at social gatherings, might smile and laugh when she saw you but would always "look over your shoulder" to see if there was someone else around to talk to who could help advance her career. In looks and attitudes, she later would be considered "the antithesis" of her daughters, recalled entertainer Bobby Short. Once Dorothy attained stardom, industry insiders would find it hard to believe Ruby was her mother, especially since Ruby's giggly aggressiveness was so different from Dorothy's delicacy and ladylike manners. Mostly, though, behind her mirth and merriment, Ruby Butler had a fierce drive and ambition.

That drive is what carried her, by the late teens of the century, out of Kansas to Cleveland. In Ruby's mind, life in Wichita was too slow and static. At first, Cleveland must have looked to her like a major metropolis with its busy streets and streetcars, its industries, shops, restaurants, theatres, and parade of people. When she arrived, the city was in the midst of possibly its greatest transition.

Cleveland had long been a land of promise for African Americans. Runaway slaves flocked to Cleveland for sanctuary on the Underground Railroad. Black freedmen found opportunities for advancement there. Oberlin College—the first American institution of higher learning to admit Negroes—was also nearby. A Negro community sprang up quickly. During and after the First World War, Cleveland became one of the principal destinations of the Great

4

Migration of Southern Negroes to the North. In 1917, Cleveland's *Gazette* reported that migrants were "vainly 'running the streets' in the Central Avenue vicinity, seeking rooms last week worse than ever before, two carloads more having arrived from the South, Sunday evening." By 1919, the Black citizenry had soared to over 30,000, then doubled in the 1920s

With a growing Negro population came changes in a city that had once been fairly open with Colored and Whites attending the same schools, eating at the same restaurants, and staying at the same downtown hotels. Now restaurants, theatres, hotels, amusement parks, and other public accommodations all became restricted. Some restaurants gave Blacks poor service. Others posted "Whites Only" signs in their windows. Some theatres shut their doors to Negroes. Or forced them to sit in segregated balconies.

Colored sections of town also suddenly appeared. Negroes now lived mostly on the east side, the hub of which was Central Avenue, once an enclave for affluent Whites, that is until the first Blacks moved in. Others saw dollar signs on the Black faces at their doors. Onetime Cleveland resident Langston Hughes recalled that "the white neighborhoods resented Negroes moving closer and closer—but when the whites did give way, they gave way at very profitable rentals."

Upon her arrival, Ruby Butler looked around and found herself in a segregated city. But like most Black residents, aware of racial codes and discrimination throughout America, she added up the score and still believed Cleveland was a place where Black advancement was possible; where there were still jobs, activities, advantages. Ruby settled into a home on Cleveland's east side at 2269 East 40th Street, most likely living for a time with a cousin. Setting her sights on a new life for herself, she also set her sights on a young man she met named Cyril Dandridge.

Cyril Dandridge was a Cleveland resident, who was born there in 1895 and would live there all his life. For him, Cleveland represented security and order. He was an only child, fawned over and pampered by his parents. His father Henry Dandridge was a cook; his mother, the former Florence Locke, a hairdresser born in Canada in 1873. In Cleveland's Black community, Florence Locke Dandridge was a figure of intrigue and curiosity, something of a haughty mystery, known for her brisk manner, her open adoration of her son, and her striking appearance.

"She looked *completely* Caucasian," said Cleveland-born Dorothy Hughes McConnell, whose mother knew the Dandridge family. "She wasn't. I think she was mixed. But you couldn't tell that she was not Caucasian."

The Dandridge family lived comfortably at 4710 Central Avenue for several years. As a young man, Cyril worked as a clerk, later a mechanic, and then as a draftsman.

Slightly built and fine-boned with curly woolly hair, Cyril "was very attractive" with sharp features and a light brown color, recalled Geri Branton, who later became Dorothy's closest friend and confidante. Around Cleveland, he was known as an easy-going, good-natured, decent fellow, who was also a devoted son. For years, his mother Florence was the primary focus of his life; the woman whose approval he always sought, whose comfort concerned him most, and whose welfare was the source of his motivation. She in turn believed Cyril was hers and hers alone; her private, treasured property that she was unwilling to share with anyone.

"She worshiped that boy," said Dorothy McConnell, who recalled the stories that circulated about Cyril's mother along the grapevine in Cleveland's Black community. "They said that Old Lady Dandridge was quite a tyrant. Cyril's mother absolutely ruled him. Everybody said he was just a mama's boy."

After the death of his father Henry, Cyril and his mother moved to a home at 2180 East 103rd Street. Life went on as before. Everything was still Cyril and Florence. Florence and Cyril. Nothing of much consequence seems to have occurred in his life until surprisingly, while in his early 20s, he turned his attentions away from his mother to Ruby. Most were surprised, not because Cyril Dandridge finally had a serious girlfriend but because of his choice of girlfriends. From the beginning, anyone could take one look at Ruby and Cyril and see immediately that they were an improbable pair: a study in contrasts—in looks, attitudes, energy, and aspirations. For the sensitive and unassuming Cyril who was content with his lot in life, stability could have been his middle name. All he ever seemed to want was a happy family life (that included mother), a pleasant home with mother, of course, and a little peace and quiet.

Ruby, of course, was just the opposite. Always eager to talk, she was, as in Wichita, unendingly social. Energy and confidence were stamped all over her. While Cyril was pliant, Ruby was bossy. Yet, differences aside or perhaps because of them, the two were drawn to one another. Her optimism may have been the trait that attracted him and put some kick in his life, rousing him from his basic inertia. His relaxed sincerity—along with his good looks—may be what won her over. On

September 30, 1919, the two were married in a ceremony performed by the Reverend J. S. Jackson. Ruby Jean was 20. Cyril was 23.

Having been with his mother all his life, Cyril Dandridge naturally saw no reason to alter his living arrangement. He moved his young bride into the house he shared with Florence on East 103rd Street. The homes in the neighborhood were modest two or three story dwellings with comfortable parlors, dining rooms, kitchens, and bedrooms that were roomy and airy. Outside were small front lawns and a patch of green in the back. They were good, solid homes in which to raise a family.

The house on East 103rd Street should have been perfect for a young couple on its own. It might even have been fine for newlyweds and an in-law were the young wife more docile and the mother-in-law less demanding. But living under the roof of her husband's mother grated Ruby. By most accounts, Ruby's presence grated Florence as well. Neighbors really didn't blame Cyril for the problems in the home, said Dorothy McConnell. "They blamed his mother."

No one will ever know what transpired daily in the home, but Ruby knew it would never be her place. Here she had to live with her mother-in-law's furniture, her rugs, her curtains, her dishes, her linens, her time for getting up, her time for turning in, her diet, her opinions, her beliefs, and her unending control over Cyril. Ruby couldn't move without fear of breaking something. She couldn't rearrange one thing in the house without fear of a sharp rebuke from Florence. Ruby had become a nonperson without any say, and nothing she did could please Florence. At least, that was how she described the situation to her friends, and later to her children.

Given the sentiments of the times, Florence must have wondered what her good-looking son saw in this gabby, dowdy girl. What had come over *her* Cyril?

The marriage was headed for trouble in a short time. Ruby openly complained about the time and attention Cyril gave to his mother rather than to her. She maintained that he was not a good enough provider and was precisely what everyone knew him to be, just a mama's boy.

Still, Ruby stayed and coped with the situation. Less than two years after the marriage ceremony, Ruby was pregnant. On April 22, 1921, she gave birth to her first child, Vivian Alferetta Dandridge. Afterwards it looked as if the Dandridges might now settle into blissful domesticity.

Ruby, however, felt nothing had changed. Neither Cyril nor

Florence could understand her. She in turn appeared not to care to understand them. Unlike most wives who were expected to enjoy the fruits and pleasures of their families, to find satisfaction in their household responsibilities, and to take pride in their husband's ambitions and achievements rather than their own, Ruby, although a good cook, showed no interest in the home and little in Cyril. She must have wondered too how she could focus on her husband's goals when, in her eyes, Cyril didn't have any. She, on the other hand, had many. To stay stuck inside a house twenty-four hours a day—saying yes to her husband while always walking on eggshells around her mother-in-law—was not one of them.

Their conflicts grew. Cyril complained that the house had become filthy. The same was true, he said, of Ruby's personal habits.

The real friction between Ruby and Cyril and his mother grew out of differing views on life itself. Their lives were settled, fixed, stagnant. Not much would ever change for them. Ruby, on the contrary, was bursting with energy, interests, and enthusiasms. She wanted adventure, change, diversity, freedom. And even in the early years of her marriage, she also wanted to perform.

Finally, exasperated with her mother-in-law, Cyril, and the entire domestic set-up, Ruby did something few women would have then dared. She packed her bags, picked up two-month-old baby Vivian, and moved out. Just up and *abandoned* him, as Cyril was to say later. Gone for six weeks, she most likely stayed at the home of her cousin.

She might have stayed away longer, but with no money, no training, and no profession, she was just a Colored woman out on her own with a young daughter and not much of a future. Cyril persuaded her to come back.

The two attempted a reconciliation, and by the spring of 1922, Ruby was pregnant again. But—for her—this was probably the worst news of all. The idea of being homebound in a household with two children, a meek husband, and a testy mother-in-law scared her. She also had to admit that Cyril did not excite her and could never answer her basic needs. She decided once again she had to get out.

And so in July, five-months pregnant, Ruby Dandridge picked up baby Vivian and walked out on her husband for that second time. On November 9, 1922, she entered Cleveland's City Hospital where she gave birth to her second daughter, Dorothy Jean Dandridge, a name her daughter would later sign on official papers and documents but never officially appeared as such on the birth certificate. It was simply Dorothy Dandridge. That name seems a special gift to the newborn girl for it was the very type of simple, elegant name that would be perfect for a movie marquee. Now Ruby had made up her mind to survive without Cyril. She wanted nothing more to do with him. If it were possible, she would have erased him completely from her memory. For many years, she managed to erase him from the memory of her daughters, who as children never saw their father, and for years would never know some of the more complicated reasons why their mother had left him. The girls were raised believing Cyril had no interest in them. And for some years, Ruby even told them that he was dead. Later she admitted he was still living but claimed he had deserted them.

Ruby also appeared to have severed other people and events from her memories. Years later, Dorothy would say she had never met her maternal grandfather or her mother's brothers. Cut off from family and all that entailed—family history as well as family customs and connections—both Dorothy and Vivian were raised in a familial vacuum in the belief that Ruby was the center of their world and their only support. That simply meant that later when Dorothy felt rejected by Ruby she would feel all the more insecure and lost.

Ruby moved into an apartment on Cleveland's Central Avenue and looked for work to support herself and her daughters. A friend named Genevieve Hughes, who also had a young daughter named Dorothy and lived nearby, agreed to watch the children for Ruby, who took a job as a maid.

Dorothy Hughes McConnell, who as a little girl played with Dorothy while her mother Genevieve baby-sat for the Dandridge girls, retained vivid memories of young Dorothy's delicate beauty, and the response it elicited from her.

"I used to give Dorothy beatings," said McConnell, "because when my mother took care of her, people would come and stop by and talk about 'Oh, isn't she cute.' I can remember this girl that was so cute with this pretty hair, and whenever she got all these compliments, I'd beat her up."

Within the next few years, Ruby moved several times, perhaps because of money problems. Or perhaps because she was still on the run from Cyril. But always she remained on Cleveland's eastside.

On East 103rd Street, Cyril Dandridge was in a panic. He knew of Dorothy's birth. But his wife and children had vanished and he launched a search to find them. Once he finally located Ruby, Cyril pleaded with her to come back, but Ruby remained adamant. Under no circumstances would she live as his wife again. But she insisted

9

that he provide support for the girls. Their relations turned stormy and ugly. During one particularly nasty altercation, Ruby contacted the police and had Cyril arrested. She also took him to Juvenile Court where he was ordered to pay $10 a week in child support.

To anyone who would listen, Ruby continued to complain that Cyril was nothing but a mama's boy without any backbone. She also told friends that when she had become pregnant with Dorothy, Cyril had not wanted her to have the baby, and that *he* had left her when she did. Of all the accusations that Ruby made against Cyril, that one was doubted later by most who knew her, especially during her years in Los Angeles. If anything, Ruby appeared to be the one who didn't want to be burdened with the responsibilities of child-rearing.

Hurt and resentful, Cyril finally accepted the fact that Ruby would never return to his home and that their marriage was over. But he refused to stand by and let Ruby take his two daughters away from him. He found an attorney, John P. Green, and in June of 1924, he filed for divorce.

A Colored man seeking a divorce was not a common occurrence in those years. Divorce itself was still frowned on in most of the country. A Colored woman who dumped her husband and ran away with her little children was not an everyday occurrence either. But so much bad blood had passed between Cyril and Ruby that each ignored the acceptable social codes of the day and each, rather boldly, set out on his and her own paths. Cyril's lawyer issued Ruby a summons.

In his divorce suit—a "Petition for Divorce, Custody of Children and Relief"—Cyril's anger and impatience boiled over. Ruby was guilty of "Gross Neglect of Duty," he charged, "in that she has ever since said marriage refused and neglected to perform her proper household duties." He argued that she had not prepared meals for him and, worst, was "filthy and unclean about her person and likewise about her home."

Also charging her with "Extreme Cruelty," Cyril accused Ruby of lying, saying she "has made all manner of false and untrue statements" to friends and relatives about his conduct toward her. Ruby had caused him great humiliation, Cyril complained, by having him arrested on false charges and "grossly misrepresented him in every way all to his mental distress and agitation." His suit stated that Ruby was "not the proper person to care for and nurture" the children. Cyril wanted custody of Dorothy and Vivian.

Ruby decided to fight him on her terms. She hired the law offices of Clarke and Costello to file a counter suit in August 1924. She denied Cyril's allegations and requested that his complaint/petition be dismissed. Instead *she* sought a divorce from him. Cyril had not been "a faithful and dutiful husband," she charged, and was guilty of Gross Neglect of Duty. She also stated that he failed and refused to provide her with a home; that she was compelled to live with relatives; that about two years earlier, the plaintiff had deserted her; that he refused to come back to her and the children; that for a considerable period, he had contributed nothing to the support of the children; that for a short time, he paid her $10 a week for the support of their daughters by virtue of an order of Juvenile Court.

She also charged that rather than provide for her Cyril gave his money to his mother. And she stated that for the past two years—ever since the break-up with Cyril—she had been "compelled to work to support herself and their children." She requested an "absolute divorce" from him and asked to be "awarded the sole care, custody and control" of Vivian and Dorothy. She also asked to be granted "a reasonable sum as and for alimony; and that she may be given such other and further relief as may be just and equitable."

The suits, counter suits, charges, countercharges, petitions, complaints, and accusations between Cyril and Ruby dragged on for years, probably longer than either had ever expected. Just weeks after Dorothy's fourth birthday in November 1926, Cyril filed a new amended divorce petition. He accused Ruby of deserting him shortly after Vivian's birth in 1921 and just months before Dorothy was born in 1922. The next month, Ruby's lawyers filed a cross petition and again asked for custody of the children and alimony.

Cyril, however, probably still hoped for a reconciliation with his wife. He made plans to visit Ruby's home at Christmas. On the evening of the visit, "Vivian and I were sleeping," Dorothy remembered, "and Mother had to put both of us up in the attic so our father wouldn't find us. He was looking for us to take us away and Mother didn't want this, so she hid us." Ruby told her daughters to be quiet because Santa Claus was coming. Upstairs, Dorothy and Vivian heard Cyril arrive. The two crept to their door and listened intently to the man—who they believed was Santa—talking to their mother. But when the voices downstairs became loud and angry, culminating in a heated quarrel, "Vivian and I began to cry," said Dorothy. "We cried because it was fearful and violent below, and we didn't know what was going on or why."

When Dorothy heard the door slam, she and Vivian realized that the man downstairs had not been Santa Claus but their father. Cyril left that night without seeing his daughters, and this was to be Dorothy's earliest memory of him; a mysterious man who had suddenly surfaced and then abandoned her without ever showing his face. In her mind, he hadn't been strong or forceful enough to walk past her mother, come upstairs, and hold her in his arms.

While the court battles continued, Ruby began to forge and fashion a new identity for herself. To keep food on the table and stay two steps ahead of the landlord, she still worked as a domestic. But away from those fancy homes where she cleaned, cooked meals, and washed windows, Ruby restlessly sought a way to express herself, to release all the creative energies knotted up inside her. Having always dreamed of a life in show business, she was determined to do something about it. She believed there must be a way to *begin* at a career and right there in Cleveland.

Looking around, she could see that Cleveland offered some promising dramatic and cultural venues to its African American residents. Already there was Karamu House, the cultural center that provided excellent opportunities (and an excellent training ground) for Blacks in theatre and the arts. The city could also boast of the Gilpin Players, a popular theatrical group founded by six actors in Cleveland in the 1920s. Cleveland also remained the home of the distinguished African American man of letters Charles W. Chesnutt.

Cleveland's movie houses could also feed Ruby's fantasies. She often slipped into the balcony or the segregated section of a theatre and sat spellbound as she watched Hollywood's early gods and goddesses flicker across the screen: Valentino, Pola Negri, Garbo, John Gilbert, Ramon Novarro. But what struck Ruby's imagination most were the Black faces.

Negroes in films appeared mainly as funny servants. Sometimes they stood, often grinning, in the background. Other times they inched forward to perform a comic antic or two. Sometimes wide-eyed. Sometimes scared-out-of-their-wits. Or, as in D.W. Griffith's *The Birth of A Nation* in 1915, they stormed across the screen in a panting rage, lusting for power and White women, emerging as the embodiment of White America's nightmarish fears about Black male sexuality and assertion. In the early years of silent cinema, the Black characters were all the more outrageous caricatures because they were so often played by Whites in blackface.

But by the 1920s, a few African American actors worked regularly in films and became known to audiences. Black child star Sunshine Sammy, whose real name was Ernest Frederic Morrison, appeared in several films with Harold Lloyd and later performed in Hal Roach's comedy series about children *Our Gang*. Also in that series was Allen Hoskins, who was cast as a spunky, sometimes dazed little fellow called Farina. Actors like Sam Lucas and handsome James B. Lowe, who each played the stalwart hero Tom in the early movie versions of *Uncle Tom's Cabin*, briefly came to prominence. Other Negro actors like Noble Johnson and Carolynne Snowden also found work in the movies.

Johnson was also one of the actors who recognized the potential of film, and the searing power of images, to inform or to distort. Convinced that Negro audiences should have their own entertainment in the form of Black cast movies with Black stars and storylines, he and his brother George Johnson established the Lincoln Motion Picture Company in Los Angeles in 1916. Producing such films as *The Realization of A Negro's Ambition, Trooper of Troop K*, and *The Law of Nature*, Johnson helped launch a movement of independent African American filmmakers that later included such directors as Oscar Micheaux and Spencer Williams. All scrambled to gather financing, formed production companies, and then, on shoestring budgets, produced quickly-made Black-cast films, known later as *race movies*—Black romances, Black westerns, Black comedies, Black gangster stories, and steamy Black melodramas, all produced especially for the African American audience.

As much as Ruby was drawn to the movies, she realized that the best opportunities for her to perform lay in Cleveland's network of churches and social groups. The city's Colored churches, of which there were some fifty-three at that time, were lively social, cultural, and sometimes political centers. Activities of all sorts flourished in them. Special performances were given by the church choirs. Women's Day functions, which helped raise funds for the churches, included bazaars, dinners, picnics, and evening entertainments. Special Men's Day events did the same. Some afternoons and nights were devoted to dramatic performances and poetry readings, too. Black women's clubs and social organizations also flourished in the city. Ruby started performing at such church gatherings and at various functions of Black women's groups. Sometimes she recited poetry. Sometimes she sang.

Of the Black churches, the Shiloh Baptist Church was the city's oldest Baptist institution, and its second oldest religious establishment. In the twenties, Shiloh's congregation swelled to some 1,500 members. Among them was Ruby.

With such a large group, church life could be hotly competitive with long-standing alliances, rivalries, feuds, and hierarchies among the congregation. Newcomers often had to prove themselves and play a delicate game of church politics as they cleverly maneuvered their way around the power brokers of the institution. Apparently, none of this fazed Ruby, who became active at Shiloh and enthusiastically participated in its social affairs, dramatic programs, and outings. Again she recited poetry and sang. On Sunday mornings, she also carried her young daughters to Shiloh for Sunday School and church services. By now, Dorothy, between the ages of three and four, was becoming an anxious, insecure little girl, afraid of letting her mother out of her sight and fearful of someone else catching Ruby's attention. Among Dorothy's earliest memories were those of clinging to her mother during services and refusing to let any man sit next to Ruby.

At home Dorothy watched closely as her mother memorized and rehearsed poetry, usually by one of Ruby's favorites, African American writer Paul Laurence Dunbar. Dorothy sat engrossed in Ruby's every move, mood, gesture, vocal inflection, and change of expression.

One evening when an exhausted Ruby returned home from work, she matter-of-factly told her daughter that she was too tired to perform at a scheduled engagement. "I'll do it for you, mama," said Dorothy, who explained that she could recite the Paul Laurence Dunbar poem "In the Morning." At first, Ruby laughed. But she was surprised that Dorothy even understood that she planned to do a poem by Dunbar. Then she sat silent, unable to believe what she heard and saw. Her daughter stood in the kitchen and recited Dunbar's lines word for word and in the very manner she had watched her mother do it. Dorothy had developed, on her own, into a perfect mimic.

Ruby Dandridge, with her infallible instincts, immediately decided to let Dorothy go on in her place. At the church that evening, she observed that Dorothy was an adorable little crowd-pleaser whose letter-perfect performance delighted the adults in the audience. At that moment, she no doubt started making plans to train Dorothy to perform.

"You ain't going to work in Mister Charley's kitchen like me," was what Dorothy remembered Ruby telling Vivian and her time and again. "I don't want you to go into service. You not going to be a scullery maid. We're going to fix it so you be something else than that." Show business could be a way out. And up.

Afterwards, in the cramped quarters of her home, Ruby worked with Dorothy. When Vivian saw Dorothy's interests and Ruby's enthusiastic response, she told her mother she wanted to learn to do recitations too. Nightly, Ruby sat at her kitchen table where she wrote skits and routines for them. Then she drilled them in memorizing poetry, explaining how to punch or emphasize important lines, how to smile and laugh at certain moments, how to pull for emotion in others. She taught them to sing, dance, and perform acrobatics—just as her father had done with her.

Her efforts were fruitful. At local churches, the girls entertained with their skits and readings, which they enjoyed, perhaps mainly because it pleased their mother so much. Neither could yet read, but they memorized poetry without any difficulty. The girls were not paid for their performances at the churches. Ruby, however, had visions of taking this early training further, of professionally grooming the girls, but she didn't have enough time. Her job took up most of her day. She didn't have enough experience either. The real grooming—or as Vivian said, "The way we got started in show business"—came about with the arrival of a woman who came to live with them. Her name was Geneva Williams.

The girls watched silently as this stranger suddenly took up residence in their home. Geneva Williams was a talented musician who had studied at Fisk University in her native Nashville, Tennessee. She played the piano well, had a fine eye for spotting talent, and was an excellent teacher of both the piano and voice. "Neva was a great musical director," said Geri Branton. "She was very talented in that way." Brown-skinned, stocky, of medium height, and in the eyes of some, an attractive woman, she had met Ruby in church. The women were about the same age and discovered they had much in common with similar interests and similar disappointments.

Like Ruby, Geneva, who Ruby called "Neva," also had fled from an unsatisfying marriage. Hers was to a minister. In fact, when Neva came to live with the family, said Vivian Dandridge, she "was hiding out" from her husband. Not much more was known about the marriage. Neva was suspicious of men, and like Ruby, she never remarried.

Far more compatible with each other than with their husbands and far more in tune with one another's moods and aspirations, the two women became inseparable. While Ruby could be off on a cloud, her high-pitched voice chattering away, Neva stayed grounded. Autocratic and intelligent, she was a master of organization with a keen sense of decorum and high standards. Ruby became the family's breadwinner and handled the money. Neva, who could sew, cook, clean, and run a shipshape house, took charge of the home—and the children.

Neither Dorothy nor Vivian understood who this woman was who had entered their lives and their home. All they knew was that their mother turned them over to Neva, who was given control of the girls and allowed, even encouraged, to discipline them however she chose. Much to Vivian's and Dorothy's dismay, Ruby never challenged anything Neva said. Among the first of orders, remembered Vivian Dandridge, was "to call her Ma-Ma. Auntie Ma-Ma."

An unyielding disciplinarian, foul-tempered, and petty, Ma-Ma insisted upon neatness, good manners, and punctuality. "Auntie was the mother. She ruled the roost," said Vivian's and Dorothy's childhood friend in Los Angeles, Juliette Ball. "Auntie had the last word about everything. Where they went. Who they were friends with. And she was mean as hell. Ma-Ma did all the spanking, designated all the chores, decided who was to wash dishes, who was to make up the bed, who was to play, who didn't play, and if they played, with whom."

Neva criticized and reprimanded the girls' behavior and habits daily and she beat them regularly. Sometimes she slapped them on the hands or the legs, the buttocks or the face. The slaps were hard, swift, and often unexpected. Other times, she beat them with a hairbrush, using either the back of the brush or the bristles, whichever was most convenient. Her anger seemed to leap out of nowhere. Bewildered, the girls could never anticipate what might set the woman off.

Of the two children, Vivian, who Ruby called Vivi, was the more compliant and—surprisingly in view of her behavior in later years—the more docile. Dorothy, who Ruby called Dottie and who was about four years old when Neva moved in, was outspoken and "adventurous when she was little," said Vivian. Consequently, Dottie frequently incurred Ma-Ma's anger. Dorothy's punishments, said Vivian, were also harsher.

"Dottie got so many spankings I used to ask Ma-Ma to spank me instead," said Vivian. "And the only reason I didn't get any is that I was so dull I did the right things all the time. I was afraid of getting spanked."

At the end of a day, as the girls turned in for bed, if Dorothy had not been spanked or reprimanded, she whispered to her sister, "Vivi, I haven't gotten one today."

Vivian, who at an early age developed a sense of humor that would sustain her through many troubled years ahead, replied, "Shhh. The day isn't over."

In some respects, Neva didn't treat the children any differently than did many parents of this earlier age, who rarely hesitated to hit a naughty child. Believing that was the best way to instill discipline, most Americans lived by the adage, "Spare the Rod and Spoil the Child." But Neva did cross over the line "She was a child abuser," said Geri Branton. Neither Dorothy nor Vivian ever forgot Ma-Ma's tyranny and cruelty. Yet neither appeared to blame Ruby for her complicity in Ma-Ma's control over them. As children and even as adults, their feelings, especially Vivian's, towards Ruby were ambivalent. Both understood the pressures that Ruby endured as a working mother. "Auntie Ma-Ma presided over our home like the Rock of Gibraltar," Dorothy once said, while Ruby "worked, worried, faced fears of the landlord, and carried the burden of food-getting because she had the complete economic responsibility."

For both Dorothy and Vivian, it would have been too painful to admit that in many respects, other things were more important to Ruby than her children. Ruby could be affectionate, propping Dottie or Vivi on her lap, and she was willing to make sacrifices for them. To most observers, however, she simply didn't want the hassles or daily grind of raising them and was happy to turn over such responsibilities to someone else. As for Neva, she never appeared to pass on an opportunity to discipline the kids. Nor did she seem to want them around. The girls were in the way of both Neva and Ruby, who may have secretly or unconsciously wanted a life together without them.

On many occasions, Dottie and Vivi huddled together, frightened and confused, and wondered why their father didn't rescue them. Or why he had deserted them. Or why their mother failed to protect them from Ma-Ma. The two sisters became exceptionally close, clinging together in the belief that each was all the other could depend on. "They had no one else to love but one another," said their childhood friend Juliette Ball.

Ruby and Ma-Ma quickly assessed the budding talents and pretty looks of the girls. "Ma-Ma is the one that discovered that we had talent," Vivian said. "Dottie had a flair for reciting things. And I was more musical. So Ma-Ma started teaching me piano at 5. I gave my first concert at 6. Dorothy recited Paul Laurence Dunbar and things like that. And she was very funny as a child. She was very comical."

Now what had been a game of make-believe became a strict, highly structured, repetitive regime of rehearsals—for hours daily—in dancing, singing, and acrobatics. Not a day, save Sunday, went by without the unending drills and rehearsals. Even at night, the girls spent their time singing spirituals and hymns with Ruby and Ma-Ma. Not much time was left for anything else, including a childhood. Neva took over the education of the girls, teaching them reading and arithmetic. For some years to come, neither Ruby nor Neva saw any need to enroll the children in school.

Of the two children, Vivian was becoming the taller with a larger frame, more angular but similar to her mother's. Her color was a yellow or golden brown. She had Ruby's dark eyes and much of Ruby's optimism and energy. Her features had some of the sharp definition of Cyril's.

So, too, did Dottie's. Her eyes were also dark and magnetic, already full of promise and dazzle. They were eyes that captured light and danced and sparkled; the kind of eyes that movie cameras came to adore. Through childhood, her skin color (which friends and associates in later years described in different ways) went from a deep burnt yellow to a startling golden brown, close to Vivian's but somehow richer, neither dark nor extremely light. "It was pure *café au lait*," said Dorothy's friend Geri Branton, "absolutely gorgeous." Her skin also would take to lights, camera filters, and makeup extraordinary well, and she would be blessed, like most great film stars, in having the type of beauty that could be heightened with makeup.

During this era when light skin, keen features, and straight hair were valued in both Black and White America, Ruby considered the girls' complexions a blessing. As a dark woman who had bore subtle and blatant forms of discrimination—from Blacks and Whites—in a culture that devalued her physical attributes and viewed her as the opposite of the feminine ideal, Ruby, to her credit, appeared never to devalue herself. Her confidence was one of her most appealing and admirable traits, and it carried her a long way.

As the girls continued to perform locally, Neva, always a tough critic, dissected each performance, emphasizing that they *could* be and *had* to be improved upon. Dorothy and Vivian struggled, trying to meet her seemingly impossible standards. Neva's unceasing picky critiques left their mark on Dorothy, who as a child loved performing but became nervous and unsure of herself, afraid of some wrong move or gesture. Throughout her later solo nightclub career, she suffered from an almost paralyzing fear of live audiences, seldom believing she could meet their expectations. It was almost as if she expected the clubs to be filled with patrons as tough and demanding as Neva.

A change in Dorothy's and Vivian's lives occurred when Neva, upon receiving news that a relative had died in Nashville, made arrangements to return home for the funeral. Since Ruby had to work with no one in the house to care for the children, she decided to let Neva take them with her to Tennessee. In a few months, she planned to join them there. Of course, another matter probably determined Ruby's decision. Court proceedings with Cyril over custody of the children dragged on. With the girls out of the state, Ruby knew Cyril would never be able to find them.

All the girls were told was that they were going south with Neva and that they'd see their mother at Christmas. "So she took us to Tennessee where Ma-Ma's mother was living," said Vivian. Both children were confused and no doubt feared they might not ever see their mother again. For Dorothy, the separation, like so much else that had already occurred in her life, simply served to make her all the more insecure.

In Nashville, Neva continued to rehearse and drill the girls. Shrewdly and aggressively, Neva also found them work by using her contacts and a network of acquaintances in the city. She worked out an arrangement with Roger Williams University, a Black religious institution, for the girls to appear on a tour. "They lined up some shows and places for us to perform," recalled Vivian. "Mostly Baptist churches. Some schools." Sometimes they would also appear in halls, even in barns, just about anywhere a Black audience could be reached.

Such an arrangement worked well for the girls and the university. Dorothy and Vivian were paid for their work, which could average between $400 and $500 for each appearance. The bulk of the money paid by the organizations and church groups, however, "were chiefly for the benefit of Roger Williams University," said Dorothy.

Their act was also given a name. "We were called The Wonder Children," said Vivian, "because we did acrobatic stunts." Photographs were taken of the girls in various poses and attitudes in preparation for the tour. Then special flyer advertisements were printed. "I was shown doing these splits with a smile and some kind of a bonnet," Vivian recalled. "And Dorothy had both legs behind her neck. That's how they publicized us as The Wonder Children."

Black churches had sprouted throughout the state, in the big cities like Chattanooga, Memphis, and Knoxville, as well as such smaller areas as Clarksville, Jackson, Columbia, Greenville, and Johnson City.

On the road with Ma-Ma, the girls travelled from city to city, or from one little backwater town or hamlet to another, usually staying no more than a day before moving on to the next stop. The girls were developing into pint-sized professionals, but they were lonely and missed their mother.

Once Ruby arrived in Nashville, Dottie's fears of losing her mother forever were assuaged, at least for the time being. But she didn't want Ruby out of her sight. None of this—the children's needs as well as the affection Ruby briefly bestowed on Dottie and Vivi—went unnoticed by Ma-Ma. Yet all of these reverberating emotions and passions appeared to pass over Ruby's head. Instead she was preoccupied by the newfound success of the girls. Ruby reasoned this was only Tennessee. Surely, there were other regions—a larger market—that could be tapped.

Envisioning a new horizon for the girls, Ruby also saw a new role for herself, that of a businesswoman who had to be adept at negotiating deals, establishing contacts, and getting the most out of what Nashville had to offer. Located in the city was the headquarters of the National Baptist Convention. An independent federation of Black churches around the country that had been founded in the late 19th century, the organization disseminated religious literature for Sunday Schools and church services for its member churches, and also provided speakers and entertainment for special occasions.

Ruby and Neva contacted the National Baptist Convention about an extended tour for The Wonder Children (sometimes called The Wonder Kids) at its churches in the South. That meant practically everywhere; from neighboring states like Kentucky and Arkansas to Oklahoma, Georgia, North Carolina, South Carolina, Mississippi, and Alabama. It was an inspired idea that worked. "Having that organization as our sponsor was, for the Negro community then," said Dorothy, "like having a deal with MGM for white folks."

Ruby and Ma-Ma mapped out an entire evening's presentation, composed of a series of skits in two acts that could run for several hours. Dottie and Vivi, dressed as boys with large floppy hats and baggy pants, performed an insurance scam routine. They also performed a funny tummyache routine. Acrobatics were also part of the act: tumbles, somersaults, cartwheels, flips, and turns. Or they sang and danced. Vivian performed on the piano. Dorothy recited poetry and did an impersonation of singer Al Jolson. Neva and Ruby also joined the girls on stage. Ma-Ma played the piano. Ruby performed tumbles, which doubtless, given Ruby's size, were comic. Their act delighted the Southern Colored church-goers (especially in more rural areas), who were eager for some type of entertainment.

During the next three years, thousands of Negroes in all the Southern states came to see The Wonder Children, according to Dorothy. Traveling by train or bus, the four stayed at the homes of church goers or at local Colored boarding houses. The National Baptist Convention picked up the traveling expenses and paid all four a salary which, Dorothy said, was "several hundred dollars a month." "Vivian and I became the best-dressed little girls in the country."

The touring also took its toll, though, robbing the girls of time just to be themselves and to behave like children. Also denied were any pleasures that might have come from the travels themselves. Dorothy never forgot those occasions when, arriving in a new town or city, she and Vivian set out to explore the "Colored section." But Ma-Ma prohibited such ventures. Her voice heavy and stern, she would rattle off what became a standard litany of reasons why Dottie and Vivi shouldn't have fun: there was no time for foolishness; discipline had to be maintained and schedules kept; and they had to be fresh for their performances, without any sign of fatigue and surely none of irritability. Therefore, the girls must rest and not go roaming around. Yet the truth of the matter was that the girls never felt they had enough time for rest and were usually exhausted.

Other problems came up on the road. In the beginning, the girls had to sell religious books to the audience during intermission. Later, the sisters sold photographs of themselves and chatted with the curious. Dottie felt awkward.

"After the show," she said, "I had to stand out front and shake hands with the people who lined up and asked questions like 'How much older is your sister than you?' 'Do you prefer acting or singing or dancing?' 'Do you play with other children?'" Vivian was also embarrassed by having to smile while "people would come up and ask you what you ate. They'd ask you all kinds of questions. And you felt sort of freaky," said Vivian. "We got tired of answering questions."

Years later, Dorothy believed her aversion to interviews sprang from this childhood "question and answer routine." "Even now," she said as an adult, "when I have to do it, it's not that I don't want to. It's just that I feel something very strange about it."

Performing the same act over and over also became monotonous. And she learned that the show always had to go on. In the middle of one performance, Dorothy fell and sprained her ankle, but Ruby told her she had to finish the act. "Many years later," Dorothy said, "I heard Elsa Lanchester say, 'An actor must be indestructible.' She was right." But it was a hard lesson for a little girl to learn.

Not being settled in one place also did little to alleviate Dottie's growing insecurities, or her sense of a suffocating claustrophobia. Long restless nights were spent with Vivian, Ruby, Ma-Ma, and herself cramped together. "I remember sleeping four in a single bed," recalled Dorothy.

The heat too drained her, leaving her languid and feeling all the more trapped in a world governed by a giant eye in the heavens; a cruel or indifferent "hot sun" that threatened to descend and scorch her at any moment. Her life seemed an unending stream of "hot trains" that the family boarded, rehearsed in, ate in, slept in, and hastily departed from to arrive at a church in time for a performance. For Dorothy, the South became a haze of burning "cities of heat," one place never any different from another—where "I usually had a hot parched throat, and I was always looking to get in the cool somewhere."

The tours also brought the sisters face to face with American racism, southern-style; Jim Crow laws that led to separate water fountains, restaurants, and stores, with signs that Dottie and Vivi learned to read "For Colored" and "For White." There was no way for the girls to forget color, race, divisions, differences. To their credit, Ruby and Ma-Ma understood the culture and maneuvered their way through it. Like other African American parents, they taught the girls the tactics for survival the places they could and could not go: the things they could and could not say; the way they must stand, speak, even breathe when around Whites. The children obeyed without fully comprehending and never forgot the experiences of travelling in the South.

Like other actresses faced with unhappy childhoods, Dottie began to withdraw into a comfort zone of fantasies; a world filled with the most personal of dreams where nothing could touch or harm her, where nothing could dispel a little girl's hope for happiness. Years later, Dorothy recalled a recurring childhood dream of "disappearing into snow, of drifting into hills of cool white."

Yet, paradoxically, what also helped her escape was the very thing that appeared to imprison her. Performing enabled Dottie to lose herself in another identity. For a few hours a night, she could become a different person, who was happy, carefree, even mischievous without fears of repercussions or reprimands. Playing that other person also seemed the only way to ever win approval from Ruby and Neva. If she were good, and she and Vivi almost always were, there were hugs and kisses from Ruby and a big, happy smile. "That's my babies," Ruby might enthuse. Otherwise no one said anything encouraging to her. The only time she seemed to matter and to have any worth, so she believed, were these times that she and Vivi spent on stage. The applause of the audience, too—-that vast anonymous approval every performer seems to live for; that sign of love rushing up and over the footlights—also excited her. Real everyday life offered no such affirmation. So on stage Dottie could be funny and clever, said Vivian. But offstage, feeling incomplete and inadequate, Dottie began to keep to herself. "She was very shy," said Vivian. "She was outgoing maybe until she was age ten." Then she became very quiet.

Offstage, she also began to assume a role, a persona that made life bearable: that of the sweet, charming, obedient little girl without any discontents. For years to come, she played this role perfectly, and then followed it with other roles, that of the ideal young wife, the ideal young mother, and then the role of a Hollywood star, larger than life, glamorous, and haughty as hell. Dorothy Dandridge would always seemed one step removed from reality, able to function only when insulated by her self-protective shell, by whatever role she chose to play. Of course, problems emerged because real life didn't conform to her idea of the way it should be. Real life often turned too harsh and brutal to permit her to play her role; to live out her fantasies. Real life reared its ugly head and then everything she feared and sought to escape by playing/living a role came crashing in on her.

Nonetheless, Dottie, dreamy, vaguely distant and distracted, was developing, at a young age, into the most private of girls. Her retreat and absorption into a private sphere would be a lifelong trait. So, too, would be her need for privacy and an intense type of secrecy. If she had buttered toast for breakfast, she might not be willing to tell you. For almost the first half of her life, she appeared to open up to no one other than Vivi. Some of the secrecy grew out of living in a home where if you admitted to the slightest infraction of some rule, you might have to suffer the greatest of consequences. A violent slap. Or the silent treatment from Ma-Ma. The secrecy also came partly from the world of show business itself where rivalries and competition forced everyone to keep his or her guard up.

Much of the secrecy also seemed simply a part of Dorothy Dandridge's nature. That didn't mean she wouldn't discuss her goals or her problems with other people. She later confided in select intimates, but she didn't immediately trust anyone. Vivian developed into a far more outgoing and friendly young woman. Dottie, however, while always a creature of dazzling charm with vast seductive powers, continued to hold back on her innermost thoughts and feelings with most people.

As a little girl, Dottie's reason for guarding her privacy had to do with a secret she and Vivian shared of their homelife, which they never openly discussed with each other. Daily, the sisters observed Ruby and Ma-Ma—on the trains, on the stage, in the small boarding houses. The two women seemed to read one another's minds, even anticipate one another's thoughts, moods, plans, schemes, ideas, and goals. The girls saw all of this and the way Ruby and Neva spoke to each other, confided in one another, tenderly touched each other, and the way, when space permitted, they shared the same bedroom and bed. The children understood intuitively that the women were not merely church-going friends who had cast their lots together to survive through tough times; rather they had found in one another what no man could offer them. Had the relationship between Ruby and Neva been known, it would never have been accepted in Cleveland or most other places in America.

Paradoxically, Ruby, while daring, and oblivious to the feelings of others, was also religious and steeped in basic Christian doctrines, which she passed on to her daughters. Though Ruby appeared to enjoy gossip, she instilled in her daughters the belief that they should-n't speak ill of others and that they must also learn to forgive others their trespasses. "No one is all good and no one is all bad," was something Dorothy remembered hearing Ruby say frequently. "There is some good in everyone if you will look and find it. Even a bad one has a good spot somewhere." Throughout her life, Dorothy was rarely known to utter nasty or vindictive comments about her peers in show business. The same held for Vivian. Both adhered to Ruby's advice to look for the good in others. But such advice did not always serve the sisters well. In looking for the good, both often appeared to overlook the obvious bad.

When the stock market crashed in October 1929 and sent the nation spiraling into the Great Depression, the fortunes of Ruby, Ma-Ma, Vivi, and Dottie took a devastating turn. Suddenly, The Wonder Children were among the unemployed. Ruby and Neva, fearful and frantic, decided to pull up stakes in Tennessee and see if they could make a go of things somewhere else.

Briefly, Dorothy said, they moved to Chicago, but their situation worsened. Chicago had hard, bitter winters with a howling, ripping wind that chilled the bones. Each day, Ruby rose early, left the apartment, and looked for work. Going from one establishment to another, from home to home, asking if they needed help, Ruby sometimes walked for hours. But when nothing turned up, the family was forced to live on relief.

Dorothy recalled that her mother, "hysterical about money for rent and food," would walk "to the welfare offices with me tagging along at her side." In what looked like a huge warehouse, little Dottie saw lines of people waiting for food and then leaving the building carrying "sacks of potatoes and cans of beef." Ruby also left with sacks of food in her arms. For dinner, the Dandridge household mostly had meals of meat from the pig, like chitlins and pigs knuckles, said Dorothy. She never forgot nor lost her admiration for her mother's resiliency and tenacity in keeping the family afloat. "Don't leave none," Ruby would say at dinner. "Eat while you got it."

Ruby knew that security might be found back in Cleveland with Cyril, but she still had no doubts or regrets about her decision to leave. In the years to come, she only grew more bitter about her short-lived marriage. During this time, her optimism propelled her on. Ruby believed there had to be a way out of this economic nightmare.

She was confident of her daughters' talents and the possibility of them having careers that might generate enough income for the entire family to survive on. Two adorable entertaining children could make far more money than Ruby ever could being a cook or maid. That had already been proved.

Still caught up in the magic of the movies and the lure of the American Dream, Hollywood-style, Ruby began to think about work in motion pictures. With her intuitive senses as sharp as ever and her survival instincts honed to perfection, Ruby understood that American movies were on the historic brink of offering more opportunities for Black performers. Much had already happened in the past few years since her movie going days in Cleveland. The great change in Hollywood occurred in 1927 when an ersatz Black man— singer Al Jolson with burnt cork smeared over his face—flailed his arms and sang "Mammy" in the Warner Brothers movie *The Jazz Singer*. In one fell swoop, his song in blackface marked the death of silent films and launched the arrival of the talking motion picture.

Afterwards, the Hollywood studios wired for sound and set off in a mad search for new talents, scouring the Broadway stage to find actors—not only with faces but voices—to import to the West Coast. Unexpectedly, the new medium, which clearly demanded distinct sounds and a new type of fast-moving, energetic rhythm, indeed a new style of acting and a different type of star, now also made a place for the Negro entertainer.

Already in cities around the country Negro performers were becoming well-known and in vogue. They performed at New York's Cotton Club as well as niteries in Chicago, Philadelphia, and St. Louis. They appeared in theatrical productions like *Shuffle Along* and *Running Wild*. And they made race records—Black music by Black artists that were sold to Black people. Such African American stars as Bessie Smith, Josephine Baker, Duke Ellington, Ethel Waters, Louis Armstrong, Florence Mills, and Adelaide Hall had made remarkable inroads in the world of entertainment. They altered the very shape and scope of American popular culture with their unique talents, styles, energies, and personas. By the late 1920s, the Negro as Entertainer was becoming an acceptable presence on the mainstream cultural landscape.

Now in some circles, rumors spread that the Negro voice recorded better than a White one. Moviemakers decided to experiment with Negro sound. Short musical films were produced starring Black entertainers. Bessie Smith was a hefty, moody blues-singing mamma in *St. Louis Blues*. Duke Ellington was his sleek and dapper self with Fredi Washington as his iridescent, dying leading lady in the short *Black and Tan*. Charismatic and at the height of her vocal powers, Ethel Waters performed two unforgettable musical numbers—"Birmingham Bertha" and her big hit "Am I Blue?"—in the big Hollywood film *On With the Show* in 1929. That same year, two major Hollywood studios, Fox Pictures and MGM, released two all-talking, all-singing, all-dancing Colored pictures: Paul Sloane's *Hearts in Dixie* and King Vidor's *Hallelujah*.

In those films, the characters were familiar stereotyped figures: non-threatening docile souls who sometimes fell victim to their sexual desires or their naiveté. Vidor, however, sought to create a folk poem, a moody tale of tragedy, regeneration, and redemption, and in some respects, despite its stereotypes, his film succeeded. Most important, in both of these early Black musicals, the actors and actresses playing the clichéd roles were dazzling and innovative. In *Hallelujah*, audiences saw Daniel Haynes and blues singer Victoria Spivey and heard

the Dixie Jubilee Choir under the direction of Eva Jessyee and wit-
nessed Hollywood's first attempt at presenting an African American
love goddess: the energetic and incandescent beauty Nina Mae
McKinney. In *Hearts in Dixie*, audiences marvelled over the talents of
Clarence Muse, Mildred Washington, and a lanky comedian named
Stepin Fetchit.

Reviewing *Hearts in Dixie* in the April 1929 National Urban
League's publication *Opportunity*, critic Robert Benchley was almost
beside himself with excitement about the African American performers. "It may be that the talking-movies must be participated in exclusively by Negroes, but if so, then so be it. In the Negro the sound-pic-
ture has found its ideal protagonist," he wrote. "What white actors
are going to do to compete with it is their business. So long as there
are enough Negroes to make pictures, and enough good stories for
them to act in, the future of the talking-picture is assured."

In the same issue of *Opportunity*, Floyd C. Covington commented that

> ...with the current venture of all-Negro talking pictures,
> the Negro emerges from a somewhat obscure place in the
> industry to take a place in the center of the stage. It is hoped
> that with the increase of all-Negro pictures that the Negro
> will also develop directors and technicians that may aid
> them. A Culver City writer expresses a view somewhat
> naively, It's the day of the dark star in Hollywood....

Benchley's and Covington's comments expressed the enthusiasm,
quiet as it was kept, among some critics and a few studio executives
about the future of the Negro actor and actress in films. But when neither *Hallelujah* nor *Hearts in Dixie* was a box-office success, the studios lost interest in the Black-cast film, and seven years passed before
Hollywood launched another—the comedy *Green Pastures*. Still, the
situation in 1929 looked promising for Negro talent. For Ruby
Dandridge, who was surely aware of the new medium and the possibilities, of all the comments made, those nine words of Covington
would have been prophetic. *It's the day of the dark star in Hollywood.*

Excited and optimistic, swept up in her own enthusiasm and perhaps her own near desperation about her financial state, Ruby began
to make plans with Neva. Nightly, Dottie and Vivi overheard the two
women talking. A place mentioned often was California. Ruby and
Neva saved what money they could, when they could. "I'll get the
money. I'll get the money," was the refrain Dorothy heard her moth-

er uttering in the Chicago apartment.

Both Ruby and Neva must have realized that the odds were stacked against them; that anybody in his or her right mind would have thought the two of them were out of theirs. The quest they were setting out on was outlandish and foolhardy for anybody, let alone two African American women. How Ruby had the audacity and insight to imagine that the girls—as well as she and Neva—might find work out West is anybody's guess. But Ruby never played by anyone else's ideas of what she or her daughters could and could not do. Vivian only remembered that "Mother and Ma-Ma decided we were going into films." So that was that. There was no time for second thoughts.

Having scrimped and saved, Ruby bought four bus tickets. Ruby, Neva, Vivian, and Dorothy then boarded the vehicle that would carry them away from cold winters and dreams deferred to the land of sunshine and dreams come true. They headed for Los Angeles. Hollywood. And they never looked back.

TWO

A HOLLYWOOD
GIRLHOOD

*F*or two women accustomed to the pace of a slower, gray, winter-driven city like Cleveland, Los Angeles may have seemed a bit forbidding and perplexing, even if a magical, sensual empire flush with sunlight. But here they were: Ruby and Neva with Vivi and Dottie, in the place where America's dreams were manufactured, merchandized, and sold over the counter at movie theatres throughout the world. Ruby and Neva—along with the steady stream of go-getters, dreamers, artists, and shysters who flocked to the city saw Los Angeles's perennial sunshine beckoning like a sign of hope.

For Ruby, the adventurer, it was vast and wondrous. The city of angels offered sights, sounds, smells neither she nor Neva had known in Cleveland or in the cities of their birth, Wichita and Nashville. They found boulevards with pretty names like Sunset and La Cienega, Beverly and San Vicente, and enchanted streets lined with orange and lemon groves and tall, stately palm trees that gently swayed with a breeze. Perfuming the air were the fragrant scents of the eucalyptus, the honeysuckle, and the sycamore.

For Ruby and Neva, Los Angeles was also a sprawling, meandering maze with areas of seemingly endless turns and twists, hills, valleys, and canyons. Surely, they wondered if they would ever be able to fathom the layout of the city, to understand directions, to know for sure which part of town was east, which west. A whole new way of life, another approach to living, had to be conjured up, imagined, understood, practiced. A new arsenal of survival skills would be required, too, for it was the worst of times. The long lines in Los Angeles—for soup, for employment, for relief—were the same as those throughout the nation, now that the economy was on the brink of collapse.

Ruby and Neva could easily have been overwhelmed, but they kept their heads and charted their course. Despite the Depression, Los Angeles still meant freedom, escape, and, oddly enough, security. Ruby didn't have to worry about waking up to find Cyril sitting on her doorstep, demanding custody of her daughters. Nor did Neva have to fret about the minister husband she had left behind showing up. But more importantly, Los Angeles offered Ruby and Neva a promise that they couldn't turn their backs on; a promise of opportunities. Work could be found in the movies.

Black Americans had always been an integral part of Los Angeles's history. Of its 44 founders in 1781, there were 16 of Native American descent and 26 of African ancestry. Only two were White. After World War I, almost 16,000 Blacks lived in the city. The numbers would swell to 63,774 during the years of the Depression.

Just as moviemakers migrated West from the eastern cities in the first two decades of the twentieth century, eventually establishing the powerful studios that were to dominate American films for decades to come, many of the newly arrived Black Angelenos were lured to the city by this new phenomenon called the movies. Perhaps no city has ever represented the American Dream—for Blacks as well as Whites—as powerfully, seductively, and romantically as Hollywood. Many Black newcomers, despite the movie colony's images of African Americans, still believed Hollywood was a place where the extraordinary just might happen on any day, at any moment. After all, hadn't that already happened for African Americans in the New York clubs and theatres and in the recording industry, too?

Now in Hollywood, many hoped that at least a degree of fame, wealth, or happiness might possibly come their way, if they had the right look, the right moves, the right smile. Even Langston Hughes thought his pen might have a chance in the movie industry as he trekked West during the Depression era to write the screenplay for *Way Down South*.

Through their contacts with the National Baptist Convention, Ruby and Neva were able to meet people and find a place to live. The hub of life here was Central Avenue with its clubs, restaurants, shops, stores, and the famous Dunbar Hotel where the big stars and the Black elite like Duke Ellington, Billie Holiday, Louis Armstrong, Langston Hughes, Count Basie, Nina Mae McKinney, and W. E. B. DuBois stayed while on the coast. On Central Avenue and scattered throughout the city were also such clubs and theatres starring Black entertainers as the Club Alabam, Club Congo, Club Apex, the Plantation Club, and the large Lincoln Theatre.

They first settled into a small house on Newton Street, near a police station. Within the next few years, they made several moves, from Newton to East 55th Street, then to Ascot Avenue just north of 55th Street, then to two different locations on Fortuna Street. The neighborhoods were mixed or sometimes mostly White working class.

The homes were just about all the same. They usually consisted of a small living room, a semblance of a kitchen, and two bedrooms, everything on one level. Outside the homes a bit of grass separated one nearly identical house from another. Contrary to Cyril's divorce complaints that Ruby kept a filthy home, her residences in Los Angeles, even though sparsely furnished, were known for being immaculately kept (sometimes almost antiseptically so), thanks perhaps to Neva.

In these homes, the girls were stripped of any hopes of privacy, of escaping Ma-Ma's watchful eye and foul temper. With so little room to breathe, it is not hard to understand why Dorothy, in later years, occasionally suffered breathing problems, especially when she was tense and nervous in small or confining dressing rooms. Just as she found ways to cope as a child, she continued to withdraw into her private reveries and fantasies, finding them the only way to escape from the pressures and bouts of serious depression that began not long after she reached puberty. Another less spirited or plucky girl might have succumbed, though, to a paralyzing despair without any dreams of moving up in life, without any hopes that there might be other ways of living.

The division of labor was just as clear between the two adults in the house as ever. "Ruby was like the husband," said musician Phil Moore, who met the family in Los Angeles. Remaining in charge of the finances, "she was out everyday trying to make money. The aunt stayed at the home." Neva was still responsible for the house and the children—and their continued training: the lessons in singing, dancing, acrobatics, and proper ladylike behavior. Every minute of their day was monitored, scheduled, controlled, scrutinized, and criticized by Ma-Ma.

Ruby and Neva took stock of their situation, and they listened carefully to stories they heard of the African Americans who had first come to Hollywood. Those with dreams of acting careers often had sought behind-the-scenes jobs at the studios. Early Hollywood history was scattered here and there with figures who used domestic service to earn a living while they climbed up the ranks and found a place in the milieu of glamor and magic.

A woman like Lillian Moseley had first worked as a maid for actress May Allison and later Ann Sothern. Then she worked her way up to become a matron at Columbia Pictures where she knew just about every big star on the lot from Rita Hayworth to Glenn Ford. Moseley took pride in the fact that the stars confided in her. Lillian Moseley was a woman said to know where many of Hollywood's secrets lay.

Lula Bolden Evans was another case. When her husband died, this former schoolteacher couldn't find work to support herself and two children. She became a maid to White actress Norma Shearer and later became the head matron at MGM. Promptly, at 5:15 every morning, Lula Evans opened the building for the stars. Around the lot, the word was that Lula Evans held the keys to MGM. A day could not start without her. Later her daughter Lois studied at San Francisco's College of Chiropody and at MGM treated everyone from Lana Turner, Lucille Ball, Judy Garland, and Greer Garson to studio mogul Louis B. Mayer in her office at the studio.

Then there was Madame Sul-Te-Wan, a name that Louisville, Kentucky-born Nellie Conley grandly took on, along with a stately new persona, upon arriving in Hollywood in the teens of the century. Born in 1873, she was then no starry-eyed kid, but rather a single parent who had to support herself and her children. So she boldly approached a fellow Kentuckian, D. W. Griffith and landed work on the production of his scandalous racist masterpiece *The Birth of A Nation*. Assigned to clean the studio dressing rooms, she also appeared in a minor role, which was cut from the final version, and as an extra in various scenes.

Afterwards, Madame Sul-Te-Wan's relationship with Griffith continued for years. Apparently platonic, it was nonetheless rumored to be otherwise and consequently puzzled the film community. "She was devoted to Mr. Griffith, and he in turn loved her," said Griffith's star Lillian Gish. "Later, when Madame was having financial difficulties, he sent her money to help herself and her small sons. She was one of the few friends near him when he died years later in Hollywood."

Never an important actress, Sul-Te-Wan managed nonetheless to keep working for decades in such movies as *In Old Chicago, The Maid of Salem, Black Moon, Maryland,* and later *Carmen Jones.* Madame was also adept at self-promotion. In later years, stories circulated in Hollywood that she was the grandmother of Dorothy. By then, the Madame no doubt considered Dandridge the greatest of Negro stars, and so perhaps it seemed only fitting to her that Dorothy should have been a descendent of Sul-Te-Wan.

Others behind the scenes in Hollywood included such men as Charles Butler and Ben Carter, who were early Black casting agents for the studios.

Years passed, of course, before any performers made significant inroads. Only the most driven and tenacious got a chance. Sam Lucas, James B. Lowe, Ernest Morrison, Carolynne Snowden, and Noble Johnson opened doors in the teens and early twenties. Others like George Reed, Clarence Muse, Mildred Washington, Clifford Ingram, Jim Blackwell, Mattie Peters, and Gertrude Howard found work following *Hearts in Dixie* and *Hallelujah.* Most Black performers still found themselves, if working at all, cast in bit roles, or most often as extras in crowd scenes, or as set dressing as a shoeshine boy or a butler or a maid.

But during the Depression era (and into the early 1940s), other Black actors and actresses rose from the extra ranks and appeared regularly—playing roles with dialogue and becoming known to audiences. At first, none was more popular than that loose-limbed, slow-moving comic Stepin Fetchit, who stammered and shuffled his way to stardom.

Others followed. Louise Beavers played Mae West's maid in *Belle of the Nineties.* Later she and Fredi Washington gave moving performances in the 1934 tear-jerker *Imitation of Life.* Paul Robeson performed "Ol' Man River" in *Show Boat.* Willie Best and Mantan Moreland began playing befuddled characters in one film after another. Butterfly McQueen used her high-pitched voice to high comic effect in *The Women* and *Gone With the Wind.* Under the direction of such Hollywood luminaries as Howard Hawks, John Ford, Josef Von Sternberg, George Stevens, James

Whale, and Preston Sturges, they worked side by side (and often stole the scenes) with the era's great icons: Harlow, Gable, Dietrich, Crawford, Colbert, Hepburn, Fonda, Stanwyck, Jack Benny, W.C. Fields, and Mae West.

Though African American images hadn't changed much since silent days, the performers themselves infused their characters with unique cultural perspectives and unexpected subtexts that sometimes called a lie to what the script wanted an audience to believe. Hattie McDaniel boomed and belted her lines so forcefully in movies like *The Mad Miss Manton* and *Affectionately Yours* that audiences knew here was a strong-willed woman born to *give* orders, *not* to *take* them. Eddie "Rochester" Anderson strutted so confidently through his movies with Jack Benny that he looked as if *he* were the boss and Benny the servant. The energy, optimism, and *sound* of the new African American screen performers contributed much to the tone and texture of the new talkies, far more so than the Black performers were given credit for. These very same performers, who were struggling to maintain a foothold in Hollywood and to turn trash into art, would also watch the young Dorothy Dandridge grow up; for most, she would embody their dream of Black movie stardom. This close-knit small enclave of African Americans went on the same casting calls, auditioned for the same roles, discussed the same dreams and disappointments at the same restaurants and clubs, and met, mingled, and commiserated in one another's homes. Rivalries sprang up. So too did feuds and alliances.

At the top of Black Hollywood's hierarchy were the name performers. Mid-level were the bit players and near bottom were the extras. At the very bottom—the basement of Black Hollywood as well as White Hollywood—sat the never-weres, the people who could not find work and just hung around on the fringes, hoping for some of the gloss of glamor to rub off on them, for some of the crumbs of fame to fall their way. This was the established Negro community, something of a Black Hollywood, that had sprung up within the film capital by the time Ruby and Neva arrived in Los Angeles.

Aware that she would have to work her way up, Ruby's Hollywood experience must have struck her as not being too different from some of her church-going activities in Cleveland.

Survival anywhere demanded a quick grasp of the internecine politics of a place; knowing who to be nice to; who not to give the time
of day to. Never one to hide her ambition, Ruby was ready to court
and cajole, flatter and fuss over just about anyone in order to get
ahead.

One of those people was actor Clarence Muse, who had started
his career with the Lafayette Players and then appeared in such
movies as *Hearts in Dixie, Huckleberry Finn, The Last Parade,
White Zombie,* and later *Broadway Bill.* Versatile and ambitious, he
wrote the song "When It's Sleepy Time Down South," which became
a signature piece for Louis Armstrong. He also collaborated with
Langston Hughes on the screenplay and spirituals for the Hollywood
film *Way Down South.* Ultimately, his career spanned some five
decades. With his deep theatrical voice and imposing bearing, Muse
was regarded as a serious, dignified actor, a leading light in Black
Hollywood. Eventually, heading Los Angeles's Negro unit of the
Federal Theatre Project, he was clearly a man with some influence
and power. He was also a man who could be pompous and arrogant.

Shortly after the family's arrival in Los Angeles, Ruby finagled a
meeting with Muse. She carried Dottie and Vivi to the actor's home,
hoping he might be able to help her daughters find work. The girls
were immaculately dressed and told to mind their manners. Ruby
explained her situation to Muse. He in turn glanced at Dorothy and
Vivian, and then informed Ruby, "Go back East, Mrs. Dandridge.
They don't stand a chance. I can't help them."

"We can't go back East. We got to stay," Ruby told Muse.

"Well, good luck," he replied. "I really mean it, good luck. But
you'll never make it."

Dorothy recalled, "He was looking at me when he said it."

Muse told Ruby that the girls weren't dark enough to get into the
movies. He insisted that the studios wanted *Colored-looking* Colored
people.

Ruby knew he was wrong. But careful not to show how
annoyed she was, she thanked him for his time, then left his house
in a huff. Her daughters would get work, no matter what the
esteemed and pompous Mr. Muse had to say. Years later, all three
Dandridges—Ruby, Vivian, and Dorothy—relished telling the story
of Muse's reaction to them; of having proved him wrong. Dorothy
and Vivian appeared most annoyed, not because of the way he dismissed them but rather their mother. Still, Ruby was able to pour

on enough charm to persuade Muse to lend her some money. "I paid their first damn money for an apartment they lived in," he said years later. "And I never got my $70 back either."

In Los Angeles, Dorothy and Vivian enrolled in the Hooper Avenue School on Hooper Avenue at 52nd Street. "We didn't enter public school until we were like eight and nine," Vivian said. "We had been tutored so well that I was skipped a grade." Her little sister was not so advanced. "Dorothy never [liked] school that much." For both Dorothy and Vivian, the best thing about the Hooper Avenue School was that now, for the first time, they had classmates. Girls like Juliette Ball and Henriella Dunn would be friends of Dorothy's for the rest of her life.

Dorothy studied as best she could. If she failed to do so, she knew the nasty repercussions that would follow. Yet the years spent on the road as one of The Wonder Children had kept her moving so much that despite Ma-Ma's drills, Dorothy's education (unlike Vivian's) was spotty. She could memorize a text quickly. But for years, she could barely read.

Ruby and Neva, however, didn't fret about the education of either Dorothy or Vivian. They were too concerned about finding employment for the family. To earn extra money, Neva gave piano and voice lessons from the house. Ruby was ready to take any type of job she could find, even doing domestic work again. She didn't want to, but it was a necessity she could live with.

For Ruby and Neva, the real value of public school though was as a way of reinforcing the girls' discipline; the classes at the Hooper Avenue School, and later McKinley and then Jefferson High School, became but one part of a highly structured daily regiment.

"When we started at public school, we had to be there at a certain time or we were told we would get a spanking. That was to keep us out of trouble," Vivian said. "We didn't play that much because you see we were still into acrobatics. And I rehearsed piano two hours a day. We rehearsed acrobatics at least an hour a day. Then we went to dancing. We had to rehearse that. And then Dottie would have to stay up on her readings. So it was really work. We weren't permitted to play with other children at that time. We didn't have the time."

Ruby also enrolled them in a dancing school run by an enterprising Black woman—well-known in Los Angeles's Black community named Lauretta Butler, who taught classes to about fifty students in her home. "She had a great big house," recalled Avanelle Harris, who as a little girl studied dance with Dorothy and Vivian. "A huge living room. Great hardwood floors. And her living room, dining room, and music room were all part of her studio." Two other women, a pair of sisters named Nettle and Helen Mitchell, were employed there to teach dance.

Butler herself played piano and was a very, very commanding presence. "She was a big, tall woman," recalled Harris. "Very strict. Very professional. Everything she taught you had to do with the discipline of the theatre. She taught you about your lighting. She taught you how to come into the auditorium with your music and present it to the orchestra leader. She just gave you the whole rundown on the whole entire picture of what show business was." Once a year, Butler also gave a large recital with her students.

"You didn't go there to play," said Avanelle Harris. "You went there to work. We had our little break periods and we had a lot of fun as children. But it was school. We were there practically every day, all afternoon. But always on Saturdays."

Harris met Dorothy and Vivian on the first day that Ruby brought them to class. "There were these two little girls. And the tallest girl was Vivian. And this little tiny adorable girl, Dorothy," recalled Harris. "Dorothy was so cute and Viv was rather awkward and shy." Because of their ages, the Dandridge sisters were put into a class for the younger girls.

At Lauretta Butler's school, Dorothy and Vivian became friendly with another little girl, Etta Jones. A year older than Vivian, the daughter of a German Jewish mother and a Black postal worker father, Etta's family had moved to Los Angeles from Lake Charles, Louisiana. Now living near the Dandridges, Etta often spent time with Vivian and Dorothy after their classes.

"We would play rummy and cards and laugh," recalled Etta. "I was also taking voice lessons from Ma-Ma. So I went to their house for the lessons." Sometimes the girls practiced dance steps. Sometimes they just sat and talked about what they wanted to be when they grew up. Etta remembered, "Dorothy *always* said she wanted to be an actress." Other times they sang together. "Our singing just came naturally," said Etta. "I had the highest voice. Vivian sang the low voice or alto. Dorothy sang the lead."

One afternoon Etta's father heard the three and was impressed.

"You kids sound kinda good," Paul Jones told them. Afterwards, whenever he heard the girls harmonizing, Jones called out, "Sing some more." "He'd throw us pennies on the sidewalk," Etta remembered, "and we'd pick up the pennies and go to the candy store."

For Dorothy, the singing was just a way to have fun, to relax during days that were already too structured for kids wanting to play. But that soon changed.

When Paul Jones mentioned the girls' voices to Ruby, her ears perked up. Ruby had them sing for her and liked what she heard. So too did Neva. As could be expected, the women started making plans. Pragmatic and honest with herself, Ruby felt that now that Dorothy and Vivian were growing bigger and getting older, those cute antics of The Wonder Children would no longer be so cute. Forming a singing group might be just the way to groom the girls into a more grown-up act with a mature image that could be further refined and that might carry them through their teens into young adulthood.

"Mrs. Dandridge and Ma-Ma could see a good thing because it was the Depression and everybody needed money then," said Etta. So Ruby told all three girls they'd now be a trio that would be called the Dandridge Sisters.

Vivian and Etta were excited by the news. But Dorothy chafed at the idea of Etta, the play sister, being considered a real Dandridge girl. Vivian was her only sister. Through all the years of their young lives, the two had been a team that had comforted and helped one another on stage and at home. To Dorothy, Etta was little more than an interloper. Though annoyed and angry, she didn't say anything to anyone, except Vivian. Had she voiced any complaints to Ruby, she knew she'd be ignored. Had she said anything to Ma-Ma, in all likelihood she'd have been told she was silly and selfish—and then struck with the back of Neva's hand or a hairbrush. By now, she understood the futility of expressing her feelings to anyone other than her sister. Instead, Dorothy simply resigned herself to the fact that the name for the trio had been decided and she had no say in the matter; that what once had been fun would now become part of the daily grind, along with the dance classes at Butler's and the endless, rehearsals, drills, and exercises.

Mindful of the stiff competition and the limited opportunities, Ruby sent the girls, including Etta, to study dance at other schools, including the Covans and the Nash studios where they'd be exposed to other forms of dance and technique. "I think we took dancing from every dance teacher in Los Angeles," Etta said. "We practiced day in and day out."

≈

Eventually, Ruby found work for the girls through Black actor Ben Carter, then one of the few Black agents in the movie capital. Carter had arrived in Los Angeles in the early 1930s and first worked as an extra and as an unbilled player in movies. His acting career didn't pick up steam until later when he became one of the first Black performers to sign a seven-year contract with 20th Century Fox. He also teamed up with Mantan Moreland in a comedy act. Known for his wiry hair which practically stood on end, and his large eyes, which he frequently widened and bugged, he usually played smiley toms or comic coon characters in such movies as *Maryland, Tin Pan Alley,* and *Bowery to Broadway.*

But Carter was shrewd enough to see another opportunity for himself. He realized Black performers needed representation—someone to pound on the doors at the studios and "sell" them rather than the actors having to sell themselves. So he opened an office on Central Avenue and set himself up in the agenting business. Consequently, he became an important figure in Black Hollywood, handling such Black performers as Libby Taylor, Eddie Green, Hattie Noel, and Oscar Polk. He eventually helped cast the Black actors in *Gone with the Wind,* supplying, so he said, every Negro role in the film except Prissy, Mammy, and Uncle Peter.

As soon as Ruby heard of Carter, she set out on a campaign to win his friendship and his help. A steady flow of people were always in and out of Carter's home, and now the smiling, chatty Ruby went into action and became part of the crowd.

"She would come over to Ben's, and sometimes the girls would be with her, sometimes not," recalled actor Lennie Bluett. Ruby seemed to thrive on the rush of show business, the new people, the new contacts, the social affairs, and the opportunity to always be *on,* on stage and off. At Carter's and other gatherings, her girlish laughter and high pitched voice could be heard throughout the room. Usually, she was engaged in chatter about her daughters. She joked, she mimicked, she parodied. Anything was done for a laugh, for attention, or for a job.

"She was always trying to get the girls in vaudeville or anything she could get for them," said Bluett. "Pushing. Pushing. Pushing.

Ruby was a typical stage mother," he said. "She wouldn't trust any-one near them."

Carter thought the girls were cute and talented and brought them into a group of about fifteen kids he had organized. Known as Ben Carter's Pickaninny Choir, the group performed locally and in parts of northern California.

The act would open with Carter standing before his young Pickaninny Choir. "Good morning, little children," he would address them. "And the good Lord's blessing. Have the little chocolate drops learned their Sunday lesson?" In unison, the kids answered, "Yeah, man. Yeah, man. And how we've learned our lesson."

They would be followed by the Boys Quartet. Then the trio, the budding Dandridge Sisters, who were often dressed alike with ribbons and bows in their hair, sang and danced.

Carter's material itself was, of course, little more than soft Old-South-docile-*negra*-style imagery. Just the type of thing that Dorothy would have absolutely no part of once she reached adulthood. But being a part of the choir worked well for the girls. Their appearances with Carter's group lasted about two years. Afterwards the three girls teamed with two brothers, Eugene and Freddie Jackson, to form a quintet called the Five Rhythmatics. The five kids rehearsed among themselves, usually under the direction of Eugene Jackson, who was older than the others and had already appeared in the *Our Gang* series and *Hearts in Dixie*. "We had a good act with the Rhythmatics," Etta recalled. "The trio would sing and Freddie and Eugene would do most of the dancing and we'd have like little skits in between and then we'd do something together, the three of us and the two boys togeth-er. And we'd have a grand finale."

The five got bookings in outlying communities like Bakersfield, Victorville, Santa Barbara, and Long Beach. They also played at the-aters in Los Angeles and occasionally in other states like Arizona. The girls would pack their gear into a car while Ruby drove them to the engagements. At the theatres, Ruby dealt with the managers or pro-prietors, checked on the layout of the places, and made sure the kids were paid. The work was steady. "We wouldn't work too much dur-ing the week," said Etta. "But we'd work on weekends." The Five Rhythmatics appeared together on and off for the next five years.

These were still hard, lean times for Ruby, but she remained deter-mined. She found employment for herself through the Negro unit of the Federal Theatre Project of the Works Progress Administration (WPA) program, which kept her going for years and further helped her extend her social contacts. She also sang with the Hall Johnson Choir, the Black choral group whose voices were heard in such films as *Green Pastures* and later *Tales of Manhattan* and *Cabin in the Sky.*

❦

An important break came in 1934 when the trio entered an amateur radio show contest along with over 25 White contestants in Los Angeles. "We were the only Blacks that I can recall in the contest," said Etta. Heard throughout the city on the broadcast, the three little Dandridge Sisters came in first place. "At that time, when there was a great deal of prejudice," said Vivian, "we were shocked that we won. It gave us the inspiration to keep going ahead as the Dandridge Sisters."

Afterwards, Ruby pushed even harder to find movie work. She sought the help of Black casting director Charles Butler, who was employed by Central Casting, the agency that acted as a clearing house in employing extras for all the studios, to cast most of its Black extras. "To get bookings in the movies," said Etta, "you would have to go through Butler, who would have you go out and audition at the studios."

Accompanied by Neva, Ruby carted the girls over to Butler's office. Like Ben Carter, he believed they were talented. He also found work for Ruby and Neva, as extras or in bit parts. Neva appeared in the Shirley Temple movie *The Little Colonel,* as a mammy-like servant. About all Neva proved was that she was a terrible actress: overdone and hammy. But it was work.

More importantly, Charles Butler recommended the girls for a spot in a musical called *The Big Broadcast of 1936.* Being filmed at Paramount Pictures, the movie was little more than a pastiche made to cash in on the popularity of famous radio and vaudeville stars. But it was a big production featuring such headliners as Bing Crosby, George Burns and Gracie Allen, Ethel Merman, Bill "Bojangles" Robinson, the Nicholas Brothers, and Amos 'n' Andy, played by its White creators Freeman Gosden and Charles Correll, in blackface.

The children were hired to perform in an elaborate song and dance sequence with Bill Robinson. The girls would not have a great deal to do, but Ruby knew it was a plum assignment that, because of Robinson, would guarantee them some attention, at least within Black Hollywood. Bill "Bojangles" Robinson had first become a major entertainer—a dazzling master of tap—on the vaudeville circuit and later in such movies as *The Little Colonel* and *The Littlest Rebel*, opposite Shirley Temple. Bojangles was the man who taught little Shirley to tap-dance up a staircase in a sequence that remains a classic in the history of the American movie musical. By this time, he was about to become Hollywood's biggest Black star, possibly bigger than Stepin Fetchit. The girls were starting off at the top.

The Big Broadcast of 1936 is probably the earliest record of Dorothy Dandridge on film. She was barely thirteen years old at the time. With Etta to her right and Vivian to her left, Dorothy joins a singing Bojangles as part of an exuberant street crowd in a long, intricate shot. Dressed alike with big bows in their hair, the girls looked perfect; nothing out of place and full of energy and optimism. Though the trio wasn't billed in the credits of *The Big Broadcast of 1936*, their movie career had begun. At Paramount, the girls also appeared—unbilled—in *Easy to Take*.

A highlight of the film was the famous pair of young tap-dancing brothers, Harold and Fayard Nicholas. The girls had no scenes with the Nicholas Brothers but would meet them within a few years at New York's Cotton Club.

Shortly afterwards, The Dandridge Sisters were booked by E. K. Hernandez Productions to perform for several months in Hawaii with the circus. "We were there during Christmas," recalled Etta, "from the latter part of 1935 and the first part of 1936."

Because the job was too good to pass up, Ruby had taken them out of school for several months. Unlike the movie studios where tutors were required for children, the circus made no such provisions. The three girls did visit different high schools, where each did projects. "We thought that would be satisfactory for us once we got back to school in Los Angeles," said Etta. "But when we got back, our school in Los Angeles said that the projects wouldn't give us enough credits. Because of that, I ended up graduating a semester later. But Vivian and Dorothy didn't graduate at all."

Once back in Los Angeles, Ruby found new engagements for the girls, most of which were one night stands in one city or another in the area. At theatres and clubs, they appeared on bills with entertainers like Mantan Moreland, Nat Cole, and dancer Marie Bryant, whom the girls, according to Etta were startled to see "smoking reefer. Men at the clubs were also starting to eye the sisters. "When I think about it now," said Etta, "I wonder how we worked those clubs. We were so young." Though school remained secondary, Dorothy and Vivian were still expected to attend their classes. But it was tough. "The one thing that got me were the night gigs," Etta remembered. "You're so tired the next day in school."

Ruby and Neva—still striving to give the girls an even more polished and professional image and sound—eventually enlisted the help of two young musicians and arrangers. One was Nat Cole, a tall, lanky, Alabama-born fellow, who was then struggling to make a career for himself in show business. The other was an arranger/composer named Phil Moore, who had recently come to Los Angeles from Seattle.

Moore was immediately struck by Dorothy. "She was very pretty even then and very different," he said. He saw that she was a dreamy romantic without much time to be a little girl. "The hardest thing about rehearsals," said Moore, "was pulling Dorothy off her bicycle to come inside and rehearse." He also observed the way Ruby pushed her daughters. "She never let up," he said. "All Dorothy and Vivian really knew as kids was work. It was their whole life."

If it ever occurred to Ruby that her daughters might prefer playing with other children or cuddling a doll or hopping on a bicycle, she quickly brushed such thoughts aside. What she never took into consideration was how the girls felt about show business, if all of this was indeed the kind of life that *they* desired. Already Dorothy was beginning to have serious doubts and questions—and a growing ambivalence about this thing that Ruby and Neva called a career. She and Vivian swore that once they were grown, they would get out of show business for good. "We never told our parent, of course," said Vivian. "but we both said, no way." Ruby, nonetheless, appeared oblivious to their feelings. Dorothy and Vivian were "pretty much expected to be successful," said Jeanne Moore Pisano, who years later married Phil Moore and befriended Vivian Dandridge. "I get the sense that there was manipulation going on. There was nothing that had to do with being a kid and having a home and people who love you and take care of you. I never got that sense."

Away from Hollywood and all of Ruby's hopes for movie work, there was Cyril Dandridge, still living in Cleveland with his mother Florence and bewildered by the turn of events in his life. The past few years had left him frustrated and frantic. In court, he had continued his pursuit of Ruby, still trying to have his marriage dissolved. But by 1930, he had lost track of his wife, who seemed to have completely disappeared. He questioned Ruby's cousin and other relatives but without any luck. If they knew Ruby's whereabouts, they were not saying. Worst of all, for Cyril, there was no trace of his daughters.

In June 1933, he returned to court with a new divorce petition. But with no address for Ruby and no idea where she had gone, Cyril was advised by his lawyer to take out an advertisement in a newspaper, publicly notifying Ruby of the divorce. If she failed to reply, a divorce would automatically be granted him. The advertisement, ran in *The Daily Legal News* for six consecutive weeks and mistakenly listed her as Ruby E. rather than Ruby B. Dandridge, it read:

> *DIVORCE NOTICE*
> *Cyril Dandridge vs Ruby E. Dandridge*
> *Ruby E. Dandridge, whose place of residence is unknown, will take notice that on June 6, 1933, the undersigned Cyril Dandridge filed his petition against her in the Court of Common Pleas of Cuyahoga County, Ohio, praying for a divorce and relief on the grounds of gross neglect of duty and wilful absence for more than three years last past. Said cause will be for hearing on and after the 21st day of July, 1933.*
> *Cyril Dandridge*
> *By John P. Green, his attorney.*
> *June 8-15-22-19; July 6-13*

When no response came from Ruby, Cyril finally won his divorce. But it came, of course, at a price.

In the years that followed, Cyril Dandridge, sensitive and saddened, sought to find Ruby and to establish contact with his children, whom he believed had been stolen from him. He remained frustrated. But had he slipped into a movie theatre in 1937 to see the Marx Brothers' feature *A Day at the Races,* he would have been truly startled. There he would have briefly glimpsed two pretty teenage girls performing right along with Groucho, Harpo, and Chico and a group of others in a musical sequence. The two pretty girls would be none other than his daughters Vivian and Dorothy.

By then though Ruby had won. He had lost his daughters. They in turn had lost him.

By the mid-1930s, Ruby secured the services of a Hollywood agent, Arthur Silver, who agreed to become the girls' representative and help find them more movie work. They reported to Columbia Pictures for a musical sequence in *It Can't Last Forever*. The entertainment paper *Variety* dismissed this comedy starring Ralph Bellamy and Betty Furness as trite and "nothing of much note save for the comedy team of Aramanda and Lita" and "a quintet of Colored kids who are spotted in a street dance." The kids were Dorothy, Vivian, and Etta along with two adolescent boys—their friend Eugene Jackson from the Five Rhythmatics and his partner Charles Bennett—billed as The Jackson Brothers.

But the great excitement came when Ruby learned of MGM's plans for *A Day at the Races*, starring the Marx Brothers. Scheduled for this major film was a production number set in a Black shantytown and featuring the song "All God's Chillun Got Rhythm." When Harpo Marx insisted that Black performers be used in the sequence, the Black newspaper *The Pittsburgh Courier* reported that over 1,500 Black applicants showed up to audition.

Ruby pulled out all the stops to get the girls in the movie. First, she spoke to Ben Carter, who handled the casting with Freita Shaw and could be counted on to push for the girls. But the ace up Ruby's sleeve was Phil Moore, who was hired by MGM to arrange music for the film. Finally, the girls were signed to perform as part of a singing/dancing crowd scene in the big musical number featuring the Marx Brothers and vocalist Ivie Anderson.

Growing up in a household where almost every conversation had centered on show business, the girls knew the significance of this film and arrived at MGM barely able to contain their excitement. Sitting on 167 acres in Culver City, MGM was like a city unto itself with executive buildings, star bungalows, a private zoo and schoolhouse, a hospital, park, and private lake. Here was the studio of Hollywood's most glamorous gods and goddesses: Garbo, Spencer Tracy, Jean Harlow, Mickey Rooney, Joan Crawford, Norma Shearer, Wallace Beery, and Clark Gable.

"I remember how thrilled we were about all the big stars," recalled Etta. "When I saw Clark Gable on the lot, I just ran over to him and asked him for an autograph and told him I loved him. He smiled at me, and I just melted. Dorothy and Vivian were excited about being on the set. But there were so many people in the picture. You just more or less did what you're told. I don't even remember meeting Ivie Anderson."

The shantytown sequence appeared late in the completed film when Harpo, Groucho, and Chico end up in a backwoods Colored section of town. In the midst of this poverty, there are happy faces and high spirits. The Blacks shoot craps and are ready to sing and dance. Life just can't keep these folks down. And so Ivie Anderson with the Crinoline Choir performs an exuberant version of "All God's Chillun Got Rhythm." Dorothy, Vivian, and Etta are among the free-spirited group, and are also seen briefly among the group singing with the Marx Brothers during the film's racetrack finale.

Both sequences were a perfect antidote for gloomy Depression audiences in need of signs and signals of optimism and endurance; pure hokum that was a lopsided tribute to an old cliché: the joyous resilience of the downtrodden, in this case, the Black downtrodden. Nonetheless, the sequence would live on in the memories of generations of moviegoers. In her adult years, Dorothy would always speak proudly of having appeared in the movie, no matter how brief that appearance had been.

The trio returned to MGM to shoot a sequence for a two-reel 1938 musical short *Snow Gets In Your Eyes*, and starring Virginia Grey and Roger Converse. Again Phil Moore, who arranged music for the short, helped the girls get on the picture. Dressed as if they were Swiss milkmaids and with Moore in a Tyrolean hat in the background, they sang "Harlem Yodel."

The girls were also signed to appear in Warner Brothers's *Going Places*, which featured Louis Armstrong. In this racehorse comedy, which starred Dick Powell as a salesman who pretends to be a world-famous horseman (partly to impress a young woman played by Anita Louise), Armstrong was cast as a groom to a very eccentric horse. The animal could gallop at lightning speed, but only to the sound of music. Consequently, Armstrong sings "Jeepers Creepers" to the horse in one of *Going Places*'s most famous scenes. Dorothy, Vivian, and Etta appeared in a musical segment where they joined Armstrong, jazz singer Maxine Sullivan, and a host of other Black performers to sing "Mutiny in the Nursery."

Both Ruby and Neva hovered around the set of *Going Places*, watching out for the underaged girls, and also looking out for their own interests. Neva landed a bit part—as a laundress carrying a laundry basket, who is frightened out of her wits by the sight of the galloping racehorse.

All these early films—*The Big Broadcast of 1936, It Can't Last Forever, A Day at the Races,* and *Going Places*—required the girls to adapt to the rigors of filmmaking. Before the shoot, they endured lengthy rehearsals to block the musical sequences. Afterwards, they had to be up by dawn and into the studio for makeup and costumes.

On the set, they were expected to know what marks to hit and the importance of remaining within the frame. Sequences often had to be repeated. But peak energy levels were required as much on the fourth or fifth takes as on the first. Almost overnight, the girls mastered the art of maintaining their concentration and harnessing their energy. Again their training had prepared them.

For these teenagers, learning the ropes at the studio also meant understanding the industry's covert social and racial codes. At the studios, race was both an issue and a non-issue. Some big stars could be pleasant and liberal, in fact more liberal than most other Americans. But the men who ran the studios were another matter. So, too, were the grips and technicians working on the set. Once the cameras rolled, talent was respected. Once the cameras stopped, the Black performers were confronted with the familiar biases and prejudices.

Working on a movie like *A Day at the Races*, the teenage Etta Jones didn't remember any instances of discrimination. But Black actor Lennie Bluett recalled that the studios sometimes could be unexpected hotbeds of racism. During filming of *Gone With the Wind*, Bluett, working as an extra, said he was so shocked to see signs for lavatories that were marked "Colored" and "White" that he and other Black actors protested. Their efforts went nowhere until Bluett approached Clark Gable, whom Bluett said was outraged by this treatment of the Colored performers. Once Gable voiced his anger, the signs, said Bluett, were removed.

At the studio commissaries, the girls discovered how socially and professionally stratified Hollywood was. Stars dined only with other stars; executives, producers, and directors, only with their likes. Extras were seated apart. Even within that stratification, race further delineated a place for performers. Always at lunchtime, Black performers ate among themselves, usually by choice.

But they were keenly aware of the unspoken rule that relegated them to a certain section of the commissary. Black actor Mel Bryant described the commissaries as being "partitioned off. They didn't have a sign, but it was implied that you didn't go beyond this point." Even big-name Black performers like the Nicholas Brothers in the 1940s were seated in a cafeteria with the grips and carpenters. That is, until they complained. Thereafter they were permitted in the stars dining quarters where they indeed belonged.

In the years to come, there would also be talk about Hattie McDaniel who, after having given a powerful performance in *Gone With the Wind*, wasn't invited to the film's glittering premiere in

Atlanta. The studio believed Southerners would be enraged at seeing a Black woman at the festivities.

A precocious and perceptive Dorothy picked up on these industry attitudes, never permitting herself, even as a little girl, to suffer from any illusions about the barriers and parameters—both overt and covert—for African Americans in the movie capital. "I didn't see the racism then," said Vivian Dandridge. "But Dottie did. And she talked to me about it. Even then." Yet, precisely (and ironically) because of her awareness of the racial lines, codes, and policies, she believed, perhaps idealistically, such old attitudes could be broken down.

Ruby, however, seemed oblivious to the racial situation. Not that she was unaware of it. She wasn't. She was far too shrewd for that. Instead she didn't appear to let the racism affect her, or to make any serious dent in her consciousness. And she was certainly not going to let her feelings about Hollywood and race upset the apple cart. Work was primary to Ruby's survival. She had no time to concern herself with social or racial inequities, or with any questions about African American images in the movies. Any racial slights or incidents at the studios were ignored by her.

By the late 1930s, Ruby could take satisfaction in having achieved some of her goals: she and Neva had ushered the girls into the movies and also created an act that would lead her daughters and Etta to successful careers as young women. The Dandridge Sisters were known by all of Black Hollywood. As teenagers, the girls had worked more than many twice their ages. They were not stars, but Ruby knew— and Dottie and Vivi understood too—that they were on their way somewhere. Ruby also knew that a very important contact had been established for the girls during the filming of *Going Places*. Louis Armstrong had become fond of them and taken an interest in their careers. "He was so kind," said Vivian. "He went out of his way to help us. To an extent that he interested his [manager] who was in New York." The manager was Joe Glaser. Known as being crusty, sometimes crude, and often enough obnoxious, Glaser was not an easy man to please. But he too liked the girls and worked out an arrangement with Ruby, thereby becoming their manager. Ruby, of course, still made all the decisions and handled the money, but she was happy to let Glaser, with all his push and pull, handle engagements for the trio. She was even happier when Glaser said he wanted to bring them to New York.

But while Ruby and Glaser discussed the girls' future, Dottie and Vivi still complained between themselves of being weary with show business. The same grueling schedules, the dulling rehearsals, the try-outs, the costume fittings, the constant demands on their time, and the unvaried backbreaking discipline it required were becoming too much for them. Yet as ambivalent as they were about continuing their careers, the sisters knew no other life.

As Depression-age teenagers who had always had it drummed into their heads that they had to work for the family, they never openly complained or questioned anything. They also dutifully turned their earnings over to Ruby to put into the household kitty; a habit that Dorothy kept for years afterwards.

By now, both Dottie and Vivi had also developed glistening exteriors, charming personalities, and lovely manners. Dorothy, with her surface calm and delicacy, and Vivian, with her carefree extroversion, bore no outward signs of discontent. But the discontents were there, and they ran deep. Those like actor Lennie Bluett, who saw the family up close, knew that "there were a lot of personal problems between Ruby and those girls."

By the time Dorothy was fifteen and Vivian sixteen, their emotions had become all the more guarded; their fears, all the more concealed; their family secrets, all the more kept to themselves. Their professionalism served as a mask, a protective shield, for the underlying tensions and the ebbing pangs of adolescence.

In the tight quarters of their home at 5516 Fortuna, where one walked from the street right into the small living room, where the small dining room was converted into a bedroom for Ruby and Neva, where Dottie and Vivi shared a small bedroom, where the small kitchen was the only other room, where the tiny bathroom was the one private area, where the linoleum that ran throughout the house gave the place a cold, artificial feel, where the spotlessly clean and neat rooms that were without any untidy corners concealed a deep set of dark emotions, Dorothy still felt barricaded and near suffocation.

Theirs was a home without relief or refuge for either Vivian or Dorothy. The sisters were frank about their feelings for Ma-Ma. Simply stated, they loathed her. Yet Dorothy seemed more aware and articulate about the state of their lives, more resentful and questioning than Vivian. Why was most of their time spent working? Weren't she and Vivian really supporting the family? Why was Ma-Ma given such control over them? Why hadn't Ruby remarried—surely many men would want her, Dorothy reasoned—and gotten away from Neva? Listening to her sister's questions, Vivian never had answers and admitted to rarely thinking about their domestic situation as deeply as Dorothy.

"The childhood affected her one way and affected me another," said Vivian. "She didn't like her childhood. She felt that as children, we were exploited, which we were. Not because they wanted to exploit us because they were just mean or horrible people. I hate to say it. It's a mental state. But my sister, Dottie, didn't like being exploited. At the time I didn't agree with her that we were being exploited. Dorothy was ahead of her time. Mentally. Things that she used to tell me I found out [later]. About people. About racial problems and things. About family."

Yet despite her resentment and despite her mixed feelings about show business itself, Dorothy still harbored dreams—very intense, very concrete—of becoming an actress. That was pretty much the single fixed goal throughout her life. She was one of those rare people who early on knew exactly what she wanted to do. And surprisingly under her delicate exterior, she was highly ambitious. Somehow she also understood that show business itself, with its demands for schedules and performances, kept other feelings at bay and offered some escape from her miserable homelike. At least at the studios or even at the clubs, she was in larger open spaces and not cramped in a few tiny claustrophobic rooms with Ma-Ma and her far too accommodating companion Ruby.

By the late 1930s, Dorothy and Vivian no doubt fully understood the nature of Ruby's and Neva's relationship. Neither sister used the word lesbian to describe that relationship. They would grapple with fully accepting it for years to come. Their difficulties were simply exacerbated because of Ma-Ma's cruelty and her power over them. Both Dorothy and Vivian were still regularly beaten by Ma-Ma. As their bodies changed and they developed into pretty teenagers with figures that young men started to notice, the girls were plagued with additional problems. "I have a feeling that Dorothy blossomed very early," said Jeanne Moore Pisano. "She must have been a beautiful little girl and became a stunning woman very quickly in a system that could care less about having any respect." Ma-Ma became obsessed about the adolescent girls' virginity, or the fear of the loss of that virginity. Especially Dorothy's.

Daily, Ma-Ma pulled Dorothy aside, forced her to remove her upper garments, and then tightly bound up the girl's budding breasts with heavy muslin cloth. She did the same to Vivian, although Vivian later joked that Ma-Ma had done so without much success. Vivian became an amply endowed young woman with large, full breasts and full hips. But Dorothy was Ma-Ma's main target. During Dorothy's teenage years, if she appeared even mildly interested in a boy, Ma-Ma became enraged and questioned her relentlessly.

Ruby never intervened to speak up for either daughter. "She agreed with everything Ma-Ma said Dottie and Vivian should do," said Dorothy's friend Geri Branton. "Everything. The things that went on in that house must have been so horrible that it's a wonder Dottie could even sleep at night. It had to be just awful for her."

Vivian had other problems. Her childhood friends knew, recalled Avanelle Harris, that Ruby "made a definite difference between the girls and it was a very bad thing. It was frowned upon throughout the city. Ruby raised her daughters with Dorothy as the little princess and Vivian as her handmaiden. It was just obvious that Vivian had to be in the background and that Dorothy was Cinderella." Juliette Ball remembered that Ruby "had pictures of Dottie all over the house."

"All her hopes and dreams were tied up in Dorothy," said Etta Jones, who recalled an incident that had occurred during the filming of *Going Places*. When the director wanted one of the girls to dance with Louis Armstrong, he decided Etta would be best. But Ruby, sitting on the set in typical stage mother fashion, sprang to her feet and protested that Dorothy should be the girl to dance. When the director insisted on still using Etta, Ruby told him, "Well, if Dottie D. don't do it, ain't nobody going to do it."

"That got her nowhere though," said Etta, who recalled that the director stared at Ruby and told her, "Look, you go take your seat and sit back down."

"She favored Dorothy in everything," said Etta. "Ruby didn't care not one blessed thing about Vivian."

The manner in which Ruby slighted Vivian was ironic because Vivian was so much like her: outgoing, spontaneous, blessed with a sense of humor, and able to function in a world that could be insensitive and cruel. Yet by ignoring Vivian, Ruby appeared to want to stamp out a part of herself, as if she believed her own assets were Vivian's flaws. Dorothy, on the other hand, was still like Cyril, the husband Ruby had rejected: sensitive, basically quiet and withdrawn, gentle. She had also fully inherited Cyril's looks. Every time she looked at Dorothy, Ruby must have seen all the qualities she had once loved in him, or perhaps the qualities, especially the delicacy, she might have wanted for herself.

But what ultimately appeared to draw Ruby to her younger daughter was Dorothy's talent and her drive and focus. The young and pretty Dottie might one day have the kind of career the middle-aged and dowdy Ruby knew could never be hers. Then, too, Ruby took comfort in the fact that Dorothy (despite her resentments and ambivalence) never rebelled, never confronted her, never tried to force her to look in the mirror, as Vivian eventually did. Ruby's preference for Dottie may also explain why Ma-Ma was so unrelentingly cruel towards the girl, whom she must have perceived as a rival for Ruby's affections.

Yet Ruby's feelings about her daughters were more complicated. Others who observed the Dandridge household felt that Ruby didn't care but so much about either daughter.

"You would have never known that Ruby was their mother," said Juliette Ball. "Ruby never wanted either one of those girls. Ruby told everybody she never wanted children. She told the kids, too."

From Vivian's comments, Jeanne Pisano concluded that Ruby "was clearly incapable of any kind of maternal feelings or instincts, which had to have been from day one. The daughters had to be strong to survive. That's clear. The rest is just really very sad. There was clearly no ability or interest in actually raising her children. It appears as if she just abandoned them to the wolves and cleaned up later on being the mother of a famous daughter."

Or as Clarence Muse put it bluntly, "She didn't care a damn about those kids."

During these years, Ruby seemed frustrated by her own profession-al disappointments. Though she was willing to battle with anyone to insure that her daughters found work, Ruby, unlike most stage mothers, wasn't content to sublimate all her ambitions into her children and to recede into the background as the girls became more successful. She also yearned for the spotlight and pursued her own aspirations.

"She wanted to be up there herself," recalled Lennie Bluett. "She wanted to be on stage. To hell with Dorothy and Vivi." Yet what work Ruby found in the 1930s brought her no attention and took her nowhere. Only later, in the 1940s, did Ruby's career flourish. In the house on Fortuna, even Dorothy and Vivian may have realized that other than Neva, Ruby's main focus was always herself. Rather than favoring either daughter, Ruby most favored Ruby.

More and more during her teenage years, Dorothy withdrew, slip-ping comfortably into her private dream world to forget how miser-able she felt at home. She had gone from being a friendly, funny little girl to becoming a dreamy, melancholic adolescent on the brink of an uncertain womanhood. Vivian noticed the change. Dorothy's moodiness—and the bouts of serious depression that were beginning and would simply grow within the next few years—sometimes made her snap at her older sister. "She always wasn't that pleasant with me," said Vivian. Yet she trusted no one else.

Regardless, in 1938 Dorothy was about to have her first escape from the house on Fortuna Street when manager Joe Glaser informed Ruby and Neva that he had secured a booking for the Dandridge Sisters at the Cotton Club in New York. Ruby and Neva knew it was an extraordinary opportunity. So did the girls. Fortuna turned alive with excitement over the news.

Immediately, schedules had to be lined up. Music had to be arranged. Phil Moore was called in to work on new numbers for the trio. Rehearsals were set up. Then bags were packed. Discipline as always, the girls were reminded, had to be strictly maintained. The fact that Dorothy and Vivian, now attending Jefferson High School, would miss the first part of the school year, was never an issue for Ruby. The girls could always catch up on their education at another time. Etta had already graduated from Jefferson that past year. Dorothy and Vivian planned to catch up on their studies later and graduate from high school within the next two years. Of course, that never happened.

Amid all the plans and excitement about the Cotton Club, the only problem was, as always, Ma-Ma. Ruby decided not to make the trip. "Ruby was with the WPA and she needed her job. They had a place downtown where Ruby studied drama," recalled Etta. Plans were made for Neva to travel with the girls to New York as guardian and chaperon.

But even that news, awful as it was, was secondary to Dorothy. The Cotton Club promised a taste of freedom and a fresh adventure that she, Vivi, and Etta eagerly set out on.

THREE

THE DANDRIDGE SISTERS

*I*t was late summer in 1938 when Dorothy, Vivian, and Etta, and the omnipresent Auntie Ma-Ma arrived in New York City. The nation's great slump was easing and the girls were ready to kick up their heels, have some fun, and take in the splendors of the city, much of which came from something as simple as rushing for the subways—those roller-coaster modes of travel.

The girls spent some of their free time exploring Manhattan with a gregarious singing trio called the Peters Sisters—Anne, Virginia, and Mattie—who happened to be staying in the same apartment building on Seventh Avenue in Harlem, not far from 125th Street. They had gotten to know Virginia in the days when they worked with Ben Carter's Pickaninny Choir, so they already felt at home with the young women who, like themselves, had successful show business careers. The Peters Sisters had appeared in clubs, theatres, and musical sequences of such Hollywood films as *Ali Baba Goes to Town, Love and Hisses, Happy Landing,* and *Rebecca of Sunnybrook Farm.* All three sisters had beautiful voices, but specialized in a kind of musical comedy based on how they looked. Each of the young women weighed over two hundred pounds. Still fun, with or without friends, would still be in short supply for Dorothy, Vivian and Etta. Most of their time would be used in preparation for their engagement at the Cotton Club.

Neva took them downtown to shop for gowns that would make them look like young women, rather than girls. Roger Segure was hired to do new musical arrangements. His would work better for the Cotton Club than the music previously arranged by Phil Moore.

Tutors were brought in so that Vivian and Dorothy could keep up on their studies. Because she had already finished high school, Etta was permitted to skip the lessons but nothing else. Their days were crammed with rehearsals, fittings, and meetings. It was exciting, but most exciting of all for Dorothy, Vivian, and Etta was finally seeing the Cotton Club. "We were ecstatic about the Cotton Club," said Etta.

Already in business fifteen years, the Cotton Club was still the night spot for fast-moving, glitzy, talented Negro entertainers; the place that Whites rushed to and that gangsters ran; and still steeped in legend and lore, unlike any other club anywhere or anytime before. The original Cotton Club had opened in the fall of 1923 and was located in Harlem on 142nd Street. Dorothy, Vivian, and Etta appeared at the new downtown location at 48th and Broadway. They didn't know that they were walking through its door towards the end of the club's illustrious history. It was soon to close up shop: June 10, 1940.

In many respects, the Cotton Club was the cradle of a new brand of popular culture that spread throughout the nation. *Crossover* wasn't a word then used, but the Cotton Club's great Black stars did cross over and invigorated American nightlife and entertainment with a whole new style.

This was the club where Ethel Waters moved audiences to tears, singing "Stormy Weather," a tale of love gone wrong; where Bill Robinson, a cool emblem of urbane savoir faire, breezily tapped circles around other performers; where Ellington and Calloway led their legendary bands; and where a lineup of "tall, tan, and terrific" chorus girls stomped, sashayed, and showed off their wares. Patrons streaming into the club held the belief that here the unexpected and the extraordinary could happen any moment.

The club offered the girls a new world of personalities, sensations, and experiences. Backstage was a steady flow of gossip, laughter, stories, intrigues, and nasty rivalries. Chorus girls were courted by aging sugar daddies, while well-heeled, sexy, young "White boys" prowled the club, looking over the fresh lineup of beauties. Handsome male singers and dancers also had beautiful women fawning and swooning over them. Most of the chorus girls were high up on what African Americans called "the high-yellar pole," and all originally required to be at least 5'6" tall and under twenty-one. All were giddy at the prospect of being appreciated for their unique beauty.

Only five years earlier, within the ranks of the chorus line, a copper-colored teenager named Lena Horne had first sought to make a name for herself. Stories abounded of the way the young Horne's mother sat on guard outside the chorus girls' dressing room, to make sure none of the gangsters got near her daughter. The girls learned that some dressing rooms were to be avoided. Those with the aroma of marijuana wafting out from them. Those known to be occupied by horny old dudes.

The girls were excited to be assigned a dressing room with singers June Richmond and Mae Johnson. "We thought we were so grown," said Etta. But they were also shocked by Johnson. "She was neurotic and some things she said were just so vulgar."

Also appearing on the bill that fall of 1938 were headliner Cab Calloway and his band, guitar-strumming Sister Rosetta Tharpe, the contortionist Jigsaw Jackson, and three dance teams. Timmy and Freddie. The Berry Brothers. And most spectacular of all, the fabulous Nicholas Brothers. Just seeing these faces was a heady experience for the girls.

Away from home and the heat of Los Angeles, the sisters were pumped up with an exhilarating feeling of freedom. This was in part due to their New York City surroundings and in part due to the fact that they were developing into—even prettier—young women. Auntie Ma-Ma, hovered over them to make sure that nothing untoward took place. She remained hard on Vivian but still even harder on Dorothy, who delighted in the exposure to this brave new city and its unique urban rhythms. Here, as in the years to come, when traveling through Europe, Asia, and South America, she soaked up as much of the new cultural wells as possible.

Pixieish and girlish, she was not yet the womanly "knockout killer beauty" that singer Bobby Short said he encountered in Los Angeles in the early 1940s. But with her magnetic dark eyes, her lush golden color, and a beautifully developing figure, she could enter a room and literally have it turn silent. Everybody had to take at least one quick peak at her.

When she strolled with Vivian and Etta along the avenues of Harlem or in downtown Manhattan, all eyes fell on Dorothy. Sometimes, Vivian recalled, people actually stopped and stared. "My sister was just gorgeous," said Vivian. "When she woke up in the morning, she was gorgeous."

On the day that the girls arrived at the Cotton Club for their first rehearsals, Vivian remembered that Ma-Ma quickly assessed the young men in the club and admonished them, "Do not come near these girls. They are flirtatious. They are silly. They are virgins." She let the fellows know if there were any hanky panky, "I'll have you thrown in jail."

Ma-Ma stayed by the girls' sides during rehearsals and even during casual conversations the girls might have when taking breaks for meals—to make sure the wolves didn't get too close. Because Etta was older, she was given more leeway. Yet Etta too understood that Auntie Ma-Ma's orders had to be followed. Ma-Ma, however, still appeared obsessed with Dorothy's looks; she was relentlessly fearful and paranoid about the girl's virginity.

In Los Angeles, Dorothy hadn't quite understood Ma-Ma's suspicions and fears about men pursuing her. But in New York, she became aware, for the first time, of the effects her looks had on people, but not yet the power it could give her. "I have a feeling that she never knew how pretty she was," said Vivian Dandridge, "or how beautiful. You know other people did. But she never really did." Only later in adulthood, said Dorothy's close friend Geri Branton, did Dorothy *use* her beauty, as she began her fierce and determined climb to stardom.

On that first day, Dorothy also came face to face with Harold Nicholas. He was the younger of the Nicholas Brothers, the show business act who many felt were America's greatest dancing team and perhaps later its most underrated.

Harold was on stage rehearsing with his older brother Fayard when Dorothy walked by. He practically stopped dead in his tracks. "I met her right away," Harold recalled. "It was like instant-wanting-to-be-with-her. To get close to her." He couldn't take his eyes off her. Nor could Fayard Nicholas.

"My brother and I," said Fayard, "saw these three pretty little girls. And we said, 'Ah, they're lovely.' And I looked at Dottie right away and said, 'Ooh! That's a lovely girl.' The other girls were lovely too. But Dottie had something. Personality and everything. And my brother was looking at her too. She was just 15 years old then. But she was blossoming."

Despite the Nicholas brothers' impressions of her, Dorothy was far more impressed by them. In the world of Black entertainment of the 1930s and 1940s, the Nicholas Brothers were certified princes. Gifted with style, presence, and a superlative talent, these young monarchs were already well on their way to becoming legendary performers.

Like Dorothy and Vivian, the brothers had spent their lives in show business. Bred and weaned on entertaining, they knew little else.

Their parents Viola and Ulysses Nicholas, both talented and accomplished performers themselves, led a band at Philadelphia's Black vaudeville theatre, The Standard. Viola played the piano. Ulysses played the drums. The couple had three children: Fayard, the oldest; a daughter Dorothy; and then Harold, the youngest.

By the age of three, Fayard, precocious and observant, sat in the Standard Theatre fascinated by the performances of many of the greats: Louis Armstrong, singer Adelaide Hall, dancers Buck and Bubbles, and comic Dewey "Pigmeat" Markham. Confident he could have an act of his own, Fayard became a self-taught dancer and mimic, who entertained the neighborhood kids with his deft impersonations of all the Black stars he had seen. An inveterate movie-goer, he was also enamored of Hollywood talents. His favorite comedian was silent screen star Harold Lloyd. When his mother gave birth to a second son, Fayard asked that the infant be named after the comedian. Harold Lloyd Nicholas was the new baby's full name.

When Harold was five, Fayard took him under wing and taught him everything he knew, which was already quite a bit. Fayard was a brilliant teacher: imaginative, patient, thorough, enthusiastic, eager to experiment with dancing styles and dedicated to perfecting his technique.

Recognizing the boys' talent, the parents Viola and Ulysses were encouraging and eager to promote them. They were convinced that their sons could become stars on the vaudeville circuit. Harold and Fayard made their professional debut in 1931 on a radio show, no less, "The Horn and Hardart Kiddie Hour." It may seem odd and unlikely to feature dancers on radio now, but listeners were then content to listen the sound of their magnetic taps.

The next year, when Fayard was eighteen and Harold ten, they made their first appearance at the Cotton Club. By then, they were quite a team; an incomparable, perfectly coordinated pair that could execute elaborate lightning-speed turns, spins, and splits. Fayard was lean and taller with an innate elegance, a smooth effortless style, and the ability to expressively use his hands as forms of dramatic flourish and punctuation for his dance. Harold, shorter, cuter, impish, and playful, had a youthful sexiness, and like Fayard, joyously mastered style and technique. The audiences loved them.

For the next seven years, they worked at the Cotton Club, performing with the great bands of Duke Ellington, Jimmie Lunceford, Lucky Millinder, and Cab Calloway. Harold also played the drums and did crackerjack impressions of Bill Robinson, Louis Armstrong,

Josephine Baker, and Cab Calloway. To accommodate the demands of their sons' careers and to better manage their engagements, Ulysses and Viola moved the family from Philadelphia to a large apartment in New York at 321 Edgecomb Avenue.

In a short time, the brothers' accomplishments extended beyond the Cotton Club. In 1932, they appeared in their first movie, the musical short *Pie Pie Blackbird* with Eubie Blake's orchestra and that doomed goddess of *Hallelujah* fame, Nina Mae McKinney. Two years later, they were back before the cameras in Hollywood in the Eddie Cantor movie *Kid Millions*. While in Los Angeles, they also appeared at the Cocoanut Grove. The next year they appeared in the movie short *An All Colored Vaudeville Show*. Then came *The Big Broadcast of 1936*, in which—unknown to the brothers—the girls had also appeared. And another musical short *Black Network*, again with Nina Mae McKinney. On his own, Harold performed in the movie *Stoopnocracy* and also *The Emperor Jones*, which starred Paul Robeson and Fredi Washington.

But tragedy struck the Nicholas family when Ulysses Nicholas, traveling by car to join his boys in California, suffered a fatal heart attack. Viola Nicholas, a strong and shrewd businesswoman, then managed her sons' careers.

Afterwards Harold and Fayard performed on Broadway under the direction of George Balanchine in the *Ziegfeld Follies of 1936*, along with Fannie Brice, Bob Hope, and Josephine Baker, who had just returned to the United States eleven years after becoming one of Europe's most famous stars.

The brothers also sailed abroad to appear in London in Lew Leslie's *Blackbirds of 1936*. Then George Balanchine cast them in another Broadway production *Babes in Arms*.

By 1938, much of the greatest work of Fayard and Harold still lay ahead of them. In such 1940s films as *Tin Pan Alley, The Great American Broadcast, Orchestra Wives,* and *Down Argentine Way*, the Nicholas Brothers invigorated the American movie musical and turned dance inside out with their highly kinetic style.

Within the Negro community, the brothers were talked about, fawned over, and, of course, spoiled like crazy, living in a world of privileges and comforts. During the height of the Great Depression, Harold and Fayard were squired around town in a chauffeur-driven car. When they crossed the Atlantic for their first European appearances, they carried their own movie camera and documented the trip with a series of lively home movies, which have remained one-of-a-kind historic glimpses into the past lifestyles of the young Black rich and famous.

Harold and Fayard were also free to roam amongst the patrons of the Cotton Club when it was taboo for other entertainers there to do so. Management policy dictated that the Black entertainers be seen only onstage, never in nor near the audience. But "we were just kids," said Fayard. The leniency of the Cotton Club management paid off for the boys in some very particular ways. On one occasion, Tallulah Bankhead was so charmed by the brothers that she asked Harold if there was anything he wanted. When he told her that a bicycle would be grand, Bankhead promptly had one delivered to him.

"I was in awe of these kids who as kids were making more money than most adults," remembered actor Joe Adams, who later appeared with Dorothy in *Carmen Jones*. "They were such perfectionists. When I was a kid, I used to go to the barber shop on Central Avenue [in Los Angeles], and they went to the barber shop when they were in town. They would pull up in their limousine and get out. Every Black kid was trying to be one of the Nicholas Brothers or something like that because that was what was going on. Then Joe Louis came along and everyone had to be a prize-fighter."

At the clubs, the chorus girls adored Harold and Fayard. And Harold and Fayard in turn adored them right back. Throughout most their lives, both brothers would always have devoted, glamorous women by their sides. In the romance department, Harold, even as a teenager, was a precocious sophisticate, a boyish Lothario, with few equals, who was capable of seducing women older and seemingly more experienced.

Unusually close, the brothers, however, were quite different. Fayard, sometimes called Big Mo, was the more outgoing: friendly, peppy, optimistic, funny.

Harold, sometimes called Little Mo, was a party creature who loved the vast network of friends, associates, gatherings, happenings that were so much a part of show business life. Though he possessed great charm, he was nonetheless considered remote, snobbish, and cold in the eyes of some.

"He was a great talent but arrogant," said Etta Jones, "and spoiled by all those showgirls at the Cotton Club." Said Fayard Nicholas, "A lot of people had a hard time knowing my little brother."

People always had to come to him. He rarely seemed interested in initiating friendships. Unless, of course, it was a woman he was pursuing. Though he knew how to please and satisfy women sexually, his interests usually stopped there. Emotional attachment did not appear to be part of the equation. When he did feel attached, he did not readily admit it.

Harold kept a tight lid on all his feelings. His private fears and pain remained exclusively his. Perhaps in the world of show business where everybody was always *on* and eager to articulate, dramatize, and perhaps even trivialize his or her feelings, he found the best route to sanity and survival was by opening up *only* when he danced. No one really knew what was going on in his head.

Well-aware of the phenomenal success of the Nicholas Brothers, Dorothy was not aware of, nor prepared for, their reputations as ladies' men. Or to be more precise, for Harold's reputation. True that backstage in the dressing rooms, the chorus girls dropped hints. But Dorothy was too young to take such comments seriously. Nor was she in any way prepared for Harold's emotional distance. About all she knew that first day of rehearsals at the Cotton Club was that Harold Nicholas was watching her and that she was flattered. He didn't have to open his mouth because his eyes—locked on her—said everything.

The two quickly became friends. "We'd just play around. I'd ask her questions," Nicholas recalled. "Make her laugh." He took to calling her the Duchess. Years later, he admitted to being struck most by her beauty, and the ripples it generated among the sea of men, young and old, at the Cotton Club. But he was drawn to her in a way he hadn't been to the other women who paraded in and out of his life. Maybe it was her sweet temper and wholesomeness. Most girls and women were eager to accommodate him, not giving a second thought about "putting out" for this little potentate. But Dorothy's ladylike demeanor and impeccable manners set her apart. Perhaps her most endearing quality was her sensitivity. Time and again in later years, he emphasized that "she was *very* sensitive." That acute sensitivity, he believed, ultimately caused her unbearable pain.

Dottie liked Harold from the start. Fayard recalled, "I was trying to get to know her better. And my brother was trying to get to know her too. And he won out. Dorothy and Harold hit it off fine. They became very good friends. And so I just backed out. I started going out with Etta."

Of course, the Dottie/Harold budding courtship did not go unnoticed by Ma-Ma, however. She permitted the two to see each other but only under the supervision of a chaperon, almost always herself. Obviously, she was a bit more tolerant because the young man in question was, after all, the famous Harold Nicholas. But she kept her guard up. Never at this time, said Harold, did he and Dottie have *dates*. Harold and Fayard visited the Harlem apartment where Dorothy, Etta, and Vivian stayed. The girls in turn visited the Nicholas family home on Edgecombe Avenue.

"We would invite them to our apartment. Of course, Ma-Ma would be right there with them," said Fayard. "She was really firm. And she wouldn't let anyone get too close to the girls. It was all right if the girls would go with us. But she would be right there too. We were never alone with them in New York. They were lovely girls and they listened to everything Ma-Ma would tell them." Harold recalled, "Auntie Ma-Ma was pretty rough on Dorothy, I think, because Dorothy was the prettiest of the three, and Ma-Ma knew all the guys were going to try to get next to her. So she was very strict. I mean *extremely* strict with Dottie."

Still, despite Ma-Ma, Fayard remembered that he and Harold had wonderful times with the girls. When together, the five teenagers talked and kidded around. On some occasions, "Harold and Dottie hit the subways," Etta said. The two were thrilled with these fast-moving vehicles. Etta and Fayard spent time together, often riding around town in the car driven by the brothers' chauffeur Lorenzo Hill.

Other times at the Nicholas home and also the apartment where the girls stayed, the brothers brought out their movie camera. Fayard concocted melodramas for them to act out. Then as their chauffeur Lorenzo operated the camera, the five performed as if on a Hollywood sound stage.

One cowboy saga, partly filmed in Central Park, featured Etta as a pretty damsel in distress, being accosted by some hooligans. When she cried out, Fayard came to the rescue, backed up by Harold with a pistol in his hand and a huge cowboy hat on his head!

Another featured Dorothy as a pretty well-to-do girl in her apartment. The brothers soon start fighting over her but are interrupted when her maid shows up to announce, "Dinner is served." The maid was played by Vivian. These home movies forever capture a radiantly young Dorothy Dandridge, whose eyes are alive with joy and promise.

Otherwise Ma-Ma's grip remained as firm as ever. After all, the girls were in New York to work. They had to produce and make something of themselves. There couldn't be a lot of time for playing around. Nothing was much different from the tours as The Wonder Children. During the day, Neva saw that the girls were tutored, or she rehearsed them.

Then on September 28, 1938, The Dandridge Sisters opened at the

Cotton Club. On that evening and those that followed, the trio was a fabulous sight with a wonderful sound. Three pretty young Black girls—transformed into junior league divas—beautifully gowned and coifed, who sent spirits flying and set hearts a pitter-patter when they sang "A-Tisket A-Tasket," "Swing Low, Sweet Chariot," and joined Cab Calloway for "Madly in Love."

On stage, the Dandridge Sisters represented one glamorous girl in three. Etta was the lively one with the highest voice, who seemed as if she were ready in a split second to outdance and outmaneuver the others. Vivian was the dishy one with the lowest voice; the most aggressively sexy of the three and also the funniest, with a cute naughty girl twinkle in her eye and her smile. Dorothy, singing lead, was the soft, young one, warm, sensitive, sincere, not as knowing as the others. Together they were all things to all the men in the audience. For women watching them, they were fetching symbols of progressive young Black womanhood.

The critics liked them too. "Their style is refreshingly unique," wrote *Variety* in its October 12, 1938 review of the new Cotton Club show. In a second review of the girls' act, the paper's reviewer commented: "Dandridge Sisters, introed [sic] by Cab Calloway as from the Coast, are something of a sepia edition of the Andrews Sisters. They swing the pops and nursery rhymes in much the same rhythmic style, also giving a jeep interpretation to 'Swing Low Sweet Chariot.'" The reviewer added, "Girls are light-skinned and nice-looking, with the middle femme especially strong vocally."

Now their work schedule grew more demanding. Daily, Neva had the girls downtown at the club by late afternoon. Usually, they were allowed to take a subway by themselves. It was a huge show, Vivian remembered. "Just fantastic. We had to do three shows a night. And that was a bit grueling. Seven o'clock supper show. Then the next show was maybe around ten. And then we'd do a show after midnight." That later show, said Fayard, was at two in the morning, nightly. Afterwards they were whisked away by Ma-Ma. "We were never permitted to socialize at the club," said Etta. "Ma-Ma was stricter about that kind of thing than Ruby, who could be lenient. Ma-Ma came to the club and took us home on the subway."

Nightly, as she sang with Vivian and Etta, Dorothy discovered even more how to gauge a crowd's attitudes and perceptions. She learned to extend something the audience liked, be it an expression or a movement; to cut back on something that didn't work. Her training taught her that on some occasions, she had to skillfully or subtly take the audience in a direction it had not anticipated. Movement was important. Never would she stand motionless on stage. The use of her dramatic eyes and smile also helped her punctuate a lyric's meaning. From this point through the 1940s, her work was much like that of a playwright still testing the waters with an out-of-town, pre-Broadway production.

During this time, she was also discovering how to perform for an audience with a different set of cultural expectations and references. Until now the girls had entertained for mostly Black audiences with whom they could use vocal or body shorthand to sum up an attitude or mood. A hand on the hips immediately meant one thing to a Black audience. A shimmy of the shoulders meant another. But at the Cotton Club, the clientele was usually all White. Unless a famous Black American arrived at the club, the establishment had a strict policy of not admitting Black patrons.

That meant Dorothy had to communicate with them in ways they could understand. It also meant that as a Black woman, she had to lead them around to her point of view. Later when she performed for audiences, Black and White, her performances could be a delicate balancing act. Her choice of material—pop standards or show tunes—said one thing. Her playful attitudinizing said another. But never with a White audience could she let any feelings of cultural dislocation or isolation affect a performance. That was quite a feat in this era before American society had become fully integrated; a time when most Black performers still found mixing with a White audience an alien experience.

For a woman who later hated nightclub work, Dorothy had few pains at this time. But then while performing at the Cotton Club, all expectations didn't fall solely on Dorothy Dandridge. She had the support of Vivian and Etta—psychologically and physically—who were right there by her side. Still, even this early, she began thinking of performing on her own. She still hoped to become an actress, too.

Backstage at the Cotton Club, Dorothy also learned to contend with the men, Black and White, who hung around. "She liked the attention," Harold Nicholas recalled. But she *always* kept her distance.

"All the guys at the club were talking about her even at her young age," Harold recalled. "Everybody liked Dorothy. *Everybody*." But all those hot and horny fellows at the Cotton Club knew that no matter how much they might salivate or how strong they might come on, she was not one of those easy overnight conquests. In fact, not a conquest at all. If a fellow enjoyed the chase, then Dottie was perfect because a chase was all a guy would get.

She had been raised so strictly that sex was acceptable only when accompanied by a wedding ring. But a little flirtation here and there never hurt.

The Cotton Club engagement drew the attention of the press, not only in New York, but in other parts of the country. One of those places was Cleveland. Cyril Dandridge learned of the girls success and was determined to see them. Perhaps he might explain to them who he was and what had happened so many years earlier.

At a theatre in Cleveland where Bill Robinson was performing, Cyril made a bold move. He managed to speak to Robinson, whom he knew had worked with Dorothy and Vivian. Cyril explained who he was. Then he pled his case. And a good plea it must have been because Robinson placed a phone call from the theatre to the Cotton Club.

Dorothy remembered her surprise upon answering the phone. Robinson told her that he had just met her father, who wanted to speak to her. Cyril was put on the line. He told Dorothy and then Vivian that he wanted to see them.

But Dorothy and Vivian were puzzled and confused. "They had been lied to by their mother and Neva," Dorothy's friend Geri Branton said. First the girls had been told he had died. Then they were led to believe he had deserted them.

"My mother had not mentioned him in ten years," Dorothy said. "He was dead to her, dead to us."

Not knowing what to think or feel, Dorothy and Vivian agreed to see him. Informed in Los Angeles of the call, Ruby apparently realized it was foolish to forbid the meeting.

Soon afterwards, Cyril came to New York. For a man accustomed to a quiet, restrained existence, the noise, the rush, and the crowds of New York must have been jarring. So, too, must have been the emotional experience of finally reaching his daughters. At the New York station, he was met by Dorothy, Vivian, and Etta, who arrived without Ma-Ma.

"I knew him when he got off the bus," Dorothy said. "I guess it was because of his smile."

"He was not tall," recalled Etta. "He was nice looking." But Cyril was confused by seeing three girls. "We were all dressed alike in black and white outfits. We did it on purpose," Etta recalled. "He didn't know who was who. He couldn't tell us apart. He didn't know who to go to."

"Not me," Etta told him. "Those two over there."

Then his excitement showed. "But it was a very strange feeling being with your father, a man you don't know, and you're 16," Dorothy said. "Then he wanted me to turn around because he wanted to see what I looked like. I was embarrassed. I can't tell you how strange I felt. All I know is, I just wanted to get away. So I just made some kind of excuse and disappeared."

Cyril was not, however, about to disappear. "He came to the house," said Etta. There he tried his best to get to know his daughters. During the visit, Dorothy introduced him to Harold, now openly acknowledged as her first boyfriend. Not long afterwards, he returned to Cleveland. For Cyril, the visit must have been a heartwrenching experience. After all this time, contact with the daughters he loved so much had been established, but he still had no real relationship with them. For Dorothy, who was still more like him than Vivian, he was a stranger.

For years to come, the situation with Cyril remained awkward, troubling, and emotional for all involved. Later, in therapy, Dorothy struggled to work out her anger and also her feelings of abandonment and betrayal, as well as her unspoken desire to love him. She always felt something was "missing because I never really had a father, even though Mother was both mother and father to me and my sister." Vivian later saw more of her father and established a relationship with him, but said little about Cyril to Dorothy and their mother Ruby. Ruby, whose animosities and bitterness remained deeply ingrained, did all she could to thwart any rapport or affection that might have developed between her daughters and their father.

When the Cotton Club season ended, Dorothy said goodbye to Harold. But they promised to stay in touch. The Nicholas Brothers went off to perform in South America. The Dandridge Sisters, having been so successful at the club, were booked for another season.

In January 1939, their schedule became even more hectic and tiring. The girls began performing—with Bill Robinson and Louis Armstrong—across the street from the Cotton Club at the Strand Theatre, where the film *Going Places* had just opened. The girls appeared in the stage show before screenings of the film. There could be several shows a day. Daily, they were shuttled back and forth between the Strand and the Cotton Club. Eventually, all three lost their voices.

"It was strenuous," Etta said. "We'd come off the stage at the Strand and have to go in the room with this vaporizer to get our voices together to do The Cotton Club show. Oh, it was just a mess but we loved it."

By the spring, the Cotton Club engagement came to an end. Afterwards the girls embarked on yet another phase of their young careers.

Joe Glaser met with Neva and spoke to Ruby in California about the trio's future. Having seen their success in New York, Glaser believed work could be found in Europe, which since the glory days of entertainers like Josephine Baker and Florence Mills, offered Black performers great opportunities often denied in the States. He began plans for engagements in England, Ireland, and Scotland, which would start in June.

Ruby remained in Los Angeles, where she worked in the race movie *Midnight Shadow*. Again Ma-Ma was left in charge of the children. Soon their bags were packed to set sail for England on the Queen Mary. Three teenage Black girls on a world-famous oceanliner.

Their first stop was London for performances at the Palladium. Headliners were American comedian Jack Durant and Jack Harris' band. Because the girls arrived late in England, Ma-Ma felt they didn't have enough time to rehearse and refused to let them open with the new show on June 12th. Instead they appeared a week later to good reviews. "Dandridge Sisters, harmonizers," wrote *Variety*," worked nicely with the band."

Their arrival occurred just as the threat of war loomed over London. Only a couple of months before, in March 1939, Hitler's troops had occupied Czechoslovakia. In April, Italy seized Albania. Great Britain and France then abandoned their policy of appeasement, and Europe stood on the brink of another world war.

Despite the fears of war, the girls were surprised to discover that, strangely enough, a festive air permeated London, allowing the girls to feel even more liberated than they had in New York. The Peters Sisters, who were very popular with European audiences, were again the girls' neighbors at the hotel where they stayed. They spent more fun times with the sister act.

"They would tell us, 'Don't worry about cooking or anything.

Come on and eat with us,'" Etta recalled. "Our meals at the Peters were like a banquet."

Some afternoons, Dorothy, Vivian, and Etta strolled down West End, where passersby were often surprised at seeing these three little sepia girls. "Heads were turning," Etta said. When they went for a walk with the Peters Sisters, even more people stared. "The Peters Sisters dressed alike and we dressed alike and when we walked down the street," Etta said, "the people just went boom, boom, boom, boom. Cause we were real little and they were real big."

London-born jazz critic Leonard Feather, then still living in England, was also impressed with the trio, on stage and off. "I caught the Dandridge Sisters' show at the Palladium," said Feather, "and one night, at a club called Elma Warren's Nut House, met them: Dorothy and Vivian Dandridge, sixteen and seventeen years old, protected by a chaperon who was on hand to preserve their virginity and keep them out of the clutches of predatory males."

In Europe, as at the Cotton Club, Dorothy was again the focal point of attention. After her opening at the Palladium, a line of would-be suitors lay in wait. "You couldn't get anywhere near Dorothy," said Feather. "She was unapproachable. Everyone was rushing to meet her."

The irony was that while Vivian and Etta were ready for fun and frivolity, the prettiest girl in town didn't appear to be interested in anyone. "She didn't have a whole lot of friends." said Etta. "She would rather be by herself."

Vivian understood her best. "You didn't get to know her that easily," said Vivian, who believed many people mistook Dorothy's aloofness for arrogance about her looks. "She was very shy. She wasn't outgoing. She wasn't conceited, which many people thought because she was so gorgeous. But Dottie really wasn't conceited at all because I would have to get after her about getting new clothing and things like that, many times. Even later when she was wealthy."

"One of the reasons that she wasn't overly friendly is because she had a certain insecurity, strange as it seems," Vivian said. "Dottie was always a little bit afraid of people."

She struck up a friendship with a young British girl her age but otherwise still preferred Vivian's company to anyone else's. Around her, she never flinched from revealing her moods. Or her anger about the discipline the act required; about the fact that their lives were nothing but work, appearances, travel, and tight schedules; about the fact that they still had to answer to Ma-Ma. But while she was never at a loss for words with Vivian, Dorothy otherwise withdrew from most people.

While Dottie kept to herself, Vivian began seeing Leonard Feather, who recalled that they had "an immediate affinity." A romance bloomed between the two. At the time, the twenty-five-year-old Feather wondered what his parents would have thought. His previous relationship with an older woman had been kept secret because he knew his family would disapprove. "She wasn't even Jewish, for God's sake," he said. But the relationship with Vivian, "brief and innocent though it was, would have struck them as doubly dubious: she wasn't even White, for God's sake." Feather's parents were one matter. Ma-Ma was another.

"Somehow she was permitted to go out with me," Feather remembered, "and we spent a series of pleasant evenings together which we felt, in our self-deceiving way, were romantic. That was not hard to understand, at least from my point of view. I had felt isolated from the girls of my own social group: the nice, middle-class Jewish types who thought alike, acted alike, married alike. They had nothing to say to me, nor I to them. Vivian and I had something in common immediately—music—and mutual friends."

One evening Vivian and Feather organized a farewell party for musician Coleman Hawkins, who was heading to New York after a five-year stay in Europe. Held at a Chinese restaurant in Piccadilly Circus, the party was a lively affair with guests that included a couple of the Mills Brothers and the Heralds of Swing, the guitarist Norman Brown, Ken Johnson and trumpeter Dave Wilkins, and of course, Etta and Dorothy. "We were high more on the music than the liquor," Feather said. How Ma-Ma ever let such an evening slip past her is anyone's guess. But as Etta recalled Leonard Feather fell "madly in love with Vivian when we were in Europe."

Yet Ma-Ma continued to monitor Dorothy's comings and goings, and if something displeased her, she still struck the girl. "She beat me till I cried, and then she beat me because I cried," said Dorothy. In time, Dorothy managed to block out the abuse, which could occur two or three times a week, and accepted it without showing any emotion. Ma-Ma was more careful in London though, said Dorothy, to "choose occasions when she would turn on me. She couldn't do it when people were around, when we were onstage, or when we were in transit. It was a privately done and timed performance of her own." That would explain why Etta never recalled seeing either Dorothy or Vivian abused.

During the tour abroad, however, an incident occurred that left Dottie shaken. One day as she and Vivian relaxed in their London flat (Etta had apparently gone out), Neva suddenly told Dottie to go to her bed. As Dottie, puzzled, did so, Neva questioned her about her virginity. At first Dottie couldn't understand why she was being grilled. Then she realized the cause of the urgent questioning was because the young unmarried British girl (around Dorothy's age), with whom Dorothy had grown friendly, had become pregnant. Apparently, paranoid that Dottie might be in the same predicament, Ma-Ma wanted proof that the teenager was untouched. Dottie protested that she had done nothing. But Ma-Ma was not satisfied. As Dottie lay on the bed, Neva suddenly lifted Dorothy's dress and ripped off her undergarment in order to examine her vaginally.

Dorothy was shocked and frightened, unable to understand Ma-Ma's behavior. Having been taught to obey and respect this woman, she felt emotionally paralyzed and unable to defend herself. Ma-Ma, however, said she wouldn't hurt her. But when Dorothy cried out for her to stop and then tried to get off the bed, Ma-Ma pushed her back on the bed and then forcibly examined her. Amid Dorothy's screams and struggle with the woman, Vivian became so frightened that she fled into another room.

Finally, Dorothy raised her fist and slapped Neva's face. Surprised and enraged, Ma-Ma hit the girl again "across the face, the back, anywhere her hands could reach. I didn't cry out, but held my hands to my head," said Dorothy. Then Dorothy struck Ma-Ma just as forcefully. In these fevered moments, she decided never again to endure the punishments and humiliations that Neva dished out. "I was in a rage. I had never struck her before, nor anyone, but it felt good." She hit her repeatedly until Ma-Ma called for Vivian to help her and then fell on the bed exhausted. Dorothy ran from the room in tears. But she had won.

"That was the last time she ever put her hands on me." Dorothy said.

Later, though, Dorothy told Harold Nicholas and her friend Geri Branton about other incidents with Neva, which seem to indicate that her bizarre psycho-sexual behavior may have resumed in the States. Vivian, though, appeared to escape such examinations, even though by her own admission, Vivian was far more outgoing with boys than Dorothy.

Ruby learned of Neva's actions but apparently said nothing. "She saw nothing wrong with it. She thought it was right that Neva did that!" said Geri Branton.

Dottie, however, felt as if she had been raped. Though her rebellion against Neva signaled a newfound assurance, the incident left her emotionally scarred, and understandably, even more resentful of Neva and determined to get away from her.

Vivian recalled her younger sister's new resolve: "She told us that someday she was going to do a single." Vivian said. "We asked, 'Why?' because we were sort of leaning on her. And she says 'Because I think I'd like to.'" Vivian understood that Dottie's attitude also had something to do with the fact that she still bristled at the thought that Etta was billed as a Dandridge sister.

No love was lost between Dottie and Etta. "The two of us weren't friendly," said Etta, who found Dorothy "erratic" and "highly emotional." "But being in the trio with Viv and Dorothy, it was a job. In the act, we got along. We never fought and argued. But she was a strange person."

After appearances in London and such cities as Birmingham, Liverpool, and Manchester, the Dandridge Sisters departed for their engagements through Ireland and Scotland, but their tour was cut short by the start of the Second World War. Europe was terrified as Germany invaded Poland that September 1, 1939. Two days later Great Britain and France declared war on Germany. Everywhere the girls went, they saw warning signs of the impending hardship. People were hoarding food. They avoided coming outdoors after dark. Fear was etched in the faces of the people they saw. Then came more air raids, blackouts, and then the bombs.

"They were blowing up all the train stations and everything in Europe," Etta recalled. "Ma-Ma had to go and change our plans." She quickly arranged passage home on the *Ile de France*.

"We went over tourist. But Ma-Ma changed to first class in order for us to get back to the United States because we were caught in the war over there," Etta remembered. Throughout the trip back, Dorothy, both exhilarated and frightened, became seasick and was mostly confined to her cabin.

Once the girls returned to the States, they had little time to reflect on their experiences because Joe Glaser put them to work. In the fall of 1939, they were booked into the Cotton Club again with Bill "Bojangles" Robinson headlining. Again they performed three shows a night.

Then they went into rehearsals for the New York musical *Swingin' the Dream*, which was a swing adaptation of Shakespeare's *A*

Midsummer Night's Dream.   Changing the Elizabethan comedy's locale from ancient Athens to New Orleans in the year 1890 (at the time of the "birth of swing"), this lavish production, described as a "jitterbug extravaganza," had an impressive lineup of talents. Directed by Erik Charell and written by Charell and Gilbert Seldes, *Swingin' the Dream*'s choreography was by Agnes de Mille and its music by Jimmy Van Heusen and Eddie de Lange with "musical supervision" by Benny Goodman and Don Voorhees. It starred Glaser's client Louis Armstrong as Bottom.

Dorothy, Vivian, and Etta, cast as three pixies who performed the title number, found themselves working in a huge cast that included Maxine Sullivan (as Titania), Butterfly McQueen (playing Puck), Jackie "Moms" Mabley, comic Nicodemus (known later in his career as Nick Stewart), Dorothy McGuire, dancer Bill Bailey (brother of Pearl Bailey), Oscar Polk, and Juano Hernandez. The production also boasted some 120 musicians and scenery designed "after cartoons by Walt Disney."

Backstage at rehearsals, Ma-Ma appeared agitated and even more suspicious than usual. This time it wasn't because of some handsome young man hotly chasing after the girls but rather because of a female cast member. "She was skeptical because of Moms Mabley," Etta recalled. Throughout Black show business circles, Mabley was known as a woman without any qualms about showing her preference for women. Fearful that the girls might be approached by the comedienne, Ma-Ma warned them, "I don't want you anywhere *near* that woman. Don't go anyplace where she is. Don't go anywhere near her."

"Moms Mabley stayed away from us," said Etta. "I guess Moms was afraid of the evil eye of Ma-Ma herself."

During rehearsals, word spread among jazz aficionados and fans that *Swingin' the Dream* was a progressive production that made excellent use of its often underemployed Negro talents. But upon opening at Radio City's huge Center Theatre on November 29, 1939, *Swingin' the Dream* flopped. In *The New York Times*, Brooks Atkinson praised Benny Goodman and his musicians, notably Lionel Hampton, but otherwise labelled the production a "hodge-podge of Shakespeariana" that failed to make good use of Shakespeare or its Black talents. The other critics agreed.

But one reviewer, writing for a Chicago publication, had a different view, calling the production "a worthwhile evening's entertainment." He was quick to point out not only the performance of Armstrong as a "brilliant actor" but other cast members.

"Nicodemus, Oscar Polk, the sweet Dandridge sisters, Bill Bailey and Troy Brown all provide good interludes," he wrote. The critic was Leonard Feather, now in the United States and just as fascinated by Vivian Dandridge as when the two had met a few months earlier.

After just thirteen performances and reportedly at a loss of over $100,000, *Swingin' the Dream* closed, becoming, according to *The New York Times* reported, "one of the costliest failures of recent years." But now that The Dandridge Sisters had played legitimate theatre, Joe Glaser quickly lined up even better new engagements. Plans were afoot for a South American tour. Bandleader Jimmie Lunceford was also interested in hiring them as vocalists with his orchestra.

Other bookings followed. The Regal in Chicago. The Howard in Washington, D.C. When the trio was back in New York at the Apollo Theatre, Etta remembered, "In walked Leonard Feather chasing after Vivian." Their romance apparently continued for quite some time, and they eventually became lifelong friends.

Once Harold and Fayard returned from their South America tour, the brothers spent time with the three girls in New York. Dorothy and Harold continued their courtship. But they didn't have long to do so. The brothers were signed to appear in the Twentieth Century Fox film *Down Argentine Way* and soon left for Hollywood.

Ma-Ma also suddenly had to go to Los Angeles for some business, though no one was sure what her trip was all about. Years later Etta believed, in retrospect, that Neva had rushed to California because of fears of Ruby's involvement with another woman. At the time though, Etta didn't know anything about the sexual nature of Ruby and Ma-Ma's relationship. Whatever the reason, Ma-Ma's absence meant that for a brief spell the three girls would have the best time ever in New York. When Etta's father learned his daughter was in New York unchaperoned, however, he insisted she return to Los Angeles.

"I was eighteen and old enough to handle myself," said Etta. "But Viv and Dottie were not out of high school yet. So we had to go home. We had to call off the South America tour. All the advance publicity had been completed. It was a big deal."

Back in Los Angeles, Dottie saw Harold again, and their courtship picked up. Ruby liked both Harold and Fayard. Certainly, she relished the idea that her daughter's boyfriend was one of the biggest Negro stars in show business. Following *Down Argentine Way,* Twentieth Century Fox signed the brothers to a five-year contract, which was a rarity for African Americans in films. None of this was lost on Ruby or Neva.

The Dandridge Sisters then worked locally. In 1940, they reported to RKO Pictures for an appearance in the romantic comedy *Irene,* starring British actress Anna Neagle and Ray Milland. They turned up in a musical segment that occurred when Neagle goes off to the theatre for an evening of fun. As she waits for the show to begin, Neagle opens a program that lists the evening's entertainers. Here appeared the name of the Dandridge Sisters, which was the girls' only billing in the film. They were listed in neither the opening nor closing credits. In the sequence, the three are perched on a window sill—singing while looking down on a street parade of Black performers, led by robust Hattie Noel. The sequence was played mostly for gentle humor (with fun being poked at Noel's hefty size) and high spirits. But the voices of Dorothy, Vivian, and Etta were heard in perfect harmony, and the three had a couple of brief but solid closeups.

The great opportunity, however, came when the Dandridge Sisters were hired to tour with the band of Jimmie Lunceford, who had not forgotten their performance in *Swingin' the Dream.* Known as a polished, sophisticated performer who was a graduate of Fisk University, Lunceford conducted an orchestra that was considered one of the country's finest. A smooth showman, he understood how to dazzle audiences not only with his sound but also with an image. His big band was composed of a troupe of talented, well-bred gentlemen musicians, who were always impeccably dressed and perfectly groomed.

"The Lunceford band was the top drawing Black band in the world at that time," recalled Gerald Wilson, then the trumpeter with Lunceford. "We played everywhere. We were the first Black band to play the Paramount in New York City. It was a very suave band. If there were seven shows that night, we changed costumes seven times from top to bottom. Everything was big with the Lunceford band."

The fact that Lunceford wanted the Dandridge Sisters was an acknowledgment of their talent as well as their image. On stage, the three still dressed alike and harmonized beautifully with Dorothy still singing lead. They were the perfect stylish complement to his orchestra.

"They were good," said Wilson. "Sang real nice with nice orchestrations for the accompaniment. They were top notch. Bigtime. Very professional."

The girls were also still protected. Like everybody else in the orchestra, Wilson became aware of Auntie Ma-Ma's presence. His comment echoed those of everyone else: "She was very strict." Ma-Ma arranged that the girls, who played only certain venues with Lunceford, did not travel with the band itself.

"If they were going to be with us, they would meet us there," said Wilson. "I think Lunceford hired them for special theater dates," said Wilson. 'I don't remember them playing any dances, any nightclubs or ballrooms. They just did theatres."

When Lunceford played theatres, he put on an entire show with vocalists, sometimes dancers like the Berry Brothers, and also comedians, some of whom later became famous within the African American community. "Slappy White appeared. He was once a member of the Zephyrs," said Wilson. "Dusty 'Open the Door Richard' Fletcher might appear. Another was Tim Moore who later was Kingfish on television's *Amos 'n' Andy* show. He was just a comedian around New York then. Another comic was Johnny Lee who played Calhoun on *Amos 'n' Andy*. They were very good."

Once the comics and dancers warmed the audience up, the highlight was Lunceford—always urbane, elegant, and glamorous—as he conducted his orchestra of impeccable musicians. The trio's appearance simply capped the shimmering glamor and romance of the evening's entertainment.

The period with the Lunceford band was grueling but short. "We weren't with Lunceford that long," said Etta. "About a year and a half. We travelled so much. And us being young, doing all those one-night stands, it wasn't good."

But the Lunceford tour proved important to Dorothy's growing ambitions. Playing such cities, large and small, as Chicago, Boston, Baltimore, Kansas City, Washington, D.C., and Evansville, with Canadian appearances too, she reached a broader audience. The trio's style itself became smoother, more defined and polished to perfection.

"Dandridge Sisters trio have not been a regular part of the troupe, *Variety* wrote of the group's appearance with Lunceford at the Tower Theatre in Kansas City in April, 1940, "but their work on 'South American Way,' 'When' and 'Jumpin' Jive' falls right in line with the Lunceford style." By the next month, when the trio appeared with Lunceford at Chicago's State-Lake Theatre, *Variety* reported, "Dandridge Sisters are a neat little vocal trio, who sing three numbers pleasantly enough, doing best with their swing tunes."

In June 1940, the trio also went into a New York studio to make lively, well-orchestrated and arranged (some by Phil Moore, some by Roger Segure) recordings with Lunceford: "I Ain't Gonna Study War No More," "Minnie the Moocher Is Dead," "You Ain't Nowhere," and a big hit, "Red Wagon."

Years later critics sometimes wrote that Dorothy's range was narrow. Competitive rivals liked to say that she couldn't sing at all. But the Lunceford recordings remain testaments to her vocal talent. Hers was a mellow, inviting sound with a dreamy, girlishly sexy quality that blended beautifully with Vivian and Etta. Phil Moore thought she had a great sound and style.

Despite Ma-Ma's precautions, Etta began to date Gerald Wilson. The two fell in love and talked of marriage.

Dorothy had a short-lived crush on a member of the Lunceford orchestra, but Ma-Ma need not have worried. She still preferred Harold Nicholas to all the other young men surrounding her. Mostly, though, she remained a quiet, sensitive girl immersed in private fantasies, many no doubt about her future career rather than a romance.

In London, neither Vivian nor Etta had taken Dorothy's comments about leaving seriously. But by now, Dorothy's resolve to be on her own was firm and unalterable. Everything about her life had been managed and orchestrated by Ruby. Or monitored, checked, questioned, examined, judged, and criticized by Neva. Having constantly been pushed to meet their expectations, she sometimes was confused about her own hopes and aspirations. But one thing that she knew she wanted was the freedom to work on her own terms.

"I think she got tired of our rehearsals because there were three and you have to harmonize," Vivian said. "I don't think she realized that you still have to rehearse a lot. Let's face it, she was young." Vivian added, "This was just what Dottie *had* to do."

The trio itself no doubt came to represent another form of imprisonment in a suffocating and humiliating domestic situation. To break away from the group also might mark her first step in breaking away from the home on Fortuna Street and the control of Ma-Ma. To break away from the trio might be the crucial step toward understanding herself. "Dorothy was intelligent," said Phil Moore. "A bit dreamy at times. But always intelligent and sure of certain things she wanted."

"So she did have an ambition," said Vivian, "even though she was a shy person."

If she paused to review or reflect on her experiences, young Dorothy might have realized that already for an African American teenager, and a female at that, she had done some remarkable things. By the age of ten, she had toured the South and proven herself a thorough professional. Able to memorize lengthy material and perform the dance steps and acrobatics taught her by Ruby and Neva, she had mastered the discipline crucial to the success of any important career. She had also learned to smile and chat and be charming in public— and in private, to control her temper and to mask her most personal feelings.

By the age of fifteen, she had appeared in movies, played the Cotton Club, and worked with such top professionals as Armstrong, Robinson, Calloway, Maxine Sullivan, June Richmond, Sister Rosetta Tharpe, and, of course, the Nicholas Brothers. Then at sixteen, she had travelled through parts of Europe and seen the onset of a war. At age seventeen, she had appeared on the stage and also made recordings. If she ever seriously thought about it, she might have realized how heady an experience her life had already been. But Dorothy Dandridge appears to have been too focused on the future to look back.

Now this experienced young woman kept her eyes open for a way to break free and perform on her own. That happened following the Lunceford tour when the trio returned to Los Angeles. Etta and Gerald Wilson decided to marry, which meant that Etta most likely would have to live and travel with her husband. The trio would have to disband, so Dorothy assumed. Etta, however, felt otherwise. She believed she could be married and still perform.

Dorothy, however, was being considered for a low-budget Black film called *Four Shall Die*. She also auditioned for a stage production called *Meet the People* that had already opened in Los Angeles. The producers were looking for a replacement for an actress who had left the cast. That Dorothy sought a role in a White revue indicated her emerging belief that she could play any part; that indeed Negro actors and actresses should have a chance to be fully integrated into the theatre. And to do so without playing maids, butlers, or dimwits. Even now, she was venturing into new professional territory. The producers of *Meet the People* liked her and signed her on. Afterwards, she broke the news to Vivian and Etta.

"Dorothy's aspirations broke up the Dandridge Sisters," said Etta said. "Dottie always said, 'Well, I'm going to be a star.' Then she got the notice for *Meet the People*. Her first solo break. And she cut us loose." The last performance of the trio was with the Lunceford band at the West Coast Cotton Club in Culver City. For Vivian and Etta, it was a sad occasion. But for Dottie, it was the beginning of a new phase of her life.

CAREER, COURTSHIP, AND MARRIAGE

*N*ow Dorothy was on her own. A girl of eighteen. Ambitious, confident, focused. Her work was cut out for her. She had crossed an important threshold in the Hollywood Theatre Alliance's production *Meet the People*. Not only was she appearing by herself for the first time, but in a show with a White cast. It was quite a different experience from performing in a Black production with people whose rhythms, tones, attitudes, and language, she was so familiar with, but she adjusted quickly.

When it was announced that she would perform the role originated by comedienne Virginia O'Brien, many were dubious. Few thought Dorothy could be funny and successfully follow the hilarious, deadpan performance that had earned O'Brien critical kudos. But once center stage in this cast of thirty unknown performers who sang, danced, and poked fun at politics and Hollywood itself, Dorothy surprised all the cynics. When she sang her big number in the precise poker-faced style of O'Brien, she claimed the part as her own. It was a clever and deft performance. Harold and Fayard were in the audience as well as *Colliers* magazine writer Robert Andrews. He was bowled over by Dorothy, though heretofore he was not sure who she was or even how to spell her name. Andrews wrote that "a young Negro girl named Dorothy Dandrich [*sic*] did the [O'Brien] number. Wild arguments sprang up all over town as to which was better—and certain families are still a feudin.''

"She did it well," said Fayard Nicholas.

No longer known as one of the Dandridge Sisters, she was establishing a name on her own a new professional identity. But her home life was another matter. No one would have imagined that at home this well-mannered, sweet-tempered girl, who mixed well with the cast of *Meet the People*, still endured the reprimands and humiliations of Ma-Ma as well as the relentless stage-mothering of Ruby.

Ruby eyed her younger daughter's success in *Meet the People* and realized she had the stuff to succeed on her own. That meant that Dottie would have to be pushed. That also meant that Vivian would be moved aside even more by Ruby. The situation was not easy for either sister. Just when Dottie thought she had really broken free, Ruby was hovering over her as much as before.

"My overall impression of Dorothy is as a very sweet, naive, gentle person, who always wanted to please and be liked," said Dorothy Nicholas Morrow, the sister of the Nicholas brothers. "And I'm never too sure whether her ambition stemmed from her own inner desire or whether it was because of her mother and her distant aunt that she was living with."

Harold and Dorothy dated steadily. Now permanently based on the west coast, he and Fayard lived with their mother Viola Nicholas on 28th Street, near Adams Boulevard and Arlington Street. Usually, the brothers had heavy tour schedules but their contract at Twentieth Century Fox provided them with enough movie work to spend significant time at home.

Harold often breezed by Dorothy's house to pick her up in his blue Chevrolet. Energetic, optimistic, full of fun, still spoiled and self-indulgent, he was also clearly in love. Dorothy's attraction to Harold had grown strong as well. Curiously, some of the very qualities that drew her to him contributed to their later problems. Growing up with the belief that Cyril Dandridge had been weak and ineffectual, Dottie didn't want anything to do with someone she thought anemic, passive, or meek. "Dottie didn't like wimps," her future friend Geri Branton said. Instead, she would always be attracted to strong-willed, sometimes headstrong men like Harold.

Luckily for Dorothy, Ruby and Neva continued to eye Harold's courtship with approval. He was the perfect catch, not only successful but perhaps able to advance Dorothy's career. The women were eager to please him. Ruby—still outgoing, funny, and engaging with her high-pitched voice and seemingly scatterbrained personality—could prattle on and on about her Dottie and her Vivi. Or she could excitedly discuss the latest piece of casting news or the newest film scheduled to go into production. Anything that pertained to the world of show business was of interest to her. Neva too sought to make

Harold feel comfortable. Both women were fine cooks, who delighted in preparing meals and entertaining the young man.

"It was just a happy situation when I was around," he recalled. But he wasn't blind to the way that Ruby left Ma-Ma in charge of everything in the home. "She wouldn't dispute anything with Ma-Ma," Harold said. No longer was Neva binding Dottie's and Vivi's breasts to conceal their young womanhood. But as before, she unyieldingly set all the rules.

"We'd be schooled," Harold remembered of his courtship days with young Dorothy.

"Don't come in too late," insisted Neva, who set a curfew for their dates. Dorothy had to be home no later than eleven or sometimes midnight. Ruby never uttered a word.

Harold's and Dottie's dates were innocent. They were just two Southern California kids heading out to the movies; or visiting friends; or going for drives in the hills; or dropping in at the Black clubs in Los Angeles that Harold loved.

Harold saw Neva discard her mask of congeniality at least on one occasion when he and Dottie missed their curfew. As he hopped out of his car and hurriedly ushered Dorothy into the house, he suddenly saw Ma-Ma was waiting at the door. Furious that one of her cardinal rules had been broken, she openly expressed her feelings. "If you can't do any better than this," she told him, "I'm gonna have to stop you from coming around." She saved her stronger words for Dorothy.

At times like this, Dottie usually didn't say anything in defense of herself. "I know that sometimes Dorothy didn't particularly like all this strain that Ma-Ma put on her, about doing this and being like this and all that," Harold said. "I know that she didn't like that all the time." Yet she obeyed the rules of the house.

Harold recalled one evening, though, when Dorothy showed her anger. He believed the argument started because, once again, they got home past curfew. At first, the scenario seemed typical, but suddenly Dorothy raised her voice and actually "talked back to her," Harold recalled. "That's the only time I remember that anything happened in front of me. But for Dottie to talk back, it had to be something strong."

Dottie said little about her home life to Harold. But eventually, she described to him her most humiliating experience: the vaginal examination that Ma-Ma had given her. Otherwise she kept silent about her feelings for the woman and about the treatment she received from her for years. But she yearned to get away. She saw a chance to escape when Harold began to talk of marriage. But she held off;

despite the fact that like most young women of her generation, she was encouraged to accept marriage as her manifest destiny. She told Harold she wanted to wait.

"I think she figured we were too young, which we were," Nicholas said. "I was anyway." But too much was happening in Dorothy's life for her to consider marriage.

Always on the run, harboring dreams of an acting career, searching out for roles even while appearing in *Meet the People*, she kept herself working, often at a feverishly productive pace. During the early 1940s, she rushed from one movie studio to another for a bit part here or maybe a supporting role there. Helping to navigate her through Hollywood's rough waters was the agent Arthur Silver, who handled Ruby and had also represented the Dandridge Sisters.

In the fall of 1940, she won her first leading role in *Four Shall Die* at Million Dollar Productions, the company that specialized in producing race movies. Operating in Los Angeles, Million Dollar Pictures was run on the cheap by two White entrepreneurs, the brothers Harry and Leo Popkin, along with Black actor and Apollo Theatre emcee Ralph Cooper. All saw the possibilities of profits from Black movie entertainment for Black audiences. There were already between 800 and 900 Black theatres around the country showing such films.

Race movies—largely unseen by general White audiences and Blacks outside urban areas—were cheaply and quickly made. Horne, as well as other Black performers who worked in them, remembered low budgets, short shooting schedules, poor lighting or unflattering camera angles, and no assurance of getting paid.

Ralph Cooper had already written and starred in the 1938 race musical *The Duke Is Tops,* which Leo Popkin directed. A very pretty and then rather chubby young singer, who had recently had a baby, Lena Horne, was also featured. "Making the picture was no fun," Horne remembered. "First of all, there was trouble about money. The producers apparently had not completed their financing before starting up and they were paying off in promises of what we would make later, when the picture went into release." Shot in about ten days, the movie did so-so business, but later was re-released and retitled *The Bronze Venus* with Lena Horne's name blazing above the title on splashy full-color movie posters. It was the Popkin brothers' effort to capitalize on her new fame and success when she was at MGM.

Horne's director, Leo Popkin, also directed Dandridge in *Four Shall Die*. It too was re-released and retitled a few years later as *The Condemned Men.*

But *Four Shall Die* was a more ambitious movie making project for Million Dollar Productions. Even before production began, there were hopes that this film might become a breakthrough in the race movie market. The company boasted of having spent three months in preparation and research on *Four Shall Die*. Twelve special sets were constructed for the drama, which was conceived as a spectacle with large-scale action sequences. Four full camera crews, as opposed to the usual one, were used to rush through production and achieve a better look. Determined that *Four Shall Die* and its other features were to be shown nationwide, the company audaciously set out to establish a new distribution system with offices in Atlanta, Dallas, Chicago, and a special East Coast exchange in New York.

When shooting began on September 26, 1940, Los Angeles's Black newspaper *The California Eagle* announced, "Just about the biggest and hottest news this week, so far as sepia Hollywood is concerned is the fact Million Dollar Productions started their new mystery melodrama *Four Shall Die* last Thursday morning."

"The story by Ed Dewey, is a horror thriller of the Boris Karloff order, with a Haitian background," reported *The California Eagle*, "of mysticism, supernatural manifestations, weird in explicable climaxes, and Zombies or the 'walking dead.' This will be the first picture of its kind made with an all-colored cast."

Four Shall Die centered on a character named Pierre Toussaint, the fictional great grandson of Haiti's real-life legendary general Toussaint L'Overture. He is a detective trying to unravel a mystery. Playing the role was former Morehouse College and Wiley College football star Neil Webster. Also appearing was comic actor Mantan Moreland, best known as the chauffeur Birmingham Brown in Hollywood's *Charlie Chan* movie mystery series.

Dorothy was cast as the pretty ingenue, which didn't require much. But the fact that Million Dollar Pictures starred her in the production was a sign, even at this early date, of the strong impression she had already made on Los Angeles Black entertainment circles. Shot in about a week's time, the film was completed by October 2.

Convinced that *Four Shall Die* could broaden the appeal of race movies and reach a large audience, *The California Eagle* urged its readers to think seriously about the future of Black films and the importance of movie exhibitors willing to show such features. A columnist for the paper wrote:

> I just finished putting in 20 hours out of each 24 on the
> sound stages of Million Dollar Productions, watching them

make *Four Shall Die,* the most unusual picture ever filmed with an all-colored cast. . . .

But it has been brought to the attention of this race-proud scribe that recently there is a growing tendency on the part of the theatre managers who depend on colored trade to ignore their judgment as to movie fare....
If your neighborhood theatre boycotts all-colored cast pictures then boycott the theatre.

Despite the pre-production enthusiasm, *Four Shall Die* became something of a disaster. Million Dollar Pictures, even with its new distribution system, couldn't get the film into theatres. It didn't open in Los Angeles until almost two years later, in October 1942, at the Lincoln Theatre.

Four Shall Die, however, managed to get an earlier New York release, thanks no doubt to Ralph Cooper. Playing at the Apollo Theatre in December 1941, it caught the eye of mainstream critic Archer Winston at the *New York Post,* who wrote:

After a decent interval has elapsed, say once every three years, this department begins to hope that all-colored pictures may have come of age. True, the old ones were made on ten-cent budgets, no retakes, with nature's make-up, a stationary camera, and sets borrowed from deserted vaudeville houses. But after waiting three years and a few tantalizing glimpses of talented colored performers in what pictures, hope springs up again.

This article is by way of inviting hope to lie down flat for another three years. *Four Shall Die,* the all-colored picture at the Apollo Theatre on 125th Street, shows progress. That's all. The rate of progression is such that it must be inspected with a microscope.

That Winston didn't think much of the film wasn't as important as the fact that by reviewing it, he afforded the melodrama a distinction seldom reserved by the White press for race films. More significantly, he focused on young Dorothy. Remembering her recent appearance in *Sun Valley Serenade* (which actually was made after *Four Shall Die*), with the best of camera angles, lighting, and makeup, Winston called her a "pretty miss." But he noted that in *Four Shall Die,* she "doesn't look or act like the same person here. You would not think that direction, makeup, and photography could make such an amazing difference. This is by all odds the most interesting fact to be derived from the film."

No doubt those words struck home with teenaged Dorothy, who within a few years devised a striking *look* for the camera. But the experience of making the film must have been frustrating because few people saw it or even knew of its existence. Whatever Dorothy herself thought of it, she never mentioned the film in later years. And prints of *Four Shall Die* virtually vanished soon after its limited release. Still Dorothy had made an impression on Winston, who, like various other critics during these years found her presence unforgettable, even when she played small roles in forgettable films.

Million Dollar Productions remained excited about her too. The company began plans to star her in another race movie *The Dancer from Brazil*. That film was never made, but for a spell, she looked as if she might become race movies' next important leading lady.

In her scramble to keep working, Dorothy took singing engagements, too. At the close of 1940, she performed, along with Bing Crosby, Frankie Darro, Mantan Moreland, Sunshine Sammy, and the King Cole Trio, in a special Christmas benefit at which gifts were distributed to needy children. In February 1941, she appeared at the Cafe It in Los Angeles and also at the Orpheum theatre on a bill with the Floyd Ray orchestra and the Rayettes. Ray's wife Maggie Hathaway recalled that Dorothy later did scattered tour dates with the orchestra leader in San Francisco, Seattle, and other cities. Often, Dorothy spent her days on tour in tears because she hadn't heard from Harold, who was then on tour himself.

The next month, she was in front of the cameras again, this time at Republic Studios, which specialized in low-budget films. Ruby also worked at Republic and, along with Arthur Silver, helped get Dorothy cast as a servant girl in *Lady from Louisiana* with John Wayne and Ona Munson.

During the early forties, Harold Nicholas—just as Ruby and Neva had hoped and pushed for—netted a big break for Dorothy. Set to appear in a musical sequence in Twentieth Century Fox's *Sun Valley Serenade,* the Nicholas Brothers were to sing and dance to a new song by Mack Gordon and Harry Warren called "Chattanooga Choo Choo." Neither Harold nor Fayard thought much of the song. Both felt if the number were to work, it needed a little kick, perhaps "some femininity," as Fayard said, to liven things up.

Unlike Fred Astaire who danced with such beauties as Ginger

Rogers or Rita Hayworth, the brothers performed with one another. Their dance numbers weren't intended to be romantic or even vaguely suggestive of their sexuality. Now both Fayard and Harold thought that the act could benefit from some romance and that Dorothy could provide just the right tone and sex appeal. Nick Castle, the choreographer for the number, liked the idea.

Dorothy's agent was contacted. Then she went to Fox for the first rehearsal. But when she and the brothers listened to the song, Dorothy looked over at Fayard in disbelief. "We all felt the same thing, 'What the hell is this song?'" said Fayard.

Rehearsals began, nonetheless. Harold, Fayard, and Castle were careful not to put on Dottie the same kind of rigorous athletic dance movements that the brothers were known for. "We arranged things that she could really do with us," Fayard recalled. "We didn't tell her to do any splits or anything like that." Harold and Fayard remembered Dottie's excitement about working with them. Throughout, she was comfortable and controlled.

Filmed at Fox, the sequence took only a few days. During rehearsals, Fox's head of production Darryl F. Zanuck, who liked the brothers, dropped by the set with friends, eager to show off his prized Negro talents. "We had just started rehearsing this number with Dottie," recalled Fayard. "And we weren't sure of it at that time. So we went through it. And we were making mistakes."

Fayard apologized, "Mr. Zanuck, sorry, it's not complete."

"That's all right," Zanuck told him. "I know it's going to be fine."

The brothers introduced Zanuck to Dorothy. He took one look and told her, "You're very pretty." Zanuck did not forget her.

Sun Valley Serenade was a light and breezy musical directed by H. Bruce Humberstone and starring the ice-skate diva Sonja Henie, John Payne, bandleader Glenn Miller, Milton Berle, and Joan Davis. Most of the film chronicled Henie's adventures as a Norwegian war refugee adopted by a big band.

The film's best known sequence occurred when Glenn Miller and his orchestra first perform a spirited version of "Chattanooga Choo Choo." Then as the band completes the number, the camera glides left where Dorothy stands, wearing a snug dark satiny dress with sequined spaghetti straps, a glittery broach, and a feathered hat perched on her head. One hand demurely rests on a hip, and the other holds a little parasol. As she moves further left, she passes, without letting on that she even sees them, two young men waiting outside the back of a caboose. Her smooth glide immediately snaps the guys to attention.

They are, of course, the Nicholas Brothers, dressed in jaunty sports jackets and slacks, with snazzy bow ties and rakish straw hats. With a pert, girlish flirtatiousness, she then asks, in song, "Pardon me, boys, is that the Chattanooga Choo Choo?"

Thereafter the brothers flirt with her with their feet as they join her in singing the number. With their taps, spins, splits, and flips, the sheer joyous thrill of dancing is written all over the faces of Harold and Fayard. Dorothy has to keep up with the fellas. And with her beautifully modulated shoulder shimmeys and hip glides and her enduringly sweet smile, she does so splendidly. Then she waves to the guys as she disappears into the caboose while the brothers perform in their trademark acrobatic style. She reappears with them at the end of the number.

It was a deliriously enjoyable sequence, an often unacknowledged classic in the history of the American movie musical, that officially gave the brothers sex appeal in a film and drew the attention of the critics. "The dusky Nicholas Brothers and Dorothy Dandridge," wrote the *Dallas Morning News*' critic John Rosenfield, "make a killing with a Harlemesque dance and song number."

The reviewer for the *New York Sun* was quick to comment on the "Chattanooga Choo Choo [number] with the Nicholas Brothers and Dorothy Dandridge that reeks with rhythm. Your feet tap, your pulse rises. You swing." In the *New York Daily News*, Kate Cameron wrote that "the Nicholas Brothers and Dorothy Dandridge put over a specialty act effectively.'"

The song "Chattanooga Choo Choo" went on to become a national hit for the Miller Orchestra. But quiet as it was kept, it was the Nicholas Brothers and Dorothy who had really put the song over.

Upon the completion of *Sun Valley Serenade*, Harold pressed Dottie again about marriage, but she still wanted more time. In June 1941, she signed to do the film *Sundown* and shortly afterwards *Bahama Passage*, to be shot later in the summer.

With both films scheduled, a new opportunity came that Dorothy could not pass up. Word went out that Duke Ellington was about to do a stage musical. One of the few created and produced on the West Coast, *Jump for Joy* was to be an unusual production: a collection of songs and satirical skits that in many respects challenged the traditional racial stereotypes of Hollywood and Broadway. One sketch was called "Uncle Tom's Cabin Is a Drive-In Now." In the original script, there was a skit which depicted Uncle Tom lying on his deathbed while a Hollywood producer and a Broadway producer hovered about and tried to revive him by injecting adrenalin into his arms!

Ahead of its time, *Jump for Joy* was, as Ellington once said, an "attempt to correct the race situation in the U.S.A. through a form of theatrical propaganda." It signaled the start of a shift of attitudes about African American roles and images in popular entertainment of the era.

Among the financial backers were producer Joe Pasternak and actor John Garfield. Among the writers contributing lyrics for the show were Langston Hughes, actor Mickey Rooney, and Sid Kuller. Billy Strayhorn also contributed to several compositions. Eventually, the production would also boast an all-star Black cast that included Ivie Anderson, Herb Jeffries, Marie Bryant, Wonderful Smith, Paul White, Avanelle Harris, the comic trio Pot, Pan, and Skillet, and later Big Joe Turner. Almost every Black actor in Los Angeles was excited about the show's possibilities and hoped to get in the cast.

When it was announced that Nick Castle would stage the production and that Ben Carter—who, of course, had worked with the Dandridge Sisters as little girls—would be *Jump for Joy*'s casting director, Ruby's ears perked up. Dorothy had to be considered for the show. Despite her film obligations, she auditioned and won the plum young female lead, with top billing. Ellington, Castle, Carter and the others were all excited about her. "If I'm not mistaken," said Avanelle Harris, "they all wanted Dorothy because she just fit right in." *Jump for Joy*'s producers wanted her badly enough to agree to let her come into rehearsals late because of her commitment to appear in *Sundown*.

Almost immediately, Dorothy left for Acoma, New Mexico, where *Sundown* was partly shot. Produced by Walter Wanger, directed by Henry Hathaway, and starring Gene Tierney and Bruce Cabot, *Sundown was* an adventure tale set in a British outpost in Kenya during World War II. There the natives are being secretly armed. The British search for the arms suspects, one of whom is a young seemingly half-caste woman, played by Tierney. Of course, any possible native uprising is squashed by the film's end. And also by the conclusion, when the young hero has fallen in love with the half-caste, it is revealed that in actuality she is as "all" White as he, and therefore free to waltz off into the sunset with her. Dorothy was cast as a native girl, identified merely as Kipsang's Bride, who marries and then loses a "heroic" African aide to the British.

Some sixty other Black actors and actresses, including Jeni Le Gon, Jester Hairston, and former football players Woody Strode and Kenny Washington—also travelled to the location.

There the shoot, while short, was exhausting and often brutal. "I thought it remarkable what a motion picture company can do with a patch of desert," recalled actress Gene Tierney. "They had hundreds of people to feed and house. We were almost like a little city sprung up overnight, living at the foot of the hill in barracks that were temporary. Donkeys were used for loading and hauling equipment. And the presence of the camels, along with our isolation, encouraged the feeling that we could just as well have been in North Africa."

Dorothy immersed herself in the dreamy unreality of this Arizona version of an African village. Yet working in the sun with the temperature over 100 degrees, she often felt fatigued and drained. Especially grueling were scenes in which she was required to go barefoot. The hot sand and rocks scorched her feet. She feared the effect this could have on her performance in *Jump for Joy*, which required some dancing. Finally, director Hathaway permitted the wardrobe department to create a special pair of sandals that were painted so that she still looked barefoot.

Afterwards, when the rehearsals for *Jump for Joy* began for Dorothy, they also began for Ruby. She wasn't there to perform, but rather to keep an eye on her daughter.

Ruby would sit in the back of the theatre and watch Dorothy's every move. The fact that her presence might embarrass Dorothy meant nothing to her. "Ruby was with her all the time," said singer Herb Jeffries. She was there to make sure none of the guys in the cast got too close to her daughter.

By now, Dorothy, at eighteen, had developed a stunning figure, slim, curvy, and perfectly proportioned. "Dorothy was physically built as beautiful as any living female that you'd ever seen in your life," recalled Herb Jeffries. He remembered the small waist, the "beautifully formed" legs, even the tiny, delicate feet. "She was in my estimation the most beautiful woman I had ever seen in my life. By all standards."

Ruby didn't ease up, said Jeffries, until she felt that Dorothy "was in good, safe hands, when she felt that the members of the orchestra were mature and understood Dorothy as being a very talented lady but still not experienced with worldly ways."

But Ruby couldn't do much to shield Dorothy from the real headache during the rehearsals: singer Ivie Anderson, who had worked with young Dorothy in *A Day at the Races*. Despite all her talents and the fact that she was probably Duke Ellington's favorite vocalist, Anderson appeared threatened by Dorothy and "didn't like the fact that Dottie was getting so much attention," recalled Fayard

Nicholas. "Because she wanted the best songs. She wanted to know why they were giving Dorothy Dandridge all the best material. Ivie talked to the producers and Duke. Ivie wasn't friendly to Dottie. Ivie would give her one of those looks."

"Well, Ivie Anderson was one of those old time Ethel Waters chicks in show business," recalled Avanelle Harris. "Jealous. Ivie could be *evil*. She was mellow and all. But she could be *evil*. All of us, the younger glamour girls, we steered clear of her. She had a little *side* to her."

Dorothy's predicament wasn't helped any by the pre-opening buzz about her. On the morning before the show's premiere, an article appeared in *The California Eagle* predicting, "Scheduled to be [the] hit of the show, according to inside reports, is petite Dorothy Dandridge."

Trying to ignore Anderson, Dorothy concentrated solely on her work and kept to herself. She would be performing skits and such numbers as "Brown Skinned Gal in the Calico Gown," "Cindy with the Two Left Feet," "Cymbal Sockin' Sam," "If Life Were All Peaches and Cream," and "Hickory Stick."

"Dorothy didn't let anyone get close to her. She was definitely a loner," said Avanelle Harris. "I liked her because she minded her own business. She wasn't with a catty group of girls. She was friendly. Very friendly. But she just wasn't one of the people that I went around with. None of us hung out with Dorothy. On *Jump for Joy*, she didn't socialize with us and go out and all that good stuff."

By the time she was working on *Jump for Joy*, Dorothy had developed the working habits and demeanor she maintained the rest of her professional life. The aspect of show business that could be most upsetting to her was the petty jealousies and the backstage bickerings. In theatres, clubs, and on film sets, one's every move could be scrutinized, examined, exaggerated, and criticized. Whenever possible she removed herself from the fray. Never did she participate in group sessions of backstage gossip, which theatre and film people often reveled in. Rarely did she discuss her feelings about working conditions or personal problems with her colleagues. Almost always she backed off from disputes and confrontation.

Dorothy did strike up a friendship with Herb Jeffries. Tall, good-looking, light-skinned, with slick wavy hair and a deep baritone voice, Jeffries represented for many in Black entertainment circles the essence of the smooth, debonair, Black dude, who could woo and wow the ladies. Already, he had starred in race movies; such Black westerns as *Bronze Buckaroo, Harlem Rides the Range,* and *Two-Gun Man From*

Harlem, in which he dashed about in fancy spurs and tight riding clothes, performed action stunts of derring do, and became America's first Black singing cowboy. Eventually, Jeffries became best known in the States and later Europe as a balladeer, whose most famous recording was "Flamingo" with Ellington's band.

Together Dorothy and Jeffries looked like the perfect pair. But despite Jeffries's reputation as a ladies' man, he and Dorothy became friends, not lovers. For a young woman who had grown up without a father, she looked to Jeffries as a big brother with whom she could talk and exchange ideas, aspirations, and opinions. Sometimes, surprisingly, their talk turned to makeup. A wizard with the makeup brush who had given suggestions to Lena Horne, Jeffries understood the use of a foundation base, lipstick, rouge, mascara, and lighting for dramatic effect. In time, he became the man who helped Dandridge early in her career to make the visual transition from girlishly cute ingenue into young glamour goddess.

Jump for Joy's opening at the 1,600-seat Mayan Theatre on July 10, 1941, drew a glittering Hollywood turnout. Langston Hughes flew to Los Angeles for the event. Marlene Dietrich sat in the audience. Fayard Nicholas attended. "The audience itself was of unusual composition," Duke Ellington said, "for it included the most celebrated Hollywoodians, middle-class ofays, the sweet-and-low, shuffling-type Negroes, and dicty* Negroes as well (doctors, lawyers, etc). The Negroes always left proudly, with their chests sticking out."

For Dottie, *Jump for Joy,* much like *Meet the People,* meant further exposure to the more sophisticated, progressive edge of the film/entertainment community. But the reactions to her performance were mixed. "Dorothy Dandridge and Marie Bryant are definitely the hits of the show," wrote Sam Abbott in *Billboard.* But Harold felt her performance lacked the sparkle of her work in *Meet the People.* "Her part was amply done," recalled Avanelle Harris. "She was good. She wasn't sensational. But she was good."

Most reviewers and audiences focused more on her looks. Of Dorothy, *The California Eagle*'s reviewer John Kinloch commented,"Don't know whether she can sing or dance or wot [sic]! But she's beautiful. YEAH MAN!"

During the musical's three-month run, Dorothy began work on the film *Bahama Passage.* Nightly, she performed in the show, usually not returning home until the early hours of the morning. Then she had to

---

* dicty: African-American vernacular meaning upper-class or snobbish.

9 1

be up by five in the morning in order to be at Paramount Pictures by six a.m. The strain showed.

"She was making the film and they had promised to let her off for the matinees," recalled Avanelle Harris. "And Nick Castle threw me in her spot. And old Mr. Ellington was so grateful to me for it." Harris substituted for her on Wednesday and Saturday matinees, until finally Dorothy left the cast and was replaced by Juanelda Carter. "Doubling in Paramount's *Bahama Passage* was reported to have been too strenuous," *The California Eagle* reported of Dorothy's departure. "Besides the picture's more important for the future." Afterwards, rumors spread that she had been fired. Harris and other cast members denied such stories. It was the conflicting schedule, not the quality of her work.

Her movie résumé grew. Between 1941 and 1943, she also starred in soundies—short musical films (distant precursors to music videos)—which were shown on jukeboxes with special tiny screens. The soundies offered employment to a number of African American performers. Today they are startling documents on the work of some legendary stars. No one took soundies very seriously, however, when they were being made.

Avanelle Harris remembered that performers usually went to "one of those small studios in Los Angeles. It wasn't a major studio at all. I know how long it took us to do it. One day. You did all those soundies in one day." For the young Black women, it was very competitive. "There are a whole lot of girls there to be picked. There were a lot of dancing girls in LA in those days,"said Harris. "Practically everything you did, you auditioned for or you showed up and maybe you have to read a line. Or the man just looks at you. The man just went down the line and picked the faces he wanted."

The pay was $25 for the day's work. "You get paid for just one day," said Harris. "Great when you needed the day's work and you're honored to be picked."

Some of Dandridge's soundies conformed to the then acceptable movie images of Blacks at the time. In *Jungle Jig*, Dorothy found herself dressed and made up to look like something of a sexy native girl as she sang and danced in an African jungle setting. *Congo Clambake* and *Lazybones* teamed her with Hoagy Carmichael. *A Zoot Suit* used her as the pretty foil of jivey Black comic Paul White. She also worked with White in *Birdland Fantasy*.

Other soundies moved in other directions. In the church setting of *Yes Indeed*, she led a congregation of her Black brothers and sisters as she performed a swing style number about the shout that leaps when the spirit hits you, *yes indeed*. In *Swing for Your Supper,* dressed in a sweater and skirt, she looked like a demure, well-brought up coed at Spelman or Bennett College as she stood by a piano and energetically sang.

Cow Cow Boogie starred her as a sexy cowgirl, with short skirt, boots, and cowgirl hat, who crooned about a cowboy who "was raised on the local weed/he's what you'd call a swing half breed." Here in coded language, her lyrics directly addressed a segment of the Black community, particularly the entertainment segment, that was quite familiar with what the weed reference was all about. Tumbleweed it was not.

Perhaps the soundie that best expressed her position in Black Hollywood of the early 1940s was the Mills Brothers's *Paper Doll.* She was featured as the dreamgirl of this then very popular Black singing group. Here while three of the Mills Brothers sit with a bevy of beauties including Avanelle Harris, Juanita Moore, and Lucy Battle, another lovestruck guy gazes at a photograph of a pretty girl. As the brothers sing about their hope to find the right girl who will be just theirs and theirs alone, the girl in the photograph—Dorothy—becomes a cut-out paper doll, who springs to life and dances. It's an innocently romantic number that clearly touched on the Black community's desire for its own glamour girls.

Most poignant of her soundies was *Easy Street,* in which she sang of searching for a place without cares or troubles. All these short films helped establish Dandridge's name within the African American community. Usually free of the rigid stereotyping that entrapped so many Black performers during this period and perhaps because she felt at home in a cast of fellow Black actors and actresses, she emerged as a relaxed, wholesome young woman; just the type Mom and Pop would want their young sons to marry; just the type of soothing symbol for a generation of young Black soldiers that soon found itself in the grip of the Second World War.

In later years, she rarely spoke about much of her early work. Like *Four Shall Die,* the soundies seemed to have vanished from her memory. The same held true for many other African American performers who worked in them. But the young Dandridge was clearly honing her talents and developing the discipline, style, and technique that would be so valuable for the films to come. Her ability to find work also set her apart from the grim statistics for Black performers in Hollywood at this time. The 1940 United States Census reported that of the 2,426 actors in Los Angeles, only 51 were Black. Of the

910 male dancers, showmen, and athletes, a mere 33 were Black. Of the 1,271 experienced actors in Hollywood, 42 were Black. Most significantly for the women in the Dandridge household, of the 743 actresses working in the film capital, only a paltry 15 were African American. Among those women were Hattie McDaniel, Louise Beavers, Theresa Harris, Butterfly McQueen, and Lillian Yarbo.

Hollywood itself was about to undergo an important evolutionary shift in the depiction of Black Americans. Once the nation entered the Second World War, young Black men found themselves shipped abroad to fight for the freedom of others. They did so in segregated troops. Back home far reaching issues and questions arose among African American leaders, who spoke out about the basic freedoms such soldiers, as well as other Black citizens, were denied in their own country, this land of the free and home of the brave.

The NAACP's executive secretary Walter White, aware of inequities in Hollywood as much as anywhere else in America and also acutely cognizant of the power of Hollywood's images, journeyed from New York to the West Coast in 1942. With the help of his friend Wendell Willkie, the 1940 Republican candidate for President, who was then the chairman of the board of Twentieth Century Fox and a special counsel to the National Association for the Advancement of Colored People (NAACP), White met privately with such industry leaders as Twentieth Century Fox production chief Darryl F. Zanuck and producer Walter Wanger.

White protested against the Black stereotypes that prevailed in Hollywood. The giggling, silly maids. The lazy roustabouts. The obsequious butlers. The bug-eyed bootblacks. The NAACP grew particularly critical of Hattie McDaniel's mammy characters—those heavyset bossy and sassy women whose chief goal in life was to nurture and nourish the "good" White folks for whom they worked (or *slaved*, some might say). White urged industry leaders to delineate "the Negro as a normal human being and an integral part of human life and activity." Even in crowd scenes, Hollywood had traditionally presented a lily-white world with not a Black face in sight, as if the Negro (truly the Invisible Man and Woman) did not exist as just an ordinary everyday citizen. Black extras were still used mostly in jungle films or in Black "specialty" segments of movies. Not only more developed Black characters but also more Black extras—in scenes of "normal" daily life, in train stations, department stores—had to be used in films in order that the Negro be depicted as a part of the nation's social fabric.

The Negro press also addressed the situation. Articles in such Black newspapers as *The Pittsburgh Courier, The Chicago Defender, The New York Amsterdam News,* and *The California Eagle* already had been critical of Hollywood's images, especially around the time *Gone With the Wind* was filmed. The Black press, however, was usually supportive of Black actors and actresses, aware of the talents and the tremendous obstacles such performers surmounted to find work. But such writers as J. A. Rogers, along with a group in Los Angeles that included *California Eagle* publisher Charlotta Bass, Maceo Sheffield, Fay M. Jackson, and producer/promoter Earl Dancer (who later became the second husband of Viola Nicholas and thus the stepfather of Harold and Fayard) denounced certain films and the repeated stereotyping of African Americans.

During the war years, the government's special Motion Picture Bureau of its Office of War Information monitored Hollywood films to insure that the right images and messages were being sent to the American people, especially at a time when it was believed important to promote America as a fully free and open society. While the Bureau did not express great interest in insuring that the movies addressed festering and longstanding social, racial, or political problems, it did examine stories and images that were less than flattering to the nation's prestige, patriotism, and morale; on occasion, that included images of Black Americans. Generally, the feeling was that African Americans had to be presented in a more favorable (and less caricatured) light.

Slowly, changes came about. John Huston's *In This Our Life* was the story of a wealthy, spoiled young woman (Bette Davis) who has a hit-and-run car accident, then lets the Negro son (Ernest Anderson) of her family's maid (Hattie McDaniel) be blamed for the crime. He is an intelligent, sensitive young man who aspires to be a lawyer. Here Huston incorporated a race theme in an otherwise standard movie melodrama. Departing from the image of the cheerful servant figures of the past, he also afforded McDaniel the opportunity for a moving and quietly powerful sequence in which she spoke of her son's innocence.

Another major film that featured a new style for a Black character was *Casablanca*, in which Dooley Wilson played Sam; the man at the piano who understands hero Humphrey Bogart's torment for Ingrid Bergman. When Sam plays and sings "As Time Goes By," he not only touched at Bogart's emotional base but also performed a number that became an anthem for young lovers during the war years. Viewed by later generations, Sam might seem like the friendly, kind-hearted servant figure, but at the time of *Casablanca's* release, Sam too was a step above the old grinning servants of the past.

By 1943, Hollywood released two all-star Black musicals: *Cabin in the Sky* and *Stormy Weather.* Both starred New York-born newcomer Lena Horne who, after signing a contract with MGM, then the most powerful movie studio, became the first African American woman to be fully glamorized and publicized in Hollywood. Walter White, a friend of Horne's family in Brooklyn, took a keen interest in the movie career of the young singer, whom he did not want to see end up playing maids. That never happened.

Except for *Cabin in the Sky*, MGM used Horne exclusively in musical sequences of films that starred White performers. Usually, she might sing a song or two, perhaps in a nightclub setting, then disappear from sight. When the films were shown in the South—a segment of the country the studios did not want to offend—her scenes could easily be cut without interfering with the plot lines.

Another performer arriving in Hollywood in the early 1940s was pianist Hazel Scott. Having become a star in New York nightclubs, Scott's movie contract stipulated that she could not be cast in maid roles. Instead she simply appeared as herself—usually beautifully dressed and coifed—in musical sequences, which, like Horne's, could be cut when the films were shown in the South.

Older Black actors and actresses in Hollywood grew fearful that the NAACP's campaign for new roles might mark the end of their careers. Because of this attitude, Lena Horne found herself at the center of controversy and hostility among Blacks in Hollywood, who viewed her suspiciously as an uppity outsider (the NAACP's darling) who could upset the applecart. Ironically, one of Horne's greatest allies was Hattie McDaniel, who understood the Hollywood system and her place in it.

"She sent a note to me to come to her house," said Horne. "She had the most exquisite house I've ever seen in my life. The best of everything."

Horne found McDaniel to be "an extremely gracious, intelligent, and gentle lady." "She explained how difficult it had been for Negroes in the movies, which helped give me some perspective on the whole situation. She was extremely realistic and had no misconception of the role she was allowed to play in the White movie world."

McDaniel told Horne, "I have a family I have taken care of very beautifully. I'm a fine Black mammy [on screen]. But I'm Hattie McDaniel in my house."

McDaniel also understood the image changes that were destined to come about. "You've got two babies. And you've got to work," she told Horne. "Just do what you have to do." Horne recalled, "Miss McDaniel's act of grace helped tide me over a very awkward and difficult moment." She offered her support to Horne, who indeed helped lead the way to the new depictions that ultimately signaled the end of the talented McDaniel's career. Thus Horne as well as jazz pianist Hazel Scott, presented images of sophisticated, polished Black women in films. Like her predecessors Nina Mae McKinney and Fredi Washington, Horne also had the "mulatto" looks that Hollywood treasured: the lighter skin, the keen features, the straighter hair. Yet, despite her talent and beauty, Lena Horne never got the big Hollywood prize: the major dramatic roles that could put her in a league with White female film stars. The one role Horne yearned to play, the mulatto Julie in MGM's 1951 remake of *Show Boat*, ended up going to White actress Ava Gardner.

This was the atmosphere in Hollywood that the young Dandridge now maneuvered her way around. As she started out on her own, the important changes were just beginning. But, even as a teenager, Dandridge struck most as being far too sophisticated and bright for the traditional roles. Still, she had her share of such parts. In *Lucky Jordan,* she appeared in only one scene; as a pretty young maid with a snippet of dialogue as she answers a door for Alan Ladd. She received no billing in the credits. In the jungle film *Drums of the Congo,* she played a native girl. The same was true, of course, of her appearance in *Sundown,* although *Variety* called her one of the film's standouts. In it she was able to delineate her character without speaking any dialogue—first as an idealistic young bride, and then as a distraught widow, grieving over her young husband's grave.

Then there was her role as the servant girl Felice in the late-19th century, New Orleans-based melodrama *The Lady from Louisiana.* Here Dandridge had to contend with a trite script that called for her to utter inane lines in just about every scene; the standard type of simple-headed dialogue for movieland servants in period pictures. "The boys just naturally loves us, Miss Julie," her Felice tells her White mistress played by Ona Munson. "Good thing I went to the conjure man last night, lammy. He fixed me the bestest conjure for to keep my man. I can get him to fix one for you too," she adds, pulling a small dark voodoo doll from her pocket. In another sequence, she advises her headstrong mistress, "Honey, ladies don't go into gentlemen's places of business." But Miss Julie pays Felice no mind, which causes the servant girl to pout, "Um mm mmm. You'se the most scandalizing female in the whole of New Orleans."

Her performance in *Lady from Louisiana* was neither inventiven or clever. In fact, Dorothy looked as if she had been coached by Ruby, who played such ditzy characters all the time. At no other point in her acting career would Dandridge ever come across in such a light-headed way. Yet the great irony was that despite the silliness of the character, she retained her charm and ladylike style.

During this period, though, she sought fresh interpretations. In very subtle, unconscious, quiet ways, Dandridge used her own evolving *personal* screen persona to break down barriers and preconceptions about Black characters in films. That's what saved her in films like *Sundown* and even *Lucky Jordan*. Rarely, too, was that more apparent than in the sluggish melodrama *Bahama Passage*. In this Edward Griffith-directed, Technicolor tale of love, intrigue, and power plays in the West Indies, the central characters on the "dark" isle were White performers Sterling Hayden, Madeleine Carroll, Flora Robson, and Leo J. Carroll. Cast as the friendly servant of the island's ruling White family was Black actor Leigh Whipper. Dorothy played Whipper's daughter, a servant girl named Thalia.

Not a large or impressive role, Dorothy nonetheless made the most of her scenes in a wholly natural, spontaneous way. Wearing a blue checked dress with a spotless white bibbed apron and white cap, she usually entered a room, performed a function, then exited, forever consigned, like most Black screen servants, to the sidelines of the action and the culture, without their own lives explored.

In one sequence with blond Madeleine Carroll, whom Thalia tends, the young woman tries on a pair of high heels. But as a naive native unaccustomed to such shoes, Thalia loses her balance and falls on the floor but laughs at herself. "I just can't wear them," she says in sweet exasperation. "Nobody can. What's that got to do with it?" says Carroll.

The two have an exchange of dialogue in what appears to be the most innocuous of scenes. Yet when compared to what usually transpired on screen with Black movie servants during the period, the teenage Dandridge never lets her character become clownish or achingly servile nor overly optimistic and cheery. At times, she gives a suggestion of a West Indian accent but always Dandridge speaks English, not some trumped-up phoney movieland dialect. Throughout she looks at and speaks to Madeleine Carroll with a direct simplicity. Here with a minimum of strokes, she created a character, not a caricature, that was textured with reserves and underlayers of charm and intelligence.

～

Dorothy kept working, and so did Harold. Their courtship continued, but their demanding careers often kept them apart. The Nicholas Brothers continued the hectic, grueling tour schedule, which was essential to their livelihood. "Every year we did the Roxy Theatre in New York because that was Twentieth Century Fox," said Harold. "We'd play that every year for about two or three weeks." The brothers also appeared at such other major theatres as the Capital, the Paramount, the Palace, and Loews State. "We'd travel around the country all the time," Harold recalled. "When we weren't doing a movie in L.A., we were working. Or on the road. Or something. We had three months out of the year where we could travel."

Otherwise their Fox contract stipulated that they be available for work nine months of the year, which they spent in Los Angeles. If they were not appearing in a film there, they accepted dates in the area at such top theatres and clubs as the Orpheum, Los Angeles' Paramount, Ciro's, and the Cocoanut Grove. They were also expected to perform at Fox theatres.

While on tour in December 1941—just as the Japanese bombed Pearl Harbor and America entered the war—the brothers appeared at the Regal Theatre in Chicago. One night a young woman sat in the audience in rapt attention. But she was hardly the typical star-struck fan. Nor was she like so many young women who were eager to make themselves available to Fayard and Harold. Later in the lobby of the Regal Theatre, she was introduced to Fayard Nicholas. Her name was Geraldine Pate, but everyone called her Geri.

Slender, dark-haired, light-skinned, with a quick sense of humor and an even quicker intellect, she was a native of Jackson, Tennessee. Educated first in a New Orleans convent, she later studied at DePaul University in Chicago. She once wanted to be a chorus girl but abandoned the idea because she did not think she was sexy enough. For years, Geri Pate had loved the work of Harold and Fayard. Once Fayard met Geri, he could not resist her. In January 1942, they were married in Nevada. Shortly afterwards, Geri was in Los Angeles.

The brothers were eager to introduce her to Dottie, about whom she had heard much. But frankly, Geri said, "Harold had so many girlfriends, I was confused." She also was introduced to the

Dandridge family: Vivian, Ruby, and Ma-Ma. Geri liked Dottie immediately. Ruby and Neva, however, viewed Geri—a young woman who had suddenly turned up out of nowhere—suspiciously.

"They were frightened," Geri said. "They were threatened. Because they were trying to push Dottie." By now, Dottie's work in films and theatre had made her the Dandridge family's breadwinner. She "took care of the family," said Geri. "And she got bit parts all the time." Whenever Dorothy made any money, "The first thing she'd do, she would [give] it to her mother."

Neither Ruby nor Neva wanted anything or anyone to interfere with Dottie's career. Or her relationship with Harold. Everyone now knew Dottie and Harold would marry. As Mrs. Harold Nicholas, Dorothy—so Ruby and Neva understood—would be in a privileged position in the culture of Black Hollywood. Secretly, Ruby and Neva even thought she might also establish herself as a dancer with the brothers. The plum musical spot in *Sun Valley Serenade* might have been to them a prelude for many professional riches to follow.

"When I came on the scene, they thought that I would join the Nicholas Brothers as a dancer and then that would cut her out," Geri said. So Ruby and Neva "tried not to be friendly with me." "Dottie didn't have those feelings," said Geri. There was nothing cold or calculating about her. "Harold and Fayard were so close that we went out every place together and so she didn't see me as a threat." Still Ruby and Neva did whatever they could to prevent a friendship from developing between the two young women. As a dutiful daughter, Dottie followed Ruby's advice to keep her distance from Geri.

Ruby Dandridge, however, was not the only watchful, guarded, ambitious stage mother.

Both Geri and Dottie had to win the approval of Harold's and Fayard's formidable mother, Viola Nicholas. As manager of her sons' careers, she was long accustomed to managing other aspects of their lives, too. The brothers could not have asked for a more adoring mother. Nor a more attentive one. Fayard Nicholas remembered as a boy, being awakened every morning by his mother, who would gently put a moist wash cloth to his face. "Then she would lead me to the bathroom," said Fayard, "and would start brushing my teeth, would bathe and dress me, while I was still half-asleep." His mother continued to bathe him until he was thirteen years old. "Then I said, 'Mother, I think from now on, I'll do it myself.'"

Viola Nicholas travelled with her sons until the time the family set-tled in California. But still cushioning Harold and Fayard from the demands of the world outside show business, Viola handled their money, paid the bills, oversaw all the household matters, made sure their meals were cooked, their clothes were laundered, and their suits were pressed. "She even made sure our shoes were shined, even if she had to do it herself." said Fayard. "Mother did everything for us." With no responsibilities other than giving a brilliant performance, the brothers remained shielded from having to learn to express their feel-ings or emotions (except on stage). Fayard remained outgoing and friendly while Harold was still considered an emotionally distant young man.

Regardless, Viola Nicholas didn't want anyone tampering with her sons' lives. She was well aware of the eager, adoring chorus girls, who flocked around Harold and Fayard. That she was prepared to deal with. But these two young women, Dottie and Geri, were so different from the other women in the brothers' lives. They caused her concern.

Even after Geri and Fayard set up their own household in LosAngeles, Viola was reluctant to surrender her reins. "She went everywhere with us," said Geri Pate Nicholas. "She wouldn't let Fayard out of her sight. She wouldn't let him go."

Ultimately, Geri confronted her mother-in-law. "Tonight you're not going out with us," she said. "You simply aren't going out. We have a life. And you have a life."

"Well, they're my sole support," Viola told Geri.

"You will be supported," Geri told her mother-in-law. "And you're going to be supported better as a result of my being with you. But you're not going to take our lives." Geri recalled, "So I cut the cord."

When asked the question "Did Viola like Dottie in the beginning?" Geri answered, "As much as she could."

But Viola Nicholas grew extremely fond of both young women and they became close to her.

Harold's pressures for Dorothy to marry him intensified. "I wasn't ready for marriage," he said years later. "But this was a pret-ty girl. Beautiful. I think it was an ego trip for me. At the begin-ning, everyone wanting this pretty woman. But she wanted me. And I felt differently about her than all those other girls that I used to go out with."

As their youthful dates grew more passionate with heavy kissing and petting, neither Harold nor Dorothy felt they could wait much longer to consummate the relationship. "It was getting close," Harold said. "And that's why, I guess, she eventually said yes. She didn't want to go home to Ma-Ma, you know, and tell Ma-Ma that she. . . whatever. . . without being married."

By all accounts, the young Dandridge had fallen deeply in love with Harold, whom she believed in and trusted. Marriage to Harold also offered a release from the house on Fortuna Street.

Even though she was working and often out of the house, nothing at home was any better. Daily friction was a way of life. Ruby and Neva still constantly hovered about. Sometimes the older women argued, like husband and wife. Their spousal roles could be reversed with Ruby (usually the aggressive one out trying to earn a buck) assuming the more submissive role. If Neva grew too irritated, "She would beat Ruby," said Geri. "Just spank her, like you do a child. I saw that once." Apparently, Neva still struck both girls if they disobeyed her or did the slightest thing to provoke her, and both Ruby and Neva continued to lie to Dorothy and Vivian about their father Cyril. He had no contact with them since their meeting at the Cotton Club. Never was a kind word said about him.

Since the breakup of the trio, Dorothy and Vivian were still close yet aware of a distance slowly growing between them as their lives, personal and professional, veered in very different directions. For Vivian, it was no doubt difficult to watch the upward swing of her younger sister's career.

Vivian found some club and movie assignments, though. In the late summer of 1942, she and Ruby both worked on the MGM lot in the studio's all-Black musical fantasy *Cabin in the Sky*, which starred Ethel Waters, Eddie "Rochester" Anderson, and MGM's then new Black beauty on the lot, Lena Horne. Ruby had a small speaking part while Vivian turned up in the film's climactic cabaret sequence where she performed a curbside jitterbug with actor Lennie Bluett outside Jim Henry's nightclub. The film was released in 1943. Both mother and daughter also did voices for the animated characters in Bob Clampett's Black cartoon takeoff on the Snow White story, *Coal Black and the Sebben Dwarfs*. Ruby supplied the voice of the mammy figure at the film's opening and also, it is believed, that of the wicked witch. Vivian, however, was the voice of the sexy lead character called So White. Vivian was also an extra in *Stormy Weather*.

By now, Vivian had developed into an attractive young woman. Tall and big-boned, she was not a small delicate beauty like Dorothy, but she was considered sexy with her full hips and breasts. Often self-conscious about her voluptuousness, she ultimately did something about it. In later years on a visit to Los Angeles, Vivian took a male friend aside, pulled up her blouse, showed him her "new" breasts. She was excited by the results of a breast reduction operation she had had.

Outgoing, lively, sometimes loud, usually outspoken, with a sharp, sometimes raunchy sense of humor, she was quick to deliver an intelligent retort when a situation called for it. Composer Phil Moore always believed Vivian might have had an important career had she become a comedienne, perhaps on the order of the young Pearl Bailey. Vivian's humor, which was often enough directed at herself, helped her survive through many a lean year to come.

By her own admission, Vivian was "fast;" far more forward with men than was Dorothy. She was hellbent on breaking loose from the rules of Ma-Ma. Ruby was angered by Vivian's behavior and, said a friend considered her sluttish.

Once America went to war, both Vivian and Dorothy, much like so many young women of the period, may have felt a sense of urgency to get on with their lives. No one could be sure of anything in the future. Time could be running short. Dorothy even considered getting out of show business altogether. But marrying Harold would give her a chance at a new kind of life. Ruby may have had reservations about a marriage at this time because her daughter was still so young. But once Dottie made up her mind, said Vivian, "there was no talking her out of it." Finally, a wedding date was set for early September 1942.

Vivian wed first, though. On June 28, 1942, she married Jack Montgomery, a handsome young welder, whom most of Vivian's family and friends liked. But the marriage appeared to be, for Vivian, one of impulse. By January 1943, little more than six months after the wedding, Vivian left Montgomery and later divorced him.

The hasty, short-lived marriage marked the beginning of a recurring cycle in Vivian Dandridge's life. Other impulsive romances and marriages followed. So, too, did other quick separations and divorces. Often impetuous and sometimes erratic, she would become swept up in a fast, swirling, romantic swing and later find herself enveloped by the pressure just to survive in a tough show business atmosphere. She was also aware of standing in her sister's shadow in the business, but Vivian was usually too busy living her own dramatic professional and personal life to think much about Dorothy's.

On September 6, 1942, Dorothy Dandridge and Harold Nicholas were married. For a young woman bred in Hollywood, theirs was an ideal fairy tale wedding. The ceremony was performed at the home of Harold's mother Viola. Harold looked boyishly dashing in a dark suit. His best man was brother Fayard. Dorothy's matron of honor was Vivian.

The family and friends of the bride and groom were present: Etta Jones and her husband Gerald Wilson and her parents, Vivian's husband Jack Montgomery, Fayard's recent bride Geri, such luminaries of Hollywood as Hattie McDaniel and choreographer Nick Castle, and, of course, that formidable trio of mothers wondering about the destinies of their children—Ruby, Viola, and Neva.

Radiant with her hair brushed back, a string of pearls around her neck, dressed in a modestly low-cut, white gown covering her shoulders and arms and highlighting her small waist, Dorothy had a luxurious smile and luminous glow. If ever a young woman appeared as if she walked in a magical world of endless promise and hope, it was the 19-year-old Dorothy Dandridge on her wedding day.

The couple moved into a small home in a mostly White neighborhood on 27th Street between Arlington and Cimmarron, not far from Viola Nicholas's home. Their modest dwelling looked more like an enchanted cottage than a house. They had a small yard in the front of the house with hedges and trees that shaded a small porch. Inside the rooms were all on one level: a living room; two bedrooms; a bath; a dining room and kitchen, facing the backyard outside.

Soon after the marriage, Dorothy enthusiastically began decorating her home. In the years to come, her homes were to be marvels of taste and elegance as well as telling metaphors for her state of mind and her ambitions. Blessed with a keen eye for detail and design, she furnished the house simply, almost starkly with a minimum of furniture; a home symbolically free of the cumbersome emotional weight of the house on Fortuna. Geri remembered that in her home, "She had thick white carpeting. Lovely drapes."

"They fixed it up beautifully," said Fayard. "They spent a lot of money on redecorating it. It was a beautiful little house. It was just made for them."

She indeed became a model homemaker. The house was spotless with nothing out of place. Taught by Ruby, Dorothy became an excellent cook, who enjoyed entertaining and favored a traditional African American "soul food" diet: collard greens, potato salad, fried chicken, and on special occasions, chitlins. Conscious of her weight and figure, she was careful not to eat such a diet daily and usually set aside only one day a week for true soul food feasting. She was determined never to let herself become heavy and matronly like her mother and put herself on a daily exercise regiment that continued throughout her life. Still working occasionally, she returned to Republic Pictures to a musical sequence in *Hit Parade of 1943* with Count Basie and his orchestra and then with her old friend Louis Armstrong in a musical number in *Atlantic City*. She also did an unbilled walk-on in David O. Selzneck's *Since You Went Away*. At Universal, she appeared in *Drums of the Congo*.

During this time and in the next few years to follow, a whirl of famous faces in Black entertainment walked through the doors of the cottage at 27th and Arlington. One evening Count Basie and his whole band came over. On other occasions, Sammy Davis Jr., Herb Jeffries, and Louis Armstrong stopped by. Some times Vivian and Jack, during their short-lived union, joined them. The actor Joel Fluellen, who had become a close friend of Ruby's and sought a friendship with Dorothy, also came by. Geri and Fayard were, of course, also frequent guests.

In some ways, Harold proved to be a fine husband. Happy to be handling his own money, he was an excellent provider and spent freely. "I didn't want for any comforts," Dandridge said.

Yet despite the comfortable home, the handsome, successful husband, the stream of guests and friends, Dorothy soon discovered herself in a marriage fraught with problems. Harold found it impossible to accommodate himself to someone else's schedule or needs. Still caught up in the rush of entertainment life—the clubs, the personalities, the parties, the gatherings, the constant attention, and the continual flow of new faces—Harold was always on the move. A restless extrovert, he was forever in search of something away from home, and he still had an eye for other women.

Within days of their wedding, Dorothy was convinced Harold was seeing someone else. He denied it. But he could not deny that later there were girlfriends. Women did not stop looking at him, and he did not stop looking at them. With her storybook view of marriage, Dorothy couldn't cope with the idea of his infidelity. Nor was she prepared for another household filled with tensions. She was an incurable romantic, and this was a period, in her mind, when romance should prevail in her marriage and home.

Dorothy and Harold argued. Not about money. Not about his selfishness. Not even at first, said Harold, about his having girl-friends. Mainly, the arguments centered on the fact that he was just not spending time with her. He sometimes stayed out until the early hours of the morning with buddies. Then there was the sport of golf, which became a consuming passion, perhaps the only way he was able to relax and to be himself; or perhaps the only way he was able to escape himself. He spent hours on the golf course.

Soon daily quarrels flared up between the two. "I instigated the arguments because of my actions," Harold Nicholas admitted. "So they would start and naturally it was done back and forth. But it never got to the point where we were so furious with each other that it could come to blows or something like that. That never happened."

"Your brother isn't doing right," Dorothy told Fayard one after-noon. "He should be home more."

"Dottie was between marriage and golf," was the way Fayard summed up the situation. His brother "would get up real early in the morning to go out and play golf with his friends. And she wanted him there more with her." He added, "That's when the marriage started getting shaky."

Some nights Dorothy, crying and tired of waiting up for her hus-band, returned to Fortuna Street, to stay with Ruby.

Shortly after their marriage, the couple was also in a car accident with Harold at the wheel. "A drunk driver ran into us and knocked her out of the car," Nicholas said. "She fell on the pavement." Though not seriously injured, Dorothy was hospitalized with back problems. Most of her days at the hospital were spent alone. Harold was back on the golf course. Ruby was busy with career assignments. But on several occasions, Dorothy's new sister-in-law Geri visited her. The two women had known each other now for almost a year.

Lying in her hospital bed, Dorothy began to question Ruby's and Neva's admonitions to avoid Geri; she discovered facets of Geri's per-sonality that she had only caught glimmers of before. Geri was an altogether remarkable young woman. Well-read. Political. Independent. Outspoken. In the most polite fashion, Geri Pate Nicholas could tell anyone she found to be a pain to go straight to hell. To top it off, Geri was attractive with a great sense of style.

For Dorothy, having come of age in a heady movieland atmosphere where the talk was always about show business and little else, Geri's range of knowledge and varied interests were stimulating. Never had she heard anyone talk about books, politics, or the arts in such a thoughtful way. Fayard had been lucky to take Geri for a wife. Dorothy understood she was lucky to have Geri for a friend. By the time Dorothy left the hospital, she told Fayard, "Geri is my best friend."

This marked the beginning of an extraordinary friendship between two remarkable African American women that endured for decades. The women changed husbands and boyfriends, had families and careers and sometimes were separated by great distances, but they always confided in one another. In a profession where trust could lead to betrayal and disillusionment, Dorothy realized Geri, unlike so many others in her life, was someone she could depend on.

They talked woman to woman about things too painful for Dottie to discuss in great detail even with Harold. About her past. About the beatings from Ma-Ma, the humiliating vaginal inspections, the constant pressures, and the relationship between Ma-Ma and her mother. On one level, she came to accept Ruby's lesbianism. On another level, it troubled her.

As Ruby became better known as an actress, so, too, did the stories of her sexual proclivities. In the Hollywood community, whether Black Hollywood or White Hollywood, despite the fact that no one really cared about anyone else's sexual orientation, that didn't mean people didn't talk. Gossip flourished and flew like mad in the movie capital. Dorothy McConnell, who as a little girl had played with Dorothy in Cleveland, said that upon later moving to Los Angeles in 1957, she heard stories all over town that Ruby was a lesbian. The comments and terms of the era that were bandied about, words like "dyke" and "bull-dagger," could be harsh and cruel.

"For a while, Dottie was in denial about Ruby and Neva," said Geri. "She was scraping around for answers. She couldn't face it."

She would ask Geri, "Why does my mother accept this relationship and treatment?" Or "Why does Ma-Ma try to be my father?" Or she said, "There are plenty of men who would marry my mother."

"As time went on, she was trying to face up to some reality," said Geri. Dorothy "could intellectualize the fact and accept it. But she couldn't accept it *emotionally*. And this was a different day. Our day was different. Mores of people were different."

But then, too, had Ma-Ma not been such a terror, had she not monopolized so much of Ruby's attention and affections, Dorothy and Vivian both might have felt less tense about the relationship. In their eyes, their mother conspired with their jailor and that bred ambivalent, conflicting, and unresolved feelings towards Ruby from both daughters. Ultimately, Ruby's sexual preference didn't bother the sisters. Instead it was her particular choice of partners that disturbed them.

Dorothy's family situation was a complex, troubling one that took her years of reflection and psychiatric treatment to work through. Still Dorothy worshiped her mother, Geri said, and she "absolutely adored Vivian."

The friendship with Geri enabled Dorothy not only to express some of her innermost feelings—and in a sense also to begin to really define herself—but it also helped broaden her perspective and stretch her intellectual horizons. Long curious about a multitude of topics, Dorothy found in Geri the ideal friend with whom to sift through ideas, to debate, to hash out opinions and theories. Not only could she share her interests with Geri, she could learn from her, as well. "She depended on me. She had missed a lot," said Geri. "She had a hunger for knowledge. A real hunger. When [she realized I had] read a lot, she would just, for hours, talk to me and make me analyze [the books] for her. And we'd analyze together and so on. This thirst for knowledge was just insatiable."

Geri also discovered another of Dorothy's well-kept secrets. Until she was sixteen, Dorothy still struggled to learn to read. "She didn't read until she was quite old, about four years prior to my meeting her. She was in the process of learning," said Geri said "But she memorized. She had a tremendous memory. And she fooled everybody. But she was so charming, she could get away with it with the teachers. And they just pass you. And she even did radio scripts which she'd make people read for her. But when Neva caught her and started to point out words, she was about fifteen."

Dorothy's strong desire for knowledge fired her to push herself to improve her reading skills and learn on her own. Within a short time after meeting Geri, she was devouring books on her favorite subjects: psychology and psychiatry. "She just went mad over psychology," Geri said. She read as much Freud as possible and later attended psychology classes at UCLA. It was in part her evolving, ongoing struggle to decipher her past, to understand her family, to explore her present relationships, and in short, to know herself.

Like many other actors, she relied on others to fill in, through conversation, the gaps in her knowledge, to supply the information on the subjects she deemed important. In later years, Dorothy's nightclub pianist Nick Perito saw that despite her intellectual interests, she was often so overworked, overextended, and overbooked that she didn't have the time to read and reflect as she wanted. "She, for instance, wouldn't read novels and books on Black history," Geri recalled. "She wouldn't bother with Langston Hughes and poetry and other things. She would depend on people like me to discuss it with her. And, of course, she would remember it. And [later] she'd go to dinner with people like Samuel Goldwyn and sound off as though she had read it."

"That was a weakness and a strength," Geri said of Dorothy's reading habits and her reliance on others. "It got her through." In later years, her dinner table discussions (which no doubt were also dramatic performances) of Langston Hughes or whomever, would dazzle White Hollywood, which often enough was just being introduced to a certain Black author or subject.

Once Dorothy opened up, Geri discovered, she could talk nonstop, sometimes hours at a time on the telephone, often about herself. She was "totally self-absorbed," said Geri. "But she had to be self-absorbed to achieve what she did. One must understand that." Like almost every other major star in films, Dorothy's career would have gone nowhere without her unending attention to and concentration on self.

Clear to Geri was Dottie's immersion in a personal fantasy world, which was crucial to her well-being. While a sense of humor proved the key to self-preservation for Vivian, Dorothy's survival still came from her ability to withdraw into her own realm of dreams, hopes, and mostly, order. Only in this private dream world—and her acting roles—did the life seem ordered enough to make sense. Or for her not to be afraid.

Like everyone else, Geri saw that Dorothy was undeniably pretty, with the most beautiful color imaginable. "There is nobody that I've ever seen who had that coloring." She was about 5'4" tall, though people invariably thought of her as being taller, with measurements of 36-24-36½, and she weighed about 110 pounds. But the young Dorothy Dandridge, at age twenty, had not yet emerged as the magnetic beauty whose looks would be world-famous. Dorothy's sister-in-law Dorothy Nicholas Morrow remarked that Dorothy became more beautiful as she grew older.

The flip side of Dorothy's self-absorption was her generosity. "I never met anyone who had the same kind of generosity," recalled Geri. "She was the sort of person that if you were in need, she'd get out of her bed and [help] you. Or if she had a coat and somebody didn't have a coat, she'd jump out of the car. She would do everything she could to give you that coat. She took a stove out of her house once because somebody got put out of their apartment and they were going into another apartment. She gave them the stove. It was a spirit. It was the heart." And Dottie also "didn't talk against people," which was rare in the competitive, back-biting, back-stabbing world of show business. "She praised other actors," said Geri. "She was generous of spirit. She had supreme honesty."

Dorothy's problems with Harold continued. To Vivian, to Geri, and to Fayard, she voiced her complaints, her feelings of desertion and rejection by him. Aware of Harold's penchant for nightclubs, Vivian kidded her, "Maybe he finds you dull. You know you don't want to go out. And he likes to go." Vivian suggested that Dorothy try to participate in some of the activities that Harold enjoyed. Dorothy tried. She accompanied her young husband to Los Angeles' jazzy Black night spots. "But when she would go, she'd get sleepy or she was bored," Vivian recalled. "She never did care for the nightclub scene. I thought it was fabulous. Different type."

Now that the war raged on, Harold and Fayard became eligible for the draft. But while they toured, their draft board in Los Angeles had been unable to catch up with them. Twentieth Century Fox also didn't want either brother drafted until they had first worked in two Fox films.

In early 1943, the brothers returned to the city to shoot their most famous film sequence: the startling staircase number in *Stormy Weather*. The brothers' leaps, splits, and sublime dual co-ordination would astonish audiences for decades to come. Choreographed by Nick Castle, their number was rehearsed and shot quickly in only a week, said Harold, because the draft board had finally contacted Fayard, who immediately afterwards was enlisted into the army. *Stormy Weather* proved to be their last film for Twentieth Century Fox. The sequence may well have also marked the final high point of their careers in America, for within the next few years, the Nicholas Brothers, once the great headliners, would see their fortunes in the States decrease and their careers gradually suffer a decline.

In March 1943, Fayard was sent off as a young private to Fort Hunchia, Arizona. He spent thirteen months in the army. Harold, however, was exempt from the draft. At 5'2", he did not meet the military's height requirements. The thirteen months that Fayard spent in the army marked the first significant time the brothers had ever been separated.

By that March, Dorothy also learned she was pregnant. She turned radiant with expectations of motherhood. A child might also change Harold's habits, she believed; fatherhood might make him grow up and accept his responsibilities.

Though Harold was excited, the news did little to alter the pattern of their daily lives or his behavior. Most of his spare time was still spent on the golf course. Or playing cards with buddies. Or club hopping. Or flirting. The arguments continued unabated. During the advanced months of Dorothy's pregnancy, a quarrel in their home grew so heated and upsetting that an emotional Dottie suddenly became dizzy and swayed. Nicholas then saw her collapse on the floor of their bedroom. Alarmed and frightened, he rushed "to lift her up and put her on the bed but she was too heavy," he recalled. But finally he was able to revive her. He never forgot, however, the sight of his young wife lying on the floor.

As the delivery date of the baby drew near, Dottie awoke on the morning of September 1st in great pain. Though she was convinced that the baby was on the way, Harold assured her it was a false alarm. Having already made plans for the day, he didn't think it necessary to take her to the hospital. She called Ruby, who tried to calm her. Harold suggested she spend the day at Geri's home, about a half mile away. As he dropped her off, he said he would return later in the day. But, so Dorothy recalled years later, an angry Geri confronted him. Where was he going, she asked, when he should be with Dottie, who might have the baby at any moment? Shortly afterwards, a friend drove by and picked him up, and he was gone. He left the car but forgot to leave the car keys.

As the day progressed, Dottie's pain and then contractions grew stronger. She went into labor. Geri and her sister Rose, who was also at the house, knew they had to get her to the hospital. But with no car keys, the women were stranded without any means of transportation. Nor did they know how to reach Harold. They guessed that he had taken off for the golf course. Time dragged on. Fearful, upset, and dripping with perspiration, Dottie, much like a little girl, cried out for Harold. She was after all but twenty years old, having her first child, and she wanted her husband with her. When Vivian learned of her sister's state, she too became alarmed and believed there had to be some way to reach Nicholas. But "we couldn't find Harold," recalled

Vivian. "And Dottie said she was going to wait until he arrived before she delivered the baby."

"She was holding back because [of] the little bastard [who] took the car keys," said Geri.

Then the pain overtook Dorothy.

"Her water had broken. And she was afraid. And we finally found a neighbor," said Geri, "[but] she kept on saying she wasn't going." Finally, the women convinced Dorothy that she couldn't remain in the house.

But "we simply didn't get to the hospital on time," Geri remembered. "By the time we got there, the baby was coming." Once in the hospital, there was another delay before Dorothy was taken into the delivery room.

With her emotions at a fever pitch and her fears escalating, it was a painful, difficult birth. Geri remembered that the doctors "used forceps" during the delivery to pry the child from the womb. At 2:42 a.m. on September 2, 1943, at Los Angeles' Rose Maternity Hospital, Dottie gave birth to a little girl. For weeks after the birth, the infant bore the marks of the forceps on her head. And the memory of those forceps would haunt Dorothy for the rest of her life.

She named her daughter Harolyn Suzanne Nicholas after the young husband she still loved so passionately. The family called her Lynn.

Harold, Geri recalled, "got to the hospital about an hour after Lynn was born."

But soon spirits were high as Harold, Ruby, Vivian, Viola, and Geri all marveled over this precious little girl who looked so much like her father: she had his rich reddish brown color, his large eyes, and his full face and forehead. "She looked perfect," Geri said. "She looked perfect."

For young Dottie, a few days later as she left the hospital with Lynn, the wide, open California skies must have looked very blue and bright. Surely, Lynn represented another chance, a new hope, a fresh beginning. Now her residence at 27th and Arlington might really become the enchanted cottage she fantasized about.

LYNN

*D*orothy contentedly settled into motherhood. None of the mundane day-to-day activities that might have driven some women to distraction ever bored, tired, or exasperated her. She assumed her problems with Harold and the tensions she had grown up with were now safely behind her; all objects of a past that could be discarded and forgotten.

Now she had Lynn. And in her mind, everything about her life had changed. Harold had been transformed into the perfect husband to fit the dream image she had so lovingly created. "Really, she wanted to have a white picket fence and really be a wife," said Geri. "She really did."

She decorated Lynn's room and filled it with toys and stuffed animals. Throughout the house, she could be heard laughing as she performed the daily rituals of bathing, drying, powdering, and pampering her newborn. She shopped at an exclusive boutique at Farmer's Market where she bought special dresses, outfits, and matching pinafores for Lynn and herself.

Family and friends came to see the darling infant often. Ruby beamed when she held Lynn in her arms and posed for pictures with her daughter and granddaughter. Harold was all smiles as he hugged and played with his beautiful baby girl. These home-centered, quiet times were, Dorothy later said, the happiest years in her life. Indeed they were the very incidents that might have sprung out of her fantasies about married life.

She found a nanny for Lynn, an older woman called Jonesy. Described as elegant and warm, she had worked for many years for other Hollywood families. Both Jonesy and her husband seemed as enchanted by Lynn as everyone else, even during those long, strange nights when the little girl became unusually restless and cried loudly.

Not long after Lynn was born, Geri became pregnant and gave birth to her first son Tony. Now the two young women were mothers and not only compared notes on their husbands' busy careers but also on the growth and activities of their children.

Elevated to the top of Black Hollywood's social life by her position as Mrs. Harold Nicholas, Dorothy became a prized member of an elite circle of upwardly mobile young Negro women in Los Angeles. There came a steady round of social affairs, gatherings, clubs, groups, and organizations, chief of which was a Black women's horseback riding group called Crop 'N' Tails. The activities of these young women were covered in the pages of *The California Eagle* by its society editor Jessie Mae (Brown) Beavers.

They were all "pretty girls," recalled singer Bobby Short, who temporarily settled in Los Angeles in the early 1940s. "The other girls were all students at UCLA or someplace, the *university,* you see. And they had this little social club. And Dorothy was just floating around being a housewife and a mother."

Bobby Short met both Dorothy and Vivian during an appearance at a club in Hollywood. The two came to see him perform on several occasions. He was already aware of Dorothy's impact with the Dandridge Sisters as well as her other appearances. "I knew the name Dorothy Dandridge," he said. "Every now and then, she would work some place. I remember going down to the Lincoln Theatre, which was like the Apollo in New York. . . and seeing her on a vaudeville bill. And every now and then you'd see Dorothy in one of those little [movie] roles where [someone would] arrive at Miss Ann's house and Dorothy would open the door and say, '*Just one moment please.*' Or '*She'll be right down.*' Looking pretty as a picture. Of course, looking just *knockout* pretty because she was some kind of beauty. My Lord, she *was* pretty." But she was best known at this time, Short recalled, as being "married to Harold. She was Mrs. Harold Nicholas." During these years, a mix of familiar and new faces came into her life. She and Geri, sometimes with, sometimes without their husbands, attended parties given by the then still reigning doyenne of Black Hollywood, Hattie McDaniel. They also were friendly with Billy and June Eckstine, and Eddie "Rochester" Anderson.

Geri entertained. Dottie did, too, but infrequently. One guest at her home was the young Nat Cole, then performing with the King Cole

Trio, who came with his first wife Nadine. Other frequent guests were Bill "Bojangles" Robinson and his young new bride Elaine, whom everyone called Sue. Dottie and Geri especially liked her. Billie Holiday, Dizzy Gillespie, Hazel Scott, Duke Ellington, Cab Calloway, and members of the singing groups The Charioteers and The Delta Rhythm Boys "were the ones that came to my house or Dottie's," said Geri.

Racial lines remained tightly drawn in Los Angeles, making the Negro community all the more cohesive and unified. "In those days of segregation, you only had each other," said Geri. "Los Angeles was totally segregated. Totally."

Despite the segregation, racial lines were crossed when it came to such big stars as the Nicholas Brothers, who were recognized by the White Hollywood elite, some of whom ignored the traditional racial codes and mixed socially with whomever they chose. Dorothy and Geri often went to hear jazz at Billy Berg's club in Hollywood on Sunday afternoons. "It was a White-owned club with mainly White people. Black people could come as long as they were show people, musicians, and their friends," recalled Geri. "They'd have the finest jazz artists. And all the musicians and show people would be there."

"Every once in a while, people like Tyrone Power and of course, Carole Landis and Rita Hayworth and a few daring Whites would mingle with us. We would hang out in the clubs." Places like the Club Alabam—which was "totally for Black folks," recalled Geri—and the Plantation Club were packed with entertainers seeking entertainment. "A lot of the White movie stars would come to the Plantation Club. George Raft was a frequent visitor there. Betty Grable and Lana Turner would go to the Plantation Club, too. After entertainers finished work, they'd come over to the Dunbar Hotel on Central Avenue. And the Club Alabam," remembered Geri. "It didn't serve food. Just had a bar. And they had a chorus line and Slappy White and Redd Foxx had a team there. And we had what you call after-hours spots."

None was as popular with the hip, young entertainment crowd than a place called Brother's. The club was run by a Black male diva, who was given to wearing flowing robes and a touch of mascara and who was known simply as Brother as he floated about greeting his guests.

"Brother was legitimately employed at the Dunbar Hotel as a bartender. That was the hangout on Central Avenue," said Bobby Short. "Central Avenue was like Lenox Avenue in New York. Brother would quickly leave that job when it closed and rush to his house. A nicely furnished house, which operated all night long as an after-hours club."

"That's one reason I'm sorry that there's integration because when there was segregation, you just met with everybody," Geri said. "We'd end up at Brother's. Sitting in a room with pillows around. And they'd sell breakfast and everything. All the show people would gather there."

"Everybody knew about it. And Brother himself came to the front door to greet you. And if he didn't like you or know you, you didn't get in," said Short. "There was a piano. And there might be someone playing the piano. Mostly people just sat around. In those days, you got dressed up. But *really* got dressed up. People were sitting around during the war in furs and jewels, you know, and dresses and dark suits. *Dressed*! Heavy perfume. Sitting in there smoking and drinking and having a little plate of food if they felt like it. It was grand. It was marvelous."

Dottie occasionally saw Lena Horne at Brother's. By this time, Horne had become the most publicized Black woman in movies. For Black Americans of her generation, Lena Horne stood as a glittering symbol of glamour and sophistication. Moreover, by not playing maids in films, Horne—just as the NAACP's Walter White and others had hoped—represented a new kind of dignity for audiences clearly ready for a fresh set of Black movie images. It was Lena Horne that Dorothy—because of her looks—was already being compared to.

The essence of Horne's appeal as an icon was her aloof, sometimes brilliantly cold, emotionally distant, contemplative beauty. You could look but you dare not touch Lena Horne. Dandridge's essence would be a classy elegance coupled with a compelling vitality and vulnerability that just seemed to rush towards the audience. The idea with Dandridge was: Here she is. You can *try* to touch if you dare. Later she would represent haughty glamour and then tragic mystery. But both women had such presence that the patrons at Brother's probably didn't know which way to look.

They'd be friendly with each other, Geri recalled. "But nothing big." Geri liked Horne whom she thought was an intelligent woman. "I would get invited to her house. But they didn't invite Dottie." The two goddesses would never be close friends.

Missing from this social scene though was Dottie's sister. While Vivian remained her confidante, she was cut off from the top circles of the Black entertainment world. The snobbishness of show business, said Geri, relegated Vivian's social life and contacts to the other end of Black Hollywood's stratified social spectrum. "She was working at the Swanee Inn and places like that on La Cienega Avenue. Small clubs," Geri said. "Vivian hung out with chorus girls. People like that. And that wasn't our crowd. It wasn't by choice. But it was just the way people separated."

Supportive and sympathetic, Dottie always made a point of attending her sister's performances. She worried about Vivian, who through the years was continually beset by some problem or hassle or illness.

Once Vivian's marriage to Jack Montgomery soured, she fell "madly" in love with Babe Wallace, the smooth, handsome entertainer who played Chick Bailey in *Stormy Weather*. Some thought Vivian and Wallace married. Others said they didn't. But when she gave birth to a son, she named him Michael Wallace.

Vivian married again within the next few years. On February 18, 1946, in Yuma, Arizona, Vivian wed a young musician named Ralph Bledsoe. Their marriage lasted eight months and nine days. By October 1946, the two separated. By December, Vivian began divorce proceedings. By June 1947, an interlocutory divorce was granted by the Superior Court of Los Angeles County.

Bledsoe surprised everyone by turning to medicine and becoming a prominent physician. Of course, that happened after he and Vivian had parted. Years later on a return visit to Los Angeles after having vanished for years, Vivian learned of his success as a doctor. She confided in good humor to her friend Etta Jones, "If I could turn my foot around and kick myself for leaving Ralph Bledsoe, I would."

Be the crisis small or great, Dorothy came to the rescue, usually with money. A very dramatic Vivian might rush into Dorothy's home in a maddening dither, angry or hyped up about some matter or another. "If she needed a new hat," said Geri, "it was a big tragedy. And she'd fall down and have a tantrum. And Dottie would say, 'Oh, Vivi, here's the money. Go get a hat.'"

"Dottie always felt guilty that she was the pretty one. And she always tried to compensate. I have known times that she did everything for Vivian," said Geri. "Vivian was always in trouble. And Vivian really played that guilt thing out. She had accidents and Dottie would send money for her operations. She always looked after her. Dottie hadn't even started making money then."

Dorothy and Geri bought a house together on 51st Street in Los Angeles, primarily to provide a place for their respective sisters— Vivian and Eloise—to live. "Vivian was always moving about because she hadn't paid her rent. The house was a triplex with two apartments

117

in the front and one in the back. "My sister lived in one and Vivian lived in the other," said Geri. "They stayed until it was convenient for them to leave. My sister bought a house later. And Vivian went on tour and just forgot. But she lived there with Bledsoe."

While Vivian's career was a series of hits and misses, gigs in this club or that, Ruby's career in the 1940s was on the rise. With both her daughters out of the house, and, so she may have felt, also out of her hair, she paid full attention to her own aspirations. She performed in the stage play *Hit the Deck*. From 1942 to 1959, she appeared in such movies as *Tish, Corregidor, Ladies in Washington, Junior Miss, Home in Oklahoma, Three Little Girls in Blue, Tap Roots, My Wild Irish Rose,* and *Father Is A Bachelor,* as well as others. Surprisingly, she played comic servant roles at a time when such parts were slowly being viewed as passé. Even as late as 1959, she turned up as the maid in the Frank Sinatra comedy *A Hole in the Head* and later as the family maid Delilah on the television series "Father of the Bride" in 1963. Always Ruby endured.

More importantly, she worked with remarkable success on radio, again usually playing ditzy maids. With her high-pitched comic voice, Ruby became well-known to American radio listeners for her role as the maid Geranium on the long-running *The Judy Canova Show*. "She was a scream on that one," remembered Dorothy McConnell. She also played Raindrop on *The Gene Autry Show*, Ella Rose on *Tonight at Hoagy's*, and the neighbor Oriole on radio's *Beulah* with Hattie McDaniel. Later when the *Beulah* series went to television, Ruby went along with it, reprising her role as Oriole for a new generation.

Appearing in guests shots on radio's *Amos 'n' Andy, The Lux Radio Theatre*, and other shows, Ruby also aggressively used her contacts to help Dorothy find radio roles too, both Black and White. Dorothy did spots on *Beulah*. Actor Nick Stewart, who played Lightening on radio's (and later television's) *Amos 'n' Andy Show*, also recalled once suggesting to the show's producer that something different be done with the series' characters. "The next few weeks," said Stewart, "he put Dorothy and a young boy in a love relationship."

Dottie and Geri became good company for each other when they accompanied their husbands on tour. These trips were always adventurous excursions, a series of encounters with the famous and not-so-famous, the arrogant and the demanding, the giddy and the despairing; a fascinating round of musicians, comics, dancers, choreographers, producers, all trying to keep their grip in the slippery world of show business.

During a tour that took Harold and Fayard to Philadelphia, Dorothy and Geri ran into their friend Billie Holiday, who by then, said Geri, was drinking and in "a sad mood." They saw her often in Los Angeles because Holiday kept an apartment not far from Dorothy's and Harold's home. On those occasions when "the cops were after her, shaking her down," recalled Geri, "she'd stay at Dottie's house until we'd pick her up and get her out of town. And Billie would be so high, she wouldn't even know what was happening."

In Philadelphia, they visited Holiday in her hotel. Dorothy "went over to her and gave her money and a lot of beautiful wardrobe. And she spent a lot of time talking to her," Geri recalled. Both women were talkers, eager to express all their pent-up tensions. On these occasions, though, Dorothy did most of the listening.

"She also introduced Billie to a lot of people who could help out. To agents and different people," said Geri. "That was another kindness that Dottie showed. But she appreciated Billie. Really appreciated her and everything that she did."

Once after a prominent bandleader had made advances to Holiday, she went to Dorothy in tears. "Billie acted like a sixteen-year-old," said Geri. "She went out of her skull."

"He made a pass at me. He doesn't respect me," Holiday told Dandridge. "And you know what he told me? He said, If the band men could do it to me, why couldn't he. So I'm going to tell his wife."

Dorothy sat down with Holiday. "Please don't do that to yourself," she said sweetly. "You're a big girl. You can get rid of it better than that."

Holiday listened and didn't say anything about the matter to anyone else.

Dorothy was still happy with married life but began to toy with the idea of getting back into show business. When she ran into her old manager Joe Glaser, he told her she *had* to come back. She held off. But show business was too much a part of her to ever leave it completely behind. She went out on calls, performed, kept her ears open for word of new shows, and still kept herself in shape, too. She was doing aerobic exercises decades before it was fashionable.

She also kept updating her photo portfolio. One of the photographers to do portraits of her during this time was a young Black woman named Vera Jackson, one of the first professional Black female photographers around, who took photographs for *The California Eagle*. Jackson was familiar with the Dandridges, having grown up in Wichita near Ruby's family. Whenever she ran into Dorothy at social affairs, Jackson thought she "was very sweet and friendly. But she always seemed like she was on the defensive. Kind of shy. She really didn't overwhelm people."

The afternoon Jackson arrived at Dorothy's house for the photo shoot, she was a little early and caught Dorothy off-guard. She was just coming out of a bath. "When she came to the door, she was wrapped in a white towel. Water was dripping all over her," Jackson recalled. "With her beautiful skin, it would have made a beautiful picture. I didn't have sense enough to take advantage of it."

Dorothy quickly dressed and Jackson began snapping away. "She was very friendly to me. Very sweet," Jackson said. Throughout, Dorothy was relaxed and eager to please the camera, to strike various poses and moods, and also to present herself as a mature, sedate, demure young woman. Jackson's photographs are among the very few of Dorothy during this time when she was wife and mother with secret hopes of again being an actress.

Jackson took other pictures of Dorothy: as a bridesmaid at Jessie Mae Beavers' wedding; and also family scenes with Lynn, Geri, and Geri's son Tony. At another shoot, she observed the growing Lynn with other children. "She was snatching things from the children around her. Kind of a little nuisance. Nervous like," Jackson said. "Nothing to be alarmed about. But it was unusual." On another occasion, Jackson photographed a romantic Dorothy and Harold out for a horseback ride.

In early 1944, Dorothy appeared in the Black musical revue *Sweet 'n' Hot* which opened at the Mayan Theatre. She worked with a cast that included Marie Bryant, Mabel Scott, the comics Miller and Lee, dancer Freddie Gordon, and emcee Leonard Reed.

Later in the year she worked again with Louis Armstrong. The previous year she had appeared with him in a musical sequence of *Atlantic*

City and now in a musical sequence in a Warner Brothers' film, to be released the next year, called *Pillow to Post*. They went into a studio in August to record the number "Whatcha Say" for the picture as well as other material, "Groovin" and "Baby, Don't You Cry."

Dandridge and Armstrong had remained friends since her childhood years. They got along well and even shared a ritual of sorts when they went to the studio together. Armstrong's driver would pull the car in front of the house on 27th Street to pick up Dorothy. Just as she was about to get in, she was usually put off by Armstrong puffing away on his weed. Dandridge, who never smoked, would tell him, "Pops! Pops! I can't get in this car with all this smoke."

"Get in the car, girl," he'd tell her without flicking an eye or an ash. "You make me miss my draw."

Their performance in *Pillow to Post* remains striking for two reasons. In their earlier film *Atlantic City*, Dorothy energetically sang "Harlem on Parade," which served mainly as a prelude—a pretty woman as a sort of decorative embellishment—for the arrival of Armstrong, who performed "Ain't Misbehavin.'" Her appearance also gave Armstrong some sex appeal.

In *Pillow to Post*, however, performing "Whatcha Say?," Armstrong just about turns the sequence over to Dorothy, almost as if handing her a gift of prime exposure. And what exposure it was.

By now, Dandridge understood—from her experience in *Four Shall Die*, if nothing else—the importance of lighting, camera angles, and makeup for both dramatic effect and star power. At Hollywood's studios, she might have no control over the position of the camera or the lights or what transpired in the editing room, but she could maintain control over the way she looked: the style of her hair and the definition of the contours of her face.

At the studios, make-up and hair were tended to by White artists who were unaccustomed to working with African American skin tones and hair textures. When Lena Horne arrived at MGM, the studio went through conniptions on how to light and make her up. MGM created a special pancake base for Horne called Light Egyptian. But it was so dark, Horne claimed, that only White actress playing mulattoes or Blacks could wear it. Ultimately, the studio just made her up in much the fashion it did White stars.

When it came to Horne's hair, said Hollywood's great hair stylist Sydney Guilaroff, "No one would touch her. Except me." Guilaroff tended to the locks of female stars from Dietrich, Crawford, and Garbo, to the new stars of the postwar era Ava

Gardner, Marilyn Monroe, and Elizabeth Taylor. He remembered well MGM's attitude about makeup and hair for Black performers. Because he created Lena Horne's hair styles but couldn't be with her while she shot a film, Guilaroff persuaded the studio to hire a Black hairdresser to work with Lena daily on the set. He believed the studios should have Blacks working on hair and makeup anyway. Later Hazel Washington, a former actress who had worked as an aide in the 1920s for Garbo and later Rosalind Russell, was the licensed Black hairdresser assigned to the Black actors on Lena Horne's two big films of 1943, MGM's *Cabin in the Sky* and Twentieth Century Fox's *Stormy Weather*.

Some years later when Guilaroff worked with Dorothy on the MGM releases *Remains to Be Seen* and *Bright Road*, he did the same. First he created, with her, the look they felt appropriate for the character (or in the case of *Remains to Be Seen*, the nightclub setting). Then to execute the look during production, a Black hairdresser was assigned daily to the set. On later films, Dorothy met privately with Guilaroff to create hair styles. "Then we took pictures. And then Dorothy would take it to the new studio and tell them this was just how she wanted to look. I did this with other stars too," he said.

Dorothy also listened to the beauty advice of her friend, singer Herb Jeffries. During this era, Hollywood had very set notions about beauty standards, to which all female stars were expected to conform. It became almost a generic beauty look, without much room for variety. Upon Greta Garbo's arrival in the States from Sweden, for example, MGM mogul Louis B. Mayer insisted that she have her teeth fixed (to eliminate spaces between them) and more importantly, that she should lose weight. "In America, men don't like fat women," he said.

Later when Columbia Pictures signed a young Hispanic dancer named Marguerita Cansino, it was decided that in order to become an important star, she had to have a new look. So her hair color was lightened and a widow's peak that gave her face a distinctly "ethnic" look was removed hair by hair by the then painful process of electrolysis. She also slimmed down, and, of course, her name was changed. Margeurita Cansino became a less ethnic, more British sounding Rita Hayworth. As such, she emerged as a major box-office star at Columbia Pictures during the 1940s.

Given the social climate of the times, neither Lena Horne nor Dorothy Dandridge, despite their talents, would have made the cultural impact that they did if their looks had not suggested—at the very least—that they were racially mixed. The studios were eager to emphasize the more Caucasian aspects of their looks in order to insure their appeal to the mass White audience. The irony is that it was the ethnic aspects of their looks that provided the spice that made them more intriguing and exciting than the typical White goddesses. They were the forbidden, *yet oh so delicious*, fruit in the imaginations of the same people who racially rejected them. Thus, they were racial yet non-racial looking in the eyes of the mass audience.

As far as the mass Black audience was concerned, Dorothy and Lena, as they were known, were simply golden goddesses. *Fine sisters.* Mixed? Well, maybe. But then all Black people were. And in the long run, their color, along with their attitudes and styles, bonded Black America to them in the most intense personal and communal manner.

Much like Elizabeth Taylor and Ava Gardner, Dorothy was a natural beauty who, Jeffries explained, looked beautiful without makeup. "But there's a theatrical look," said Jeffries, who had experimented with makeup for Black Americans. At the time, the cosmetic companies hadn't developed products for browner and darker complexions. He sought out the industry's innovative makeup maven Max Factor. "I sat with him personally," said Jeffries.

Under Jeffries' tutelage and relying on her own instincts and experiments—darkening the eyes, highlighting the cheek bones, emphasizing the lips, later using a pancake base to even out and enhance her magnificent skin color—Dorothy ultimately devised a stunning visual image that worked splendidly for the camera and also for personal appearances.

"Dottie was pretty," said Geri. "And she had the makings," said Geri. "But Herb Jeffries taught Dottie and Lena to make up. It took hours to make up. And Dottie wore makeup like a *dream*."

In *Pillow to Post*, Dandridge emerged as a glamorous looking young woman. Not yet a mature beauty, but her look was now changing. It's no wonder that Armstrong appears to be almost beside himself in the sequence. *Can I really have this pretty child with me?* he must have been thinking!

As Dottie thought more seriously about a return to her career, she discussed it with Harold and Vivian. Harold's reaction upset her. "Dorothy told me that he said she couldn't sing and that she never had any talent," said Vivian. "And I was surprised because when he met her, you know the trio was working. And we had a marvelous reputation for being an excellent trio. So, I don't know if he was ridiculing her or teasing her." Years after the fact, Nicholas denied mocking her efforts, but Dorothy always insisted that he made light of her aspirations.

But others were enthusiastic. "She was a tremendous talent, a greater talent than anybody really had the opportunity to realize," said Herb Jeffries. During this period, he worked with Dorothy in three short films: *Flamingo* (also known as *Flamingo Isle*), *I Don't Want to Cry Anymore*, and *Basin Street Blues*.

"Dottie used to come to the house quite frequently and rehearse with Eddie Beale because she liked the way Eddie played piano. She always had some cute little jokes that she would come up with and if little jokes were told around her, she would laugh. She was always clowning and kidding around, or she would be doing some funny thing on Pearl Bailey. Or some funny thing on Lena. She would create these funny little bits on them." Jeffries remembered, "She imitated Lena, I mean till you could hardly tell that it wasn't Lena. Her whole personality and everything. She was a great impressionist. Just about any woman that she wanted to do, she could imitate."

The Nicholas Brothers' careers still flourished in the mid-1940s. Their representatives at the William Morris Agency persuaded them to embark as headliners on a new tour through the south. Called *Hepsations 1945*, the tour group included Dizzy Gillespie and his newly formed band, as well as Charlie Parker, the comedians Patterson and Jackson, shake dancer Lovey Lane, and vocalist June Eckstine (the wife of Billy Eckstine and also a friend of Dorothy's).

The road show traveled through Alabama, Tennessee, and Georgia. Dorothy and Geri joined the group for a visit in Texas. To avoid any racial problems that might flare up on the segregated trains in the South, the two women hired a driver and motored from Los Angeles. Staying with the tour on its leg into Mississippi, they then traveled with their husbands on the Nicholas Brothers' tour bus. Throughout the South, huge audiences turned out to see Harold and Fayard, who now, especially since *Stormy Weather*, were more popular than ever. Usually, they gave separate performances for Black audiences one night and White ones the next.

Just as the tour reached Arkansas, word blared from radios and newspapers around the country that finally the Second World War had ended. The Allies had triumphed. The Arkansas date, however, was canceled, Geri recalled. "It was sold out and everyone was excited but the promoter felt he could not control the crowd. Not enough security. People were so drunk and so happy with the War being over. And we left there and came back here to Los Angeles."

Like so many other Americans, Dottie was buoyed with the optimism of the dawning postwar era. A new day was coming. Black Americans were beginning to look at their nation—its opportunities, its lack of them, its segregated culture and cultural life, its voting system, its promise of freedom—from a new perspective.

By the start of 1946, Harold and Fayard signed to star in a new Black-cast musical headed for Broadway called *St. Louis Woman*. Produced by Edward Beck with a score by Harold Arlen and Johnny Mercer and a book by Black writer Arna Bontemps and the late Black poet Countee Cullen (based on Bontemps novel *God Sends Sunday*), the show also starred Rex Ingram, Ruby Hill, Maude Russell, and Pearl Bailey. After the pre-Broadway engagements in New Haven and Boston, its director Lemuel Ayers was replaced by Rouben Mamoulian.

Just before *St. Louis Woman*'s Broadway opening, Dorothy and Geri traveled by train to New York. "We took the Super Chief and the Twentieth Century," said Geri Nicholas. "There were bedrooms, drawing rooms, and dining cars. It was so exclusive that they didn't have too much trouble with integration on the line because there were so few Black people riding it."

Once in the city, Dorothy and Geri with their husbands "took over a floor in a hotel downtown near the theatre," recalled Geri. Dorothy and Geri took in the sights in New York, did some shopping, and spent time with Bill Robinson and their friend Sue, his wife. They also attended rehearsals, where Dorothy met *St. Louis Woman*'s director, Russian emigré Rouben Mamoulian, who over a decade later would be the original director of her film *Porgy and Bess*.

At rehearsals, she also met the spouse of one of the show's other stars—none other than comic Slappy White, then married to Pearl Bailey. Both Dottie and Geri, who liked him, were amused by the antics of White and Bailey, a mismatched pair if ever there were one. Pearl was clearly ambitious, en route to mainstream stardom. But White would make his mark as a ribald fixture on the "chitlin circuit," those small venues—clubs and theatres, joints and dives—for Black entertainers that were scattered around the country.

When Dottie grew bored with sitting around at rehearsals in a cold theatre, she and Geri went out to lunch. "Slappy would want to come with us," Geri recalled. He was just as anxious to get away as they were. "Now Slappy didn't have any money." So Dorothy and Geri would both tell him, "Well, Slappy, you've got to get *some money*. At least pay for a *hamburger*."

White would answer, "Well, I'll go and tell this woman." Then he headed for Pearl's dressing room. "This was better than the show," Geri said, "because he'd go in there and you'd hear Slap! Slap! Kick! Bang! *You So and So and So and So! You Sit Down! You Do What I Tell You to Do!* I couldn't tell which it was. And it was Pearl whipping Slappy!"

Afterwards Pearl would storm out of her dressing room. "You're taking him away from me," she would tell Dorothy and Geri. "You're taking him to lunch. Well, then you all just pay for it. Goddammit! Just pay for it!" Then the dressing room door would slam shut.

"That would just shock me in those days," said Geri.

This marked the first real meeting of Dorothy and Pearl, whose paths would cross in subsequent years when they appeared in *Carmen Jones* and *Porgy and Bess*. Bailey had no problems with Geri. "She got along with me okay." But she never hesitated, said Geri, to "make little comments about Dottie." Indeed, Bailey told Geri, in reference to Dottie, "You're the one with the brains."

"She was jealous from the get-go," Geri remembered. "That was Pearl's main motivation for living. It was jealousy."

Like Ethel Waters and Bill "Bojangles" Robinson, both of whom had warm, sweet-tempered personalities on stage but otherwise were holy terrors to be around, Pearl—also good-humored on stage—was already becoming known as a performer who could be difficult and mean as hell to work with.

"Evil won't begin to be the word for her! She was *evil*. She was one evil lady," said Geri. Bobby Short commented that Bailey was "as mean as a hornet." Geri always felt Slappy "put up with her because she was making good money."

Dorothy, however, glided past her encounters with Bailey without so much as batting an eyelash or making any comment on Bailey. She did so, partly because "she didn't hold grudges," said Geri, which in show business, was "completely out of the ordinary. But I seriously think that she had no viciousness or jealousy towards anybody. And people did her in *all of the time*." Dandridge also ignored Bailey because of her preoccupation with other matters, namely Lynn, who was brought to New York during rehearsals by the nanny Jonesy. Geri's son was also brought to the city at the same time by her sister.

"We'd take the kids to the park and walk down Broadway, which was really a joy," said Geri. "And we'd go to matinees and take them. And then we'd go uptown to the Apollo. They thoroughly enjoyed that."

"We were like a family at that time," said Fayard. "We would go out to dinner with the two children. Dorothy, Geri, and my brother. Just like a nice family." But Dottie was troubled by Lynn's behavior. "She responded if you hugged her. She liked to sit on laps," Geri recalled. "She played with Harold. He'd play ball with her, and she'd laugh. She was very sweet." But often Lynn was very quiet and very much to herself. Worse, Lynn "didn't recognize anybody," said Geri. She didn't seem to know her mother at all.

St. Louis Woman opened on Broadway at the Martin Beck Theatre on March 30, 1946 to mixed reviews. The musical ran for 113 performances. Its run might have been longer but Harold and Fayard, now that the War was over, decided to leave New York and, once William Morris could make the arrangements, embark on a tour that would take them out of the country.

Once back in Los Angeles, Dorothy had the familiar problems with Harold. When Harold traveled on the road, stories about his infidelities (Fayard's too) could be dismissed. But now in Los Angeles, she couldn't ignore the fact that Harold was rarely around, again spending time on the golf course and apparently in the bedrooms of other women. It was common knowledge throughout Black Los Angeles that Harold had girlfriends. It was common knowledge, too, that Dorothy's illusions about Harold, the perfect husband, were shattered and that the marriage was on shaky ground. Even their arguments were public knowledge and gossiped about.

"Nothing serious," Harold Nicholas said of the women he saw during these years. "But I was pretty bad."

Dorothy couldn't understand Harold's restlessness. He probably couldn't understand it either. She tried reaching him, in hopes of salvaging their marriage, but Harold was complicated and perhaps unable to admit even to himself how much he really loved her. Perhaps he feared needing her too much and becoming too emotionally tied to her.

On many nights, she was still alone while Harold joined his cronies for fun and card games.

"Hey, man," his buddies asked on many nights, "when you going home?"

"Ah, everything's cool," he would answer.

Years later he admitted, "That was wrong. I know it now. I didn't know it as much then as I know it now. But I was trying to be a man when I wasn't. I'm sure it must have been like hell for Dottie."

"Look," Fayard said to Harold one day, "things aren't working well with you and Dottie. Now why don't you. . ."

Before he could finish the sentence, Harold let out a familiar growling sound, which indicated always that the discussion was to end. *Now.* But Fayard tried again. "Listen to me," he said. Again the growling sound came.

"I couldn't talk to him," Fayard recalled. "He didn't want to talk to me. So I did my best. I couldn't get them back together."

Years later Harold said simply, "I don't think to this day I was ready for marriage, even after we had the baby."

The marital problems were temporarily pushed aside when, not long after their return to Los Angeles from their appearance in *St. Louis Woman*, Harold and Fayard embarked on an ambitious tour that stretched into 1947 and carried them to Miami Beach, Mexico City, Panama City, Havana, and Kingston (Jamaica). Dorothy occupied her days with her women's groups and activities, most of which helped take her mind off the domestic situation.

In early 1947, the brothers came back to Los Angeles where they reported to MGM for work in the Vincente Minnelli musical *The Pirate* with Gene Kelly and Judy Garland. Their big dance sequence with Kelly was shot in one day on July 9th. But because they appeared throughout the film, they worked on the production, which dragged on because of star Judy Garland's emotional problems, for some four months.

Around this time, Dorothy grew more concerned about Lynn. She admitted to having first sensed "that something was wrong" when Lynn was about two years old. "She couldn't speak, although other children her age were speaking," Dorothy said. "She did begin to walk at about eight months, which was a little ahead of when most children walk." By the time Geri's son Tony, who was younger than Lynn, turned two, he was talking. But Lynn still couldn't talk. "And her frustration made her have temper tantrums," recalled Geri.

For a time, Dorothy took comfort in the advice of her pediatrician as well as friends who assured her that some children took longer to express themselves. "Don't worry. Einstein didn't talk until he was six years old because he was a genius. So your child is a genius," she remembered being told. "I wanted to believe they were right because I didn't want to face reality."

But when Lynn was almost four and still didn't speak or seem to know anyone, when she still had loud crying fits and was unmanageable, Dottie became distressed and then frantic.

"I took her to psychoanalysis for children. I started to study psychoanalysis to see if I could understand what was wrong," Dorothy said. "We traveled a lot. People would say the child was emotionally disturbed because of the traveling. Others said she would be disturbed if we left her at home without her parents. It seemed that whatever I'd do would be wrong."

"I finally had an electroencephalograph taken of her," said Dorothy. "That's a brain wave test to determine whether the brain is functioning as it should."

The electroencephalograph or EEG was used to measure the electrical activity of the brain. Metal plates were secured around Lynn's scalp. A normal "awake" brain has a particular pattern of electrical activity, which indicates the brain is functioning properly. Lynn's physicians were searching for signs of pathology or abnormal brain wave activity that affected her cognitive status or the level of her awareness. But, according to Dorothy, the EEG revealed no abnormality.

Said Dorothy, "Then I had an air encephalograph made."

Before the age of more sophisticated ways of imaging the brain (such as the computerized axial tomography, known as the CT scan), this was a technique of great importance for visualizing inter-cranial pathology. Air was injected into the lumbar region of Lynn's spine and allowed to ascend to outline the ventricular system of her brain. A picture was then taken to delineate Lynn's brain structure. Based upon the shape of the ventricles, a diagnosis of abnormal brain structure could then be made. But this very risky, painful test also uncovered no structural abnormality. The physicians' efforts to establish the etiology of Lynn's mental condition were frustrating.

Dorothy then sought the opinion of other physicians, enduring what she called her "odyssey of despair" in her search for a "cure."

A new ritual was established. She'd rise, bathe Lynn, dress her, and comb and braid her hair, often tying on bows. She'd put the girl in the car. And off they'd go to see a physician. Usually, Geri went with her because now Dottie's emotional state worried the family. But her visits to the physicians usually ended in the same way, with Dottie in tears.

"There was no doctor that could say anything definite," Harold recalled. "They couldn't tell you *why* she was like that. Or they didn't know what caused it. It was just pitiful."

Nicholas admitted he wasn't much help as Dorothy searched to find a physician with an optimistic diagnosis. "It was a heavy load I left on her. Cause for her to be there alone to do all this, that was a heavy toll," said Nicholas. Having been protected all his life, Harold seemed emotionally incapable of facing Lynn's problems. He, with his emotional withdrawal—and even Dottie, in the minds of some, with her round of physicians—appeared to deny what was becoming increasingly clearer to everyone else. Lynn's problems were serious and irreversible. She was not learning. She never would. "This was a little girl I wanted to take out and show to everybody and have fun with her," recalled Fayard. "Maybe teach her how to dance and just have fun with her. And I couldn't do that. Cause I tried to talk to her. But she wouldn't talk. She wouldn't talk to me. And I'd say, something's really, really wrong." "[Lynn] developed up to about three-years-old," Geri said. "And she couldn't go beyond that. But she still couldn't talk. And everything would make her have a temper tantrum. She could wash dishes. And she liked to. But if you moved the soap on *this side* rather than on *this* side, she'd just blow up."

Lynn soon required "a twenty-four-hour watch," said Geri. "She didn't sleep. And if you'd give her sleeping pills, they'd wake her up. She'd get more energy. And she'd run away. Or she'd try to run through a window or jump out of a window. And she'd laugh about it. She was very sweet. But just out of it."

Every day seemed to present a new problem with Lynn. "I took her once to get her teeth pulled," Geri recalled. "She had a double set of teeth. And they gave her more anesthesia than they'd give a grown man. . . and she just got stronger. It took six men to hold her down. No anesthesia would work when they pulled her teeth. She got out and she was as strong as a bull."

That afternoon as they arrived home, Lynn "opened the car door and was running down the street laughing with me chasing her. It was just terrible. She didn't know rain or sunshine. She'd just as soon jump out of a window. You couldn't leave her with a child. She'd probably hit them. And yet other times in other ways she was very affectionate." Suddenly, she might reach her arms out to Dottie and just throw them around her. "There was no feeling like that," Dorothy recalled.

Perhaps the irony was the one manner in which Lynn seemed capable. "She had a real thing about dressing and looking pretty and changing clothes. And she'd go get clothes and bring them to you," Geri recalled.

As Vivian sat in the home on 27th Street, she saw Dorothy in a panic. Dorothy tried to play with Lynn, tried to teach her words and communicate with her. And the strain was starting to show.

During this era of confusion and ignorance about developmentally disabled children, parents found themselves burdened by guilt and shame. Little information was available on the causes of retardation, and there was limited effective treatment for such children. Like any other parent, Dorothy agonized and felt herself responsible in some way, even though Lynn's condition still hadn't been diagnosed in any concrete way.

Never could Dottie forget the circumstances of Lynn's birth. Never could she "be certain that there was a direct relationship between a delayed delivery and the kind of child that matured," she said, "but in my deepest heart I think there was some connection. In a way, all of this was my fault."

What everyone knew now was that Lynn suffered from severe mental retardation; that there was no "cure."

"Dottie didn't want to believe this child was retarded," said Vivian. "It was something that she just never really wanted to accept. Now this was something that she didn't recognize after we even had recognized it."

She "just took her everywhere. Took her to everybody you could think of," said Geri. Later Dottie tried to place Lynn in school, hoping that there the child would conform. But it didn't work out.

"Every doctor would say she's retarded," Fayard recalled. "I was shocked when I heard that."

On occasion, Dorothy completely withdrew from the reality of the situation. Perhaps dance lessons in Switzerland would help Lynn, she decided one evening. Most times though she found herself crying, depressed, and struggling just to leave the house or to see people.

At the same time, her marriage continued to deteriorate. She couldn't talk to Harold, who was sullen and uncommunicative. Or out on the golf course. Or, so Dorothy believed, with other women.

Dorothy continued to speak to Fayard about Harold. "Here I am with my daughter," she told him. "And her father's not here." Then she broke into tears.

"I'd try to caress her and make her feel better. I did what I could," recalled Fayard.

Again, Fayard spoke to his brother about Lynn's condition and Dottie, but he pulled back.

"Harold couldn't stand it at all," Fayard said. "He'd go away and stay for many hours cause it really hurt him. Cause he was so in love with this little girl. And we were all in love with her. And it just broke Dottie up. It just broke her up completely."

Harold, Fayard explained, "always held things back. When something upset him, he wouldn't express himself and say what was bothering him. I knew what was bothering him. His daughter Lynn. That was on his mind because Dottie was almost divorcing him at that moment. All those things were on his mind. So you couldn't get to him somehow. And I did my best to try. It just didn't work. It didn't work." Like Dottie, Harold questioned one incident after another, searching for answers. He recalled the argument with Dorothy during her pregnancy, when she had become so distressed that she fainted and fell. He asked himself if that had caused Lynn's condition. He also wondered about a day when, while playing with Lynn on the bed, she had fallen on the floor and hit her head. But he said nothing to anyone at the time.

Fayard did much the same. He questioned if Lynn's condition was the result of the time he saw the girl hit her head on a concrete pavement.

Everyone in the family was confused by Lynn's behavior and asked questions. But it was left to Dottie to find solutions for the treatment of Lynn.

Soon Dorothy began seeing a psychiatrist. From then on, "She was never without therapy," said Geri. She questioned everything about Lynn, her own family history, her relationship with Harold, all of which troubled her for years to come. She wondered what had she done wrong and if she were in some way inadequate for Harold. When they married, Harold had been a sexually experienced young man of the world. She had been a virgin. Often she felt she didn't satisfy him sexually. Then, too, she questioned her feelings about sex and men. Had Ma-Ma's obsessive concerns about virginity made her feel sex was something to be ashamed of? Had Ma-Ma—and Ruby too with her critical comments about

Cyril's weaknesses—made her forever suspicious and untrusting of men?

She also used therapy to work through her feelings about Ruby and Neva. Dorothy struggled with her contempt and inability to forgive Neva for the way she had treated her as a child.

Dandridge's psychiatrist recommended that she let someone else care for Lynn. "[Dorothy] was told that if she kept the child, she would end up in an institution because she couldn't deal with it. That's what the psychiatrist told her," Vivian said. "So she had to give the child up. And she was also told, 'Don't see the child for awhile.' I mean it's sad. But I used to see the child sometimes because I didn't have any kind of hang up. She was my niece. So I would have the child over. And we would treat her like there was nothing wrong with her. But it was pitiful." Sometimes Dottie left Lynn with the nanny Jonesy. But a new crisis emerged when Jonesy, then in her 70s, became ill and couldn't care for Lynn any longer. Dottie searched for another nanny, without success. Then Ruby and Neva offered to take care of Lynn.

Dottie consented. Some questioned how she could have turned her daughter over to Neva. But her decision grew out of desperation. Of course, Neva made it clear that she was to be paid for the care of Lynn. Geri volunteered to watch over Lynn to make sure the girl was handled properly at Ruby's home. Neva and Ruby also found a day nurse to come in.

Attempting to focus on something other than Lynn's condition or the sad state of her marriage, Dorothy threw herself into other activities. Most of her free time was spent with Geri, who also had problems with Fayard and *his* girlfriends. "Women would have cut off my arm to get near Fayard," she said. Apparently, he didn't pass them up either, yet Fayard was always attentive to Geri.

Geri, though, became active in social and political causes in Los Angeles. As a consequence, Dorothy became active as well. *The California Eagle* was among the causes they took on. The paper was in such financial trouble—its publisher, the ever-resourceful Charlotta Bass, was struggling to stay in business—that Dorothy and Geri, along with another woman named Jean Seroity, stepped in to help. "Every week she [Charlotta Bass] couldn't get it out of the printer's," said Geri. "So Dottie, Jean, and I would pool money in order to pay. About $700." They did this on a week-by-week basis.

Dorothy also threw a party at her home to raise funds for the newspaper. "We made everybody pay $30 to help us with *The Eagle*,"said Geri. Paul Robeson, who was in town for a concert, attended the affair, just at a time when his political problems were mounting. His allegiance to the Soviet Union had made him a target for the growing conservative anti-Communist forces in America.

Dorothy attended other political affairs, sometimes with Harold, sometimes with Geri. Most were civil rights rallies or benefits. Actor Byron Morrow remembered that she sang a number from *Meet the People* at one such fundraising party. "Any progressive person of the industry was involved in such activities," said Morrow, "and therefore suspect. Dorothy and other entertainers attended all types of parties for the budding civil rights movement. White stars like Ava Gardner came too."

She also joined other progressive acting and social groups, including the Hollywood Democratic Committee, which was composed mainly of Hollywood liberals with some "radicals" and Communists. To Dorothy and many others actors, the organization's purpose during the War Years had been to support victory abroad and the presidency of Franklin Roosevelt. Usually, Dorothy's work with this group and others was to help with fundraisers, bond sales, blood drives, and also the election of "honest and responsible" public officials. Later the Hollywood Independent Citizens Committee of Arts, Sciences, and Professions grew out of the Hollywood Democratic Committee. During the war years, however both the Hollywood Democratic Committee and the later organization were viewed suspiciously by conservative politicians and conservative members of the film colony, who sought to weed out subversives in the entertainment industry.

Upon learning of Dorothy's activities, Ruby became upset. Politics, she knew, could wreck a career. "You got to be careful," she warned Dottie, adding, "Look out for that Geri. She's gonna get you in jail. You ain't never gonna get no more work."

Ruby was just a "damn Aunt Jemima," said Geri, and in reference to her own political activism, she added, "It didn't make me no-never-mind."

Politics for Dorothy, though, were never a major part of her life. Given her ongoing tensions with Harold, focusing on such activities was often difficult for her. Later, though, her political activities, as minor as they were, were enough to affect her career. Dorothy was unaware that some of her activities put her name in the files of the

Federal Bureau of Investigation. Many of her appearances at rallies and benefits would also be questioned during the era of blacklisting and the witch hunts in Hollywood in the late 1940s and early 1950s.

Dorothy also began to concentrate on her career again. Aware now that comedy was not what she wanted to do, she still enjoyed singing and tried working up a nightclub act. She had also enrolled in the Actors Lab in Los Angeles, becoming one of its first African American students. This was a progressive, new style of acting school on the West Coast, similar to the Actors Studio in New York. She began to think seriously of a career as a dramatic actress, which she had dreamt of since she was a little girl. For her, that meant being an actress not on the stage but on screen.

In the mid-and late-1940s, such an ambition for a Black woman was considered a folly, pure foolishness. There was almost no history of Black dramatic actresses in Hollywood films. Early on, Nina Mae McKinney's soulfully dramatic Chick in *Hallelujah* had presented the *possibility*. But despite the praise of director King Vidor and MGM producer Irving Thalberg, McKinney afterwards scrambled for work and didn't have another significant film until 1935's *Sanders of the River* with Paul Robeson, in England, not the States.

Then there had been iridescent Fredi Washington, who played the light-skinned young Black woman who tries to cross the color line, in the original 1934 *Imitation of Life*. Very few screen actresses of the Depression era were as striking as Washington. She made another film in the movie capital, *One Mile From Heaven* with Bill Robinson, then headed back to the East Coast. No films followed that. Still acting on the stage, she became committed to the state of the Black actor in America. She helped found the Negro Actors Guild, and wrote articles and reviews for the newspaper *The People's Voice*, run by her brother-in-law Adam Clayton Powell. Interestingly, one of Fredi Washington's favorite actresses in the 1950s would be Dorothy Dandridge, whom Washington had first met at the Cotton Club in the 1930s.

Black women like Lucia Lynn Moses, Ethel Moses, and Bee Freeman (called sometimes the sepia Mae West) appeared in such race movies as *Scar of Shame* and the Oscar Micheaux features *God's Step Children* and *Underworld*. Nina Mae McKinney also worked in such race films after her brief Hollywood heyday. But race movies were not viewed as plausible alternatives. By the late 1940s, this film category would be on its last leg and vanish.

Dorothy's studies at the Actors Lab were interrupted when she and Geri made plans to join Harold and Fayard in Europe. The William Morris Agency had set up an extensive tour for the Nicholas Brothers that would ultimately keep them out of the country for several years. They were scheduled to travel through England, France, Switzerland, and Portugal. It was decided that the brothers would leave immediately. Their wives would join them later in England.

This tour eventually proved a turning point in the career of the Nicholas Brothers. *Stormy Weather* marked the end of their contract with Twentieth Century Fox. And MGM's *The Pirate* was the last Hollywood film in which the brothers worked together. During the dawning years of the civil rights movement, postwar movie audiences would come to view many of the African American dancers and singers of the first half of the century as passé. Television became the venue for such Black performers as moviemakers gradually created more dramatic, realistic depictions of the Negro. The heady days of the Nicholas Brothers' success in America was about to come to an end.

Dorothy and Geri departed from Los Angeles in need of some relaxation. Their first stop was London where the brothers were playing the London Casino. For Dorothy, memories floated back to the time she, Vivian, and Etta had appeared in the city just as Europe had first entered the war. Now, as the wife of a famous entertainer, her role would be to insure his personal affairs were in order and to keep track of his social obligations. Harold and Fayard were much sought after and operated in a seemingly privileged realm where they were free to mix with the moneyed and the titled. Daily, Dottie sorted through the invitations that came in for luncheons, dinners, and receptions.

One evening Harold, Fayard, Geri, and Dorothy were invited to a party at the home of one of London's most famous Black entertainers, a very attractive American-born expatriate who sang and performed on the piano in some of the city's posh dinner clubs and cabarets. In a home filled with priceless antiques, imported carpets and drapes, fine silver and linens, she was at the center of a very sophisticated, moneyed crowd. Known for her elegance, she was also known to be the girlfriend of a powerful politician.

Fayard, Geri, and Dorothy—without Harold—arrived at the woman's home where she graciously greeted them and introduced them to the roomful of other guests, all beautifully dressed and groomed. It looked as if it would be one of those glamorous elegant evenings that they would never forget. As it turned out, the evening was memorable but for some unexpected reasons. Once everyone was seated for dinner, Geri found herself not far from her hostess. The two began talking about politics. Dorothy and Fayard were at the other end of the long dining room table, out of earshot of the conversation between Geri and the hostess. Geri was surprised to learn that the woman's politician boyfriend, her benefactor, was Jan Smuts, the South African leader who became known as the father of apartheid.

As the woman prattled on about Smuts, praising his political acumen and the deft manner in which he was handling South Africa's "nasty" political situation, Geri became infuriated. Had Smuts been there, she informed the woman, she would have told him to go straight to hell. Suddenly, the expression on the hostess's face changed. "This woman turned livid," said Geri.

Indignant, the hostess told Geri, "You're dining, my dear, at a table Jan Smuts bought. And he paid for all this food. And I adore him."

Geri stared at her hostess in disbelief. She had no intention of spending another moment in this woman's house. Rising from the table, she looked for Dorothy and Fayard. Dorothy was engaged in an animated conversation and apparently enjoying the evening.

"Dottie, let's go!" said Geri. "Fayard, let's go!" Both Dorothy and Fayard, still unaware what all the commotion was about, rose from their seats, excused themselves, walked with Geri to retrieve their coats from the butler, and then walked out of the woman's townhouse.

Dorothy was confused but laughed at Geri. "My best friend is getting me in trouble again!" she said. "What conversation were you having with that woman?"

After Geri explained the situation, a fired-up Dorothy exclaimed, "Well, let's go back there and tell her a few things, and get thrown out of there all over again!"

Geri recalled, "That was Dottie! If you started the fight for Dottie, she'd help you finish it."

～

From London, the two couples traveled for several months throughout the British provinces, including Liverpool, Blackpool, and Birmingham. Huge and adoring crowds packed the theatres. The Nicholas Brothers' movies now had been shown worldwide.

An odd and troubling incident occurred one evening when Dorothy and Geri attended a performance at a music hall either in Liverpool or Blackpool, as Geri recalled. An elderly woman in a rocking chair was brought onto the stage. She was a fortune teller who stared poker-faced at the audience as she asked them to take out a picture of someone they had questions about.

"Dottie opened her purse and took out a picture of Lynn. She held it in her hand," recalled Geri. For a few minutes, the woman on stage said nothing. Then still staring out stone-faced at her audience, she said, "There is a lady here with a child who has a birth defect. She is worried about the child. The child will never speak."

Dorothy was stunned. For a few minutes, she did nothing and looked as if she could neither speak nor move. Then she quietly put the picture of Lynn back in her purse and began to cry. "It broke Dottie up," remembered Geri. "She was just devastated. She cried. Afterwards she went to the hotel. She wouldn't eat. She didn't want to talk." Everywhere she went, there were reminders of Lynn's tragedy.

Yet for much of this hectic, non-stop tour, there was laughter and excitement and a never ending gallery of personalities, especially in Paris, which was the next stop for the brothers who performed at the Club des Champs Élysées. As Europe was rebuilding and lifting itself out of a wartime economy and frame of mind, everyone seemed ready to kick up their heels and have some fun. "We'd get up when we'd feel like it," Fayard remembered. The two couples would spend the early part of the day dining and sightseeing, absorbing as much of the culture and customs as possible. Dottie and Geri especially liked to visit museums or galleries, or to shop for clothes and gifts.

Harold was a genius with languages, sharp enough to quickly pick up foreign colloquialisms, inflections, and expressions. After one day in a city like Paris, he was able the following night to introduce their act in French. A day in Italy and he would be speaking

Italian. Wherever they went, he could speak the language, order their dinners, and give instructions to bellhops or a concierge. Throughout the stay in Paris and the other European capitals, his spirits were high.

But while Harold and Fayard were the center of attention on stage, off-stage all eyes were on Dorothy. Harold recalled that in Paris, the Frenchmen went "crazy" for her, literally following her down the street or stopping to stare and engage her in a conversation. Geri too saw the extraordinary, almost unreal effect, Dorothy had on everyone who met her, male and female.

Geri was reminded of the times when she and Dorothy went to the Farmer's Market in Los Angeles, with its outdoor restaurants and its quaint boutiques where the two sometimes shopped for children's clothes. Dorothy gracefully walked through the spacious open area looking serene and gorgeous. Men—White men—would a catch a glimpse of her and then literally push aside chairs at their tables and turn around just to look at her again.

The response in both Europe and the States was partly to Dorothy's beauty, partly to something else.

"It was Dottie's vulnerability," said Geri. "This is what I think they responded to. And I saw that before she was on stage or famous in Europe. People were so *drawn* to her. And everyone wanted to protect her. Of course, she used that tremendously. And you can't blame her. But that vulnerability was the key."

Usually, around seven in the evening, the foursome would make its way to the nightclubs or theatres where the brothers were performing. Dottie and Geri always surveyed the audience, to see if it was a full house and if the patrons were in good humor. After the shows, there came more socializing as they hit the late night spots with friends and new acquaintances.

"We were having a good time over there," Fayard said. "And so we didn't have time to be thinking about any hardship. We were there in Europe and we wanted to see it. So those days were good. With the four of us. We really had fun."

"We used to have such good times laughing together," Harold remembered, "that we kept people up [at our hotels] because we were up late and were laughing and having a good time, I mean the people couldn't go to sleep and they would call into the office. And the owner would call us and ask us to keep it down."

While in Paris, their Hollywood friend White actress Carole Landis flew over and joined them. Egypt's King Farouk, who knew

Landis, flew her, along with Harold and Fayard, Dottie and Geri, to Egypt for some fun. Later Dorothy, Geri, Fayard, and Harold were shocked to hear that Landis returned to Hollywood and committed suicide.

They also saw Josephine Baker, who Harold and Fayard had appeared with as children in the *Ziegfeld Follies of 1936*. In other cities, American stars like Bob Hope and Milton Berle saw the brothers perform and came backstage afterwards. It was a heady, fast-moving time.

During the tour, whenever Dorothy had some extra money, the first thing she did was to wire some to her mother. Ruby was now a well-established character actress in movies and radio and certainly making a very good living, but, said Geri, "Dottie never forgot them." She would also send $25 or $30 to Vivian.

Along with the fun and excitement, however, there were still the problems with Harold. The ugly reality of his philandering always came crashing in, usually the minute Harold entered their hotel suite after having been gone for hours.

There were quarrels, mainly about his girlfriends. Angered and dejected, she finally told him she was leaving and made arrangements to return to Los Angeles. "I'd cry with her," said Geri, "and she'd get up and leave and come back to the States." But once in Los Angeles, confronted with another situation that had not changed at all, a daughter whom she seemed unable to do anything for, a charming but now deadly silent house that she had once decorated with visions of a secure family life, Dottie found herself often alone. She thought about Harold and, whether she liked it or not, she missed him.

Harold also missed her. He called, apologized, and asked her to come back. She was hesitant and still angry, but he continued to call. She still loved Harold and still hoped for a happy ending; a sweet romantic resolution of their marital woes in which Harold was miraculously transformed from spoiled, self-indulgent playboy to a devoted, attentive husband. She returned to Europe.

Once the Nicholas Brothers completed the first leg of their sprawling European tour, both couples returned briefly to California. Then the European tour resumed. The brothers opened at London's Palladium with Duke Ellington and Pearl Bailey for a command performance in June 1948.

Dorothy remained in Los Angeles for a spell and later joined Harold, Fayard, and Geri in Sweden where the brothers traveled as part of a tour starring the legendary Swedish performer Karl

Gearhard. Once again there came the familiar cycle of fun and excitement followed by strain between Harold and herself.

"They'd have a big making up and so on," said Geri. "But then it would start all over again."

Nothing could camouflage Harold's escapades with other women. Nor Fayard's. On numerous occasions when Dorothy and Geri prepared to spend an evening with their husbands, the women were told by Fayard or Harold, "Oh, no, this is not a party for wives."

On such nights the two women stayed in their hotel rooms to read or talk. Often they analyzed problems. Or they played checkers. Or Dottie discussed renewed career plans. "We'd wait. And they'd come home like five or six in the morning," said Geri. "No point in fighting about it because this was their life."

During one such evening in Stockholm, the brothers attended a party where they met two pretty young women, who returned with them the next morning for breakfast in their hotel's restaurant. As Harold and Fayard sat with their lady friends enjoying their morning meal, who should walk into the restaurant but Dottie and Geri. The brothers felt they had had an innocous night on the town. "We didn't do anything," Fayard said. So they simply waved to their wives who sat at another table.

The young women with the brothers became nervous. But Harold and Fayard brushed aside their anxieties. Neither Dorothy nor Geri said anything to their husbands or the women. They ate their meal, then left the dining room, and returned to their rooms. Both were furious though and later gave their husbands a piece of their minds. Still, neither Harold nor Fayard felt any guilt pangs because they believed themselves innocent of any wrongdoing.

On another occasion, Harold and Fayard smuggled their girlfriends into the hotel where the two couples were staying. All was fine until their cover was blown by a bellhop. He entered their suite and asked a question in French, which, unfortunately for Fayard, Geri understood but he did not.

Fayard asked suspiciously, "What's the fool saying? Hurry up and get out of the room."

"The fool is saying 'Where do you want to put your girlfriend?'" Geri told him. "She's in this hotel. But did you want her to go to another hotel?"

Fayard was so annoyed with the bellhop, according to Geri, that he took off his shoe and threw it at the poor guy!

"It's comical now," Geri said years later. But at the time both women were upset and depressed by the repeated behavior of their husbands.

Of her relationship with Fayard, Geri said, "I knew that the marriage wouldn't work. You should never marry an artist. And he was a womanizer." Early on, she had resigned herself to the fact that Fayard might never grow up. But she loved him and always valued the world of opportunities—the travel, the people, the experiences—he gave her. For her, it was just a question of when the marriage would end, not if. As it turned out, the couple stayed together for fourteen years.

Geri buried herself in books and classes, which she took at universities in Switzerland and later Italy to cope with Fayard's infidelities. But Harold's womanizing "broke Dottie's heart," said Geri. "It destroyed Dottie, whose ego was weak. And any rejection of any kind destroyed it."

"Nothing really drastic" happened between Dorothy and him, Harold once said. "But there were times when we got into arguments, Dorothy and I." Dorothy's temper would flare up and then Harold would tell her she was overreacting and being too sensitive. Their shouting matches escalated to the point at which Harold would leave or Dorothy would cry. "She was very sensitive," Harold said. He never physically abused her. But he said, "I guess the words *hit* her. The way it was done. Perhaps that was what was hurting her."

Disappointed in him and the drift of her marriage and her life, still preoccupied with Lynn's condition, she frequently withdrew. More and more, she fantasized about a career and, of course, a cure for Lynn. But those reveries could comfort and cushion her only so much.

Looking for some release from the emotional tensions with Harold, Dorothy performed one evening, apparently at a benefit. Geri was surprised by what she saw. Standing on stage alone, Dorothy was a haunting presence as she sang an old-world tale of the three stages of a woman's life. First there was youth and all the hope it offered. Then came middle age as hopes diminish and fears set in. Then old age when hope has vanished and despair taken over. Quickly altering her makeup and using a scarf and wig while performing, she transformed her appearance right on stage. The entire audience turned silent as this lovely vision performed a wistful song of change and the vicissitudes of life. "She was so good that night and so moving," said Geri. "She really understood something about living. It was just beautiful."

In Sweden, though, the pressures, the arguments, the nights she was left alone overwhelmed her and she slipped into a debilitating depression, which she couldn't snap out of. Geri didn't know what to do. Then one morning, Geri entered Dorothy's room—the couples usually had adjoining suites—to discover Dorothy still in bed, dazed and disoriented; her face was pale and swollen. Geri tried to get Dorothy up. Then she realized her friend had taken an overdose of sleeping pills. She called for help and got Dorothy to a hospital where they pumped her stomach.

Afterwards, Dorothy shrugged off the incident, saying to Geri, "Well, I made a mistake. You know, I couldn't sleep."

But it was clearly a suicide attempt; as such, it was partly crying out for help, and being a performer, it may have been partly using dramatic effects in hopes of saving the marriage. Yet as the years ahead proved, underlying that attempt was Dorothy's fundamental sense of futility.

She made another suicide attempt when the tour took the group to Switzerland not long afterwards. Another trip to a hospital. Again her stomach was pumped. In Zurich, Dorothy consulted a psychiatrist. Described by Geri as a "wonderful" and "marvelous man," he worked with Dorothy and shared his conclusions with Geri: he believed Dorothy was an artist who wouldn't be able to cope without the safeguard of her strong interior fantasy life. Otherwise realities, which he tried to help her to deal with, were too much for her to bear.

"He told me that *by no means* would he ever bring Dottie to reality and get her out of her fantasy. Nor would he do that to any actor because then they would be finished because they are not of this world." To tamper with her dream world was dangerous and futile, he concluded. Her creativity sprang from it.

But recovering from the suicide attempts awakened her in another way. If she was to live, then she had to live on her own terms; not Harold's. She probably considered divorcing him, but her feelings were too conflicted and remained so for years to come. Harold excited and moved her with his strength and daring. The very qualities that others found arrogant and snobbish, she admired. To her, Harold was a man who wouldn't take any guff from anybody, who spoke his mind, and went his way. He was also the first person to offer her an escape from her past and provide her an opportunity to start a new life.

Then, too, she was always in awe of Harold's talent. Every time she saw him dance, she had to forgive him for his transgressions. She also understood how Harold's talents were fully appreciated in

Europe, which offered him a way of life and freedom that were denied him in the States. He "saw and experienced less of the rejection that was the lot of Negroes," she said. "Even there you couldn't escape some feeling of alienation, but it was not as extreme as in the States."

The careers of the Nicholas Brothers had cushioned them from American racism, to some degree, but not completely. Neither Dottie nor Geri could forget an incident that occurred during an appearance by Harold and Fayard on a show in Los Angeles prior to the European tour. Backstage at the theatre, a famous White American comic "came in and saw Harold and went over and rubbed his head," Geri said. It was an old racist custom to touch a nigger's head for luck.

Harold stepped back. "Look," he told the comic. "You're White. I'm a Negro. But I'm talented. And don't you ever put your hands on my head. I know the meaning of that." "What's wrong?" the comic asked. "What the hell is wrong with you? You're not big enough to talk to me?"

"Yes, I am. Talent gets me everywhere."

When the comic stated that the then up-and-coming performer Sammy Davis Jr. let him touch his head in such an "affectionate" way, Harold bristled, "That's Sammy. I'm an aristocrat. He's a peasant. Don't ever do that!"

Angered, the comic said that Harold would never work again.

"They put the blacklist on him," Geri said. Not an official blacklist. The industry didn't have to do that for this kind of behavior. But word spread that Harold could be aloof, difficult, and unfriendly. *Stormy Weather*'s director Andrew Stone once said that Harold "was the only Black actor that I've ever known that I felt was a bit snotty." Others in the industry had the same impression. According to Geri, following this incident with the comedian, the brothers "*had* to go to Europe, which was just great. They worked there for years."

During the years Harold spent abroad, Sammy Davis Jr. indeed rose to great success at home. Geri and others believed he did so by stealing Harold's act. Harold was not only one of the world's greatest dancers, but also a fine singer, a wonderful impressionist, and a talented drummer. Ultimately, Sammy would dance, sing, and do impressions, too.

But with all that Dorothy admired and understood about Harold, ultimately she couldn't cope with his steady parade of girlfriends. Hurt and embarrassed, she no doubt felt as abandoned and betrayed by him as she did by Cyril. Harold also still couldn't express his emotions, his needs. Nor was he the kind of man to show any vulnerability. Still a very young man, he was too much at the center of his own universe to comprehend someone else's needs or pain, to be able to open himself up enough to understand Dorothy's fears and point of view, to truly share with her. "Harold was a victim of himself and having grown up in an entertainment world where he was always prized and always made over and always the cutie pie. Always loved by women regardless of who he was or rather *because* of who he was," said his sister Dorothy Nicholas Morrow. "And there was not enough balance there. Which helps to develop your personality. He was just taken in by it. So with falling in love with Dorothy and Dorothy falling in love with him, he was happy to find this lovely young woman to fall in love with him. But it never stopped him from doing all those things he had done before."

Morrow summed it up by saying, "It's sad. I'm speaking quite honestly, and I'm as disappointed with him as I am with anybody for treating people the way he did or did not treat Dorothy."

Harold himself admitted, "I didn't treat her like I should have, as a loving husband should have treated his wife. Someone that he cared about and someone that he wanted to be with."

Finally, Dorothy decided to call it quits. On a flight from London to the States, she seemed lost in her thoughts until she suddenly sprang forward in her seat, looked at Geri, sitting next to her, and said, "I'm going back to London."

"But we're over the ocean, Dottie."

"Well, when we get to New York. I'm getting a flight back."

She wanted to tell Harold everything was over. Geri knew from the look in Dorothy's eyes that her friend had made up her mind. But once back in the States, she did nothing to dissolve the marriage.

Ultimately, what appeared to have prompted a decisive move was a visit Dorothy made in California to a new doctor named Ethel Harrington to discuss Lynn, who was then about five years old. Dorothy grilled the woman for answers about Lynn, as she had done with doctors in the past. Dorothy still wanted to know if something could be done so that Lynn might learn to talk and care for herself. Up until then the doctors "would not tell her that Lynn would never talk," Geri said, by now, Dorothy believed she was getting the runaround, that the doctors were not leveling with her.

To all of Dorothy's questions, the new physician Harrington answered in medical terms. Finally, frustrated, desperate, but determined to confront the truth whatever it be, Dorothy looked directly at the physician and said bluntly, "I want to know. Something is wrong and I want to face it now. I have to face it sometime."

"Mrs. Nicholas, your child has a brain damage," Harrington explained. "The best thing for you to do is give her up and have another." "[She] said it just like that," Dorothy recalled years later. Then the woman repeated what she had said. "I think the reason [she] did is because people had been telling me so many different things just to make me feel good." The doctor wanted her to finally accept the fact that Lynn was irreversibly retarded. Then Dorothy felt all the more guilty about the delayed delivery and the use of forceps to pry out Lynn's head. But her guilt appeared to be unfounded, so Harrington indicated. Sometimes forceps could cause brain injury. But the use of forceps, contrary to what Dorothy wanted to believe, was not uncommon. Most children delivered in this way grew up perfectly "normal." Instead, in all likelihood, Lynn suffered from anoxic brain damage. During Dorothy's labor and delivery, not enough oxygen had traveled to the baby's brain. In a sense, it was as simple as that.

Stunned, Dorothy now had an explanation. Or perhaps now for the first time she could accept an explanation.

"I just sat there for a while. Finally, I heard what [she] had said. I just said, 'Thank you, doctor.'" Quietly, Dorothy left the physician's office with her daughter. "I just didn't want to stay and hear anymore. I took [Lynn] by the hand and put her in the car. She had been sitting there listening to every word. She began to make strange little sounds and do things she had done before."

"Later people told me they had seen me driving down the street with her," Dorothy said. "Some said I stopped at a stoplight and didn't speak to them. I guess I was so preoccupied with my thoughts that I just didn't see them."

Geri believed that the conversation with Harrington was the turning point. Fayard said that "it took Dottie a long time" to finally accept Lynn's condition. Now she did.

Once Dorothy fully accepted Lynn's condition, indeed Lynn's fate, some of her tension eased. Or so it appeared. Certainly, the frantic, unceasing, nerve-shattering search for a new diagnosis ended. Certainly, the hopes for Lynn to attend school, to have playmates, to learn to read, to one day look at her and say Mommy, vanished. But, she once said, "Inside I never gave her up. It was myself that I began giving up."

The acceptance affected Dorothy's view of life itself, its meaning, its purpose, its sense or senselessness. Always Dandridge had a gorgeous, poised exterior. Now that calm poise seemed firmly reserved for all her public outings. It served as a magnificent shield. Rarely did she discuss Lynn with anyone outside her family or the friends she had known from childhood. She even stopped permitting photographers to take pictures of Lynn. Seldom did she say publicly anything about Ruby or Vivian. Certainly never was a word said about Ma-Ma. A profound resignation about life set in. It enabled her to endure her circumstances, but, ultimately, it took a toll on her spirit.

Now hers was a classic case of the dichotomy of appearance versus reality. Her exterior signaled classic haughty beauty while her interior was all torment. It was something Sidney Poitier said, almost twenty years later, he was stunned to discover about her from his experience on the set of *Porgy and Bess*.

As Phil Moore, who soon came back into Dottie's life, once observed, her whole existence seemed like a shiny red apple. Absolutely luscious and perfect to view. No flaws. No faults. But inside the red apple was full of worms.

Inside were self-recriminations always about Lynn. She had "nothing to do with that child's condition," Vivian said. "But you could never convince her that she didn't have something to do with it. She blamed herself." Now "she felt she failed as a wife. And she felt like she had failed as a mother."

"Rightly or wrongly," Dorothy said, "I date much of what was to happen to me thereafter—in my personal life and in my career—from the incident of the delayed delivery. Whatever happened, I blame only myself."

Her agonizing preoccupation with Lynn's condition endured for years. As Geri said, "It motivated her entire life."

"That was something that was tearing her up because she blamed herself," Harold said years later. "And she shouldn't have. If anything, if there was anyone to blame, I should be blamed because I wasn't acting right.

Though Dorothy knew the marriage meant nothing by 1948, it would take her almost two years to formally begin to end the union. No matter what had happened, she found it agonizing to live away from Harold. "I don't care what anybody says," Geri said of Dorothy. "I don't care what anybody tells you. She *loved* that little bastard. She *really* loved him. And look what it got her."

On a brief return to Europe in 1949, she let Harold know of her decision that the marriage must be dissolved. "Well, actually, it happened after she left me in London to go back to America," Harold said. "After a few months, then I heard from her where she said that she was going to go back to try to get her life going and do her *act* or whatever, to get it together. And that's when it happened."

"I wasn't happy at all," Fayard said of the breakup. "And Geri wasn't happy that this marriage was going to break up. But I said, 'If it breaks up, I'm still Dorothy's friend.' And Geri said, 'Yes, I'm still Dorothy's friend.'"

Accepting Lynn's fate may have psychologically freed Dorothy from the marriage, just as it allowed her to turn her full focus on a career. But for the duration of her life, despite the fact that she believed a career could give meaning to her life, she carried a deep private sadness within her that only those closest to her understood.

3. Kansas beginnings: Ruby Dandridge with a friend, Hilda Ruth, in Wichita in the teens.

4. Hollywood calling. A lobby card for the film Going Places: Maxine Sullivan, Etta Jones, Vivian Dandridge, Dorothy, and Louis Armstrong (l. to rt.).

5. The Dandridge Sisters: Etta Jones, Dorothy and Vivian; around the time of their appearance at the Cotton Club.

6. With Ona Munson and John Wayne in *Lady from Louisiana*.

7. A dream come true, dancing with the Nicholas Brothers—Harold and Fayard—in "Chattanooga Choo Choo," the classic number from *Sun Valley Serenade*.

8. Happy times: Dorothy and Harold cutting their wedding cake.

9. Joined by Gerald Wilson, Etta Jones, Geri Branton, Fayard, Hattie McDaniel, Jack Montgomery, Vivian (front row l. to rt.), and other guests.

10. The newlyweds.

11. With Harold, Fayard and Geri.

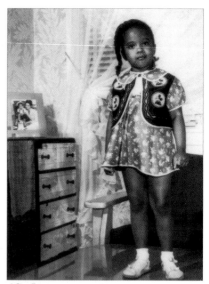

13. Lynn

12. With Ruby and daughter, Lynn.

14. Problems ahead. With a restless Lynn, Geri and Tony.

15. Ruby Dandridge, at the height of her career.

16. With Harold, Viola Nicholas, Fayard, Geri, and Herb Jeffries (l. to rt.).

17. With Joel Fluellen and Geri at the *California Eagle* fundraiser Dorothy held in her home.

18. Dorothy (sitting 2nd from rt.) and her sister-in-law, Dorothy Nicholas Morrow (standing far rt.) and other members of one of her social clubs in the 1940s.

19. Prepping for stardom.

20. California dreaming: with Geri and actor Jack Holt on the Warner Bros. lot in the late 1940s.

21. Young career woman. On her own, at last.

22. With Anthony Quinn on the set of his film, *Ride, Vaquero*!

23. Rehearsing with Phil Moore. "My sister worked 24 hours a day to be a star," Vivian Dandridge said.

25. With Phil Moore outside the Mocambo.

24. Advertisement for the appearance at the Mocambo.

26. Making a specta-
cular entrance at
London's Café de Paris.

27. At Café de Paris
with Phil Moore, on
piano.

29. Back in Cleveland for a nightclub appearance. With childhood friend, Dorothy Hughes McConnell, and her husband, Woodrow.

30. With director Gerald Mayer on the set of *Bright Road*.

28. As Melmendi in *Tarzan's Peril*.

31. Vivian Dandridge, struggling to keep a foothold in show business in the 1950s.

32. With her friend Ava Gardner and director John Farrow on the MGM lot. *Carmen Jones*.

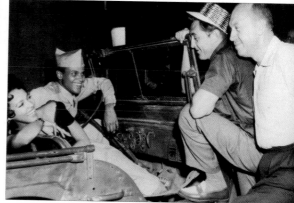

34. Dorothy and Harry Belafonte with Otto Preminger (rt.) and actor Robert Mitchum on the set of *Carmen Jones*.

33. The Philippe Halsman photo that ran on the cover of *Life*.

PART II

CAREER THRUST

$\mathcal{B}$ack from Europe, Dorothy returned to Los Angeles and the house on 27th Street. Lynn remained in the care of Ruby and Neva. It was 1948, and for a time, she invited her sister-in-law, then Dorothy Nicholas, to move in with her. Having been around show business all her life, Dorothy Nicholas was aware of its highs and lows, its demands and disappointments. Yet, she had managed to keep a clear head and unlike her brothers, hadn't been cloistered from the outside world. Bright and attractive with a wide range of interests, Dorothy Nicholas had graduated from Howard University. Dorothy Dandridge was feeling lonely and enjoyed Dorothy Nicholas's company.

Dorothy was excited yet full of doubts, entering this new phase of her life. She approached it not as Harold's wife or Ruby's daughter or Vivian's sister, but as a focused young woman, ready to channel her ambition and energies into a career. Once before, at 18, she had asserted her independence, leaving the Dandridge Sisters to join the cast of *Meet the People*. She was sidetracked then by her love for Harold, but that wouldn't happen again. She couldn't afford either short cuts or distractions. Whatever amount of time or focus the creation of Dorothy Dandridge, the actress, demanded, she was willing to give.

"My sister worked twenty-four-hours a day to become a star," Vivian Dandridge said. Her days were spent in an ongoing round of classes, interviews, auditions, benefits, politicking. Given Dorothy's great desire for privacy, almost every public encounter—every smile, every bit of charming small talk—must have been something of a performance, perhaps a painful one, as she met with agents, casting directors, nightclub managers, and tried to please them.

Throughout her life, Dorothy lived *and* behaved like an actress. Never would she be like any ordinary worker who at the end of the day left the job behind. She exuded drama and intensity at every turn. People seeing her, whether or not they had any idea that she was in show business, knew immediately, from the presence and the aura, that here was a woman who *had* to be an actress. It would be that very quality, of always being dramatic, being like an actress, that would eventually help win her the respect of Hollywood itself. A real star always looks like a star, moves like a star, speaks like a star, *acts* like a star, even when she's living in a small cottage and is daily trying to make ends meet. Young struggling actress became both the role and the reality of Dorothy Dandridge's life; the definition of her newfound identity.

Her continuing studies at the Actors Lab were most important to her now. Located behind Schwab's Drugstore at Sunset and Laurel in Hollywood, the Lab had been founded by some of America's most respected actors, including former members of the Group Theatre in New York. One of its administrators, who also studied and directed there, was an energetic, ambitious young man named Joseph Papirofsky, who later became known as Joe Papp. Offering classes in acting, directing, criticism, and movement, the Actors Lab introduced West Coast actors to new theories, techniques, and approaches to the art of acting.

Having taken classes in the past, Dorothy read Stanislavski, studied Michael Chekhov's concept on "the center of energy," performed "sense memory improvisations," worked on perfecting the "telling psychological gesture," and diligently practiced exercises in concentration, scene study, and the tricky, and sometimes emotionally draining, technique of using life experiences as the foundation for building a character.

This last approach to acting—finding the key to a character's motivation furthered her interest in psychology and in untangling more about herself and her family history. The technique used in this school of acting had to do with the actor's ability to recreate a character's behavior by understanding the motive behind the behavior. The Lab was a crucial training ground, the foundation of her developing attitudes and ideas about acting, technique, and character development. She participated in such Lab productions as *The Doll's House*, *The Philadelphia Story*, and *Gaslight*.

The Lab, by late 1948, prided itself on having opened its doors to students of all races, on being fully and fairly integrated, just before the time when integration and cultural assimilation would lie at the heart of the emerging Civil Rights Movement. Other Black students at the Lab included Juanita Moore, who later appeared as the stoic Annie in the

1959 remake of *Imitation of Life*, actor Bob Davis, Dorothy's childhood friend Juliette Ball, and for a brief time, Vivian Dandridge.

At the Lab, Dorothy was enveloped in a hotbed of lively discussion, not only on acting and drama but politics as well. The war years had stripped America of much of its innocence and kindled a new awareness of social problems inside and outside the performing arts world. Already Americans had witnessed a great change in popular culture. The world of sports, in particular, took a big step forward. In 1947, Jackie Robinson made history when he integrated major league baseball as a player for the Brooklyn Dodgers. These Group Theatre expatriates and Dorothy, at the time, believed that, like sports, other aspects of popular culture such as movies and theatre should begin to address and examine social issues in a different way.

The Lab reverberated with such talk and debate. Many artists thought that the very fabric of American life, from the high arts to the low, had to be rewoven and redesigned. Many believed entertainment should not be just frothy escapist fare. Instead it should be about *something*. The arts should have a conscience. This was not a completely new idea in artistic and intellectual circles, but now it was expressed with a peculiarly American brand of optimism.

For Dorothy, the heady exposure to new theories, attitudes, and ideas was invigorating. The acting school introduced her to the up-and-coming new young White Hollywood, many of whose members during these postwar years were free of the prevailing ideas and attitudes about race and interracial friendships. Thus far, her work and social activities had been grounded almost exclusively in the African American community. Even when appearing in *Meet the People* or in bits at the major Hollywood studios, her life at the end of the day always carried her back to the Black community, its social contacts and cultural references and perspectives. But now that changed.

Among the instructors, at one time or another, were Morris Carnovsky, his wife the actress Phoebe Brand, Hume Cronyn, Aline MacMahon, Sam Levene, Phil Brown, and Anthony Quinn. Her classmates included Charles Chaplin, Jr. and a young blond named Marilyn Monroe, with whom Dorothy struck up a friendship. Young veterans of the war attended the Lab tuition-free on the G.I. Bill. The studios also sent some of their young contract players to study there.

Despite the Lab's liberal attitudes, Dorothy saw that the acting school wasn't as free of the familiar racial codes as it might have wanted to think of itself. When she won a role that traditionally would have been played by a White actress, some at the Lab feared that audiences might not accept a young Black woman as the lead in a cast of White actors. Dorothy lost the part shortly before the play was to be performed for the public. She said Anthony Quinn was given the difficult task of telling her the role was no longer hers. "The rejection caused a deep frustration I can't deny," said Dorothy, who never forgot the incident.

Dorothy and the other students discovered that the Lab's interracial mix and liberal politics were viewed suspiciously by Hollywood's older conservative generation. It was considered left-wing and radical. By 1948, the Tenney Committee went so far as to label it a communist front. This committee, headed by politician John Tenny, had been established as California's arm of the House Committee on UnAmerican Activities and set out to expose Communism or Communist influences in Hollywood.

Actors such as Juliette Ball felt, "It was when the Lab started taking Black students that they called the Actors Lab *communist*."

It was a social gathering, not work, that brought Dorothy to the center of a racial controversy at the Lab. The school held a benefit, a carnival called *Exuberanza*, in a parking lot in back of Schwab's Drugstore. It was on Labor Day, 1948. The public was invited to the event, which was intended to raise money for the Lab and provide an opportunity for its patrons to meet and mix with the school's instructors, students, crews, and casts. Planned for the day was a program of skits, songs, and other activities along with food stalls and a bazaar.

Everything was casual and festive as students, patrons, and staff laughed, talked, and swapped stories and jokes. People danced, as well. Geri Nicholas recalled that during the evening, actor Anthony Quinn walked over to Dorothy and asked her for a dance. She accepted, and they took to the floor.

Other Whites and Blacks apparently danced together, too, but little did they know they were being watched. At the end of the evening, Dorothy and Quinn went their separate ways, like most who attended, and thought that it had been a pleasant summer's afternoon and evening.

But a ruckus grew out of it. A few days later, Dorothy was stunned to pick up a copy of the September 9th the trade paper *The Hollywood Reporter* and read an item in Jim Henaghan's "Rambling Reporter" column about the event. Henaghan wrote:

> We've been swamped with protests from the Sunset Strip area the last couple of days objecting to the "impromptu" show put on by Actors Lab Players. . . in the back of the theatre Labor Day night. The report has it that mixed dancing,

Colored and Whites, and the overall tenor of the program was pretty party-linish. There is also a report that the studios which subsidized the so-called school for actors by sending them youngsters for training are mulling dumping the group before too much more unfavorable attention is drawn to the industry by this and similar activities."

The Lab actors—Black and White—including Dorothy, couldn't believe it. Bad enough that the article twisted reality to fit someone's political agenda, but matters were made worse by the fact that this was the paper routinely read throughout the movie industry.

But the situation didn't stop there. Another item about the event appeared four days later in *The Los Angeles Times*. This time in the column of gossip Hedda Hopper, who wrote:

> . . . Out of Character. The Actors Lab made no friends when they gave an open-air barbecue, which included dancing between Whites and Negroes. They used a parking lot on Sunset Blvd for their dancing space where one and all could see. This group's corny idea of being liberal will eventually lead them into trouble. The situation has nothing whatever to do with racial prejudice or discrimination; every man in the world is as good as he is in his heart, regardless of race, creed or color. But that doesn't mean they have to intermix. Right or wrong, the great balance of the community has this deep-rooted conviction, and they were shocked at this display by the Actors Lab. That's the sort of thing that leads to race riots.

Dorothy's name hadn't been mentioned, but she knew that again Hopper's readers in the industry would know, or soon hear, to whom the item primarily referred. She became both angry and depressed. Hopper, along with fellow columnist Louella Parsons, wielded great power in the movie colony and also in the consciousness of the movie going public. Her column was syndicated in newspapers around the country.

"Hedda Hopper was in her glory. She was a vicious witch," said Geri Nicholas. "And she raised sand because Anthony Quinn danced with Dottie." Able to boost or sometimes destroy a reputation, Hopper—as Dorothy and everyone else in Hollywood knew—was a rabid, ultraconservative, who, during a time of blacklisting, believed the foundation of American society was being undermined and destroyed by Communists or Communist influences. Almost anyone whose politics veered in the direction of the liberal or, heaven forbid, the left was suspect. "She said that anybody was a Communist if you go to a Paul Robeson concert and applaud," Geri recalled.

Geri believed that Hopper probably did not mind Dorothy dancing with Anthony Quinn but so much because, after all, Anthony Quinn was half-Mexican. But rather Hopper was angered by the Actors Lab for encouraging behavior unacceptable to the larger society. Dorothy knew Hopper's remarks (even though Dorothy had not been named) could be damaging. But she wasn't sure what to do.

The Lab did have its defenders, Joseph Papirofsky wrote Frank Eng of the Los Angeles *Daily News* stating:

Mothers, fathers, kids and old folks, Catholics, Protestants, Jews joined together this day and had a good time. Certainly there were Negro people present! The Negro veterans who attend classes here under the GI Bill 'mix' every day.... There were no backdoors or separate entrances for Negroes. In the best tradition of theater and democracy, there was no discrimination against fellow human beings. We, as a theater, are part of the tremendous struggles being waged ... we uphold the fight of SAG [the Screen Actors Guild] against discrimination.

Papirofsky informed Eng that Negro artists were preparing statements in protest of the Hopper column. He contacted the NAACP, Urban League, and Black newspapers "in order to combat her unfair attack on the Lab and its Negro artists, students, and patrons."

"We were active in those days, politically active," said Geri. Infuriated members of the Lab as well as the African American and liberal White communities "put calls into Hopper's office until they were running out of her ears. We were just calling saying, 'We resent your *implication*.'" Joining the protest was actor John Garfield and former members of the Hollywood Democratic Committee.

Eng himself blasted Hopper's comments in the September 16th issue of the Los Angeles *Daily News*. "One columnist who attacked the Lab wound up with the statement that such 'mixing' would 'lead' to race riots,'" Eng wrote. "It sounds very much to our ears that precisely that point of view encourages it—or perhaps even threatens it."

The Black press also protested. "Hedda Hopper Joins Ranks of Race Baiters," read the headline in the September 16th edition of *The California Eagle*.

Dorothy felt herself in a quandary. She had to take some kind of action, but could she do so without drawing even more unwanted attention? Finally, following the advice of friends, she contacted The *California Eagle*, which published a letter from her on September 23rd.

> I am outraged by the slanderous statement made by Jim Henaghan. As an actress and student at the Lab, I am anxious to know if Mr. Henaghan considers the democratic policy of the Actors Lab wherein students are selected on the basis of ability, rather than on the color of their skin, a subversive policy. If he does, then he advocates a policy which is inherently un-American and subversive and fans the flames of race hatred. I have just returned from Europe where I was received with cordiality and respect both professionally and socially. In answering queries about the Negro artist in America, I was ashamed to admit the humiliation to which we are subjected. Europeans are suspicious of pious mouthings about Democracy for other countries when right here in America the most abominable discriminatory practices and ideas are still being perpetuated as reflected in the Hollywood Reporter column.
> Very sincerely,
> Dorothy Dandridge.

Dorothy didn't mention Hopper, whose comments were far more damaging than Henaghan's. Hopper was too powerful. But Dorothy didn't forget the incident and never considered Hopper a friend. Afterwards, it looked as if the matter had passed and was over with. But within a few years, when it appeared she might be blacklisted from work on a film, she would discover she had to comment on Hopper's words.

Black actor Joel Fluellen served on the board at the Lab and was known as a fighter in the battle for new roles for African American actors. Fluellen brought eighteen young Black performers, primarily Black women, into the Lab in the summer of 1947. Once they got there, he charged that the Lab, by establishing special evening courses for them, had continued a form of segregation.

Fluellen also stood before members of the Screen Actors Guild in 1946 and 1948 and called for better treatment of African American performers in Hollywood. He asked for the creation of a permanent committee that would meet with representatives of guilds and producers to establish "a policy of presenting Negro characters on the screen in the true relations they bear to American life." Under the leadership of Ronald Reagan, the Screen Actors Guild ignored Fluellen's concerns. But Fluellen remained vigilant and eventually founded the Negro Art Guild. It was his effort to provide better opportunities for Black actors and actresses on the West Coast.

Of all the young Black actors and actresses in the postwar years, none ever interested Fluellen more than Dorothy. He had first seen her during the early 1940s in the lobby of the Dunbar Hotel. She was wearing ballet shoes and was so fine-boned that he thought she was sure to be a ballerina. He set out to become her friend. Already he knew Ruby. But to strike up a friendship with Dorothy, he understood, might be more difficult. She was completely unlike her very social, extroverted, cheery mother.

Fluellen had already mastered the social art of getting to know people. He himself had arrived in Hollywood not too many years earlier. Tall, broad shouldered, dark, handsome, and drawn to the theatre, Fluellen had been born in 1908 in Monroe, Louisiana. As a young man, he moved to Chicago where he was a milliner and also a store clerk. But he wanted to get out of Chicago and move forward with his life. Opportunity came his way when, in the mid 1930s, he met Black actress Louise Beavers, then nationally known for her performance in the 1934 *Imitation of Life*. Fluellen impressed the older Beavers with his looks, polished manners, and gift for gab. He flattered and fussed over her. Beavers took a motherly liking to him and suggested he come to California.

He did just that. In 1936, he moved to Los Angeles and fumbled around in hopes of getting into films. The closest he came was a spot as an extra in the Black-cast comedy *Green Pastures*. Discouraged, he returned to Chicago, spent some time in Texas, and then came back to the West Coast. Beavers helped him again. He even stayed at her home.

Keenly ambitious and given to social climbing, Fluellen was an excellent cook and a fabulous host who always knew just when a drink should be refilled or when a special delicacy should be prepared. Of Fluellen's culinary skills, Sidney Poitier said, "I carry two extra inches on my waist because of that man." A lively, intelligent conversationalist, he used his knowledge of everything from theatre to politics and gossip to charm his way into the Los Angeles Black movie colony.

Once he moved from Louise Beavers's home, Fluellen lived at the

Dunbar Hotel. Known as a consort for mythic divas in distress, he comforted both a self-destructive Nina Mae McKinney and a troubled Billie Holiday. Josephine Baker became a friend as did Louise Beavers's rival Hattie McDaniel. It was his friendship with Ruby and Ma-Ma that led to his introduction to the young Dorothy. Over the course of his long life in Hollywood, he managed to strike up friendships with both the old guard and the new lights of postwar Hollywood and afterwards, from Poitier to Ivan Dixon, Gordon Parks, Bernie Hamilton, and Judy Pace.

But with all his social skills, Fluellen worked for many years mainly as an extra and in bits. A few minutes in a crowd scene in *Cabin in the Sky*. A native in *Mighty Joe Young*. His career did take off when he turned in well-crafted performances in *The Jackie Robinson Story* (as Jackie's older brother; Beavers played Jackie's mother), *Friendly Persuasion*, and Gordon Parks' *The Learning Tree*. He also appeared in *Riot in Cell Block 11*, *Run Silent, Run Deep, Lucy Gallant*, the 1959 remake of *Imitation of Life*, *The Great White Hope*, and *The Bingo Long Traveling All-Stars and Motor Kings* as well as scores of television programs from the 1950s through the 1970s.

In lean times, Fluellen worked as a caterer. He later even served at some of Dorothy's parties in her Hollywood Hills homes. When close friends of Dorothy who knew Joel might speak to him at these gatherings, Joel would shush them and then give a dead-cold blank stare. "I'm working tonight," he would say. It was his way of helping Dorothy impress the big shots: the Gary Coopers or the James Masons or whomever. This was no time for him to be familiar with any of the guests. When he catered, he catered. But once the guests left, he and Dorothy would have their own after-party, discussing everything that happened. Joel never missed a thing as he worked the party and kept track of the various guests. On other occasions when Fluellen was a guest in her home, no servant dared approach him with familiarity!

Fluellen's social skills extended into other areas of the Hollywood community. He was a key figure in gay Hollywood, privy to the secrets of various White male stars and industry executives. One lover was one of postwar Hollywood's most virile and athletic young leading men. Another lover was an older man who provided Fluellen with the right clothes, expense-paid trips, and privileged dinner invitations.

Fluellen's homosexuality, like that of other actors in Hollywood, including Ruby, was an open secret. It would be discussed but privately, never publicly. Discretion was valued in the industry, especially at this point in Hollywood history. As long as the moralists were not breathing down the industry's back, as long as no scandal disrupted box office receipts, people in Hollywood could do precisely as they wanted. Besides, the sexual proclivities or romantic peccadilloes of this person or that made for juicy, sometimes malicious gossip, which the industry thrived on.

Neither Dorothy nor Geri discussed Joel's sexual interests with him for years, but they were aware. When Joel broached the subject, they listened, but said nothing unless he spoke about the matter.

Joel's friendship with Dorothy grew largely out of Harold's absences. Joel, aware of Dorothy's loneliness, would often spend time with her when Harold was on tour. Geri watched as Joel shrewdly manipulated his way into Dorothy's life. "When she was tired from coming home, he'd massage her with castor oil," Geri recalled. "And he'd go shopping with her. They'd cook together. Since 27th Street. He was always over there. He'd sit up late at night and talk to her. And he gave her a lot of attention."

He also played on, as time went by, Dorothy's constant need for reassurance. "First of all, with Dottie, you could never compliment her enough," said Geri. "And Joel was a flatterer. He knew other people in the business, and he'd say, 'Oh, you're better than she.' This and that. And he'd do the same thing with Lena Horne, who he was close to. When you're a name in the business, you can get in doors and you can get in parties and you can get in places where other people can't get into. So he flattered her."

On those occasions when Dorothy wasn't around, he pursued Geri, whose love of politics intrigued him. "He would come around me and go to the kind of parties I'd go to with [actress turned congresswoman] Helen Gahagan Douglas," Geri recalled. "I could get in a lot of those places because of the Nicholas Brothers. People wanted me around. They knew that I knew other stars. And they would use that. This is a *using* town. You have no worth if you can't produce."

No one claims to know exactly what drew Fluellen to Dorothy, but in the late 1940s, his friendship with her grew. Aware of her sensitivity and her fatherless upbringing, and perhaps sensing her desire for advice from older men, he established, some say by clever manipulation, an intense friendship with her.

Fluellen understood that coupled with her ambition were her growing self-doubts. Her childhood, the failed marriage to Harold, the problems with Lynn—all had left their marks, making her question everything about herself. Having failed, so she believed, in so many other respects, she feared she might fail at acting. Then, too, while the

Lab stimulated her, she didn't always feel comfortable joining in on all the heady intellectual talk.

"There were a bunch of people around there who were very erudite and very arrogant and they were so glib," said Dorothy Nicholas. "But you begin to feel extremely inferior around these people whose extreme knowledge goes way beyond your own intuitive instincts. Those things almost negate that way of working because hers was an intuitive way of working. I can understand how they had an effect on her for a long time, and in terms of that kind of security as a performer."

Fluellen knew how to reassure her and shrewdly understood how to play on her needs. The two were the subject of many conversations by the people who knew them. Theirs was a close and complicated relationship, more so because of Fluellen's motives—his fixations and his obsessions—than Dorothy's.

"I'd see Joel at Dottie's, and sometimes I had the feeling that Joel Fluellen thought I was intruding even though I was her sister," said Vivian.

No one ever questioned Fluellen's loyalty and affection for her. Still, respected as he was by many in Hollywood (especially a later younger generation), those close to Dorothy, who were well aware of his reputation, viewed him with some caution. Dorothy's friends asked each other how could so private a woman become friendly with so public a man? And so public a gossip?

"He knew everybody. Knew everything about everybody," said Dorothy Nicholas. "If you wanted to know anything, ask Joel. And he would or would not tell you. Joel was just that kind of guy. Fine artist. Fine chef. But he was a gossip."

"He would fall in love and out of love with people who had been friends with him for years at the slightest provocation," said Dorothy Nicholas. "You would not know when Joel was out of love with you. All of a sudden he was talking about you. And you're saying, 'Joel, what's the matter? What did I do?' and Joel would say, 'I'm not talking to you. Shut up.'"

"That was the kind of person Joel was. If you knew Joel, you knew how to take him. But the point is he would upset you to no end. That was Joel's own eccentricity and idiosyncratic nature or whatever you want to call it. You could get fun from Joel. But Joel would talk about you at a moment's notice."

Yet Byron Morrow observed the positive effect Joel's presence had on Dorothy. "There's a difference when Dorothy can be free, comfortable, not having to compete with what you're doing and what you're saying," said Morrow. "That was obviously what she needed. And Joel was perfect for that."

Though Dorothy and Harold had separated, she had not begun to date. When she needed an escort at some event or affair, Fluellen accompanied her. Dorothy was accustomed to maneuvering her way around men who made unwanted advances or tried to put their hands on her. Like just about every other major female movie star, she felt relaxed, accompanied by a man like Joel who showed an interest in her other than sexual.

Otherwise Dorothy tried to maintain social engagements with the young Black middle-class set in Los Angeles. On occasion, she played hostess. Dorothy Nicholas remembered a pajama party that Dandridge gave at the house on 27th Street during the time she lived with her. Among the guests were singer Herb Jeffries, Bob Davis, who was a young actor from the Actors Lab, the performers The Treniers, as well as Byron Morrow, whom Dorothy Nicholas had begun dating. Everyone was required to wear pajamas to the party, and most of the guests also performed. Jeffries did magic tricks. The two Dorothys sang "There's No Business Like Show Business" for their guests. "We really hammed it up," said Dorothy Nicholas. It was a rare night of relaxation for Dandridge.

Within a few months, though Dorothy Nicholas moved out of Dandridge's house. They remained friends but she fell in love with Byron Morrow and eloped with him in Mexico during Christmas of 1948. "We married there because of the anti-miscegenation laws here," said Dorothy Nicholas Morrow. Byron Morrow was White.

Alone again on 27th Street, Dorothy reflected on her future. Despite the auditions and interviews, her efforts to advance her career were not leading very far. She tried to put together a nightclub act. Her old friend, the agent Arthur Silver, booked her into some small clubs. But her performances were disappointing, at best. After she opened at a Seattle club, the owner took her aside, said her material wasn't worthy of her, and then fired her. Club failures aside, the frustrating fact was that she wanted to act, not sing.

She no doubt felt herself running in circles. Adding to her frustrations was her awareness of the changing tide in the industry. In 1949, she stepped into movie theatres and saw four startling films— *Home of the Brave, Lost Boundaries, Intruder in the Dust,* and *Pinky*—that left her feeling both elated and depressed.

Most were the work of a new generation of filmmakers, who were often influenced by the neorealism of the postwar Italian cinema. The new filmmakers were convinced, like her classmates and instructors at the Lab, that movies should now not merely entertain but also say something. In this case, they were saying something about the Negro Problem. The films exposed racism in America and presented serious, leading, dramatic African American characters who, rather than simply smiling as they carried a tray or sang a tune, were brooding and bruised, troubled and perplexed by their place in American society.

The first of these "Negro problem pictures" was *Home of the Brave*, directed by Mark Robson and produced by Stanley Kramer. It looked at racism within the American military. Here Dorothy saw a talented new-style Black dramatic actor, James Edwards. Alfred Werker's *Lost Boundaries* explored racial dynamics in a New England community where a light-skinned Black doctor and his wife are passing for White. Veteran director Clarence Brown's *Intruder in the Dust*, based on a William Faulkner novel, and newcomer Elia Kazan's *Pinky* uncovered racism in the Deep South. Though flawed and compromised, the films were all worth seeing, so Ralph Ellison wrote in his essay "The Shadow and the Act." "And if seen," he wrote, "capable of involving us emotionally. That they do is testimony to the deep centers of American emotion that they touch." Each gave Dorothy hope. But of the four films, only *Pinky* focused on the dilemmas and conflicts of an African American woman.

Pinky told the story of a light-skinned young Black woman who, after having lived as a "free" White during her years as a student in the North, must decide whether to cross the color line once she returns home to the South. *Pinky* drew mixed feelings from Dorothy.

She reportedly had been considered by Twentieth Century Fox for the title role. That might seem hard to believe because while Dandridge had a "mulatto" look, she also had *color* and was not light enough to be plausible as a woman passing for White. But she was already known throughout the industry. Darryl F. Zanuck, who produced the film at Twentieth Century Fox, remembered meeting her on the set of *Sun Valley Serenade*. So there might be some credence to the stories that said so.

Fox's New York office was said to have had anxieties about the public response to Dorothy, an unknown dramatic Black actress; that indeed her presence would "kill" the picture. The script called for the Negro character Pinky to have a love affair with a White doctor. Had Dorothy played opposite a White actor, Fox surely would have had problems from the film industry's self-regulatory Production Code Administration, which prohibited miscegenation on screen.

Interestingly, in *Pinky*, the heroine's interracial relationship ends when she makes the decision not to pass for White. It was an adroit way not only of infusing the character with racial pride but also adhering to Production Code requirements.

Ultimately, Zanuck cast *Pinky* with a young White actress then under contract to Fox, Jeanne Crain.

Playing the role of the older, traditional self-sacrificing Black grandmother in *Pinky* was veteran actress Ethel Waters. She walked off with an Oscar nomination as Best Supporting Actress of the Year, the first time an African American woman had been nominated for the Academy Award since Hattie McDaniel's Oscar win for *Gone With The Wind*. Significantly, though, the leading role, the young heroine of intelligence and drive in *Pinky*, who represented postwar Negro ambition, was not played by a Black woman.

The irony wasn't lost on Dorothy. No one will ever know precisely what thoughts ran through her mind as she sat in a darkened theatre and watched *Pinky*. But the casting of this film added to her depression and made her question whether there would be ever be a place for a serious young Black woman in motion pictures, even when the script called for a Black character.

So, too, did the appearance of the remake of *Show Boat*—just two years after *Pinky*—in which once again another pivotal Black female character in Hollywood cinema, the role of the mulatto Julie who crosses the color line in the remake of *Show Boat*, was also played by a White actress, Ava Gardner. For Dandridge, this period represented one frustration after another. "If I were Betty Grable," she told Geri, "I could capture the world." At times her disappointments were so great that she seemed, said Geri Branton, to resent "her Blackness." She was keenly aware that her color or rather the industry's attitudes about race held her back—if she had blue eyes and perfectly straight hair, everything would be different, Dorothy said. "Let's face it," recalled Branton. "It was hard to be Black."

"It was very difficult for her," said Bobby Short. "I mean what did you do in those days. There were a number of very pretty girls out in Hollywood. Colored girls who just never got off the ground because they could only get so far," Short observed with sympathy. "She had been sitting around. This pretty, pretty girl, full of ambition, full of energy, dying to just do something," he recalled. "Nothing terrific ever seemed to happen to her."

But then came a new development. "The turning point in Dorothy's career," said Short, "came about through Phil Moore."

By chance, one afternoon Dorothy ran into Moore, the arranger/composer she had known from her days with Vivian and Etta as The Dandridge Sisters. The two had not seen each other for a few years. Dorothy explained to Moore that she was working again, hoping to find acting roles and to put together a nightclub act.

Shortly afterwards, Dorothy was desperate for work. With mounting expenses for Lynn and a home to maintain, she didn't always have money coming in from Harold, still in Europe. She had put in a call to an agent she had met. He managed to set up an interview for her with Charlie Morrison, the owner of the Mocambo nightclub. Known as a shrewd businessman, capable of spotting talent, and aware of Dorothy as the wife of Harold Nicholas, Morrison agreed to see her. She auditioned for him and told him that she was seeking nightclub work. As they talked, she was honest about her aspirations to be an actress. As they both knew, there wasn't anything around for a serious young Black actress and they agreed that nightclubs might offer an easier route to a career than film work.

Dorothy was but one of countless young women who approached Charlie Morrison for a job. But she must have struck him as somehow different, perhaps not only prettier and more ambitious than most but also highly charismatic. Then too she was a charmer, who also seemed fragile. Whatever it was that impressed Charlie Morrison that day, he couldn't just dismiss her. Morrison made an unusual move. Dorothy had mentioned Phil Moore, so he telephoned him. "There's a girl here says she knows you," Charlie Morrison said. "Maybe you'd make some arrangements for her because she wants to get back in the business."

"It was Dorothy Dandridge on the telephone," Moore recalled. Over the phone, she quickly told him that "the man at the Mocambo said he would put her in there if I would do her arrangements and handle her stuff, which worked out."

Fortune seemed to be smiling on Phil Moore. He remembered Dorothy's presence on stage with the Dandridge Sisters, recalled her gentle quality and energy. Over the years he watched her grow into womanhood, and he heard about her marriage, her problems with Harold, and her subsequent separation. In truth, he had never really lost track, and was likely carrying a torch for her, all along.

Moore's career had progressed well since the old days. He had come from a unique, rather privileged background. Born in 1918 in Portland,

Oregon, he was adopted by George Moore (who some say was actually his father through a relationship with a woman outside his marriage) and his wife, who everyone called Jimmy. The elder Moore helped manage Black boxing champion Henry Armstrong and also was an investor in the Black musical *Shuffle Along.* Despite the Depression and his father's financial losses, young Phil still grew up comfortably.

He learned to play the piano and was a child prodigy. He made his debut at age 12 with the Portland Junior Symphony, and at 13 was playing in speakeasies. Later he studied at the Cornish Conservatory and the University of Washington. In the 1930s, he left Seattle to move to Los Angeles, and worked on the 1938 Black cast film *The Duke Is Tops* (with Lena Horne) and also MGM's *A Day at the Races.*

Afterwards, he pounded on the doors of the big studios, trying to land a position as an orchestra arranger, but none budged. Most were doubtless surprised that a Black man would even have the presumption to apply for such a position. Finally, in 1941 Moore was hired by MGM as a rehearsal pianist; as such, he became what is believed to have been the first Black musician in a Hollywood studio music department.

At MGM, he contributed to the music of some fifty films, as a composer, arranger, and vocal coach. Although he broke the color line and was employed on major films with major stars, Moore was never permitted to work without supervision with White female performers. "Judy Garland was always accompanied by a chaperon," he said. "No way a Black guy could be alone with her in a rehearsal bungalow." During that time, he also did freelance scoring jobs at RKO, Columbia, and Paramount on such features as *The Palm Beach Story, This Gun For Hire,* and *My Favorite Blond.* Rarely did Moore receive screen credit for his work. But he was becoming known among musicians, directors, producers, and major studio stars.

He left MGM in 1945 and established a reputation within the industry as a master musician, coach, and arranger. Moore was the composer of such popular songs as "Shoo Shoo Baby," which was a hit for the Andrews Sisters and also Nat King Cole, and "A Little On the Lonely Side." He also formed the popular group The Phil Moore Four and singed an exclusive record contract with RCA Victor.

Within Black show business circles, responses to Moore varied. Some found him pretentious. Others believed he was aloof and a snob. Still others found him genuine, imaginative, easygoing. But one thing everyone agreed on was that Phil Moore was a major talent and a real pioneer who broke down racial barriers in Hollywood.

Women also found him attractive and sexy, perhaps because of his cerebral, sophisticated manner rather than his looks. Of medium height, heavy, balding, and forever puffing on a pipe, he was hardly a Billy Eckstine or Herb Jeffries romantic type. But Moore in time had several wives, one of whom was actress Jeni Le Gon, and any number of other women who clamored around him.

Phil Moore listened to Dorothy talk about her aspirations and frustrations. His instincts told him she could succeed in nightclubs, not only because of her singing talent but because of her presence. Like Charlie Morrison, he saw that her innate charm glowed at every turn. Her soft-spoken demeanor, as well as the simple, casually elegant way in which she dressed, stamped her as different, not only from most nightclub singers, but also from many other women in show business.

Moore also saw that Dorothy's difficult years growing up and her troubled years with Harold surprisingly had not toughened her. While her past had fed her ambition, it had not robbed her of her gentle, sweet-tempered quality.

Sex appeal was crucial, that she had. There was nothing forced about it. Her classy manner combined with a heated sexuality could make her a truly distinctive woman on the nightclub scene.

Moore knew, having seen the direction of Lena Horne's career, that Dorothy had the makings of what later would be termed a "crossover style." Her looks and manner would appeal to White audiences as well as Black. Her material would have to do the same. As with Lena Horne, with whom Moore had worked closely, there would be no gritty blues songs for Dandridge. Certainly no raunchy rhythm and blues. Mainly, she would have to perform American standards and popular tunes. He would arrange material that would enhance her assets and steer her clear of any vocal limitations. The elements for club stardom were there, but it would take work to put them in place. She needed grooming, styling, and imaging. She needed direction.

During a career which spanned some six decades, Moore coached or did special arrangements for a gallery of stars, including Mae West, Ethel Waters, Ava Gardner, Frank Sinatra, Louis Armstrong, Marilyn Monroe, Lucille Ball, Ann Sothern, Count Basie, Dinah Washington, Charlie Mingus, Bobby Short, and later Diahann Carroll, The Supremes, Leslie Uggams, Goldie Hawn, and Johnny Mathis.

But of all the talents he worked with, none ever affected him as strongly as Dorothy Dandridge. Not Lena Horne. Not Marilyn Monroe. Not Ava Gardner. Not the male stars like Sinatra and Perry Como.

Because he understood Dorothy's real ambition was to be a film actress, Phil Moore said he decided to use nightclubs for Dandridge "as a forum, a place to show her off. And we tried to do things that would excite film people, which we finally did." Completely enthralled by Dorothy, he would always consider himself her Svengali.

Moore selected, arranged, and composed material for her. He also looked over the gowns she selected for her engagements, her hair styles, and make up. He preferred her in tight, slinky gowns, which he called snaky, that showed off her figure. Yet they had to be subtle with a relaxed elegance; nothing about them could ever be vulgar or obvious. Moore's suggestions on all matters were important. But again Dandridge knew when to take his advice and when to stick to her instincts.

Working so closely with her, Moore, perhaps better than anyone else at this time, saw what lay beneath the surface of Dandridge's extraordinary drive and ambition—and also the source of some of her tensions. "She was interested in her career," he said, "because she had this child to support. We had to use that as a positive thing. That she had to make it in order to make this child happy."

But despite his insights, Moore remained puzzled by her professional insecurities. She was often literally terrified of performing. And that terror affected her vocal abilities. He remembered hearing varying reports about her performance some years back in *Jump for Joy*.

"Everybody said she was beautiful. But she couldn't sing," he recalled. "I wondered why she couldn't sing because I'd known her as a child and maybe from thirteen to sixteen or seventeen, somewhere around there, and she could sing her butt off. She could just *sing*. So something must have happened to her psychologically in that in-between time." But he didn't know what.

Ironically, it seemed that the more firmly career-directed her life became, the more her insecurities were mounting and intensifying. "She always doubted her voice," Moore said. When he saw her slip into a despairing mood, he kept her busy and focused with rehearsals on new material and routines. He understood how therapeutic work could be for her, but he was also aware that work was no foolproof way to break her out of her depressions.

One day he told her candidly, "I don't know how this system of working is going to solve the three-o'clock-in-the-morning times when you wake up and you really think about things. But we'll try to keep you so busy you don't have too many of those times."

Daily rehearsals and work on arrangements, their concentration on her movements and her singing, their exhaustive attention to the most minute details of her style and image drew the two the closer. Phil Moore was convinced that he had to have control of her career in order for it to work. "I became her manager," Moore said. But, of course, he became more than that. He also became her lover. "Phil took Dorothy under his wing. And they began having an affair," said Bobby Short. "I think Phil was also nurturing her spirit and intellect."

Nurturing, he may have been to her, but it also appeared she completely dazzled him. For a man like Moore—and later Otto Preminger—Dorothy, whom he called Dottie Mae, was the kind of woman he couldn't stop watching or thinking about. Not simply because of her beauty. But because of everything else about her: the way she thought, the way she moved, the way she smiled, the way she made decisions, the way she reacted, the way she *was*.

For Dorothy, Moore answered many needs. He provided perceptive professional advice and emotional stability. She continued to look to strong men, and he was that. Just as Joel Fluellen gave her fatherly support, so, too, did Moore. She once even said, "He looked the way I imagined a father ought to look."

She also believed he helped her achieve a sexual maturity. "From Phil I was able to learn about physical intimacy," she said. "I became passionately involved but never in love. I had been too hurt by Harold to let myself go that way with anyone, as yet."

But Moore was wildly in love with her. Bobby Short observed that the relationship—certainly from Dorothy's perspective—was rooted in the "training and preparing of her for her reentry in show business." Moore, however, may not have been willing to accept that. Most important to him was his love for her.

"Obviously, Phil Moore had her basic interests at heart in promoting her, what he saw in her as a performer," said Dorothy Nicholas Morrow. "And he helped her through that period which I observed after. I saw the results, not the process. But the results were beautiful, what he did with her, because we saw them. We saw her perform."

Money continued to be a source of worry for Dorothy. Despite their relationship, she paid Phil for coaching her. When she ran low on money, ledgers were kept with the amounts she owed Moore. She also had to pay an accompanist for performances. There were traveling expenses, too. She had to be dressed to the nines. Always she looked for deals on clothes—gowns, dresses, suits—and sought out young, talented designers whose clothes she could afford. Among her early favorites were Black designer Zelda Wynn and Rudi Gernrich. Later she sought those *couturiers* of the Hollywood elite: Oleg Cassini, Don Loper, and Travilla. Her overhead and the care of Lynn left little in the way of profits. She wondered monthly if she had enough even to make ends meet.

Slowly, she started getting club bookings, often at clubs in and around Los Angeles that were, she said, "adjuncts to hotels. A date might be in an old hotel where the phones were in the hall and several people used the bathroom. They were one-night appearances." Not every gig worked out.

Moore recalled an engagement when Dorothy began so upset about her performance that afterwards she rushed to her dressing room. There she started hyperventilating. Moore got her to the emergency wing of a nearby hospital. "The person on duty said, 'Well, it's just excitement.' She hadn't done as well as she wanted to and was feeling depressed," Moore recalled. "They gave her oxygen."

He and Dorothy returned to the club where she had to do another show that night. "She was terrific," said Moore. But when she came offstage and went to her dressing room, "she was hyperventilating" again. Moore was stunned. Aware of her past years in therapy, he felt something was seriously wrong. "It's all right to have this kind of thing when the ship is sinking," he told Dorothy, "but when it's going over great to have this same symptom, that's not very good." He spoke to his secretary whose husband was a therapist. Dorothy began undergoing treatment.

Her work improved though, more so than she realized at first. When Moore learned that Desi Arnaz, then appearing at the Mocambo, needed a last-minute replacement for his girl-singer, who had suddenly taken ill, he jumped at the chance. With his vast contacts, Moore began making phone calls. He reached both the Mocambo's Morrison and Arnaz. He suggested they let Dorothy go on as the replacement, and they agreed. She was hired to do so and, despite her nerves, performed for several days with Arnaz's band. Soon other dates followed.

In late 1949, Moore landed Dorothy a booking at a small supper club in Las Vegas called The Bingo. The headliner would be White comic Jim Ames. She would receive good billing, and ads for the engagement were taken out in the Vegas newspapers. The importance of an appearance in Vegas wasn't lost on her. Up-and-coming, as well as established, performers were appearing there on the ever-expanding "Strip."

In the late 1940s, Las Vegas was still in the midst of a transition from a small sleepy desert town to the sprawling neon empire it would become in the 1950s and 1960s. Sammy Davis, Jr. made his Vegas debut at El Rancho in 1945. The Mills Brothers headlined at the

Nevada Biltmore in 1946. That same year Dorothy's friends the Delta Rhythm Boys appeared at El Rancho Vegas. But the tide really turned when in 1946, gangster Benjamin "Bugsy" Siegel opened his sweeping high-rise, the Flamingo Hotel. Its first headliner was Jimmy Durante. Next came Lena Horne in early 1947. At the end of 1947, Bill "Bojangles" Robinson appeared there too. For other Black stars such as Ella Fitzgerald, Pearl Bailey, and Ethel Waters, Vegas became an important venue.

Dorothy and Moore rehearsed and prepared strenuously for her appearance. Moore found a young musician named William Roy to work as her accompanist.

Barely 21 years old, Roy was thrilled at the opportunity to work with Moore and newcomer Dorothy. After having acted as a child in such movies as *The Corn Is Green, Passage to Marseilles,* and *It Happened In Brooklyn* and having also worked with Ruby Dandridge in the Los Angeles stage production of *Hit the Deck*, Roy was at the start of a promising new professional career.

At rehearsals, he became entranced and charmed by Dorothy. He noticed her insecurity about her voice, and he also observed the shrewd manner in which Moore maneuvered his way past her doubts. "Phil was very gentle with her in the sense that she wasn't singing any arias," said Roy. "He saw to it that she was able to get around every piece of material she was assigned. And he did that very well."

After the long period of rehearsals, gown fittings, and experiments with hair and makeup, Dorothy left Los Angeles for Las Vegas with Phil and Roy. Moore went along simply to guide the two through additional rehearsals and opening night at The Bingo. Afterwards he planned to return to Los Angeles for other work.

Vegas held promise for Dorothy, but it also brought her face to face with familiar problems. Postwar Las Vegas was openly segregated and bigoted. When such major stars as Lena Horne, Nat "King" Cole, and Sammy Davis, Jr., were hired to play the top casino hotels, they were informed—in no uncertain terms—they had to adhere to the racial codes of the day. That meant they were not to mingle with the White audiences and could not use front entrances. It was a humiliating experience to be a headliner at a hotel and not be able to ride in that hotel's elevator. Or, to have to stay in some cheap hotel miles away because the hotels on the Strip where they performed wouldn't accept them as guests. Likewise at the casinos, Black entertainers were fine, but the clubs did not welcome Black patrons unless, on rare occasions, the Black person was a celebrity.

From her girlhood days with The Wonder Children, to her teenage years with the Dandridge Sisters, and then her young adulthood on the tours of Harold and Fayard, Dorothy had become a sophisticated traveler. She was well-versed and perceptively attuned to racism, in this country and abroad, in its varied and most subtle forms. In the past, though, surrounded by Vivian and Etta or even Ma-Ma or later Geri, she had been shielded by their support. She had also played Black establishments in the States, which insulated her in other ways. She never ventured into places where she was not wanted. Even when she played the Cotton Club, her youth had protected her from certain racial indignities. Like Harold and Fayard, she was freer to mix with the White patrons at the club, if she chose, than she would have been as an adult woman.

Although Moore was with her on her arrival in Las Vegas, she was on her own once he left. While Dorothy was to be beset by other problems during her career, few experiences were as emotionally jarring as those on the nightclub scene where she was exposed to blatant racism.

Young Roy, who was White, was caught completely off-guard and shocked by his "first real introduction to Jim Crow behavior."

"We had a terrible time trying to get her a place to stay," Roy remembered. Moore and Dorothy "knew we were going to have difficulty." Roy stayed at the same hotel as Dorothy "on the outskirts of the city proper" in a room across the courtyard from her.

Dorothy quickly filled Roy in on the rules of game—what she, as a Black woman, could and could not do—and he quickly mastered the technique of entering a restaurant and asking point blank if they served *Colored*. "I learned to know from the look on the face from the answer whether yes meant *yes* or yes meant *no*," he said. "And I would see to it that she wasn't embarrassed. Because I could have easily gone out, got her, and brought her in, and have them say, 'Sorry, we're full.'" If he felt they did not serve African Americans, Roy would purchase meals to take back to their hotel.

The Bingo was segregated, too. Opened in 1947 on Las Vegas's Strip, The Bingo was a small club with a three-hundred seat parlor for bingo as well as the usual gaming pleasures: slot machines, blackjack, and poker. But The Bingo was already considered ahead of other clubs because it offered first-rate entertainment. The patrons in 1949 and some years to come were exclusively White.

Dorothy was permitted to be in the lounge where she performed *only* when she performed. Under no circumstances, management informed her, was she to socialize with any of the patrons at the club, even if she were invited to their tables. She could not dine there, either.

She didn't even have a formal dressing room. She was to dress in a small abandoned manager's office where she also was to take her meals. She looked the room over and realized she had to make the best of the situation.

"There were lots of cartons and crates and God knows what around," Roy recalled of the office that served as a dressing room. "They brought in a table that was just a plywood top. That's what they brought in for us," said Roy. "So we dined together in this old abandoned manager's office." Roy would have been granted certain privileges. But he stayed with her, he said, "because I adored her so, and I certainly wasn't going to let her dine alone."

When she dressed, Roy was also in the office. Usually, she asked him to help zip up her tight slinky gowns, so tight in fact that once she was dressed, she couldn't effectively raise her dress to use the bathroom. One night as she waited to go on stage, she had to urinate in a glass.

"I can't imagine that [the proprietors of The Bingo] would have let her use the public facilities because she couldn't use any of the other public facilities anyway. They literally did not let her in that room unless she was performing," said Roy.

"After the initial shock of seeing where we had been banished to, we really had fun. We had a wonderful time and we laughed and carried on and were silly."

Sometimes she was in a funny and playful mood. Whenever the phone rang in the tiny carton-cluttered office, Dorothy picked up the receiver and said—in a grand theatrical manner—"Hello. Yes, this is *Miss* Dandridge." If the caller on the other end was a friend, her tone and language immediately changed. "Hi, honey. How are you!"

"It would just knock me out," he said. "I would laugh after that. She was just adorable. She was just as cute as she could be. Really a very sweet girl. I just loved her."

As close as the two became in those two weeks, Dorothy remained private. Roy didn't remember any mention of Lynn, Harold, or Vivian. Ruby might call, but not often. Roy had the impression that Dorothy and Ruby were not close. Whatever she felt about the people in her life and her personal problems, that was never discussed.

"I knew she wasn't terribly happy," he said. "At least I didn't think she was. She didn't think of herself as a smashing musical performer. There are so many people in the business who are terribly important who haven't enough talent to get out the front door but it doesn't stop them. Dorothy wasn't like that."

"And I think being as gorgeous as she was, at a time like that can be a handicap too. Because in a sense, she knew that was why she got hired, why she was going from here to there because you could just sit and look at her and it wouldn't matter whether she opened her mouth or not. I think she had a sense of that. And that's very painful and difficult, I think."

Roy also understood the effects of Las Vegas's segregation on her. "Dorothy was very philosophical about being treated very badly at The Bingo Hotel," he said. "But I don't think she was the kind of person who said 'Goddammit! I'm not going to take this shit!' I don't think she did that. She did the best that she could. But I don't think she tried very hard to fight it. I don't mean to say she wasn't a crusader. I don't mean that." She just kept it all in.

Dorothy mostly spent her days alone in her hotel room. Like most performers, she slept late, then had a meal, then began concentrating on the evening's performance. If she had any spare time, her energy had to be conserved. So she read. Rarely, did she venture into the city proper.

The exception came when she heard from Sammy Davis, Jr., who was also in Vegas, appearing at El Rancho down the way on the Strip. He was with the Will Mastin Trio, which was composed of Davis, his father, and his uncle Will Mastin. Happy to have a friend around for a little fun and moral support, Dandridge and Davis arranged to meet whenever possible.

One afternoon when Sammy stopped at Dorothy's hotel, the establishment's landlady caught sight of him at the front desk inquiring about Miss Dandridge. Immediately, she went into a dither. She rushed to Roy's room and loudly pounded on his door. He asked if anything was wrong.

"That Sammy Davis is visiting Miss Dandridge," the landlady said. "You've got to get him out of there."

"Why?" Roy asked.

"You know why," the woman replied.

"Well, you knew Miss Dandridge's race when you rented the space to her," he said.

Her response was, "I know. But she's so beautiful and he's so ugly."

Another time, Dorothy and Davis planned to meet at the Bingo after her show and his at El Rancho. They planned to go out on the town and do some socializing at a club in the Black section of Las Vegas. Though her figure didn't show it, Dorothy still loved soul food.

As soon as she finished her last set, she rushed back to the small office at The Bingo and changed her clothes. But she waited almost an hour with no word from Sammy. Finally, she called his hotel. They informed her that he had left some time earlier. Suspecting something was wrong, Dorothy turned to Roy and said, "Go to the door and see what's happening."

"So I went to the front door of The Bingo. And he was waiting there. He been waiting outside for forty-five minutes. They wouldn't let him in. They wouldn't deliver a message. They wouldn't tell us that he was waiting there."

When Dorothy saw Sammy, neither had to say anything. Neither let their anger or frustration interfere with their plans. The threesome ended up having a great time that evening at the Black club. Roy, for one, remembered it to be a highlight of the trip.

There were the indignities because of race, and also the indignities suffered in being a woman. Night after night at The Bingo, Dorothy sang before a White audience, including "guys who wanted to come and look at Dorothy to have their little fantasies. Whatever they were," said Roy.

Like so many other Black female singing stars, she had to learn to detach herself from the audience's misconceptions of her as a Black woman. Lena Horne used aloofness and her icy image as a shield in her act. Dandridge was just learning how to cope with club audiences. She chose to focus on her power to tease and flirt. She never singled out any particular patron in the audience as some female stars did, but rather addressed the entire room. She learned to move as she sang. Her dramatic dance-like movements gave her singing performances dramatic punch and power, but sometimes she appeared to be moving in an attempt to get away from the audience's gaze and desires. Eventually, she learned how to control the nightclub floor.

While The Bingo management was ever watchful and insistent that Dorothy not talk to White patrons, Phil Moore was protective and sensitive to possible problems she might encounter from men who tried to talk to her. So, as her manager, he made sure that "very good care was taken that she wasn't approached in any way that she shouldn't be," recalled Roy, "because that was the first thing that would have been likely to happen. But I think that was well seen to by him." No doubt he laid down the law to The Bingo's proprietors; that they had to prevent any males in the audience from making any advances or comments.

Despite her nervousness, the discrimination that faced her, Dandridge made an impact at The Bingo.

"Club Bingo Draws Top Crowd with Dandridge-Ames Show" read the headline of the review in the November 18, 1949 issue of the *Las Vegas Review-Journal*. The reviewer wrote:

She (Dorothy Dandridge) is billed . . .as an 'international singing beauty.' He (Jimmy Ames) is billed as the 'frantic comedian.' When both opened Wednesday night to a capacity crowd . . .it was very evident that . . .the billings [were] absolutely correct. But had we been writing the billing for Dorothy Dandridge we would have been inclined to say 'the sepia songstress who is headed for musical stardom.'

The review praised her performance as simply "terrific."

At the end of the engagement, Moore met Dorothy and Roy in Vegas and, ecstatic about the response to the engagement, they motored back to Los Angeles. Moore and Dandridge dropped Roy off at home where he lived with his parents. Roy's mother went out of her way to be friendly. Yet Dorothy, ever sensitive to racial or social nuances, asked, "Your parents never had any [colored] people in their home before, have they?" He admitted that they hadn't, and he and Dorothy laughed. "We both had a sense of humor. I guess that's what made us so fond of each other. There was no pretense."

Back in Los Angeles, Moore's and Dorothy's efforts at building her club career continued. Moore was not a man easily impressed. Nor was he a man who wore his heart on his sleeve. But his devotion to Dorothy, to the creation of her as a major new Black talent in night-clubs, began to touch on obsession.

A new decade, the Fabulous Fifties, was approaching. Dorothy pondered the future. Her career was slowly moving along. But there were loose ends in her life that needed tying. She had to make some decisive move about her marriage to Harold and her relationship with Phil. She resolved to get a divorce. Within a few months, she contacted the attorney Robert Butts of Butts and Grosenbaugh in Hollywood. By June, Butts served papers on Dorothy's behalf against Harold for divorce on the grounds of extreme cruelty. On September 29, 1950, an interloctury judgment of divorce was granted for Dandridge by the Superior Court of Los Angeles County.

She received custody of Harolyn as well as $300 a month in child support to begin October, 1950. Harold was also responsible for the legal and court costs for the divorce, which amounted to $250. The terms of their property settlement stated that Dorothy receive the cou-

ple's home, their furniture and furnishings as well as personal property, and their 1946 Buick. Harold received the property on 51st Street,
which was the home Dorothy had bought with Geri. Dorothy waived
and relinquished any claims against Harold for alimony.

Upon receiving the papers, Harold didn't want to sign but felt he had
no choice. "I signed them over in Europe because I realized it would
best," said Harold, "because the way it was going and the way I was
going, which was crazy, it would be best to sign those papers and not try
to fight it. So that's what I did." Their union was officially ended.

The divorce became final in October 1951.

The issue of the marriage was settled but not the matter of the welfare of their daughter. Ruby and Neva couldn't handle the girl any
longer. Viola Nicholas intervened and for a time, tried to watch Lynn.
But Lynn was too difficult and needed professional care. Dorothy had
to find someone who could be on call to provide round-the-clock
supervision; someone who was capable of controlling her daughter's
fits and crying spells. It had to be someone who knew when to comfort and cuddle Lynn, when to discipline her.

Dorothy considered a special school. "But prejudice ruled that
out," said Geri. Most of the best schools of the day still excluded
Black children.

Dorothy recalled, "I thought, 'I just can't give her up, really, to an
institution.' Somehow at that time that seemed like the worst thing in
the world to do. I felt that, well, I'll make money and put her in a private institution with someone I know—someone who would groom
her properly and treat her nice. I thought of an institution as a place
with a lot of beds and where they just sort of throw you around like
animals. I just couldn't see her there."

Finally, Dorothy believed she found just the right type of attendant
for Lynn when she met a woman named Helen Calhoun, who already
cared for other children. Dorothy and Calhoun came to an agreement.

"So I moved all the little mother and daughter pinafores out and
let my daughter go to this wonderful woman," Dorothy said. Lynn
was moved into Calhoun's home. Weekly payments for Lynn's care
were made by Dorothy to Calhoun for the next thirteen years.

Having worked so closely with Phil, Dorothy ended up living with
him as well. Couples were not open about such living arrangements without the sanction of marriage during this era. But Phil urged her to move
out of the house on 27th Street to Hollywood, a more central location for
interviews and auditions. Dorothy found an apartment, really a house, on
Hilldale right off Sunset Boulevard with two separate dwellings. Whereas

her home on 27th Street had been warm, homey, cozy, the ideal setting for her fantasies about a magical family life, the apartment on Hilldale was another metaphor: it was something of a 1950s-style bachelor girl pad, the perfect setting for a young career woman.

The building on Hilldale was a duplex. Phil lived upstairs on the top two floors. Dorothy had the downstairs one bedroom apartment, furnished modestly but impressively. There was a fireplace in the living room and a large piano. There was a small kitchen, in which she frequently cooked her favorites—greens and chitlins—and experimented with French recipes. Outside was a large garden where she entertained her friends whenever she had the time.

Dorothy made her move to Hollywood, got her divorce from Harold and hired her new caretaker for Lynn, all in the same week. "I just thought I'd make a clean sweep of the whole thing," she later told the press. Yet, Geri remembered, despite the move, Dorothy held onto the house on 27th Street for a long time.

Her life with Phil was harmonious and filled with an assortment of interesting people, conversant about books, music, art, politics, and of course, about show business.

"They used to have musicales on Sunday afternoons," Bobby Short recalled. "Phil always liked to do that. With a house full of piano players and singers. They'd all sing things. And somebody would recite. And I think it was a very, very happy relationship."

In what free hours she had, Dorothy tried maintaining ties with her loved ones. She had few new close friends. But Ruby and Vivian still knew her comings and goings. She talked to both, especially Ruby, almost every day. And she and Geri were still close. But everything really revolved around the people she worked with. Geri was in and out of the States. In 1950, she and her son Tony travelled with Harold and Fayard on a tour through North Africa. Then she came back to Los Angeles for the birth of her second son Paul. Then she returned to Europe. But Dorothy kept in touch with other old friends and family with telephone calls that went on for hours.

"Oh, but she loved to talk," remembered Dorothy Nicholas Morrow. "She had so much that she had to get out."

She also saw Marilyn Monroe, her friend from the Actors Lab. As two aspiring young actresses enduring the hassles and disappointments of the business, Dandridge and Monroe talked about their careers, ambitions, and aspirations. And sometimes the talk turned to men.

Dorothy's friend Juliette Ball remembered Marilyn's visits to Hilldale. "Dottie had a little white rug in front of the fireplace," Ball said. "And Marilyn used to lie on that rug. And many a night she cried. Mostly about her relationships."

"Oh, they were friends all right," recalled Geri. "They spent all day at the Lab. They had exercise class there. And sometimes Marilyn forgot to bring her leotards. And Dottie would lend her hers. Marilyn wasn't as neat as Dottie. Dottie was a perfectionist, and if somebody used something like that, she was through with it." Dorothy discarded the leotards. But now she also saw Marilyn frequently because she also took lessons from Phil.

Moore coached both Monroe and Ava Gardner at the Hollywood duplex. Geri and Juliette both believed it was Dottie who persuaded the actresses to study with him. Their presence on Hilldale though made for some funny evenings and encounters. On some occasions, Moore remembered that Dottie, rarely the jealous type, raised concerns and an eyebrow about each woman.

Gardner studied with Moore in preparation for MGM's big-budget Technicolor remake of *Show Boat*. Gardner planned to sing, rather than be dubbed, although after all her training, that was precisely what the studio did: used the voice of a professional singer for Ava's numbers. She looked to Moore to give her the right phrasing and inflections; no doubt to help her bring a certain cultural sound and tone to Julie's songs.

Because of Gardner's tight shooting schedule at MGM, the actress always stopped by Phil's in the evening for her lessons. Nervous about her voice, she refused to go anywhere near the microphone that Moore had set up in the apartment. She did not even want to look at it. Consequently, they rehearsed "with only a small piano light on because she got 'spooked' seeing the microphone," Moore said.

"This made things a bit rough for me since I was 'going steady' with Dorothy," Moore said. "She'd pop up through my backdoor every evening, and catch us performing in the dark. Needless to say, this didn't set too well with Miss D."

At the time, Gardner was also undergoing psychoanalysis. "Man, she was 'acting out' everything," Moore said. "Short short dresses. Being rather coarse and loud in her speech. Cursing whenever she felt like it. Sitting in unfeminine positions with dress up to here! And no drawers. And in comes Dorothy! You see, there are problems in every field."

Marilyn often stayed at Phil's just to talk after coaching sessions. He could see that she was lonely. One afternoon when Marilyn didn't seem ready to go home, he told her to just keeping talking while he prepared for an evening out on the town with Dorothy.

Dorothy "had a habit, which I enjoyed, of popping up the back-stairs to visit me whenever she was at home," Moore said.

On this evening, when she ran upstairs, "Here I was, bare to the waist, trying to shave in the bathroom, getting ready to go out with her, and there, standing in my bathroom doorway, was Marilyn—watching me shave," Moore recalled. "It's kind a hard to remain cool in that sit-uation when your girlfriend walks into a promising but innocent scene like that. It took Miss D a couple days to get over that one."

Another time Marilyn arrived at Moore's obviously upset about something. Finally, she confided in Phil that there had been some "risqué" photographs taken of her a few years earlier. Now that she was beginning to find work and becoming known, the photographer threatened to release the pictures. Phil asked to see them. She ran out to her car to get them. When she handed the pictures to Moore, he saw the famous Marilyn nudes, which he thought were beautiful. So, too, did Dorothy when he showed the pictures to her. Both tried reas-suring Marilyn. "We couldn't imagine these shots impairing her career if they were published," said Moore. "They would certainly generate some scandal and notoriety, but we also thought the public as a whole, would not be offended." Ultimately, the pictures did no damage, even when Hugh Hefner published them in *Playboy*.

"Between the time with Monroe, and the instance when Dottie came in and Ava Gardner was singing with me, in the dark," Moore later said, "Dottie got a dose of what could have been her own medicine. Perhaps these little events were serendipitous for our relationship. In fact, I believe it helped 'D' and me get on quite well for a couple years. Guess ladies feel that if someone else beautiful 'digs' you, hey, you gotta be somethin' special."

For Dorothy, who always felt her happiest years were the early ones of her marriage to Harold, this period with Phil Moore was a very ordered, balanced time. She appeared more secure and less anxiety-rid-den. At home, she loved relaxing, cooking, or even rehearsing in jeans and loose blouses, often a large roomy man's shirt; quite a contrast from her public outings where she was known for wearing gloves and a string of pearls. Moore said the two didn't discuss marriage. But the thought of marriage clearly crossed Dorothy's mind. Living with a man was not her idea of a proper relationship. Always a romantic, she believed mar-riage represented a happy ending. On one occasion, she presented Phil a set of expensive cuff links with a card signed by her that read: "This is for when we get married."

Still, her feelings were mixed and she had to face certain facts. She cared for Phil Moore, who may well have been one of the most decent men in her life. But her primary objective now was still the molding and building of a solid career. Without a profession, she knew she would be adrift. As insecure as the life of an entertainer could be, the pursuit of a career kept her anchored and focused; helped her, as Moore understood, to blot out the reality of Lynn's condition. Dorothy understood the career boost that grew out of her relationship with Moore, but she never used Moore solely to get ahead. It's doubtful though that their relationship would have become so intense had Phil not been able to help her professionally. For Dorothy, here was a man as absorbed in her as she was in herself. Yet at times, she found him possessive and too controlling.

As her nightclub engagements continued, she hired a publicist to drum up interest, especially in the entertainment columns. And always, in an effort to become known to important people who might come to see her act, she attended social gatherings where industry people saw one another. Moore did the same. Hollywood was a town where socializing was as almost as important as an audition. In some cases, an appearance at the right social function *was* an audition.

As she hoped, the club dates indeed brought her to the attention of the film community. By the spring of 1950 when she performed at Larry Potter's Supper Club in Los Angeles, the buzz was already starting in the Hollywood columns not only about her club appearances but the possibility of movie jobs.

"Very secretly Twentieth Century Fox has been talking to Dorothy Dandridge about one of the top roles in George Jessel's *Cotton Club*," Louella Parsons reported in her May 9th column in *The Los Angeles Examiner*. Parsons also added a comment that, to Dorothy's dismay, was often repeated over next three years, at least. "Dorothy looks very much like Lena Horne." The *Cotton Club* movie with Jessell never materialized. But the buzz had started.

In July, she and Moore opened at the Tahoe Village Club in Lake Tahoe. Like Vegas, Tahoe was an important city on the big club circuit. During the engagement, a band leader named Daniel Terry asked if she would pose for a picture with him. Dorothy complied, as she did with innumerable others with the same requests at various engagements. Some years later though the "uneventful" Tahoe date reared its ugly head and became the center of a lawsuit that would make headlines around America. Dandridge and Moore, however, left Lake Tahoe, assuming it was just one more rung on the ladder.

Back in Los Angeles in the late summer of 1950, talk of movies continued. The September 1st issue of *The California Eagle* carried a picture of Dorothy and reported that she was being considered for a top role in *The Well*. But when *The Well* was finally filmed, it was not Dorothy but Maidie Norman who played the young mother whose child has fallen down a well. Still, between the club dates came offers for roles in two low-budget films. In the scheme of things, neither movie amounted to much. But each offered Dandridge more exposure and experience. Because each had a mid-October starting date, her schedule had to be juggled in order that she could work on both films at the same time.

At RKO, she was cast in producer Sol Lesser's *Tarzan's Peril*. American writer Edgar Rice Burroughs's Tarzan character had been a movie fixture since the days of silent films. Having never set foot in Africa, Burroughs's view of the "dark savage continent" was pure European exotic romanticism. Pure bunk, too. His Tarzan reigned as the lord of the apes. As he strutted through the jungle, Tarzan could mow down savage spear-chucking natives and certainly, even in a loin cloth, trumpet the cause of law and order, mighty-White-man-style. The proper Jane was, of course, usually by his side. So, too, was his faithful companion, the chimpanzee Cheetah.

Playing the title character in *Tarzan's Peril* was Lex Barker, a handsome Princeton-educated hunk with a patrician family back-ground, a fine jaw line and, of course, the requisite sturdy physique. Because producer Sol Lesser wanted greater authenticity than in previous versions, he made arrangements to shoot this Tarzan movie in color in Kenya under the direction of Phil Brandon.

Dorothy was not yet cast in the film, but that proved to be fortu-itous timing because the location shoot was, in most respects, a disaster. The film crew arrived during the winter season. Heavy clouds wrecked the lighting. The color footage was ruined during the filming, and final-ly was discarded. The film was then converted to black and white.

The crew left the continent discouraged. But they brought back some striking footage: realistic scenes of native tribal dances and chants as well as striking animal sequences and sweeping vistas of African scenery.

In the States, producer Lesser hired Byron Haskins, who had directed *Treasure Island* and later *War of the Worlds*, to direct the rest of the movie. Lesser mentioned the project to Phil Moore who, when he learned of a role of a young African woman, suggested that Dorothy test for the picture. Lesser liked the idea.

A Tarzan movie was not Dorothy's idea of a strong dramatic vehicle. But she read the script and knew she had to be realistic about her options. Her character was Melmendi, the recently coronated young queen of a village. Surprisingly, it was a dramatic role with a touch of dignity and without the standard jungle-style dialogue. She could do the role without losing her self-respect. Moore agreed. It might lead to something else.

The film was to be shot quickly. The cast included character actor George Macready as the villain, Alan Napier, Virginia Huston as Jane, and Black actors Frederick O'Neal and Bob Davis.

Tarzan's Peril's storyline was a familiar one with stock characters and predictable plot turns. There were the warring African tribes, the Good White Man, a commissioner who is kind to the natives (like "our father and our mother," Melmendi says), and the Bad White Man, who sells guns to a corrupt African chieftain, Bulam of the Yorango tribe. But guns are not the only thing the chieftain Bulam is after. He also hankers for the pretty queen Melmendi of the Ashuba tribe, whom he has kidnapped from her village and then carried off to a hut where he has her tied to the stakes. As she lies on the ground, twisting and turning in efforts to free herself, the audience knows Melmendi wants desperately to be rescued. Of course, who does ultimately rescue her but good old Tarzan!

This sequence drew attention even before it was filmed. All Hollywood films had to be cleared by the industry's self-policing censorship bureau, the Production Code Administration which was headed by Robert Breen. Breen's office was always on the lookout for any sexually suggestive or morally offensive scenes or dialogue. Scripts were sent to the Breen office before production began. Rough cuts of films were shown to the office for its approval. A film could not be released without the Production Code seal. When the Breen office, as it was called, read the script for *Tarzan's Peril*, it commented on the rescue scene with Tarzan and the native queen.

"Care must be exercised lest Bulam, by his looks and gestures appear too lecherous as he has the young queen dragged away to his quarters," stated the letter from the Breen Office to producer Sol Lesser. It was also pointed out that: "In this scene where the young queen, Melmendi, is shown staked to the floor, it will not be permissible to have her staked out in such wise that her legs are spread-eagled. Such a position, in view of the foregoing action on the part of Bulam, would be offensively sex suggestive."

The irony, of course, was that while Melmendi was not shown spread-eagled, the sequence itself still reverberated with sexual tension. The camera panned over Dandridge's body, from her legs to her waist and breasts and a quick glimpse of her face. As she lay bound, gagged, and pinned to the ground, the scene was a sadist's dream of bondage, though it might appear quite innocent to today's audiences. Once Tarzan arrived in the tent, the sequence became sexually charged simply because of the two actors on screen.

Certainly, director Byron Haskin and writers Samuel Newman and Francis Swann were toying with audience perceptions once Dandridge and Barker were cast. In their brief scenes together, she's so implausibly pretty and sexy (it was one of Dandridge's few sex-kitten roles) that no one could imagine Barker's Tarzan, for once in his life, thinking much about Jane. And one can be certain he is not thinking about Cheetah. The subtext of *Tarzan's Peril* titillated audiences with the suggestion of an interracial romantic attraction.

It is significant that in this, her first quasi-lead role in a Hollywood film, Dandridge is indeed cast opposite a White actor. Lena Horne usually had been kept isolated in her film work. She was always something of a poised beautiful object, a fantasy in a musical sequence. Dandridge portrayed a character, thus becoming touchable flesh and blood. Director of photography Jack Whithead shot lush closeups of her. Both he and director Haskin were clearly enamored of her, far more so than they were of the leading lady Huston. When released in Great Britain, the film's title was *Tarzan and the Jungle Goddess*.

Although more Hollywood than African, the character Melmendi nonetheless is presented as a woman with power and certainly, by the fact that she is glamorized and well-shot, allure. Dandridge played the character amusingly like the beautiful, healthy, all-American Black "girl" next door. When she uttered dialogue like "Stay, Tarzan," she gave an enticingly playful Hollywood-style performance, knowing precisely how to send a signal underneath a line.

She got the media's attention. *Variety's* reviewer commented," Virginia Huston has only a few scenes as Tarzan's mate, Jane, in the footage. There's more emphasis on Dorothy Dandridge, queen of a tribe that is saved by Tarzan from its warring rivals."

Her appearance in *Tarzan's Peril* landed Dandridge her first *Ebony* magazine cover on the April 1951 issue. Though her role was not a starring one, *Ebony* proclaimed her "Hollywood's New Glamour Queen." The article and cover portrait marked the start of the magazine's love affair with her.

Thereafter, John H. Johnson's publications *Ebony* and *Jet* both chronicled her career achievements at every opportunity. While White female stars traditionally looked to *Photoplay, Modern Screen,* and *Motion Picture,* not to mention the ultimate celebrity status symbol *Life,* for publicity and exposure, Dandridge was celebrated by the Black press. Soon other African American publications like *Our World, Tan, Hue,* later *Sepia,* as well as newspapers like *The Philadelphia Tribune, The Pittsburgh Courier,The New York Amsterdam News, The Norfolk Journal and Guide,* and *The Chicago Defender* traced the spiraling rise of her career and then the problems of her private life.

Dandridge's other film was Columbia Pictures's low-budget quickie *The Harlem Globetrotters*'s. Its screenplay was by former sports writer and journalist Alfred Palca, who came up with the idea of doing a story around the legendary basketball team after he noticed the extraordinary reaction of audiences, full of laughter, cheers, applause, to a Globetrotters newsreel. At the time, the all-Black Harlem Globetrotters was a nationally famous team known not only for its basketball skills—dazzling basketball spins and magical fake passes—but also the humor they displayed on court.

As conceived by Palca, *The Harlem Globetrotters* would be a decently made B-movie melodrama with tautly shot court sequences. Its wrap-around dramatic story was of a spoiled athlete, who leaves college to join the Globetrotters, only to be dropped because of his lack of team spirit. Of course, he has to learn the error of his ways, repent, and then redeem himself in a climactic sequence with the team at their big game. Helping the young man him find himself was his college sweetheart.

The male lead was played by real-life athlete Bill Brown, who was also the husband of Dorothy's childhood friend Juliette Ball. Dorothy played the athlete's girlfriend, whom he marries, and the Harlem Globetrotters played themselves. It was a Black-cast film with only one important White character, the Globetrotter's feisty manager Abe Saperstein.

Columbia was testing the waters. Great profits were not expected of the film. The idea of dealing with multi-dimensional aspects of African American life was still novel and daring. But the studio felt it might attract sports fans as well as the Negro audience, and therefore make a profit. The director was Phil Brown, one of the founders of the Actors Lab, who shortly afterwards was blacklisted because of his politics. Brown recalled the disdain of Buddy Adler, who Columbia assigned to produce the film. "He was horror-stricken," said Brown.

Adler wanted to work only on the studio's big productions. "He had nothing do with the casting. Nothing to do with the script. He had nothing to do with anything. He just sat there."

Shot on a low budget of approximately $400,000, the dramatic sequences, as well as some in studio game sequences, were shot in eleven days on the Columbia lot. Footage from actual Globetrotter games in various cities was shot under the direction of Will Jason. In all, the movie would be completed in some twenty-three days.

"I didn't know her before at all. I knew *of* her," director Phil Brown said of Dorothy. Maybe their paths had crossed at the Actors Lab. "I probably met her at the Lab and thought that this was a very beautiful girl and thought that she'd be perfect for the part. I'm sure that's the way it happened." He remembered that she didn't test for the role and that she was paid about $500 a week but wasn't certain how Dorothy came into the picture.

Screenwriter Alfred Palca recalled, however, that producer Buddy Adler, who otherwise appeared to have no interest in the production, clearly had an interest in Dorothy. It was Adler, said Palca, who brought her into the movie.

An aggressive, up-and-coming producer determined to make his mark, Adler was a tall, virile, handsome man with a thick mane of prematurely gray hair. He was very much married to actress Anita Louise, who co-starred in the movie *Going Places*, which teenaged Dorothy also appeared in.

Adler, according to Palca, was openly infatuated with Dandridge. Palca even wondered if Dorothy was Adler's girlfriend. "I thought he had an affair with her," said Palca. "Or *wanted* to have an affair. Or maybe it was Columbia writer Sidney Buchman who told me that Buddy made a play for Dorothy Dandridge."

Dorothy must have caught Adler's eye at an audition or a social function. By now, she was becoming better known throughout the industry, not yet as an actress, nor a singer, but as a beauty. Adler was but one of many powerful film executives, including Columbia mogul Harry Cohn, who became interested in her. Dorothy apparently kept Adler at bay. By now, she was as aware of her looks as everyone else, and she was learning, as Geri Branton had said, "to use her beauty." But she wasn't interested in him. Besides, Phil Moore was always around to make sure neither Adler nor anybody else got too close to her.

"Buddy tampered with everything about her," said Palca. "She's supposed to be a working girl in the movie. But Buddy had her dressed in the movie like she was a millionairess. All this makeup. And expensive dresses. It was like he was determined to make her a star. I thought Dorothy was very sweet. But even she seemed to be embarrassed and to think that Adler was overdoing it."

On the set, Dorothy was "simply marvelous" to work with, despite the fact that she was "relatively new to acting at that time," said Phil Brown, unaware of Dorothy's years of apprenticeship in bit roles in those early films like *Lucky Jordan* and *Sundown*. But he saw that she was a "natural" on screen and also an asset in helping to coax a performance out of her co-star Bill Brown.

"The thing that I found marvelous about her is that she had to play love scenes with Bill Brown, who was a big handsome basketball player. He never thought about acting in his life and she was just wonderful with him. They played these scenes beautifully together. And I think it's important to note. I think this was one of the first [Hollywood] films to have a young romantic love interest between two Blacks. Because heretofore Blacks were playing servants or comic acts. But this was a story about some Black athletes and it had to have a love interest. So here were these two people. Dorothy Dandridge and Bill Brown. All I can say is that she made him feel completely at ease."

She also made the executives at Columbia Pictures feel at ease when they saw the completed film. "It was Columbia's pattern to have a showing in the studio's projection room which seated about three hundred people," recalled director Phil Brown. Once a week, there were screenings of two films. "And everybody had to go because [studio chief] Harry Cohn had his spies out, which meant the secretaries and everybody else had to go to these things because if they didn't, Cohn would ask, 'Why didn't you go to the picture last night?'"

Such standard studio screenings usually opened with a B-picture, then finished with a glossy A-picture. "But Harry Cohn's policy was the opposite," said director, Brown. "The A-picture, which was Robert Rossen's *The Brave Bulls*, was very big budget and prestigious. And the audience responded tepidly at best. A few people even got up and left afterwards. And then the Trotters film went on and the audience adored it. They clapped and they applauded. They thought it was a great picture and that *The Brave Bulls* was a stinker." Producer Adler took notice.

"The next day Buddy Adler calls me into his office and sits me down in a chair," said Brown. "And he said, 'Look, Phil. I want to tell you something. This picture's going to be a big picture. It's going to make a lot of money and what I want you to remember is that I discovered you.'"

"Commercial possibilities are obvious, either in the regular twin bill market or for special handling to attract eager fans or colored audiences," wrote *Variety*, which saw the potential of tapping the African American movie-going public, a segment of the audience which Hollywood rarely took into consideration.

While *The Harlem Globetrotters* didn't soar to the top of Variety's Top Ten list, it turned a decent profit. Unlike Hollywood's Negro problem pictures, *The Harlem Globetrotters* had the tone and feel of the race movies, which by now had vanished. Without presenting race as a problem, the film was standard movie fare that provided a fresh glimpse at middle-class African American life. Black character actor William Walker played a supporting role as a dedicated professor at a Black college. The movie sets him up as a role model for the young athlete. The older man is also the father of Dorothy's character.

Though Dandridge's Jane was the basic good woman trying to help a wayward man, she was wholly new and wholly refreshing in the world of African American mainstream movie images: simply stated, here was a bright, educated, articulate, normal everyday (albeit idealized) young Black woman trying to make a marriage work and to bring her restless young husband to a sense of responsibility. In the past, Hollywood didn't seem aware that such a Black woman existed.

"Brown plays the role unusually well for an acting novice," wrote *Variety* of Dandridge's co-star. But the paper added that "Dorothy Dandridge helps his performance while making a topnotch impression herself. The two characters, as well as those of a college professor done by Bill Walker and the playing-themselves contributions of the Globetrotters, foster a very good impression for the Negro race."

Tarzan's Perils and *The Harlem Globetrotters* helped create a place for Dorothy within the industry. By this time, Black actresses Ruby Dee and Mildred Joanne Smith had appeared in supporting dramatic roles in such features as *The Jackie Robinson Story, Tall Target,* and *No Way Out*. Dee would go on to a series of impressive dramatic performances, primarily as a character actress. But in cinema, Dandridge already suggested a larger-than-life romantic quality not yet exhibited by an African American woman in Hollywood films.

Dorothy returned to the club circuit. On December 6, 1950 she was in Vegas, opening at the El Rancho Hotel. Columbia Pictures mogul Harry Cohn, already impressed by her, pulled strings to get her booked into the club, which led to gossip of a romance. But their relationship was professional, never anything more.

At one of her El Rancho performances sat actress Marie Wilson, who was to become best known for the television series "My Friend Irma." Excited by Dorothy's performance, Wilson visited her backstage. Later Wilson contacted a friend from *Life* magazine, which resulted in Dorothy being photographed for a layout in the magazine. Nothing appeared, though, until the next year.

At the start of 1951, Dorothy's work had proven therapeutic. She had been able to focus on something other than Lynn. Her ambition and her career were holding her together. Tied into both, of course, was the relationship with Phil, which helped her professionally, emotionally, and psychologically. Even though her love life may not have been exactly as she might have wanted, she didn't have time to think about that.

Yet, with this career that had become so all important to her psychological well-being, she knew she still didn't have the type of big club date that could make her nationally known. Something important, however, was about to happen soon.

Perched on a little hill on Sunset Strip at Horn and Sunset Boulevard was a tiny club called the Gala. (The Gala's site would later be occupied by the restaurant Spago's.) Owned by Jim Dolan, the Club Gala had once been a private residence. The ground level consisted of a dining room and a salon with French doors that opened onto a garden. The color scheme in the main room was red and white: striped walls, table clothes, and banquettes. "The Gala was very small," said Bobby Short, who appeared there in the early 1950s. "It relied upon cachet to make it." Its patrons were a lively mix of the important and the up-and-comers, the gay and the straight, the young and the old. Among them were some of the movie colony's biggest stars and moguls as well as exiled royalty and socialites. "It was a very, very chic little club and there's been nothing like it since," said Short. "It was a White crowd and a very, very hip crowd. Very hip crowd."

Searching for new acts for the Gala, owner Dolan contacted Phil Moore, whom he hoped to persuade to perform there. Phil asked Dolan to take a look at Dorothy. She was known by now but still had not proven herself as either a great draw or a great presence on the L.A. nightclub scene. Dorothy auditioned and was hired mainly on Moore's recommendation and the fact that he would accompany her for the engagement.

Dorothy's nerves flared up. Despite her success now in Vegas and other clubs, she hadn't lost her terror of live audiences. She was no more confident than she had been two years earlier. Besides, it was not lost on her that this would be a tough, trendy movieland audience. To fall on her face in front of them could be a disaster for her club career. And also any possibility of a movie career.

Moore rehearsed her carefully. Again he wrote special material, which would not make "big demands upon her voice but upon her personality and the way she looked," said Bobby Short. Her gowns, again slinky, were shrewdly selected. She and Moore meticulously eyed the small room, relieved that it would not require great voice projection. "Of course, it was an ideal place," said Short. "No microphone. Two grand pianos. Intimacy personified."

To keep Dorothy's fears of the audience at bay, Moore created a special routine in which Dorothy was to flip a coin and catch it. It was meant to keep her focused on the coin rather than the stares of the audience. But in rehearsals, she couldn't get it right. Moore then shrewdly suggested that she should intentionally miss catching the coin, then just shrug her shoulders and smile. He knew it would be a crowd-pleaser.

Dandridge's opening night, however, was a near disaster. She was so frightened and nervous that she could barely get her first songs out. But Moore, so enamored of her and so assured of her talent, sat at the piano not far from her and coaxed her into relaxing, right before the audience. Sometimes he playfully used sexual innuendoes to make her laugh and loosen up and also to heighten the sexy atmosphere of the club itself.

Although Dandridge didn't feel comfortable with the innuendoes and later complained about them, Phil's banter worked magic on this night. Here was a personal psychodrama being played out before a room full of people. Smoothly and expertly, he led her through her repertoire of such songs as "Harlem on My Mind" and "A Woman's Prerogative." She kept getting better. Between shows, she retreated to her dressing room where she tried to maintain her composure and concentration, but she was frightened of having to perform again. Yet by the end of the evening, she was relaxed and performing well.

Within the next few nights, a more confident Dandridge, now fiery and dramatic, became stirring and glorious. She used her hands expressively as she sang, to help explain, punctuate, and intensify the lyrics. And her movements in this tiny club were those of a highly trained dancer. Few women on the club circuit ever used their bodies as dramatically.

"She was perfection!" said Dorothy Nicholas Morrow, who attended the Gala performance with her husband Byron. Both

thought the coin routine Moore had devised worked beautifully and
was a shrewd dramatic effect.

"She was just peaches and cream," remembered Bobby Short.
"She really was. There was nothing threatening about her. Nothing
at all that was aggressive. She was just so *frigging* pretty that when
she walked out in front of the audience with that low-cut dress and
those boobs and that little waist, she was just a *killer*. Just a *killer*. She
was always nervous though, I think. And maybe a little insecure."

Soon within the tough, competitive realm of Los Angeles nightclubs, word of mouth spread that this new gorgeous gal on the block
was worth seeing.

Shortly afterwards, Dick Williams, the entertainment editor for
The Los Angeles Mirror, sat in for a performance. He was mesmer-
ized, not just by Dandridge's beauty but her sexy intelligent delivery.
She showed no signs of unease that night.

Under the headline "Satiny, Sexy Songstress Has That Starlight
Aura," in the February 24, 1951 weekend section of the *Mirror*,
Williams raved about Dandridge's performance.

> It's on nights like last with the rain splashing against the
> black windows and the candles on the big grand piano glow-
> ing steadily that you should climb the hill above the Sunset
> Strip to hear Dorothy Dandridge.
> She leans there on the piano at the end of that room that
> has the feel of a Manhattan style intimate supper club, eyes
> closed, lips parted, her hands thrown in front of her, the
> fringe of her tight white dress flying as she huskily intones
> 'Got Harlem on My Mind.'
> ... This is Dorothy Dandridge, the most exciting new
> sepia singer I've spotted since Lena Horne.

A series of striking photographs accompanied Williams's review and
attracted the attention of the club-scene aficionados. But more importantly, the review brought her to the attention of directors, writers, producers, agents, and stars—movers and shakers within the industry.

The tiny Club Gala was her first important breakthrough. *Variety*
covered the show with a glowing review that read: "A new showbiz
career looms brightly for Dorothy Dandridge. She's been around
before, but never with the window-dressing and guidance Moore has
dished out and she looks like a cinch click. . ."

"Within days, the news got around about Dorothy Dandridge,"

said Short. "That was the first time she had ever really been important on her own because she got press that you would not believe. And there was talk about a great Negro beauty like Lena Horne and Ada Ward and all the pretty women who had gone before Dorothy. It was a big, big moment. And very exciting for her."

Crowds lined the street nightly to see her. "You couldn't get in. And she stayed there, I think, for a long while. Then, of course, a lot of great things began to happen to her."

For Dandridge, it was a happy time. The start of a whole new phase in her life. Had she remained a fixture in a club like the Gala, she might have been a cult favorite, known only to a select group of patrons. But she understood, as did Phil Moore, that she had to take the next step, that hers was an appeal made for a large audience.

Not far from the Club Gala, on Sunset Strip itself, stood the Mocambo. Its owner, Charlie Morrison, who remembered the nervous "girl" who had come to him not that long ago in search of work, attended her performances. He sat as transfixed as everyone else. Now she was ready for the greatest of West Coast nightclubs, the Mocambo itself. Morrison approached Phil and Dorothy with his plans to bring her to his club.

Afterwards, a jubilant Dorothy and Phil celebrated. Not much else in her life had gone well. But the career she had invested so much focus on was delivering. Everything she had been working for was beginning to happen. He basked in the glow and glory of *his creation*.

As Charlie Morrison made plans for Dorothy's debut, as he discussed and hashed out details, Moore realized that the talk now was *only* about Dorothy. He didn't say anything to acknowledge it, but, already in the perceptions of others, he was receding into the background. Already it was becoming difficult to watch Dorothy go forward while he remained on the sidelines. His role as Svengali had ironically robbed him of a certain professional identity that he needed.

Dorothy was too excited about the future to notice. She had always looked at the union as primarily professional, anyway. There was too much she wanted out of life to focus on him more than her career.

The Mocambo, the great career boost, ultimately marked the ascension of Dorothy into the major ranks of nightclub stars but it also signaled the beginning of the disintegration of her relationship with Phil Moore, perhaps the most stable romantic relationship she was ever to have.

SEVEN

RISING

$\mathcal{T}$he Mocambo remained at the top of Hollywood's nightclubs in the early 1950s, along with Ciro's, the Trocadero, and the Cocoanut Grove. Located on the Sunset Strip, that stretch of Sunset Boulevard that had become fashionable among the wealthy, the famous, and the trendy, the Mocambo first opened its doors in 1941. It had been the brainchild of former agent Charlie Morrison and Felix Young, who spent $100,000 to create the exotic, colorful nitery, once described as "a cross between a somewhat decadent Imperial Rome, Salvador Dali, and a birdcage." The decor as well as the club's Mexican name was planned to suggest the exotic, the sensual, the glamorous. On the walls were lush paintings by Jane Berlandina. Against those walls were huge tin flowers. Throughout the room were lacquered trees as well as brilliant red columns emblazoned with dancing harlequins. It was a "medley of soft blue, flamboyant terra cotta, and scintillating silver." The Mocambo's centerpiece was an aviary filled with exotic birds: parakeets,lovebirds, macaws, and a spectacular cockatoo.

Seated at the club's tables and banquettes were the movie capital's gilded, glamorous elite of the 1940s and 1950s. The Mocambo bore witness to the great stars and personalities of the age. The fan magazines and gossip columnists loved reporting on the club's stream of famous names. Gable and Lombard. Dietrich perhaps with French actor Jean Gabin one night, and with another suave escort the next. Barbara Hutton and Cary Grant. Cole Porter. Lucille Ball and Desi Arnaz. Lana Turner. Judy Garland. Hedy Lamarr. Henry Fonda. Louis B. Mayer. More than simply being a place to see and be seen, the Mocambo was also a pleasure palace of fun, energy, intrigue, adventure, and the entertainment matched the sophistication of the clientele.

Charlie Morrison believed that Dorothy, in the space of only a few years since he had first sent her off to Phil Moore, now exuded the sexy glamour his club was famous for. Under Moore's hand, she had developed excellent material and her delivery and presence were exciting. So he was now prepared to give her a major promotional campaign. Her name would appear in big, bold letters on the banner above the nitery's famous canopy. The club's public relations office would do all it could to insure that the press covered her engagement.

For Dorothy, that meant another strenuous rehearsal period. As before, she worked daily with Phil. She studied modern dance and ballet with dance instructor Olga Lunick. Most importantly, she took vocal exercises from a voice coach, which reflected Dorothy's determination to put a song over in the best way possible.

Dorothy was aware of the other women performing in clubs with whom she'd have to compete. Billie Holiday was now known for her moody, brooding emotional intensity. Ella Fitzgerald was praised for her sturdy technical virtuosity. Carmen McRae drew attention because of her soothing mellowness. Sarah Vaughan—one of the two female recording stars Dorothy liked best—was on her way to being acclaimed as a consummate jazz innovator. Dinah Washington— Dorothy's other female favorite—was known for her haunting sounds of resignation, which bore the marks of an emotionally well-traveled woman. Lena Horne was hailed primarily during these years as a great beauty who sang popular ballads rather than the blues or jazz. Horne had not yet assumed her place with the critics as a major stylist, but she was most appealing to White audiences.

Dorothy came to believe her primary hope of competing with such women and succeeding in the clubs was by emerging as an absolutely dazzling visual creation: totally magnetic, totally appealing, her beauty and sex appeal shrewdly showcased. Ironically, though, the emphasis placed on her appearance led even more to her feelings of inadequacy and insecurity about her vocal skills and her very worth as a performer.

When Dandridge opened at the Mocambo on May 7, 1951, celebrities flocked to see her. Talk continued within the entertainment colony about Dandridge as a dazzling new discovery.

Phil was by her side once again, and was thrilled by her success. His ego, however, remained bruised by all the attention continuing to be lavished on her.

Other people were being brought in to help manage her growing career. At one of Phil's earlier Sunday musicales at his apartment on Hilldale, a certain young man who would become a key figure in Dorothy's career, made her acquaintance. His name was Earl Mills. Raised in an orphanage in Chicago, Mills had studied at Northwestern. He became a musician with his own band, and later began managing performers. He had been an associate of Berle Adams, who later went to the Music Corporation of America (MCA). Mills was then on his own. He was currently managing some of Phil's affairs.

Mills asked who she was. Moore told him that she was one of the performers he coached, and also said, to the amusement of Mills, "She won't sing for just anybody." For months, Mills urged Phil to persuade her to sing for him. Finally, on another Sunday at his musicales, Phil said, "Well, Dorothy's agreed to sing something for you. So if you hang around after everybody's gone, we'll try to get her to do something." The song would be "A Woman's Prerogative."

After what he had seen and heard, Mills said he wanted to manage her. He and Phil worked out an arrangement whereby Mills assumed management of more of Dorothy's day-to-day activities—the interviews, the meetings, the auditions—as well as club bookings. Later publicist Orin Borsten was also hired to feed the press and the powerful columnists information on Dorothy's engagements and activities. But Moore still kept control of most matters pertaining to Dorothy.

During the early part of the summer, Phil, his hands forever in various pots, helped put together a half-hour musical program for local television in Los Angeles. Called "The Chicks and Fiddle," it was the "first all-Negro TV show on the west coast," according to *The California Eagle.* Featured were a quintet of Black women, headlined by the trumpet player Clora Bryant. She was a cousin of singer Joyce Bryant, another of Moore's clients.

Clora Bryant had known Moore since the late 1940s in San Francisco. As a member of an act called The Queens of Swing, she and others in her group had been asked by Moore to be a part of a quintet called The Sepia Tones that he was putting together solely for the television show. After she agreed, she learned one of the vocalists for "The Chicks and the Fiddle" would be Vivian Dandridge. The other would be Evelyn Royal, wife of musician Marshall Royal. Bryant never knew how Vivian came to be hired. "When we went to our first rehearsal for the show," Bryant said, "she was there."

Bryant already knew Vivian. She had seen her on the outskirts of

Los Angeles at various small clubs where patrons could legally gamble. Mostly, they gambled by playing cards. By now, Vivian's career seemed almost like a thing of the past. But she, for one, had not forsaken it. A gritty, fun-loving quality in Vivian made her plow ahead, taking her knocks and bruises as they came while trying to enjoy herself along the way.

Bryant remembered Vivian's stormy romance at the time with a piano player. "They fought like cats and dogs," said Bryant. "In fact, we were coming home one day from one of the [card] clubs, and she and I were sitting in the back seat of the car. My husband was driving. And her piano man friend was sitting up front. They got to fussing and arguing. And, man, she got mad. She had on high heels. And she cracked him in the back of his head with her shoe."

"Even when she was drinking and would get kind of raunchy with some people, Vivian was a very nice person," Bryant said. "We had fun together. We were very compatible."

Apparently, Dorothy had persuaded Moore to help Vivian. She didn't have to say much to convince Moore, though. He had always liked Vivian. "The Chicks and the Fiddle" ran for six weeks in Los Angeles. To boost the program's appeal and also to provide Dorothy with yet more exposure, Moore brought her in for an appearance.

At the rehearsal, Dorothy "came wearing these little short shorts," Bryant recalled. "I think she had been playing tennis. She had on these little jewel sandals. They had jewels around the sole. She had on what we call a tank top now, with the straps. A sweater was tied around her neck. She had her hair tied back with one of those little white tennis caps with the visor on it. Her skin was flawless. Kind of cream colored like a cup of coffee with about three things of cream in it. To me, that was her color. Olive with enough red to give it a glow. She was a yellow complexion. But it had enough red in it that it would take the sun and make a beautiful tan. She had a tan that day."

Bryant concluded, "I don't know how Dorothy came out looking like she did because she was like perfection. She personified class. She was a lovely lady. And kind of like a little kitten to me. She had a demure way of looking at you. That's why I say she was like a little kitten. A little kitten comes up to you and purrs. Dorothy would, you know, say 'Hi, Clora,' in a soft tone. You'd just be glad she was talking to you. With that persona of hers, you knew you had been graced with something wonderful. The perfect lady." Bryant added, "It seemed like she was vulnerable to the male species too."

During the rehearsal and telecast, Bryant watched Dandridge.

"She had these small expressive hands," Bryant said. "The way she moved her hands was like poetry in motion. For me, she was a role model. When I started doing an act later, I did try to emulate her."

It was evident to Bryant that Dorothy relied on Moore's advice. "When she'd look at Phil Moore," Bryant said, "you could see that there was adulation and admiration there."

But Bryant detected a strain in the relations between Dorothy and Vivian. "I never noticed a real closeness there. I really didn't. They were completely different people as far as I'm concerned," Bryant said. "Dorothy might be standing with Phil Moore. I don't remember Vivian going over there to see them. And Vivian never talked about Dorothy."

For Dorothy, it was an exhilarating, fast-moving period. But she was troubled by the predicament with Phil. She grew resentful of his control and came to loathe some of his playful, suggestive banter when she performed. Mainly, though, she wanted to be fully on her own, something she had been struggling for all these years, without someone else assuming the credit for her success. Or calling the shots. As far as she was concerned, she had created herself.

Yet, she still was in no position to walk away from him. For one thing, he had invested financially in her career. Moore still kept records of her debts to him for his professional work. She owed him money for the coaching sessions, the arrangements, the management, even her therapy.

Following the Mocambo engagement, the two were booked for another important club. During her run at the Gala, a British club impresario named Maurice Winnick, as mesmerized by Dorothy as everyone else, made an offer for her to perform at London's Café de Paris. Such a booking could be the launching of an international career. The Café de Paris was the exclusive, tony nightclub where such sophisticated stars as Noel Coward and later Marlene Dietrich played to the international crowd: the monied, the privileged, the titled.

Dorothy accepted the date and then was both excited and anxious. Plans were made. Rehearsals and changes in the act began. Elaborate new gowns were ordered. But during preparations, the problems with Phil escalated.

One morning, Bobby Short, then living in Los Angeles, received a phone call.

"Bobby, it's Phil Moore," the voice at the other end announced.

"Hi," Bobby said casually.

"I'll get right to the point," said Moore. "Do you want to go to

London to accompany Dorothy?"

"What?" Short asked, not quite believing his ears. "You want me to go to London with Dorothy to be her accompanist?"

Short was surprised. "We knew each other *en passant*. We were not close friends or close buddies," said Short. The two ran into one another at various times, always spoke, and always were respectful. "But never any more than that."

Short wondered, Why on earth would Phil Moore pass up an opportunity to appear with her at the Café de Paris after all the time he'd put in with Dorothy?

"The Café de Paris! It was a very important room. *Very, very grand*," said Short. "So for Dorothy to go over and do that, that was a great thing. And Phil wanted to pull out. And I'm sure, knowing Phil as I got to know him later, he probably said, 'Look, Dorothy, I'll find you a piano player. But I'm not going to go with you.' Which tells me that there could have been some problems of ego because she was suddenly getting more attention than she had ever gotten before in her life. And she was really on the crest. People fighting to get her to come to work. And she had yearned for this for so long. They'd obviously had a really important disagreement. It could have been about billing because when they went to Mocambo from Café Gala, it said, 'Dorothy Dandridge and Phil Moore.' It was a disagreement, one of their first, that came to a serious point."

People around the couple recognized that the problem appeared to be more than the matter of billing. "He was very, very controlling," recalled singer Joyce Bryant. "When he found people with talent, I guess he wanted to be in control of that and I think he wanted to be the one you gave the credit to. It's almost as if you didn't have the talent. But he did. He had a huge ego. So if you had a strong personality, you would clash."

East Coast designer Zelda Wynn, who designed clothes for Maria Cole, had first met Dorothy during a trip to Los Angeles at the time of the birth of Nat and Maria Cole's daughter Natalie in 1950. Once she began designing for Dorothy, the two established a good working relationship. "She had a gorgeous figure. She was a person you could fall in love with. Just a lovely person," said Wynn. "She was easygoing, sensitive, never difficult. She seemed to be a private woman. She and I got along so well together. I'd make suggestions for her gowns. She'd take the suggestions. She was good on fittings. She very seldom wanted me to change things." But Wynn realized that her designs had to please not only the client but the client's Svengali.

One afternoon, a nervous Dorothy took Wynn and the designer's sketches to Phil for his approval "I was over there all afternoon listening to music," said Wynn. "But he never wanted to agree on anything she suggested." Dorothy pleaded with him to reconsider some of his rejections. But once he'd made up his mind, that was that.

"Sometimes she would say to me, 'I wish he'd let me do so and so. I don't think he will though,'" said Wynn, who could see the effect Moore's control had on Dorothy. " She lacked confidence in herself. That was her only problem. That was because of Phil Moore. He just criticized her for everything she did."

Ultimately, Moore ended up going to London with Dorothy. They opened at the Café de Paris on July 9, 1951. With its red velvet trappings and gold-leaf rococo columns, the Café de Paris was an elegant setting, perfect for announcing Dandridge's arrival on the international scene. Wearing a glittering sequined gown that exposed her shoulders, she made her entrance at the top of the club's curved staircase. There she stood briefly with a spotlight on her. At first, patrons could only gasp, then they applauded as she was escorted by two bewigged attendants down the stairway to the floor. Phil was already at the piano, waiting to play one of his own compositions, "Blow Out the Candle." By the end of the evening, she had dazzled the aristocratic London crowd and the media. It was another triumphant engagement.

Despite the tensions before the trip, Phil and Dorothy spent most of their time in London together like reunited lovers. They somehow knew that the second time around probably wouldn't end any differently from the first time, but they wanted to give each other a second chance anyway. They strolled through Trafalger Square and posed for pictures. They dined and socialized in restaurants and at the homes of London's powerful, its socially prominent, its musicians, and its artists.

But soon Dorothy saw that nothing had really changed. She still resented some of Moore's behavior. "When we were on stage, Phil would be at the piano playing as I sang," Dorothy said. "He would talk sweet talk to me, and I'd give him a hard look that told him to cut it. It seemed to me that there were double entendres in the way he handled me. It dawned on me that he was conducting himself in a manner that said to the audience, 'This gal is mine.'"

Harold and Fayard, who were still working and living in Europe, attended one of the performances. Both were impressed. "She was *good*," said Harold. For Dorothy, the meeting with Harold was surprisingly subdued. She neither broke down in tears nor did she want to rush back into his arms. Her passion for him had died. She still felt a bond and a love, but she was no longer emotionally under Harold's grip. The two were friends, despite the fact that within a few months their divorce would become final.

Seeing Harold and Fayard turned out to be a welcome respite from Moore. Fayard could always make her laugh with his jokes and funny observations. He was aware that Dorothy and Moore were romantically involved and wondered how she endured Phil's domineering, arrogant manner. Moore obviously wanted Fayard and Harold to know that Dorothy was *his* now.

"He had some kind of an ego. He was always smoking a pipe," said Fayard. "A lot of guys who smoke pipes, that makes them feel important or something, doesn't it? Well, he had that *air* about him, flipping it and carrying on with that pipe. And I wished he would stop because I didn't like that smell. He would talk about Dottie and what he was doing for her and everything. And I'd say, 'Well, that's great. Great.' He was going to make her a big star."

Before the engagement ended, Dorothy and Phil had a terrible blowup at a London club. Startling the other patrons, Dorothy told him she could no longer endure his banter, his control, his ego. By the time the two returned to the States, they were barely speaking. Yet they tried putting their differences aside in order to keep the momentum of her career going.

Around this time, Moore and Earl Mills looked for an additional accompanist for Dorothy. Moore knew he would be working with her less in the future. He and Mills liked pianist Morty Jacobs. But they explained that he had to win Dorothy's approval. She herself was taking more control over her affairs. "Don't be concerned about meeting her. She's going to be a giant," the men told him. "So you go and prepare to enjoy her because this is a big talent."

Phil Moore also took Jacobs aside. He alerted him of Dorothy's insecurities and mentioned the puzzling change that had overcome her.

"Look something's happened to her," Moore said. "She used to have the greatest sound. She used to have a beautiful quality. She had a lovely timbre. But now she's kind of choking it off."

When Jacobs arrived at Dorothy's apartment on Hilldale for his first appointment with her, she greeted him at the door. "Come on in.

Make yourself at home," she told him. "Would you care to have something?"

She went through the social amenities and then got down to business. First she asked about his background. "She had heard that I had certain mentors in the world of jazz. So she asked me about them," he remembered.

Then, leafing through some sheet music, she told him, "Okay, I have some stuff here." Then she pointed to the piano. "I want you to fool around with this while I go into the kitchen." When she returned, she asked him to play. "Apparently, she thought I was rough," he recalled. She then told him, "I want you to play chords, sustain them and keep time without playing oom-pah, oom-pah." Then she sat at the piano and demonstrated the sound she wanted. Jacobs noted that she played piano very well. He also realized that she knew exactly what she needed. "She wanted a pianist who could be extremely impromptu, unrehearsed, if necessary, and that was where I came in because I had that facility." She did end up hiring Jacobs.

Working with her, Jacobs came to believe that "she developed some kind of obsession, which probably came from some pseudo-sophisticated, pseudo expert people who got it into her head about diction. She got nervous about her intonation." But "she was perfect diction-wise."

"She had a wonderful metrical sense," Jacobs said. "She had a very good, easy, concept of time and pulse, which is not something every singer in the world has. And she secretly wanted to scat sing." He added, "I prefer singers who have been curious enough and have enough love to want to be better, more creative, richer. More concept. More dimension. And there are not too many of those. Dorothy had it. She didn't know how to use it. But she had it." She also had the makings of a fine stylist. But Jacobs added, "For some reason she was being touted to being more of a visual performer." Jacobs saw that her own talents as a vocalist were becoming lost to her.

November 1951 was a special month for Dorothy as she garnered important national publicity. *Life* ran an article on her in its November 5th edition under the headline "Shy No More: Singing beauty sheds inhibitions and squirms her way to success." Its opening sentence called her the "most beautiful Negro singer to make her mark in nightclubs since Lena Horne" and pointed out that Dorothy's newfound success had come about "under the tutelage of the same man who coached Lena Horne [Phil Moore]."

As Dorothy became better known, the comparisons with Lena became more frequent—and in time a headache for Dorothy. The December issue of the national Black publication *Our World* ran a feature titled "Dorothy Dandridge Learns to Dance." "Everywhere Dorothy goes, the comparison with Lena Horne follows," the article read. "She has the voice, looks and sophistication to rival Lena's. And she has something La Horne lacks—pretty legs. What's more, they're dancer's legs that can high-step Dorothy into musical comedy."

The *Our World* article pointed out, "There's something else Dorothy and Lena have in common—musician Phil Moore. He groomed Lena into a polished performer. Now he's shaping Dorothy's career as her pianist and song arranger." *Our World* also commented on Moore's open fascination with Dandridge: "In London this summer, they teamed up to introduce his new ditty 'Blow Out the Candle.' Instead of following the advice of his song title, Moore is carrying the torch for his pretty singer."

Six months later, *Our World* ran another piece—a cover story—on Dorothy with a photo insert of Horne and a headline that read, "Can Dandridge Outshine Lena Horne."

This media-created rivalry between Horne and Dandridge was carried out for the next two years in publications as diverse as *Ebony, Life, Time, Jet,* and *Look.* It was not a new phenomenon. Black female stars of the past had been known for feuds. Josephine Baker drew the ire of Ethel Waters in the 1920s. Later Ethel Waters became angry with Lena Horne during the filming of *Cabin in the Sky.* The stories of Baker and Waters and of Waters and Horne, however, were not covered by the press and became known mainly in show business circles. But now, as never before in mainstream American popular culture, two glamorous and desirable Black goddesses were pitted against each other. The media coverage of the Dandridge/Horne rivalry suggested that only one African American goddess at a time could reign.

Their common connection to Phil Moore added fuel to the fire, suggesting a personal as well as a professional rivalry between the two beauties. In the popular imagination, they were two women fighting for the attentions of the same man. Moore may have secretly relished such a prospect.

"Word came from Lena's camp something like, 'She [Dandridge] ought to be doing something, *she's got my arranger!*'" recalled Phil

Moore. "And Dorothy D. was saying, 'I can't see how Lena would say that. *No one could ever take her place.*'"

Both women may well have been annoyed with the fact that one man, Phil Moore, was being credited with their success. For Lena Horne, the comparisons were often back-handed compliments, depicting her, at the age of thirty-four, as the older, now disposable star, who had to make way for this young beauty. To Horne's credit, she never allowed the silly hype to eat away at her confidence.

When interviewed by the Los Angeles *Daily News* in March, 1951, Dorothy had said, "Who can improve on Lena Horne?" Privately, though, Dandridge was flattered but uneasy with the comparisons. They merely added to her sense of self-doubt.

In November, Dorothy also had a chance for further national exposure when she was booked by agent Berle Adams of MCA to appear on television with the comedians Dean Martin and Jerry Lewis. They were among the rotating hosts of "The Colgate Comedy Hour." Having first been impressed with her performance at a club in Redondo Beach, Adams had been following Dorothy's career for the past year. "I was so taken by her beauty," he said. Aside from that, Adams felt she had the talent and presence to be a major sensation on the already crowded nightclub circuit. "When I saw her, I was ready to sign her."

He, too, was surprised by her insecurities. "I was so accustomed to talent with egos that needed restraint," Adams said. "But Dorothy needed an ego. She needed to be coddled. I wasn't used to that. I had a reputation of being a stickler. I didn't take any nonsense. She was difficult for me in that way. I had to always reassure her."

Excited about the prospect of being on the Martin and Lewis program, Dorothy immediately went to inform Phil. But Moore didn't share her excitement. She was not ready for national television, he insisted. He thought this could be a disaster in the making and that she should not do the program.

Just days before the Martin and Lewis show, Dorothy passed on Phil's sentiments to Adams and declined to be on the show. Adams was incensed.

"This guy," said Adams, "was determined that he be her Svengali. He wanted to have all this control over her. She was already insecure. He was just adding to that insecurity. And I wasn't going to have it. He was a pain in the neck. I felt he would just tear her down. She was so dependent on him that she wouldn't listen to anyone else. But I couldn't get angry with her for fear of destroying her. She was very delicate."

Convinced that the popular Martin and Lewis show, which aired opposite Ed Sullivan's "Toast of the Town" and featured the top names in entertainment, could be important to Dandridge's career, Adams was infuriated that Moore was holding her back. He paid a visit to his office. When Moore insisted that Dorothy still was unprepared for the booking, Adams hit the roof. He told Moore he was flat-out wrong. The two men got into an angry and loud shouting match. But Adams wouldn't back down. When he left Moore's office, an arrangement was worked out for Dorothy to appear on the show.

"I worked with her," said Adams. Despite her nerves, Dorothy kept herself focused. She had only one day of rehearsal at the television studio. Then on Sunday, November 4th, she appeared live on the program.

"She was the standout attraction! She was fabulous!" Adams recalled.

The next day, *The Hollywood Reporter* wrote, "It marks Miss Dandridge's first [national] TV appearance, but certainly not her last. She is her own sparkling answer to Lena Horne." *Variety* proclaimed that she "clicked handsomely."

She had reached a larger audience and proved to herself that she could function without Phil.

Before Earl Mills could begin to function as her manager, a formal agreement was worked out with Phil. It was a testament to what their personal relationship had become. Dated November 17, 1951, its text stated in precise terms what his fees were to be for his work past and future. But like it or not, it was also a sign that the Dandridge/Moore alliance was on its way to becoming all business, nothing more.

The agreement, written from Dorothy to Phil, opened, "This letter will confirm our prior oral understanding and will be evidence of our binding written agreement." It continued,

> You have heretofore coached, aided, and counseled me in the development of my professional career as a singer and public entertainer. You have prepared and composed musical compositions, arrangements and orchestrations and have developed for me a complete repertory which I have used in the past and which I contemplate using in the future. I acknowledge the extremely valuable services, aid, assistance and guidance which you have furnished to me in

the development of my career. As heretofore orally agreed between us you are entitled to compensation for the services, aid and assistance which you have heretofore rendered to me.

The agreement stated that Moore would be paid ten percent of Dorothy's weekly earnings "from any source whatever in excess of a base amount of $500.00 per week and continuing for a period of two (2) years commencing as of July 9, 1951."

Their agreement was to be in effect for two years, though Moore would dissolve it within less than a year, on March 7, 1952. By early 1952, he had also moved to New York. Among the stories that circulated as to why Moore made the move, foremost was that he was fleeing the situation with Dorothy.

Berle Adams also signed Dorothy to a contract with MCA, then one of Hollywood's most powerful agencies. At the huge compartmentalized MCA, agents in various departments were assigned to cover her nightclub bookings, television appearances, recording contracts, and possible movie appearances. "The Band and Act Department of MCA had a star on its hands," said Adams. "The Motion Picture Department of the agency also got very excited."

Dorothy's coordinating agent, in charge of handling her affairs with MCA's different departments, would be Harold Jovien. Unlike most Hollywood agents, Jovien had a relaxed, mild-mannered, charming style, although he was firm, protective, and unyielding in business matters. He had grown up in Chicago, had written for *Downbeat* and *Billboard* as well as African American newspapers around the country, and moved west to open *Billboard*'s Los Angeles office. Later he became an agent for the General Artists Corporation. Then Berle Adams brought him to MCA.

Both Jovien and his wife Mildred became personal friends of Dorothy's. Jovien was the agent she came to depend on for insuring that MCA not only follow through on incoming offers but also initiate others, especially those concerning movie projects. He was a troubleshooter, who learned to quickly assume control over any problem that might arise for her within the agency.

Manager Earl Mills complained that at first MCA didn't know how to book her. "They were putting her in clubs where rhythm and blues acts appeared." But important engagements followed as MCA rushed in to set up a tour: the Triton Hotel in Rochester, the Town Casino in Buffalo, and the Prince George Hotel in Toronto. Her pianist for these appearances was Ernie Freeman.

Amidst this great upward surge of her career came an engagement at a new club called Ciro's in Miami Beach. Dorothy was booked there, along with the entertainers Tony and Sally de Marco and comedian Larry Storch. She was set to open on Christmas Eve, 1951.

Miami was a segregated city with restaurants, hotels, department stores, whole sections of the city, all closed to African Americans. When Josephine Baker had played the Copa Club in Miami in January of the same year, she became the first entertainer to play to a non-segregated audience in the city. In her long contract negotiations, she had insisted that Black patrons be admitted to her performances and turned down the $10,000-a-week booking until management agreed. But other performers often found problems awaiting them. When Joyce Bryant appeared at the Algiers Hotel in Miami Beach, the Ku Klux Klan burned a cross on the lawn.

MCA's East Coast representative informed Dorothy that she could not stay in a Miami Beach hotel.

"Dorothy was furious. She wanted to cancel out," Earl Mills remembered. "She was fit to be tied."

But Mills and others prevailed upon her to honor her contract at the club. They reasoned that it might help break down racial barriers for other Black entertainers to follow. Mills recalled that the owner of Ciro's even offered Dandridge his home during the engagement. But she flatly turned it down. Since he was not married, she feared a stay at his home might be misinterpreted. Mills finally made reservations at a Black hotel for Dorothy, her pianist Ernie Freeman, and himself.

Resigning herself to make the best of the situation, Dandridge arrived in Miami, asserting herself in a new way. Having decided she wanted a different look, she had acquired a new wardrobe of more traditional evening wear with wide skirts and crinolines. Gone were those slinky gowns.

But rehearsals went badly. She found it difficult to get any sense of the acoustics and dynamics of the space she'd be performing in because construction was still underway. Workmen were still rushing to prepare the room for her. The problems beforehand impacted on her performance and her Christmas Eve opening was less than stellar. The room was all wrong. Her voice didn't carry. Phil Moore got word of it. "The reports from Florida were terrible," he recalled.

Dorothy couldn't help but think that Phil's presence might have made her feel less awkward. One thing could always be said in

Moore's defense: he understood her in some of the most important respects. He never would have let the construction workers distract her or the musicians give her any flack. He would have taken care of matters so that she could concentrate solely on her work.

Nick Kelly and Nat Harris, two important bookers, were sitting in the audience at Ciro's. They were associated with Monte Proser, who owned the New York nightclub La Vie En Rose. They saw her dismal performance, but they were aware of the construction problems at Ciro's. It did nothing to deter them from making Dorothy an offer to play La Vie En Rose but only at a nominal fee. The nightclub was in dire financial straits and actually close to folding up.

Dorothy accepted. She wanted this chance at playing New York. The Manhattan nightclubs were still considered the cream of the crop. They were the most important to the national press, and the sophisticated audiences there demanded the best. Exposure and success in New York could open the door to major club appearances throughout the country.

Swallowing her pride, Dorothy arrived in New York and immediately consulted Phil. He had already been contacted by Proser, who had questions about Dorothy. "The owner was really depending on my word that this girl was going to be terrific and was going to keep the joint in business," said Moore. The news of her failed performance made him nervous. But Moore assured Proser that Dorothy was a powerful talent coming into her own. He promised that the engagement would be a success.

Despite the changes in their personal relationship, Moore still loved her and believed in her talent. When he questioned Dorothy more about the Ciro booking, he "found out that some guys out there," said Moore, "had given her gowns with yards and yards of material. Party gowns like she was going to see royalty."

He then asked her, "Where are those old snaky things we used to have?"

"Oh, they're back in California," she told him. "I've retired that."

"Well, you better get those things out with the fringe. We got to sell everything you got to get in this joint," he told her. "And so we sent for the costumes," he said.

The rehearsals began again, like old times. The constant attention to every detail, every note, every inflection, every move of her hands or body. This time, neither had romantic illusions or fantasies. This was strictly business: the business of creating a major new presence in the most important of nightclub venues.

"All the songs had to be really right, top drawer for New York," said Moore.

Proser wanted an act that ran forty-five minutes. But in the end, the act would be only a little more than a half hour because that was the length of the material Moore felt would satisfy the tough New York critics. Moore informed the club's technical man that the last song would end after thirty-two minutes. Then the curtains were to be closed.

The night before the scheduled opening, Dorothy paid a visit to the club and gave an impromptu performance for the patrons. They cheered her. That should have relaxed Dorothy. But it didn't.

On January 21, 1952, Dandridge rushed around her dressing room at La Vie en Rose in a panic. This was her opening night. "That's when I first learned she had this terrible fear," said singer Joyce Bryant, who visited backstage before Dorothy went on. "I don't know how many people knew of her great fear. Maybe the people closest to her. And you know that this is very interesting because it wasn't as if we were tight friends or anything like that. We were acquaintances. Friendly ones. Just really nice. But I think that she wanted to know from me how I managed it."

Bryant remembered Dandridge asking her, "What do you do? How do you get up? How do you walk up on that stage and stay as calm as you are? It seems to be so easy for you."

Bryant recalled, "She was so fearful. She would just throw up. I could see and feel her fear. I just cannot begin to tell you how frightened she was. I didn't even think that she was going to go on. That's how scared she was."

But just as she was about to go on, Dorothy took deep breaths and narrowed her focus. Phil, at the piano, struck the chords. Then Dandridge, in a form-fitting gold lamé gown, "came wriggling out of the wings," so *Time* later wrote, "like a caterpillar on a hot rock." Her voice was strong and, of course, sexy as she sang "Love Isn't Born, It's Made." Again her training and basic instincts as a dancer enabled her to move about sensually and dramatically. Knowingly, she played with the song's suggestiveness. "Love isn't born on a beautiful April morn/Love isn't born, it's made/And that's why every window/Has a window shade." The house went crazy.

As other songs followed, including "Blow Out the Candle" (in which she purred "So there won't be any scandal") and "Talk Some Sweet Talk to Me," patrons sat spellbound by her hot/cool style, her intelligent and sophisticated interpretation of the lyrics. Throughout the performance, she was goddess-like but with a suggestion of fear.

She breezed through though—one number after another.   By the evening's end, the New York club scene had witnessed a dazzling new presence.   And Monte Proser had the hottest act in town. "They closed the curtain," said Moore, "and the people were screaming and hollering."   Dandridge herself felt she had hit her stride for the first time.

New York, the toughest of cities to crack, fell in love with Dorothy Dandridge. The day after the opening, *New York Post* columnist Earl Wilson called Dandridge "a singing sexation."   In its February 4th issue, *Time* ran an important piece on her. It opened on a familiar note: "Dorothy Dandridge is the most strikingly good looking Negro singer to come along since Lena Horne."   Yet it pointed out, "But 'everyone' told her she still had to prove she could be a success in New York. Last week singer Dandridge proved it emphatically. The management of Manhattan's La Vie en Rose could not supply tables enough for the customers who crowded in."

The following week, *Look* magazine ran a full cover photo of Audrey Hepburn with a small photo of Dandridge on the side. Inside she was featured, along with Lena Horne, Jimmy Durante, Sophie Tucker, Martin and Lewis, and Tony Martin, in an article on the big money-making stars of the current nightclub scene. *Cue* magazine carried a piece on her, too.

The two-week engagement at La Vie En Rose stretched into fourteen weeks with Dorothy, doing as many as three shows a night. She singlehandedly saved the club from financial ruin and accomplished one of her greatest nightclub triumphs.

But Joyce Bryant said, "I don't think that Dorothy believed it. She was so terribly insecure that I just don't think she believed that she was who she was. I heard it was the same thing night after night. She was just always frightened to death. I'm really serious when I tell you how tremendous her fear was and then to think that she lived all her life with that kind of fear or turmoil."

During the run at La Vie En Rose, Dorothy's work didn't end after a performance. "The thing I do to earn my living," she told the press, "consists of more than singing a song and parading around a stage. The interviews and the picture-taking and all the rest of the business of staying on top, of staying in the public eye, can become very tiring. Sometimes you just have to call a halt."

But there was no time for that. On February 19th, she joined the city's Mayor Vincent Impelliterri at City Hall for a special Brotherhood Week rally. She also did a round of interviews, luncheons, and receptions with disc jockeys, reporters, and columnists.

Theatre Arts ran a short article about her in its March issue. *Ebony* interviewed her for a feature that was to be run in its May issue. *Our World* reported on her for a cover story in its June issue. *Quick* also did a cover story on her in June. Other television appearances also followed: Ed Sullivan's "Toast of the Town," Jackie Gleason's "Cavalcade of Stars," and Steve Allen's "Songs for Sale."

Phil Moore made preparations for a major tour that MCA set up. He considered various pianists to accompany her and serve as a musical director, to rehearse and conduct the orchestra. Out of all the musicians he spoke to, Moore was most impressed with a dark-haired, handsome young man named Nick Perito.

Moore explained to Perito that he was grooming a young woman who needed special attention and the absolute perfect accompanist. Having already read Dorothy's La Vie en Rose reviews, Perito knew this was a golden opportunity. He deliberated over it, though. He was ambitiously working his way toward becoming a studio musician. He and his wife were comfortably based in New York. A tour would take him away from his family and also possible important career contacts. But he loved the idea of conducting an orchestra, and ultimately told Phil he would be happy to take the position. Before the deal was complete, Dorothy had to approve it. Moore knew she wouldn't do so unless she felt comfortable with the young man. So a meeting was set up.

By now, when it came to planning her performances, she was able to maneuver around her own doubts. She understood that she had to call the shots, direct herself, know when to listen and when to speak out. She had fought with Phil to get this freedom. She had no intention of giving it up.

"I met her in Phil's apartment one afternoon. And we ran down the music that we were going to be doing in her nightclub act," Perito recalled. "It was all very exciting. And, of course, she was lovely and very courteous. I was impressed with her. Naturally, she was a beautiful woman. And she had a lot of energy and a lot of vibrancy." He saw that she could be very strong-willed. "Never obnoxious. Never rude. But never shy or retiring about what she wanted. She knew exactly what she wanted to do and how she wanted to look. She could be quite firm." After the meeting, Perito was more confident than ever that he was making the right decision to do the tour with her.

Dorothy appeared to take to Perito immediately. He was just the type of assertive and gutsy young man she responded to. But Phil must have taken notice of the way Dorothy related to Nick, because he offered some words of advice to Perito. "Don't forget," he said. "She's my girl."

Dandridge and Perito soon made plans for the MCA tour. She would make her first stop May 2nd at the Chase Hotel in St. Louis. She would be the first African American performer to appear there. Next would be Cleveland, the city of her birth. She had not seen the place since Ruby and Ma-Ma took Vivian and her away as children.

Trouble began the minute Dandridge and Perito arrived at the Chase Hotel. Dorothy insisted that the Chase management afford her the same courtesy and professional dignity it would grant any White performer and asked Earl Mills to reserve a suite for her there. "They reluctantly allowed her to stay in the hotel, which I understand was also a first," Perito recalled. "They would have preferred that she stayed somewhere else. I don't know how that happened. But she did stay at a suite upstairs."

There were some unique and specific conditions for her staying there though. She was told she could use only the service elevator. Even after she was gowned and made up, she still was to use the service elevator to get downstairs to the club itself.

"I can understand that from the theatrical point of view," Perito said. "You don't want the audience to take a look at your star prior to her entrance on stage. But, after her performance, they insisted that she go back to her room via the service elevator as well. They wanted her to stay in her room for her meals and have room service. And she was not allowed, definitely not allowed, to come downstairs and eat in the restaurant or the coffee shop. She was supposed to be seen and heard, so to speak, on stage only."

Her opening night was nonetheless a hit. Early the next evening, before showtime at the hotel, she was a guest artist on CBS Radio's "Saturday at the Chase." But the irony of her success, however, wasn't lost on her. After having triumphed here at her first major New York nightclub appearance, after having been written about in *Life*, *Time*, *Cue*, and a slew of other publications, she was in a situation not much different from her engagement at Las Vegas's The Bingo club in 1949.

In this era marked by the rise of the civil rights movement and of the push for an open, fully integrated society, Dandridge understood the great emotional cost of leading the way for others. Jackie Robinson had paid a price on the baseball diamond. As White spectators taunted him with shouts of "nigger" and "jungle bunny," he had had to emotionally hold back, to always be on guard, to remain focused on the game. She, too—as she endured a multitude of indignities, great and small—had to learn to channel anger to improve her craft.

Before and following her performances, she usually preferred being alone, away from the crowds and stares. She had no desire to socialize with strangers. "Dorothy always made good use of her down time," said Nick Perito.

Still, to *want* to sit in her hotel room and read alone was one thing. But to *have* to sit in her hotel room and read alone was another. The situation grated on Dorothy, and her anger grew.

Perito was also angered by the treatment of the Chase Hotel. After the first night's performance, he decided to toss caution aside. "She was a big smash," he said. "All these Southern folk really applauded her and took to her in a great manner. So I insisted if they were able to applaud her on stage, they were certainly able to see her walk through the lobby and go right to the front elevator and go up to her suite. Well, this was unheard of prior to this time. And Dorothy was apprehensive."

After the second night's performance, Perito told her, "You will go through the main lobby with me."

Nervous and tense, she told him she didn't want a confrontation with management nor a scene in the lobby. She just wanted to be done with her work and head back to the seclusion of her suite.

"Bullshit," Perito told her.

"When it was time for her to go back to her room, much to the chagrin and anxiety of the management," Perito said, "I just walked her around the corner and down the main lobby and up to the main bank of elevators and calmly waited for the elevator to come down." They took the elevator and Perito escorted Dorothy to her suite.

"Well, the management took a dim view of this," Perito recalled. "It was an awkward moment for them. But I didn't make it appear awkward at all because it certainly wasn't. They didn't know how to quite tell me that this was inappropriate as far as they were concerned. And I was not giving them any indication that I would listen even if they intended to. So it was one of those stand-off-ish things. They were treating me kind of with kid gloves because here I was just killing them all with kindness, assuming nothing was wrong. And certainly, it wasn't wrong. But in their eyes, it was Mayday."

Despite the Chase's discriminatory polices, the hotel's manager appeared to have a crush on Dorothy. "He didn't know how to handle the whole thing," said Perito. "And there was nothing to handle because here was a gorgeous woman performing magnificently in their room and not allowed, by their previous standards, to walk through the lobby. Well, of course, we changed all that for two weeks."

For the rest of the two-week engagement at the Chase, Dandridge and Perito nightly walked through the lobby as he escorted her upstairs to her room on the guest elevator. He dropped her off at her suite and then went back downstairs. For Dorothy, it was partly a bold defiant adventure.

During the two-week engagement, she started to open up to Perito. She talked about Lynn and America's racial situation. In time, she confided her growing feelings about the irony of her career: as she integrated clubs and brought a new image of Black women onto the nightclub floor, she also found herself being cut off from the Black community. Often her audiences were almost exclusively White.

Perito grew to like her immensely, and on their last day at the Chase, he insisted that Dorothy break another taboo. He wanted her to join him for brunch in the hotel coffee shop before the two left for the airport. Dorothy was again hesitant. Nick told her again, "Bull shit. We're going to do that."

He entered the place and sat down. Afterwards Dorothy entered and joined him. "And we had brunch in the nice coffee shop," Nick said. "And the manager joined us. I think he joined us for fear that maybe some Southern cracker might come over and start to create a fuss. However, they didn't, of course, because they were delighted to have us in the room. And Dorothy had created quite a stir in the press. And the hotel received quite a bit of publicity. And we walked out, got in a cab, and went to the airport. And that was breaking the color barrier at the Chase Hotel in St. Louis. And I feel very proud to have been a part of that."

After St. Louis, Dorothy and Nick traveled to Cleveland for a two-week engagement at the Alhambra Tavern. Her return to her hometown was reported by the city's Black newspaper, *The Cleveland Call and Post*. Weeks before her arrival, items, articles, and photographs appeared in the paper. A local Black organization, the Women's Civic League, had contacted her with a request for Dandridge to participate with other performers in an evening of entertainment at Cleveland's 3,000-seat Music Hall. Proceeds would go to various charities. Despite her hectic schedule, Dorothy accepted the invitation.

No doubt the group had reached Dorothy through Ruby, who during these years away from Cleveland had remained in contact with several friends. Periodically, Ruby even returned to the city for visits. Dorothy Hughes McConnell, the daughter of Genevieve Hughes, who had babysat for Dorothy and Vivian as children, remembered occasions in later years "when Ruby sat in my mother's living room in Cleveland, talking about Cyril." Ruby, in turn, invited old friends like Genevieve Hughes to visit her in California.

"My mother and Ruby had a close relationship and Ruby would come back and forth to Cleveland. And my mother had been out there. She spent one entire winter at Ruby's home in California," recalled McConnell.

Dorothy thought her mother needed a vacation, so she invited Ruby to come east for the Cleveland engagement. Or so she said. The truth of the matter may have been that Ruby planned the visit herself. Ruby may have been fearful that Cyril Dandridge might try to reach Dorothy just as he had done when The Dandridge Sisters played the Cotton Club.

On Sunday, May 25th, Dorothy joined entertainers "Sugar Chile" Robinson, Russ Carlyle, and Tito Cavalaro for the All-Star-Revue at the Music Hall. Phil Moore flew in for the event. Ruby also attended. Afterwards, Dorothy posed for local photographers with her mother and also members of the Women's Civic League. A few days later, *The Cleveland Call and Post* announced her return with the headline: "Dorothy Dandridge Makes Hometown Hit."

One day at her hotel, Dorothy received a call from a woman who identified herself as Cyril Dandridge's second wife Thelma. Just as Ruby and Dorothy had anticipated, Cyril Dandridge read of his daughter's arrival in the city. Thelma Rudd Frazier Dandridge, whom he had married in 1946, told Dorothy that Cyril wanted to see her. Dorothy tensed up and wasn't sure what to say at first. But Ruby's presence set her at ease. She then agreed to meet her father. Cyril and Thelma came to her hotel. The meeting was awkward but relatively pleasant, thanks in part to Ruby, who appeared friendly with the two and was her usual talkative, outgoing self. One might have assumed Ruby had completely recovered from her unhappy marriage to Cyril, that all was now forgiven. But this adroit, jolly, social performance by Ruby simply masked her ongoing animosity toward Cyril. She really had neither forgotten nor forgiven him for anything.

Ruby may also have been angry about stories that made the

rounds in Black Cleveland: that Cyril had fathered a daughter by another woman, outside of marriage, before he wed Thelma. This meant there was a third Dandridge sister, which neither Vivian nor Dorothy knew anything about.

Dorothy, with Nick Perito as accompanist, opened at the Alhambra Tavern on May 27th to great notices. "Just about everything they've said about Dorothy Dandridge is true. This writer voices only one objection; they didn't say enough," declared *The Cleveland Call and Post*. "The girl has charm-plus, she sings and she 'sells' her songs and she is 'just about pretty enough.' Charm, voice and looks all wrapped up in one bundle, she represents the best bill of entertainment."

As Ruby left Cleveland to return to Los Angeles, she suggested that Dorothy contact family friend Genevieve Hughes. Hughes invited Dorothy to her home for lunch with family and friends. Dorothy received another invitation for the same day. This one from Cyril. Eager to see her again, he invited her to come to his church the next week. Dorothy agreed. But she backed out at the last minute and spent the day instead at the home of the Hughes family. Among those present was Genevieve's daughter Dorothy Hughes McConnell.

It was McConnell who, as a little girl, used to pick on Dorothy "because she was just so pretty."

The room turned silent as Dorothy entered. No one knew what to expect. "Everyone naturally was delighted to meet her because she was a star. But she was such a down-to-earth sweet girl," said Dorothy McConnell. Dorothy had asked McConnell's mother to fix "chitlins and corn bread and that type of thing. She loved soul food."

The day went well. But the mood changed when the subject of Lynn came up. "The one time she spoke about her in my presence, Dorothy cried," said McConnell. "She was talking about her little girl and her past marriage and how sorry she was that things hadn't worked out. And tears just welled up in her eyes."

Then the topic turned to Cyril, whom the Hughes family knew. "He was very proud when his daughters became famous and I'm sure very sorry about the past," said McConnell. "When Dorothy came to Cleveland, he wanted so much to be Daddy. But he hadn't been Daddy. He wasn't afforded that pleasure, I guess."

Dorothy explained that Cyril had asked her to come to his church. But she didn't want to go. "I don't know this man," she told McConnell. "I mean he wants to be my friend. But I don't even know him. But he's a nice little man."

In the end, she couldn't face her father. "So she sent him a telegram and told him she was sorry that she couldn't make it. And he had all these people waiting to meet his daughter," said McConnell.

McConnell and her husband Woodrow attended a performance at the club and visited Dorothy in her dressing room afterwards. Later Dorothy called McConnell about clothing stores in Cleveland. "I remember we went shopping one afternoon. And she was fitting jeans because she was going out on a boat ride that night. And so we were down on Euclid Avenue shopping," McConnell said. "She was just a regular wonderful gal."

Dorothy made a quick trip to New York after closing in Cleveland on June 8th. Afterwards she and Perito arrived in Pittsburgh, quickly rehearsed, and settled in at the Jackie Heller Club for a week's engagement that opened on June 23rd. But she seemed unusually nervous and tired. Then one night during her performance, she suddenly fainted on stage, Perito recalled. People rushed to help her, and she quickly recovered. Nick didn't think her collapse was serious. He simply thought that "she had been working hard and had been to New York to see Phil and came back and didn't have enough rest or something." The New York trip had taken a lot out of her.

Her relationship with Phil was still unresolved, at least from his point of view. *Jet* even reported rumors that he was so stuck on Dorothy, that he was stalking her around town. As much as she valued and trusted Moore, Dorothy felt she might have to completely sever their professional relationship. She may now have also wanted a formal break with him in order to free herself for any new relationship that might come.

In New York, Dorothy was also most likely presented with another dilemma. MGM was about to make a new Black-cast film, originally to be called *See How They Run* but later retitled *Bright Road*. *See How They Run* was a classroom drama based on a short story by Black writer Mary Elizabeth Vroman that was first published in *The Ladies Home Journal*, June 1951. It centered on a young schoolteacher's efforts to reach a wayward student. These were Negro characters in a Negro community with everyday interpersonal conflicts just as non-Blacks might experience. Dorothy was being considered for the role of a young teacher. It was another low-budget feature. But it gave her a chance at a dramatic lead.

Within the industry itself, there was a great deal of talk about her since the Mocambo and La Vie En Rose. At MGM, production chief Dore Schary and other executives had also noticed all the attention she had garnered in the national press. Many remembered her from *Meet the People* and *Jump for Joy*. Hollywood actually had watched her grow up.

MGM was the studio that had Lena Horne under contract. It was a long-known fact that Horne yearned for dramatic roles. But now as the studio prepared for its first Black-cast film in ten years and its first Black-cast dramatic movie since King Vidor's *Hallelujah* in 1929, Horne was out of the running. No doubt, the studio wanted a younger lead.

Dandridge's experience in *Tarzan's Peril* and *The Harlem Globetrotters* as well as her warmth and that unusual, inexplicable essence the industry always called "star quality" put her at the top of the list. So, MGM began discussions with MCA.

There was a problem at the studio, however. By now, America was in the grip of Senator Joseph McCarthy's witch hunts for communist infiltrators and influences in American government and society. Hollywood came under the eye of Congressional leaders' scrutiny during hearings initiated in 1947 to purge the entertainment industry of political subversives.

Tension and paranoia tainted the atmosphere in the movie capital. The studio heads like Jack Warner of Warner Brothers announced they would do all they could to insure that their products were free of communist influences. In 1950, under Ronald Reagan's tenure as president of the Screen Actors Guild, the organization's board drafted a loyalty oath, which would reinforce the studios' determination that employees were not political radicals but patriots. While the Guild professed to "fight against any secret blacklist," it stated that "if any actor. . . has so offended American public opinion that he has made himself unsalable at the box office, the Guild cannot and would not want to force any employer to hire him." In essence, the Screen Actors Guild condoned blacklisting.

The blacklist did not become effectively organized until after the 1951 House Un-American Activities Committee hearings on infiltration of communists in the motion picture industry. By 1952, the Committee constructed an alphabetical list of 324 people who had been named as Communists by cooperative witnesses. Other lists of artists suspected of being Communist or Communist sympathizers as well as organizations labeled "Communist fronts" were circulating, including those issued by private groups like *Red Channels* and *Counterattack*.

Now the studios paid careful attention to the backgrounds of all performers, writers, directors, producers. Numerous film artists found their careers jeopardized because of what many viewed as innocuous activities. They could have merely attended a rally. Or a party, as well as have been a member of a particular organization.

Lena Horne, Fredi Washington, and Hazel Scott were among the Black entertainers listed in *Red Channels*, primarily because of rallies they had attended or organizations which they joined. Because of the listing, Horne later said she was blacklisted from television appearances. Surprisingly, Paul Robeson—despite his political problems during these years—was not listed in *Red Channels*. But his career was destroyed as Communist accusations were hurled against him.

Among the organizations listed in *Red Channels* were the Actors Laboratory, the Actors Laboratory Theatre, and the Hollywood Democratic Committee, which, according to *Red Channels*, had changed its name to the Hollywood, Arts, Sciences, and Professions Council just as it faced exposure as a Communist front.

During this postwar era, just when African American actors and actresses believed the Hollywood system was finally about to open up and offer them more significant roles, many performers were pressured to denounce political groups, activities, or their peers if they hoped for any chance of work. An actor like James Edwards, who seemed en route to movieland stardom following his performance in *Home of the Brave* in 1949, publicly aired his feelings about the political pressures.

At a meeting of the Arts, Sciences, and Professions in Hollywood in 1950, Edwards told his audience that he had been visited by three FBI agents who "had come to convince him that it was his duty as a citizen and as an artist to appear before the House Un-American Activities Committee to denounce Paul Robeson. Edwards said he gave the agents a firm *no*." So reported *The Daily Worker*.

Other performers dealt with their problems in other ways. To get her name removed from the blacklist, Lena Horne was advised by an agent to speak to a representative from one of the theatrical unions and later to the powerful political columnist George Sokolsky. "Some people, of course, had to go before a Congressional Committee to clear themselves," said Horne, "but some could clear themselves through this more informal process." Horne assumed Sokolsky was able to speak to the right people in her behalf because shortly afterwards she was hired for television appearances.

At the same time, Sidney Poitier was asked to sign a loyalty oath just before he appeared in *Blackboard Jungle*. But through the intercession of director Richard Brooks, Poitier was able to do the film without the oath. He was asked later to repudiate Paul Robeson and African American actor Canada Lee. He refused to do so, but that was not known to the public until years later.

Though Dorothy wasn't listed in *Red Channels*, MGM had raised questions about some of her past political affiliations and social activities. The press had already made references to all of this as well as some of her comments. Paul Robeson had also been a guest at her home, a fact known to some in the industry. Moreover, her membership in the Hollywood Democratic Committee and its offshoot the Hollywood Arts, Sciences, and Professions Council; her appearance at certain rallies; her participation in a function of the National Negro Congress; and of course, her studies at the Actors Lab—these facts of her life were now considered suspect. Dorothy learned that MGM might withdraw her from consideration for *Bright Road* if she did not make some statement about her past activities.

Her engagement at Jackie Heller's club ended on June 28th. She had a week off to think about the *Bright Road* situation before she arrived with Perito in Lake Tahoe for a three-week engagement beginning on July 7th at the Sahatis Stateline Casino.

Upset and nervous, but also fired up during the Lake Tahoe rehearsal and the opening, Dandridge knew she had to face the situation head-on. With *Bright Road* scheduled to begin production in early August, little more than a month away, she had no time to agonize over what to do. Her manager Earl Mills stressed the urgency of the matter. So she agreed to answer any questions MGM might have about her activities. There was one thing, though, Dorothy refused to do: she would not sign a loyalty oath. "Pressure was put on her about that," said Geri Branton. "So Mr. Earl entered and denied everything and spoke on her behalf. But it was not her attitude because she wouldn't take any loyalty test. I know that. She would not do that."

During her engagement, she invited her MCA coordinating agent Harold Jovien and his wife Mildred to come to Lake Tahoe to see her act. It was not unusual for Jovien, who represented such other stars as Liberace and Gordon MacRae, to travel to see a performer at work. But Jovien knew something was amiss. At MCA, he had already caught wind of problems concerning *Bright Road*. From Lake Tahoe, Dorothy confided in Jovien and his wife during a telephone conversation. "She told us of being on a blacklist," he said. "She was very shaken by this."

"Please come up. I've got some questions I have to answer and I want your help with it," she said. "We'll be together for two or three days, however long it takes."

In Lake Tahoe, following Dorothy's first show at the casino that evening, Harold and Mildred Jovien went backstage. Once her dressing room was cleared of admirers, Dorothy sought Jovien's advice.

Dandridge was determined to survive this, and she respected the Joviens, whom she viewed as an intelligent couple attuned to both the subtleties and the ruthlessness of the industry. She had had long conversations with Mildred Jovien, who was an early fighter for the rights of women. Dorothy admired Mildred's political convictions. She sought the couple's help in writing a letter that clarified her position and spoke truthfully about her activities.

As the three sat down to work, Dorothy presented the Joviens with a list of precise accusations against her that had to be addressed. Among the questions about her past were her involvement with the Hollywood Arts, Sciences, and Professions Council. Questions also were asked about specific political gatherings she attended, but mainly, she was considered suspect because of her studies at the Actors Lab. Even now, questions were raised about Hedda Hopper's comments about the Lab.

Dorothy had to respond to Hopper's comments. Yet, she didn't want to appear to attack Hedda Hopper outright. Her syndicated column was still read by millions throughout the nation. Dandridge had to challenge and refute Hopper's comments as diplomatically as possible.

"We spent forty-eight hours with her, two days—working day and night—going over the questions." Jovien said. "At one time, we were up to about six in the morning. We would write. Then walk away from it. Then come back to it." They went over all the items in question, a number of which grew out of questions about comments published about Dorothy in *The Progressive Worker* (PW) and *The Daily Worker* (DW).

"All this wording had to be weighed over very carefully," said Jovien. "We wanted to get her off the blacklist without running away from the whole thing." Mainly, she wanted to stress that many activities and social gatherings in which she participated were done not with any intent to overthrow the government but rather to challenge

America's racial policies.

At the end of the second night, exhausted but exhilarated, the three completed the letter. It read:

July 11, 1952

Mr. Nicholas M. Schenck, President
Loew's, Inc.
1540 Broadway
New York, N.Y.

Dear Mr. Schenck:
Certain newspaper reports have been brought to my attention which I would like to comment on. 1. PW 3/14/47—One Dorothy Dandridge will appear at a party Saturday night, March 22nd at 2118 Hobart Street, Los Angeles, auspices National Negro Congress.

I appeared at this party believing that the National Negro Congress was associated with the National Association for the Advancement of Colored People (NAACP), a well recognized organization. I went with my husband, Harold Nicholas. I went for social reasons and because I was interested in the Negro community. I honestly can't remember who asked us to attend.

2. PW 6/30/47—Dorothy Dandridge among those who spoke at a series of rallies sponsored by the Progressive Citizens of America protesting the Taft-Hartley bill.

I did not speak, however, I might have been considered a member since I was requested to make a donation and I donated a small amount. I was asked to sing by a member of the program committee, whose name I can't remember. As an entertainer, I have been asked by hundreds of organizations during the past seven years to appear at benefits, the names of the individuals requesting my appearance have long since been forgotten with this event as well as numerous others such as the Catholic Youth Organization, B'nai B'rith Brotherhood Week, Red Cross, Cerebral Palsy, Heart Campaign, Pittsburgh Courier, women's clubs that I appeared for. I only remember this as one of over a hundred benefit appearances I have made and just another benefit. All five of these newspaper articles greatly magnify my appearance with these organizations and it is my feeling that they used my name for their own particular advantage and without any authorization.

3. PW 9/17/47—One Dorothy Dandridge, actress, on ballot for executive board of Hollywood Arts, Sciences, and Professions Council.

I was a member of the Hollywood Arts, Sciences and Professions Council. I voluntarily became a member when I read that several prominent personalities in show business were active, such as Al Jarvis and Norman Corwin. I believed it would further my career and that it would help members of my race. I never held nor sought an office with this organization nor was I an active member.

4. PW 9/10/48—One Dorothy Dandridge student of Actor's Lab.

Yes, I joined the Actor's Lab because this workshop was one of the few outlets available to a young actress of my race seeking actual workshop training. Attending the Lab was in direct relationship with my theatrical ambition.

5. DW 9/4/51—One Dorothy Dandridge, young Negro actress, student at the Lab has commented 'As an actress and student at the Lab, I am anxious to know whether Hedda Hopper considers the democratic policy of the Lab, wherein students are accepted on ability, a subversive policy. If she does she advocates a policy which is un-American and fans the flames of race hatred."

I noticed the date of this alleged quotation in 1951. First of all, I was not a student at the Lab at this time and to my knowledge the Lab was no longer in existence at this date. I recall one incident regarding Hedda Hopper while I was a student at the Lab. What Hedda Hopper said did affect me and I did express concern. However, the exact wording of this particular quotation is not the kind of language I use but I'm sure no one could object to my expressing concern.

I would like to close by saying that I am not now or ever have been a member of the Communist Party or Communist Party Political Association nor have I ever made any donations to these parties. Had I known that any of the above organizations would later be cited as Communistic and or subversive I would never have participated. I have at no time been active politically. My sole interests are towards having a successful career and aiding my people.

Sincerely,
/s/ dorothy dandridge
Dorothy Dandridge

P.S. I would be most agreeable to meet and discuss the above with anybody that you may designate.

What Dorothy did not appear aware of or perhaps chose not to address was that the comment attributed to her about Hedda Hopper in clause number five had actually been made by her in reference to Jim Henaghan of *The Hollywood Reporter* in her letter to *the California Eagle* on September 23, 1948. MGM did not appear aware of this fact either.

"MGM accepted the letter and after that no one bothered her on the matter," Jovien recalled. "The studios were always concerned but they eased up on her after that."

Jovien recalled, "No one at MCA knew about this letter. No one. I never reported back anything about this because frankly, they were more interested in their buyer than their client." Having paid attention to various comments casually dropped around the agency, Jovien understood that the agents "wouldn't really go out and fight for her. That's why she asked us do it. She trusted us implicitly."

Dorothy understood the symbiotic relationship of the agency and the studio. To MCA, she was expendable, just an up-and-coming actress who could be sacrificed in a minute. MCA would never jeopardize its position with a powerful studio to defend or even help her. That was the cold, hard truth.

EIGHT

THE SALOONS

*C*hanges were taking place at MGM, and Dorothy, like everyone else in Hollywood, was aware of them. Louis B. Mayer had brought in producer Dore Schary, a talented filmmaker who would help to usher in a new era in commercial films. But Mayer and Schary had clashed. Schary had talked Mayer into letting the studio produce the problem picture *Intruder in the Dust*. When Mayer saw the drama—portraying a strong-willed Black man brilliantly played by Juano Hernandez—it did not meet the mogul's favor. Mayer was incensed by what he saw as the "uppity" Black character. "He ought to take off his hat when he talks to a White man," Mayer told Schary. *Intruder in the Dust* was one of the reality-based type movies that Schary wanted to do at the studio. His ambitions along theses lines created a rift between the men, but eventually, Schary replaced Mayer as head of MGM.

Schary believed that unusual topics could be tackled in quickly made, low-budget films. These were the type of films that usually ended up on the lower half of a double bill, so if such movies failed, the studio was no worse off. If such movies succeeded, the studio was ahead of the game. With this in mind, Schary selected screenwriter Charles Schnee, who had recently won an Oscar for his script for *The Bad and the Beautiful*, to head a special unit that would make modestly budgeted films, using the talents of some of the younger writers, directors, and producers on the Metro lot. Budgeted at $490,000 and to be shot in seventeen days, *Bright Road* was among these films.

The story itself was unusual simply because it was not a drama about the "Negro Question" or "Problem." In this respect, *Bright Road* bore a resemblance to the film *The Harlem Globetrotters*. Exploring "everyday" aspects of African American life, it would be a "little" picture about seemingly "ordinary lives," portrayed with meaning and importance.

Charles Schnee gathered a mix of veterans and ambitious young people to make the film. Sol Baer Fielding was set to produce. Emmett Lavery, who had written the scripts for *Hitler's Children* and *The Magnificent Yankee*, wrote the screenplay. The director was a young man known to everyone at the studio, mainly because of lineage. He was Gerald Mayer, the nephew of MGM's recently deposed Louis B. Mayer.

Dorothy's costar would be a newcomer, New York folk singer Harry Belafonte. He would play the young elementary school principal in this, his film debut. Eleven-year-old Philip Hepburn, who had appeared on Broadway in *Finian's Rainbow*, *Peter Pan*, and *Green Pastures*, was signed to play the restless student C.T., whom the teacher must try to reach.

Gerald Mayer knew about Dorothy, but had not met her. By the time he came on the film, MGM had already signed her at a salary of $1,500 a week. "Dorothy was a wonderful actress," Mayer said. "but I had nothing to do with casting her or Belafonte."

Also cast was Barbara Ann Sanders, the ten-year-old daughter of actress Lillian Randolph, who became best known to television audiences for her performances as Birdie on *The Great Gildersleeve* and as Madame Queen on *Amos 'n' Andy*. Maidie Norman, Jeni Le Gon, and a veteran from *Belle of the Nineties* and other films of the 1930s and 1940s, Libby Taylor, also won roles. And in a brief sequence, thanks to Dorothy, Vivian Dandridge was hired to play a schoolteacher. Her son, billed as Michael Stead, was also set to appear as a grade-school student.

Before filming began, writer Mary Elizabeth Vroman arrived in Hollywood for a six-week visit to consult with the producers and screenwriter Emmett Lavary. Born in the British West Indies, Vroman's teaching experiences at a school in Montgomery, Alabama, had served as the basis of her drama. Despite the fact that she had never written a short story before, she wrote this 7,000-word story in twenty-four hours and later submitted the typed single-space copy, along with an earnest letter, to the *Ladies Home Journal*.

To her surprise, the magazine accepted the story, which was published in its June 1951 issue. "It was a story I had to write," she said. "I merely thought—if people could know these children as I do, they would be certain to love them all." She added, "Love solves more problems than anger. That's why this isn't an angry story." Later the story won the prestigious Christopher Award. In Hollywood, Vroman was the first Black woman to become a member of the Screen Actors Guild.

Director Mayer assembled his principal players during the pre-production period, rehearsing them at the studio or, in some cases, at his home. Dorothy was, of course, among them.

"I met with her a few times beforehand because obviously we had to have the same feeling about the part. The main thing I had to be sure of was that she had to play it with simplicity. That she would not get too deeply involved with a part that was meant to show that all people are alike. But I didn't have to tell her that because that's the kind of person she was in real life. She was as I knew her. She was simple, direct. We came to an understanding about the part very quickly."

From the beginning, Mayer was impressed. "She certainly was one of the most absolutely ladylike people I ever met," he said. "She never boasted about how good she was. She never complained. I think she was probably shy. But it didn't show up. If you would meet her, she was pleasant and personable with great charm. The shyness didn't show. But you know, she was an actress, too."

The Hollywood press took note of the film, then still called *See How They Run*, when it went into production in early August. "It's a current Hollywood maxim to take no chances," wrote Bob Thomas in Hollywood's *Citizen-News*. "There is one exception to this movement to satisfy the known public demands for orthodox film entertainment. Oddly enough, the picture is being made at MGM, home of glossy musicals and star-packed spectacles.

"The film is called 'See How They Run,' and it is the first non-musical made by a major studio with an all-Negro cast. Its producer, Sol Fielding, admits that the venture is a financial gamble."

"The Negro audience will just about pay for the cost of the picture," Fielding estimated. "If it has enough quality to attract a segment of the White audience, it will make a profit."

"Part of the attraction and why they were willing to take a risk," said Gerald Mayer, "was because of its very low budget. So much of it took place on one set, one scene. The classroom. The exterior of the school was existing on the lot. The kids cost nothing. They all were amateurs. Dorothy was not terribly expensive in those days. And Harry was almost unknown."

Everyone at MGM seemed aware of the picture. Dorothy's old friend Ava Gardner stopped by to wish her luck. Filming went smoothly for the most part. But the early dailies revealed that Dorothy had photographed too light. They decided to re-shoot her scenes, using different makeup. MGM's makeup supervisor William Tuttle devised a new pancake base to give her more color. Later *Ebony* wrote that this had been done so "she will be readily recognized by audiences as a Negro teacher." She looked darkened, not greatly so, but not quite as natural as she was to look in her later black-and-white films *The Decks Ran Red and Malaga*. Natural or not, the base heightened her pristine beauty.

With the help of maestro Sydney Guilaroff, she also created an appropriate hairstyle for the character. Her hair was parted in the middle and pulled back. That served only to make the face look all the more perfect. Watching *Bright Road*, audiences must have felt there was no schoolteacher anywhere in the world who looked as lushly beautiful as this one.

Excited about playing the role, Dorothy felt that little could dim her optimism now. Her training at the Lab showed. She proved herself a highly disciplined, hard worker, curious about everything that concerned her schoolteacher character Jane Richards: from the manner in which Jane spoke and walked to the way she dressed and wore her hair. As a true film actress, she understood that the dialogue was only a route to understanding the character. Film acting was not acting. Film acting was being. She knew she must push her own anxieties and self-doubts aside to create a wholly natural woman on screen.

Some days were troubling, though. The very subject matter of the film brought Lynn to her mind. She was now almost nine years old, just the age of the children cast in *Bright Road*. But her Lynn would never sit in a classroom, never be this vibrant, certainly never work with her mother in a movie. Arriving on the set some mornings, Dandridge felt much of the sorrow she had so successfully evaded with her hectic schedule for the past two years. Though no one on the set knew it, she sometimes fought back tears.

Other days brought other tensions. While Guilaroff had designed the style of Dorothy's hair, Vivian was hired to work as the on-set hairdresser. Little may Vivian have realized it but her new profession as a hairdresser—she had taken classes and even worked in a beauty salon—was the same as that of her paternal grandmother Florence Dandridge. But one morning as Vivian worked on her hair, Dorothy exploded, screaming that Vivian had done it all wrong, that her hair looked terrible and would have to be redone. What might have been a minor rift between any other two women escalated into a major one for the sisters.

During this time, the two sisters sometimes could forget the differences in their social positions. Both seemed aware that they had to get beyond the pressures and attitudes of show business in order to maintain their relationship. "There was a kind of armed truce between them," Nick Perito recalled. But "you could tell they loved each other."

But never before was the exact nature of their positions in Hollywood's hierarchy so obvious to Vivian. At best, she was recognized only as Dorothy's sister. At worst, for the major agents and talents that Dorothy now came in contact with, Vivian was nothing.

Dorothy always felt freer in expressing her emotions—and her anger—with Vivian than anyone else. The two argued in that fierce, open way that only family members do with one another. But Vivian was defenseless in fighting back on the set that day. She had to take what Dorothy dished out and do as she was told.

Vivian never forgot the argument about Dorothy's hair. For years afterwards, she mentioned it to her friends, as an example of Dorothy's growing arrogance. "Let's face it, she could be nasty," Vivian said, and many took Vivian at her word. What they did not always understand was that, despite any misunderstandings, despite tensions which would grow to a feverish pitch over the next two years, these women remained sisters with ties and binds too tight to ever be undone.

Vivian's feelings on *Bright Road* weren't helped by the arrival of Ruby on the set. To friends and acquaintances alike, to almost anyone who would listen, a bubbly Ruby praised and fawned over Dorothy, luxuriating in her success. Her youngest daughter was going to be the biggest Black star in Hollywood history.

Her daughter's success wasn't the only reason Ruby had to be in particularly high spirits at this time. She was appearing on the weekly television series *Beulah* and was a name in her own right. Someone new had also come into her life.

While content filming *Bright Road*, Dorothy also appeared happy to be back in Los Angeles. She had longed to be around familiar objects in familiar surroundings and near familiar faces. Geri had returned from Europe. And many nights, Dorothy drove to Geri's home for dinner. Geri's Aunt Sis and Uncle Gus, who lived with her, would join Dorothy at the dinner table.

"She'd drop by on her way to or from work. She was just very dependent on me and my family. She loved my sister and my aunt. She'd eat with us most of the time. Dinners, before she was going to a night club. Or if she was working on a picture, she'd stop by after work, tired and complaining."

They were touchstones, a sense of family and community for a young woman who, with the continual traveling, the constant necessity of always pleasing people and being "on," felt herself uprooted and cut off from things that were permanent and real. Even when working on a movie set and immersed in the fantasy world she luxuriated in, the dinners at Geri's grounded her in a reality she could cope with, could feel at ease with, could feel less isolated and alone with.

"I talked to Dottie every day and night," recalled Geri.

Dorothy and Harry Belafonte developed a friendship on the set that would take various twists and turns in the coming years. Belafonte would be her costar in her next two films. They were similar. Both were just beginning to make an impact in their chosen careers. Both were working in areas of show business previously denied African Americans. Both were ambitious. Both were beautiful in similar ways.

Tall, muscular, and in good shape, Belafonte's coloring was close to Dorothy's. With his dark eyes, his classically handsome face, and his perfect profile, Belafonte could have been her male counterpart. The temptation to see them as the ideal couple was irresistible. Like Dorothy, Belafonte had started making a name for himself singing in clubs, mastering folk ballads and spicy calypso tunes, performed in his inimitable husky, "honey-coated" style.

Dorothy had first met him in New York at La Vie En Rose. Nightly, he came to see her perform. "He stood against a wall and waited for me to go on," Dorothy said. "In the succeeding months, Harry and I saw each other regularly."

Now that they were working together, her romantic streak as strong as ever, Dandridge indulged in a flirtation with the singer. "Dorothy thought the world of Harry," said Vivian. Dorothy confided to Vivian her romantic fantasies about Belafonte. Wouldn't it be something if they married?

"Oh, Dottie!" Vivian would say, urging her to forget such far-flung notions. Vivian always thought the two had incompatible temperaments. Aware that Belafonte was already married to a striking young woman named Marguerite, Dorothy tried to keep her emotions in check. Yet Dorothy's manager Earl Mills said that an on-again, off-again romantic relationship between Dandridge and Belafonte—a relationship she took seriously for a time—went on for several years.

Otherwise, while filming *Bright Road*, Dandridge struck up a friendship with Gerald Mayer. She was amused and intrigued by Mayer's style. With his casual suits that he wore with shirts buttoned at the top without ties, Mayer looked like a polished Ivy Leaguer. He was different from most men in show business Clean-cut, smart, broad-shouldered, and handsome in a relaxed, unstudied way, he was easy-going, patient, often soft-spoken, and perceptive. But he also had a strong inner resolve that she found reassuring and attractive. Without a show of temperament or attitude, Mayer quietly did things his way.

Bright Road was an important crossroad in his career. It was an opportunity to prove himself. Born in 1919 in New Brunswick, Canada, he was brought to Los Angeles by his parents at the age of two. There his uncle Louis B. Mayer ran Hollywood's mightiest studio. Mayer's father took a job at MGM and eventually became the Studio Manager, which entailed handling all the business details of productions. After finishing Los Angeles High School, young Gerry Mayer graduated from Stanford with a major in journalism and with plans for a career in journalism. Then came the Second World War, when as a young recruit, he was stationed in the Pacific.

"When I came back from the war, my father was dying of cancer," Mayer said. "I had a job at a Chicago newspaper. But I had been gone long enough—for three years—and I thought I should be around for the last years of his life. So I went to work in the studio and became a test director at MGM. That was the first step of my career." *Bright Road* was the third film he directed at the studio.

By the time the picture was completed, the friendship of Dandridge and Mayer had turned into a romance. "The relationship between a director and actress frequently leads into affairs," Mayer said. "It just happens. But in our particular case, it was certainly a lot more than physical attraction. We really liked each other."

For Dorothy, having felt herself cocooned for so long, first within the marriage to Harold and then the relationship with Phil, now was a time to free herself and embark on a romance that while important, did not have to be an all-consuming involvement. The two were fairly open about their mutual attraction. Yet Dorothy, concerned about her privacy, managed in a gossip-mad community to keep their affair out of print. She especially didn't want to give Miss Hopper another opportunity to rail against interracial relationships. Mayer and Dandridge mostly spent quiet, romantic evenings together, sometimes at her apartment on Hilldale where he always felt at home. "She had wonderful taste," Mayer remembered. "She decorated it very nicely. It was impeccable. Not show businessy in any way. Because she was not what you would consider show businessy. She was not in on show business lingo."

"We would go to the movies, and then we would go out to dinner. Quiet dinners," Mayer said. In public, the two knew there might be disapproving stares. Other times they were surprised by reactions. "I took her to a restaurant called the Windsor. A really nice restaurant," Mayer recalled. "There was a table across from us with about six or eight people, and they were looking at our table and then there'd be some laughter and then there'd be some more looking and then they'd be talking."

The couple braced themselves when they saw a man get up from the table and walk a bit unsteadily across the room to their table. His face was red. "Oh, Christ, what's going to happen here," Mayer wondered. Was this a drunk who would try to insult them?

Dorothy sat with a fixed smile on her face. The man stopped at the table and looked directly at her and said, "Madam, I'd just like you to know you're one of the most beautiful women I've ever seen."

Then the man "turned around and went back to his table," recalled Mayer. "It's kind of a nice story. It's such a different story than what you might expect under those circumstances." Mayer and Dorothy managed to avoid trouble most of the time. "We went to places where that was not liable to happen," he said. "Whether we did it consciously or unconsciously, I can't tell you."

She trusted him and was therefore able to share some of her most private concerns. She even told him about the frustration she felt at not meeting professional Black men. "I never meet a Black attorney or a Black doctor," she said. "All I meet are people in show business. You can't put together a good marriage with people in show business." It was to be a constant lament in the years to come, and one that a later generation of Black women would share, in and out of show business.

"I always felt," said Mayer, "she would have been just as happy to marry an attorney and settle down somewhere and just raise children and lead a social and pleasant life. I never got the sense that she was driven by her career. It was survival and she had to do it. But if she was driven, it was hidden from me."

Mayer also believed that "a big problem for her was the relationship between Whites and herself. I think she had some unhappy experiences." She was conscious of now operating more and more in a White world, whether it be in the nightclubs or on a movie set or the social affairs to which she was invited. "She was a victim of the problem," he said.

As much as the two liked each other, they didn't discuss or consider marriage. "It was not a thing that seemed likely," said Mayer. "The race thing did not even enter into it because I was just starting my career. I was directing low budget films. I didn't know whether I had a career. I couldn't think ahead to marriage. And after the picture, she was traveling. She was gone much of the time."

But Mayer did take Dandridge home to meet his mother, who liked her. Dorothy, though, never introduced him to Ruby.

"I remember a party we gave at a house I shared up on King's Road in Hollywood," Mayer recalled. "Not very far from where Dorothy lived. And there was my mother. Billy Eckstine was there. June Eckstine was there. Harry was there. But neither Vivian nor Ruby were there, and I have no idea what the reason was." Mayer felt that Dorothy "was a little embarrassed about the characterizations Ruby Dandridge was forced to do. I don't know why I'm saying that. But something sticks in my mind."

Respectful of her privacy, he never pushed her to discuss Ruby or other aspects of her personal life. Like so many others who came to know her, he realized there were certain doors Dorothy was not ready to open. "She never talked to me about personal relationships. For instance I knew she worked with Phil Moore. But I didn't know she was intimate with him. You know that's all part of being ladylike. I mean, who talks about their affairs? She never did. I had no way of knowing who had been with her except her husband."

He sensed a private hurt, which didn't have to do so much with her past relationships as with some other matter that nagged at her and prevented her from fully enjoying life. "The only thing I always felt was locked inside was her daughter," Mayer recalled. "She didn't talk much about her. I knew she was in touch with the child. I knew she was taking care of the child," he said. "But it seemed obvious to me that she didn't want to talk about that. That was too painful."

Among those close enough to observe Dorothy's relationship with Mayer was her manager Earl Mills, who by now himself had joined the roster of men enamored with her. For years, he would have to stand by silently and watch the parade of admiring men pursue her. "He seemed a very uptight fellow," Mayer recalled. "He was so much in love with her that he resented every other man who might have been in her life."

Dorothy was aware of Mills's feelings, but she kept her relationship with him at a distinct professional distance. "She often complained about the way he fawned over her," Geri Branton recalled. "'Will you please tell Earl,' she'd say, 'to keep his hands above the covers when he *thinks* of me!'"

Once *Bright Road* was completed, Dorothy packed and was back on the road, but she and Mayer remained in touch and saw each other whenever she was in town. When she appeared at the posh Venetian Room at the elegant Fairmount Hotel in San Francisco in the fall of 1952, she invited Mayer up. It in fact turned out to be a telling experience for him.

While she played to a jammed house, complete with fans cheering and applauding, Mayer recalled, "It seemed to me that she was unduly concerned about how she was going over. In her own mind there was a decibel level of applause that was satisfactory and a decibel level that was not satisfactory. And I thought the audience was accepting her very well. But she thought it was not going well. And she was very tense about it." The Fairmont's president Benjamin Swig, however, was so bowled over that he took out a half-page ad in the October 15th edition of *Variety*, announcing that Dorothy had broken all records for attendance in the Venetian Room. According to some, she had also broken the hearts of the owner Swig *and* his young son.

More and more men were on the prowl, whether it be the club

owners and managers or the patrons or the city officials who met her at public functions in the cities where she appeared. Flowers were sent to her dressing rooms, along with cards, gifts, and invitations. The men crossed all age, class, and economic lines. Dandridge was flattered and amused by it all. But no one could have predicted, not even Dandridge who had been accustomed to the admiring eyes of males since she was a fifteen-year-old at the Cotton Club, that this kind of attention would only intensify.

The relationship with Gerald Mayer continued for about a year. "But she was gone much of the time and just eventually the nature of things led it to drift apart," Mayer said. "The total memory is of really a nice relationship. A warm relationship," he said. "In my life, she's one of the people I remember most with love. That was a very nice year of my life and, I hope, of her life."

When later released in April 1953, *Bright Road* won warm reviews. *Cue* called it "a tender and profoundly understanding story of and about children—one of the finest of its kind." *Saturday Review's* reviewer wrote that, "Negroes are all too often shown as stereotypes rather than as human beings. *Bright Road* is an attempt to head in another and, I think, better direction." The critics singled Dorothy out, including *Saturday Review's* reviewer, who wrote that she was "a beautiful young woman, known heretofore more for her night-club singing than for her acting, [who] does well as the teacher."

"The most touching and genuine reflections are in the scenes of dual conflict, wherein Dorothy Dandridge as the teacher tries to communicate with Philip Hepburn, as the boy," wrote Bosley Crowther in *The New York Times.* "Miss Dandridge is a trim, intense young lady who prettily and earnestly portrays the bewilderment and anxiety of a schoolmarm who wants to do a full, intelligent job. And Master Hepburn is a lad with an open and naturally guileless face, upon which the play of emotions and resentments flows readily. In the scenes between the two, some glints of tension and frustration most piercingly emerge."

But while most White mainstream critics viewed it as a "nice," "little" picture, *Ebony* saw *Bright Road* as a cause for celebration. The April 1953 issue ran Dandridge on the cover with a feature article on the film inside.

In some respects, *Bright Road*, like *The Harlem Globetrotters*, looked like a mainstream race movie. With only one White performer in the picture, Robert Horton as a doctor, its characters appeared removed from the tensions and conflicts brought on by the dominant White culture. The movie was really about a community holding itself together, dealing with its own problems on its own terms.

Throughout, director Mayer's infatuation with Dorothy, as well as that of so many on the MGM lot, is apparent. At the very opening of *Bright Road*, Dandridge walks into a classroom, closes the door, and is heard in voice-over saying, "I'm Dorothy Dandridge and I play the role of Jane Richards, a teacher." This simple, unprecedented introduction in a feature film was MGM's way of announcing the new star it had on its hands. From that moment on, audiences would find it impossible to take their eyes off her.

In cinema, beauties were not supposed to be troubled or isolated. Nor were they required to be particularly sensitive. Their drop-dead looks were usually symbols of their power and their destructiveness. But in *Bright Road*, she played against such traditional concepts of female beauty and delivered instead a performance of great subtlety.

Dandridge's character—a new teacher who finds herself alone among her colleagues in trying to understand a troubled student—was an oddly affecting portrait of a beauty-as-loner, the gorgeous female who is isolated from her community because of her sensitivity. While the character was not written with a set of complex drives and motivations, Dandridge managed to suggest a woman moving to her own beat.

The film's script says nothing about its heroine's life apart from her experiences with her students. The film never indicates where this woman lives or what occupies her thoughts and actions during her off-school hours.

There is one brief scene that suggests the personal lives of the teachers and adult emotion. Belafonte's principal, noting that Jane looks tired at the end of a long day at school, offers to take her out for a soda pop. Belafonte eyes Dandridge with a tender yearning, and she looks at him dreamily. They express here much that the script has ignored: namely, any notions of romance. On one level, the script doesn't want to call the audience's attention to African American romance and sexuality. But the two performers and their director Mayer allow the sparks to fly even if they aren't allowed to ignite on the screen. Surely, though, the film proved frustrating for Black audiences.   Why was it that these two spectacular-looking African American characters never fell in love and into each other's arms?

Bright Road proved that Dandridge, if given the opportunity, could become a unique screen presence.   Even before the film's release, MGM was so impressed that it offered her $3,000 for one week's work in another production.   In a musical sequence of the June Allyson/Van Johnson movie *Remains to Be Seen*, Dandridge, swathed in a tight, satiny dress with her hair shoulder-length, appeared in a nightclub setting where she sang "Taking A Chance On Love."   As she moved around the nightclub floor, the sequence captured on film possibly the closest approximation to Dandridge's actual electric nightclub appearances.   The *Los Angeles Daily News*'s critic Howard McClay wrote that "the vocal hit of this piece is lovely Dorothy Dandridge."

Dorothy began 1953 feeling exuberant.   Plans were now under-way for a new nightclub tour that would take her to Pittsburgh, New York, Philadelphia, Las Vegas, and St. Louis.   There were some return engagements at clubs where she had already performed.   All of them wanted her back.   There was also talk of engagements in South America and a return to the Mocambo.

The new tour had to outdo the previous one in every respect.   Her days were spent reviewing new arrangements and searching for new material.   Bobby Short recalled that she came to see him perform one evening at a club.   Because he was known as an entertainer who select-ed unusual material, Dorothy appeared eager to see what he was up to.   "Dorothy sat there openly with a pencil and paper and wrote down the song titles," he said.   "She's not the only one!   Performers always do things like that."

By this time, Dandridge also acquired a sumptuous collection of fifty-six gowns that were insured for some $250,000.   Included were glamorous, revealing dresses by top designers such as Hollywood's Don Loper.   Loper was then known for providing Loretta Young with the dresses she wore as she twirled through a doorway every week at the start of the episodes of her television series.

The voice sessions, the dance classes, and the aerobic exercises continued, too.   From January 29th to February 5th, she worked with Nick Perito on new material.   Every minute of her day was planned. What little free time she had, she spent shopping with Geri.   She also socialized with Maria and Nat 'King' Cole, and was friendly with women like June Eckstine and Mamie Robinson, the wife of boxer Sugar Ray Robinson.

〰

First stop for Dorothy and Nick Perito was Cleveland, where Dorothy again played the Towne Casino, opening on February 6th. She also avoided Cyril again. The Cleveland date closed on February 12th. A few days later Dandridge arrived with Perito in Pittsburgh for a new one-week engagement at Jackie Heller's club, The Carousel.

Then it was off to New York where Dorothy had a spectacular four-week return engagement at the club that had made her nationally famous, La Vie en Rose. This time around Phil was not at the keyboard. But he attended the opening-night performance, along with Eartha Kitt and Joe Louis. The next night, Harold and Fayard came to the club, accompanied by a petite young woman. Whatever emotional pangs she felt about seeing Phil or Harold didn't interfere with her performance. She was at her best.

The critics and the patrons still loved her. "She's achieved a more striking sense of the dramatic, her presentation is more knowing, and her couturiering is expert," wrote *Variety*'s reviewer. "She is excellent for sight and sound."

Great publicity followed. The pages of the March 23rd issue of *Life* carried a splashy photo layout of Dorothy, the most striking a photograph of her in a tight gown with hands reaching out as if she had been caught in the middle of a performance. The March 25th issue of *Variety* ran a full-page ad that mentioned her upcoming club dates, films, and a South American tour scheduled for June. Closing in New York on March 25th, Dorothy, with Perito, next appeared in Philadelphia at the Latin Casino from April 2nd to April 8th.

By then, she was exhausted. But from Philadelphia, it was on to Las Vegas for an important two-week booking, set to open on April 13th, at the Last Frontier Hotel. Now no longer the unknown girl playing The Bingo club and living in an out-of-the-way little hotel, she returned to Vegas as a golden goddess headliner on a bill with actor Eddie Bracken. By now, she traveled with a maid, who was assigned to tend to her gowns, ensure the hotel room was in order, arrange the flowers that were sent, answer the phone, and ward off all the eager men in pursuit. On some occasions, Mills showed up to make sure arrangements were in order, and as always Dandridge traveled with her own arranger and accompanist. In this case, it was again Nick Perito.

Upon her arrival in Vegas, there was much excitement. Millions of television viewers had seen her. Magazine readers had ogled over her photographs in *Life*, *Look*, and *Ebony*. Once settled in, Dandridge nonetheless found the city as rigidly segregated as before. As on so many other occasions, she realized, despite her extraordinary success, not much had changed in terms of race. Miami Beach. St. Louis. Las Vegas. They were all the same.

When Gerald Mayer sensed that she had experienced problems with Whites, surely it was the "wildly successful" club dates that were at the forefront of those experiences. They were the settings that still brought her front and center with bigotry and discrimination. No matter how high she climbed, no matter that she had already broken down racial barriers in previously segregated nightclubs and cities, no matter that White audiences saw her as an exception—unlike the "others"—in the world of African Americans, no matter that club owners and managers secretly, or sometimes openly, longed for a night with her or that society figures scrambled for an invitation to meet her, she was still a Colored girl in a White man's domain. The unrelenting racism of the nightclub circuit coupled with her growing distaste for the oversexed club atmosphere was driving her to hate them, to dread ever going anywhere near what she came to call "the saloons."

MCA took precautions, though, to insure her comfort in Vegas. They wanted her to perform at pitch level. The Last Frontier was a major hotel/casino on the Strip. As always, Mills, following Dorothy's instructions, insisted she be allowed to stay at the hotel itself. The hotel agreed. This was a rarity for Las Vegas. The Last Frontier no doubt assumed it was granting special privileges that she should feel grateful for. But Dorothy reasoned since she would be bringing in streams of patrons and cold hard cash for the hotel, she had the right to stay there and also to be treated with a modicum of dignity. "She was very adamant about things like that," said Mills.

MCA thought all arrangements were smoothly worked out for her and expected no hassles. But word leaked out from the club to MCA that while she was granted hotel privileges, Miss Dandridge was not to be seen anywhere near the hotel swimming pool. Knowing Dorothy and spotting trouble, Harold Jovien immediately went to Vegas. Having witnessed the changes that had come about in her within the past year, Jovien understood that he not only had to deal with the hotel management, but he also had to calm Dorothy down.

He spoke to the Last Frontier representatives and found himself appalled by their position. Hotel management declared that if she went anywhere near the pool, said Jovien, "they threatened to drain it."

Jovien discussed the situation with Dorothy, who did a slow burn. These were the rules she was being told to live by, if she wanted to work, and angrily, she accepted the conditions. It was said though, perhaps to rattle management, that she sometimes "indicated that she was going to take a swim," said Jovien. The hotel responded immediately, saying, "'The pool's under construction.' And they'd put a sign out. And *nobody* could swim."

Jovien tried reasoning with the hotel, but even he knew that that was a losing battle. "Nevada was one of the most ugly places," Jovien said. "I saw the terrible way the American Indians were treated in Las Vegas. As absolute scum. We're talking about the early 1950s when there could hardly be a worse place. Coming from Chicago and all the problems there, I saw that Chicago was heaven compared to the whole Nevada state. And the whole West there. Montana. Wyoming. And Nevada, which was more prominent because it was part of show business. It was ugly, ugly."

"They gave her quite a rough time," he said. "Always you had to be careful though because Dorothy, at this point, didn't take any crap. She reacted!" She would storm through her suite, lashing out her anger and her despair. Here she was in the land of the free and the home of the brave—and she couldn't use a swimming pool. "I would have to be around trying to psychologically keep her as cool and calm as possible," said Jovien, "for her own sake, her health, and for doing a nightly performance. When she drained herself with these terrible side things, then she wouldn't be able to continue doing her job."

"Hers was really a normal reaction of great resentment that she was being treated that way," said Jovien. "The most common, ordinary situation for anybody else. But she had to fight for a lot of little things."

Finally, just when it looked as if the situation might be resolved, Jovien was shocked to see that the hotel swimming pool was actually drained to prevent her from taking a swim.

Like most Black entertainers of the period, she remained frustrated but tried looking philosophically at the situation of racial discrimination that she faced. During the Eisenhower era, the appearances of such entertainers as Sammy Davis Jr., Pearl Bailey, Joyce Bryant, and Nat 'King' Cole at the big clubs and on national television programs like "Toast of the Town" or "The Perry Como Show" were considered a major breakthrough and a sign of progress in the fight for civil rights. But they were still relegated to the back of the bus: the back doors, the freight elevators, the out-of-the-way hotels.

It was difficult and unfair and the philosophical approach didn't work with all performers all of the time. Some artists in these supposed "high" places couldn't contain their anger at the racism. When Josephine Baker heard a man say, "I won't stay in the same room with niggers" at the Biltmore Hotel in Los Angeles, she called the police. Told they could not do anything because they had not heard the remark but that she could make a citizen's arrest, she did precisely that. She arrested the man. Later a municipal judge sentenced him to ten days in jail or a fine of $100 for disturbing the peace.

Even in the worst situations, Dorothy rarely engaged in direct confrontation. It didn't appear to be a part of her nature. She usually had the agency people or Mills fight the battles for her. She felt that that was what they were being paid for.

Dorothy opened on April 13th to raves. She made her entrance, again moving like a dancer. "She was sensational," remembered actor/comedian Eddie Bracken. "The applause was thunderous. People just went wild over her." Patrons clamored just to get a better look at her.

"There'll Be Some Changes Made," she sang, this opening number probably best expressing her feelings about Las Vegas. She followed with familiar songs in the Dandridge repertoire: "Taking A Chance on Love," "Talk Sweet Talk," "What Is This Thing Called Love," "It Was Just One of Those Things," and the Phil Moore song that always captivated audiences, "Blow Out the Candle."

"One of the top shows of all time for the Last Frontier," wrote *Variety*. "Since her quiet entry into Vegas nitery circles over two years ago, Miss Dandridge has skyrocketed into that strata of rare mesmerizers. She looks gorgeous, wears stunning gowns, has a bewitching sexiness."

In the *Las Vegas Review-Journal*, Alan Jarlson exclaimed:

> While events of atomic proportions—including the detonations themselves—have been rocking Las Vegas during the past two weeks, it isn't extraordinary (for this neck of the woods anyhow) that the night club firmament should feel the

quake of the bombastic personality of Dorothy Dandridge.
Since opening at the Last Frontier, Miss Dandridge has woven
a spell with her unique style of singing to such an extent that
with the final notes of her encore she is pelted with roars from
the audience of 'bravo! bravo!—more! more!' With her
signally outstanding local engagement, Dorothy has taken
another long step up the stairway to the stars.

Show after show was packed. As she had done at the Fairmont,
she broke all existing box-office records at the Last Frontier.

Her days were full. The Vegas press pursued her for interviews or
photo shoots. With Bracken, she performed for the troops stationed
at Desert Rock. Most poignantly, she helped publicize a special
all-star show for the benefit of the Variety School for Handicapped
Children. A photo in the *Las Vegas Review-Journal* touchingly
captured her with her arms wrapped around the one Black child in the
group. Her thoughts had to be on Lynn.

Nightly, she performed two shows. Afterwards, she sometimes
ate with Bracken and others from the club. The Joviens came up
from Los Angeles to see the show. So, too, did Geri and other
friends.

Before the engagement ended, she was in a romantic swoon over
a young man she had often seen in films but had never met. Having
come to Vegas for a little fun, actor Peter Lawford, like everyone else
in the city, had heard about her act and went to see her. With a
group of friends that included June Allyson and Van Johnson, he
showed up at the Last Frontier. On the spot, he wanted to meet her.
He wrangled an introduction. And sparks immediately flew between
the two.

Later that night, he invited her for a drive through Vegas. When
they passed a late-night restaurant, Lawford suggested they stop and
go in for a bite. Dorothy explained that Blacks were probably not
served there. Lawford couldn't believe it. His naive incredulity struck
a defiant note in Dandridge.

"Let's give it a try," she said.

The two went in. No one noticed them. They were served. But
she didn't want Lawford to dismiss her concerns about Vegas's racism.
She wanted him to understand what America's Jim Crow laws meant
to its Black citizens.

"I didn't want any question in Peter's thinking about how I regarded myself or who I was," she said. As a star in Vegas clubs, she was

as subject to and as affected by American racism as any other African American in the country.

That evening marked the beginning of their friendship and very soon their romance. "Out of the restaurant and back in the car," Dandridge said, "we motored through the night. We halted in a lover's lane. Peter put his arms around me and began kissing me in a delightful, gallant English style, if kisses can have nationality. I liked being with him."

In the Hollywood community of the 1950s and 1960s, Peter Lawford, by no means a major star, was a well-known and well-liked figure with vast social contacts and a set of credentials that impressed the film colony. He had been born in London in 1923. His father was a highly decorated British army officer Brigadier General Sir Sydney Lawford, who had graduated from Sandhurst and served in World War I as a brigade commander and later in India. His mother was a born snob and social gadfly, who made it known that she was to be referred to always as Lady Lawford.

Young Peter, an only child educated by private tutors, appeared on the British stage at age seven. A year later, he won a role in the British film *Poor Old Bill*. Once his father Sir Sydney retired from the army, the family globe-trotted, and Peter ended up in Los Angeles. For a spell, he worked as an usher in a movie theatre. Then he turned to acting. "My mother was very keen that I meet the right people," he once said, "and getting into the movies seemed a logical way."

With his dark wavy hair, his chiseled figures, his taut and lean physique, his impeccable manners, and, of course, his British accent, he looked as if he were born to be a movie star. In 1938, he appeared in *Lord Jeff*. A role in the 1942 Oscar-winning *Mrs. Miniver* brought him attention. Soon there came work in such popular films as *The White Cliffs of Dover*, *Good News*, and *Easter Parade*. Not one to take himself too seriously, he once made light of his career by saying, "I was a halfway decent looking English boy who looked nice in a drawing room standing by a piano."

A bachelor for a long time, always in demand at dinners and parties, Lawford became a member of the Hollywood elite. In time, he became a close buddy of Frank Sinatra, Sammy Davis Jr., and Dean Martin, who called themselves the Rat Pack as they hung out and fooled around at clubs in Los Angeles and Las Vegas.

Though he squired a lineup of beauties, including Elizabeth Taylor, Judy Garland, and Lana Turner, with whom he had a sizzling love affair, and later befriended Marilyn Monroe, rumors circulated for years that he was bisexual. This didn't stop women from adoring him. Perhaps it was because of his gallant manner or his good looks or his worldly sophistication. Maybe it was the English accent. Regardless, Lawford had his pick. And he chose Dorothy.

"Peter was very fond of Dottie," Geri said. "And at that time, she was a bigger star than he was. So that impressed him, too. Just the fact that he could be with her."

"He was very smitten with her, and she was very taken with him," said Lawford's friend Molly Dunne.

Just as Dorothy's homes were metaphors for her view of herself and her place in the world, the men in her life also became symbols of some of her personal dreams and ambitions. Her marriage to Harold revealed the romantic in her that believed everything should be sun-shine and harmony. But he represented an emotional challenge because she felt she could never reach him, nor make him love her. Phil Moore revealed her ambitiousness. He challenged her intellectu-ally and artistically, pushing her to extend herself professionally. Gerald Mayer, both firm and gentle, was an entirely different experi-ence. His upbringing contrasted so sharply with hers. His sensitivity, his willingness to give her some space and to listen to her even when she did not speak, was so different from what she had experienced with other men.

Lawford seemed to represent classic Hollywood glamour. With him, she could be playful, flirtatious, and romantic without fears of rejection or domination. She appeared attracted by his manners and fun-loving nature along with his intelligence and good looks. Lawford also seemed to represent adventure and freedom for Dorothy, who had worked so hard in the last few years but found herself restrained and inhibited by her own success and growing fame. Moreover, here was a courtly, suave "pretty White boy" who bought her flowers, told her clever jokes, showered her with attention and affection, and was just mad about her. Aside from all of this, she also knew she was playing with fire.

During this era, interracial relationships were still openly frowned on. Indeed, interracial marriages were still illegal in parts of the United States. In Alabama, an interracial union was a felony that was punishable by two to seven years in prison. In 1947, Lena Horne had married White arranger/composer Lennie Hayton, but Horne later admitted the pair was so concerned about public reactions to their union that they kept it a secret for three years. In 1952, Pearl Bailey made headlines when she married White drummer Louis Bellson. Some feared her career might suffer afterwards. America was not at ease with such unions.

If Dorothy was seen in public places with Gerald Mayer, it didn't matter as much. Few would have recognized him, and if they did, she could always give the impression that they were discussing a film project over a meal or a drink. Lawford, however, was famous, visible, and a commodity in the industry. The gossips would have a field day with them. Damage could be done to both their careers. For Dorothy, there was something delicious about this kind of danger; so forbidden that every moment they spent together was a risk. She enjoyed it, and in her quest to still discover herself, she seemed to grow defiant. Defiant but still on guard. Caution couldn't be completely tossed to the wind.

They spent many quiet, playful evenings at Dorothy's apartment on Hilldale. It was a sharing of enthusiasms and an exchange of cultures. On one occasion, Dorothy even fixed chitlins for Lawford. Sickened by the odor, he asked what on earth she was cooking. She laughed and told him that chitlins were the intestines of a pig. It sounded awful to Lawford, who wanted no part of them.

On another evening when Peter visited Hilldale, he brought Gary Cooper's sophisticated wife Rocky along. Dorothy told them that she was preparing a special delicacy. But she was careful not to say what it was. She served the *chitterlings*—sprinkled with paprika and other seasonings—in an elegant, long-stemmed crystal glass. She had already cooked them earlier. Lawford and Rocky Cooper couldn't get enough. What a wonderful dish! When Dorothy went back to the kitchen, Peter came traipsing in to find out what she was up to. He couldn't believe the superb hor d'oeuvres he had just devoured were that god-awful-smelling stuff he had had before. Dorothy just laughed.

Dandridge's friends liked Lawford, too. On occasion, Joel Fluellen cast the British actor a *very* admiring eye. Herb Jeffries found Lawford "a nice man, an elegant man" who "treated [Dorothy] with respect and decency." "He was good to her," said Geri. "As good as he could be. He didn't have anything. He had a title. His mother was some kind of phoney grande dame. His father was an English officer. That's all they had. But he treasured it."

When Dandridge and Lawford visited Rocky and Gary Cooper on a film location in an area known as "redneck territory," Rocky Cooper remembered "playing the beard" for the two, leading people to think Dorothy was her friend. "I had to sit in the front seat with Peter while he drove through town," she said, "and poor Dorothy had to crouch down in the backseat, out of sight."

On numerous occasions in Los Angeles, where no one cared about interracial relationships as long as they were carried out discreetly, Lawford invited Dorothy to Hollywood social affairs. But "Peter didn't have the courage to take Dorothy Dandridge to parties. He'd have me pick her up and I'd walk into the party with her. Then she'd hook up with Peter," said Lawford's friend Peter Sabiston.

One evening, Sabiston, at Lawford's request, escorted Dorothy to a huge gathering at the home of the Hollywood agent Charlie Feldman and his glamorous wife Jean Howard. At this star-packed event, Peter may have wished he had come through the door with her. "When we walked in," said Sabiston, "every man in the room started paying attention to her—Richard Burton, William Holden, David Niven, all of them. She was a gorgeous woman and a very nice person."

On May 19, 1953, Hedda Hopper's column in the *Los Angeles Times* reported: "The Villa Nova had an interesting trio the other night when Dorothy Dandridge entered with Peter Lawford on one arm and Keenan Wynn on the other." For the general public, the comment meant little. But for industry insiders, always eager to decode items in the columns and get at the revealing subtext, Hedda Hopper was sending the word out on either one of two secrets: that either Peter Lawford and Keenan Wynn were having an affair or that Dorothy and Lawford were lovers. Despite the rumors about Lawford's sexuality, industry readers knew that Hedda was announcing the Dandridge/Lawford relationship.

Dorothy may have wanted to marry him. "Peter Lawford was so beautiful and such a beautiful human being," said Vivian. "I can't speak for him but I know at one point she was in love with him. She had a respect for him which she didn't have for too many people." But, recalled Vivian, "There was no way Lady Lawford was going to let him marry Dottie. That wasn't going to happen."

For Dorothy, the affair was so romantic and exciting that she didn't want it to end. Yet she wondered, Hollywood being what it was, America being what it was, what would become of her and this dream prince. Lawford saw her anxieties and decided they had to face facts—and he had to level with Dorothy. Lawford sat down with her to talk about the realities of the society—Hollywood society, American society—in which they lived.

"Look, I love you," he said. "I would like to marry you. But let's face it. I've made it a long way on this phoney English title. But I wouldn't work another day if we married. And neither would you."

Geri remembered, "It was a rejection. She didn't like it. But I think the relationship was more important to him than to her." Lawford saw other women, including Judy Holliday. Yet he and Dandridge continued the affair almost up to the time that he married Patricia Kennedy, the sister of the then future President of the United States, John F. Kennedy.

Her accompanist Morty Jacobs believed the relationship troubled her more than she was always willing to admit. An angered Dorothy once told him, "I asked Peter if I could meet his mother. And he lied and he postponed. And I never met her. It was one of the biggest insults I've ever had in my life. He's afraid of his mother." Geri, however, said that Dottie did eventually meet Lady Lawford.

She returned to St. Louis for a three week date at the Chase Hotel on June 18, 1953. This time, she registered at the hotel without any incidents. No, this time around, problems came not from the White hotel management but from the Black community in St. Louis. Members of the city's branch of the NAACP announced that they would picket the hotel in protest because Blacks were not being permitted to enter the front door of the Chase Hotel nor be served in the hotel's restaurant. Dorothy immediately spoke to the hotel management, and the hotel met her demands that Black patrons would be seated during her performances and also be permitted to use the hotel's main entrance. Despite her success in confronting the hotel management, some local NAACP members protested anyway.

"She was very defiant," recalled Geri Branton. "Black people picketed her and that hurt her very much."

Shortly after Dorothy's opening, the NAACP's annual national conference was held in St. Louis at the Kiel Auditorium. Honored at the conference was the Los Angeles-based, African American architect Paul Williams, who was presented with the organization's prestigious Spingarn Medal. Following one of her performances at the Chase, the NAACP's Walter White and architect Williams came to Dorothy's dressing room to congratulate her. Not missing the irony that while she was being picketed, she was also being praised by the head of the NAACP, Dorothy spoke to White about the protests. "Well, what are you going to do about it?" she asked him. His reply surprised her. "Oh, just forget it," he said. Recalled Geri, "That's what Walter White told her. And that disillusioned her very much."

Following the Chase engagement came the South American tour. Dorothy would appear at the Copacabana in Rio de Janeiro, then in Sao Paulo at the Boite Lord Hotel. Because Nick Perito's schedule had become hectic and prevented him from travelling with her for all dates, her accompanist for South America and other West Coast dates would be Morty Jacobs.

Arriving in Rio, Dorothy was given a star's greeting. Representatives from the Copacabana came to meet her. Photographers snapped pictures and passersby were curious about this beautiful foreign woman, with a color so much like their own. Throughout much of her stay in Brazil, she was literally followed by throngs of people, openly fascinated by her.

After being formally welcomed to the city, she was rushed to the hotel. She had a lot on her mind, including Peter Lawford, but she had to attend to the myriad details of the engagement. Jacobs remembered the rehearsal with the orchestra "didn't go off [well] because I didn't communicate too well with them, although some of them spoke English. And the drummer was a nervous wreck."

Dorothy had to check the sound system and especially the lighting to ensure it expressively captured the mood of the songs and enabled the audience to see her from all angles. She also had to make sure the space gave her enough room to move and breath, and be seen by the patrons. Her clothes had to be unpacked. Her gowns had to be pressed, fluffed, hung. Her dressing area had to be set up with her makeup, all in place as she wanted.

"She was very particular," said Jacobs. "She was nice. But she was demanding. But ladylike, sweet, almost little girlish. She got what she wanted. She'd say, 'Well, that's not quite it.' 'I have a different idea.' 'Something in a blue or magenta or white.' She was fussy but she was not abnormal. Of course, she had to do this."

Rio turned out to see her. During the run, amid the swarm of people vying for Dorothy's attentions was an intense and striking-looking gentleman who invited Dorothy and Jacobs to his table. There he sat with several other people, some apparently family members or friends. Charmed and fascinated by Dorothy, he complimented her performance and asked her questions about herself.

Dorothy learned that this elegant, gaunt, rather pained-looking man was the scientist J. Robert Oppenheimer. The two talked and appeared to get along well.

"She thought he was a fascinating human being," said Jacobs. "He liked and admired her. I would say that he had a real, legitimate, non-sexual kind of love-appreciation for her." Observing Dorothy during this engagement and so many others, Jacobs recalled, "There were little things about her that were just darling. She was so beautiful, so vulnerable, and so politically curious and politically well informed."

But because of the conversation with Oppenheimer, "We came under FBI and State Department scrutiny and investigation," said Jacobs. Jacobs was approached by some men who identified themselves as representatives of the United States government. They questioned Jacobs about the gentleman Dorothy had been seen talking to the previous evening. J. Robert Oppenheimer was the nuclear physicist who helped in the development of atomic energy for the military but fell from grace and found himself considered a national security risk after opposing the development of the hydrogen bomb on technical and moral grounds in 1949.

"We're interested in anybody whom he knows or who seems to know him," Jacobs said he was told by one of the men, "because if we know anything about them, then it's important to the government."

Then the man posed a question that angered Jacobs. "He asked me if Dorothy Dandridge and I were lovers, and if we had separate rooms." Jacobs answered bluntly that they were not lovers and that they did have separate rooms.

Not long after her Rio opening, Dandridge was introduced to two other elegant men who had seen her perform. One was "the biggest automobile importer in Brazil," said Jacobs. The other was a suave and extremely wealthy banker. Muscular with "a good, strong black moustache, somewhere between forty and fifty with a healthy tan," he was not, said Jacobs, "a movie star type of guy but nice looking without being handsome or a pretty guy." He was also "very polite" and "immaculate," said Jacobs. "Dressed, I would say, in a most elegant Brazilian style, which is very hep."

The banker hotly pursued Dorothy. For her, he was like another prince. He filled her hotel room with flowers. Courtly and attentive, he had his chauffeur-driven limousine carry the two of them throughout the city to his luxurious home. Dorothy was dazzled. It was all so romantic—Rio's brilliant colors, its grand architecture, and its lush sensuality. It captivated her, but she was appalled by the poverty and despair she saw in the streets, which reminded her of parts of the South in the United States and was enough to bring her back to reality.

Within days, though, the fantasy returned and Dorothy was completely swept up in a new romance. One evening, she confessed her feelings to Morty Jacobs. "She thought she was in love with him. But had conflict about it. She was supposed to be in love with Peter Lawford," Jacobs said. But taking her mind off Lawford might have been what the whole thing was really about.

"She got secretive," said Jacobs. "There are ways to have your rendezvous and to have your dates and to have your assignations without anybody knowing. If you're smart, you're pretty shrewd."

Dorothy believed she might start a new life with the banker. She could leave her career behind. He seemed to be offering her the world.

He seemed almost too good to be true. And he was. Later she learned he was married, and the life he was offering her was that of his mistress. She couldn't believe what she was hearing. And she didn't want to believe that she had fallen so hard. She slipped into a depression. Still, the banker continued his courtship for the rest of her Rio stay and into her engagement at the Boite Lord Hotel in Sao Paulo.

The affair left her nerves frayed and her temper short. On the flight to Sao Paulo, Dorothy appeared nervous and agitated. "Two Brazilian men started talking with her. They were doing very well until all of a sudden she became very, very upset." Dorothy argued with the Brazilians. Then she told Jacobs, "You keep those men away from me."

In Sao Paulo, Dandridge's emotions reached a fever pitch. Unsure how to handle the situation, perhaps unsure how she really felt about the banker, and perhaps still distressed about her relationship with Lawford, she fell into a deep funk. On stage, she was fine, able to brilliantly sublimate her distress. But offstage she was distracted, nervous, panicky, and unable to sleep.

Frantic in the early hours of the morning, she placed a call to Jacobs in his room at the hotel. She needed to talk to someone. She told him she was sitting on the window ledge of her suite and was about to jump off. "I'm not afraid to die," she said. "but I feel terrible because I want to die."

Jacobs rushed to her suite where he tried calming her. She was exhausted and frightened. But she was too distraught to sleep, too restless to stop talking. She rambled on, yet made sense. There was logic—and pent-up frustration and pain—beneath the non-stop conversation. She talked about her Brazilian lover, but oddly enough, she talked about other matters just as much.

"What do you think about this race situation?" she asked Jacobs.

"I try not to think about it," he replied.

"I'm suffering every time I have anything to do with guys who are not Black," she said. Then she added, "I have trouble with Black guys who are *sweaters*." She used the term *sweaters* whenever she referred to someone who was not honest, who was attempting to put something over on her and lead her on, who were, to use the term favored by African Americans in the 1950s for such behavior, *just jive*.

"Morty, I tried to end this situation," she said. "I think I'm going crazy." When he attempted to offer some homespun advice, she told him bluntly, "Don't be a psychologist. Everybody is a seventy-five cents paperback psychologist."

She talked to Jacobs almost until dawn. Finally, after she appeared composed and also promised to get some sleep, Jacobs left the room.

When he saw her later in the day, Dorothy said not a word about the previous night. But she saw a Brazilian doctor, who prescribed medication for her.

Dorothy also called Earl Mills in Los Angeles and told him of her emotional state. The romance with the Brazilian, the fact that in her eyes it could not work out, triggered some deep emotional response in Dorothy that forecast many of the tensions and the ever-growing sense of futility that within the next few years would rise to the surface and send her spinning in a self-destructive whirlwind. For the time being though, Mills knew, as did Dorothy, that it was essential to get through the rest of the engagements in Sao Paulo—and then immediately after in San Diego—and return as soon as possible to Los Angeles for sessions with her therapist. Emotionally drained, she completed the South American tour and boarded a plane, anxious to get back home.

En route to California, however, another problem emerged.

"Let me tell it to you the way Dorothy told me," said Madeline Jacobs, Morty's wife. "They got off the plane from South America and they had a layover in Dallas and had to change planes. Back then, nothing was desegregated in the South. And they were exhausted and starved. And they started to go into the airport restaurant. And the hostess proceeded to tell Dorothy, 'You can't come in here.' It was a White restaurant.

"Dorothy looked at Morty with tears in her eyes and said, 'Morty, what are we going to do?' He said, 'We're going to eat.' He took her by the arm. He brushed passed the hostess and sat her down. And the manager came over. And Morty said, 'We are ready to eat and I want a waitress with menus.' There must have been something in the way he said it. They did it. They brought the menus."

Before returning to Los Angeles, Dorothy had to do the San Diego engagement. She didn't permit herself the luxury of relaxing, or—in essence—collapsing, until her final arrival back in Los Angeles.

There she stayed for a time at the home of her psychologist John Berman and his wife. Then she was back on the road.

Her nightclub engagements were booked solid now through the rest of the year. As emotionally upset as she was, she maintained her professional schedule, which satisfied her need to still be in control of herself. But she was afraid about her emotional well-being, and her success added to the tension. She seemed to question even more the meaning of her existence. The constant travel, the tight schedules, the new people, the incessant demands of her professional life, had continued to blot out her memories of Lynn, except perhaps as Phil Moore had told her "during those three-o-clock-in-the-mornings times" when she would feel so alone. She wasn't first and foremost in Dorothy's mind, but Lynn, said Geri Branton, was always somewhere in the back of it.

Her career gave her life its definition and structure. But as successful as she was, she still had not arrived at the professional plane where she wanted to be, or where artistically she knew she had to be. Her deepest goal remained to become a dramatic screen actress. The experience on *Bright Road* reaffirmed that and the fulfillment acting brought her. Acting enabled her also to escape and to extend her knowledge of herself.

Her professional dreams of becoming a full-fledged film actress, however, seemed to be growing slimmer. In November, she would turn thirty-one years old. That fact, said Geri, did not bother Dorothy. But she knew that being thirty meant she didn't have a great deal of time left to be cast as a leading lady. She felt that all she needed was the chance; that was all she was asking for, that somehow America, Hollywood, give her the opportunity to prove she could be a dramatic movie actress. Little did she know then that a film called *Carmen Jones* was already being talked about. It would soon change her life.

NINE

MAKING CARMEN

*W*ith the panache and vigor of a true showman, impresario Charlie Morrison launched a splashy publicity and promotion campaign for Dorothy's return to the Mocambo in the late summer/early fall of 1953. Dorothy's new star status prompted Morrison to roll out the red carpet for her with an avalanche of media hype that played on America's new open fascination with sex.

Morrison decided to use Indiana zoology professor Charles Alfred Kinsey's recently published *The Sexual Behavior of the Human Female* to promote the engagement. The book had shocked many Americans by its detailed documentation of the sexual attitudes, habits, customs, preferences, and rituals of the American female. Of course, for Morrison the Kinsey study served as an attention-getting device to promote a "sexy babe."

Morrison linked the book directly to Dorothy, saying in the advertising copy for the show that she was "a volume of sex with the living impact of the Kinsey report." But the hype didn't end there. On Dorothy's September 8th opening, Morrison had cigarette girls— young women who were fixtures in nightclubs of this era, selling cigarettes and matches from trays strapped in front of them—peddle copies of the Kinsey book at $15 apiece, right along with their packs of Camels and Lucky Strikes. It was a deliriously effective gimmick.

By the time, Dorothy appeared center stage, the Mocambo crowd was in a state of near frenzy, ready to openly cheer this new-style sex goddess of the Eisenhower Era. Now she represented a dawning day when the old attitudes and inhibitions on female sexuality were replaced by a new sexual candor.

Every night of her performance, the Mocambo filled with celebrities. Maureen O'Hara, Peggy Lee, Gordon MacRae, Joel Grey, and Ella Logan were among the first-night crowd. Black actor William Marshall, who would soon draw attention with his appearance in *Demetrius and the Gladiators*, came to the club to see her, as did Black comic Timmie Rogers. Dorothy's and Geri's old friend Slappy White was also in the audience. He was no longer Mr. Pearl Bailey, but a successful comedian on the Black club circuit.

The reviews were raves.

"That Dorothy Dandridge came through with colors flying," wrote *Variety*, "was plainly evident when her last encore brought a tumultuous ovation that must still be ringing in her ears."

"The songstress has picked up a lot of poise and assurance along the way, and with her nifty looks and sexy delivery she had this opening-night audience with her," wrote Nick Kahn in *The Hollywood Reporter*. He also noted, "there is the inevitable Lena Horne comparison, of course, with Miss Dandridge doing similar type numbers to point up the similarity, but the current Mo headliner has enough individuality to get by on her own."

The Mocambo marked her full ascension to the top rung of the nightclub/supper club circuit in America. Unlike the singers who just sang, Dandridge's club appearances now were startling dramatic performances. Dorothy used lighting, gowns, dramatic pauses, physical grace, and knowing reading of the lyrics to tell a tale of a woman in the throes of romance and passion. With her vitality and playfulness, she had created a brilliant club persona. Unfortunately, she never fully saw the value of it.

She was unsettled, too, by so much emphasis on sex. After her first Mocambo appearance, *Ebony* had covered the event with a headline that read, "Don't Be Afraid of Sex Appeal...Says Dorothy Dandridge." Much of the article concentrated on a discussion of her sexiness and her feelings about it. Now during this new appearance, *The Hollywood Reporter* wrote, "The Dandridge doll looked sexier than [stripper] Lili St. Cyr without her bathtub."

In past eras, Black women like Josephine Baker, Billie Holiday, Lena Horne, and even dancer/choreographer Katherine Dunham were seen as powerfully sexy and desirable women. Yet they were rarely openly acknowledged as such by the American press. Patrons didn't see them as female ideals or above-the-table goddesses, to be fawned over like Rita Hayworth, Hedy Lamarr, or Betty Grable. Rather, in the dominant cultural and market mainstream, the Negro goddess was only to be appreciated or desired on the sly. Dorothy Dandridge satisfied its taste for an exotic and covert sex symbol.

Things began to change in the fifties, though, as the Black women making an impact in show business found themselves openly saluted as sex goddesses. Following her appearance in Broadway's *New Faces of 1952*, Eartha Kitt became known as a sex kitten, who could purr, scratch, or snarl her way like mad through such provocative, sexy records as "C'est Si Bon" and "Santa Baby." Orson Welles called Kitt "the most exciting woman in the world" and also cast her as Helen of Troy in a theatrical production based on the Faust legend.

At the same time, Joyce Bryant used her eight-octave range and had national hits with her sexy Phil Moore-arranged recordings "Love for Sale" and "Drunk with Love." But it wasn't until the magnetic dark-skinned beauty came up with a gimmick that she made it in show business. One night in her dressing room, she painted her hair with silver radiator paint. She then walked on stage dressed in a skin-tight gown with a silver fox stole. It drove patrons mad. She became Black America's bronze blonde bombshell.

Most people chose to see it as a part of social progress—that Bryant, Kitt, and Dandridge were considered sex ideals and that the national press covered their appearances. But the constant emphasis on sex—in the media and in the way a male audience perceived female sexuality—was as disturbing and damaging to Bryant and Dandridge as it was to that other sex goddess of the era, Marilyn Monroe.

As far as the club owners and other men who controlled show business were concerned, Joyce Bryant said, "I was nothing...a pound of flesh. And I was a money-making something. Nothing. I knew that these people did not care about me." Bryant ended up fleeing from show business at the peak of her fame. "Because I was afraid for myself," she said. She went on to devote herself to a religious life. She entered Oakwood College in Alabama where, according to *Ebony*, "no one smokes, drinks or utters a profanity," where the "use of makeup, beyond powder is banned," and where, too, Joyce "is learning to serve God in the manner she feels is right."

Dorothy handled the sex symbol business better, aware of its importance in creating a viable nightclub image. Yet she was never wholly comfortable with it. "They keep saying I'm sexy, sexy, sexy," she told Geri Branton. "But I don't feel sexy. I just wish they'd stop."

She later complained to her publicist Orin Borsten, refusing to do the kind of cheesecake photo layouts that many other young women in show business used to climb the next rung on their way hopefully to stardom.

"I don't want to be sexy Dorothy Dandridge," she told Borsten. "Why are they saying this about me?"

Borsten told her, "It's a misinterpretation. They come and sit in the nightclub and they're drinking and there's smoke everywhere and dullsville and then the lights go up on the stage. And what they see is a sexy woman but a woman brimming with vitality. Now you summon up this vitality from the depths of your beauty."

Borsten remembered, "This was to pacify her, to calm her down. I know that she's sexy. That she exudes sex. But I had to calm her down so that she would not be confused about this sexy thing because she had a thing about this. She had a fixation about it."

"This is a thing a lot of people didn't understand," said Vivian Dandridge. "She really loved dignity and elegance. Almost to a fault. This is the thing that she abhorred about the nightclub scene. . . that she had to get up there and just be strictly a sex symbol. That's why she loved doing *Bright Road* because it got her away from all that."

"Ella Fitzgerald is one of the most talented people in the world," Dandridge told Geri. "And it embarrasses me that she cannot work the rooms that I work. The reason for it is so horrible. She's not sexy. The men in the audience don't want to take her home and go to bed. And yet she's up there singing her heart out for one-third of the money they're paying me. And I resent being in that category."

Branton recalled, "I liked Dottie for saying those things."

Yet in Nick Perito's mind, her club act represented "mature sex. Adult sex," he said. "Never vulgar. Never coarse. A *lady* who sang sexy songs." The groundwork that Phil Moore laid insured that the audience had to respect her.

During the Mocambo run, Peter Lawford showed up and posed with Dorothy for photographers. That night they looked into each other's eyes and didn't seem to care what the rest of the world thought. He was thrilled with her success. And she was still thrilled by his sophisticated romantic aura.

Within weeks after the Mocambo engagement, Dorothy left Los Angeles for a series of other engagements that began with an appearance in Las Vegas at El Rancho Vegas's Opera House. Harold and Fayard were playing on the Strip at the Sands on a bill that headlined Frank Sinatra. The brothers had returned to work in the States. But Black tap dancers, with their bright smiles and vigorous optimism, were going out of vogue as a new age sought more serious, edgier representations of African Americans in the movies. Of course, the Nicholas Brothers were always more than just tap dancers. Their highly imaginative, innovative, and brilliantly stylized performances were an art form. But a new generation did not realize that. It would be several decades before the Nicholas Brothers's extraordinary screen dances would be reassessed by the cultural historians, the dance critics, and yet another new generation.

Dorothy moved on from Vegas. She remained busy, and her club dates were booked into the next year. Exhilarated by the schedule and her success, she was also often tired and was sometimes lonely. When not on stage or in rehearsal or at an interview, she was plagued by memories of Brazil, the affair with Lawford, and then her mother Ruby's domestic situation.

By now, Ruby Dandridge had become quite successful. Somehow she still managed to maintain a career of playing maids when other actresses who had done so had fallen by the wayside. Careful with money, she and Neva had accumulated a solid nest-egg together. They moved out of the house on La Fortuna into a larger dwelling and then a still larger one. Aside from show business, the women had made shrewd, lucrative investments in California real estate. Ruby was living a comfortable life.

But not so comfortable that she —now in her fifties—was not willing to try something new. She became involved with a well-to-do White woman who was a real estate agent. Neva had also become friendly with her, but not like Ruby who began to see the woman frequently without Neva. The friendship between these two blossomed without Neva's awareness of what was happening. Ruby had made up her mind that her life with Neva was over.

Neva had visited her mother in Nashville, and her stay proved to be longer than she had anticipated. Indeed, it seems she stayed too long. By the time she returned to Los Angeles, the real estate agent had moved into the home of Ruby and Neva.

"Then they put Neva out," said Geri. "When she came back from Nashville, Mrs. Dandridge threw her out and kept her things. Just like that."

Not knowing where to turn, Neva tried to contact Dorothy for help. But Dorothy was traveling so much that it was impossible to reach her directly. It occurred to Neva that she might have to contact Dorothy through MCA, Earl Mills, or close friends. So she asked Geri Nicholas to intercede and persuade Dorothy to speak to Ruby on her behalf, or to persuade Dorothy to lend her money.

Aware of Neva's cruelty to Dorothy, Geri spoke to Dandridge nonetheless. But Dorothy was adamant and let Geri know that she didn't want to see Ma-Ma.

"Look, I've been in therapy all these years trying to work out my problems," Dorothy told Geri. "I do not want to be bothered with that woman. Keep her away from me."

Geri said, "I couldn't blame her."

Neva, however, kept up her pursuit of Dorothy. Ruby Jean, as Neva called her, had to be persuaded to return her items and investments. Otherwise, she would lose everything.

Ruby, that warm friendly woman known to millions of radio and television audiences of the sitcom *Beulah* as Beulah's endearing friend Oriole, remained detached. Just as she had once excised husband Cyril from her life, she now did the same to Neva. To those who knew her, Ruby appeared never to think twice about her decision.

Word spread through Black Hollywood of Ruby's new relationship. It must have seemed for both Dorothy and Vivian a shocking replay of their early troubled years. As it turned out, Ruby had selected a new partner who could be just as cold and forbidding to her family as Neva in the past. Ruby's new companion, didn't appear to care for either Dorothy or Vivian. Some years later when Vivian, with her friend Juliette Ball, tried to visit Ruby on Mother's Day, the woman stood at the door, blocking Vivian from entering. "What do you want?" She asked. When Vivian explained she had brought her mother flowers, "She still didn't want to let her in," recalled Ball. "But when she opened the door and saw me there with Viv, she let us in. We stayed briefly. Then Vivian came down to my house and Viv cried. My mother tried to soothe her," said Ball. "To think that her own mother could let this happen."

Each daughter still tried to maintain contact with Ruby, perhaps to prove themselves worthy of her love. Like the young girls they once were, the sisters knew that they were bonded as family and ultimately had only each other to depend on, even as Dorothy's rising fame appeared to be pulling them even further apart. Ruby was not completely detached from her daughters' lives. She tried to help Vivian through some difficult times and reportedly showed an interest in Vivian's son Michael. And she, of course, reveled in Dorothy's success. But otherwise, she led a separate life in an emotionally distant way. She indeed would never win any Mother-of-the-Year awards.

Her daughters, even now, couldn't turn away from her. Vivian eventually came to blows with Ruby, but Dorothy's love and devotion to her never wavered.

Dorothy remained in therapy with the psychologist John Berman. Without it, she might have been lost. She talked to Berman about her family, her romantic disaster in South America, her relationships with Lawford and, even at this late date, Harold. When on the road, she called the psychologist as she fought off her depression. He in turn would write to her.

Mainly, though, her work remained her best therapy. "I think Dorothy loved to perform," said Perito. "Her whole persona was just so dynamic. Dorothy moved with great ease. Like a cat. Smoothly. Never erotically. A total class act. When she walked out on that stage, she was a very beautiful classy woman."

Yet "she was uncomfortable and insecure about her performances," said Perito. "She lived in the shadow of Lena Horne. Lena was and is magnificent. And Dorothy had to fight this constant image of Lena, Lena, Lena. And that was a hell of a thing for her to overcome. I would say to her, 'You have another energy to give. You're another person up there on that stage. You give something that Lena doesn't give. Lena doesn't move like you do. She doesn't have the youth that you've got.' I constantly supported her. I just asked her to look out and see the audience reaction. She was doing something that was getting people to smile and applaud. I had to constantly deal with that as a source of inspiration."

All sorts of invitations arrived in her backstage dressing room. All types and ages of men still sought to meet her. It was enough to overwhelm Dorothy. She was constantly fending someone off, and it was beginning to tire her.

"This is where her behavior of being a recluse was really extreme," said Earl Mills, "because she wouldn't even sit and have dinner with a club owner because someone would think she might be having a romance with the club owner and that was how she got her job. She also was concerned about the myth a lot of people had about Black women and their sexual activities." But she had to be careful. Powerful men like the club owners and managers who might become angered and damage her professionally had to be dealt with diplomatically. Nothing, she learned, was more fragile than the male ego.

The saloons were still meant to be a means to an end for her. She had hoped by now, though, that they would open the door to films. The release of *Bright Road* garnered more attention for Dorothy than the movie itself. So the industry was aware of her as an actress. The question was: would American movies ever open up the way for a dramatic Black actress?

Otto Preminger thought so.

In December 1953, not long after Dorothy's engagement at the Mocambo had ended, Otto Preminger signed an agreement with Twentieth Century Fox chief Darryl F. Zanuck to produce and direct the film *Carmen Jones*. It was an unusual agreement in Hollywood history because it would be a studio-financed film produced and directed by an insider-turned-independent filmmaker. As such, *Carmen Jones* marked a long-held dream of Preminger.

He had been a part of the Hollywood system since the 1940s. Born in Vienna, Austria, in 1906, Otto Ludwig Preminger and his younger brother Ingo were the sons of Marc and Josefa Preminger. His father was a prominent lawyer who at one time was the Attorney General of the Austro-Hungarian Empire. The elder Preminger envisioned his sons would follow in his footsteps and become lawyers. But by the age of nine, Otto was stagestruck. Upon graduation from the gymnasium, Preminger won an apprenticeship at the legendary Max Reinhardt's Theater in der Josefstadt. At first Otto hoped to become an actor, but because his father wanted him to pursue a career in law, he also attended law school while working at the theater. At the age of twenty, this *wünderkind* had his law degree, but by that time, Preminger had lost interest in acting and decided to become a director instead. He also realized something else was happening at age twenty: he was losing his hair. Within a few years, his crown would be bare, and later in life, he would daily shave his head so that he was completely bald. It would emphasize the massive size of his head, which no doubt corresponded with the massive size of his ego and his larger-than-life tastes and attitudes.

By age twenty-three, he was made a producer-director by Max Reinhardt. Three years later, Preminger succeeded Reinhardt as manager of the theater. Not yet thirty, he was at the top of Vienna's theatre world. Brash, daring, and engaging, he directed a series of successful productions. Then in 1935, he met Hollywood's Joseph

Schenck, who was in Europe on a talent hunt. Schenck offered him a job in Hollywood at Twentieth Century Fox.

A few months later, Preminger sailed for the United States on the Normandie. Later he would bring his parents and brother Ingo to America, too. His first stop was New York where he directed the play *Libel!* Then he went to the West Coast where he directed the 1936 film *Under Your Spell* for Twentieth Century Fox.

At first, he was a favorite of studio head Darryl F. Zanuck, but later clashed with him and soon returned to New York to direct in theatre. His 1938 revival of *Outward Bound* with Laurette Taylor was a hit. In 1939, he directed Claire Booth Luce's wartime drama *Margin for Error*. During rehearsals when the German actor signed to play a Nazi consul left the production, Preminger, with a strong Germanic/Austrian accent, decided to cast himself in the part. It was a brilliant stroke. The play *and* he were a hit.

Hollywood called again. Only this time the offers were for acting roles. He accepted a part in *The Pied Piper*, and then was asked to repeat his stage role in *Margin for Error* for Twentieth Century Fox's movie version. Darryl F. Zanuck was away serving in the Army. So Preminger saw the offer as an opportunity to charge back onto the Fox lot as a director. He agreed to play the role if he could also direct the film. He was willing to direct for free. His offer was accepted.

Margin For Error, released in 1943, put him back in Hollywood's favor. The irony was that while the film helped make the proud Austrian Jew an internationally famous movie director, it also typecast him as a Nazi—in the imagination of people inside and outside the movie industry. He became known for his portrayals of menacing Nazi officers in such movies as: *The Pied Piper, Margin for Error, They Got Me Covered*, and later Billy Wilder's *Stalag 17*. His frequent brutal treatment of actors and his hot temper also helped earn him nicknames like the Prussian, Otto the Terrible, and Otto the Ogre.

He fared well at the studio, at least until Zanuck returned to Twentieth Century Fox. Then Preminger sought to produce an unusual romantic murder mystery at Fox. "I took one story nobody else wanted called *Laura*," he said, "and got Zanuck to let me produce." Zanuck, however, would not let Preminger direct. Instead he hired director Rouben Mamoulian. But when Mamoulian's direction proved disappointing, he was fired, and Preminger was assigned to direct the film after all. His smooth, cool direction of *Laura* in 1944 turned it into a classic, one of Hollywood's enduring romantic mysteries and considered by many his best film. His relations with

Zanuck improved, and there followed such films as *A Royal Scandal* with Tallulah Bankhead, *Centennial Summer*, the highly publicized *Forever Amber* with Linda Darnell, *Whirlpool*, and *Where the Sidewalk Ends*.

Restless during the postwar years and fed up with a suffocating studio system, Preminger yearned to break away. Determined to dramatize unusual and adult themes, he did not want some studio head or Wall Street executive having control, telling him how to direct. So determined was Preminger to do his films his own way that he did not even want a producer hovering over his shoulder.

Otto had decided he would answer only to Otto. He would produce as well as direct his films. Though Otto Preminger was to be disparaged by the critics in his later years, his career marked a major shift in the way movies were made in Hollywood. He became one of the first of the powerful independent directors/producers. Along with Alfred Hitchcock, he was also one of Hollywood's most famous directors in the 1950s and 1960s.

His first step toward breaking away from the Hollywood system was a return to New York where in 1951 he directed the highly successful stage comedy *The Moon Is Blue*. Afterwards, *The Moon Is Blue* became Preminger's first independent film production in 1953. Having secured financing from Arthur Krim and Robert Benjamin at United Artists, he shot the movie version on a budget of $240,000.

A mild little sex comedy, the film version of *The Moon Is Blue* became controversial in the Eisenhower Fifties, mainly because of its use of such then shocking words as "seduce," "virgin," and "pregnant." The movie industry's Production Code Administration refused to grant the picture a seal of approval. It was condemned by the Roman Catholic Legion of Decency. Preminger sued local censorship boards and took his case to the United States Supreme Court which ruled that the boards could not prevent showings of *The Moon Is Blue*. Preminger became known as a provocative filmmaker and afterwards tackled such taboo subjects as drug addiction in *The Man With The Golden Arm*, rape and sexual candor in *Anatomy of a Murder*, and insider Washington politics and scandal in *Advise and Consent*.

Preminger's reputation as a ruthless tyrant with actors swelled to legendary proportions, and in time, he was more famous for his outbursts than his films themselves. While on location in Israel for the film *Exodus*, he lived up to his reputation while directing a group of Israeli children, who were to cry in terror during a key scene. Unable to get them to perform as he wanted, Preminger was heard repeatedly and angrily shouting, "Cry, you little monsters! Cry, you little monsters!" When that command failed to elicit tears, he instructed his assistants to have the mothers of the children, who stood nearby during shooting, immediately moved out of sight. Then he threatened the youngsters. "You see, your mothers have been taken away," he screamed in his loud guttural voice with his thick, menacing accent. "You are never going to see them again. Never!" He got the effects he wanted. The children burst into tears.

Following the film *The Moon Is Blue*, Preminger returned to the studio system. Still under contract to Twentieth Century Fox, he filmed *The River of No Return* with Marilyn Monroe and Robert Mitchum. Upon its completion, however, he resumed his independent position and became even more determined to keep it that way.

"I decided not to work ever again as a studio employee," he said. "I sold my house in Bel Air and settled in a New York apartment. I returned to California, where I kept an office, only occasionally on business and to see my parents and my brother." He also paid Twentieth Century Fox $150,000 to get out of his contract.

Now with plans for *Carmen Jones*, Preminger was intent to work the rest of his life as an independent but with backing from the major Hollywood studios. The fact that his new independent venture would be a Black-cast production made his career move seem all the more risky. Preminger, however, believed there was power and vitality in *Carmen Jones*, which had been a Broadway musical during the war years.

The story of Carmen had originated in the 1845 novel of that name by French writer Prosper Merimée. Later this tale of lust, love, betrayal, and murder served as the basis of Georges Bizet's opera *Carmen* in 1875. Bizet's Carmen was a sexy worker in a cigarette factory. First she lured a young soldier named Don Jose into her web of passion. Then she dumped him. When Don Jose discovered that she had taken up with a toreador named Escamillo, he murdered the woman he had loved so passionately.

At first, the French critics hated Bizet's opera because of its violence and its low rather than high-born noble characters. Critics aside, *Carmen* won a whole new following when it toured the French provinces. A people's drama with soaring, memorable arias, and gritty, realistic, sexy characters, it became one of Europe's and later one of America's most popular operas.

A new version of the Carmen tale came from lyricist/librettist Oscar Hammerstein II in the early 1940s. When he came upon the idea of modernizing the opera *Carmen*, using Bizet's music but with new lyrics and Black characters, no one believed Broadway audiences would shell out money for such a Black show. Finally, producer Billy Rose liked the concept and backed the show, which opened on Broadway on December 2, 1943.

Now *Carmen* as *Carmen Jones* was set in Jacksonville, Florida, during the years of World War II. There the sexy parachute worker Carmen Jones seduces a young soldier named Joe. Once Joe has left his true love, the good girl Cindy Lou, Carmen abandons him to take up with a prize-fighter called Husky Miller. The musical ended with Joe strangling Carmen Jones, the ultimate seductress/betrayer. Hammerstein's *Carmen Jones*—-in which Bizet's "Habanera" became "Dat's Love," the "Seguidilla" became "Dere's a Cafe on De Corner," and "The Toreador Song" became "Stand Up and Fight"—was an instant hit with audiences of the war years.

Preminger believed now was the time for a new *Carmen Jones*. Shrewd and attuned to the changing tastes of the public, he noted the various shifts in attitudes about African Americans since the war. He had seen the huge crowds that went to the major clubs to see the new Black performers and felt that audiences were also ready for new-style Black film stars. Having observed the reactions to the "problem pictures," he believed that movie audiences would accept African Americans in more adult roles and more mature settings. Though *Carmen Jones* might strike later generations as having enjoyably dated African American characterizations, it represented a major step forward during the Eisenhower era. Preminger also believed *Carmen Jones* had a powerful role for a Black actress, perhaps the most daring thus far in Hollywood's history.

Preminger observed too that television—that tiny tube now popping up in homes throughout America—was eating away at the motion picture audience and would continue to do so unless movies began to offer viewers something they couldn't get from the box in their living rooms. Movies could compete by dramatizing themes people could not see in their homes. Television was for the family. Movies, as he planned to direct them, were for grown-ups. Preminger also was fascinated by the technical changes coming about in film, mainly the use of the wide screen, and saw them as a way of providing the audience with a visual experience it could not get in front of the TV set. He also planned to film his movie in the new wide screen process called CinemaScope, which Twentieth Century Fox had already used to splendid effect in the Biblical spectacle *The Robe*.

His *Carmen Jones* would tap all these changes. His film would present Black characters simply as human figures with tragic dimensions. The film would also—through the choice of the right actors—spotlight African American energy, sounds, movements, and of course, crucial to understanding the heroine of *Carmen Jones*, African American *attitude*. The performers and certain changes in dialogue would give, so he believed, a traditionally non-racial story racial dimensions and specific racial/cultural references. His film would not be about being Black, which in Hollywood terms was starting to mean living in the grip of festering social problems. Preminger believed films should address social issues. But cinema had to depict African Americans in diverse ways. *Carmen Jones* would just be another portrait. In this respect alone, the film's perspective would be similar to *Bright Road*'s.

He hired writer Harry Kleiner to draft the script and then approached Arthur Krim and Robert Benjamin at United Artists for financing. He assumed that they would be as supportive as they had been in helping him independently produce *The Moon Is Blue*. But the two men backed off from an all-Black film. "Sorry, Otto, this is too rich for our blood," they told him.

"I could do anything else I liked for them but not this," Preminger recalled. "I soon discovered that most other companies would not touch it either."

Then, while Preminger was editing *The River of No Return* at Fox's studio in Hollywood, Zanuck, of all people, approached him. Having heard about Otto's struggles to get *Carmen Jones* off the ground, Zanuck asked if Preminger had a script. When Preminger answered yes, Zanuck asked, "Can I read it?" Two days later, Zanuck committed Fox to the picture. "I was surprised," said Preminger. "Twentieth Century Fox had hardly ever backed an independent producer."

Immediately, Zanuck contacted Joseph Moscowitz, Fox's vice president of business affairs in New York. Later Preminger flew to the East Coast to meet with him. Then negotiations dragged on for months. First Moscowitz wanted a complete script. Then he said there were other details to be ironed out. *Carmen Jones* did not seem headed anywhere. It was obvious Moscowitz had no interest in seeing Fox produce the musical.

In the end, Zanuck interceded. Preminger had flown to Paris to show the studio chief the rough cut of *The River of No Return*. "How is *Carmen Jones* coming along?" Zanuck asked. "When are you starting?" When Preminger recounted the difficulties with Moscowitz, Zanuck exploded. He placed a transatlantic call to New York and informed Moscowitz in no uncertain terms, "Joe, you will be on the next plane to Paris. You will bring with you the necessary papers and sign that contract with Preminger right here."

Two days later Moscowitz was in Paris, where he worked out the deal with Preminger. But there was still a snag. He would give only $750,000 for the budget. Preminger knew this meant he would have to shoot *Carmen Jones* quickly, perhaps in about four weeks during the summer of 1954. He also knew he had no choice but to accept. Fox's distribution system was something he needed desperately, as well as its promotion, advertising, and marketing expertise.

Then Preminger found himself confronting his old nemesis the Production Code Administration. Kleiner's script had to meet code standards. Yet, as with *The Moon Is Blue*, Preminger understood there was no way of making more sophisticated, adult films without challenging the code in some way.

On April 19, 1954, Preminger sent the script to the Breen office for its approval. Ten days later, Preminger and Fox executive Frank McCarthy met with Joseph L. Breen to discuss the script. Breen's overriding concern was "the lack of any voice of morality, properly condemning Carmen's complete lack of morals." He was also concerned by the script's "overemphasis on lustfulness."

Afterwards he wrote Preminger a letter in which he listed specific dialogue and action in Kleiner's script which would have to be changed. Among the objectionable dialogue was Carmen's comment, "Only reason she ain't never late is 'cause all the men kick her out soon as they sober up long enough to get a look at her." He also found "unacceptably lustful" a scene in which Carmen, standing on a table, was lifted by Joe, standing on the floor; Carmen was then to slide down Joe's body. What came to be one of the era's sexiest movie scenes was strongly opposed. Breen objected to an intimate sequence in which Joe was seen without trousers, and likewise, he was opposed to a sequence in which Joe woke up in Carmen's bed.

The script's dance and fight sequences also troubled him. He stressed that the dance sequences must not be too suggestive or vulgar. The fight sequence was not to be too violent. Breen urged that Preminger "make certain to omit any unacceptably brutal actions, such as kicking, kneeing, or gouging." His letter specified, "Great care will be needed with this scene of the razor fight, to avoid making it unduly shocking."

But again and again, Breen was disturbed by the film's handling of the sexuality of the characters, specifically Carmen. He stressed that in a "scene of embracing, as in other intimate scenes, please make certain that none of the kissing is open-mouth or unduly lustful." "As discussed," he wrote, "this sequence seems unacceptable by reason of overemphasis on both lust and immorality. Specifically, we cannot see our way clear to approve detailed scenes of passion, in bedrooms, between unmarried couples." Throughout, he wanted the sexuality dramatized less directly and less explicitly. "We suggest toning down this action of Carmen adjusting her stockings in front of Joe," he wrote. Among the other comments made by Breen were: "Carmen's reaction to the nearly naked Husky should not be overly lustful." Finally, Breen strongly objected to the prize fighter Husky Miller's lyric "stand up and fight like hell."

With a shooting date to commence on June 9th, Preminger agreed to some suggested changes but objected to others. Along with Oscar Hammerstein, he felt the lyric "fight like hell" was a colloquialism "that can be heard every day in any type of society." By now, the song in which the lyric was heard had become a "classic" that was well-known to audiences. There followed a series of letters and memos to the Breen office and also within the offices at Fox. Eventually, Preminger appealed to the Board of Directors of the Motion Picture Association for "liberalization of the Code" on use of the word "hell." In the end, the expression stayed in the film.

Preminger also decided to film two versions of the Chicago hotel sequence with Joe and Carmen: first as he felt the scene would be most effective and then in the manner that would satisfy the production code office. In a memo to Zanuck, he explained, "I intend to shoot scene 130, which they are still questioning, two ways and show them the finished picture first with the original scene." Preminger added, "For this version I shall fight hard. However, if I should finally lose, I shall have a completely harmless scene in reserve." As it turned out, Preminger's version, of the undershirted Joe, was the one used in the film.

At the same time, Preminger filmed another sequence which the Production Code office originally found objectionable: that of Joe playing with Carmen's legs, and her dialogue; and the action of Carmen biting Joe's cheek; and Joe's line, "What a mosquito bite!"

The script of *Carmen Jones* also raised concerns about the response of the African American community to the film. Zanuck suggested that Preminger send the script to Walter White of the

NAACP. He wanted to be sure in advance of shooting that there was nothing about the film's subject that might prove offensive to Black Americans. Preminger asked Oscar Hammerstein II who was on the board of the civil rights organization, to contact White about the script. A Preminger memo to Zanuck explained White's response. "While White indicated that he principally is opposed to an all-Negro show as such, because their fight is for integration as opposed to segregation in any form," wrote Preminger, "he likes this particular script very much and has no objection to any part of it." Preminger and Zanuck now felt confident that *Carmen Jones* would be well-received by the African American audience.

While Preminger volleyed with the Breen office, he also began gathering his cast and crew. His director of photography would be Sam Leavitt. Musical direction would come under the knowing ear of Herschel Burke Gilbert. Choreography would be by Herbert Ross, who was then working on his first such movie assignment. Later Ross became a successful director of such films as *The Turning Point*, the 1981 *Pennies From Heaven*, and *Steel Magnolias*.

For his cast, Preminger relied primarily on New York performers. He selected Harry Belafonte, who was still known mainly as a folk singer, for the role of Joe, and Pearl Bailey for the role of the fast-talking, quipping Frankie.

Newcomer Brock Peters, whose first name was then spelled Broc, was considered for the role of the prize-fighter Husky Miller but finally signed to play the troublesome Sergeant Brown. It was the first film for Peters, who had formerly appeared on stage in *Anna Lucasta* and a stage production of *Carmen Jones*. He also had been an Arthur Godfrey talent scout winner on television and had won a recording contract with Columbia Records.

Another performer making her movie debut was 19-year-old Diahann Carroll. She was cast in the role of Frankie's friend Myrt. Local Los Angeles disc jockey Joe Adams, who had just completed a tour entertaining the American troops in Korea and Japan, was finally set to play Husky Miller.

Such Hollywood veterans as Nick Stewart—also known as Nicodemus—and Roy Glenn were added to the cast. So, too, was Black Hollywood's 81-year-old grande dame Madame Sul-Te-Wan, still in the movie capital since the days of silent films and her friendship with director D. W. Griffith. She was signed to play a small role as Carmen's superstitious grandmother Hagar. Perhaps it was because of this role that stories sometimes circulated that she was in fact

Dandridge's grandmother. Without a grey hair on her head, she had said to Preminger of her grandmother role, "I guess you want me to play her like an old woman."

Among the film's sixteen dancers who were signed, some of whom were recruited from Lester Horton's troupe, were Carmen de Lavallade, James Truitt, and a young Alvin Ailey. Veteran dancer Archie Savage, an alumnus of the Katherine Dunhan dance company as well as other films and such theatre productions as *South Pacific* and *Kiss Me Kate,* helped choreographer Ross line up the performers for *Carmen Jones'*s big dance numbers. Drummer Max Roach would play in the big cabaret sequence.

As Preminger's cast started falling into place, he still had not settled on an actress to play the good-girl Cindy Lou. But most important, he had not found an actress for Carmen. Among those considered were Joyce Bryant, stage actress Elizabeth Foster, and Muriel Smith, who had played the role to critical praise in the Billy Rose stage production. Diahann Carroll also recalled that when she first met Preminger, he had her read for the lead role, but he quickly dropped the idea. Carroll herself said, "I never thought I would get it—I knew that I did not have the kind of sexuality needed to play Carmen."

Hollywood's trade papers reported on the plans for *Carmen Jones.* Within Black Hollywood, excitement spread because it would be Hollywood's first all-star Black musical since *Stormy Weather* and *Cabin in the Sky* in 1943. *Carmen Jones* would be the first Hollywood Black-cast production shot in Technicolor. With it following so closely on the heels of the dramatic *Bright Road* as well as the recent films featuring Sidney Poitier, *Carmen Jones* signalled even in its preproduction stages the possibility of more important dramatic roles for African Americans. Not lost on anyone was the fact that, of the new films, it was the only one, save for *Bright Road,* that offered an African American actress a lead role.

No one in Hollywood was more aware of the oncoming production than Dorothy. Since *Carmen Jones* had been announced at the end of 1953, her tour schedule was as tightly booked as the previous year with engagements in Toronto, Buffalo, and Boston as well as a three week return to New York's La Vie En Rose, two weeks at Sans Souci in Miami, and another booking at the Last Frontier in Las Vegas. Some producers had also talked of casting her—as a white character—in a film called *Embrace,* written by Philip Yordan. Negotiations had begun and it looked as if the movie would get financing. Nothing was set, though.

By the spring of 1954, Dandridge was distressed that no one had contacted MCA about the possibility of her playing Carmen. While it was no secret that various other women had read for the part, she had not even been asked to do that. "Preminger started having an open casting and he talked to all the theatrical agents about whom they could recommend," said Earl Mills. "Dorothy was completely overlooked." Angered at not even being in the running, she told Mills that something had to be done so that at least she would be considered. "I checked with MCA," said Mills. "They said that Otto Preminger thought that Joyce Bryant would be the best choice. Dorothy was very upset. And we were trying to think of what to do about it."

She was upset but was not to be outdone. The story of how she eventually won the role of Carmen reads almost like a press agent's dream. But it did happen.

At the time, Mills occupied office space on Beverly Drive in Beverly Hills. Across the hall from him was the office of Otto's brother Ingo Preminger, then a Hollywood agent. Mills went to see Ingo Preminger and prevailed upon him to intercede to see if an interview could be arranged for Dorothy with Otto. Ingo spoke to Otto, who agreed to see her. But he did so more as a friendly gesture, a professional courtesy to a woman he already knew a great deal about, than as a meeting in which she would be seriously considered for the role.

The morning of her appointment, Dorothy carefully dressed and made up. Vivian was at Hilldale with her. "She had asked me to stay there. And I had moved in because I figured she had some reason. Maybe a little loneliness or something," Vivian recalled. "I didn't know what it was. So while I was there, this opportunity presented itself for *Carmen Jones*."

That morning Vivian was surprised by the way Dorothy dressed for the appointment with Preminger. "I saw her leave the apartment," she said. "She had on a navy blue dress with a white Peter Pan collar. Now the dress fit her. She had a gorgeous figure. It fit through the waist. But it flared. Her hair was back in a pony tail. Not too much make-up on." Vivian thought her sister was dressed inappropriately for an actress about to discuss the role of fiery Carmen.

"Dorothy had this thing about dignity," said Vivian. "She was always careful to dress in a way that would never be suggestive. It wasn't even that she thought about it. That's just the way my sister was. Always ladylike. Always dignified. Me. I was different."

Vivian, however, said nothing to Dorothy that morning. She did not want an argument.

When Dorothy and Mills stepped into Preminger's Los Angeles office, they came face to face with a man—tall with large shoulders, a large chest, and piercing blue eyes—who exuded power and assurance. Diahann Carroll recalled during her interview that Preminger, in an office the size of a hotel ballroom, "was seated behind the longest desk I had ever seen. The light from the window shone down on his bald head, making him look absolutely formidable." She "had never before encountered power on such a grand scale. It made me so nervous that I found it almost impossible to answer Preminger's quite ordinary and impersonal questions."

With Dorothy, Preminger was very gracious. Quickly, he went through the cordialities. But when the discussion turned to the role of Carmen, Preminger looked directly at her and asked, "Now, Miss Dandridge, what makes you think that you can do Carmen?"

"Well, Mr. Preminger, what makes you think I can't?" she answered.

Still, he was adamant as he expressed his feelings. Having seen her perform at La Vie en Rose and even once glimpsing her walking down Fifth Avenue looking like a dream in a red coat, he felt, "You're very sophisticated. You're the epitome of high fashion. But this role of Carmen is one of an earthy girl that's entirely different than you are. Every time I look at you, I see Saks Fifth Avenue."

Later Dandridge recalled, "Mr. Preminger told me I seemed too sweet, too regal, that he didn't think I'd do."

That afternoon, Dorothy told him, "Mr. Preminger, I'm an actress. I can perform any kind of role. It can be a prostitute or a nun. I'm an actress, more than a singer. It's my goal. I know you'd be satisfied with my work."

But Preminger still could not envision her as his Carmen. Then Preminger explained there was a role in *Carmen Jones* which he would consider her for and which she might be just right for. It was that of Cindy Lou. "I'd give you the opportunity to test for that part," he said.

Dorothy was immediately angered, but she held her temper in. She and Mills prevailed upon Preminger to let her test instead for the lead. But the director wouldn't budge. "I just cannot visualize you for the role of Carmen," he said.

Then Mills interjected, "Well, we will take a script, Mr. Preminger. We'll come back and do some reading for you." He made it sound as if Dorothy indeed would be willing to test for Cindy Lou.

Once out of the office, Dorothy was furious. She and Mills ended up sitting in a car on the studio parking lot for about three hours. "I'm an actress," Dorothy said. "Why can't that man understand that?" The two wrestled with ideas that might convince Preminger to test her for Carmen.

That night back at her apartment, Dorothy's anger hadn't abated. So annoyed that she couldn't sit still, she stormed through the apartment. "She screamed and carried on," recalled Vivian. Dorothy asked her sister, "Do you know the man had the nerve to offer me the other part of Cindy Lou!"

Vivian was frank with her sister, even though she knew she was risking an argument. "It's because of the way you look," she said.

"What do you mean?"

"He couldn't imagine you, with the way you probably talked to him and the way you went and sat down with *this—this* dress like a schoolteacher's. Or like you're going to church or something." Vivian suggested Dorothy do something about her look. "Put makeup on like you're going to do a nightclub show," she advised. "Just look trollopy. And get a rose. And fall through the door and put that rose through your teeth and say breathy, 'Hi.'" Vivian also told her sister she should have no problem playing the part because, "Dottie, now you know you can be very bitchy!" "Oh, Vivi!" was Dorothy's response. That evening, the two sisters, despite any other disagreements they may have had through the years, were united in one common goal: getting Dorothy the role of Carmen.

Mills also went to see the publicist Orin Borsten for advice. Afterwards when Dorothy came to his office, Borsten was surprised by her manner. "She always was a very gentle, highly refined young lady. Soft spoken. No hard edges to her." Once they discussed the role of Carmen, Borsten also asked how she'd been dressed when she had seen Preminger.

"Look, I know Preminger," he told her, "and I know what he sees is what he gets. He's got to see it. You can't project yourself and say, 'Oh, well, I'd be a good Carmen Jones.' He's got to see you as Carmen Jones." He also suggested that she should look "wild" when she went back to his office.

"Go back there and be sexy," he said.

But she bristled at his use of the word *sexy*. "You can't say that word to her," Borsten recalled. "It was offensive. But I said it to her."

Later Dorothy and Mills discussed the situation with Ruby. Still the stage mother, Ruby's door was always open for talks about career matters, if nothing else. Like Vivian, she didn't want to see Dorothy lose out on the role of the decade. In this respect, the Dandridge women were of one mind.

"I'll tell you about how some of those girls who are factory workers behave," Ruby said, becoming animated as she talked about the character Carmen. "You've always lived a different kind of a life. You're a different kind of person." Then Ruby rose from her chair to show her how Carmen would move. She strutted and sashayed around the room and, according to Mills, "showed Dorothy how to walk, you know, swinging her hips."

After mulling over the suggestions of Vivian, Ruby, Borsten, and Mills, Dorothy decided on the next approach to Preminger. With Mills, she visited Hollywood's Max Factor. She selected a wig that could be tousled. Then she picked out a skirt with a slit as well as a low-cut peasant type of blouse.

Then she told Mills, "We're going to go in. And we're going to see Otto at the appointment for the Cindy Lou part." But she planned on taking Otto by surprise.

At the next appointment, Preminger sat behind his massive desk, expecting once again to see a demure girlish Dorothy. In she walked, though, with the tousled hair, the dark makeup, the tight skirt, the revealing blouse, and the sexiest swing of hips in town. She did not even have to open her mouth.

"My God," said Otto Preminger. "It's Carmen!"

Mills remembered, "He couldn't reach the phone fast enough. He arranged a screen test for her."

He handed her the script, which he instructed her to read carefully with a particular scene in mind, and then scheduled a screen-test for mid-May.

Leaving the meeting, Dorothy immediately immersed herself in the script and the world of Carmen Jones. She continued to talk to Ruby and Vivian about the part. But she also had to prepare for a trip to St. Louis for another engagement at the Chase Hotel on May 3rd. There was no way for her to get out of the commitment.

Around the same time, Dorothy also heard news from New York. Peter Lawford had announced his engagement to Patricia Kennedy. Then on April 24th, Lawford and Kennedy married. Dorothy's very romantic romance had now come to its end.

On the same day as Dorothy's Chase opening, *The Hollywood Reporter* announced that Preminger had signed young Olga James, a graduate of the Juilliard School of Music who sang in several languages, for the role of Cindy Lou. A former teacher had arranged an audition for her at the Alvin Theatre in New York. Years afterwards, Vivian Dandridge, in reference to the later delicate performance of Olga James as Cindy Lou, "It was a beautiful role as Olga did the part. But it wasn't Dorothy."

The Hollywood Reporter also announced that Preminger was set to start shooting the film on June 9th.

Dorothy closed at the Chase on May 10th. Two days later, *The Hollywood Reporter* announced, "Film makers hired Phil Yordan and Sid Harmon to script *Embrace* in which Dorothy Dandridge will play a white gal." But the movie never materialized.

Dorothy's mind was now set on the screen test for *Carmen Jones*. Joyce Bryant and Elizabeth Foster also tested. Working opposite Dorothy in the screen test was actor James Edwards in the role of Joe. It must have been a bittersweet experience for him. Had this film come only a few years earlier, the role of Joe would surely have been his. But talented as Edwards was, his career was beginning a decline from which it would not recover.

Her test scene was a sequence with Joe in a shabby Chicago hotel. They are still at the height of their love affair. And at one point, Carmen, having just polished her toenails, raises her leg in Joe's direction. "Blow on 'em, sugar. Make 'em dry faster." In the scene, she would have to convey the mood of a highly sexual woman, aware of her sexual power, while casually giving love orders to a man who is almost literally at her feet.

Upon viewing the screen test footage, Preminger knew he had found his Carmen. "It's the best screen test I've ever seen," he exclaimed. Excitement spread through the industry almost instantly about Dandridge's performance. *Ebony* took the unprecedented step of running an article in its September 1954 issue on the test itself, treating it as a major event in African American entertainment history.

The day after the test Dandridge immediately shifted gears. She had to begin auditioning piano accompanists because Nick Perito planned to work on Perry Como's TV show and wouldn't be able to travel with her.

It was finally announced on May 26th that Dandridge had signed to star in Otto Preminger's *Carmen Jones*. Shortly afterwards, she entertained members of the Black press at a dinner party. Preminger was a special guest that evening. Even though their work on *Carmen*

Jones had not yet begun, Otto Preminger already seemed entranced by Dorothy Dandridge.

With his Carmen signed, Preminger released the names of the other performers set for the film, many of whom had previously been locked in place. The salaries of the performers indicated just how tight Preminger's budget was. Dorothy received $1,800 a week for ten weeks of work. The same was true of Belafonte, whose contract also stipulated that he would receive first-class airline tickets from New York to Los Angeles for himself, his wife, and young child. For six weeks of work, Pearl Bailey was contracted to receive $1,666.66 a week with the stipulation that should her work exceed those six weeks, she would receive $2,000 a week for any additional. Diahann Carroll's salary was $250 a week for four weeks of work. Olga James was signed for $500 a week for ten weeks. Joe Adams received $450 a week for three weeks. And Brock Peters earned $250 a week for five weeks' work.

The contracts of Dandridge and Belafonte were very specific concerning the billing each was to receive on screen and in advertising. Belafonte's representatives were able to secure top billing for the actor in the screen credits. Dorothy's were not. Already the press was hunting for trouble to report. They wrote of a reported rivalry between Belafonte and Dandridge. Despite the fact that the dispute was between the actors' representatives, it was reported in a different way; that the stars themselves had clashed over the billing. "I hate the way these things get started," Belafonte was quoted as saying. "The outcome was a tie. She got top billing in the advertising and I got it on the screen." Actually, while Dorothy was prominently featured in the advertising graphics, with nary a glimpse of Belafonte, his name still appeared before hers in the copy.

Dandridge's contract stipulated that no more than one name could be billed above hers. It also stated that no performer's name could be "in larger size type or with greater prominence" than hers. This latter clause may have been inserted by MCA to insure that Pearl Bailey's agents did not manage to snare her billing above Dandridge. At this time, Bailey was considered better known; some might have thought she was even a bigger star at the time the production began. Bailey herself appeared to have such feelings. In the end, the credits wouldn't matter much because all anyone would think about when discussing *Carmen Jones* would be Dorothy Dandridge.

Shortly before production began, though, Dandridge, riddled with doubts, considered dropping out of the film. Part of her anxiety sprang from questions about the film's images. Ironically, after all her anxieties about her sexy club persona, her great acting opportunity now came by playing a character most might view as a whore. Few seemed to consider during these years that a free-thinking woman, living on the terms men had always lived by and free enough to pick her lovers as she chose, could be something other than a whore. Dandridge would bring her own interpretation to the role of Carmen. Yet, aware of the Black community's sensitivity to its portrayal, she felt uncomfortable and pressured. In a movie colony where envy and competition ran rampant, she also grew uneasy about the mounting jealousy among other performers. Some friends who weren't cast asked if she could get them work in the film. Others were openly resentful because she indeed had won the plum role of the new era.

As she often did when depressed, she took to her bed and decided not to see anyone. Mills persisted, trying to persuade her to go through with the film and the role. When word reached Preminger that Dorothy was having doubts, he drove over to Hilldale. Surprised to see him, she may have realized at that very moment that Otto was interested in her not only as an actress but as a woman. The two talked quietly and personally. As she expressed her doubts, he gently reassured her that everything would be fine and that he had faith in her talent. Reminding her that he would be there to guide her through the filming, he convinced her to push all doubts aside. *Carmen Jones* could be a great film, he explained, that would firmly establish her as a major motion picture actress. That night both Dorothy and Preminger probably knew that very soon their relationship would also change.

Preminger soon began three weeks of rehearsal with his cast and crew. Because of his budget, every detail had to be worked out in advance. Each day the cast rehearsed on the actual sets, which had already been completed. The necessary props were also at hand. He held dress rehearsals in which the actors were blocked and the camera movements planned. There could be no mishaps. He also wanted his actors familiar with one another and the motivations of their characters. Although brutal with actors, Preminger realized their importance nonetheless. He was not the kind of director who concentrated on visuals at the expense of characterizations. His pictures always boasted some impressive performances.

Under the musical direction of Herschel Burke Gilbert, the music for *Carmen Jones* was recorded at Fox Studios on June 18th. The film was to be shot, however, at RKO Studios. Dandridge and Belafonte both studied with voice coaches in anticipation of recording the music for the film. For Dandridge, this meant carving out time amid her other commitments for long sessions with vocal coach Florence Russell.

But Preminger soon had a different idea. For his principals and others, he believed Bizet's music was best served by trained operatic singers. "Because this was to be a black movie," Belafonte said, "and because blacks were still exotic to Europeans—and the movie had to be a financial success in Europe as well—Otto had to find a way to please the Bizet estate, which did not like what Hammerstein had done to the original work. They felt turning Carmen into a folk opera was not servicing the best needs of the opera, so Otto appeased them by hiring two opera singers to dub the main voices."

For the singing voice of Belafonte's Joe, he hired Le Vern Hutcherson, who had starred in the national company of *Porgy and Bess*. Marvin Hayes performed the songs of Joe Adams's Husky Miller. For the brief sequence in which Roy Glenn as Rum performed as part of the quintet, Brock Peters's voice was substituted for Glenn's. Among the few performers whose voices actually were used was Pearl Bailey, who did a spirited version of "Beat Out That Rhythm On A Drum." Olga James also recorded her own stunning arias as Cindy Lou.

In her contract, Dorothy had agreed to have her voice dubbed. For the crucial voice of Carmen, Preminger originally hired an older established singer. But he quickly became dissatisfied. "She just wasn't doing what Preminger wanted," recalled Olga James. "He would yell at her. And it constricted her vocally." He fired the woman and then hired an unknown 20-year-old mezzo-soprano who had dropped out of the University of Southern California with aspirations for an operatic career. Her name was Marilyn Horne. In these years, her first name was spelled Marilynn. Later, of course, she became an internationally famous opera star.

Marilyn Horne was excited at having the chance to record Carmen's arias. "Even though I was at that time a very light lyric soprano," she said, "I did everything I possibly could to imitate the voice of Dorothy Dandridge. I spent many hours with her. In fact, one of the reasons I was chosen to do this dubbing was that I was able to imitate her voice had she been able to sing in the proper register, that is, high enough."

Horne listened to Dandridge's speaking voice and set out "to match the timbre and the accent, so that when it came time for me to record the songs, there would be a little bit of Dandridge in my throat," said Horne. "She sang in a register comfortable for her, then I mimicked her voice in the proper keys."

Dorothy also carefully studied Horne. "Dorothy watched Marilyn as she performed in the studio," said Earl Mills. She made note of the movement of the soprano's neck muscles and facial expressions when hitting certain notes. "She copied them perfectly," said Mills.

"Later, she filmed her scenes with my recorded voice blasting from huge loudspeakers," said Horne. "The tendency in dubbing is to overdo your mouth movements. Dandridge didn't and was sensational." Even though Horne received credit on the film, many people believed for years that Dandridge had done her own singing, so expert was her lip-synching, among the finest in the history of the American movie musical.

Before filming, the fight sequences and the choreography also were worked out for the camera. For three weeks, Joe Adams trained with Johnny Indrisano to get in shape as Husky. For the dances, choreographer Herb Ross recalled, "I put together the blocking of all the sequences. And I staged the quintet and the road house sequence. After it all was rehearsed, Otto went through everything with a cameraman." Said Ross, "Everything was pre-rehearsed, pre-recorded, and then shot on a tight schedule."

The Hollywood Reporter announced on June 30, 1954, "Producer-Director Otto Preminger puts his picturization of Oscar Hammerstein's *Carmen Jones* before the cameras today at RKO-Radio Studio."

And so the filming began.

For the most part, *Carmen Jones* moved well. For Black performers in Hollywood, it represented yet another chance at moving forward with plenty of work not only for the principals and supporting players but also the dancers, musicians, and extras.

"The significant thing about the picture," said Belafonte, "and this is something I would say without fear of contradiction is that prior to *Carmen Jones*, there was never a film that could be considered all-Black, as opposed to a film in which Black characters played. I'm even talking about movies like *Cabin in the Sky* and *Stormy Weather*. I think *Carmen Jones* marked the introduction to an era of filmmaking that engaged employment of Blacks in a more favorable environment."

For New York performers like Diahann Carroll and Olga James came the thrill of being in Hollywood. Both young women stayed at a hotel on the Sunset Strip. Also there, ensconced in a suite, was Sammy Davis, Jr. He was not in the picture, but it was there that he developed a crush on Carroll.

At the studio itself, Carroll soon saw the ways of Hollywood. When she was sent over to hair and makeup, said Carroll, "they slicked down my hair with a quart of Dixie Peach Pomade [a sort of Vaseline that was then used to straighten hair]." Olga James remembered that she and Dandridge wore hairpieces in the film. A Black hairdresser was also brought in for the picture.

A decision was made early on that, rather than dress Carmen exclusively in the traditional red that was always associated with the character and the character's passion, Dandridge's Carmen should project a different visual statement. With the exception of Dandridge's red skirt in her first scenes, costume designer Mary Ann Nyberg dressed the actress in a softer, pink, orange, and in the climactic scene, white. In the Chicago hotel sequence, however, Nyberg selected for Dandridge a polka dot robe, black bra, and zebra-striped panties that would startle movie audiences for years to come.

Throughout filming, Dorothy was clearly the production's focal point. It would be this way with all of her future films, with the exception of *Island in the Sun*. She usually rose each morning at five. Daily, as she drove onto the studio lot in her snazzy white convertible, she was a startling presence. With people scurrying about on the lot busy at work on other films—the grips, technicians, extras, studio executives, and other stars—there was little time to stop and stare at anything, but most did a double take upon seeing Dorothy step out of her car. They would ask, "Who is that?" And the response was usually, "It's the Colored singer on the Preminger film."

On her first day at the studio, Earl Mills accompanied her to ensure that everything was in order. But afterwards Dorothy instructed him not to come any more. The same edict was given to Vivian. "I never went to the set," said Vivian. "She told me I would make her nervous." Sometimes Dorothy would call Vivian on the phone to ask her opinion about various matters. "She would talk to me about things on the production," said Vivian. "And I would tell her what I thought. But I wasn't allowed on the set."

Once she left the studio and was back at Hilldale, she might fix a light dinner and make phone calls at her apartment. But she mostly spent her time with the script, studying every line and move of Carmen Jones. Sometimes Dorothy sought Ruby's advice. "I am sure that mother helped her with some of the dialogue," said Vivian, "because my mother was a very good actress. I'm sure that she helped her sometimes with some of the script. She was afraid she wasn't doing it well enough."

Before long, though, Dorothy's evening routine changed. Otto Preminger began visiting her apartment at Hilldale.

On the set, all the attention she received sometimes made her feel edgier, but Dorothy was too focused to allow herself any distractions or diversions. She had to call on her powers of intense concentration in order to mold a vibrant Carmen and also, in doing so, to keep her insecurities at bay. To the cast, she seemed withdrawn.

"I couldn't figure her out," Brock Peters recalled. "When I looked at her, I wondered what she was like. And I suspected that she might be introverted. That she might be a little bit removed because she, after all, not only was the star of the film, but she was doing the night-club circuit. And that meant that she was already having a level of success. I don't know. Maybe it was my own insecurities. It was my first picture. Here I am. There's a Dorothy Dandridge and a Belafonte. Belafonte and I had been close friends before *Carmen Jones* so I was not uptight where he was concerned. But with her I just thought, 'Well, she's probably going to be distant to us all. And I can understand.'"

Only on rare occasions did she let her guard down. Then Peters observed that she could be warm and playful. A few years later he would observe another side of Dandridge when he appeared with her in *Porgy and Bess.*

Mainly, she kept to herself as she had done when she appeared in *Jump for Joy.* "She had very few friends in the cast," recalled Diahann Carroll, who realized that Dorothy, who often looked strained and uncomfortable, "was painfully shy and self-absorbed, concerned only with improving her performance. So much was riding on it that she seemed to be living in a constant state of anxiety. Her vulnerability touched me deeply."

Diahann Carroll found herself wanting to comfort and protect Dorothy, whose "looks made the other actresses jealous." Said Carroll, "She had the most beautiful face and the perfect body, and her smile and eyes were totally mesmerizing."

Between takes, Dorothy never sat around and talked with the cast and crew. She studied her lines and rehearsed by herself. "She disappeared. And so she kept her mystique," said Olga James. "She behaved like a star. And I mean that in the *best* sense. That she was simple. She was elegant. She was well-mannered. She was disciplined. She was focused on the work." Appearing in her first film, James looked up to Dandridge and used her as a model. "Without being given direct instructions, I found that's what you're supposed to do, that was professional behavior and that's how a star is supposed to behave."

But Olga James, like Diahann Carroll, recalled that some cast members misunderstood Dorothy's sense of privacy and called Dandridge cold, which James said was not true at all.

"I think that Dorothy was basically shy even though she'd been a performer for most of her life. But the shyness made her seem aloof," said James. "Under it, Dorothy was probably basically friendlier and basically kinder than a lot of people who came off like people-people. You know the type who say, 'Hi, I'm one of the guys.' Dorothy was not that. She was aloof and ladylike and kind of hard to know. But I think her intentions may have been more benign than the intentions of the people who came off as being 'one of the boys' and all of that stuff." James added, "I thought that Dorothy was gracious. Very sweet and never forthcoming. I thought she was retiring."

Choreographer Ross, who worked closely with Dandridge on the quintet sequence in the roadhouse scene, was surprised by what he observed. "She was quite solitary," he said. "My impression of her was that she was always alone. She didn't go out or socialize with the others. Olga was much more friendly. Alvin [Ailey] and Carmen and Olga and I were friendly. I remember Diahann was always going out to a jazz club on the Strip. I'd see Diahann walking down Sunset Boulevard in a white dress. But Dorothy was always somber and more serious."

"She was very intelligent," said Ross. "But I thought Dorothy was not a happy woman. She was gifted and talented and beautiful. At that time, it was not easy for a beautiful intelligent Black woman."

What always shone through, though, was Dorothy's great discipline. When the cast and crew broke for lunch, Dandridge usually ate in her dressing room. "I believe she had her lunch brought in," said James. "She used that period to re-group or to rest or think or to stay focused." But James recalled an unusual day when Dorothy had lunch in the studio commissary. She sat at a table with James. "I ordered a big, big, big, big lunch," said James. "And I remember Dorothy having a couple of eggs for the protein. Nothing else because she had to watch her weight. She was working. That was total discipline."

Watching Dandridge at work in her steamy scenes, Olga James also noted something else. "Looking like she did was a sensual thing in itself," said James. "But the kinds of things that she did as the character Carmen, I always thought was acting, which makes the acting all the more remarkable, because I don't think that *that* was her personality from what I observed. I don't think that innately was her personality." James added, "I don't think a real appreciation of Dorothy's acting skills came for me until years later."

Dandridge's work was often demanding with a great deal of physical action in some scenes. In the cafeteria scene when Carmen flirts with Joe while singing "Dat's Love," Dandridge had to master the intricate blocking that took her through the cafeteria doorway, to the counter, and throughout the room itself as she lip-synched to the music. What made the sequence all the more demanding was Preminger's use of dolly shots with only two cuts. Another cut did not come until she completed her song.

Another sequence called for Carmen to run away from the hapless Joe, then be chased atop flatcars of a freight train, and finally, be caught by him. Then her legs and arms are bound. She performed the sequence despite great discomfort. Having had her ears pierced for the film, Dandridge suffered an infection. She recalled that her ears felt as if on fire. Finally, a special tape was used to secure her large earrings in place without them having to go through her ear lobes.

The chase sequence itself was shot on location in Simi Valley where Belafonte was required to pursue Dandridge while the freight train was actually moving. The two then had to fall down a rocky hill. Surprisingly, the actors performed their own stunts, which added to the film's realism and excitement. It was a dangerous and difficult sequence to do.

Most of her scenes were with Belafonte. By now, after their appearance in *Bright Road*, the two understood one another's work habits. Her continued infatuation with him surely accounted for some of their on-screen chemistry.

"They seemed to work well," said Brock Peters. "I think there was a lot of little horseplay. You know, kibitzing around on the set and laughing. So I took it that they were getting along. I didn't have any sense of difficulty between them."

Away from the set, Dorothy still asked her sister, "Vivi, what do you think? Should I be married to Harry Belafonte?" She would always have a dreamy schoolgirl expression on her face.

"You have to be kidding!" was Vivian's response.

"Oh, Vivi!" she'd say. "Well, you never know."

Publicist Orin Borsten recalled that around this time Dorothy and he had both seen Belafonte perform in a club. Afterwards, she and Borsten talked about his performance over the telephone.

"God, that Harry Belafonte's gorgeous," she said in a dreamy, romantic manner. "He's beautiful. I can't get over him. I want to just think of him!"

"He's good," Borsten said, "but I don't like that choking, that grating in his voice. I look for purity in a singer."

"Oh," she interrupted, "he was just absolutely divine!"

Borsten could never recall hearing her talk about any man in this way.

Vivian, however, still didn't take such rhapsodizing about Belafonte seriously, but in later years she said that Dorothy would have been very happy to have married someone *like* Belafonte. Dorothy herself even commented, "I would have been happy to have been Mrs. Harry Belafonte." Such romantic notions started to unravel later when Belafonte divorced his first wife and married a young woman named Julie Robinson.

Nonetheless, it must have been exhilarating for Dorothy to have an on-screen male/female relationship where she was in control. The scenes in the film that drew the loudest applause from women viewers were the ones where Carmen fully asserted herself with her men.

Pearl Bailey, whom she knew from Harold's days in *St. Louis Woman*, was the only real friction for Dorothy among the cast. Unlike Olga James and Diahann Carroll, who looked up to Dandridge, Pearl Bailey didn't view her with such admiring eyes. Bailey appeared not to like the idea of having to play second-fiddle to Dorothy's lead.

"I think there was a little jealousy on Pearl's part," said Olga James, "because first of all, Pearl came to this film with a reputation from Broadway. I would say she was the biggest star on that shoot.

Harry was just about to happen. And after the film, then his career really blossomed. So Pearl was the biggest star, and I don't think that anybody at that time realized how good a cinematic actress Dorothy was because everybody else came from different orientations. Most came from live performances on stage, like Pearl."

Consequently, Bailey griped whenever possible. She complained about her dressing room and grew upset because she believed Olga James had better accommodations than hers. But Pearl's took up more space than all the others. She came onto the set with an entourage: a hairdresser as well as people to assist her and run errands. Whatever she believed was out of order, she let be known. Frequently, the target of her anger was Dorothy.

From a distance she would glance over at Dorothy on the set. "She's pretty. But she really can't sing like Lena," Bailey was heard saying on various occasions.

Herb Ross recalled an incident that erupted with Pearl as he worked with Dorothy and her. "There was one nasty moment when we were doing the quintet sequence," said Ross. "Dottie was to push Pearl. And Pearl got angry. She thought Dorothy had pushed too hard. Pearl called Dorothy a Black bitch."

Throughout the production, Ross knew that Bailey had to be approached cautiously. "Pearl was a tricky character," said Ross. "She was slightly paranoid and very jealous of her territory. She was very competitive. But she couldn't compete with Dorothy on any level. And the picture was called *Carmen*, wasn't it? And Pearl wasn't Carmen. Pearl was just jealous of any woman. She was that way with Diahann later in the play *House of Flowers*. She was a troubled woman." All things considered, it remains a tribute to Bailey's talent that in the film she was convincing enough to come across as Carmen Jones's good friend.

Throughout, Preminger was a stern, demanding taskmaster. "He was a bully who bullied everyone," said Herb Ross, "with the exception of Pearl Bailey." "Preminger liked discipline," said Joe Adams. "I was never anything but Mr. Adams. And Dorothy was never anything but Miss Dandridge. He was like that with everyone."

One day a fierce argument broke out between Preminger and Brock Peters. "He chewed me out in front of a lot of people. Crew and cast and extras. He said something about, 'This New York actor. . .' Some disparaging things. And, of course, I was on the spot. It was my first picture. I was wanting desperately for it to work. I lost my temper. And I went for him. And Pearl Bailey and somebody else grabbed me."

"You'll never work again," Bailey told Peters. Once Peters had calmed down, she added, "Honey, I just saved your life."

On another occasion, Preminger lashed into Joe Adams during the "Stand Up and Fight" number. Adams wasn't doing the scene as Preminger wanted. After some six takes, Preminger stopped him and blasted over a megaphone in his Austrian accent, "Mr. Adams. What exactly is it you call yourself doing? I've got a milkman that's a better actor than you."

Adams became angry. But Pearl Bailey, much as she had done with Brock Peters, held him back. "She was squeezing my arm so tight. I could feel her nails coming through my coat," Adams said.

"Now, honey, you just be cool," Bailey told the actor. "You're being paid a whole lot of money to do something that a whole lot of people would pay money to do."

Adams's attitude, however, was, "I don't need this." He did the scene again, however, this time to Preminger's satisfaction. "Fantastic!" the director said. Adams always believed Preminger's temper was a way of provoking the best performance out of his actors. "He was just as great to rave about you when you got it right," said Adams.

Preminger also had a couple of incidents—one that he brushed aside, another that caused him to explode—with Olga James, who later said her naivete got her into trouble. During preproduction when the original soprano for Carmen was having difficulties, none of which were helped by Preminger screaming at her, James calmly walked up to him and said quietly, "I think we could get it right if you would leave." She didn't realize the mikes were still open and that their voices could be heard in the control room. "Preminger very gently told me that he wasn't going anywhere. This was *his* film," said James. "So that day I didn't get invited to lunch with everybody else. And Harry told me never to do that again."

Later, though, Preminger was less gracious. "I didn't understand anything about making films," said James. "I didn't understand anything about the power hierarchy. I didn't understand how important time was to lighting, to other costs. I didn't know at that time that actors were probably the least costly thing on the shoot. You know that all of these people standing around doing other things are what eat up the money. So he lost his temper once with me when it was towards the end of the day, and the light was changing, and we were doing an outdoor thing and he wanted to get the shot before the light changed. And I kept messing up. And he yelled at me. And I got it right after that."

Mostly, though, James recalled that Preminger was restrained and that his temper was directed more at the males in the cast—Peters and on occasion Belafonte—than the women.

Sometimes, his temper was directed at Dandridge. Diahann Carroll remembered that "Dorothy wanted success desperately and worked hard to give him everything he asked for. He often screamed at her to force her to rise above her inexperience, and she always accepted his abuse." But on an occasion when it became too much, Dandridge simply walked off the set. "She went to her dressing room and cried," said Olga James. "Which I thought was a very good tactic."

Joe Adams recalled the incident. "She turned and walked to her dressing room and wasn't coming out," he said. "She let him know in very definite terms." Preminger quickly made amends. Adams also recalled that when Dorothy returned to the set, she did the scene perfectly. "I mean she *did* it," said Adams. "Which is exactly what he wanted her to do. He made her angry deliberately. She was doing more than she knew that she could do. And he brought it out of her. And then, of course, she was very happy. He had a way of that doing that."

Geri recalled the incident and its aftermath when Dorothy and Preminger were later alone. "He had yelled at her on the set," she said. "And boy, she gave him hell for two weeks. She didn't yell back on the set, but I'm telling you she gave him hell."

As he shot the film, Preminger realized the power of Dandridge's performance. "They worked together very well," said Earl Mills, who received daily progress reports. "Dorothy, the perfectionist, just had to be told once if something was wrong. The only comment Preminger made was for her to slow down because the film was in CinemaScope and the actions might look a little exaggerated on the wide screen." Often Preminger and Dandridge sat together as they viewed the rushes from the previous day's work. "Otto became just thrilled with the work he was getting out of Dorothy," said Mills.

By then, Otto Preminger had also fallen in love with her.

"There were rumors on the set," recalled Carroll, "that Preminger was involved with her and had made her success his personal goal."

Herb Ross also observed, "Dorothy had certain privileges the others didn't have, like driving her car on the lot."

To Ross, it was obvious. "Otto seemed besotted with her."

Otto Preminger, the demanding and intransigent autocrat, who was eager to confront the most powerful studio executives; Preminger, the far-sighted and sometimes bull-headed individualist who was unwilling to yield any of his own power to anyone; Preminger, the man who prided himself on control and authority, was, away from the set, willing to be putty in Dorothy's hands.

"Preminger became absolutely fascinated with her," said Geri.

"He was seriously in love with her," said Earl Mills.

The attraction no doubt had started the day she first entered his office. From then, it grew and intensified. Dorothy possessed many of the qualities that Preminger respected most: intelligence, drive, boldness, and a determination to succeed and a willingness to put all her focus and energy into her performance. For Dandridge, there were never any shortcuts as far as her career was concerned. If it took hard, unending, time-consuming work to perfect a scene, be it the intricately blocked cafeteria sequence at the opening of *Carmen Jones* or the chase on the flatcars, she was up to the challenge and ready to go the full distance.

Then, too, like everyone else, he was drawn to her vulnerability. Moved by her perpetual nervousness and underlying despair, he couldn't figure out what troubled her so deeply. But he wanted to try. And, of course, as a sophisticated man who always enjoyed the company of desirable, glamorous women, he couldn't take his eyes off her.

Something else also attracted Preminger to her. He believed that Dorothy Dandridge could become a major star. Like Hollywood's classic prewar directors, Preminger appreciated stars. He understood the value of their appeal, and that appeal's importance to cinema. This was during the period before stardom became completely devalued; a time before a growing cynicism led to the belief that stardom was but the end product of the studio factory system. Later it was believed that stars were people who were first prettified and glamorized by the makeup and wardrobe staff; that a suitable product was then constructed around them; and that they were then processed by the studio's high-powered publicity machine—turning ordinary mortals into gods and goddesses. They were merely the end-result of a skillful hype.

Such cynicism about stardom, some of which was justified, increased in the late 1960s and lead to the false assumption that anybody could attain such star status, that stars were not artists, that they didn't have to possess any special qualities, that they didn't have to be charismatic or compelling, that they weren't important to a film's aesthetic and perspective. Instead, with the spread of the French auteur theory, the director—and that, also meant the male authority figure on the film—was elevated to the position of the true and sole artist, the shaper, the molder, the controller, the visionary.

As much an auteur as Otto Preminger actually was, as much as his ego demanded total control of his cinema, as much as he loved that era when the auteur theory helped him win the attention and praise of the critics, he understood the aesthetic of stardom. He still saw the star—who had to be supported by a good story and solid craftsmanship—as a dominant force in a very important type of cinema.

During his career, Preminger would work with some of Hollywood's great stars: John Wayne, Joan Crawford, Henry Fonda, James Stewart, Robert Mitchum, and Paul Newman. He also thrived on discovering and spotlighting the unexpected or the unusual personality. He selected the girlish Maggie McNamara for *The Moon Is Blue*. Later he would invest much of his reputation into turning Jean Seberg into a star. Always he expected his stars and his actors and if lucky, a star/actor, to bring dimensions and insights to the script, to bring his or her vision to the screen as his camera recorded it.

The star was the embodiment of the audience's wild hopes for itself, its dreams of power, charm, threat, and beauty. She or he was also a reflection of the audience's very human vulnerability, affecting it in the most intense and personal way. The aesthetic of classic movie stardom and genuine talent were at the heart of Dandridge's appeal, especially to African American audiences. They had not yet had the pleasure of seeing Hollywood movies with such a magnificent, charismatic figure (who looked like them) at the center. Dandridge came to touch on a dream of Black America for itself. No matter how Preminger mistreated and abused her later, he considered Dorothy Dandridge at this time in a league with those two other great Hollywood icons of the Eisenhower era, Marilyn Monroe and Elizabeth Taylor.

Preminger had just completed work with Monroe, whose neurosis and dependence on her drama coach had turned him irritable. He never thought of her as a great actress. But he did believe, especially in the years following her death, Monroe was a great star. Taylor, of course, was an extraordinary beauty with a dramatic temperament that made her seem larger than life. In the early and mid-1950s, both women were not yet full-fledged legendary stars, but they were ascending. In Preminger's eyes, Dandridge was capable of ascending with them. As Diahann Carroll had said, he indeed did feel it his *personal goal* to see that she rose to the top.

The idea that Hollywood would have to make a place for a Black goddess in its pantheon fired Otto Preminger's imagination and sense of daring. Even more, his ego was fed by the thought that he—Otto Ludwig Preminger, the European/New Yorker outsider, so he sometimes believed—was the man who could create that place and make those fools in Hollywood accept this woman. To that end, Preminger was a man transfixed. Much like Phil Moore, he saw himself as a Svengali to Dandridge's Trilby. Perhaps it was no mere coincidence that just at the time, on June 22, 1954, *The Hollywood Reporter* announced that the director had plans to do a film called *Galatea*, the story of a man, Pygmalion, who sculpts a statue of a beautiful woman that later comes to life as his ideal creation, Galatea. It was yet another tale of a woman transformed by a man.

The Dandridge/Preminger story was an age-old one of the powerful man who feels all the more empowered by reshaping a woman into his image of her. Both Preminger and Moore appeared to take pride in showcasing Dorothy's talents, which they believed in. Once that talent was valued by others for its great worth, the men felt their own perceptive genius was validated.

Dorothy balked, though, when the control these two men exerted grew too tight. Her view would always be that no matter how great an opportunity Preminger or Moore presented her, no matter how much she respected their talents, she ultimately was the one who had to deliver; she was the one who had to win the audience over. She was the one who answered the audience's needs or wants.

But Preminger, during the filming of *Carmen Jones*, was on an exciting adventure.

"He came to Hilldale every night," said Earl Mills.

"She told me practically everything," said Vivian, who watched the budding Dandridge/Preminger romance develop. Attentive and courtly, a born raconteur, he could regale Dorothy—and anyone else—with stories about his past. Vivian liked him but knew, as did Dorothy, that he was still married. His first marriage had ended, and he was currently estranged from his second wife Mary Gardner Preminger. Vivian also questioned Dorothy about the stories of his terrible tirades and moods, his foul temper and cruelty. Dorothy's response to that was, "He is so marvelous to me. I can't believe he'd hurt anybody."

"Well, it's probably because you're doing your job," Vivian said.

Vivian also realized that Dorothy and Preminger, like Dorothy and Peter Lawford, had to keep the relationship under wraps. "It was no secret," said Vivian, "although she tried to keep it as secret as possible. She knew she had to lay low with any kind of interracial relationship at that time. But Otto was crazy about my sister."

Still, Vivian warned Dorothy. "You know," she said, "this man is never going to marry you. He couldn't afford to." Dorothy ignored her.

For an African American woman working in an industry that seemed to keep doors closed, no matter how much it celebrated her, Preminger represented a power that would open those doors for her. Here was a man who believed wholly in her talents, as much as Phil Moore had. But now the stakes were higher and the opportunity was in the arena she had been struggling to enter for years. Otto was willing to say, in essence, industry attitudes be damned.

Dorothy responded to Preminger's intelligence and worldliness, his wide-ranging knowledge of theatre, art, history, and music. He was politically liberal and a keen observer of the American political scene. Performers—Dorothy included—who found him such an overbearing, impossible director at the studio were surprised to discover that in social settings, dinner parties, benefits, even press receptions, he could be witty, clever, and disarmingly agreeable.

"He was a charming social personality and very warm," said Brock Peters. "And I was surprised to learn that he was a life member of the NAACP. He put up his $500 or whatever for that. And he hated being called a Nazi or a German or Prussian. He would make the point that he was Austrian as opposed to German. And, of course, everybody who could manage an accent would imitate him all over the place."

When Dorothy said, "He put champagne into my life," she meant it literally and figuratively. "Cases of champagne arrived," she said. "That was his drink. He was to make it mine. Otto drank it. I sipped it." He told her, "Drink the richest and the best. Never settle for anything less." He was ready to introduce her to an ever-expanding world of glamor, wealth, and international sophistication.

While Dorothy was enveloped in fantasies of romance and success with Otto Preminger, the other members of her family were continuing to grapple with unresolved domestic issues. Auntie Ma-Ma was still shut out of the home she had shared with Ruby. By now, desperate, she wanted her furniture and other belongings. She also needed money and went so far as to contact Cyril Dandridge in Cleveland. "Neva was trying to gather everything that she could," recalled Geri. She hoped he would speak to both Ruby and Dorothy.

Cyril Dandridge found himself in the position of having to help the woman who had usurped his place in Ruby's life, who had reared the daughters who had been taken from him. Already, unknown to Dorothy, Vivian had been in contact with their father. It stood to reason since Dorothy was their mother's favorite, that she would look to her father for the affection Ruby had denied her. "She would write to him and see him," said Geri. "She didn't let Dottie know, as though she wanted to keep him for herself."

Cyril made the trip to Los Angeles, not to help Neva, but in hopes of establishing a relationship with his younger daughter. He tried to track her down but made little progress. Dorothy remained closed off from him. "She thought he was too soft," said Geri. "She was rather hard on men in that regard. She blamed him for subjecting her to this dysfunctional family life that had been abusive. She was very resentful. That was the reason for her therapy."

"Neva told him that he should see me. He had my phone number and address," said Geri. Cyril paid a visit to Geri.

"He wasn't bitter. He wasn't arrogant. He just wanted to see her," recalled Geri. "It was obvious that he didn't want to see her because she was a star. It was strictly on the basis of fatherhood. He wanted to explain that he didn't purposely dodge taking care of her as a child."

Dorothy finally agreed to meet with her father. "She had been in therapy and she had decided to talk to him because she was very bitter. She thought that he had abandoned her because that was what she had been told all these years," said Geri. Dorothy met him, however, on neutral territory, not at her home but at the studio. "He went down to see her. She talked to him that one time."

"I was a little more mature by then," said Dorothy, "and we talked and had a nice time."

"But then he didn't see her any more," recalled Geri. "Afterwards, she was very busy traveling all over again." But Dorothy had allowed a door to open with her father.

Auntie Ma-Ma, however, was another matter. Dorothy consented to see her, but refused to give her money. "Nothing?" the woman asked. "Not anything," Dorothy said again. Later Dorothy said, "I took pleasure in turning her down. I wasn't that much of a Christian."

Dorothy had money concerns of her own. For more than two years, Harold had not sent child support payments for Lynn. Ordered by the court to pay $300 a month for Lynn's care, he was now behind in his payments for the amount of $8,350. Her entreaties to him had gone unanswered. Finally, feeling she had no choice, she contacted her attorney, who later filed a court claim. It happened around the time of the Thursday, July 29, 1954 *The Hollywood Reporter* announcement, "*Carmen Jones* scheduled to finish shooting at the end of the week will be ready for release through Twentieth Fox by Sept 15th, according to producer-director Otto Preminger."

By the time the production drew to a close, Diahann Carroll was feeling that, despite all her movie-star fantasies, none of the cast was likely to have much of a future in movies. "We were the only Black people on the lot," she said. "The producers, production staff, and crew were all quite polite and professional, but there was absolutely no camaraderie on or off the set, no sense of shared purpose. The unspoken assumption seemed to be that we were outsiders, in town for only a short while to do our 'Black' feature film." Afterwards, Carroll said, it was assumed by most at the studio that the Black performers "would go back to wherever we came from" and not be seen again.

The one possible exception, Carroll believed, would be Dandridge. "She had such presence and incredible beauty," she said, "that it was difficult to believe she wasn't going to become a star."

Carmen Jones was rushed through its post-production, quickly edited and scored, in time for a late fall release. At Twentieth Century Fox, where questions lingered about the profitability of Negro pictures, screenings went well. Otto Preminger had put together a stirring, energetic piece of entertainment with a superb cast. Preminger's direction kept the action moving at a fast clip. He had made not so much a musical in the old tradition as a realistic dramatic story with musical components. The arias vividly introduced the characters and expressed their motivations and then were used to highlight their emotions. Best were the musical sequences like "Dat's Love," "Dere's A Café on De Corner," "Beat Out That Rhythm on a Drum," and "Stand Up and Fight."

As the film proceeded, he managed to abandon the music in some instances, notably in the scenes with Dandridge and Belafonte. Here were a contemporary Black woman and Black man in a struggle for power and love. It was so powerful in and of itself that the music in the later segments of the film would strike many as corny. Enjoyably so, but corny nonetheless. In fact, *Carmen Jones* would have been far more effective had he dropped the music altogether in the last half.

But most importantly at the core of *Carmen Jones*—its heart, its soul, its drive—was Dandridge's performance. At Fox, Darryl F. Zanuck was engaged by the woman on screen. Like Preminger, he understood she could signal a new era for Black performers, that indeed she was movie-star material.

When released, *Carmen Jones* would have a great impact on the critics and audiences, Black and White. For the African American community, Dandridge emerged as Hollywood's first distinctive, modern heroine. While the movie, like Bizet's opera, was tied to a long-held male concept of the alluring, sexually potent woman who has the power to enslave and destroy men and who therefore must be destroyed, Dandridge transcended it.

Her Carmen was a mercurial heroine who could be strong, independent, warm, and vibrant. Dandridge's playfulness saved the character from old-style vulgarity. In her very first sequence, as she flirts in song with Joe in the cafeteria while also asserting her power in a room full of her compatriots, she provided another comment through the use of her expressive hands. At one point, Dandridge simply throws her hands in the air and shrugs her shoulders. Yes, she wants the innocent Joe. But if she does not get him, ah, so what. That's life. Dandridge subtly communicated Carmen's fatalism and also her resignation.

Later, as Joe drives Carmen in a jeep to be taken before her jailors, she is all coquette as she sings and plays with him by offering the invitation for him to join her for a good time at the café of her friend Billy Pasteur. Throughout, she smiles and laughs, never losing her high spirits or sense of fun.

It is a very adult depiction of female sexuality. At times the script and Preminger's direction lapse into the coarse and the obvious, notably in the sequence when Joe, after catching up with Carmen who has tried to run off, throws her to the ground and ties her feet. Dandridge appropriately tries fighting him. This very physical sequence almost objectifies her.

Dandridge's Carmen is a woman, despite her view of fate, who makes her own choices. Once she has Joe in her grandmother's home, as she polishes his shoes and adjusts his belt, she is completely in control. She is ready to seduce but will do so at her own bidding.

Dandridge's Carmen is relaxed and unafraid of passion. For an age in which women not expected to show an interest in or enjoyment of sex, she was securely up-front about her desires.

And she was an independent thinker. "Look boy, don't go putting me on no stand. I don't answer to nobody," she defiantly tells Belafonte's Joe, after he questions her whereabouts. When Joe expresses his idea of the male-to-female contract they've drawn, he says, "You're accounting to me. I love you. And that gives me the right..."

"That don't give you no right to own me," Dandridge's Carmen cuts him off. "There's only one that does. That's me. Myself." Joe then asks, "Where you going?" As she stands by the door, she quickly looks him over and says, "I *might* come back."

In the following scene, as a frantic Joe wonders where Carmen, now dressed for the evening, is going, she ignores him by humming distractedly as she prepares to go out on her own. When he persists in questioning her, she tells him flat-out, "Look, boy, I don't have to keep the truth from nobody. I can't stand being cooped up in this alley no more." Later she adds, "Maybe you ain't got the message yet. But Carmen's one gal nobody puts on a leash. No man's going to tell me when I come and go. I got to be free. Or I don't stay at all."

Finally, Joe, realizing it is a losing battle, musters up enough nerve to tell Carmen, "Get back soon. And remember I'm waiting."

She looks him over. "You just keep a light burning in the window, boy." Then she is off.

Preminger wisely understood the power and isolation of Dandrige's Carmen, whose individuality and sense of emotional/sexual freedom set her apart from her community. It is another Dandridge portrait of the beauty-as-loner. In some respects, in part because of her look, she seems to play out the concept of the tragic mulatto, which depicts the mixed-race character as not being able to function as a part of any community. That may well, strangely enough, explain some of Dandridge's appeal and the complexity of her screen persona.

Preminger seemed to be getting at something else in his direction, though, perhaps at Dorothy Dandridge's own personal isolation, spotlighting it in the stirring roadhouse sequence. As the crowd excitedly rushes outside to greet the champ Husky Miller, Preminger's camera stays on the seated Dandridge and then—in a long shot—as the chords to the music start to soar, she walks alone up a few steps and outside onto a balcony to watch Husky's arrival by herself. Once Preminger has cut to Husky singing "Stand Up and Fight," his camera often keeps Dandridge in the frame on the side, observing, not participating, and then there is a lush, medium shot of her as she still looks on. Preminger understood that this type of distant woman, who does not appear to be reachable, can drive men insane. It is Carmen's emotional aloofness as well as her sexuality that makes her the object of male desires.

For Dandridge, the role was a dream: a full chance to live out her own desire never to be under the grip of the men in her life. It was a chance to be fully confident and in charge and to do so without losing her femininity and without having feelings of guilt. For a generation of Black women watching her, it was also a dream come true. Dandridge exuded throughout the film a larger-than-life glamor and allure that had never been accorded Black women in Hollywood cinema before.

As *Carmen Jones* was being previewed at the studio and for the exhibitors, before it opened for the critics and audiences, Dandridge, although nervous about the movie's reception, knew it would launch a new phase of her career. *Carmen Jones* would be a defining marker in her life.

From Dorothy's vantage point, the definers had been of frustration and disappointment in the past. There was the failure of her relationships with her mother and father. The collapse of her marriage to Harold. The birth of Lynn. The romance with Peter Lawford. Even the very fruitful working and personal relationship with Phil Moore. Though her nightclub appearances had been extraordinarily successful, she never viewed herself, as Joyce Bryant had put it, "as the [extraordinary] person who she was." So much of what had been important in life had been, in her eyes, failure.

Carmen Jones helped her, for all too brief a time, to reconfigure her definition of herself. It would be a bonafide triumph that she could take pride in. And once it was released, the various people at the studios in the years to come—the grips, the technicians, the makeup and wardrobe assistants, the extras, and the other stars—would again stop to stare as she came onto the lot for a day's shoot. Never again, though, would she be viewed as simply "the Colored singer." She would now be Dorothy Dandridge, a star.

TEN

STARDOM

"*D*orothy Dandridge has put off her Fairmont booking," announced *The Hollywood Reporter* on August 27th, "and will take a rest until the first of the year while she prepares an entirely new act."

That she was preparing for the new act was true; that she was taking a much needed rest was not. There was no time for that. Dorothy was making adjustments in her schedule so that she could be available for the splashy buildup and launching of *Carmen Jones*.

She knew that once the movie was released, additional tour bookings were guaranteed. Even if returning to the nightclub scene was not her idea of career advancement, she would do it in order to keep working and remain in the public eye until the movie offers came. Otto assured her that her film career would take off and make her a kind of Black movie star unprecedented in Hollywood. But in the meantime, arrangements were made to fly Nick Perito in from New York to work with her on the act, which was to include engagements in Mexico City, San Francisco, Las Vegas, Miami, Chicago, and New York.

Perito also agreed to accompany her on an elaborate television special called "Light's Diamond Jubilee." Scheduled for October, the broadcast was to be a celebration of the 75th anniversary of Thomas Edison's invention of electric light. Perhaps not the most exciting of ideas, the production was nonetheless being produced by David O. Selznick, Hollywood's legendary producer of *Gone with the Wind*. He was lining up a host of major names. It was the kind of production too important to say no to. She had to do it, no matter how exhausted she was.

Her affair with Otto continued full steam. Contrary to what people assumed about the fleeting nature of a director/actress relationship, Preminger still courted her with gifts, champagne, and flowers. His marriage to Mary Gardner Preminger seemed to mean even less to him.

He appeared, like Phil, obsessed with every facet of her career and her life. He even wanted to dictate how she dressed. "He liked her in white and beige," Geri Branton recalled. Those colors, Preminger thought, highlighted her color. Concerned about her financial security, he talked about investments for her, primarily in New York real estate.

Preminger also held distinct opinions about her living situation. Phil Moore had persuaded her to relocate to Hollywood, seeing the move as an advancement in an age when integration was an important social goal. But, in a sense, it had taken her away from the Black community. Now Otto believed Dorothy should leave Hilldale and her cozy 1950s-style bachelor-girl pad. *Carmen Jones*, he knew, would put her in a new league. Her home should reflect that and should be in the Hollywood Hills.

The clothes and the living arrangements were one thing. But Preminger also believed she could have an even greater nightclub career. His schedule was full with the editing and scoring of *Carmen Jones* and preproduction work on a television drama as well as the film *The Man with the Golden Arm*, but he began giving suggestions on her new nightclub act. Dorothy listened enthusiastically as he elaborated on his ideas for making her act even more glamorous and elegant, more theatrical and dramatic.

It was a glorious time for her. But within the industry word became more widespread about her affair with Otto, which seemed like another tale of Beauty and the Beast. Or Beauty and the Tyrant. Whether she really loved Preminger is debatable, but Otto's drive and power excited her. Every minute with him seemed dramatic and eventful. It's doubtful if anyone ever reached her emotionally as Harold had. However, Otto was an expert at either playing or being the consummate, attentive lover. If they had a spat, he apologized. If he were going to be late for an engagement, he called. If Dorothy were dramatically expressing her plans or her dreams or her anger—about show business or race or America or anything else—Otto listened and seemed to understand.

He offered her security. He was like a rock of emotional stability, solid and unmovable. Nobody scared him. Nothing deeply troubled him. Nor did any problem ever seem insurmountable. He was able to assure her, as had Moore, that everything would work out.

Carmen Jones's premiere date was set for October 28th, 1954 at the Rivoli Theatre in New York. It was bound to draw extensive coverage by the national press. Preminger closed a deal for RCA-Victor to release an album based on the movie soundtrack. Then he received good news from the Breen office, which had approved the final cut of *Carmen Jones* without a single deletion.

Before September ended, the Black press also started its pre-*Carmen* focus on Dorothy. *Jet ran* an article titled "Hollywood's Newest Love Team"—Dandridge and Belafonte—in its September 30th issue, which commented on the importance of the film.

> For the first time in the nearly 25 years that the klieg-lighted Hollywood world of celluloid and sound tracks has attempted all-Negro films, movie makers are now casting a Negro couple as a love team that does not tax the imagination. Today, the names of handsome Harry Belafonte and luscious Dorothy Dandridge are taking their places alongside those of Clark Gable and Lana Turner, Spencer Tracy and Katharine Hepburn as screen lovers.
>
> The Belafonte-Dandridge team thus breaks the tradition begun with the first major all-Negro movie, *Hallelujah*, in 1929 in which beauteous Nina Mae McKinney began a long-suffering career of playing opposite males who were a far cry from the 'leading man' type. Through the years, Hollywood moguls who made millions coupling White stars of comparable age and equal physical attraction fostered such glaring miscasting of Negroes as the improbable May-December romance between Bill (Bojangles) Robinson and Lena Horne in *Stormy Weather*....
>
> But the instant jingle of box-office cash that greeted MGM's *Bright Road* in which handsome Harry and glamourous Dorothy had starring roles probably ended the obtuse miscasting of Negro talent and launched the young stage and night club stars on fabulous careers as Hollywood's newest love team.
>
> Shrewd, box office-conscious Otto Preminger, commenting that 'Belafonte and Dandridge go together like apple pie and ice cream,' cast the handsome couple as lovers in the soon-to-be-released *Carmen Jones*.

Jet added that plans were afoot for a film in which Belafonte and

Marlon Brando would vie for the love of Dandridge.

The September *Sepia* also published a feature on the Dandridge women titled "Family of Talent: The Dandridges, Ruby, Vivian, and Dorothy are about the busiest family in show business." Reading the article must have been difficult for Vivian. The success of Dorothy and Ruby was a concrete fact, but Vivian was discussed as being on the comeback trail. "For Vivian, who dropped out of the entertainment picture for a while," *Sepia* stated, "the demand for her unusual blues and jazz stylings has got her booked heavily for supper club engagements." But there were no such bookings that the magazine could actually report on. The truth was that with but four club engagements in 1954—one in Long Beach, California; another in El Monte, California; a third in Portland, Oregon; and the fourth in Butte, Montana—Vivian's singing career looked as if it was headed nowhere. She didn't even seem to do much work as a hairdresser now. This may have marked the beginning of one of the most painful periods of Vivian Dandridge's life.

Dorothy also was photographed by Allan Grant and then Philippe Halsman for a possible spread on the movie in *Life* magazine. Halsman had already photographed seventy covers for *Life* as well as portraits of Elizabeth Taylor and Marilyn Monroe.

This was not Dorothy's first meeting with Halsman. He photographed the sensual, dreamy shot of her for *Esquire* when the magazine selected her as Lady Fair for June 1954. For the *Life* pictures, Halsman wanted her dressed as Carmen. Some shots were taken of her in the black blouse and red skirt. Others were of her in the white gown and fur stole she wore at the movie's climax.

Halsman also photographed Dandridge for an *Ebony* spread on the "Five Most Beautiful Negro Women in the World," which was to run in the January, 1955 issue. Selected with Dorothy were Lena Horne, Joyce Bryant, Hilda Simms, and Eartha Kitt. While photographing her for *Ebony*, Halsman grew impatient with Dorothy's nervousness. So tense and extremely self conscious did he find her that he publicly called the shoot one of his most difficult assignments. "Besides beauty and elegance, Dorothy has an unusual intelligence," he said. "Intelligence is an admirable quality but in a studio it can be a hindrance. It is hard to reach the real Dandridge hiding behind the iron curtain of her intelligence."

Part of Dorothy's unease with Halsman may have sprung from an incident around this time with a world-famous photographer. Dorothy had wisely arrived at the studio for the shoot with a female friend. Once Dorothy was made up and dressed, though, her friend had left the studio, waiting outside to allow the photographer and Dorothy to work in privacy.

After awhile, the friend saw Dorothy rush from the studio. She said she wanted to leave immediately. Then the photographer, looking agitated and annoyed, came to the door. Dorothy glanced at him but said nothing, as she ran out of the building with her friend. Angry and shaken, she explained to her friend that during the shoot, it occurred to her that the way in which the photographer was giving her directions for various poses was a bit strange. He had so much equipment around him that she couldn't quite see him at first, but she saw enough to realize that this world-famous photographer was masturbating. She quickly began to gather her belongings. He tried stopping her, but she left the studio telling him the shoot was over. It was a terrible experience for her and a classic example of the downside of being a woman in the business.

Before *Carmen Jones*'s release, Dorothy had anxiety attacks, fearing that the film—and her performance in particular—might be a disaster. Her fears weren't helped any when she invited a group of friends, some new, many old, to a Fox special screening of *Carmen Jones*. By the time she arrived back at her apartment on Hilldale with a smaller group, she became upset because no one expressed much excitement about the film. She reflected on the reactions, and finally concluded that the lethargic response grew out of something she should be familiar with: movieland envy and jealousy. For those at the screening, Dorothy had in fact been too good.

On Sunday, October 24, 1954, Dorothy made a live appearance on David O. Selznick's two-hour long "Light's Diamond Jubilee" extravaganza. Unable to produce anything on a small scale, Selznick had lined up impressive talents that included Lauren Bacall, Kim Novak, Eddie Fisher, Helen Hayes, Judith Anderson, David Niven, Walter Brennan, Brandon de Wilde, new comic George Gobel, and Joseph Cotton. Part of the program featured filmed dramatic sequences by such Hollywood directors as King Vidor, William Wellman, and Norman Taurog. The sketches were written by such celebrated writers as John Steinbeck, Irwin Shaw, and Max Schulman. Also making an appearance was President Dwight David Eisenhower. Dorothy was the only Black American performer in the production.

For Selznick, the evening proved to be a bomb. "Not in a month of spectaculars will you come across the kind of marquee values as were superimposed over this $1,000,000 (and plus) jumbo," wrote *Variety*. "More's the pity, then, that it had to wind up largely as a glorified paean of faith in the American individual suggestive of 'Voice of America' programming. And it seemed to go on interminably."

The program, however, worked splendidly to Dorothy's advantage. Her two numbers "You Do Something to Me" and "London Town" were well-received by the critics. The program also, thanks to Selznick's promotional skills, aired on all three major networks, as well as the fourth network of the time—the Dumont station. In the end, Dorothy was seen by an estimated 60 to 70 million people. For Fox, her appearance marked an ideal way to launch the national promotion of *Carmen Jones*.

The next day, on October 25th, the November 1, 1954 issue of *Life* hit the newsstands. On its cover was Philippe Halsman's photograph of Dorothy, dressed as Carmen in red skirt and black blouse, with hooped earrings, a red rose pinned in her hair, and her hands dramatically posed. She almost seemed to spring alive from the pages.

"Of all the divas of grand opera—from Emma Calve of the 90s to Rise Stevens—who have decorated the title role of Carmen and have in turn been made famous by it," wrote *Life*, "none was ever so decorative or will reach nationwide fame so quickly as the sultry young lady at right and on *Life*'s cover this week. She is Dorothy Dandridge, star of 20th Century-Fox's exciting new musical drama *Carmen Jones*."

Hollywood was abuzz. In the movie capital, and in the mythology of Hollywood, no magazine cover was so coveted or considered so great a status symbol as *Life*'s. Dorothy Dandridge at that very moment achieved true movie star/goddess status. Her face was seen by every film, television, and music executive in the entertainment business. It was a perfect launching for a new-style icon. Her achievement was all the greater because she was the first African American woman to appear on its cover. Yet, in the minds of the executives, the cover lifted her out of the "Black woman" category. The *Life* cover also brought her to the public's attention in a broader, more sweeping, and defined way. Her cover portrait sat in living rooms throughout America: the East, the North, the West, and that area of the country that so concerned the film industry, the South. Jackie Robinson had graced *Life*'s cover in 1950. Their portraits indicated that their achievements had made them both a significant part of the nation's cultural life; the covers, a testament to them as cultural pioneers, charting new territory within the popular imagination of the average citizen. The *Life* cover also alerted the rest of the press in America. In the cities she traveled to for club engagements, the local reporters and photographers would be eager to see the cover girl of this wholly American publication. So propitious an occasion was the *Life* cover that a crew from *Movietone News* joined Dorothy and Otto in *Life*'s offices to record the event. A jubilant Dorothy, dressed in pearls and a dark dress with a hat that wrapped around her face and tied at the neck, was seen smiling with Otto and a *Life* executive as she held a copy of the magazine. Reminding her that this was only the beginning, Otto beamed and glowed at the precedent-breaking success of *his* creation.

After *Life* appeared, Dorothy arrived in New York to begin the promotion for *Carmen Jones*. All was well with her except for one thing: the portrait Fox was using in the ad campaign for the film. It was the drawing of her in the black blouse with red skirt, with hands on hips and head tossed back. She thought the image was too sexual.

Some of the ad copy was too. It played on Carmen's image of the Black woman as an alluring "primitive" exotic. "The name Carmen will sing in your brain and the songs pound in your heart," read one advertisement. "That man crazy, dazzle dancing gal—sultry and savage—incendiary—whirling through a jungle world in Bizet's pulsing beat and blood surging musical!"

All of this struck Dandridge as being the complete antithesis of what her Carmen was about. In some scenes, she indeed had hands on hips. But that was always meant as a sign of Carmen's independent spirit and control.

Dorothy asked Vivian to accompany her on the New York trip. It would give the sisters a chance to spend time together. Dorothy checked into the Warwick Hotel, the New York establishment she always preferred. "She was always nervous about how she might be treated at hotels and restaurants," said Vivian. Even now with a hit movie about to be released, with a cover portrait on *Life*, with sensational nightclub engagements around the country, she remained guarded and jittery, unsure if she risked the embarrassment of being turned away at an establishment.

As preparations were being made at the Rivoli Theatre for the splashy premiere, Dorothy and Vivian walked down to the theatre arm-in-arm and watched workman put up a large placard of Dorothy. Vivian burst into tears. Dorothy laughed loudly and hugged her sister. "Oh, Vivi!."

"I was crying and she *loved* it," said Vivian. "She was so dramatic." Later back at the hotel, "She told *everybody*! She'd pick up the phone and say, 'You know Vivi was crying when she saw my body going up in front of the theatre.'"

On October 26, 1954, she attended a reception, hosted by actress/singer Juanita Hall, and given in her honor by the *Pittsburgh Courier* and the National Negro Network at the Hotel Theresa in Harlem. Arriving at the event, she was taken aback by the large crowd. Five hundred invitations had been sent. Over fifteen hundred people turned up. And every one of them wanted to get a look at Dorothy Dandridge in person.

Also honored with Dorothy were Pearl Bailey and Otto. Animated as ever, Bailey no doubt didn't relish the idea of sharing the spotlight with Dorothy again, but she was all smiles at the gala.

Then came the opening itself on October 28th. First was a dinner, with Dorothy as guest of honor, hosted by the National Urban League. Proceeds from the benefit premiere of *Carmen Jones* would also go to the organization. On hand at the Rivoli premiere was a host of glittering stars and personalities, including Count Basie and his wife, Sammy Davis Jr., Olga James and her manager Abe Saperstein, Diahann Carroll, Joe Adams, Pearl Bailey, Oscar Hammerstein II and his wife, crooner Johnny Ray, singer Billy Daniels, producer Billy Rose, radio talk show personalities Jinx Falkenburg and husband Tex McCrary, and Lena Horne and husband Lennie Hayton.

Each female guest received a red rose—a dark crimson color "never previously seen," so the press releases said, and developed by the I. W. Gianchi Greenhouses. Of course, Otto was there too. Vivian entered the theatre early with a group of friends. Plans to light flares atop the Rivoli Theatre were dropped for fear of a fire. Instead, a battery of specially designed red kleig lights—the color to symbolize Carmen's rose—illuminated the sky. Airports, police stations, and firehouses were alerted not to be alarmed by the brilliant red.

Amid the lights and the crowd, Dorothy arrived at the theatre alone and was surrounded by a flock of photographers. If ever Dorothy looked happy, it was this night. Afterwards, she appeared on "The Tonight Show," then hosted by Steve Allen and at a party where Dorothy and Preminger, mindful of the gossips and the New York press, were careful not to appear too chummy.

The next morning, Dorothy awoke to dazzling reviews. "Crowded with fiery music and blazing passion! Dorothy Dandridge is a bewitcher!" proclaimed columnist Walter Winchell. In The *New*

York Post, Archer Winston, who had first written about her in *Sun Valley Serenade* and *Four Shall Die*, exclaimed that she "comes close to the edge of greatness." *The New York Herald Tribune*'s critic Otis Guernsey called hers "an incomparably seductive performance."

Newsweek hailed her as "an incandescent Carmen, devilishly willful and feline. She is one of the outstanding dramatic actresses of the screen." At the center of the film, *Time* saw only Dorothy, who "holds the eye—like a match burning steadily in a tornado. Actress Dandridge employs to a perfection the method of the coquette: by never giving more than she has to, she hints that she has more than she has given—and sometimes even more than she really has to give."

Time's critic also saw *Carmen Jones* as a rallying call for future Negro pictures. Wrote the critic:

> The rattle of the cash register does not often serve as the drum roll of social progress. With this picture it may. Otto Preminger's Hollywood version of Billy Rose's Broadway version of Georges Bizet's grand opera seems sure to be a big hit. It also seems likely that the picture will somewhat widen the gates of opportunity for Negro entertainers in Hollywood. For in this picture the actors present themselves not merely as racial phenomena but as individuals, and they put across a Carmen that may blister the rear walls of many a movie house.

Later, following *Carmen Jones*'s November 1st opening in Los Angeles, the West Coast critics also praised her. The *Los Angeles Mirror*'s Dick Williams, who had written the pivotal review of her performance at Café Gala, now took great satisfaction in seeing her promise fulfilled. He wrote "there never has been as sexy and beautiful a Carmen as Dorothy Dandridge. She makes the screen seethe." *The Hollywood Reporter* gave a six-word review of her performance: "Dorothy Dandridge in *Carmen Jones*...WOW!"

Joining the praises was columnist and one-time foe Hedda Hopper. "It's a terrific picture!" she exclaimed. "Hope you won't repeat my experience when you see *Carmen Jones*. I got so excited I burned a big hole in the front of my dress. Yes the film is that hot." Elizabeth Taylor, who also fell into disfavor with Hopper and found herself criticized at every turn by the gossip columnist, once said that there is no deodorant like success. It was the one thing the movie capital really respected. Attitudes changed overnight with a triumph.

Now Dorothy could bask in the satisfaction that her triumph in *Carmen Jones* had made even Hopper at least publicly regard her in a new light.

Mindful of industry protocol, Dorothy sent the gossip columnist a hand-written message:

Dear Miss Hopper—

Just a note to say thank you so very much for the nice things you have said about me. It means a lot, and I am most grateful.

Sincerely,
Dorothy Dandridge

Throughout the country, the African American press, which had long followed Dorothy's career, praised both Dandridge and the film. "*Carmen Jones* is simply out of this world!" *The New York Amsterdam News* proclaimed. *The Los Angeles Sentinel*'s theatre editor Hazel Lamarre wrote that the production contained "exciting dramatic scenes, good acting and singing." Lamarre ended the review stating that the "show is Dorothy Dandridge's, she is truly the star."

Other African American reviewers were equally as excited. "I am so prejudiced in favor of Dorothy Dandridge that I have lost perspective and I'm glad," George F. Brown wrote in *The Pittsburgh Courier*. "*Carmen Jones* requires true acting talent. Dandridge proved that she had it when the rushes of the picture were shown. If this lovely doesn't reach the status of Lena Horne in the movies, or better still, eclipse gorgeous Lena (who seems to be happy earning ten grand a week and up in supper clubs), I will eat two porterhouse steaks on Broadway in broad daylight."

The Pittsburgh Courier also called the film "a wonderful one-year milestone for CinemaScope, and with its success hopes must rise that others will follow where Otto Preminger has had the courage to lead." Perhaps the world of moviemaking itself would be turned inside out, so the paper hoped. "Another rumor has certain Italian movie directors interested in making an all- Negro picture. A silver screen version of *Porgy and Bess* continues to be a topic of conversation. And who knows, maybe somebody'll finally get around to writing an acceptable 'original' for the movie cameras wherein Negro artists will get an opportunity to shine. At any rate, '55 promises to be a burning year for the movies and CinemaScope and the Negro, and *Carmen Jones* will have started the fire."

There were some dissenting critical voices, including James Baldwin, who in *Commentary* called the film a "stifling" production in which "Negro speech is parodied out of its charm" and which represented a "total divorce from anything suggestive of the realities of Negro life." But he did praise Pearl Bailey. In *The New York Times*, Bosley Crowther criticized Preminger's production for failing to comprehend "the depth of the hero's inevitable suffering or the nature of the woman who leads him on." He also stated, "What we can't understand is why a musical about American Negroes has to have a nineteenth century French opera score. Is this the best that could be found for Negro talents? Has anybody thought recently of *Porgy and Bess?*"

Of all the reviews, however, few could have touched Dorothy more than the one that appeared in *the California Eagle*.

> The exciting movie of *Carmen Jones* finally opened its L.A. run—Twentieth Century Fox really has something this time, a gigantic improvement over their last attempt with an-all Negro cast (*Stormy Weather*). This time they use the talent of sensitive Actor-Director Otto Preminger to put this brilliant cast through its paces...It is apparent that a lot of work and study has gone into her [Dandridge] version of Carmen, and she apparently liked and sympathized with the gal and consequently makes you do likewise—Carmen is a tramp, but with such dignity that you have to respect her right to the end. Certainly it was one of the biggest thrills I've experienced viewing a movie.

The reviewer was Geri Nicholas, now identified as the "ex-wife of Fayard Nicholas."

A congratulatory letter also came later from Berle Adams at MCA. "I guess I get a bigger boot out of your success than most people would," he wrote. "I can well remember the fears and frustrations that you once had. After this performance even Dorothy Dandridge should be convinced that what we have all known all the time will be—that Dorothy Dandridge is destined to be one of the great stars in our industry."

The glowing notices continued for months. Audiences and critics alike seemed unable to stop talking about Dorothy's performance.

But in Los Angeles, no one beamed and basked in the glory of

Carmen Jones more than Ruby, who showed up at a private screening. Laughing loudly, chatting, waving to friends, and energetically accepting congratulations for her daughter's success, Ruby let everyone know that she always knew her "baby" had the stuff of stardom. Observers that evening whispered comments to one another not only about Ruby's behavior—even more outgoing than usual, and that was saying a lot—but also about her companion. The Black press even felt compelled to report on Ruby's appearance.

"Like the 'Queen Mother' visiting here from England, Ruby Dandridge, charming mother of screen star Dorothy, attracted as much attention here as did her daughter in New York," wrote the correspondent for *The Chicago Defender*. "Mrs. Dandridge and her Caucasian friend and business associate, Dorothy Foster, was accompanied to the private showing by Harry Levette."

Levette, of course, was Ruby's "beard" that evening, a decoy escort. By now, Black Hollywood knew that Ruby's life had changed. So, too, had her lover.

Three days after the New York opening of *Carmen Jones*, on Sunday, October 31st, Dorothy made an appearance on Ed Sullivan's "Toast of the Town." Pearl Bailey had performed on the program the week before. Dorothy, rather than perform, would be shown in a clip from *Carmen Jones* that would highlight her dramatically. Then from the stage, Sullivan, as he often did with major stars who presumably just happened to be in the theatre during the broadcast, would introduce a radiant Dorothy who sat in the audience. It was an indication of her new star status. She was being asked only to be Dorothy Dandridge. It was also a shrewd piece of promotion. Now for the second week in a row, she was seen by a national television audience of millions. Also performing on the show that evening was Dorothy's friend Nat 'King' Cole.

While in New York, Dorothy received an offer to appear at the Waldorf Astoria's Empire Room. The French chanteuse, Patachou, who had been set to open in early November, had taken ill in France. The hotel besieged MCA with panicky requests that Dorothy step in as a last minute substitute. Dorothy knew this was an opportunity of a lifetime. The Empire Room had never in its seemingly illustrious history had a Negro performer. She agreed to perform and immediately began rehearsals, working with an arranger and also selecting a new collection of gowns.

But the strain and pressure proved too great. So, too, did her insecurities. Believing it was too important—and socially significant—a booking to go into without the most thorough of preparations, she wanted at least three to four weeks to break in a new act. She also balked at the idea that she was being booked at the Waldorf only as a substitute and only at the last minute. She believed that the hotel assumed she should be grateful that it was opening its doors to her. Finally, she informed the Waldorf that she couldn't do the engagement after all.

The Empire Room was so eager to have her perform, though, that its management said it was willing to wait; to book her at *her* schedule. Still, she hesitated to make a commitment. Negotiations, however, began with MCA, and in late November, the Waldorf announced that Dandridge would make her debut at the hotel in April for seven weeks. She would be paid $3,500 a week plus fifty percent of all supper covers in excess of $2,500 a week. MCA considered the booking a major coup for Dorothy.

With the attention and her new level of stardom, Dorothy now discovered that the press asked more personal questions. In the past, reporters, mainly for the Black publications like *Ebony* and *Our World*, had enthusiastically charted her rise to prominence without probing deeply into her personal affairs. Now the reporters and interviewers wanted more details. True movie stardom demanded a story, some type of personal drama on which to peg the myth or the legend. Some tale of struggle. Or adversity. Something that cast the star in a heroic or larger-than-life light.

It was difficult for Dorothy to open up. Usually, she stressed her career goals to reporters. "If *Carmen* succeeds in really establishing me," she explained to *The New York Times*, "perhaps I can build up the kind of balanced career I've always longed for—a few pictures a year, recordings, and some sort of permanent social life there at home."

Inasmuch as Dorothy tried to keep the journalists focused on her career, the press she received, in some ways, uncovered the emptiness she felt at the core of her personal life. So hard had she been working the past few years that she hadn't had time to consider the loneliness she felt. Those the gods bless, they also curse.

"Before you can get seriously interested in anyone," she explained to *The New York Post*'s interviewer Nancy Steele, "you have to have a chance to share things with him, to really get to know him. When you're on the road as much as I have been, there's no opportunity. You meet people, you go out occasionally, you have fun—but you don't have time to really get acquainted before you're off to your next engagement."

"The kind of man I'd like or who would like me seriously," she added, "would never be the one who sends a note backstage saying he'd like to take me out. When I get one of those notes, I always think, 'This man has dated or tried to date every entertainer who ever came to town.' You have to decline that kind of invitation or you demean yourself professionally."

In the *Post* article, she also discussed her career. "I don't want to be typed," she said. "People who've seen me as Carmen have suggested that I should do *Porgy and Bess,* but I don't think that's for me now. People would say 'um-m-m, this is all this girl can do.' And I know I can play other parts."

In an unusual kind of moment for Dorothy, she revealed a motivating factor behind her career. "I think it was really the heartache over my child and the failure of my marriage that forced me to make a success of my career," she said. "I had to keep busy. I threw myself into my work. It's wonderful therapy. You don't have time to feel sorry for yourself."

Always everything seemed to come back to Lynn and Harold.

She also spoke to the *Post*'s interviewer Steele about race. "When you reach a certain position, people accept you more. And there are places where you are acclaimed as a performer, yet you know the doors would be shut if you walked in as plain Mrs. Sally Smith." She added that prejudice saddened her; it was "such a waste. It makes you logy and half-alive. It gives you nothing. It takes away. And it is superficial, like so many of our reactions today." She might easily have skirted the race issue by saying America was progressing, that inequities between the races were being addressed; but for a woman who still worried about the reactions when she signed the register at a hotel anywhere in America, she had to speak the truth as she saw it.

The *Post* interview ended with a Dandridge comment on happiness. "What makes you really happy is when you love and give and understand, when you look at beauty and really see it," she said. "We are so busy watching the road under our feet we forget to look up at the beauty all around us."

She grew more relaxed with the press and sometimes appeared unable to *not* talk about Lynn, race, or romance. The conversation—with Mr. and Mrs. John Q. Public of the time—seemed cathartic and therapeutic.

She explained to Sidney Fields of the *New York Daily Mirror* that Lynn "was injured at birth, and the speech centers of her brain were damaged. Otherwise she's normal and a very beautiful child." When asked if there was any hope for Lynn, Dorothy responded, "We never stop hoping, but the doctors know and they say the damage to her brain is beyond repair." The interviewer noted that Dandridge paused, perhaps to keep her emotions in check, before she added, "How terrible it is never to be able to really speak to your own child."

Dandridge also told the reporter that during the filming of *Carmen Jones*, she would rush home at the end of the day's work to cook dinner for Lynn and the woman who took care of her. Whether the interviewer misunderstood something Dorothy had said or whether Dandridge indeed did make such a statement, it was, of course, not true.

Nonetheless, the *Mirror*'s interviewer saw the poignancy in Dandridge when she explained the line of communication she sought to establish between herself and her audience. "I have something I want to do for you," was how she expressed her feelings about performing. "Please let me." Fields commented that Dandridge was "articulate as well as lovely. And strange that an actress, still a struggling actress, would say things that bite your thoughts."

Carmen Jones did well at the box-office, too, grossing almost $60,000 in its first week in New York. The next week it grossed $47,000. Once it opened in Los Angeles, the film took in $38,500 the first week, followed by $28,400 the second.

"*Carmen Jones* was among the few of my pictures that succeeded with both the critics and the public," said Preminger. "Its triumph was proof of what I had tried to explain first to Krim and Benjamin and then to other doubting executives like Moscowitz. There are no rules like 'pictures with black actors won't make money.' Just because black films hadn't made money in the past it didn't mean that they would not in the future. A good story is a good story, even if a similar one failed in the past."

Otto, of course, wanted to continue working with Dorothy. She in turn attempted to find her own projects, hoping for studio financing. On November 3rd, Hedda Hopper reported that Preminger planned to film a modern version of *The Barber of Seville* with Dorothy and Belafonte. Dorothy and her manager also toyed with the idea of producing a musical version of *Scarlet Sister Mary* for Dorothy's own production company.

Preminger was jubilant that his faith in her had proven justified.

She would be the great star he had predicted. He told her now they must chart her course and make all the right moves to insure that her stardom took full root. Their promotion work for the movie continued. Both attended the film's openings in various cities. Preminger also considered taking *Carmen Jones* in the spring to the Cannes Film Festival in France. Otto also made another prediction: that Dorothy would win an Oscar nomination.

Vivian also felt that way. "While she was doing *Carmen Jones*," said Vivian, "I had a dream that she would be nominated for an Academy Award. It was so ridiculous because no Black person [in a leading role] at that time had been nominated. I used to have dreams. And something would happen behind them."

She told Dorothy about the dream, but added, "Don't tell anybody. They'll think I'm crazy."

"You are crazy!" said Dorothy.

But the Oscar talk sprang up within the movie colony. The Black newspaper *The Los Angeles Sentinel* ran an article on November 25th with the headline "Dorothy Dandridge May Get Academy Award Nomination," which reported on the industry buzz and the support Dorothy was getting from key press figures. Among those urging that Dorothy be nominated were gossip columnists Louella Parsons, Sheilah Graham, and—a woman who seemed to want to be Dorothy's new chum—Hedda Hopper.

She was now Black Hollywood's greatest symbol. No African American woman in the history of films, not even Hattie McDaniel and Lena Horne, had garnered such attention. She marked a bridge between two generations of African Americans who had been working in films.

Here was a young woman known by all of old Black Hollywood, the established Black entertainment world of the pre-World War II era. Duke Ellington, Louis Armstrong, Louise Beavers, Mantan Moreland, Ethel Waters, Bill 'Bojangles' Robinson, Count Basie, Eddie 'Rochester' Anderson, Madame Sul-Te-Wan, Slappy White, Cab Calloway, all had watched Dorothy from the time she was a girl. They had seen her mature and develop, had sometimes worked with her, had observed her study, struggle, and progress, had been aware of her extraordinary perseverance and drive. She was one of theirs. In a sense, she validated some of their efforts in films, the idea that the right role could come, that a statement could be made in Hollywood motion pictures, that dignity, style, and class could be brought to mainstream movies by a Black performer in a serious role.

But she was also an integral part of the new postwar generation of African Americans who worked in Hollywood: James Edwards, Bob Davis, Sidney Poitier, Harry Belafonte, Nat 'King' Cole, Maidie Norman, Ruby Dee, Mildred Joanne Smith, and Diahann Carroll. She was one of theirs, too; again the idea being that films might finally be opening up. For old Black Hollywood and the emerging new Black Hollywood, Dorothy had become the jewel in its crown, its proudest achievement.

Her triumph couldn't have come at a more socially significant time. 1954 was the year of the Supreme Court's groundbreaking decision in the case of *Brown vs Board of Education* that segregation in public schools was unconstitutional. Afterwards, America's educational institutions underwent sweeping changes as school desegregation in such states as Alabama and Arkansas made headlines throughout America. One year later, seamstress Rosa Parks refused to take a seat at the back of the bus in Montgomery, Alabama. There ensued the Montgomery bus boycotts, led by a young minister, Dr. Martin Luther King Jr. He was part of a new crop of African American leaders coming to national prominence that included Thurgood Marshall and Medgar Evers. Following Montgomery, other boycotts, sit-ins, demonstrations, and protests began to spring up. America stood on the brink of extraordinary social change now as the civil rights movement was galvanizing itself to have a startling impact on American society.

Now as Black America stood on the eve of its bright new day of an integrated and open society, Dorothy Dandridge assumed her place with Jackie Robinson as a symbol for the future. Her presence indicated that now dramatic mainstream motion pictures *had* to make place for a remarkable African American dramatic actress. The movies, like the rest of American life and culture, had to fully integrate themselves.

Within Black America, there was tremendous excitement and optimism about Dorothy. Quite simply, said actress Nichelle Nichols, "She was our queen."

In the December issue of *Cosmopolitan* magazine, Hollywood power broker Louella Parsons wrote a feature titled "Dorothy Dandridge Stars in a Great New Movie." Parsons's tribute was one more sign of Dandridge's arrival into the upper ranks of movie stardom.

But while *Cosmopolitan, Life,* and *Look*, all major mainstream publications that often covered show business, acknowledged Dorothy's presence on the entertainment scene, the movie magazines like *Photoplay, Modern Screen,* and *Motion Picture* chose not to do features on her. *Photoplay* reviewed *Carmen Jones* and also included Dandridge and Belafonte in its list to poll America's favorite stars, but there were no glamorous photo layouts. No visits to the star's home. No features detailing the star's love life. No pieces that traced the arc of the star's climb to fame. Significantly, these publications went into the homes of young moviegoers around America, mostly women at the time. That may have been an early sign that the vast moviegoing public was not really ready for a Black movie star. Or so the industry believed.

Upon Dorothy's return to Los Angeles, requests rolled in for appearances at social affairs and benefits. In December, she agreed to be one of the sponsors of the National Urban League's annual Winter Ball, which was held at the Deauville Club in Santa Monica. Its theme was a "Salute to the Supreme Court." It was a glamorous evening with the movers and shakers of both the Black and White communities in Los Angeles. Other committee sponsors included Los Angeles's former Mayor Fletcher Bowron; Mrs. Fleur Cowles, the associate editor of *Look* magazine; MGM chief Dore Schary; and Samuel and Frances Goldwyn. Goldwyn no doubt took one look at her this evening and knew someday she would be his Bess in a production of *Porgy and Bess.*

The evening also marked the start of Dorothy's involvement with the Urban League. Shortly afterwards she accepted the League's National Chairmanship in a funding campaign for a new headquarters building for the civil rights organization.

Now Dorothy socialized with Samuel and Frances Goldwyn or spent more time with Gary and Rocky Cooper. She operated in a more rarefied Hollywood atmosphere; a notch above even the glamorous and the beautiful set. Now she floated among some of the industry's megapowers. Of course, in this forward-looking, integrationist-oriented civil rights era, a Black entertainer was expected to aspire to such upward social mobility. Such doors had been shut for so long. Now that they opened, the performer was expected to march right through. Dorothy did.

It was becoming increasingly harder for her to balance profession-al demands and personal desires, though. Black Hollywood was her base, but she was being pulled away from it by her need to hobnob with the White power brokers. She was moving so fast that there was no time to deliberate over the situation—the fact that she was being absorbed more and more into a White world and the emotional toll she might have to pay in doing so.

Other changes were coming about. Seeing her face magnified thousands of times on the screen, travelling through the nation's air-ports where she was recognized and stared at, being courted by the press, being pursued for social engagements and benefits, finding her-self catered to and openly adored, Dorothy inevitably couldn't contin-ue her life as before; couldn't escape being affected by her fame; and couldn't help but look at herself differently.

Geri noticed that Dorothy was becoming *very grand*. Her stan-dard pose now was with her back held ramrod straight and her head arched high with the chin lifted, her face assuming an imperial expres-sion of a cool and even disdainful distance, like that of royalty, albeit it movieland or otherwise. Even when she spoke, she sounded like a woman who felt above it all. Behind her back, Joel Fluellen sometimes referred to her as The Queen.

Sometimes Dorothy would stop in front of a mirror. Gazing at her reflection, she would ask whomever was nearby, "Do you like what you see?" Then she would answer herself, "I do." She would suck in her cheeks and hold her head higher while inspecting the image in the mirror more closely. "Of course," she would say, "I could change this. And this. But then... why?"

In the past, she had been naturally aloof; a defense mechanism against a world she feared; she withdrew, as Vivian understood, to insulate and protect herself, mainly from people. But now her haugh-tiness, perhaps partly just her pride in finally having risen above so much that had depressed her, and perhaps still a protective shield from the world, was interpreted by many as being pure arrogance. Yet it was never really arrogance at all.

Often she played with the perks and privileges of stardom. Charlotte Sullivan, the sister of Maria Cole, recalled an evening when she, Dorothy, and June Eckstine went to a restaurant for dinner. The three were about to enter without any to-do when Dorothy suddenly stopped, according to Sullivan. She told the two to go in and sit. Then she went back out. "Before I knew it," recalled Sullivan, "I look up and Dottie was draped in the doorway making an entrance." Her head lifted dramatically high, she was every bit the movie star as she joined Sullivan and Eckstine at their table. Dorothy told her friends, "Well, you know, what it is being a star!" Then she broke into laughter. Their service that night was excellent.

Her self-absorption and constant need for attention grew and became all-consuming. "She'd call me," said Geri. "She stayed on the phone like two or three hours. That was too much time being taken from my children. But you couldn't get her off the phone. And the entire conversation was a very intellectual discussion about her sessions with the psychiatrist. You [could] say, 'Dottie, I broke my toe.' And she'd say, 'Oh, that's nothing. Forget that. I broke my fingernail.' And then she'd go on to all the things that had happened to *her*. The greatest tragedy ever in the world. *Her* tragedy. She could never ever deeply understand somebody else's tragedy. She did. But she didn't. The conversation had to be around her tragedy. It would always come back to her. So you were becoming a listener totally. And yet she was a giver of things. She'd just take the coat off her back and give it to you. But she couldn't really give herself. And that's not unforgivable. She was in a fantasy world."

When Dorothy became too grand, Geri would simply tell her, "Now sit your black behind down and stop it!"

Arching her shoulders and lifting the head even higher, Dorothy would say, "*Tan*. Teasing tan, darling!" Usually, that was followed by laughter between the two women. Geri knew that Dottie had worked so hard, so long over the years that now if being grand brought her pleasure, she deserved it.

Dorothy began her search for a new home that would reflect her new status. She was still hesitant about moving out fully on her own, though. Once she considered buying a house in the hills on Mulholland Drive. Next door to it was another home for sale, which she urged Geri to buy. But Geri had no desire to change residences. Dorothy ended up not buying the home.

A variety of other people came into her life. They clamored to reach Dorothy, to invite her out, to ask her opinion, to flatter and cajole her, to tell her simply how marvelous she was, to do anything simply to be in her presence. Some begged for an invitation to a big event. Some asked for a loan. Others implored her to intercede with a producer or a director about a part for them.

"Dottie always did whatever she could," said Geri Branton. "Then if they didn't get a part, they felt it was her fault."

Amid all these people—the phone calls and visits from agents, the press, the friends and acquaintances—there remained Vivian. The two sisters had united in Dorothy's pursuit of Carmen and afterwards enjoyed the flush of her success. But the familiar distance between them returned as Vivian found it hard to cope with Dorothy's rising star status.

"Naturally, there were people that started swooping in. You see the star is always the center. Everyone wants to get close to that center. And if you're there, closer, you have to be moved," Vivian said. Daily, she saw "the hangers-on" trying to push her aside and away from her sister.

"These were people who before this great success didn't really voice any opinion about her career," said Vivian.

"I don't know how to handle it when so many people are always on my back for money," an exasperated Dorothy told Vivian one evening. "They get angry."

"Well, if it's a friend, you want to help," Vivian told her. "But there are people that are just trying to use you. Send them to Earl Mills. Let him deal with them. Then you don't have to go through the abuse."

But Vivian found it hard to reach her sister. Becoming even more susceptible to the unending flow of attention, Dorothy appeared to need even more reassurance, even more praise and adulation.

"She really started to listen to some of these people," Vivian said. "And they really didn't have her interests at heart. I think she didn't hear anything I said any more. But with all these people flattering and catering and being phony, she bought it."

"She would choose the wrong people who would do her in. Or do something that would be against her. Or put her in a difficult position or whatever," Dorothy Nicholas Morrow said. "Because you're always surrounded by people who want to take advantage of you, unfortunately. And you've got to know when to back away and when to accept."

"All kinds of people got in to her," said Vivian. "I don't think maybe they did it on purpose to try to destroy her. But that's what was happening. I could see it."

"They would do her in every single time," said Geri.

The year 1955 opened with more media coverage. *The Sunday New York News* magazine *Coloroto* featured Dorothy on its cover in late January. That same month *Ebony* ran its "Five Most Beautiful Negro Women in the World" photo layout. Then while working with Nick Perito on material for her new act, word came on February 2nd that the *New York Herald Tribune's* critic Otis Guernsey named her the finest dramatic actress of 1954. But the accolades didn't stop there. The Hollywood Foreign Correspondents Association nominated her for their Golden Globe Award as Best Actress in a Musical. In a poll taken by the Hollywood trade publication *Film Daily*, she was selected as one of "Filmdom's Famous Five" for 1954. Talk about an Oscar nomination continued and by now, she had begun to believe, like Otto, that it could happen.

She also entered into negotiations for a three-picture contract with Twentieth Century Fox. Darryl F. Zanuck took a special interest in her career and discussed her future with Preminger. He believed that Dorothy could be a major movie star. Of course, Otto prided himself on having known that all along.

Meeting with Zanuck at Fox, Dorothy walked through the corridors of Hollywood power that few Black performers had ever seen. Zanuck was gracious and charming, even solicitous as he explained that he did not intend to handle her like past Negro stars. He believed she could be cast in any type of role. She could portray a Brazilian, a Spaniard, a Mexican, an Italian. Of course, what Zanuck really meant was that Dorothy could play any type of ethnic role.

Yet Zanuck saw her, as did Preminger, as being able to transcend the limited roles offered to Black performers. In the past, White women had played these ethnic types—the gypsies, the "half-breeds," the Asians, the pretty Native American squaws, and, in movies such as *Pinky* and *Show Boat*, the tragic mulattoes. Zanuck considered it a step forward for Dorothy to play such roles. That in itself was perhaps fine. But by considering her mainly for non-Black ethnic roles, Zanuck, and the industry in general, paradoxically seemed to be denying her a place as a contemporary Black woman in cinema. The prevailing idea was that Dorothy Dandridge could star in movies but in no way was Hollywood ready to star her in films in which a Black woman was the central character.

This was a new professional dilemma that she was aware she would have to cope with. The chance to play ethnic types was unprecedented for an African American film actress. Light-skinned African American actor Frank Silvera was able to cross ethnic lines, successfully playing a variety of supporting roles in films. But Silvera was an exception. In general, such an idea didn't take hold.

During Dorothy's negotiations with Fox, Preminger insisted that she play hardball; she should ask for more money than Zanuck intended to offer. Knowing and understanding Hollywood culture and power struggles, Preminger stressed that she must, in all ways, behave like a star. Her performance in *Carmen Jones* as well as her success in the clubs and the media attraction all validated her star status; now star behavior would be expected from her.

She had grown up in the industry and understood the facts of life in Hollywood in her own right. But she listened. Otto became the dominant force and influence on her career. "When Preminger came in, Earl was kicked out. Totally!" said Geri Branton. "Preminger took over her career." Still devoted, Mills no doubt felt sidelined by Otto, yet another man who drew her attention away from him.

"She appreciated [Earl] for what he did," said Geri Branton. "And he did many things for her. He was a little lapdog. He was going with her when she had no escort to premieres. He really tried to help her in her career." But, added Geri, Dorothy deeply "resented his having that kind of romantic feeling for her."

"Earl was a very nice man," said Perito. "He was almost like a little puppy dog around Dorothy. He just took whatever she said. He was compromising. Whatever Dorothy wanted, her wish was his command. And I always got the feeling that Dorothy didn't really have respect for him as a real ballsy kind of guy."

"He did everything he could for her" and "took a lot of guff" from Dorothy who could be "complaining" and "impatient" with him, said Morty Jacobs. "Earl was in love with Dorothy. He just told me he loved her. Once she told me that Earl wanted to marry her, and she couldn't marry him."

Nick Perito traveled with Dorothy on her tour, opening February 4th at the Park Lane Hotel in Denver. Denver was Perito's hometown. His mother still resided there. He talked to Dorothy about her and told her the Italian soul food his mother cooked, like greens and neck bones, was similar to that of African Americans. "You're kidding," Dorothy said. "Your mom makes greens?"

Nick answered the question by bringing her food from his mother's kitchen. "Here I am," remembered Perito, "in a fancy hotel, on the elevator, carrying a pot of greens." After that "Dorothy was convinced I was a soul brother. My mom came to the show and it was love at first sight" between her and Dorothy.

But Perito remembered that "Otto Preminger didn't think too much of greens. He tolerated them. Dorothy and I had them every night after the show." Otto arrived in Denver to spend time with her and also check on her act. The people who traveled and worked with Dorothy on tour considered Otto something of a pain, as he attempted to "make the act more dramatic." Louella Parsons reported in the *Los Angeles Examiner* that Preminger "volunteered to direct Dorothy in her night club act." But everyone tolerated him. They didn't have much choice. "He was imposing," said Nick Perito. Dorothy took his comments seriously, but most at the club were relieved when he left, soon after the opening.

"He was a bad influence," said Earl Mills. "He was a great movie director. But he didn't know anything about nightclubs."

While Dorothy was in Denver, the Academy of Motion Picture Arts and Sciences announced the nominations for the 1954 Academy Awards on an NBC broadcast on February 12th. Best Picture nominees were *On the Waterfront, The Caine Mutiny, The Country Girl, Seven Brides for Seven Brothers,* and *Three Coins in the Fountain.* The Best Actor nominees included Marlon Brando for *On the Waterfront,* Humphrey Bogart for *The Caine Mutiny,* Bing Crosby for *The Country Girl,* James Mason for *A Star Is Born,* and Dan O'Herlihy for *The Adventures of Robinson Crusoe.* And in the category of Best Actress, the nominees were Judy Garland for *A Star Is Born,* Audrey Hepburn for *Sabrina,* Grace Kelly for *The Country Girl,* Jane Wyman for *Magnificent Obsession,* and Dorothy Dandridge for *Carmen Jones.*

Hearing her name, Dorothy screamed with excitement. She ran to the phone and called Ruby first and then Vivian. "We didn't think it would happen. But when it did happen, she called me. And we were screaming!" said Vivian. Remembering her sister's dream, Dorothy told Vivian to make plans to accompany her to the Academy Awards presentation on March 30th.

It was an historic moment. Only two African Americans had previously been nominated for Oscars: Hattie McDaniel, who won as Best Supporting Actress of 1939 for *Gone With the Wind*; and Ethel Waters, who had been nominated for Best Supporting Actress of 1949 for *Pinky.*

The Academy had awarded James Baskette a special Oscar for his performance as Uncle Remus in Disney's 1946 *Song of the South,* even though Baskette hadn't been nominated for an award. Coming during the postwar era when Black movie images were changing, some Academy members opposed the special Oscar because the Remus character seemed so much a throwback to slave stereotypes of the past. Such people, fumed Hedda Hopper who favored the award, thought "that Negroes should play only doctors, lawyers, and scientists." Arguments went back and forth until four a.m. Hopper's side won. The special Oscar ended up looking like a symbolic gesture from those who wanted to hold back time and to stall more realistic and challenging roles for African Americans in Hollywood.

But for Black America, Dorothy's nomination—in the leading actress category for a performance that projected intelligence and independence and captured (even through a distorted lens) the spirit of a contemporary African American woman—opened a new chapter in motion picture history and was a cause for celebration. Throughout the nation, such Black newspapers as *The Pittsburgh Courier* and *The Baltimore Afro-American* carried the story on their front pages.

Letters, telegrams, and telephone calls came in, requesting a statement from her. She responded that her heart "swelled with pride at the thought of what this means to me as an actress and for the significance the nomination has. It is the first time a Negro performer in a leading role has ever won this distinction. It gives me courage to go on with my acting career. I note with pleasure that the members of the Academy expressed their judgment solely on the basis of the performances. In viewing this, I hope that more Negro people will be employed in the motion picture industry."

In Los Angeles, Joel Fluellen, upon learning the news, immediately hopped on a plane and flew into Denver. "All of a sudden, he was there," said Nick Perito. "I think he came in the night of the nomination." At times Joel seemed even more excited than Dorothy, almost unable to contain himself. He would run to the window, open it, and scream out, "Dorothy Dandridge! Dorothy Dandridge!"

"He would just yell in joy about Dorothy's nomination," said Perito.

A telegram came from an old love.

"CONGRATULATIONS ON YOUR WONDERFUL ACHIEVEMENT. I COULDN'T BE HAPPIER ABOUT IT. KEEPING MY FINGERS CROSSED FOR THE FINAL VOTE. ALL THE BEST=PETER."

Then Preminger flew back to Denver, ready to help her celebrate in grand style with champagne, flowers, and gifts. "He may have come in the night of the nomination, too," said Perito. Otto was beaming. Now all those doubters in Hollywood would have to recognize her star power. In the mythology of cinema, Federico Fellini later said, the Oscar is the supreme prize. In this case, for an African American woman, the Oscar nomination lifted her, as had the *Life* cover, into a special realm, another tier of movieland stardom, mythology and iconography.

Otto had other reasons to beam over Dandridge.

His observations on Hollywood culture and the dos and don'ts of stardom had proven shrewd and cunning. The outcome of Dandridge's negotiations with Zanuck was evidence of that.

Fox offered her a three-year contract with an agreement that she would do one picture a year with her salary escalating from $75,000 to $125,000. Though Fox had priority on her services, it was a non-exclusive agreement which meant she would be free to do films for other studios. If there were a conflict with nightclub or other film schedules, she would have to clear such matters with Fox first. The contract also stipulated that her name would appear above the title. Again she would be the first African American in Hollywood accorded this distinction. Zanuck was already looking for projects for her. She signed on February 15, 1955, just three days after the Oscar nomination.

Dandridge was relieved and optimistic. She had taken just the kind of crucial step an actor needed to make to keep a film career on track. She had assumed something significant would have been offered to her by now. But despite all the attention for *Carmen Jones* and the Oscar nomination, no concrete movie offers had yet come her way. The most promising project was not a movie at all but a proposal by impresario Sol Hurok to star her in a Broadway revival of Oscar Wilde's *Salome*. In the past, the role had been played by White actresses. Dorothy tentatively agreed to do the play. Perhaps with the Fox deal closed, the tide was about to turn. So she hoped.

Following Denver, Dorothy returned to the Last Frontier in Las Vegas. The hotel that had once threatened to drain the pool should she go near it now had an Oscar nominee as a headliner. Needless to say, they were just as determined in their effort to publicize her appearance as such. Outside the establishment stood huge placards of the sexy portrait of Dandridge as Carmen with hands on hips. Dandridge took one look upon her arrival and became openly annoyed. She requested that the hotel take down the placards.

"I've never been happy about the figure that 20th Century Fox used in advertising the picture," she told a reporter from the Associated Press, "but I realized that it was important in selling a film based on an opera. I don't want people who come to see me to think that they're going to see me as I was in the picture. There's no relation to the two. In night clubs, my material is highly sophisticated, I wear beautiful gowns that completely cover me. I'm not earthy and I'm not fiery."

The Associated Press reported, "She instructed the owners of the Last Frontier Hotel to yank down all blowup photos." And they did.

Yet, despite the controversy over the promotion campaign and again the interference on her act of Otto, who soon arrived in Vegas, Dorothy glided through the engagement to rave reviews from audiences and critics alike. In the *Las Vegas Sun*, critic Ralph Pearl summed up some of the excitement about her when he wrote about attending a press conference in Dorothy's hotel suite. "This was one press conference I was not only intent upon attending, but I was gonna make sure I grabbed the seat nearest Dandridge. And as luck had to have it, I did get the seat nearest to the seat she would adorn," he wrote. "Then Dorothy Dandridge came out of her boudoir and my hidden notebook felt like a slab of dry ice pressing against my rapidly beating chest bone. And my pencil felt like a live jack hammer. She wore champagne colored lace, skin tighter than tight bolero pants and skimpy top. The little hairs on my neck felt like so many ice picks while the tongue I have used so many years to conduct marathon one-way conversations seemed stuck to the roof of my mouth."

The Frontier in Las Vegas was also the site of another memorable event for Dorothy: the second marriage of her best friend Geri Pate Nicholas. Following her divorce from Fayard Nicholas, Geri developed a successful real estate career, continued her political activities, and met an ambitious attorney named Leo Branton. The two decided to wed in the same city where Geri had married Fayard years before. Dorothy was maid of honor and Nick Perito stood as Leo's best man. When the couple later gave birth to a son called Chip, Dorothy became his godmother.

From Vegas, she went to Miami's Fontainebleau Hotel. Before her arrival, she issued a set of stipulations which the hotel had to adhere to, foremost of which were her accommodations. She hadn't forgotten Miami's prior treatment of her—when she had played Ciro's—any more than she'd forgotten Vegas's. This time around, things would be different in Miami, too. She insisted that the exclusively White Fontainebleau reserve her a suite as part of her contract.

The engagement was another hit.

Afterwards she went to New York for the Oscar telecast and also, scheduled shortly later, her Empire Room engagement.

Dorothy's nerves were on edge about the award. A few weeks earlier *Jet* had run a cover story on her titled "How Good Are Dorothy Dandridge's Chances for An 'Oscar'?" The article quoted top Hollywood columnists, several of whom seemed to be pulling for Dandridge to win. "For the life of me," said Sheilah Graham, "I don't see how they can overlook Dorothy Dandridge's Carmen Jones." *Daily Variety*'s Army Archerd commented, "I think Dorothy certainly has one of the best chances." *The Hollywood Reporter*'s Mike Connolly, who was forever a Dandridge fan, added, "It was no surprise to me that she won an Oscar Nomination...This girl has everything." Even Hedda Hopper told *Jet*, "There are many people here who hope she gets the Oscar."

Otto also expressed his sentiments. "She deserves it, I feel, though I may be a bit prejudiced for obvious reasons. She worked hard and did a marvelous job in the title role." *Jet* concluded with the comment, "The Latest Hollywood report being circulated: 'This year's Oscar race maybe the biggest upset in history. People are betting Dorothy Dandridge will cop the award.'"

With this type of talk, Dorothy began to think she might have a chance. But privately, Otto expressed his doubts.

"Why not?" she asked.

"The time is not ripe," he replied.

"She really wanted the Oscar," said Vivian. The idea of winning it consumed her to the point where she was often wired and unable to unwind and sleep. By now, she took sleeping pills without any second thoughts. That, too, was yet another part of the star culture.

On March 30th, a limousine escorted Dorothy and Vivian Dandridge to the Century Theatre in New York. The awards ceremony was to be broadcast from two locations. In Los Angeles, Bob Hope emceed the awards at the Pantages Theatre. Thelma Ritter was the host in New York.

As the limousine driver opened the door, Dorothy shifted round in her seat and elegantly extended her hand for the driver to help her exit the car. Flashbulbs popped and cameras snapped as reporters and photographers rushed to get a better look at her. Dressed in a clinging gown with a fur stole wrapped around her shoulders, smiling and waving to the crowds behind the police barricades, she looked like a million dollars, magically aglow in that glimmer that movie stars somehow emit.

Vivian was at her side, at least as close to it as she could get. But to the crowd and the press, Vivian was almost nonexistent. Photographs taken that night capture Vivian standing to the side as Dorothy, still smiling brilliantly, entered the theatre front and center. It was as it had to be.

Once inside, Dorothy and Vivian sat together. As she greeted the famous faces that came up to her, she introduced them to Vivian. Dorothy laughed, chatted, and charmed. At the Century Theatre in New York were Eva Marie Saint, Karl Malden, and Nina Foch. Earl Mills also flew in for the evening's proceedings. It was indeed a night to match any glamorous fantasies either Dorothy or Vivian might ever have had.

For African Americans watching the awards on television, Dorothy's mere appearance was another historic occasion. Black faces were practically unheard of at the Academy Awards. When Hattie McDaniel won her Oscar, she became the first Black to attend the awards banquet. But for most of the proceedings at the Cocoanut Grove, except the brief time McDaniel sat at producer David O. Selznick's table, she and her escort, actor Wonderful Smith, spent the evening seated separately, actually segregated, from everyone else.

But now Dandridge, standing at the podium proud and triumphant, was the first African American actress to present an award at the proceedings—for Best Film Editing. It was a potent symbol, which *Ebony* later did a feature story on.

When William Holden came to the podium to present the Best Actress Award, Dorothy turned tense and grasped hold of Vivian's hand as he read the nominees' names. As he announced that the award was to go to Grace Kelly for *The Country Girl*, Dorothy smiled and applauded. In a matter of seconds, the evening's magic had ended. As soon as the ceremony was over, Dorothy wanted to go back to the hotel.

Vivian stayed on in New York while Dorothy relaxed and then prepared for her opening at the Waldorf's Empire Room. They had fun together. One day as they shopped, passersby stopped in their tracks.

Dorothy grew uncomfortable. "Why are they always staring?" she asked.

"Because you're gorgeous," Vivian told her.

"Well, I don't like it."

"Well, then," laughed Vivian, "wear a mask!"

"Oh, Vivi!"

But as was often the case the sisters also argued. Vivian grew restless, sitting around with nothing to do once Dorothy's Waldorf rehearsals started. But nervous and fretful, Dorothy wanted Vivian there with her.

"She wasn't happy," said Vivian.

But Vivian wasn't sure if Dorothy was troubled by the affair with Otto. Or if it were her career that bothered her. Or maybe it was still thoughts of Lynn, wondering what she was doing, how she was progressing.

"Something just wouldn't let her be happy," said Vivian.

Vivian herself was having an affair with a Canadian and needed to talk to Dorothy about it, but Dorothy was too preoccupied and jittery about the Waldorf engagement to focus on anything else. Vivian left for Canada for a few days without saying anything to Dorothy. "I made a trip there for the fellow I finally married," she said.

Dorothy went on about her business; this time appearing on "The Toast of the Town." She performed "Back Home to Joe" and "I Got Rhythm." Backstage she got a chance to see her friend Sammy Davis, Jr., who also performed that evening with his father and uncle in the Will Mastin Trio. That was Sunday, April 3rd, and within days, she was in daylong rehearsals with Nick Perito for her Waldorf opening. Bob Wells worked with her on material, as did the ever-present Otto, who had a knack for making the rehearsals grueling.

"Otto, I can't!" she'd say of his suggestions.

"But, Dorothy, you *can*!" he'd bellow.

During rehearsals, Perito didn't see any signs of a romance between the two. "They never held hands," he said. "There was never any lovey-dovey stuff. I never saw them kiss or hug."

As the two openly disagreed, Dorothy found it difficult to focus. "He was very firm and cruel in the sense that he had this oppressive Nazi attitude," said Nick Perito. "He was used to having his own way. He would tell her how she should walk on. It just wasn't Dorothy though. He would upset her. She would cry. Lots of tears."

"Preminger had a whole idea of how she should behave now that she had been an Academy Award nominee," said Perito. "He was trying to re-invent the wheel."

Perito tried to reassure Dorothy that her decisions were the right ones. She should just "go ahead and do what her gut told her," to perform on her own terms. "When you get out there on the floor, baby, just do what you've got to do," he said, "because you have to wear a song like a dress. You become that character in the music."

Still, despite the difficulties and tensions, Dorothy was determined to shape a glossy evening of entertainment. The Waldorf's Empire Room represented, as Otto was quick to remind her, the top echelon of the supper club line. She knew it demanded a different approach, in style and material, from her Vegas engagements and even the intimate setting of La Vie En Rose.

The Waldorf was the place where the most cosmopolitan of nightclub goers dallied: those very established, very wealthy men and their ladies, usually wives rather than girlfriends or mistresses, dressed to the tees in taffeta, chiffon, diamonds, emeralds, ermine, and mink. It was not that the Empire Room was a more sophisticated venue than a club like London's Café de Paris or even the Mocambo. But it was a different type of sophistication. This was not Hollywood swank or movie power people. This was not Vegas glitz. This was East Coast establishment.

Opening night on April 11th, her nerves almost overcame her. Not having heard from Vivian, she half expected her sister to come traipsing into her dressing room just before she went on. Instead she received flowers from Vivian wishing her success.

Out front was a packed house. Seated ringside was Otto. At his table were the powerful Jules Stein, who had founded MCA, producer Sam Spiegel, and Barbara Warner. Hotel magnate Conrad Hilton was in attendance with socialite Sloan Simpson. Representatives from MCA also sat in the room along with an array of socialites and New York power brokers.

On cue, Dandridge made her entrance, dressed in a simple white gown with a slit at the knee, allowing her to sensually move to the beat of the music. Taking a quick nervous glance at the audience, she then sang an energetic rendition of—what else but—"Ridin' High."

Spellbound by the vision before its eyes, these very hoity toity New Yorkers appeared at first almost unable to respond, stunned and speechless. Then two minutes later, "Miss Dandridge heard such applause as she never heard before," reported the critic for the *New York Journal American*. "Park ave. [sic] applause. Fifth ave. [sic] applause. Society applause. The usually reserved patrons of this usually reserved room—under the spell of the attractive young singer who starred on screen in *Carmen Jones*—were letting themselves go."

There followed such romantic pop standards as "You'd Be So Easy to Love," "Good For Nothing Joe," and "Just One of Those Things." She also sang a calypso tune called "Never Mind the Noise in the Market." When she removed her shoes to playfully perform a dance, island-style for this number, the audience just about went wild.

"This room has echoed to the best performers in show business and Miss Dandridge joins that elite group of glittering talent," wrote Frank Quinn in the *New York Mirror*. "After the first song Dorothy took complete command and gave her responsive audience one of the best thrills of a cafe lifetime. Few realized that the sultry singer was making nightlife history as the first woman of her race to star in this ultra nightspot."

"Miss Dandridge," wrote *Variety*, "will wind up with one of the more artistically successful seasons this inn has had for some time."

Yet along with the accolades, some reviewers commented on Dandridge's initial nervousness. Critic Frank Quinn referred to her as "a stunning and half-frightened figure." In the *New York Journal American*, Gene Knight wrote of her "shy, half-frightened manner" and her "forced smile."

The reviewers were stating openly what patrons in the clubs had responded to, often unconsciously, for the past few years: Dandridge's vulnerability and fragility; that need the audience felt to join her in the evening's festivities, so that she herself might enjoy the night all the more.

Once again New York was enraptured with Dorothy Dandridge. *Time* interviewed her a second time for another article; titled "Two for the Show," it reported on her Waldorf performance and also Eartha Kitt's engagement at the Copacabana.

Ed Sullivan wrote a short profile of her in his *New York Daily News* column. He had asked her to name the people most important in her career. She answered, "Charlie Morrison, who gave me my first break at his Mocambo in Hollywood, and told me that some day I'd be a star. Phil Moore, who made my first arrangements; Danny Kaye, who once told me something I never forgot, that you don't grow as an artist unless you grow as a human being; Otto Preminger, who taught me in *Carmen Jones* that I should sing songs that lent themselves to acting." She also named Bob Wells, who was credited with staging the act.

Shortly after the Waldorf opening, Vivian returned to New York from Canada. By that time, Dorothy was infuriated with her.

"She called me and she was really nasty," Vivian said.

She angrily accused Vivian of not showing up at the Waldorf opening just to make her all the more nervous.

"What are you worrying the hell as to whether I came to your opening night or not?" Vivian asked. "Besides, you're opening all the time. You've been opening for years."

"Yes, but this is New York City," Dorothy snapped.

Hoping to calm her down, Vivian asked, "Did you get the flowers?"

"Of course," Dorothy told her. But her anger hadn't abated.

"I had to leave," Vivian tried to explain. "I have my business and things to do too, Dottie."

"Well, when are you going to come to see the show?" Dorothy asked, abruptly ending the conversation.

Later Vivian saw the Empire Room performance with a friend. Afterwards, the two visited Dorothy at her hotel. "We called first," said Vivian. But upon arriving at the hotel, they were met in the hallway by Dorothy's secretary.

"She's very upset now," the woman told Vivian. "I don't think you should go in there."

"Are you kidding? She's my sister. What's she upset about?" Vivian asked.

She explained that Dorothy had learned of the death of Geri Branton's mother. Vivian brushed the secretary aside and entered Dorothy's hotel suite. Lying down, Dorothy was obviously upset and not very coherent.

"Well, I knew Geri and her mother and everything. But it wasn't that," said Vivian. "I think it was other things. She was very confused."

Perhaps the strain of the relationship with Otto had upset her. Perhaps she had needed Vivian to talk to just as much as Vivian had needed her. Vivian began to joke with Dorothy.

"Oh, Vivi!" Dorothy laughed.

"Then she got herself back again," Vivian recalled.

The sisters embraced.

The evening ended on a pleasant note, but not long afterwards the sisters quarreled again. Geri Branton believed it was over money. Apparently, Vivian needed a loan. Busy with her performances and interviews, Dorothy told Vivian to speak to one of her people about the money, part of her growing entourage of which Earl Mills was at the top.

"She was very nasty to me. That I was accustomed to," said Vivian. "Not to do me in or anything. I think it was because she thought she could get away with it with me. And besides she was very unhappy." Never did Dorothy think that Vivian would become so angry about the incident that their relationship would be permanently damaged. But it was.

During the Waldorf engagement, she met with Harold Arlen for discussions about his new musical *Blues Opera*, to be produced by Robert Breen. She agreed to star in the production, which was scheduled to premiere in Venice in the fall and then move to Broadway. But she later backed out of the deal.

Nothing seemed more promising, however, than the news that came from Zanuck at Fox. Having just returned from Europe where he had negotiated for the rights to the film *The Blue Angel*, Zanuck planned to remake the drama that had originally catapulted Marlene Dietrich to international fame. "But it won't be Marlene who sings 'Falling in Love Again,'" Louella Parsons reported in her column on April 13th, "it will be Dorothy Dandridge, because it's Darryl's idea to have this an all-Negro cast. His decision is undoubtedly influenced by the big success of *Carmen Jones*."

Dorothy reasoned she might have a chance for another great role in *The Blue Angel*, the tale of a sexy cabaret singer who corrupts a stodgy, repressed university professor. Zanuck believed that a Black version with Dorothy might not only be successful in the States but abroad.

Already there were signs of a large Dandridge following in important markets outside the United States. *Carmen Jones* premiered in London in early 1955 to great success and had a healthy run in West Germany where it took second prize at the Berlin International Film Festival in 1955. Dorothy's face even turned up on the cover of *Der Stern* as a dazzling symbol of a new day in international cinema. *Carmen Jones* became a hit in the Scandinavian countries and in Latin America, too.

The film also surprised Fox with its long run at a 1,600-seat theatre in Singapore. "Dorothy Dandridge has all the local cinema fans gasping for breath," *The Hollywood Reporter* announced. "Everyone is unanimous that this Dandridge girl has everything." And when the film opened in South Africa, the exhibitor advertised it by telling his apartheid countrymen "that Dorothy Dandridge was the nearest thing they would ever see to Marilyn Monroe."

She indeed was on her way to becoming the first authentic international Black film star. In the 1930s, Josephine Baker's French films—*Zou Zou* and *Princess Tam Tam*—succeeded in France but failed to win the crucial American market. The same was true of Robeson's British films of the 1930s and early 1940s.

Zanuck had other projects in mind, including Fox's planned movie version of the Rodgers and Hammerstein hit Broadway musical *The King and I*. Based on the book *Anna and the King of Siam*, it had already been filmed in 1946 with Rex Harrison and Irene Dunne. Zanuck planned to cast Dorothy in the Tuptim role first played by Linda Darnell in *Anna and the King of Siam*, that of a lovely, rebellious young woman. He believed this non-Negro part would be a breakthrough for her.

Other news excited her more. A technicality in French music copyright laws had ruled out a showing of *Carmen Jones* in France, an important market for Fox. But a formal invitation came from the French Government, inviting her to attend the Cannes International Film Festival where *Carmen Jones* would have a special screening. Because of the copyright problem, it could not be shown in competition with the other international films. To avoid problems with the Bizet estate, the festival board was prepared to show *Carmen Jones* on a United States aircraft carrier in the waters off Cannes. Of course, Otto would be going, too.

The Cannes Film Festival was still relatively young, having come into existence following the Second World War, but already Cannes was considered the most sophisticated of film arenas. Here were shown the art films that eventually played in theatres around the world and ultimately acquired classic status. Here, too, was a glittering gathering of figures of international cinema: the directors, producers, actors, actresses, writers, designers; a heady mix of the avant garde and the purely commercial that included acknowledged talents as well as the gaggle of international hucksters, promoters, and charlatans eager to strike a deal.

Otto made plans for their trip, but there was a snag. Dorothy had to depart for Cannes by May 7th, but her Empire Room engagement was scheduled to run for seven weeks until the end of May. Finally, the French Embassy in New York intervened to ask the Waldorf to grant Dorothy a leave of absence. On April 29th, *The New York Times* announced that Dandridge would indeed take a week's break from her Waldorf engagement to go to Cannes.

Dandridge and Preminger departed for France on May 7th. It was a whirlwind trip that took her some 36 hours. She arrived in Nice on the last two days of the festival.

Such American films as *Marty* and *East of Eden* were being shown at the festival. Grace Kelly, Doris Day, Esther Williams, Van Johnson, Gene Kelly, director Stanley Kramer, producer Mike Todd, and Olivia de Havilland were among the celebrities present. Some 470 correspondents, 80 photographers, and 19 newsreels from around the world covered the event. The United States, aware of the importance of the festival, poured some $15,000 into the proceedings. And now, for the first time, a Black American actress would glide through the festivities.

Upon her arrival at the Nice airport, Dorothy peered out the plane's window and couldn't believe her eyes. Greeting her was a "throng of thousands," *Our World* reported, that shouted her name and fought French police to get near her. Amid the crush of reporters, photographers, and fans, she smiled and waved but was quickly whisked into a long, cream-colored Cadillac that drove her to the famous Carlton Hotel. Once there, she saw another crowd that swarmed around the car. A police escort was ordered to shepherd her out of the car and into her luxurious suite at the Carlton. But the press demanded more. She couldn't just disappear. Otto and others implored her to go back out. And so, shortly afterwards, she reappeared to take a stroll down the Croisette and again was pursued by a horde of photographers who called out "Car-Man," "Car-Man" and "Door-Tee," "Door-Tee." They screamed, shouted, pushed, and shoved to see her as she stood, wearing a sleek form-fitting dotted skirt and blouse, in front of the Carlton.

To accommodate the photographers, she walked down to the beach while their cameras snapped away. Taking off her shoes, she gingerly kicked her feet in the water. Then they snapped her standing—with hands on hips—next to a *Carmen Jones* billboard. They even captured a shot, later published in *Jet*, of her affectionately planting a kiss on the cheek of Otto. The international press didn't seem able to get enough of her.

That evening, Dorothy, looking triumphant in a white gown and white fur stole, arrived on the arm of Preminger for the screening of *Carmen Jones*. With every ticket for the event sold, an additional screening had to be set up. As she was about to enter the theatre, she posed for the photographers, her star glow in place as she smiled, laughed, and then, true to her training, lifted her head and arched the chin in true haughty, untouchable, imperial goddess style. There they were, she must have thought, openly adoring her, openly excited about her.

Even Preminger stepped back to let the photographers inch closer. Inside the theatre, Dorothy nervously watched the film, unsure how the audience would respond. But by the end of the film, amid thunderous applause, shouts, and screams, she was besieged by a battery of artists, intellectuals, and producers, clamoring to meet her. It was an altogether glorious night.

"Dorothy Dandridge, here for the two closing days, also was a phenomenal favorite, applauded by crowds everywhere," wrote *The Hollywood Reporter*. "*Carmen Jones* was screened twice on the closing day to accommodate requests and there was applause after every song, with big acclaim at the conclusion."

Later *Jet* sent out the word for Black America. "Dorothy Dandridge, getting a bigger ovation than Oscar winner Grace Kelly, caused columnist Sheilah Graham to comment that Dorothy 'seems to have what the French want.'"

Throughout the brief trip, Preminger felt freer about his public appearances—and affection—with her. They were openly seen together at the screening, at lunches, dinners, and gatherings. He presented her with jewels. And with dreams. This was just an extension of a beautiful new ordered world that began with the release of *Carmen Jones* and that appealed to her romantic fantasies. For Dandridge, it was a promise of a today that would never end.

Six days after leaving New York, she returned to continue the Empire Room engagement. The excitement continued. So did talk of new films. She agreed to play the role of Tuptim in *The King and I*, then scheduled to begin shooting in September. *The Blue Angel* remake was being readied. Fox also prepared to star her in a remake of the Foreign Legion drama *Under Two Flags*, in which she would play the sexy camp follower Cigarette, the part which had been created by Claudette Colbert in the 1936 version. Fox was moving ahead with all three projects. But Dorothy started having misgivings about *The King and I*. She balked at the idea of playing Tuptim, who struck her as being little more than a slave. Earlier in her career, she had played servants because she had *had* to. But why should she have to play such a role now? Her publicist Orin Borsten tried to brush aside her doubts.

"It has nothing to do with Southern slavery," he told her. "It has nothing to do with Black history in America. This is a different country. It's a wonderful opportunity for you."

But he knew Dorothy wasn't listening to him. Perhaps one of the things troubling her was an interlude in the film where the slave girl Tuptim performed a Siamese pantomime version of *Uncle Tom's Cabin*.

Then Otto advised her that she shouldn't do the role, but for other reasons. Deborah Kerr would star as the governess. Yul Brynner would play the King. Tuptim was a solid, decent-enough supporting role that could be important for a young actress on the rise, he believed, but it wasn't what Dorothy needed at this point in her career.

He felt strongly that after *Carmen Jones*, she should play only leading roles, never be a backup support, especially in a film with another actress. Preminger warned Dorothy that if she accepted the part, she would designate herself forever to nothing but supporting roles in films with White female stars. The two had a heated discussion about the picture wherein he advised her to tell Zanuck that she wouldn't do the film.

Preminger had a point. He still saw Dandridge as an actress in the league of Taylor and Monroe. Had either of these women just been nominated for the Academy Award, there was simply no way they would have been offered, nor would they have played, a secondary role, no matter how big the movie production was. He refused to believe that Dorothy might be limited by the movie industry because of her race. In the grand, larger-than-life way Preminger envisioned her career and appeal, her race played no part. She was above and beyond conceptions of race. If anything, rather than a liability, her being Black was an asset because of the cultural statement she might bring to the screen through her style, energy, attitude, movement. Despite his remarkable insights into her appeal and despite his faith in her talents and the grandeur of his vision of her, Preminger, usually adroitly pragmatic and perceptive, was in this instance blind to movieland realities.

For one thing, he was not considering what Fox had to contend with: namely, the exhibitors at moviehouses around the country; and the attitudes of the mass audience. Even if Dorothy appeared in non-Negro pictures, she was still, especially in the eyes of Southern theatre owners, a Negro star. White audiences, so the exhibitors believed, would not support films that a Black actress had to carry alone. Nor would White audiences relish the idea of seeing a Black actress performing star roles opposite Whites.

Of course, Sidney Poitier had begun to work steadily in films.

Having debuted in *No Way Out in* 1950, he had also appeared in *Cry the Beloved Country, Red Ball Express*, and *Blackboard Jungle*. His great successes *Edge of the City, The Defiant Ones,* and *Lilies of the Field* were yet to come. But Poitier emerged as a star in mainstream cinema partly because his characters were often social symbols in an era that was beginning to have racial conflict—as well as civil rights—more and more on its mind. Not cast in larger-than-life romantic parts, Poitier often played the good Negro character, who was a metaphor, as had been those in the old problem pictures, for social inequities and injustices. His films were often pleas for the acceptance of the Negro.

The sexuality of Poitier's characters, particularly in later films like *Guess Who's Coming to Dinner* and *A Patch of Blue*, could be muted, almost to the point of seeming nonexistent. Poitier would never be perceived as a sexual threat to the mainstream audience. But Dorothy's vibrant sexuality couldn't be ignored. Her look itself demanded that she be cast in glamorous romantic roles. To ask her to play a social symbol in a film was like asking Elizabeth Taylor, Audrey Hepburn, Kim Novak, or Grace Kelly to perform as such. Cinema's glamorous and sensual goddesses had to play glamorous, sensual romantic roles. Preminger felt this way about Dorothy.

Fox realized it couldn't cast her only in Black-cast films because, frankly, the studio didn't plan on making a series of them. *Carmen Jones's* success was considered an anomaly, not a norm. Zanuck therefore thought he might be able to maneuver around exhibitor and mass audience attitudes with his decision to cast her as other "ethnics," in fundamentally White films. Only a few years earlier in 1952, Fox had starred Marlon Brando in *Viva Zapata*, the story of the Mexican revolutionary Emiliano Zapata's rise from peasant to the presidency of his country. Jean Peters had played his Mexican love interest. Such a role would have been perfect for Dandridge. Yet never even in Zanuck's wildest dreams of casting Dandridge in nontraditional ways would she have won such an acting coup. Zanuck—and Fox—weren't ready to go that far. Now as *The King and I* indicated, the "ethnics" wouldn't be leading characters.

Again Preminger pressured Dorothy to tell Zanuck she would not do Tuptim. The part wouldn't take her career anywhere. She vacillated and wondered what role would advance her career. Others around Dorothy, however, urged her to accept the Tuptim part.

Ultimately, the situation simply depressed her. But soon *The King and I* wasn't the only dilemma to trouble her. There was also Vivian.

Frustrated by her life there, Vivian had talked, for some time, of leaving Los Angeles. She had had it with the city, with the people, with Dorothy's clique of hangers-on, with the movie colony's social hierarchy, with her own professional difficulties. More and more, she must have felt she was becoming an appendage of Dorothy. She still relied on her sister whenever she had health or money problems. Her earnings in 1954 had been $2,020, and $300 of that came from Dorothy. Her income tax returns were even prepared for her by Dorothy's accountant. Dorothy also paid the fee for Vivian's son to attend camp during the summer of 1955. Vivian feared living completely in Dorothy's shadow and disappearing altogether. Then too, she could no longer take Ruby's emotional distance.

"To hang around and see what was going on in their lives—my mother's and Dorothy's—and what these people were doing to them. Why should I have a nervous breakdown?" she said. "I couldn't do anything. Even though Dottie and I had argued about things, she knew I loved her and that I had her interests at heart. She knew it was purely caring on my part. And then I knew the business. Let's face it."

Vivian did not make a complete break at first. Since the Empire Room engagement, she had spoken to Dorothy but hadn't seen her. In the summer of 1955, she replaced Thelma Carpenter in the Broadway play *Ankles Aweigh*. Friendly and social, she made new friends and for a time, resided at the Alvin Hotel on West 52nd Street. But she knew if she ever really wanted to break away from her family, she'd have to move further away.

"I just decided to leave completely, not just leave and be in even New York City," Vivian said. "But to be out of the country altogether and with my name changed."

"I told them both I was going to leave. I was very straight with them," said Vivian.

She began making plans for herself and her son. She also tried to explain her feelings and fears to both Dorothy and her mother, but neither Dorothy nor Ruby took Vivian's comments about leaving seriously.

Back on the road, Dorothy opened for a two-week engagement at the Biltmore Hotel in Lake Tahoe in August, 1955. For Dorothy and accompanist Nick Perito, the closing at the Biltmore was the poignant end of their professional relationship. Because of his family as well as his growing professional responsibilities in the East, Perito could no longer travel with her.

Ever since he escorted her up the elevator at the Chase Hotel, she had felt at home with him. To her, he was Nick, the good-looking guy with the big smile and the "ballsy" manner, who was always ready to come to her defense, to take on the world if necessary, and who never hesitated to tell her the truth about what he thought. She had spent long hours talking to him—about the clubs, about men, about race. She was sad to see him go. The two remained friends, and she would miss him on the road.

Fox had notified her in mid-May that she was to report to the studio on October 3rd to begin work on *The King and I*. Now she was forced to resolve the situation. Preproduction publicity had already started. "Fox plans to make a big star out of Reuben Fuentes," announced *The Hollywood Reporter* on August 25th. "He'll play the young lord opposite Dorothy Dandridge in *The King and I*."

At her request, Fox had also begun negotiations for Nick Perito to do prerecording work with her for the songs she would sing in the film. The studio was doing all it could to insure that she would be comfortable while shooting the film. She also had flown to Toronto to see a stage performance of the musical, perhaps in the hopes that she might be persuaded to take the role. Finally, however, she decided she just couldn't do it. The problem, though, was informing the studio of her decision.

When publicist Borsten heard the news, he pleaded with her to reconsider. "There are not too many opportunities for you in films," he told her. "You let these opportunities go by and all of a sudden there will be another beautiful Black woman, singer-actress who comes down the pike and you're passé. You've got to take every opportunity."

Borsten recalled, "I really got on my knees and begged her. 'Do it. You need it. You have to have it. You have to have that credit. You have to have that exposure. There's no limit to what you can play. Right now you're on the top of the heap. You turn this down and nothing is going to be coming for you in the next two years. You've got to keep Dorothy Dandridge above the title.'"

But Dorothy wouldn't budge. She looked directly at Borsten and told him again, "I don't want to play a slave. I can't play a slave."

Mills also tried persuading her to do the role. But, said Borsten, "I think Earl was not strong enough to handle her career properly, to say, 'You do this, Dorothy. You do that.' Because she wouldn't listen to him." Finally, she informed Fox, and Zanuck, as delicately as possible that she was declining their offer, using a clause in her contract that guaranteed her only starring roles at Fox. Her decision took the studio by surprise. But Fox played hardball in a letter dated September 12th:

> Whereas, since you were assigned by us to render your services in connection with our said motion picture production "THE KING AND I," you have on several occasions, either personally or through your authorized representatives, notified us that you would not render your services in your assigned role in our said motion picture production....
>
> Now, therefore, you are hereby notified that, pursuant to your contract and in particular Article Twenty-Eighth thereof, we elect to and do hereby cancel our obligation to utilize our services and/or to compensate you in connection with the one (1) motion picture which was to have been commenced during the now current one (1) year period of the term of your contact, and you are hereby further notified that we elect to and do hereby extend said current one (1) year period of the term of your contract for a period of one (1) year, during which period you shall render your services for us in connection with the full and complete production of one (1) additional motion picture upon all the terms and conditions of your contact and at the same per picture rate of compensation as specified therein....

The letter was signed by executive Frank Ferguson, Fox's first assistant secretary.

Two days later, Dorothy's attorney sent a registered letter on her behalf to the studio. It read, in part:

> You are hereby notified that Miss Dandridge does not accept your said notice of September 12, 1955 and does not acknowledge that there has been any action on her part entitling you to the purported rights which you have asserted in your letter of September 12, 1955.
>
> Specifically, it is Miss Dandridge's position that the role of "TUPTIM" in the motion picture "THE KING AND I," as described in the screenplay submitted to Miss Dandridge, is not a star or co-star role as required under Paragraph THIRTY-SIXTH of your agreement with Miss Dandridge dated February 15, 1955.

Eventually, Dorothy had to agree to an extension of her Fox contract. Tied into her contract was the need to receive permission from Fox before she could accept certain nightclub engagements. It would have been hell for her not to have made concessions. Fox could have kept her out of clubs for years.

The studio would have preferred that she had appeared in the film. "Zanuck couldn't force her to do it," said Orin Borsten. "He was disappointed. Dorothy was a bigger name than [the actress who finally did the part]."

Zanuck was also reportedly infuriated. "That was the turnaround for her at Fox," said Earl Mills. Zanuck believed he had been true to his word of casting her in a nontraditional way. He also believed she could add something to the picture. The studio hoped to convince her to reconsider, but Dorothy refused to do so.

"She turned down the role," said Geri. "Partially because of Preminger, who said, 'No, Dorothy. You've got to have the *top* spot.' Dottie could have made the part of Tuptim better. So I don't think that was too swift...to have that mindset. When you get that nomination, it's a curse. You stop the craft of acting and become an egomaniac. 'I can only do *this*. I can only do Shakespeare!' You know you sit there and have to cut off your ear like Van Gogh. You wait for things to happen."

Not until early October, however, did Fox finally resign itself to filming *The King and I* without Dorothy. Fox then announced that Rita Moreno, a Latina actress also in search of a variety of roles, would play the Tuptim part. Even then, the studio tried handling the situation diplomatically, despite the stories that already had leaked about Dorothy's refusal to do the picture.

"Reports that film star Dorothy Dandridge 'walked out' on a featured role in the forthcoming movie *The King And I* because of dissatisfaction with the part were denied in Hollywood by 20th Century Fox," *Jet* reported in its October 6, 1955 issue. "The studio said Miss Dandridge was withdrawn from the cast because of 'production schedule conflicts' with a commitment the singer-actress has at Las Vegas's Riviera Hotel. The studio added it now plans to feature Miss Dandridge in the remake of either *Under Two Flags* or *The Blue Angel*, with production starting early in 1956."

Later Dorothy agonized over her decision. She never thought much of the role. But ultimately, *The King and I* was a major box-office success that won nine Oscar nominations and was seen by millions around the world. She also would have been paid $75,000 to do the picture.

Having rejected the role, she discovered herself stranded with nothing else on the horizon. A year had passed since *Carmen Jones* and so long a time could be devastating to a rising actress's film career. Worse, in terms of industry perceptions, were stories that she had become difficult. Her departure from *The King And I* was viewed as the act of a woman biting the hand that had fed her.

She spoke to Zanuck about the William Inge drama *Bus Stop*, a Broadway hit that Fox had bought the rights to. It was the poignant story of a saloon singer, Cherie, who sees a chance to change the course of her life when she meets an innocent cowboy named Bo, who wants to marry her.

"I want to play Cherie," she told Zanuck in his office.

He looked at her in disbelief.

"I want to play Cherie," she said again. "Why not?"

Zanuck explained that her presence would inject a racial theme into the production and just wouldn't work with audiences.

But Dorothy was insistent. "No, no, no," she said. "I know I can play Cherie and I know the public will accept it."

Publicist Orin Borsten recalled, "Well, he wouldn't let her play Cherie. You see, she wanted to move ahead with a compulsion toward a world in which there were no color differences."

Fox gave the role of Cherie to Marilyn Monroe.

The plans for every other production fell through. Dorothy did not appear in a revival of Salome. Nor, of course, did she star in Harold Arlen's *Blues Opera*. Nor did the Preminger remake of *The Barber of Seville* or a Black version of *Under Two Flags* come to fruition. Zanuck also dropped the idea of filming a Black version of *The Blue Angel*. When the studio finally produced the remake in 1959, it starred Swedish actress May Britt, whose career later seemed to perish after her marriage to Sammy Davis, Jr. For Dorothy, too many projects now seemed to be a series of dead ends. In the game of movieland politics which Otto understood so well, Dorothy feared she had miscalculated. Three years would pass between *Carmen Jones* and her next big screen appearance. But Otto didn't seem worried. Something better would come along, he reasoned.

As infatuated and fascinated as ever with Dorothy, he continued the affair. Privately, he loved showing her off. At small elegant dinner parties, "he wanted her very much to be his hostess," said Geri.

"He was *very good* to her. He wanted to buy her huge real estate in New York. He really wanted her security. She would go with him once a year to Paris and London for clothes. Once a year, he would get her a wardrobe. Givenchy. You name it. Juel Park [an expensive boutique on Rodeo Drive] gowns. Hand made shoes. Magnificent lingerie that was made especially for her and signed by the designer. He'd keep her checking account balance up to like $5,000 a month. His company leased her a different car every six months. He still liked her in white and beige. He wanted to control her life."

Dorothy contented herself with this heady lifestyle. But she never failed to notice that their relationship remained secret. An open secret in Hollywood, but still a secret nonetheless. As she became more deeply involved, she wanted marriage. But Otto still hadn't divorced his second wife. Finally, she realized he would never jeopardize his career with an interracial marriage. Vivian's early warnings had proven true. Their affair would remain just that: an affair. Resentful and restless, she became querulous and openly rude to him in restaurants or at private dinners.

"He would have cared more if she had allowed it," Geri believed. "Sometimes she was so *insulting* to him. She used to say, 'Stop chewing your food. Your teeth clack. You got an ugly old bald head.' It kind of hurt him. But you know you don't say that to a *Prussian.*"

She was back on the road in late 1955 for personal appearances and engagements. In November, she flew to Rio de Janeiro where she was a guest of honor at a three-day charity festival for the benefit of Brazil's homeless and abandoned children. Arriving in the city, she couldn't escape memories of her trip there two years earlier when she had fallen so passionately in love. But she returned at the invitation of President Joao Cafe Filho, the Copacabana Club's co-owner Oskir Orenstein, and the publishers of the newspaper *O Globo*. She was the government's honored guest at a reception and cocktail party and then a lavish dinner assembling Latin American officials. Later she attended a charity event at Rio's racetrack, followed by the opening of *Carmen Jones* at the Palacio Theatre. Over 2,000 patrons packed the theatre hoping for a glimpse of Dorothy. When the film ended after midnight, Brazil's president along with the audience applauded wildly and also sang "Happy Birthday." Dorothy turned thirty-three.

During her visit, Dorothy heard rumblings of military and political problems. But everyone was so gracious and charming that she brushed any troubling thoughts aside. Once she was back home, the news of a coup d'état was breaking. "The President who sat next to us at the opening of your film," a friend wrote, "was forced to resign."

≈

Her schedule took her almost immediately to Springfield, Illinois, for a club date, and then to Las Vegas for an opening the day before Thanksgiving at the Riviera Hotel. She arrived in the city with manager Earl Mills. Upon entering her suite, she found a room overflowing with flowers. Among them was a huge bouquet from Twentieth Century Fox. But the flowers simply reminded her of her decision about *The King And I*. And that in turn made her think of Otto—and again the status of their relationship.

The constant traveling drained her and often left her wired and unable to sleep without the help of prescribed pills. Often she took Miltown, a tranquilizer that helped manage her anxieties. The work steadied her and still kept her focused, but during her down time, she felt languid and frightened yet often was unable to relax. A restlessness was growing, making her all the more susceptible to anything that promised change. While she was in just such a mood, she met Jack Denison.

Denison was a familiar presence on the Vegas scene. Of Greek descent, Jack George Denison had been born in 1912 in Montreal where his father ran a restaurant and bar. He grew up schooled in the ways of pleasing the customer. In 1934, he left Canada and settled in New York. He worked at the Waldorf and Astor hotels.

Three years later, he moved to Los Angeles. He worked as a waiter in two of the city's top restaurants, the Cocoanut Grove and the Brown Derby. He also studied business administration in preparation for the day when he would have his own place.

During the Second World War, Denison served in the Navy. Afterwards, like other ambitious young men looking for opportunities and venues for advancement, he landed in Las Vegas. Denison's slick demeanor served him well in this bustling metropolis that openly embraced shrewd resourceful fellows. "Everybody knew Jack Denison in Las Vegas," recalled musician Gerald Wilson. "He ran the Kit Carson Club."

Denison maneuvered his way about. He became the maitre d'hotel at the El Rancho. Then he worked at the Flamingo and the Riviera. All were big clubs. As was the case with so many in Vegas at this time, gossip and speculation swirled around Denison, who was said to have ties with the mob. But, of course, no one could ever prove anything.

When Dandridge arrived at the Riviera, Denison, then its maitre'd, couldn't stop watching her. Experienced enough with women to realize that she was a woman alone, he set out to meet her. "He wanted to ingratiate himself personally to Dorothy," said Mills. "But she never socialized with anybody." When he realized that she rarely dined in the hotel's restaurant, instead preferring to stay in her quarters, he began sending the staff of waiters to her room with lunches and dinners. Any request she had was immediately answered. Everything was done to please her.

Nightly, when Dorothy completed her performances, she returned to her dressing room to find flowers sent by Denison. In the beginning, she stuck to her policy of never responding to such pursuers. But Denison continued to try establishing contact with her.

When she finally met him, she found a man who throughout his life and especially in Vegas, had gotten by in part because of his looks. Considered attractive, he was tall and lean, with such well-tended silver hair that he was referred to as the Silver Fox. He also earned that name because he was considered crafty and clever as a fox. Even Preminger, when he met Denison later, conceded that he was handsome. But Otto also observed that Denison was the Whitest looking man he had ever seen. "He had long white hands and fingers," said Otto. "He had *white* hair, and *white, white* skin." Preminger's comments about the very White-looking Mr. Denison were not meant as a compliment. "He was a very shrewd, slick dude, and good-looking," said Herb Jeffries, who also knew Denison in Vegas. "The chicks were chasing him. And he was a womanizer. Everybody knew that."

To enhance his looks, Jack dressed impeccably and fashionably, although his style was more swanky than sophisticated. He had a quick, ready smile, which was also something of a give away because most felt there was a manipulative glint to it.

He flattered Dorothy and was attentive just at a time when she needed special attention. "He was very cooperative in Vegas," said Mills. "He wanted no serving during the show. He also made sure that the staff complied with that." She spent some time with him. But in the beginning, Jack Denison was no more than an innocuous diversion to keep her from being bored, and to keep her mind off Preminger.

The engagement at the Riviera went well. Good crowds. Good notices. As she prepared to leave Vegas, Denison asked if he might come to visit her sometime in Los Angeles. She told him that was fine. They would keep in touch.

※

Once in Los Angeles, other matters occupied her. Attending the premiere of Preminger's *The Man With the Golden Arm* in December, she was frustrated all over again by the relationship with Otto. They still weren't seen together in public. Their romance remained one of Hollywood's great open secrets.

Focusing again on her career, she accepted an offer to appear at the Savoy in London—a major club on the international circuit—in the spring. Negotiations began for her to appear in a French film called *Short Cut*, to be directed by American expatriate, Jules Dassin, who had recently scored an international success with the thriller *Rififi*.

Zanuck also was interested in her for a new film. He had acquired the rights to the forthcoming novel by British writer Alec Waugh called *Island in the Sun*. It was the story of love, politics, and miscegenation in the West Indies. This would be a unique project for Zanuck. Surprisingly, for a man so powerful within the Hollywood studio system, he had grown weary of that system and his life in the film capital. He wanted to break loose from it all. He resigned from Twentieth Century Fox and set up residence in France. *Island in the Sun* represented a chance at a newfound freedom for him. To be financed by Fox, the film would be his first independent production.

Now Zanuck assembled his production team. Hiring Alfred Hayes to write a script from the novel, he also intended to gather an all-star cast. He wanted Dorothy for the role of the young West Indian woman Margot Seaton, who has an interracial love affair. No other actress was even seriously considered.

Buddy Adler, Twentieth Century Fox's new production chief who had been so enamored of her when she appeared in *The Harlem Globetrotters*, contacted Dorothy about the film. Shooting was tentatively scheduled to begin in early June 1956. Dorothy knew even before reading the script she knew she had to do the picture. *Island in the Sun* would be a return to a major American production. Perhaps it would give her a chance to redeem herself with Zanuck and Fox after her departure from *The King and I*.

ELEVEN

PEAKING

*D*orothy was in an upbeat and reflective mood at the start of 1956. *Jet* included her comments, along with those of Duke Ellington, Sammy Davis, Jr., Sarah Vaughan, Jackie Robinson, Herb Jeffries, and Sugar Ray Robinson, in its list of celebrities' New Year's resolutions. Most spoke of personal goals. Jackie Robinson promised to spend more time with his family. Sammy Davis sought "to be loyal to my audiences by always making each performance better than the last." Sarah Vaughan promised to attend church more often.

Dorothy resolved "to endeavor in my own small way to widen horizons for others of my race, to try sincerely to be a credit to my people at all times."

The next month *Jet* ran a cover story titled "Is Dorothy Dandridge Afraid of Love?" The publication reported on her rumored romances with Preminger, Peter Lawford, actor Farley Granger, and Phil Moore. But the magazine concluded that there appeared to be no one special in her life. "Romance seems to have by-passed beautiful film star." How could it be that one of the most desirable women in Hollywood could be so alone?

In February, Dorothy prepared for a two-week engagement at the Sans Souci club in Havana, to be followed later by the trip to England for her Savoy performance. Musician Marty Paich, who was to be her musical director and accompanist for the engagements, met with her. "She showed me what had to be done," said Paich. "And that was it. I met Earl Mills. Then the next thing I knew, after working on the music, we were getting ready to go. We took just a drummer and myself for the piano," said Paich. Dorothy was also accompanied by

Mills and a maid. In Havana, they rehearsed for about a day, Paich recalled. Then came the performances at the Sans Souci. "They just loved her. But they loved her for Carmen," recalled Paich. "That's what they called her." Nightly, the crowds that gathered outside the Sans Souci, waiting for a glimpse of her, surrounded her once she arrived, asking for autographs. Later in the evening, upon her return to her hotel suite at the El Commodore, the crowds were so thick that there were traffic jams in the city. She broke records at the Sans Souci.

Havana didn't seem able to get enough of her. She was front page news as she reigned as honorary queen over the Carnaval de Habana. There was also a running of the Dorothy Dandridge Handicap at the Oriental Park racetrack. She left Havana exhilarated, ready for her next engagement at Philadelphia's Latin Casino.

Revved up about *Island in the Sun*, she continued negotiations and also discussed a starring role as a "fiery gypsy girl" with Italian director Giuseppe Amato in his film *Nina*. Other meetings followed about the film *Short Cut*.

She also spent hours with her therapist. In January alone, she had nineteen sessions with psychology John Berman. The next month, there were eight.

"Surprising that Dorothy Dandridge has not made a picture since *Carmen Jones*, in which she was so successful," Louella Parsons announced in her column on April 2nd. "As soon as she completes her four weeks engagement at the Savoy Hotel in London on May 15, she will head back to Hollywood to discuss *Island in the Sun* with Twentieth Century Fox. She's already agreed to play the Jamaican girl who falls in love with the British newspaper man in the bestseller by Alec Waugh. The sequences will be shot in Jamaica. Later in the year, Dorothy will go to Abyssinia to make *Short Cut* for a French motion picture company."

In London, the Savoy engagement was a smashing success. Prince Philip, Princess Margaret, Charlie Chaplin, and a bastion of other British royals and social figures came to see her. They were not disappointed. Her voice was in peak form. And her surprising confidence—doubtless because of the prospect of movie work—showed in her performances too, which were among her best.

"She was an actress who was a cabaret performer. She was a very very good singer," said Marty Paich. "Very theatrical. She moved right. She read the lyrics very, very well. She got the song across very nicely. She had an extraordinary personality to back it up. If you were watching her in the audience, her smile and her eyes would just indicate to you that she was having fun and was trying to communicate. A lot of performers don't have that."

"As a humanitarian, she was a wonderful, wonderful, kind human being," Paich said. "She always had a smile. She was very thoughtful and considerate with the players and especially myself. It was wonderful to work with her, and I thought she was a wonderful performer. She was quiet and undemanding. People can be such dogs. Dorothy was just the opposite."

"We sold out every night," said Paich. "She was mobbed with press and media. Everybody wanted to see or meet her."

A whirl of social engagements and publicity events followed. Dorothy was a guest at a Parliamentary dinner. At a reception, Prince Philip stood to the side, quietly watching her, openly dazzled. "He walked up to me," said Mills, "and asked if he could be introduced to Dorothy." Mills complied. The Prince smiled, chatted, and lavished Dorothy with praise.

Dorothy was also invited to the campus of Oxford. There she punted with students and was crowned the Queen of May.

She seemed carefree and happy at public outings. "But from my observation," said Paich, "it almost seemed that inwardly there was a sadness in her." Paich didn't spend much time with her though. "Earl pretty much shielded her."

From London, she made a trip to Paris, partly for shopping, partly to discuss new projects. Other than *Island in the Sun*, nothing had been offered her in the States, and she was beginning to think that Europe was the only place where she would find opportunities to work. Three new French films were planned, two of which were to be shot before *Island in the Sun*. Meeting with producer Roland Girard, she agreed to star in *Tamango* with the proviso that she be granted script approval. She also firmed up plans to star as a Portuguese woman in love with an Italian officer in Jules Dassin's *Short Cut*. It was to co-star her with French actor Gerard Philipe, beginning in August. Both films, however, were later delayed. She also met with French movie producer H. Bevard. Rumors swirled about a romance between the two.

By the end of her trip she was exhausted. Returning to the States on the Queen Mary, she canceled her appointments and took to her bed. She turned down offers for appearances at the Fontainebleau

Hotel in Miami Beach, and Chez Paree and the Palmer House in Chicago. Her therapist was called to her home on May 30th for a consultation. She also saw him the next day. Her primary concern seemed to be the general direction of her life, and, of course, the direction of her film career.

❧

Finally, she found a French Regency home that she liked on Evanview Drive in the Hollywood hills. Otto looked it over and thought it perhaps not as large and grand as he might have envisioned. But otherwise he could find no fault. Her taste was unquestionable. "He bought her that house," said Geri. She didn't immediately move in though. Having decided to completely remodel the place, she spent months dealing with contractors, interior decorators, and designers to get it into shape.

❧

Though Otto remained the primary man in her life, he was often working, either on location or at the studio. Or he was in New York. Dorothy, however, had no shortage of suitors. Everywhere she looked or went, men flocked around her, some behaving like hormone-driven adolescents.

As one man after another, sometimes famous, often rich, almost always in a delirious pant, pursued her, she seemed eager—for one of the rare times in her life—just to kick up her heels and have fun. Always discreet, she nonetheless threw herself into a wild series of flirtations and infatuations.

"They were at her feet then!" said Geri. "Let's face it. *Every* man who met Dottie was taken with her. I cannot say that she went to bed with every one of them. But *every* one of them wanted to go to bed with her. I didn't see anyone who wasn't interested. They were *all* interested in her. And some of them would even say, 'Oh, isn't she gorgeous!' And she'd laugh at all of them."

One suitor was Fredric March, the very elegant, very serious, and very married dramatic actor of stage and screen, who seemed unable to dispel her from his thoughts. "Here he was, an actor in a fantasy world like Dottie. He'd see her. And he just *loved* her," said Geri Branton.

Amused and flattered by March's attention, she was thrilled about the prospect of a clandestine romance. In her imagination, it would take place in secluded, intimate restaurants or candle-lit hideaways with verandas where lovers could stand and watch the ocean on a moonlit night. Dorothy began to meet him secretly. Or so she thought. Unknown to her, *Mrs.* Fredric March, actress Florence Eldridge, was very much aware of her husband's philandering—and very much prepared to handle the situation.

"Darling, Freddy gets interested in so many other people. Freddy is always fascinated with something new," Eldridge told Geri Branton one day at lunch. "But he always comes back to me." The message was meant more for Dorothy than Geri.

"Dottie, Mrs. March knows what's happening," Geri later told Dorothy.

"What *do* you *mean*?" Dorothy asked dramatically and haughtily. "What *do* you *mean*?"

"She knows that he's playing footsie with you under the table and trying to be cool," Geri replied. "Don't fall into that trap. And don't do this to her. Don't do this to yourself because you can't hurt her." Dorothy pretended to dismiss the matter. But she soon ended the relationship.

An Argentinean tin heir, suave, courtly, and handsome, also became enchanted by her. He aggressively courted her and presented her with two beautiful jewels, which either out of sentiment or forgetfulness, she left tucked away in a book.

Another South American, a well-known jeweler in Rio de Janeiro, telephoned Dorothy's accompanist Morty Jacobs, during a visit to Los Angeles, to say, "Somebody told me that they know you and that you were in town with Miss Dorothy Dandridge?"

"That's right," said Jacobs.

"I have a present for her," the man said.

Jacobs made a quick visit to see the man, who handed him a small packet of jewels and said, "I want you to give this to Miss Dandridge and tell her it is a present."

When Jacobs delivered the package, Dorothy marveled over the jewels, the most spectacular of which was a large yellow stone. "I want you to do something for me," she said to Jacobs, as she reached for the yellow stone. "I don't [really] know your wife, but I hear she's very sweet and a very loveable person. I want her to have this as a present."

She also flirted recklessly with one of Hollywood's biggest stars of the 1950s; a rugged, handsome actor with a muscular build, a strong jaw line, a dimpled chin, a good sense of humor, a huge following, and a wife. When he invited Dorothy for a rendezvous at his estate in Palm Springs, she excitedly told Geri that it would be a glorious time. She would be the hostess at a series of parties and dinners he planned. They would spend a wonderful weekend together. Her expensive gowns and Juel Park negligees were packed. And off she went to Palm Springs.

But when she arrived at his home, she was surprised to discover that his wife was there. Apparently, the wife's presence surprised the actor as well. Panicking with the Mrs. on the scene, the actor arranged for Dorothy to stay in one of the guest houses on his property. *That* infuriated her.

"Now there were other very famous directors and other people in the guest houses," said Geri. But that meant nothing to Dorothy, who in her grand movie-star manner, "thought it was utter discrimination to have her in one of the guest houses." When she got the actor alone, she "raised sand" with him, and then, from Palm Springs, telephoned Joel Fluellen. She wanted him to come immediately to get her.

"Don't pick me up at the house. I'll be out of this place," she said, giving him instructions to meet her in the lobby of a nearby hotel.

Fluellen rushed out in the rain to drive to rescue Dorothy. But by the time he arrived in Palm Springs, she was in another mood altogether. When he walked into the lobby to ask for Miss Dandridge, she spotted him and turned her back to him as if she did not know him at all. At that moment, Fluellen saw the handsome actor at the hotel. Apparently, he had come in pursuit of her, eager to apologize for his wife's unexpected appearance and to make amends. Dorothy disappeared with him, so she could grandly play the role of the imperial goddess who accepts the pleas of forgiveness from her repentant supplicant, in this case the actor.

Fluellen waited and waited, and sure enough, she reappeared and "deigned to ride back with him" to Los Angeles, said Geri, who was not surprised by Dorothy's behavior. "She was the queen and everybody was paying homage." That was clearly now a part of Dorothy's character. "She made him wait while she went through her shenanigans and finally she climbed into his Volkswagen and he brought her home. Now he was awfully put out because he thought he was pretty cute," said Geri. "But she'd very often do that."

On another occasion, Fluellen came, in the middle of a downpour, to pick her up in his car to run an errand. She became annoyed with him, for some inexplicable reason, and, after getting in the car, decided she did not want to ride with him. She got out, stood in the rain, and yelled that she never wanted to see him again, slammed the car door, and then rushed back inside her home. Fluellen was never sure what had angered her. Later she accepted *his* apology for having upset her so.

In these years, Fluellen frequently bore the brunt of Dorothy's moods. With him, she could be temperamental, haughty, demanding, and, if pushed, nasty, much as she could be with Mills, at times with Preminger, and, of course, in a far different and more intense way, with Vivian.

It was all a part of Dorothy's self-written and directed drama in which she herself starred. Her self-created drama was similar to those of other female stars who, on finally becoming major names, felt liberated after having spent years in studios taking orders from men. For Dorothy, there was no Phil or Otto or Harold telling her how to behave. There was no man who could abandon her. Instead *she* could walk out on them. And if a man proved weak, then he must pay the consequences.

Her romps, adventures, and exploits continued at a sometimes dizzyingly enjoyable pitch. She was delighted for example at being chased by the powerful agent Kurt Frings, who handled the careers of Elizabeth Taylor and Audrey Hepburn. But Dorothy had no real interest in him. Like Fredric March, he was just an amusing way for her to spend some time. He was married to the playwright Ketti Frings. But to be in her presence, Frings was devoted, willing to do almost anything. One evening, she had Frings drive her in his Rolls Royce to a place called Queen Bee's for chitlins. A little later in the evening, the Rolls Royce pulled up in front of Geri's home. Dorothy left Frings by the car while she rushed inside the house to ask for George, a man who worked for Geri.

"What do you want George for?" Geri asked.

"Well, I need some soap and water," Dorothy said. "I have to clean a car."

Dorothy then explained what had happened. As she carried the chitlins from Queen Bee's into Frings' car, she had stumbled and dropped the container. Its contents spilled all over the interior of the Rolls Royce.

"Frings got hysterical," said Geri. "He was hysterical that chitlins were all over his Rolls Royce. Then it turned out that the real reason he was scared to death was because it was his wife's car and not his car." Standing outside Geri's home, Frings was "having a tantrum. Walking up and down my sidewalk."

"Get those goddamn something. . . whatever you call them, out of my car," he said. "I can't go home."

While Frings fumed and fused, Dorothy sat on the sidewalk and broke into laughter. "She thought it was the funniest thing she had ever heard," said Geri. She was amused because she thought it a just comeuppance for a man who, not liking chitlins, wasn't showing proper respect for *her* culture!

"You just suffer, you old bastard," she told Frings. "Just suffer. Cause you're a prejudiced old bastard in the first place!"

"Now's not the time to talk to me about prejudice," he fumed. "Talk to me about getting rid of that mess out of my car. Whoever heard of chitlins riding in a Rolls Royce?"

"Well, that's what you get when you go out with me!" she told him. "And that's the end of it. And I'm not washing anything. George, you can wash it."

Dorothy took Geri on a series of other romantic escapades and encounters with the powerful men pursuing her. "She'd take me along as a buffer," recalled Geri.

"Come some place with me," Dorothy said one afternoon when she stopped by Geri's house unexpectedly. Geri knew Dottie was up to something.

"Oh, don't be afraid. Come on," Dorothy said.

"I'm not afraid. But I'd like to know where I'm going," Geri said.

"Oh, come on," Dorothy insisted. "I want you to see this house."

A producer had invited Dorothy to his palatial home for a meal. The two drove to an old home on Sunset Boulevard. "It was big," said Geri. "One of those big estates on Sunset. And so we go. We drive in. And he's there. And he's in his dressing gown. And he certainly did not expect me."

The producer was obviously irritated by having this third party around during what he hoped would be a rendezvous. But Dorothy acted as if nothing were out of the ordinary. She just talked and talked. She was completely vivacious. But the gentleman became fed up. He wanted Geri out of the house.

As the day dragged on, Geri finally said, "Dottie, I really have something to do. And I know you do too."

"Do you call the shots for what she's doing?" the producer asked Geri.

"No. Not necessarily," said Geri. "But she brought me here. And it's obvious that you and I have absolutely nothing in common. And this seems like a dud. So I want to go home."

He then said, in a huff, "*Well*. I won't even see you to the door."

"*Well*," said Geri. "Thank you very much."

Geri started out of the house. Dottie quickly followed. "Will I see you again?" the producer asked her.

"I think *not*," Dorothy responded with head arched high. She then left without even looking back at him.

Geri recalled, "So that was the end of that. She took me there because she didn't want to be bothered with him. And she thought that if I'd go, I'd have a chilling effect on his ardor. And she didn't have the guts to tell him to go to hell. So this was her way of doing it."

But Dorothy didn't want to admit this fact.

"Why would you end up with trash like that?" Geri asked her.

"Oh, you're too snobbish," Dorothy said. "He's successful."

"Dottie, look down the street," Geri told her. "Up that way. That way. Across the street. A whole lot of successful people with a whole lot more brains than he's got."

Dorothy simply said, "Oh, poopie-la-lee."

"Well, poopie-la-lee. Take me home."

The two women ended up laughing about the encounter.

But the ravenous attentions of so many males was apparent to everyone around her. At a diplomatic social gathering in Los Angeles, the Indonesian president Sukarno, who had seen and loved Dorothy on screen—he boasted of having watched *Carmen Jones* seven times—stepped out of a reception line to go over and greet her. "Apparently, she had gone to some party given by some mogul maybe the night or two before because when he saw her, he greeted her as though he knew her. He was very warm and very friendly," said Geri. "He was very fond of her. He absolutely adored her. But he wasn't trying to be on the make. He wanted to talk to her for political reasons."

Having noticed the maddening battalion of men surrounding her, Sukarno pulled Dorothy aside and said, "I want to help you. I see exactly what's happening. White men adore you. But it isn't always complimentary." He then told her to always "glory in your Blackness as I do mine."

Taken aback by Sukarno's comment, she thanked him for his advice. Then she complimented him on *his* beauty. And he beamed.

"He rather liked that. But he was a nationalist and he wanted her to show nationalism. Dottie and I talked about that together for a long time afterwards," said Geri. "She was grateful that he had given that kind of attention because she wasn't accustomed to getting that kind of caring from people, from men especially. And she very much appreciated it. And she could just analyze and analyze and analyze and analyze and ask, 'Why did he say it?'"

"There was one period in her life where she was kind of easy," recalled Geri. "But she was a tease, you know. She'd string 'em along and walk out on them."

Still, Geri advised her to watch her behavior. "You're going to get known as a nymphomaniac," she said.

Then Dorothy, in her haughty movie star manner, said, "You're the constipated one."

"Well, at least I'm my own person," Geri responded.

"*Well*, so am I," Dorothy said huffily. "You need to get a broader attitude. Why don't you go to my psychiatrist? He'll help you."

"If you're the result, baby," said Geri. "I'm going to be me."

At that comment, Dorothy "fell out laughing" and said to Geri, "You know what? You may be right. You may be right."

Later Geri said, "Dottie didn't give a damn about this kind of talk. It could go on all night. She would just laugh. She had the heartiest laugh you've ever heard. I used to enjoy it. You couldn't help but like her. Even when she did dumb things and carried on. Dottie could always laugh at herself in those days. She liked a good joke."

For Dorothy, it was all moving along fast. Yet, she still was riddled with fears and anxieties as well as feelings of loneliness and isolation. Marriage was still on her mind. Like so many other female stars, Dorothy, despite the parade of men at her feet, found it hard to establish new relationships. As Maria Cole observed, "It was a hard life for Dorothy. I'm sure there were many nights after a performance when it was very lonely. No one there to share it with."

Sometimes men who interested her were afraid to make an approach. "I remember her telling me a couple of instances," recalled Nick Perito, "where she felt like. . . okay, she was going to relinquish-and-give-into-the-amorous-attentions-of-a-particular-suitor, who was plying her with poetry and bonbons. And at the crucial moment, after the dinner and the champagne, I guess, this guy copped out. He, all of a sudden, had to leave. And they never actually consummated their love affair. And she really got upset about that. And from a woman's point of view, I think she couldn't understand it."

But Perito could understand. "I think sometimes men—White, Black, or whatever—have a fear of being involved with a gorgeous woman, regardless of her color, for fear of inadequacy. I would imagine Marilyn Monroe would have had the same kind of problem in dealing with a man's opinion as not being an adequate lover. After all, he's going to be in a bedroom situation with one of America's big sex symbols, whether it be Marilyn Monroe or Dorothy Dandridge. And a lot of guys, for fear of failure, or not being able to live up to my-God-what-this-woman-must-expect-after-all-she-is-the-love-sex-goddess, they will opt to leave. Then make any excuse at all to cop-out. And Dorothy lived with all this kind of stuff."

"She expected her guy to be a Prince Charming and have all the male attributes and sweep her off her feet," said Perito. "And these guys were frightened of her, I think, in awe of her. Or intimidated by her success, her beauty, her intensity. And Dorothy had a very frantic attitude about life. She was impatient with a lot of things."

But Dorothy also had other concerns about just taking up with certain attractive men she met. She knew that for men in show business, the situation was simpler, less fraught with guilt and the moral judgments of a society. A male star could pick up some pretty little thing and no one thought twice. A male star could marry a waitress, a stewardess, a secretary, or a chorus girl without anyone being concerned that the wife was from a different social status.

But a female star could not just pick up with anybody. She might be able to have discreet affairs, if she was lucky. But for the important public outings—the openings, the receptions, the dinners, the charity events, the parties—she needed the proper escort. And if she married, he had to be a man with a position, a clearly defined status, either in or outside the business. Otherwise she would be a joke.

Hollywood was full of fakes and hucksters, covert gigolos and cads. But the colony, while aware of chicanery, would overlook the obvious as long as appearances were maintained. The successful money-laden executive husband of a star could be down to his last dime. And everyone might know it. But as long as he did not look like he was headed for the Bowery, everyone was willing to accept the facade.

Such problems were compounded when the female star was Black. The more successful Dorothy became, the more isolated she was, the more difficult it was to find, even meet, successful, acceptable Black males.

The debilitating and draining despair that she had lived with throughout so much of her life returned. So too did her overriding sense of futility. Her unresolved relationship with Otto, the club scene, which now she hated all the more, her movie career. She was tormented by thoughts of what she should have done, especially her mistake in having turned down the role in *The King and I*. Despite the fact that Zanuck wanted her now for *Island in the Sun*, she believed something had been lost in their professional relationship.

"Artistically, I started going downhill from that moment," she said of *The King and I*. She came to believe that "my decline may have dated from that decision."

During this time, friends noticed that she seemed to become increasingly more impatient and restless. Often she was unable to sit still or relax. She exercised daily, maintaining a very disciplined schedule; partly, of course, to stay in shape and to be healthy, but also partly to ease her tensions, and to keep herself focused and not think too much about herself. Mills noticed that all she really did was exercise, rehearse, and perform. She also seemed to him to exist often in either one of two frames of mind: either very, very up and excited, or calm, languid, and lethargic. There was no in-between. In the past, she had been able to pin her hopes on her career and the idea that life still offered possibilities. But, slowly, that outlook, despite its glimmers of optimism, seemed to be disappearing.

Her sessions with her therapist, John Berman, continued. In June, she saw him for 23 consultations, often going past the usual time limit for such an appointment. She was seeing him a little over five times a week. In July, there were fourteen consultations. In August, there would be eight, and in September, sixteen.

While in this mood, she heard from Jack Denison, the maitre d' in Vegas. Planning a trip to Los Angeles, he asked if he could visit her. Later at her home, he was shrewd enough to see she was needy and obviously unhappy. Clever enough to realize she was on the rebound from the love affair with Otto, he offered her a sympathetic ear. The two had a pleasant time together. As Denison was about to return to Las Vegas, he asked her to let him see her again; assuring her that he wanted to be there for her if she ever needed him.

Afterwards, Denison sent her flowers and notes and made special trips to Los Angeles. Slowly, she came to like him, and perhaps worse, to depend on him. Although some of her friends might have disagreed, Denison impressed her as having the rugged masculine control she had always valued. Jack could get things done, could manage and maneuver, so she told herself. Secretly, she started to make visits to him in Las Vegas. Not seeing people, staying secluded there, she felt free from pressures.

In August 1956, producer Giuseppe Amato informed her that he was willing to postpone his production of *Nina* until she completed *Island in the Sun*. But in the end, plans for *Nina* fell through and it became yet another aborted project. When Dorothy learned of plans to film *Kings Go Forth*—the story of two White American soldiers in love with "a half-Negro girl" in Europe during World War II—she had Mills contact the producer, Frank Ross, asking that she be considered for the lead.

But Ross replied:

> In "Kings Go Forth" it would be impossible to use a negro [sic] in the role of Monique, because at the beginning of the picture, we must not know she is a negro [sic]. I am a great admirer of Dorothy Dandridge. She is one of the finest natural actresses I have ever seen. Maybe some day I will have a picture for her. I would like to.

She had heard such comments before. They *all* admired her. But they rarely gave her any work. *Kings Go Forth* was filmed with Frank Sinatra and Tony Curtis—and Natalie Wood as the "half-Negro girl."

In the fall, Dorothy agreed to do the film *Tamango*, which would be shot in France in the spring of 1957. Mills had negotiated a solid deal for this European production. Not the greatest of scripts perhaps, but she thought its subject—a slave-ship rebellion—interesting nonetheless. Though her character was a slave—the mistress of the White ship captain—Dorothy believed she might be able to do something with this lead role and the film's theme of Black revolt. Later Louella Parsons reported in the *Los Angeles Examiner* that "Dorothy is said to be getting a bigger salary than ever given an outside star—and that includes Gina Lollobrigida. In addition, she'll have a percentage of the picture's world gross."

She soon started preparations for *Island in the Sun*. Zanuck had gathered an impressive group of artists to work on the film. Early on, he hoped Elia Kazan would direct. But Kazan wrote his agent, saying that although "it has some strong melodrama and a good background that can be effective and interesting," the script "really and truly didn't interest me or move me in any way. I didn't like the people and wasn't interested in their fates." He believed "its got no heart-appeal" and that "this is what makes a picture have 'class.'"

Then Zanuck signed the director of the Oscar-winning *All the King's Men*, Robert Rossen, who had been blacklisted a few years earlier during the height of the McCarthy era. The cast would be an ensemble group: James Mason, Joan Fontaine, Joan Collins, Michael Rennie, Stephen Boyd, Patricia Owens, John Justin, and in the pivotal role of the island political firebrand, Harry Belafonte. Dandridge would receive third billing after Mason and Fontaine. Belafonte would have a special billing that came following the primary cast credits. The film was to be shot on the then-hefty budget of $2,250,000 in Barbados and Grenada. Later interiors would be filmed in London. Director of photography would be F. A. Young, who would shoot the film in CinemaScope and color. Costumes were to be designed by David Ffolks.

From the start, Zanuck was concerned about the two interracial love themes to be dramatized in *Island in the Sun*. Belafonte as David Boyer, the island union organizer, would become involved with a privileged, wealthy White woman, Mavis, played by Joan Fontaine. Their "romance" would not be consummated. The other relationship, that of a Black woman and a White man, would be depicted more realistically. Dandridge, as the shop clerk Margot Seaton, was to fall in love with the aide to the island's governor, played by John Justin. The two end up going to England together.

There was also another romance between a young man, Euan, played by Stephen Boyd, who was the son of the island's governor, and Jocelyn, played by Joan Collins, the daughter of a powerful White island family, who is mistakenly led to believe she has "Black blood."

Throughout, *Island in the Sun* would also touch on, but never fully examine, the drama of the island's White minority as it discovers itself confronted with political resistance and a possible uprising by the Black majority. It had the makings of a powerful, significant popular drama.

Early on there were script conferences and correspondence with the Production Code office about the race theme. The Breen office was notified in June of the way the script would address specific moral/racial issues. It was decided that the affair between Jocelyn and Euan "will be treated with proper compensating moral values." To explain Jocelyn's "immoral," pre-martial affair and her resulting pregnancy, the Production office was told, "Some reason will be given for her sin, probably the shock of the discovery that she has Black blood." Of course, the script was implying that nothing could be more devastating or disorienting than having Negro blood. It also suggested that a Black woman was sexually "looser"—less moral—than a White one.

But even before the script of *Island in the Sun* went to the Breen office, its themes and characters had been neutralized and scrubbed clean of any explosive issues or scenes pertaining to interracial unions. There would be no kissing between the races. There would be no onscreen marriages between the races. There would be very little explicit physical contact between the races, except where it concerned Dandridge's Margot.

The Black character David Boyer's chastity with the White Mavis would be explained by his political convictions. So committed was Boyer to his island cause that he had no time nor apparently any great inclination toward making any romantic passes; politics would inhibit him from being the traditional male aggressor. But what about the White male character involved with Dandridge? Was there some way of explaining his being sexually inhibited? By now, Dandridge was such an acknowledged beauty and sex symbol that Fox understood it would be totally implausible for a White male romantically interested in her *not* to make a move. In some way, he would physically have to express his interest in and desire for this gorgeous Black woman. Otherwise White males in the audience would lose all identification with him. He might even seem, in the parlance of the Fifties, "less than a man."

Zanuck also had concerns about the way the film would be received by Black America. Just as he had suggested that Preminger have *Carmen Jones*'s script read by someone of note from the African American community, now at Fox, executive Frank McCarthy sent the *Island in the Sun* script to a prominent African American attorney, Truman Gibson. McCarthy and Gibson had served together in the army during the Second World War.

On July 13, 1956, Gibson wrote a long letter to McCarthy,

explaining his feelings about the *Island in the Sun* script, which basically he liked. Yet his letter pointed out certain problem areas. He also clearly expressed the attitudes and concerns of African Americans about movie images.

In my opinion the treatment is not objectionable from a racial point of view. In this connection I hasten to add that no one can set himself as an absolute judge of Negro opinion because there is no such animal. However there are universally objectionable racial stereotypes which Negroes generally object to. When these are avoided, or if employed, used in a context that does not make them focal points, Negroes by and large react to the overall material in the same manner as others of similar economic educational and geographical backgrounds.

Since the writer of the screen play and Waugh himself has viewed a minimum of what be termed racial stereotypes the screenplay is not one that could be condemned on this score. A few stereotypes appear. Among these are the steel band players, the Calypso singers and the "forelock pulling 'typical;' peasant who retrieved the murdered Colonel Carson's wallet; they are all well integrated into the plot and hence are not used for the purpose of portraying all natives as being stupid, singing Calypso dancing dwellers of a beautiful semi-tropic paradise.

Just as I do not assume to be a final authority on Negro opinion, I likewise can make no serious pretensions as a script critic. However, I did have the feeling of disappointment in the character development of Boyer. Since the lawyer was omitted from the screenplay, the development of Boyer as a cynical exploiter of his people diverts attention from some of the basic reasons why people in that area are now actively and rapidly pushing towards dominion status; and also why the Caribbean World has so radically changed in the last few years.

Gibson's letter concluded, "Twentieth Century Fox is due tremendous credit for courage in tackling the ticklish issues in the screen play and for demonstrating an increasingly evident maturity in the selecting and treatment of screen material."

Gibson, however, was no more concerned with trouble spots in the story than was Dorothy, who had reservations about her character

Margot but was waiting to see a revised script.

Shortly before filming *Island in the Sun*, Dorothy joined her old friend Louis Armstrong, Gordon MacRae, George Sanders, Shirley Jones, and George Chakiris for CBS's "Ford Star Jubilee's" tribute to Cole Porter. She performed "You Do Something to Me" and "My Heart Belongs to Daddy." During rehearsals, though, she had a run-in with CBS. Dorothy balked at the fact that during the number "You Do Something To Me," four White male performers backed her as she sang. She asked point blank why no Blacks were included in the number. Taken aback, CBS capitulated and hired three Black dancers to accompany her as she performed the Porter number, "My Heart Belongs To Daddy."

Filming of *Island in the Sun* began in mid-October. As the cast and the British crew descended on the small island of Grenada, most seemed in a mood for fun.

But for Dorothy, much of her experience was miserable. Things went awry the minute she arrived in Grenada and settled into the Santa Maria Hotel. She had been sent the revised version of the script shortly before her departure from Los Angeles. But she had been too rushed then to look it over. Now at this late date, she found herself dissatisfied with what she was reading. It was her understanding that none of the cast had received the script until then. She learned otherwise. "They were not telling the truth," she said of the studio brass. "Everybody had seen each script except me. Harry had his part rewritten before he agreed to do it."

She was infuriated. "I hated the part," she wrote a friend. "I almost left two days after I arrived when I read the script."

The relationship between her character Margot Seaton and Denis Archer struck her as compromised and unrealistic. Here were two people who were supposed to fall passionately in love. Yet they didn't even kiss, and, more significantly, the script never let them say they loved each other. Now that Hollywood was finally dramatizing interracial love, why do it so timidly? Was the script—in order not to "offend" White audiences—suggesting a Black woman might be sexually desirable but not worthy of being *loved* by a White man? Were a White actress playing the "colored" Margot, wouldn't the script be more forthright and honest?

Margot needed greater definition. Nothing explained who this woman was or what she wanted out of life. Privately, Dorothy referred to the character as "a nothing role." "I just can't stand these nothing to do, take the chick roles," she wrote another friend.

Psychologically, she began to see her career problems not so much as the fault of the industry, but of her own failings. Just as she had always blamed herself for Lynn's condition and even had blamed herself for Cyril's "desertion" of the family, she now began to blame herself for a film career that hadn't developed as she wanted.

Her anger boiling, she met with director Robert Rossen and complained. He was evasive and didn't seem to understand why she was so upset. But Dorothy wouldn't let Rossen just dismiss her concerns. Their meeting became heated. Rossen agreed to think the matter over but refused to make any immediate changes in the script.

Perhaps believing Dorothy might become a problem on the set, Rossen decided to let Zanuck deal with the dilemma. He wrote Dorothy on October 12th:

> *My dear Dorothy,*
> *I have given our conversation a great deal of thought and I now think the only way this whole situation can be resolved is in consultation with Mr. Zanuck, who is the producer of the film and who has read and approved of the script as it stands right now.*
> *Mr. Zanuck, as I have informed you, will arrive early Sunday morning and at which time we can dispose of this matter one way or another.*
> *All the best.*
> *As ever,*
> */s/ Robert Rossen*
> *cc-Mr. Darryl Zanuck*

Dorothy wired Earl Mills in Los Angeles and prevailed upon him to contact Zanuck. Upon his arrival in Grenada, Zanuck met with Dorothy and Rossen. Still hating confrontations, Dorothy nonetheless spoke her mind.

"I lost lots of sleep and had to fight like hell," she told a friend. "It was difficult to make many changes as it was two days before shooting. Anyway, I fought and made whatever improvements I could, and decided to stick with it instead of running, and do all I can with what I have. I hate it here."

But Zanuck saw her point and promised to consider some of her suggestions for further script changes. She found the meeting with him productive. The two had also discussed the direction of her career. "I must admit that I like Mr. Z. We have become quite good friends," she said. "He understood right off the bat my objections to certain things, including the parts I've been offered." Yet she was realistic about the film. It would still be an uphill battle.

Dorothy kept her anxieties to herself. Though others in the cast also had doubts about the script, most seemed eager to forget work and have some play and relaxation during the shoot. For many of them, *Island in the Sun* was just another movie.

"*Island in the Sun* is still talked about as being one of the most enjoyable locations ever among the British film units," said Joan Collins. "It has become almost legendary. We had an enormous crew, including a second unit. Over one hundred technical men and women."

The schedule was not a tight one. Usually, shooting had to be completed before the sunlight changed, which meant that the production closed up around four in the afternoon every day. With so much time on their hands, said Collins, the cast and crew often gathered and played cards, charades, or board games like Monopoly and Scrabble.

There was also time for other games. Collins remembered the day Zanuck, always seen chomping on his cigar, grabbed hold of her in the corridor of the hotel. With his current mistress away, Zanuck thought he should avail himself of other opportunities. "You've had nothing until you've had me. I've got the biggest and the best," he told her. "I can go all night." Collins tried tactfully to disentangle herself. "Luckily," said Collins, "Dorothy Dandridge and a makeup man came walking down the corridor and I made my escape, vowing to keep out of Mr. Z's way in the future."

Participating in some of the social gatherings, Dorothy played a few games, went sailing with Joan Fontaine, Patricia Owens, and others, and attended the big brunch Zanuck tossed for a hundred and fifty of his cast and crew.

Usually, though, she felt pressured into attending events. It wasn't just the filming that drained her, she told a friend, but "all the outside things that somehow you can't say no to. Joan Fontaine's birthday party. You know everyone must be there." Then there were the parties given by residents of Grenada. If she didn't show, she believed the people would feel insulted. "Harry and I are really on the spot. You know why. The island is ninety percent Negro," she said in a letter.

"The studio has taken over the Island, and the people have been so wonderful and given so much of themselves that we just have to make their offers once in awhile."

She felt trapped by the other seemingly endless requirements and activities. "My life is not my own at this point," she wrote, and commented on the other seemingly endless requirements and activities:

> . . . . the studio press photos etc.—interviews with local press—meeting the Govenor [sic]. Rehearsing a dance with one of the girls on the Island that they have decided to put in the picture (which helps, but its [sic] still more work when you're trying to shoot too.) Fittings for the new costume for the dance, etc. Meeting and having dinner with Alec Waugh, and God knows what all else. Then up at 5 A.M. when shooting. So far I've been called every morning except 4 in 2 weeks. On location you can shoot six days a week. Even when you're not called you have to wake up at 6 A.M. because the walls are so thin that you hear everybody else's wake up call. There are no shades and the sun comes rushing in at about 6 A. M. and you can't sleep anyway. If I didn't have these pills, I don't know what I would do. . . .
>
> It just goes to show there is no easy way. There is quite a price to pay for everything. When you're in night clubs you think pictures are the answer, then you get pictures and location (still fighting for script changes—when to go out, when to stay in—heat, bugs, ants in your bed, wrong food—can't get steaks and things—no sleep. People yes, you're not alone, but now its [sic] too many people, and almost in the room with you all the time. You have to fight even harder to ever to be left alone—no telephone— no hot water, and sometimes no water at all. I can see now that 1 location trip a year (3 mos.) is about all I can take. Maybe its [sic] because I was tired when I left. And I've had so little family life. Somewhere there's an answer I must find.

Yet, with all the activities, she managed often enough to keep to herself. Or at least appeared to keep to herself.   But early on, there were whispers about a romance between her and Belafonte. "Harry Belafonte split from his spouse and Dorothy Dandridge are

Very Warm for Tobago or even Chicago," was the item that appeared in *The Hollywood Reporter*.

Without a doubt, she was still attracted to him, and, apparently, he to her. Their special, sometimes argumentative friendship had endured for several years now. And she no doubt still considered him the ideal romantic lover. Publicist Orin Borsten remembered an incident that occurred in Los Angeles. One day he had received a call from Earl Mills, who told him, "Don't call Dorothy this week." Borsten couldn't understand why. Then Mills told him, "She and Mr. Belafonte have closed the doors to the place. I bring the food to them. Leave it at the door. They are not to be disturbed for this whole week." Borsten recalled, "That was the first time I ever knew her to be linked with a [particular] man."

Dorothy confided to a friend that late one night during the *Island in the Sun* shoot, Belafonte raised the window of her hotel room and crept inside. "He's so silly," she said. "He's a child." "We were very good friends," Belafonte himself said years later, "As a matter of fact, if Julie [his second wife] hadn't been in my life, I probably would have run off with her."

But Dorothy now accepted the fact that loving Harry wasn't going to take her anywhere. The truth was, said Geri Branton, that Dorothy "was annoyed because he was never serious enough about her." She was also aware, as was everyone else on the picture, that Belafonte and Joan Collins were rumored to be in the midst of a sizzling love affair.

She turned her attentions elsewhere—in the direction of her co-star James Mason, whose wife Pamela didn't travel to the location shooting. Pamela Mason may have later regretted not being there because James and Dorothy quietly but *pleasantly* became very *friendly*. Sophisticated and witty, Mason was a likeable companion with whom she could discuss some of her problems. "There was an affair because she alluded to it," said Geri. But "it didn't last that long."

Dorothy also regularly talked to Denison over the phone.

She also had struck up a friendship with actor Michael Rennie. Like Mason, Rennie was British, polished, and urbane. He had been involved with Preminger's estranged wife Mary Gardner Preminger. That led some of Dorothy's friends to believe Rennie was attentive to her partly—only partly—in hopes of prying information from her about Otto. Such information could be passed on and used by the estranged Mrs. Preminger in her divorce suit against the director. But the two did enjoy each other's company. Rennie was always quick to sing Dorothy's praises, and once when asked by columnist Earl Wilson to list the world's most beautiful women, Rennie promptly included Dorothy.

On the set, aside from the script problems, Dorothy questioned Robert Rossen's direction. Mainly, she felt she was being asked just to smile, sit, stand, frown, say yes, say no. The carnival sequence, when she had to perform the limbo, proved physically demanding. Take after take left her feet blistered and raw.

Throughout the production, she remained in communication with Mills about other projects and problems. Most pressing was her tax situation.

As early as the fall of 1954, she had received inquiries about her taxes from both the Internal Revenue Service and the State of California's Franchise Tax Board. But as soon as one inquiry was answered, another arose. Letters and discussions went back and forth between Dorothy's accountants and the tax boards. Then in October 1956, the State of California's Franchise Tax Board contacted Twentieth Century Fox by certified mail and put a levy on the studio's pay.

The total due was $1,210.04, for taxes for the years 1945, 1946, and 1947. Dorothy countered that she had never been advised of any tax due for those years. In fact, she said she had not even earned any income during 1947. During those years, joint returns had been filed for Harold and her. It took her months to get the matter settled. Little did she know it, but her tax problems were only beginning.

From the States, Mills informed her of offers for nightclub appearances. Already scheduled were dates in early 1957 in Miami Beach, Kingston, Jamaica, and Boston. Now Mills pressed her to accept an engagement at the Cocoanut Grove, which would be almost immediately upon her return from the *Island in the Sun* shoot.

"I don't know how I will do the Grove," she informed him. "If I go the first of December and go home and start with Bob [a musical director] for the Grove I'll have no break at all," she said, then kidded, "I don't know how I can take it even with the pills."

She had mixed feelings about accepting the engagement because she needed the money. "What's the cost for the boys, gowns for me, their clothes, etc.," she wrote:

> Can I come out with enough money with the 6 weeks work? *Unless You're sure* I'm really going to *clear* lots of

money I don't think I can make it, and I don't think its [sic] worth it. Off hand it I doesn't look as if it will pay, and at the same time do it right.

Dorothy ended up turning down the engagement. But she found another offer tantalizing. Mills cabled her the news that producer Lester Cowan had optioned the rights to Billie Holiday's autobiography, *Lady Sings the Blues*, which traced her troubled life from her "illegitimate" birth to her rise to jazz star to her stormy affairs and drug addiction. He wanted Dorothy for the lead. If the film were to be made, it could be a searing role.

Immediately, Dorothy cabled Mills back:

GO AHEAD WITH LADY SINGS IDEA BUT I KEEP FEELING THERE SHOULD BE SOMETHING MIXED IN BETWEEN I WANT VERY MUCH TO DO IT BUT TIM-ING IS IMPORTANT YOU CAN CALL ME
HERE=DOTTY MAR [sic]=

Mills began negotiations on the project. The film would have to be shot sometime in early 1957 because *Tamango* was scheduled to begin in the spring. At first, Dorothy insisted on the option of using her own voice for the musical sequences but later changed her mind. "Miss Dandridge is quite sure that Miss Holiday should do the singing for authenticity and with respect to Miss Holiday, one of the great singing stylists of our time," Mills later wrote Cowans. Most important though, Dorothy was determined not to have another *Island in the Sun* situation with a script that she hated. Thereafter Mills informed producer Cowans that should she do the film, "Miss Dandridge must have billing above the title; Miss Dandridge must approve Director and SCRIPT." The project became even more promising when Dorothy learned that producer Cowans had begun discussions with Orson Welles about directing the film.

On November 12th, the production moved for three days of film-ing to Barbados. Afterwards, with the cast and crew scheduled to go to London for interiors, Dandridge requested permission from Fox to fly to New York for a few days. There she met Denison. It appears that by now, he was feeling more sure of himself. An argument broke out between the two, apparently over a pair of gloves she planned to wear. It upset Dorothy, who was surprised by the violent display of his temper over an obviously minor incident. But soon they reconciled.

What had started as a diversion from her relationship with Otto was becoming more serious. It's doubtful that she was searching for "true love" with Denison, even being the romantic that she was. But she no doubt was hoping it might come along.

Zanuck called a press conference on November 29th at the Claridge Hotel in London to discuss the progress of *Island in the Sun*. Dandridge by this time had flown to London to resume work on the picture. Otto was also in London to introduce his new discovery, Jean Seberg, who was set to star in his production of *Saint Joan*. As Dorothy heard of Preminger's predictions of a glorious future for Seberg, she couldn't help remembering the past and his excitement over her budding career. She sent him a note wishing him luck with his "new star." She still hadn't given up on their relationship even though their schedules kept them so far apart.

As filming of *Island in the Sun* continued, Zanuck and director Rossen fiddled with the script. By now, they were fully aware of its weaknesses and dramatic inconsistencies. But Dorothy's concerns were not uppermost in their minds. Rather, Zanuck was anxious about reactions and threats from movie exhibitors in the South. There was already talk that some Southern theatres might boycott the film.

Dorothy still fought for a different treatment of her character Margot's love affair. She objected seriously to the sequence in the summerhouse where John Justin was to confess his love for her.

"In this one scene where we have physical contact the whole thing is a little too self-conscious and unnatural," she said. "First of all, it must be understood that Margot, whom I play, is not an American Negro girl but a West Indian, and she would not be self-conscious about or sensitive to an interracial love affair. It happens all the time in the West Indies."

She also spoke again to Rossen and Zanuck. Her co-star John Justin agreed that the depiction of the affair seemed compromised. The two had long discussions about their characters. Then they approached Rossen.

"John Justin and I seriously proposed that two versions of the scene be made," Dorothy said, "one for American audiences without kissing and the other for Europe where people are not concerned or upset about the problem of interracial love. When two people are in love and confess their love to each other, the natural thing for them to do is kiss."

The suggestion to shoot two versions of the scene was discarded. But Dorothy and Justin still pressed for changes, which led to a battle. "John and I had to fight to say the word 'love,'" she said. "At first this line was, 'You know how I feel.'" Mills also spoke to Zanuck, who finally agreed to some concessions. "We'll do it over again," he told Mills. The line "You know how I feel" was replaced by Justin's character saying to Margot, "You know I'm in love with you, don't you?" He still hadn't been able to profess his love with the simple declarative statement, "I love you." But Dorothy accepted the change.

Still, Zanuck remained adamant that the couple not kiss. "We do embrace in the picture, but we're not allowed to kiss," Dorothy said. "Of course, I disagree entirely with the reasons for the ban."

Otherwise her pleas with Zanuck about more development for Margot—something to explain the character's motivations and make her more than just a beautiful cipher—went nowhere.

"He said he wasn't able to change all the dialogue, the way it should have been done," said Mills. Privately, Dorothy began to feel that she had hounded Zanuck so much that he must "hate" her for some of her comments.

Belafonte and Joan Fontaine were also dissatisfied. "In this movie, where the normal sequence of events would have led to romantic situations between myself and Joan Fontaine," said Belafonte, "they were played down."

Fontaine concurred. "At least I have made them agree that Harry and I can drink out of the same coconut together in a scene. But they insist no kissing, and that we give one another up at the end of the picture."

Publicly, Zanuck denied there had been any pressure from Hollywood censors. Or any fears about reactions from the southern market. "There is no scene that calls for kissing," he insisted. "There was no conscious effort to avoid it."

Once *Island in the Sun* wrapped in December, Dorothy returned to Los Angeles exhausted. Mills was instructed to cancel her upcoming club dates for early 1957 in Miami Beach, Kingston, and Boston. She did little at the end of 1956, other than agree to be honored, along with actor Glenn Ford, by the National Urban League at its annual

Winter Ball in February of the next year. Mostly, she savored the pleasures of finally moving into her new home. While she had been on location, the new home had been remodeled to her specifications. Everything had been moved in.

She didn't say good-bye to Hilldale, though, without second thoughts and fond memories. Dorothy could look at her "bachelor girl pad" and remember the dreams that had come true there. It was warm and cozy; private but accessible. She'd had good times there: cooking with Joel, having Vivian stay over and Geri stopping by to chat, or standing on the little hill north of the block to see part of sprawling Los Angeles.

The place had meant much to her. She felt she had grown up there, but now was the time to move on.

The house on Evanview Drive was larger and higher on the hill. Coming off Sunset Plaza, one had to drive through a long winding nest of avenues to reach Evanview, and it was easy to get lost. Only the very directed and the very focused could find the house on Evanview on the first drive. It took concentration. Evanview was a metaphor for her steady ascension, the next stage of her life. It was dwelling of a star on the rise. She settled in.

"It was a gorgeous house," said Geri. "Very well built. It had only one bedroom. And it was just furnished to perfection. Beautiful drapes and carpeting. She loved thick carpeting. And large couches. It didn't have an entrance hall. You just go in. And to your right was the huge living room and then across from that was a lovely library and it was beautifully done." In the terraced living room, there was a brick fireplace framed in antique gold. There also sat an ebony Steinway grand piano and an ebony television set. Plants were everywhere, and a large bay window overlooked Hollywood and Beverly Hills. The living room, dining room, and den all opened onto a covered patio where she could entertain. "And then, of course," said Geri, "her bedroom—*gorgeous*! Like a movie star's! All in white. And these heavy, heavy, thick blackout drapes. A lovely kitchen. A dining room. And den." She hired a secretary named Veada Cleveland, who also assumed responsibility for running the household.

Sammy Davis, Jr. lived across the street in the home once owned by Judy Garland. Herb Jeffries moved to the same block with his wife, exotic dancer Tempest Storm. Dorothy socialized with both men.

Often she entertained, and now her guests were Gary and Rocky Cooper, Peter Lawford (when available), Fredric March, and later

James and Pamela Mason. When she attended their parties, she was often the only Black person, except on those occasions when Joel Fluellen was her escort. But in her own home, the gatherings were an interracial mix. She invited Geri and Dorothy Nicholas Morrow and her husband Byron. Or Herb Jeffries. Or Sammy Davis. Also on hand, of course, was Joel, sometimes a guest, sometimes as a member of her staff.

Her parties were planned, blocked, story-boarded, choreographed, directed, and produced in high Hollywood style. On polished and ornate silver trays were delicious delicacies, often prepared and often served by Joel. In elegant Baccarat crystal flutes, champagne bubbled and fizzed as it was carried to guests. Throughout the room were cut flowers in beautiful vases. On the stereo, music by Ellington (still Dorothy's favorite), Nat Cole, or Sinatra sent out sweet, soothing sounds that helped create a dreamy, idyllic romantic atmosphere.

Often the guests had to wait for Dorothy's arrival. She would be in her bedroom, preparing herself to look absolutely smashing before making an appearance. Geri remembered the elaborate procedures Dorothy went through to make herself up for social gatherings and public events. It would take hours and hours "and just drive you crazy. In those days, we used a heavy pancake base, which had to dry." Then she painted on her lips. Her eyes were perfectly lined. "Dottie would take two hours to get dressed. She would change this and change that. And keep everybody waiting."

In her bedroom, Dorothy would often be attended to by Veada Cleveland, who had previously worked for Jennifer Jones or, as some in the industry liked to say, Mrs. David O. Selznick. Cleveland advised Dorothy on clothes and social protocol, always quick to let her know how Mrs. Selznick handled matters. "Veada would have her make an entrance," said Geri. Although some friends found Cleveland officious, phoney, and manipulative, "Dorothy listened to her," said Geri. "She really did."

While Joel served the hors d'oeuvres and supervised the kitchen staff, he also kept an eye on his watch. Often Dorothy's lateness in greeting her guests drove Fluellen to conniptions. Sometimes he marched to her room and reprimanded her.

"You've got all these people waiting. Now come on, girl," he might say.

"Not to worry," she might tell him, using an expression she had picked up from the British during her Savoy engagement. At such times, Dorothy seemed vague and spacey but imperial and more goddess-like than ever. She would be caught up in the giddy romanticism of the evening. Then she would appear. Making her entrance, she was naturally Dorothy Dandridge, looking sensational, smiling and vivacious, her head held high with the chin arched up as she extended her hand and greeted her guests. And, of course, the room stopped. She was not your usual Hollywood hostess, those brilliantly social wives of the industry executives or male stars who planned perfect evenings and always looked wonderful but remained *wives*, not prime movers; not the objects of attention and desire.

Dandridge was at the center of her social affairs. On such evenings, Hollywood, caught up in its own mythology, saluted Dandridge, as the goddess it knew her to be. Her beauty, success, and fame all endowed her with an extraordinary power. It was no wonder that Otto relished having her as his hostess. As an industry potentate, he had not a consort by his side, but a mythological Aphrodite or Athena.

Dinner could be a mix of soul and European haute cuisine. The table would be set with Wedgewood china, glittering silverware, Irish crystal, imported linen, and vases of flowers everywhere. Everyone smiled. Everyone was gracious and charming. Everyone at such affairs was determined to participate in an illusion of a memorable evening. Often their most spirited talk was about the industry. But Dorothy was known to prefer discussing books, theatre, and still her favorite topic, psychology. "She loved to get into lengthy intellectual discussions," said Nick Perito.

Sometimes "bad" behavior by a jealous wife or boyfriend surfaced at these gatherings, or little intrigues developed. On some occasions, both Dorothy and Geri were surprised by Joel's behavior, especially if there was a particular male guest, such as pretty boy Lawford, who might strike his fancy. "Dottie and I just could not believe it!" said Geri. "He would flirt with some of these men like there was no tomorrow." But, of course, in the long run, Joel's presence simply added to the evenings festivities.

Financially, Dorothy was now in fine shape. Her club engagements paid her between $5,000 and $10,000 a week. But while she luxuriated in certain extravagances, she was still oddly cautious about money and spending.

She prided herself on being able to take care of her bills and expenses, as she had been doing so since she was a teenager when she had been her family's breadwinner. The idea of an unpaid bill scared her, and must have been a reminder of the Depression years when

Ruby struggled to keep the family afloat. Usually when money came in, she made sure first that everything was taken care of with Lynn, and apparently, she still sent something to Ruby. Then money had to be used for new costumes, new arrangements. The house had to be properly maintained too. The rest of her money went into savings and investments.

"I wear two hats," she liked to say both with a mixture of pride and weariness. "I wear the hat of a woman. But I have to wear the hat of a man when I take care of my business because men will take advantage. I pay my own bills. I am the man of my house."

Through her new social circle, Dorothy decided to invest in a seemingly promising business venture: oil wells in Oklahoma and later New Mexico. Along with such stars as Kirk Douglas, Doris Day and her husband Martin Melcher, Billy Eckstine, and Gordon MacRae, she left her finances in the hands of the law firm Rosenthal and Norton, headed by Jerome Rosenthal and Sam Norton. They formed the Earlsboro Oil and Gas Company, of which Dorothy and the other celebrities became limited partners. Rosenthal, Norton, and New York attorney Andrew D. Weinberger were the general partners of the corporation. Advised that the wells were bound to come in and assured that she would be financially secure for life, she poured a great percentage of her earnings into the well investment.

It was around this time, in January 1957, that an article appeared in the Black publication *Hep*, titled "Dorothy Dandridge—Her 1,000 Lovers." It was a fictitious account of the supposedly innumerable men in her life. Friends had rarely seen her so agitated and angry. She felt the article was an invasion of her privacy as well as a lie. Having guarded her personal life so closely all these years, she decided she had to take action. She consulted Geri's husband Leo, an attorney, and decided to bring a suit against the publication. She didn't care what it cost.

The next month, Branton filed a $2,000,000 lawsuit in Superior Court against *Hep*'s publishers, The Good Publishing Company. It became front page news for Black newspapers around the country.

But her battles with the press were just beginning. In February, *Sepia* magazine published an article titled, "Why Dorothy Dandridge is Afraid of Marriage," which also angered her. The magazine implied that she was warned by people in the industry that the wrong type of marriage—to a White man—could wreck her career.

Dorothy wrote *Sepia* that its article had caused her "a great deal of pain and embarrassment." She also wrote an article—"I'm Not Afraid of Marriage by Dorothy Dandridge"—which she wanted the magazine to print as a form of rebuttal. In it, she explained, "I must speak up in defense of myself" and stated that she was "not a gregarious person."

> Perhaps I could be, but long years of touring from city to city meeting strangers who were not always to be trusted, have made me something of a hermit...
>
> Why did I guard myself when I might have met the man I could have found happiness with?
>
> I've examined myself over and over on that question, and I think it's always been largely a matter of a sense of responsibility to my own people. . . I was afraid, terribly afraid, of bringing disgrace of [sic] and to my people by taking a chance with all the strangers one meets in touring and on location jaunts. . . .
>
> No, I would rather be lonely, I would rather look at the walls of my hotel room than risk mingling with individuals who turn out to be unsavory characters.
>
> Above all, I wanted to keep an unblemished reputation for the sake of members of my race.

But as Dandridge made her heartfelt response to *Sepia*, another story about her—far more damaging—was soon published in *Confidential* magazine. *Confidential* was a popular publication that specialized in scandalous stories about celebrities, everyone from Marilyn Monroe and Mae West to Anthony Quinn, Ava Gardner, Kim Novak, Maureen O'Hara, and Liberace.

African American personalities like Sammy Davis, Jr., Sugar Ray Robinson, Floyd Patterson, Eartha Kitt, Jackie Robinson, Joe Louis, and Herb Jeffries were also featured in *Confidential*, which enjoyed titillating its readers with tales of reported interracial couplings. "The pages of *Confidential* were filled with innuendoes about celebrities involved in relationships with other races," Joan Collins recalled.

Confidential's Dandridge story purported to be an account of a lovemaking session between Dorothy and a male she happened upon while walking alone in the woods of Lake Tahoe. Titled "What Dorothy Dandridge Did In the Woods," the article opened:

> You ambitious wolves who set the stage with champagne, caviar and gypsy fiddles when you're on the make, have been doing it all wrong. The suave sirens are going back to nature. They're digging the trees and the birds and the bees.

> Now take Dorothy Dandridge, the talented tan songstress, who looks like the last word in sophistication. All she asks for is the open sky and some green grass on the turf.
> Up at Tahoe Village in Lake Tahoe where Dorothy played an engagement some time ago, the playboys spent most of their time plotting how to get a warm tumble from the sensuous singer. They tried all the tricks the wolf uses to snare the rich prize, but their message wasn't getting through to Dorothy.
> Then one brisk afternoon on a wooded mountain top, a guy with a little ingenuity and a lot of patience discovered that no matter how glamorous a chick is, she can be a pushover for the simple things in life.
> The article continued:

> "Would she in the woods?" he wondered. There was nothing like finding out. He let one arm snake around the famous Dandridge hips and pretty soon they were going through some very passionate preliminaries, but then old Mother Nature cued them into the main event. The birds were doing it and the bees were doing it, so shouldn't they?

"Highly, highly incensed," said Geri Branton of Dorothy's reaction to the article. Dorothy consulted Leo Branton again about suing *Confidential*. Like most stars in Hollywood, Dorothy was aware that it was a battle to win a libel suit in America. That she had already seen in her lawsuit against *Hep*. One had to prove that the article in question had been written with malicious intent or that the intention was to cause harm. During lawsuit proceedings, other personal information could be revealed. That explained why, despite the fact that *Confidential* had angered much of the Hollywood community, few were willing to make a move against the publication.

But Dorothy said that the *Confidential* article, like that in *Hep*, was another lie. Second, it depicted her as a woman who would engage in sex with anyone, anywhere. Its racial connotations also suggested that a Black woman was readily available to any White male, including a "pale" stranger in the woods.

"She was interested in correcting a wrong. She really was strong in that respect," said Geri Branton. "She was not interested in money from a suit."

In late March, Branton filed the lawsuit against the magazine for $2,000,000.

The *Confidential* article upset Dorothy for other reasons. She always feared the press reaction to an interracial romance, and the article seemed to add to an ever-growing perception that she was no longer attracted to Black males. Other publications, both Black and White, linked her with such White males as Tyrone Power (who she said she had never met), Preminger, Michael Rennie, Farley Granger, millionaire Arthur Loew Jr. (who she also said she had never met), and scores of others.

Ironically, by reporting on her supposed romances with prominent White American males, the national press viewed her differently from the African American women who had preceded her in the public eye. Despite the sexy image, the element of "class" and "sophistication" that Nick Perito said was always apparent in her club performances carried over to her general media image. Whenever seen in public— at airports, restaurants, benefits,receptions—she was photographed stylishly dressed with gloves, pearls, and matching handbag and shoes. Her manners remained impeccable. Ultimately, the national press treated Dandridge like a lady whom it perceived as being worthy of White male adoration. That was in stark contrast to the press treatment of Dorothy's contemporary Eartha Kitt, who the press delighted in depicting as an exotic and something of a tasty oddity.

The nature of the publicity Dandridge received called into question America's basic racism toward African American women. Dandridge's image signaled that Black American women, rather than being exotics, were intelligent, elegant, sophisticated, and worldly. It was this aspect of Dandridge that made her so appealing and important to Black America. Had the movie industry provided her with choice, sophisticated roles, the perceptions of Black women in the consciousness of the American mass audience might have changed all the more dramatically.

Yet, paradoxically, part of Dandridge's general media image, that of the Black woman dating White males, was also used against her. It looked to some as if she lived totally in a White world. That was partially true, but never to the extent that some might have imagined; and never without complications and contradictions that disturbed Dorothy herself.

Her friend Geri Branton was aware of this and believed Dorothy's participation in Black social functions was a way to help keep Dorothy grounded.

"I just could not let the White community absorb her life," said Geri. "I would take her to Urban League functions." Leo Branton helped her prepare speeches for such affairs. "Dottie took pride in it too," said Geri. She also became a lifetime member of the NAACP.

Still, stories circulated that she had fled her Black roots. Years later Preminger committed a terrible injustice against her with his comment that she was attracted only to White men. That was Otto, the spurned lover, trying to strike back, particularly at her relationship with the very White-looking Jack Denison.

"Sometimes people thought that Dorothy was prejudiced against Black men," Vivian said. "She discussed it with me many times. She would say, 'What can I do? I'm earning so much money. I don't want to feel I'm keeping them.' Then there was a certain amount of jealousy because she was famous."

"My sister would have been very happy to have married someone like a Harry Belafonte or a Sidney Poitier. But those men were already married. And when they left their wives, they married White women. Dottie just didn't meet Black men in her world."

Even Harold Nicholas, years later, was angered by the accusations against his former wife. "I think it's unjust," he said. "She just happened to be in contact with White men. She didn't make it that way. That was not what Dorothy was about. She was in a business where she didn't meet Black men. She couldn't establish relationships."

Through Geri and Leo Branton, Dorothy sometimes was introduced to a Black lawyer or doctor. But the lives of these men were so different from hers. Had she ever married such a man, it was likely he would have been unable, maybe even unwilling, to cope with her schedule, which kept her away from home for months at a time. Nor might he have understood the very nature of her temperament: her dreamy quality; her need to envelop herself in fantasies; her haughty glamour. It would have been difficult for a successful professional

Black male to take a backseat to his wife. Or in some cases even to function in her exclusive world. Lena Horne once explained that she married White arranger Lennie Hayton because he could take her places a Colored man couldn't. Dorothy did see Black men. For a time, she went out with a Black banker. But, those relationships received no publicity. One such relationship fizzled because of the differences in their lifestyles and prompted Dorothy to say, "I don't want to be bothered with any man that punches a time clock."

With marriage in the back of her mind, she still hoped her relationship with Otto would lead there. Then a crisis arose. According to her manager Earl Mills, Dorothy became pregnant with Preminger's child. "She believed that Otto would marry her," said Mills. "He told her that he was in love with her." An ambitious careerist, he still was unwilling to risk it all. "Otto refused to marry her," said Mills. Stunned, Dorothy became upset and frightened.

"I knew he would never marry Dorothy," said Orin Borsten, who didn't know any details about Dorothy's relationship with Preminger. But Borsten understood Preminger. "I knew he was going to marry a slender, slim, waspy White woman and that's what she was (his wife). I think he was enamored of Dorothy. Who wouldn't be? But I think when it came to marrying her, he was not going to do that. I think maybe he intended to marry Dorothy and then someone said, 'Hey, that would be trouble for you. Don't do it.'"

"Days of suffering set in," said Mills, as Dorothy took to her bed. This could give her another chance at motherhood and perhaps make up for all the trauma surrounding Lynn. Yet she was aware of the attitude about unwed mothers, not only in Hollywood, but throughout the country. They were shunned and criticized. If a woman had a career, she would see it shattered. Proof of that had been the decline of Ingrid Bergman's career, after she had given birth to the son of Roberto Rossellini before the two had married. The idea of an abortion tormented her. But Dorothy must have felt she didn't have much of a choice.

"She had the abortion," said Mills, who made the arrangements. "It was performed by a prominent doctor that I took her to in Beverly Hills."

Years later, Geri Branton emphatically said that Mills's story about an abortion was untrue, that it simply never happened. But if it did occur, Dorothy no doubt was too embarrassed and saddened to say anything to her friend.

Regardless, Dorothy's feelings towards Preminger underwent a drastic and dramatic change. "She ended the relationship with Otto Preminger at that time," said Mills. Embittered and resentful, she neither wanted to see nor talk to him.

"Otto was ugly. Truly ugly," she said later. "Many of those little men who run Hollywood are ugly. It is the folklore of Hollywood: the ugliness is much commented upon; it is known and understood that out of their ugliness they fashion an armor or toughness with which to prey and rule and succeed, and these alone are the kings of Hollywood. Maybe they are the kings everywhere. I think now that Otto never loved and never was loved."

Battles were won and lost for Dorothy in these times. The plans for *Lady Sings the Blues* hit a snag and it looked as if the film would have to be postponed or cancelled altogether. But Dorothy was committed to leave in the spring for *Tamango*, and there was talk about a starring role in a film version of Black writer Ann Petry's novel *The Street*, to be adapted by best-selling writer Harold Robbins.

The *Confidential* and *Hep* lawsuits dragged on for months. Both were settled out of court. But Dorothy became the first star to win a suit against *Confidential*. It was resolved by late May of that year when the magazine agreed to an out-of-court settlement, obliging them to pay Dorothy $10,000 and to print a retraction. The Hollywood community saw it as a victory for the whole town. Dorothy was jubilant.

That spring, Dorothy was a presenter at the Academy Awards and performed as well the Oscar-nominated song "Julie." Three days later, for whatever reasons, she made out her will. The eleven-page document specified that the primary beneficiaries were to be Vivian and Lynn. To Vivian, she bequeathed "my Thunderbird automobile and all of my silver, books, jewelry, works of art, clothing, and furs, other than my Crystal Mink fur, and other personal effects." No matter what disagreements the sisters had, Dorothy remained concerned about Vivian's welfare. The crystal mink was to go to "my dear friend, Mrs. Geraldine Branton."

Most of the document focused on Lynn. To her daughter, she bequeathed "the residue of my estate, real and personal wherever situated, including all failed and lapsed gifts, and including all insurance proceeds payable to my estate," which was to be held, managed, and distributed in a trust fund. The estate was to be used for the "proper support, maintenance, comfort, medical care, and education" of Lynn for "the remainder of her life."

Upon Lynn's death, Dorothy specified that the sum of $1,000 was to go to the National Urban League and another $1,000 to the NAACP. The remaining principal and accumulated income of the trust should then go, in equal shares, to Vivian and Ruby. Earl Mills was named as trustee of the estate.

Also specified were details for her funeral. "I direct that all expenses of my last illness and funeral be paid," the document stated, "and I further direct that I be given the least expensive casket available and that no funeral services be held. On the other hand, I would prefer a nice burial plot and an adequate and ornamental monument marking my burial place."

The will was signed "Dorothy Jean Dandridge."

Shortly afterwards, Dandridge sailed on the Queen Elizabeth for Europe to begin work on the Italian-French production *Tamango*. She was scheduled to spend a few weeks in Paris for wardrobe fittings and script conferences before leaving for the French Riviera where filming was to take place. Manager Mills accompanied her on the trip.

But it was not a relaxing shipboard cruise. In her stateroom, Dorothy picked up the new version of the *Tamango* script , which had been sent to her only a few days before her departure. "Here is the script all the changes have been made in order to get a great part for you," director John Berry wrote in a letter. "I am very excited at the wonderful adventure we are about to embark on, I believe that we can really do a thrilling picture. We must have a great performance from you. I know you will give one and I shall do all I can to make it so. Warmest regards see you soon."

But once Dorothy read the script, she became incensed. Instead of a shipboard rebellion, *Tamango* seemed a shipboard sex drama, tawdry and exploitive. Infuriated, she insisted that Mills immediately contact the director and the producer. She wanted to call the picture off.

"Tamango script not approved," Mills informed director John Berry and producer Roland Girard in a cable from the Queen Elizabeth. "Surprised and shocked script not like treatment. Role as characterized will not be performed by Dorothy. Telephone call Urgent."

The next day word came from director Berry that he couldn't meet with Dorothy in Paris until a few days after her arrival. He was presently in the south of France working on sets.

Mills tried calming her down. Once in Paris, others sought to appease her as well. Calls came from the States. Her attorney had been contacted and agreed to look into the situation to insure that the producer live up to his contractual agreement that Dorothy have script approval. But there was some discussion as to whether her contract in fact actually gave her that approval. Dorothy contended that script changes had been submitted to her late. Perhaps that would help her build a case against the producer.

Later, though, her attorney sent a Western Union wire from the States that read:

> FIRST EIGHT DAY TARDINESS IN SUBMITTING SCRIPT NOT SUBSTANTIAL DEFAULT IN MY OPIN-ION SECOND UNDER CONTRACT PRODUCER ONLY OBLIGATED TO TAKE DANDRIDGE REMARKS AND REQUESTS FOR CHANGES INTO CONSIDERATION NO CLEAR OBLIGATION TO CHANGE BUT THERE IS STRONG INFERENCE THAT DANDRIDGE HAS SCRIPT APPROVAL THIRD IN VIEW OF UNCERTAIN-TY OF LANGUAGE BOTH THE NEGOTIATED UNDERSTANDING AND RULES OF FRENCH CINEMA GENERAL DIRECTION APPLICABLE FOURTH SUG-GEST YOU RELAY ON DOROTHYS BARGAINING STRENGTH AS STAR RATHER THAN PURSUE TECH-NICAL APPROACH SUGGEST OBVIOUS NEED SHOW PRODUCER BAD TO IMPAIR DANDRIDGE CREATIVE ENTHUSIASM=

For various reasons of their own, no one wanted Dorothy to leave the production, neither the producer nor Dorothy's people. Berry agreed to other script changes before filming began on April 27th.

On the Riviera, Dorothy took up residence at the $100 a day suite at the luxurious Hotel du Cap d'Antibes. She stayed in the private suite of Darryl F. Zanuck who "made all the arrangements," said Earl Mills. "I stayed in the next room." The production company picked up the tab. One of the most spectacular settings along the Cote d'Azur, Eden Roc was the place where the wealthy Russian czars had once summered; where Marlene Dietrich rendezvoused with writer Erich Maria Remarque; where the ambassador to the Court of King James, Joseph Kennedy, had vacationed with his brood of children and his wife Rose. Dorothy's suite opened to a magnificent view of the clear blue Mediterranean.

Zanuck's feelings about her seemed ambivalent. "He was very fond of her," said publicist Orin Borsten. "The truth was he liked her a little too much," said Geri Branton. As a man who typically felt actresses should be his private property, he ironically "didn't try funny things with her as he did with other actresses," said Borsten.

Tamango afforded her all the accoutrements of stardom. With a salary of $10,000 a week, she would earn a total of $125,000 for the film. She was given $500 a week for living expenses and also furnished with a chauffeured limousine, a maid, and a hairdresser.

Her costars were Austrian actor Curt Jurgens, a handsome Black medical student named Alex Cressan, and actor Jean Servais. *Tamango*'s director John Berry, like Robert Rossen, had previously been blacklisted. No doubt he saw the film as a way to resurrect his career.

Based on a story by Prosper Merimée, the author of *Carmen*, *Tamango* cast Dorothy as a slave girl Aiche, who is the lover of the slave ship's captain, played by Jurgens. Because it was a European production, she didn't have the Production Code Office breathing down her neck. *Tamango* would be explicit in its interracial love scenes. Still, safeguards were taken with the huge American market in mind.

Early on, Mills said, it was decided the film would do what *Island in the Sun* should have: film romantic scenes in two versions; a more explicit one for European patrons; another sanitized version for American audiences. The film was to be shot mainly in French. To prepare for the role, Dorothy, who had studied French in Los Angeles, worked on the Riviera with the French coach Michel Thomas. Later though, her voice was dubbed.

Dorothy appeared less agitated by the script as the production moved along. More motivation had been developed for her character. The ending also gave her a chance for some political comment when the "White man's trash," as the promos would call Dorothy's Aiche, asserts herself and joins the rebels. Filming proceeded without great problems. Off the set, Dorothy remained as dazzling a figure for the European press as she had been during her visit to Cannes two years earlier. She flew to Paris to see the couturier collections. While there, she was pursued by a troubled young White man, who threatened to commit suicide if she didn't marry him. She tried diplomatically to explain to the man that such a marriage would never work. But still he followed her. Finally, the French police were asked to intervene.

The press also reported Dorothy's effect on one powerful and wealthy married European, known for his passion for such exciting and beautiful women as Maria Callas, Greta Garbo, Elizabeth Taylor, and later Jacqueline Kennedy. "Dorothy Dandridge," reported *Jet*, "is causing Mrs. Aristotle Socrates Onassis to steam because of her shipping tycoon husband's attraction to the star." Dorothy delighted in all the attention and fuss the Europeans made about her.

From Eden Roc, some evenings she motored to nearby Cannes or Monte Carlo. At a glittering gathering in Monte Carlo, attended by Prince Rainier and Princess Grace, she was an honored guest at the British-American Hospital's fifth annual ball at the Hotel de Paris. Another spectacular evening was spent at the Casino in Monte Carlo. There she smiled and chatted, floating through the crowd as Warner Brothers chief Jack Warner and Darryl F. Zanuck hit the gambling tables. When Zanuck broke the bank that night, the Casino went wild, and she was as thrilled as everyone else.

She returned to the Cannes International Film Festival where Elizabeth Taylor and her husband, producer Mike Todd, invited her to the huge party they tossed for his film *Around the World in Eighty Days*. Dorothy arrived with costar Curt Jurgens. Photographers snapped the couple as they danced, dined, smiled, talked. The photograph of Dorothy and Jurgens ran in newspapers around the world. Naturally, rumors sprang up of a romance. Despite her ongoing involvement with Jack Denison, Dorothy fell for the charms of co-star Jurgens. A man of immense sophistication, Jurgens, born in Munich in 1912, had been a journalist before turning to an acting career in 1935 on the German stage and in films. In 1944, he was deported to a concentration camp for political undesirables by the order of Josef Goebbels. After the war, he returned to acting and became a star on the stage and in international films such as *The Devil's General, And God Created Women*, and later *The Inn of the Sixth Happiness*. He had five marriages and was considered a romantic, dashing figure with an appealing world-weary attitude. Not much seemed to faze him. He could court a woman in high style yet he could also be emotionally detached.

Despite the early problems, work on *Tamango* became part of a glamorous, romantic reverie for Dorothy. Only a few distractions disrupted the dream. In June, she learned from Ruby that Vivian had married again. Dorothy also received a telegram from Vivian—then in Montreal—that had been sent to her in Los Angeles in late April. It read:

THIS IS TO LET YOU KNOW I WILL MARRY
MR GUSTAV FRIEDRICH TOMORROW AT ST
JAMES UNITED CHURCH

LOVE=VIVIAN

Not having seen Vivian since the Empire Room engagement, and not sure how to reach her sister, Dorothy felt relieved at hearing from her at last. She drafted a letter, which she asked Mills to have sent.

> Sorry just received your telegram. So happy that you are getting married. Being in love is the most wonderful thing that can happen to anyone. Wish I could be there. I'm shooting film at South of France. Staying at Hotel Du Cap until July. Would like much to see you and meet you in N.Y. in July on my way home.
> Let me know if this is possible. Wire me your permanent address.
> Much love. Dottie.

But it turned out that the sisters didn't meet that summer.

In June, Dorothy was visited by Leo Branton. She learned that the *Confidential* case was not resolved after all. The magazine was ready to resume a fight with her, claiming that her public statements that the settlement proved the story was untrue were in violation of the settlement agreement. The magazine said it agreed to the settlement only to avoid expensive litigation, and that the story *was* true. There was also the possibility that she would have to testify for a grand jury investigation of *Confidential* for publishing libelous and obscene material, involving many celebrities. Still angry, Dorothy was determined now to see the fight through to the end.

Taking a break from *Tamango*, she flew to London in July for a Royal Command Performance of *Island in the Sun*. Princess Margaret was in attendance as well as Zanuck and other cast members.

By then, *Island in the Sun* had been released in the States to less than glowing reviews. Dorothy's criticism of the script proved justified. Critics complained that despite its lush production values and its all-star cast, the film was static, evasive, and unformed. In *The New York Times*, Bosley Crowther commented that "it raises some Black-White racial issues that are not dramatically clarified or resolved." "Toying with its theme of race relations under the palms," wrote *Time*, "*Island* abounds in mixed-blood romances without showing any interracial kisses." *Time* also called it a "disjointed welter of plots" as well as "the sexiest West Indian travelogue ever made."

Likewise the performers suffered from a screenplay that failed to define their characters' drives. James Mason was stiff and vague as weak Maxwell Fleury. As Jocelyn, however, Joan Collins was appealing, wisely playing the role like a movie star rather than a character, since the film had not provided her with one.

The scenes between Belafonte and Joan Fontaine were flat and often dull, mainly because they just stood around and talked. Not exactly how one might expect people attracted to one another to behave. Belafonte publicly called it "a terrible picture based on a terrible best-selling book."

Time wrote that Dorothy as "a dusky lovely" had "seductively" portrayed Margot. But most critics commented little about her work. When seen by later generations, though, hers emerged as the film's most intriguing character. In her first scene, as Belafonte brings her to a government reception to which she hasn't been invited, Dandridge shows some spark. He asks what difference does it make if she crashes. He'll just tell everyone she's his cousin. "It makes a difference to me," she tells him. "If I go in, I go in as Margot Seaton. If I have to leave, I leave as Margot Seaton." "We're going," Belafonte tells her. "All right but I warn you. You may regret it."

Later at a ball that she attends with the governor's aide-de-camp, Belafonte is miffed. "So that's the reason you didn't go to the Nurses Ball with me," he says.

"I warned you, didn't I?" she says.

"About what?" "That you might regret making me go to the governor's party."

Then she coolly walks off. The scenes with Belafonte play well. His presence seems to ignite deep fires within her, and in their brief exchanges, Dandridge seems eager to speak her mind. No doubt, once again, the personal relationship of the two gives their sequences some punch and drive. The Black audience would, of course, have preferred seeing these two—one of the screen's most beautiful couples—in great romantic clinches. But *Island in the Sun* failed to develop any kind of relationship for them, despite the fact that they were to have been sparring lovers.

Her big scenes are with John Justin. Moving with grace and ease—in the shop where she works and later in the summerhouse where he lives, which remove them from society—she is full-fledged Dandridge: dreamy, romantic, and real. Having had to conduct "secret" romances with Lawford and Preminger, she understood just what such nonpublic moments of "hidden" intimacy were all about: the power of love when lovers know they are breaking a taboo.

Of course, the key sequence in the summerhouse turns absurd. Just when Dorothy and Justin embrace and one expects them to kiss, Dorothy instead brushes her face against the side of his. And that's that.

Most striking—and intriguing—was the moment when Justin asks about her past. "Funny, I don't know anything about you," he says.

"Well, what would like to know?" she asks.

"All about you. Everything."

The director keeps Dandridge in the foreground, facing the audience, her expression tense and anxious. "Well, there really isn't very much to tell," she responds in high gear. "I've lived in these islands all my life. Trinidad. Port-au-Prince. Santa Mara."

Movie audiences sat in rapt anticipation. But then just as it looks as if she is about to reveal the most private of confessions and when the film will have its most intimate moment, Margot suddenly gets off the subject and asks, "Does the gramophone work?" That is that.

Not another word in the script ever attempts to explain Margot. Consequently, Dandridge plays Dandridge. Like other great stars who, when given a good script, were at their best, and who, when given cardboard-thin characters to play, succeeded by using their own charismatic personalities, she, too, relied on her persona to make up for the screenplay's deficiencies. On screen she is the vital, appealing woman whom some in Hollywood caught a glimpse of at social affairs and functions. Not fiery. Not overly passionate. Just lovely with a suggestion of tension and deep untapped emotional waters. Almost implausibly beautiful, she is a great, glamorous, elegant icon.

Her performance again suggested the theme of the socially isolated "mulatto." Her looks and manners made her seem a woman of a mixed racial heritage. She appears removed from the Whites and other Blacks on the fictional island. She hardly appears as the typical young woman from an island culture. The White audience no doubt felt that this "perfect" looking woman shouldn't have any problems with romance. *She and this White fellow could be so happy together,* the mass White audience must have thought, *if only there was **not** that "taint" of her Negro blood.*

In *The New Republic*, Philip Roth wrote that "one would like to know what motivates this young Negress to cross the social line, or, more accurately, ignore it. Is she ambitious? Ashamed? I suggest these as possibilities because they seem faintly hinted at—the latter, perhaps, unconsciously—in Miss Dandridge's performance."

Island in the Sun's release generated great controversy. Joan Fontaine told the press she received "terrible letters" of protest against her appearance opposite Belafonte. "Most of the letter writers termed me unprintable filthy names."

Southern theatre exhibiters were outraged by the interracial love themes. The Memphis censor board banned the film. A Citizens Council and an American Legion committee attempted to halt a showing of *Island in the Sun* in New Orleans but failed.

When the picture was shown at the Springs Road Drive-In Theatre in Greensboro, North Carolina, a five-foot high wooden cross was set afire. Violence threatened to flare up in Wetumpka, Alabama at another drive-in theatre that showed it. "A man holding a shotgun sat in one of the cars blocking the gate while other men stopped prospective patrons," the Associated Press reported. "One of those halting persons approaching the theater near here said he was from a White Citizens Council."

In South Carolina, the legislature attacked the film and considered passing a bill that would fine any theatre showing it $5000. An angered Zanuck said he would personally pay any such fine. Ultimately, no such bill was passed.

Variety reported that Fox's sales department "is anything but happy with the prospect of losing the Southern market on one of its major attractions." The studio considered editing a special version for the South but Zanuck refused to make cuts. Nonetheless, in the ads for the film, Whites and Blacks were pictured separately. Interestingly, some ads, in which Dorothy was shown, along with the other major stars, also featured a drawing of a scantily dressed island woman with an arm raised and legs bent, as if she were about to perform the limbo. The drawing was intended to be Dorothy. Fox had no problems in using a sexy image of her to sell the picture. But for Dorothy, the graphic was all too reminiscent of the advertising campaign for *Carmen Jones*.

Finally, *Variety* reported that Southern theatres—roughly 20 percent of the American market—would likely refuse to show the film. And if they did show it, they would cut out offending scenes. Even in Minneapolis, a campaign was launched to boycott the film, but that fizzled out.

"They've given me the same treatment before," Zanuck told the press. "They said I couldn't show *The Grapes of Wrath* in Oklahoma and Texas, and I got scared as hell. All I won with that was an Oscar and a fortune. And the censors gave the same business with *Pinky*, but the opposition never really materialized. People are reacting, I guess, because now for the first time we have Negroes playing Negroes, which we didn't in *Pinky*. But I'm not frightened of any opposition."

But *Island in the Sun* turned a profit of a then-very-healthy $8 million. And perhaps to Dorothy's satisfaction, *Variety* reported that the film "is doing very good business, out drawing *The King and I* in many of the spots where it's opened." Its financial success proved that the general audience, despite the reactions in areas of the South, was ready for a film that examined issues such as interracial love and politics in the Caribbean, even if superficially done. A rueful Zanuck then realized he could have gone farther in his Black/White love scenes. "I never liked *Island in the Sun*," he confessed years later. "I didn't like it because they made me compromise the book." Dorothy's sentiments, though, clearly were *I told him he could have gone farther.*

Upon completing *Tamango*, Dorothy bade adieu to Curt Jurgens, but the two promised to see each other again. Departing from France to return to the States, she was in a very romantic mood. Because her flight had a layover in Copenhagen where *Carmen Jones* was then playing, Fox hoped that she would meet with the Danish press and do some promotion work for the film.

Then appearing in the city was Harold, who was contacted by Fox's publicity people. "The press knew she was coming in," said Nicholas. "The reporters called me and asked if I would go to the airport because they wanted to take some pictures." He agreed to do so. The publicity could be good for both.

Once she descended the stairs of the plane, she was met by reporters and photographers. Exhilarated, she felt very much the star.

"She looked more glamorous. She had a glamorous thing going then. Before she was just a young girl," said Nicholas. "Now she was a glamorous woman. I was just so happy because the whole world then was talking about her, so to speak. But at this time, it was a little different from the past. I could see that she was on the star side. She was posing and turning her head up and this way and that. I didn't blame her 'cause that was it. She had to play the role."

Not having seen Harold in several years, she knew this could be a vindication of sorts; a validation that all those years ago she really had had talent. Yet she was genuinely eager to see him.

The two chatted. The photographers snapped their pictures. "It was just about an hour or so," said Nicholas. Then he watched as she boarded the plane and took her flight to the States.

In Los Angeles, she had no time to rest. Once again, she had to prepare for the case against *Confidential*. Now standing by its story, the magazine identified the informant—the supposed mystery man in the woods—as a White bandleader named Daniel Terry, who said he had a tryst with Dandridge during her appearance at Lake Tahoe in 1950. A photograph of Terry standing next to Dandridge—one no different from hundreds of such pictures that Dorothy posed for with fans or workers who came up to her after a performance—was shown. He had sold the tale to *Confidential* for $200.

Dandridge did recall meeting him but the story was a lie. She had met many people during the Lake Tahoe engagement. Those who knew Dorothy understood also that the story couldn't possibly be true for two important reasons. First, such a tryst was completely out of character for her. Secondly, during the 1950 Tahoe engagement, Phil Moore had been with her. As Billy Roy had noted during his 1949 engagement with Dorothy at The Bingo Club in Vegas, Phil always took precautions to insure that no one had an opportunity to make any advances toward Dorothy. Also during the Tahoe engagement, Dorothy and Moore were still very much involved. There was no way she ever would have been out of Moore's sight.

Reporters, photographers, and television crews scrambled to see Dorothy as she was escorted to the Los Angeles courthouse by Geri and Leo Branton that September. Also testifying that day was actress Maureen O'Hara, who was suing the magazine. When Dorothy took the stand, she denied the story completely. Her testimony was not only a rebuke of a tabloid tale, but also a comment on race relations in America. Under cross examination, Dandridge was asked by *Confidential*'s attorney if she had ever walked in the woods with Terry.

"I would not have done that," Dandridge answered.

"There are trees all around Tahoe Village, aren't there?" he asked.

"Yes," she said.

"Did you ever walk alone or with someone?" he asked.

"I wouldn't have walked alone or with anyone. Negroes were not permitted to socialize with White people." She added, "I would not have ridden with Terry anyway because of the prejudice. I wouldn't have been seen with him."

With *Tamango* completed and the trial finally over, an exhausted Dorothy attempted to settle into a normal routine. She entertained at her home on Evanview, which she turned into an elegant showplace. Contrary to her usual thriftiness, she spent money lavishly. On the home. On clothes. On friends. She lent money to associates. She also bought homes for two of her employees. A large percentage of her earnings was still being invested by the law firm of Rosenthal and Norton in the oil wells, which made her feel confident about her financial security.

She didn't think much about money. She was far too excited about a romance. Denison remained in her life, but Dorothy was thinking mainly about someone else: Curt Jurgens. Making plans to visit him in Europe, she decided to buy a dazzling new wardrobe for the trip. She wanted to look like a million dollars.

Some film projects loomed on the horizon. Producer Lester Cowan was still trying to put together a deal for *Lady Sings the Blues*. That led to a meeting where her old friend Billie said that she liked the idea of Dorothy portraying her. Everyone was excited about the project.

"They really wanted Dorothy to do it," said Mills. "They planned using Billie's singing voice on the soundtrack with Dorothy lip-synching."

The Hollywood Reporter had announced the resurrected project in early August, but talks dragged on without any definite financing coming the producers' way.

Talk also began about a film starring Dorothy as Josephine Baker; and a film on the life of Bricktop, the legendary African American woman whose clubs in Paris and later Rome were the playground of the international rich set, but nothing materialized. Then rumblings started about a film version of George Gershwin's *Porgy and Bess*.

She still found it hard to believe that *Island in the Sun* had been her first movie in three years. And while the picture made money, it hadn't advanced her career. She couldn't let another three years go by without a movie. Telling friends that she didn't want to go back to the nightclubs, she privately agonized that she might have no choice. Where was the great movie career Otto had prophesied? When she asked herself if the industry had changed after all, even with all the talk of changes coming about because of the civil rights movement, the answer was that there still didn't seem to be a place for her—for a Black leading lady in Hollywood films.

"Dorothy was more political than people thought," said Byron Morrow. "Not political in going out and starting a protest. But politically savvy enough to know why her movie career wasn't taking off."

"A White actress who had been nominated for an Academy Award—who had done the kind of work that Dorothy did—would have worked constantly," recalled Olga James. "A White actress who had attained that kind of stature would have had more protection."

"They were only going to let Dottie get so far," said Geri. "They were not ready to let her become a really big star."

Fearful and anxious, Dorothy grew almost desperate for movie work.

Then she heard from director Andrew Stone, who wanted to star her in a drama. The new project was a shipboard drama originally called *Infamy* but later changed to *The Decks Ran Red*. As a sea adventure story, it could have some moments. But the role, that of the only female on board a ship that turns mutinous, was far from challenging, little more than a pretty face in the crowd role, and would do nothing for her career. Had *The Decks Ran Red* offer come right after her success in *Carmen Jones*, she would have turned it down flat. But she had few choices. At least the film might keep her off the road and out of the saloons.

She fretted about it. While she did so, Joel Fluellen stopped by her home and lent a sympathetic ear. He also saw the script. He believed she should do the picture. He also pleaded with her to intervene with director Stone to cast him as the husband of her character. Somewhat taken aback, Dorothy, even while distressed, knew she didn't want Joel in the picture. He was all wrong for the part. But he pressured her.

"It was always happening to her," said Geri.

Finally, she invited Stone over for lunch at her home to discuss the project, which was scheduled to begin filming early the next year.

Afterwards, she accepted the role.

As the summer of 1957 wore on and the fall approached, Dorothy found herself tired of the draining hectic schedule, of the relationships that had turned sour, of much of her life. She also found herself face to face with a not very pretty but undeniable fact. She began to fear she had peaked. Her film career, already a series of false starts, frustrations, and dead-end projects, would not, could not, go any higher or farther. Be it talk about the Southern market or talk about the public's fear of interracial screen romances, or talk of the mainstream audience's rejection of the all-Negro film or whatever, the fact was plain and simple: the dramatic film career she had been working for since her days at the Actors Lab might never happen.

With the possibility of a grim future facing her, she retreated into her own dreamy world. At night, she took pills to sleep. During the day, she exercised—and lost herself in fantasies. Her thoughts returned to Curt Jurgens. She would spend Christmas with him. They would look out on snowcapped mountains from his chalet in the evenings with the moon shining down, illuminating the tranquil beauty, making all look clean, bright, ordered, and at peace.

35. Love's triangle: with Belafonte and Joe Adams (l.) in *Carmen Jones*.

36. With Diahann Carroll (rt.) and a testy Pearl Bailey in *Carmen Jones*.

37. *Carmen Jones*: she really only has eyes for Harry.

38. At the New York premiere of *Carmen Jones*.

39. With Vivian (background l.) Oscar night, March 30, 1955.

40. With Otto in Cannes for the special screening of *Carmen Jones*.

41. Obliging the international press corps, as she strikes a Carmen pose.

43. Striking a pose for photographer Philipe Halsman.

42. (previous page) At the height of fame: haughty, glamorous, sophisticated.

44. With Sammy Davis Jr.

45. Off the road, spending rare moments with friends, including Geri and Maria Cole (4th from l. to rt.).

46. Rehearsing the limbo for *Island in the Sun*.

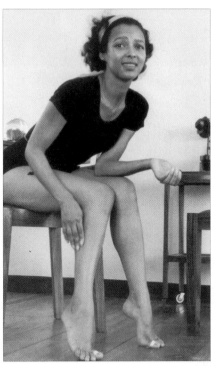

47. Rehearsal break.

48. Love and politics in the tropics. With Stephen Boyd and Joan Collins on location for *Island in the Sun*

49. The controversial summer house scene in *Island in the Sun*. With John Justin.

50. - 51. With *Tamango* co-star, Curt Jurgens on the set—and off—in Cannes.

48a. As Margot in *Island in the Sun*.

52. With Maureen O'Hara after testifying at the *Confidential* magazine trial.

53. Difficulty with Otto, the filming of *Porgy and Bess*.

54. With Poitier as Porgy.

55. The *Porgy and Bess* rape sequence with Brock Peters as Crown. Preminger said she didn't want to do it.

56. Some believed that Dorothy's Bess was too sophisticated and delicate.

57. Arriving in New York with new husband, Jack Denison, for the opening of *Porgy and Bess*.

58. As alienated as an Antonioni heroine. With Edmund Purdom in *Malaga*.

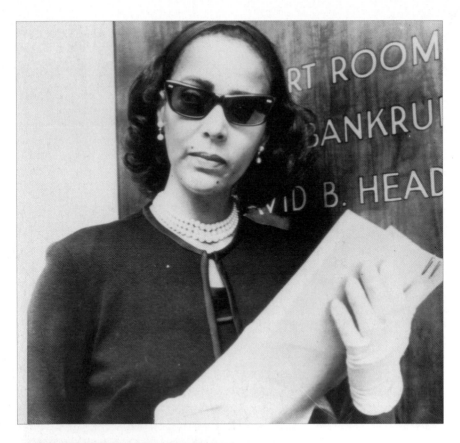

59. At bankruptcy court in Los Angeles. Dark glasses obscure a bruised eye which she said was received from a fall, United Press International (UPI) reported.

61. One of her last appearances in Mexico. A few months before her death.

60. Her body being removed from her apartment on the day of her death.

62. (next page)

PART III

MAKING PORGY

"*There* was no way I could make Bess ladylike. But I didn't know this at the time."

Porgy and Bess started filming September, 1958. But before one frame of footage was shot, it was already the most difficult movie Dorothy had ever worked on and would be her last major film. Much of the hell she caught working on it came from Otto. All at a time when Dandridge, vulnerable and fatigued, wanted to lock the door of her home on Evanview and keep the world at bay.

At least once in the past, Dorothy had publicly said she had no interest in working on a film version of *Porgy and Bess*. But producer Samuel Goldwyn had decided to do the film and he wanted her in it.

For years, Goldwyn loved the George Gershwin musical, which was a part of theatre lore and legend. Based on the 1925 novel *Porgy* by White writer Du Bose Heyward, a dramatic version of the story first appeared on Broadway in 1927 with Frank Wilson and Evelyn Ellis. Its tale of a crippled beggar and a doomed beauty named Bess struggling to survive in a Charleston ghetto called Catfish Row was directed by Russian immigrant Rouben Mamoulian, who had studied at the Moscow Art Theatre and brought to the drama the perspective of a man who felt himself as much a cultural outsider as did the Negro in America.

Eight years later, with Mamoulian again the director, the musical version of the Heyward story appeared on Broadway, now called *Porgy and Bess*, with a libretto by Heyward, lyrics by Heyward and Ira Gershwin, and music by George Gershwin. Despite some of the most haunting and beautiful music ever written for the American theatre, *Porgy and Bess* had a disastrous short run of 124 performances. But in the years afterwards, with numerous successful productions in the United States and abroad, *Porgy and Bess* assumed its place as a landmark in American musical theatre history, and proved a mainstay for African American performers. It afforded them the chance to play dramatic roles and offer a tragic view of Black life at a time when the acceptable image of African Americans on stage and film was as comic figures.

For years, too, *Porgy and Bess* attracted the attention of Hollywood. Over ninety producers tried to buy movie rights from the Gershwin estate. Columbia Pictures head Harry Cohn envisioned filming it with White actors in blackface: Al Jolson as Porgy; Fred Astaire as Sportin' Life; and Rita 'Hayworth as Bess. At another time, there were plans for a Black version with Nat 'King' Cole playing Sportin' Life.

But in May, 1957, after long demanding negotiations, Samuel Goldwyn acquired the screen rights from the Gershwin family for the then-hefty sum of $650,000. He expected to make a hit. What he did not expect were the adverse reactions to it.

Within Black America, feelings about the musical had long been ambivalent. The music was recognized as brilliant. But the images were disturbing. Throughout was an assemblage of familiar stereotypical crap-shooters, dopers, carousers, roust abouts, and a scary Black rapist named Crown. Its hero seemed an emasculated Black man, who literally spent all his time on his knees. The musical's Bess was a trollop who snorted happy dust and ran off up North with a jivey, pimp figure called Sportin' Life.

Now, during the rise of the civil rights movement, a time of bus boycotts, protests, demonstrations, and changing attitudes, the characters of *Porgy and Bess,* as well as its perspective on African American life looked like social, political, and cultural relics, if not insults. Not lost on anyone was the irony of poor Porgy singing the lyrics "I Got Plenty of Nothing and Nothing's Plenty for Me" in an age when Blacks were fighting for equal rights.

Protests started after Goldwyn's announcement. A little-known group called the Council for the Improvement of Negro Theatre Arts took out a two-page ad in *The Hollywood Reporter* that called on Black performers not to accept work in the film.

But Samuel Goldwyn—for many, a producer who embodied Hollywood—was not to be taken lightly. He was a pioneering movie mogul—a former glove salesman—who in 1913 was one of the first to migrate from New York to California where he helped produce one of the first films actually made in Hollywood, Cecil B. DeMille's *The Squaw Man.*

Over the decades since then, Goldwyn was known as a prestigious independent producer who turned out classy elegant motion pictures with the best of production values. Twenty-seven of his movies, including such classics as *Wuthering Heights* and *The Best Years of Our Lives*, had won Academy Awards in various categories. Goldwyn employed only the top writers, directors, actors, designers, art directors, sound technicians, and production staff. Among the stars who worked for him were Bette Davis, Laurence Olivier, Frank Sinatra, Myrna Loy, Fredric March, Merle Oberon, and Marlon Brando. His directors included William Wyler and Joseph L. Mankiewicz. Even when his movies were critically or commercially disappointing, they reflected his taste. His style was distinct enough to become known as "the Goldwyn touch."

Immediately, Goldwyn shrewdly fended off the early protests. He pledged the profits of *Porgy and Bess* to charity, made a donation of $1,000 to the NAACP, and won the support of the West Coast chapter of the civil rights organization. As far as he was concerned, that should have been enough to end the protests.

Now at 75, Goldwyn was moving full-steam ahead with his ambitious plan to make *Porgy and Bess* with major production talents and major stars. He wanted only the best. For director, he considered Elia Kazan, Frank Capra, and the man who had directed the early Hollywood Black musical *Hallelujah*, King Vidor. Finally, he selected Rouben Mamoulian, director of the original *Porgy.*

Next came the business of casting. With all the controversy over the images, Black actors in Hollywood were apprehensive about the production. "I didn't want to do it," Diahann Carroll recalled, because "the racial stereotypes of Catfish Row held absolutely no attraction for me, and I was offended by the story."

Still, Goldwyn, too powerful and ego-driven to let anything stop him, searched for the best cast and eyed his choices carefully. His choice for the role of Sportin' Life was Cab Calloway. But it was no secret that Sammy Davis, Jr. desperately wanted to play Sportin' Life and was waging a campaign. He urged his buddies Frank Sinatra, Jack Benny, and George Burns to speak to Goldwyn in his favor. At a party at Judy Garland's home, Davis took to the floor and entertained the guests with songs from *Porgy and Bess.*

Ira Gershwin's wife Lee was so appalled by the idea of Davis as Sportin' Life that she said to Goldwyn, "Swear on your life. You'll never use him!"

"Him! That monkey!" Goldwyn said, surprised she would even think he was considering Davis.

But when he could not get Cab Calloway, Goldwyn showed up at Davis's dressing room at the Moulin Rouge nightclub. "Mr. Davis, you are Sportin' Life. The part is yours," he said. Davis was elated.

For the lead, talk swirled about Harry Belafonte as Porgy. But Belafonte would have nothing to do with it. That hardly fazed Goldwyn. He would simply get Sidney Poitier, who was then the most respected Black actor working in films.

Goldwyn spoke to a West Coast agent, who said she represented Poitier. "I want that boy to play Porgy," he informed her. When she promised to deliver Poitier, Goldwyn announced to the press that Poitier would star in the musical.

But Poitier knew nothing of this agreement. "In my judgment, *Porgy and Bess* was not material complimentary to Black people," Poitier later said. In New York, he told his East Coast agent that he was not doing the picture. The press then reported the news that Poitier had turned down *Porgy and Bess*.

But Goldwyn did not back off. Poitier's agent Martin Baum pressured the actor at least to fly out to Los Angeles to meet with Goldwyn, who was too powerful to turn down flat. Poitier conceded. At the producer's palatial home on Laurel Lane, Poitier was wined and dined, courted and cajoled, in lavish Hollywood style by Goldwyn, who, to Poitier's surprise, was a sophisticated and charming host.

Still, when Goldwyn proclaimed, "This is one of the greatest things that has ever happened for the Black race," Poitier thought the statement was "outrageous bullshit." He still did not want to do the picture.

But Poitier quickly learned that in Hollywood, Samuel Goldwyn was not one to tangle with. On this very trip West, Poitier was approached by director-producer Stanley Kramer to do a high-voltage, dramatic tale of interracial brotherhood called *The Defiant Ones*. The ambitious 30-year-old Poitier knew the part of Noah Cullen could be a career-maker. But once negotiations were underway, Kramer informed Poitier that he risked losing *The Defiant Ones* role if he did not honor the *Porgy and Bess* agreement made with Goldwyn by the West Coast agent.

Poitier capitulated. He signed to do the picture with the understanding that first he would star in *The Defiant Ones*, which became one of his biggest hits and also earned him an Oscar nomination. Without the *Porgy and Bess* agreement, the Poitier career might have hit a snag at a crucial moment.

Still, Poitier thought he had been had. "To this day, I lean to the theory that some of it was predetermined," he said, "because I refuse to believe that Goldwyn didn't know about the Kramer project and know that I would flip for it. I'm also sure that my agents knew I would flip for it. In other words, I think I was manipulated. As smart as I thought I was, that time the White folks were smarter."

But while ever-shrewd and resourceful Samuel Goldwyn repeatedly wooed and then brass-knuckled Poitier, while he reluctantly selected Davis, while he meticulously deliberated over other roles and matters on the picture, he was aware only one actress in Hollywood could play Bess. No woman other than the industry's Black goddess Dorothy Dandridge could even be considered a contender. With Dandridge and Poitier together, Goldwyn's picture would have the marquee names, the stature, and, primarily because of her, the classy, elegant glamour he prided himself on. Goldwyn's people contacted Dandridge's agents. Talks began.

Dorothy was well aware of the controversy. Her feelings were mixed. Frankly, she felt that Porgy *and Bess* told some basic truths about "the harsh, terrorized lives of Negroes forced to live in ghettoes."

Still, she wondered why anyone would even bother to shoot a picture about such lives on a sound stage with pretty sets and pretty people. And why bother with a grim story about Negro life that took place in a mythical ghetto called Catfish Row in the year 1912? "Actually, the film should have been shot in the streets, in the shack-ridden quarters that fester throughout the South," she said.

Goldwyn used his persuasive powers and charms on her. He told her of letters he had received about the production, of his correspondence with various organizations. He assured her everything would work out. This would be an important picture. An important role. Yet she remained ambivalent and hesitant, partly because of the controversy and the bickering.

Belafonte called. "Don't do it, it isn't right," he told her. "I'm out of it."

"I'm going to think about it," she said.

Other calls came. Discussions began with director Rouben Mamoulian, whom she had met years earlier when he directed Harold and Fayard on Broadway in *St. Louis Woman*. He appealed to her artistic sense when he told her that "every actress wants to play Camille, and Bess is Camille." He also tried to put to rest her concern about the images in the musical, informing her that the film would be done in a Southern dialect—an authentic one rather than the often fake-sounding phrases and intonations of the past—because "you wouldn't play *Oklahoma* with a Spanish accent, or Sean O'Casey's plays in Brooklynese, or Shakespeare with a German accent."

"The whole point of the show is that the people involved in it are human beings—great human beings—and you don't make changes in their intrinsic values," Mamoulian informed the press. "It's the obligation of art to serve life and uplift the spectator. We would never trample on the dignity of the human being. We plan to make an uplifting film about the nobility of life and that's what we told Mr. Poitier and Miss Dandridge."

Urging Dorothy to come aboard the production, Mamoulian let her know he would be there to guide her through.

She talked to Otto. "Do it," he told her. "It'll make you as big a star as you were when you did *Carmen*."

By the time a call came from Sidney Poitier, who was then still vacillating, Dorothy had made up her mind. "Look I have spoken with Mr. Goldwyn about this," she told him. "He's going to do this picture with or without me. He will do it with or without you. Now the way I'm thinking, if I can help to bring some dignity to the role, maybe that is what it needs."

No doubt she arrived at her decision after apprising herself of some basic facts. Big-budgeted Black productions did not come down the pike everyday. Paramount would soon release the all-star, Black-cast film *St. Louis Blues*, the story of Black composer W.C. Handy, starring Nat 'King' Cole, Eartha Kitt, Ruby Dee, Juano Hernandez, Mahalia Jackson, Ella Fitzgerald, and Cab Calloway. But it had been shot on the quick and was without lush production values. *Porgy and Bess* would be Hollywood's first important Black film—and a big-budgeted one—since *Carmen Jones*, almost four years earlier. Bess was a whore. But maybe an interesting one, if played right. And frankly it was still the best role she had been offered in years.

She also had other facts to deal with. She was 35 years old. For an actress in movies, she was only five years away from the great divide, the cut-off period, the time when everything could go blank. There was not a film actress alive who had not faced a crisis at 40. Many stopped playing lead roles or just disappeared from the screen altogether. Even the toughest of survivors, Hollywood's great female stars, Davis, Crawford, Hepburn, Dietrich, and later Dandridge's contemporary, Taylor, all faced problems and career declines once they were beyond their thirties. Within a few years, her old friend Marilyn would be dead at age thirty-six.

Black women were not even in the equation. Lena Horne was still doing clubs and making a comeback on Broadway in *Jamaica*. But Hollywood never considered her a real movie star. Ethel Waters worked in movies sporadically but as a heavy matriarch, not Hollywood's idea of a viable leading lady. What could be in store for her? She could keep working in nightclubs, but that she hated. Hollywood's one Black goddess saw all the limitations.

A threatening letter came to Dandridge. "Why do you always have to play a prostitute role," the letter writer asked, "when you are supposed to be holding up Negro womanhood with dignity?"

The letter writer didn't realize that there was "a limit to the professional vehicles available to me." Nor did the writer understand that "America was not geared to make me into a Liz Taylor, a Monroe, a [Ava] Gardner. My sex symbolism was as a wanton, a prostitute, not as a woman seeking love and a husband, the same as other women."

She resigned herself. "I decided that if Goldwyn was dead set on doing the picture, he might as well do it with me," she said. Besides, she could probably do it better than someone else.

On December 10, 1957, Goldwyn held a press conference with Poitier at which it was announced that the actor would play Porgy. His salary was $75,000.

Almost a week later on December 16, 1957, Louella Parsons announced in her column in the *Los Angeles Examiner* that Dorothy Dandridge was set to do Bess. She would be paid $75,000.

As she sat in her home on Evanview, Dandridge felt that less and less of anything seemed to matter. During the past few years, she found herself tired, drawn, and depressed. She managed to keep out of the prying, scrutinizing eye of the public. Except for those occasions when she ventured forth for a planned public outing, the private goddess remained private. She had Veada to keep the house in order and Joel, who came over to gossip or cook or give her a massage or simply to cheer her up. She also talked to Geri, a sane, uncompromising voice in an environment with far too many compromises.

By now, she was in the grip of her affair with Denison, who wanted to get established in Los Angeles. Dorothy helped him with her contacts, including and especially Sammy Davis, Jr., her neighbor. Denison used his smooth charms on Davis, hoping to persuade the entertainer to invest in a restaurant that Denison planned to open on the Strip.

But Dandridge seemed preoccupied with other matters. She had much to think about. Lynn was now a teenager. Her body had already started to change. But her little girl would always be a little girl. Because of Lynn's condition and concerns that she might become pregnant, even through a rape, Lynn's physician advised that Lynn undergo a hysterectomy. He urged Dorothy to consent. But she refused at first to do anything. She hoped the situation would just go away on its own. Already she had been putting the decision off. But she was pressured to take some type of action. She discussed the matter with friends. Then in one of the most painful decisions of her life, Dandridge finally consented and afterwards was consumed with guilt.

"After Dottie signed the papers, she cried for days," Juliette Ball said. "She never got over Lynn. She just never got over it," Geri said. "Her daughter was always in the back of her mind."

Then there was Vivian. As fall came and winter approached, Dorothy went into a panic about her sister. Bad enough that Dorothy had not seen her in two years but neither Ruby nor Vivian's friends Etta Jones and Juliette Ball had heard from her. Not a phone call. Not a letter.

The last word to come was the cable from Vivian, saying she had married again. But now Vivian seemed to have vanished.

"What did I do? Why would she just go away like this?" Dorothy asked Geri and others in long telephone conversations.

"No one has any idea how Dottie suffered about Vivian," said Geri. "She suffered about Vivian to the same extent that she did about her child. It was very painful. She just couldn't imagine what she had done. Vivian was her only family. That's the way Dottie looked at it because of the way her mother treated her."

For a time, she was frantic and unable to think of anything other than Vivian's welfare, and what she had done to hurt and alienate her sister. Desperate to locate Vivian, Dorothy hired a detective to track her sister down but without any luck.

Something else that was new to Dorothy developed: the worst thing in fact for someone in show business. "I ceased to have the motivations for 'staying' that dominate many or most actors and actresses after they have arrived," she said.

The only reason she did not walk away from show business was perhaps that she did not know where else to go. Having been a performer all her life, there was nothing else she could do. Unsettled and frustrated about her place in Hollywood, she said, "I turned violent against my own career because it wasn't the career I wanted."

Norman Granz at Verve Records wanted her to go into the recording studios to do an album. During these years, a singer could survive from club dates and did not have to do recordings. Record albums were becoming increasingly important, and she had not recorded since her days with Jimmie Lunceford and with Louis Armstrong. Recordings might help to keep her off the road. She agreed to do the album for Granz and began preparations. Her old friend Harold Jovien from MCA initiated the contractual discussions. She also started to prepare for the Andrew Stone film *The Decks Ran Red*, which would shoot in February 1958. On occasion, she ventured to the home of Stone and his wife Virginia for dinner. Stone never recalled her showing up for these social gatherings with Jack. "She always came with a Black man," Stone said. The man no doubt was Joel Fluellen.

By Christmas 1957, her depression grew. Since her return from France while filming *Tamango*, she hadn't stopped thinking about her costar Curt Jurgens. She confided in Geri but was careful not to say too much. Now she was off in a fantasy about the relationship. One day she would be in a reverie about spending Christmas with Jurgens at his home in Vienna. The next day she would be upset because she had not heard from him. "She had decided that he was madly in love with her and that this was a fairyland kind of thing. And she was going to spend Christmas with him. She didn't want marriage but she had this fantasy that she was going to go to his lodge and spend Christmas and wave the magic wand and be the hostess and be the main person for Christmas vacation," Geri recalled. "He wasn't thinking about marriage. He was on the same wave length that she was. So she went out and got a whole new wardrobe. And she came back here and settled some things and she was going to go there for Christmas. And his invitation never came."

That did not surprise Geri. "Well, I knew it wouldn't because he had a girlfriend. . . a mistress there. And they just had a baby. And he wasn't going to invite Dottie to Christmas. But she just knew."

Strong as her fantasy life and romanticism were, nothing could alleviate her mounting depression. She took to her bed. She wanted to see no one. She told Geri she would spend Christmas by herself.

"Christmas with us is always family and lots of food and singing," said Geri. "And whoever wants to come in, can." As she planned her usual family holiday celebration, Geri had no intention of letting her friend spend the day alone.

"I had to go up there," Geri said of the Christmas morning that she drove to Dorothy's house and walked upstairs to Dorothy's bedroom. "She had this gorgeous, gorgeous room that she had done over," Geri recalled. But the bedroom was completely dark. "She had these thick drapes that could make her room night," Geri said. "And she was all curled up in bed. And she was crying."

Geri talked to Dorothy, insisting that she get herself together. "I am not going to put up with this," she said. She knew she had to maneuver her friend out of the house. "Well, I'm not going to worry you today," Dorothy said.

"I'm not going to put up with it," Geri told her. "You're going to get up, put your clothes on, look decent, and come, and act like a human being."

To Geri's surprise, Dorothy got up. In a short time, she was dressed, made up, and entering Geri's house, looking, of course, like Dorothy Dandridge. The head arched high. The chin thrust up. Her movie star persona intact.

"Well, nobody treated her any differently," Geri said. "She was just a part. She had to compete with everybody. She had more fun than anybody." It was a happy day that drew her out of herself and got her mind off her concerns and pressures. By the day's end, Curt Jurgens's "existence absolutely was just of no consequence," Geri said. "So that started out ugly but it came out all right."

Afterwards, with the arrival of the new year, 1958, Dorothy braced herself for the bruising schedule ahead. Work on *Porgy and Bess* would not begin until the spring. In January, she went into the recording studio to do the Verve album. The results were not her best. Her voice was listless. Her mood was languid. Harold Jovien said the arrangements were all wrong. So too was the choice of material. Dandridge got through the recording sessions, which were completed on January 21. But the album was never released. Later there was also talk of her recording an album of the music from *Porgy and Bess*. But those plans never came to fruition.

Her main social commitment was an appearance at the Urban League's Annual Winter Ball. She arrived for the event at the Beverly-Hilton Hotel, resplendently dressed in a silk brocade gown. Some 460 of Los Angeles's socialites and its Black bourgeoisie attended that night, primarily to see Dandridge present an award to the board chairman of the Standard Life Insurance company.

Shortly afterwards on February 18th, she went into *The Decks Ran Red*. It was a low-budget production (made for $593,305, of which $75,000 was paid to Dandridge) that was filmed partly on the freighter *The Liberty Ship* and partly in Catalina. It took only 21 days.

After all his badgerings, she landed Joel a part in the film, playing her husband. Her earlier protestations to Geri about him being all wrong and unbelievable in such a role proved right. The two did not make a very good or particularly convincing pair. Her co-stars were three well-known White actors: her friend James Mason, veteran Broderick Crawford, and young actor Stuart Whitman.

The Decks Ran Red focused on a ship mutiny. Two men (Crawford and Whitman) scheme to spark rebellion among the crew against the ship's captain (James Mason). Afterwards the men plan to kill everyone off and then sell the ship for salvage. Although based on a true story that took place in 1905, the film's plot was fairly implausible. Dandridge played Mahia, the only woman on board, a Maori married to the vessel's cook (Fluellen), who is killed. Not much of a picture.

But writer/director Stone was taking a chance. Though the leading lady was Black, race was not a part of the plot. In the past, Hollywood would have used a White actress in such a role, particularly since the character is the sexual focal point throughout. By casting Dandridge, Stone, of course, titillated the audience with the idea of interracial romance. One gorgeous Black woman being eyed by three virile White men.

Yet he upheld prevailing attitudes by making sure that Dandridge's character Mahia never actually ends up with any of the men on board. He was also observing the Production Code's prohibition against depicting miscegenation on screen, despite the fact that *Island in the Sun* had already challenged the Code. While she flirts with the captain, she does not fall into his arms at the film's finale. In one crucial scene, White actor Stuart Whitman also grabbed her in his arms and, forcing himself upon her, kissed her. Though Whitman's kiss was more than of a man violating rather than romancing her, it still marked Hollywood's first interracial kiss.

At the same time, *The Decks Ran Red* made no attempt to define the character in any cultural terms. Because it did not mention race, the film now looks afraid of the subject. For Dandridge, the experience was not much different from what transpired on *Island in the Sun*. For every two steps Hollywood took forward in race themes, it took another step back.

What remains striking about *The Decks Ran Red* was the way Stone and his cinematographer Meredith Nicholson treat Dandridge as a full-fledged movie goddess. Her first appearance—when she is hoisted on board the ship, surrounded by a troupe of men who look like lovesick schoolboys—established her as a feminine ideal. Throughout the closeups were lovingly, dreamily, lit and shot. For years to come, the film would be worth viewing simply to glimpse Dandridge at the height of her lush legendary beauty, which director Stone was clearly enamored with. She may never have been more beautiful on film. But Stone did not know how to work with the Dandridge temperament—the fire and humor that Otto had tapped so expertly—and she was left without much of a character to play. Apart from her goddess like presence, *The Decks Ran Red* had little else to recommend it. It was just a low-budget feature. Quickly made. Quickly released. Quickly forgotten. Except by Otto, who later criticized her performance.

Andrew Stone thought differently. "She was extremely professional. I never worked with any star that I liked better or that I thought was more competent," said Stone.

Only once did Stone detect Dandridge's nervousness and insecurity. Following the completion of the film, Dandridge held a party at her home for cast members and friends, inviting about thirty guests. Stone and his wife Virginia attended. So, too, did Dorothy's friend and co-star James Mason, who brought his wife Pamela on his arm.

"Everybody except Pamela fit in just fine," said Stone. Dandridge seemed jittery much of the evening, which Stone did not understand. "There was no reason to be nervous," said Stone. "It was the only time I saw any semblance of nervousness." Geri Branton thought Pamela might have become aware of James's infatuation with Dorothy—and their brief flirtation—which in turn may have added to Dorothy's nervousness that evening.

The Decks Ran Red wrapped on March 22, 1958. Then came the preparations for *Porgy and Bess*. By now, Goldwyn had lined up the rest of his major talents. Pearl Bailey, Brock Peters, Diahann Carroll, Poitier's buddy Ivan Dixon, and, no doubt again at her behest, Joel Fluellen. N. Richard Nash, the author of the hit *The Rainmaker*, wrote the screenplay. The director of photography would be Leon Shamroy, a three-time Academy Award-winning master of style and lighting. André Previn would conduct the music and supervise the score. Oliver Smith was contracted to design the sets. Irene Sharaff, one of the most talented designers to work in films, would do the costumes. It would be shot in 70 mm Todd-AO. Goldwyn was living up to his reputation. All the elements of his *Porgy and Bess* were top drawer. Filming was set to begin in July.

While Dorothy prepared for the movie, there was talk of a role for her in a film for an Italian company, to be called *Arrivederci* and to be shot in Italy and India. Her character would be a "high caste" Indian woman who falls in love with an Italian writer. The prospects looked promising. It was even announced to the press. Ultimately though, the film would never be produced.

Regardless, now she had to be ready for the cameras. In an effort to get in shape for *Porgy and Bess*, Dorothy went to a Chicago hypnotist in search of ways to unwind. She began a new exercise regime with the Swiss physical culturist Walter Saxer, who, like Veada, had previously worked for Jennifer Jones. At six in the morning in the exercise studio in her home, Saxer put her through vigorous aerobic motions and routines, using hoops, sticks, and rowing motions to help her develop swanlike body movements. Her Bess would not move like a streetwalker.

Samuel Goldwyn's wife Frances, who assisted him on his productions, often with suggestions and advice on costumes, was openly impressed by Dorothy's attention to keeping physically fit as well as her extraordinary physical poise. "A beautiful Negro woman carries herself better than the Caucasian does, and this we can afford to learn," Frances Goldwyn said. "There is a fineness of construction about her that I have never seen in anyone else, and believe me, I have seen plenty of bellies naked as a jaybird. After all, you get to know people's bodies pretty well."

But Frances Goldwyn also saw the tension underlying the fitness regime. "I had never known a girl who took care of herself the way Miss Dandridge does. Almost too much. I used to say to her, 'forget about taking care of yourself and have fun.' This girl gets up every morning at the crack of dawn and goes to an exercise man."

The results would be evident on screen. In *Porgy and Bess*, Dandridge cut a supremely elegant figure with not an ounce of excess flesh, streamlined and shapely as any high-fashion model. That would cause some critics to comment that she was much too refined to play Bess. Or perhaps far too chic to be a whore.

Whatever her reservations about the character Bess or the film's images, Dandridge took her work seriously. When another cast member balked about the dialogue—the use of dialect—Dandridge agreed to a meeting with Goldwyn and others to discuss the script. "Dottie was openly opposed to any dialect," recalled Geri Branton. "She could be pretty outspoken about that kind of thing." Just before the scheduled meeting, Dandridge discovered that the other cast member had failed to show up. She met with the production people by herself.

She also met with Mamoulian, whom she trusted and respected, for other script consultations and discussions on the character. Shrewd, sensitive, perceptive, and accustomed to maneuvering his way around the temperaments of talented actresses, Mamoulian's history of working with some of the screen's most fabled female stars in gilded tales of romance and power was not lost on Dorothy. He had guided a testy Dietrich through *Song of Songs*, Barbara Stanwyck in *Golden Boy*, and Rita Hayworth in *Blood and Sand*. Most famous and impressive were his closing shots of Garbo in *Queen Christina*: an enigmatic, moving closeup of the face that remained indelible and unforgettable. Working closely with Dandridge, he reassured her that her Bess could be a new interpretation.

Mamoulian's concepts and attitudes about the production struck her as sound and imaginative. He sought jazz-like arrangements for the music. He was also dissatisfied with the insulated, prettified look of the studio sets being constructed for Catfish Row. He preferred to shoot more on location, but he and Goldwyn differed over such matters.

She also understood the hassles Goldwyn, writer Nash, and Mamoulian had to contend with from the Production Code office. Having read various drafts of the script, the Breen office wanted less cursing in the film and the references to dope ("happy dust") minimized. Strongly objected to was a scene of Bess taking dope. Ultimately, all depictions of drug use were eliminated. When the Production Code people raised the question of Porgy and Bess living together without the benefit of marriage, Mamoulian and Goldwyn countered by saying that "in view of the fact that Porgy is cripple, there would be no suggestion whatsoever of a sex relation between them."

Poitier's and Dandridge's singing voices were to be dubbed by opera singers. Goldwyn felt it essential that the voices correspond to the personas of the actors. For Bess, Goldwyn considered young Leontyne Price. She reportedly said, "No body, no voice." Robert McFerrin was selected for Porgy.

After a soprano recorded Bess's music, Dandridge did a test, lip-synching to the recording. Goldwyn grew unhappy with the soprano's sound. The Bess recordings were scrapped.

New York was scoured for a new soprano. One young African American woman, Adele Addison—who had made a name for herself performing Bach with the Boston Symphony and Handel with the Philharmonic Symphony at Carnegie Hall under the direction of Leonard Bernstein—was contacted. On tour, Addison turned down the offer, saying she was too busy. She was also to be married that month. It was out of the question. The Goldwyn organization persevered, and promised her manager that the singer would be flown back to New York in time for her wedding. Finally, Addison agreed. As it turned out, she was perfect for the part.

In June, Addison flew to the West Coast where she endured what she called a "nerve-wracking experience." Accustomed to the formality and strict discipline of the concert world, Addison found the movie people very casual and slow. "We started and worked and every fifteen minutes they were stopping to drink Coca Cola," she recalled. None of her duets with McFerrin as Porgy were performed with him. The two recorded at different times on separate tracks that were later mixed. Informed that she would meet Dandridge the next day, Addison was expected to match her voice in some way to Miss Dandridge's personality as Bess.

"What she was going to do was to read through the script so that I could hear what she did," Addison said. "They made it sound as though it was going to be that I could listen to her and think about how she read these things. Then I could sing in terms as though it was coming from her mouth. Well, this was a very very disappointing affair."

The next day at the Goldwyn Studio, Addison sat in a room waiting for Dandridge to arrive. Casually dressed, Dorothy arrived with Rouben Mamoulian. "She was a very attractive woman," Addison recalled. But Addison noted that nothing was coming from inside her. It was apparent that Dandridge was very upset about something. But Addison had no idea what bothered the actress. "Hello," Dorothy said.

Addison responded, "Hello."

Dandridge did not extend herself further than that. She was "flippant" and simply "not a very cordial person," said Addison. "She wasn't on very cordial terms with anybody. She was really sort of noncommittal about it. I mean she didn't seem very involved at all. She didn't seem angry. She didn't *seem*. You got no sense of what she was feeling." Addison stressed, "There was obviously something disturbing her because she never said anything to me."

Mamoulian asked Dandridge to read for Addison.

Dorothy opened the script and proceeded to read some of Bess's lines. Addison could not believe Dandridge's attitude and lethargy.

"I have no clue what she was going through or what she was about. She said something. A few lines. And I didn't feel it was the character," said Addison. "She was reading and it would be just as though I picked up this book and said 'Book of Dried Flowers.' I thought, 'What am I supposed to do with that?'"

"Of course, I was absolutely flabbergasted," Addison recalled. "She certainly was not an inviting personality or appealing when I met her. And I thought maybe that's the way they do these things. So I just sat and I listened. I gained not any idea of what to do or how I was going to do this, and I thought, Okay, now that's the end of that."

Later in the afternoon, Addison attended a small party given at the studio by Goldwyn, who was friendly and gracious. When Addison expressed concern about how slow things were proceeding because she had to be back in New York for her wedding, Goldwyn told her to have her groom-to-be come West. "I will give you a wedding," he said. Addison thanked him but said no. Dorothy did not attend the gathering. "I never saw Miss Dandridge again at all," said Addison.

Dandridge's distraction and listlessness remained unexplained. But her distress was becoming more public and drawing more attention from on-lookers.

Pre-production continued through June. Mamoulian and Goldwyn continued to differ. On Stage 8, then one of the largest in Hollywood (some 400 by 800 feet), Oliver Smith's designs for the Catfish Row set were executed. Sharaff's costumes were completed. For Dandridge, she designed a long black skirt with a slit, a dramatic red blouse, and a wide-brimmed black hat. Mamoulian rehearsed his cast. Then a dress rehearsal on the completed set was scheduled for 9 a.m. on July 2, 1958.

Just hours before the dress rehearsal, around 4 a.m., a fire mysteriously broke out on Stage 8. Within a short time, it was raging out of control. Flames soared some three hundred feet high as the fire department struggled to contain it. By morning, Stage 8 was gone.

When the actors arrived for their 9 a.m. call, Ivan Dixon remembered seeing the police at the studio. It was then they learned of the fire's destruction. Everything—the sets, props, costumes, and costume sketches—was burned completely with losses totaling over $2,000,000. Various theories circulated about the fire's origins. One was that a Black group angry over the picture might have set it. That drew a heated response from the West Coast NAACP. Ultimately, the mystery of the fire's cause was never solved.

That afternoon Goldwyn met with the principals in the cast. Production would resume. Sets would be rebuilt. *Porgy and Bess* would still come to the screen. All he sought was their patience and support. The cast rallied around him. As the meeting ended, Pearl Bailey said, "And God's Will Be Done." Dorothy blew Goldwyn a kiss.

But the fire made Dorothy feel "like a race horse ready at the starting post, and suddenly told to go back to the table and eat some oats. I had been preparing for the picture and I was all ready emotionally. Where will I put all this energy?"

Within the next few weeks, differences between Goldwyn and Mamoulian over the conception of *Porgy and Bess* escalated. "There was a very strange thing going on between Mamoulian and Goldwyn," Ivan Dixon said. "I always felt Mamoulian was tricked into casting the movie. Goldwyn was a shrewd man. And I always felt that Goldwyn wanted Mamoulian for his artistic sense and his knowledge in terms of preparation of the picture. Mamoulian found all the Black actors in the country who were capable to play parts and brought them out for testing; and he helped put drawings together with the art director."

Regardless, Goldwyn now believed Mamoulian's services were no longer needed. He fired Mamoulian and replaced him with Otto Preminger. For Mamoulian, it brought back painful memories of the time he was fired and replaced by Preminger on the film *Laura*. As bad as it was for Mamoulian, it was the worst imaginable scenario for Dorothy; to have Otto in command.

Reactions were immediate. Mamoulian took his case to the Directors Guild of America. At a press conference, Black actor Leigh Whipper, who had played Dorothy's father in *Bahama Passage* and had originally been slated by Mamoulian for a small role in *Porgy and Bess*, announced his departure from the movie in protest of the treatment of Mamoulian. He criticized the production for now being in "hands unsympathetic to my people." He added, "I have first hand information concerning the new director which brands him, to me, as a man who has no respect for my people." Whipper was suggesting that Preminger was a racist. Shock waves rippled through Hollywood as the trade papers reported on this now very troubled production. Within Hollywood's African American community, Preminger was believed to be tough on actors, Black or White. But he was not considered racist. Pearl Bailey, Sammy Davis, Jr., and Brock Peters issued public statements in support of Preminger. But no public support came from Dorothy, despite her feelings that Preminger was not a bigot. Later she believed Preminger had not forgiven her for that.

For Dorothy, now there was no hope. Preminger—the man who had guided her through *Carmen Jones*, who had faith in her talents and delighted in being her Svengali, who became her lover as well, who brought champagne into her life—now was too much a symbol of disappointment and pain.

With new sets, new costumes, all the elements in place, *Porgy and Bess* resumed production in September. A depressed and fragile Dandridge began work. A week of rehearsals went smoothly. Otto was civil, even charming as he ran his actors through lines and interpretations. Maybe things would work out after all. Goldwyn stopped by. Pictures were taken.

Dorothy's co-workers—Sidney, Pearl, Sammy, Diahann Carroll, Brock Peters, Ivan Dixon, Ruth Attaway, and Joel—seemed to mix well. She herself remained aloof. Ironically, veteran actor Clarence Muse, the man who once told Ruby Dandridge that her daughters would never make it in films, had a small role. Also among the cast was Nichelle Nichols, a newcomer hired as a singer and dancer. Nichols became later well-known for originating the role of Uhura on television's *Star Trek*. Another dancer was Maya Angelou, who had recently toured in a stage production of *Porgy and Bess* in Russia.

In mid-September, Dandridge gave an interview to Hollywood columnist Sheilah Graham. By now, word had leaked out about her romance with Jack Denison. There was a man in her life, she admitted, but said little more. Regarding her career, she said, "It may always come first and the man I marry would have to know that," she told Graham. "With my friends, I can pick up and leave any time I want to. I couldn't do this with a husband. And that is why I am taking my time about marrying again."

She also told Graham of her disenchantment with the nightclub scene. "I started in nightclubs six years ago, and it wouldn't upset me if I never appeared in one again." Shrewdly, Jack saw her desire to get out of the nightclubs as a way for him to remain in her life. He promised her that once they were married, she would never have to work in the clubs again.

When she arrived for work at the studio, a thin and jittery Dandridge may have felt out of sorts. But for the assembled Black cast—the major performers, the supporting players, the extras—no matter that the big pictures had not come her way, no matter that as Diahann Carroll observed, "the early promise was unfulfilled" and Dorothy was now obviously "wracked with uncertainty," she was still Dorothy Dandridge. "Dorothy was the one everybody regarded as the star," Ivan Dixon said.

"On the set, there was awe of her beauty," recalled Nichelle Nichols. "This woman was a superstar. I just thought Dorothy was very beautiful, very delicate, and very, very insecure. And the reasons for the insecurity being that her relationship with Otto Preminger was very intimidating to her."

Made up and dressed in her Irene Sharaff design, she strode onto the set. "Obviously, she was always in the goldfish bowl," Brock Peters observed. "Everybody else was looking at her like here she is with this wonderful opportunity. So very little could she do on the set [without] somebody wasn't watching her and running it through their brain and deciding that it was or was not something positive." The pressure was enormous. "I had real sympathy for the state of her spirit," said Peters.

Dandridge retained her outer calm and that imperious air that some perceived, Ivan Dixon remembered, as being "arrogant," "conceited," and "haughty." In truth, it was simply a still method of shielding herself and holding herself together.

Preminger was as tyrannical as ever with his actors. Tales made the rounds of his recent treatment—some said abuse—of young Jean Seberg on the films *Saint Joan* and *Bonjour Tristesse.* In later years, Seberg never seemed to have regained her confidence after Preminger's tirades. Beset by problems, Seberg ended up dead from a pill overdose. So too did such other Preminger leading ladies as Monroe and Maggie McNamara. No one could hold Preminger responsible for the actresses' fates. But in the Hollywood system, many women still found themselves subject to insensitive, autocratic, powerful men who trampled over their identities and sense of self-worth.

Poitier and Dorothy were instructed to take their places. The set turned quiet. The cameras rolled. Action was called.

Dorothy began her dialogue as Bess. But she had not progressed very far when Preminger's anger and impatience were suddenly apparent. "Otto Preminger jumped on Dorothy Dandridge in a shocking and totally unexpected way," Poitier recalled. "She had done something that wasn't quite the way he wanted it." Dandridge froze.

"What's the matter with you, Dorothy?" he shouted. "You're supposed to be an actress. Now what kind of an actress are you that you can't do such a simple thing?"

She was "visibly shaken," said Poitier. Otto told her to start again, to take it from the top. She began the scene again. But once more, Preminger interrupted with a thundering attack.

"No, no, no—what's the matter with you? You can't even do a simple thing like that? That's stupid, what you're doing," he screamed. "You don't even know who Bess is. You call yourself an actress—you get paid to perform, not to do stupid things."

Tensions and explosions on any movie set were expected. Yet Preminger's attack struck Poitier as irrational and unfounded. But no one said anything. No one went to Dorothy's defense. Even more disturbing was Dorothy's reaction. Before the cast and crew, she broke down into tears. "Dorothy Dandridge fell apart," said Poitier.

She simply could not defend herself. She was "unable to summon up that survival sense essential to the secure person she wanted people to think she was; unable to strike back, because her defense mechanism was that of the prey, and the predator had selected her, staked her out, marked her for the kill, then struck without warning," Poitier said. "Nowhere in her anguish was there enough venom to dip her dagger into. There she was, that delicately beautiful woman whose appearance suggested many more things than her personality could deliver, stripped naked."

"On that day," said Poitier, "I learned that the serene look Dorothy Dandridge always wore only served to mask the fears, frustrations, and insecurities that were tumbling around inside her all the time. Fears about herself as a Black woman, just those were enough to overburden her sensitive personality."

He concluded, "I think that these contradictions—the appearance of serenity; the visage of a self-assured lady, accompanied by the absence of any real foundation underneath it all to fight the world with—made her the most vulnerable member of the cast. Otto Preminger smelled this, and she became sacrifice number one."

Preminger's temper and vilification were "now heaped upon me, telling me I was doing this wrong, that wrong. Now I was an idiot," She said, "The old romance was now as cold as iced cucumbers."

The following days went no better. With the exception of Pearl Bailey, Preminger was brutal with his other actors too. One day he lashed out at Poitier, who simply walked off the set. Afterwards

Preminger was more controlled with the actor. Another time he struck out so ferociously at Ivan Dixon that the actor told him, "Don't you ever yell at me again. Ever!" Dixon said he was ready to pound Preminger, who backed off.

But like the other cast members, Dixon saw that Otto unleased his foul temper most with Dorothy. "He just abused her. He treated her like a dog. She would cry. It was terrible to see." After a scene, Dandridge would retreat to her dressing room.

Also shocked by Preminger's abuse of Dandridge was Nichelle Nichols. "I think she was walking on eggshells the whole way through *Porgy and Bess*, Nichols said. Otto Preminger was overwhelming to that lady. He didn't know how to say 'Good Morning' without intimidating someone. I didn't have enough sense to be afraid of him. I laughed at him, which enraged him. He berated Dorothy in between takes. He did it loudly and in front of everyone until she was just totally incapable of doing re-takes. He took delight in destroying her because she'd crumble."

"Dorothy Dandridge was a lady," said Nichols. "She just didn't know how to handle that kind of crudeness. How she turned in the enormous performance that she did, under those circumstances, was a miracle to me. Because daily he had her dissolving into tears."

On those occasions when Dandridge walked off the set, Nichols recalled, "Otto would say, 'We'll go to another scene until Miss Dandridge is ready to get herself together.'" Nichols also remembered that "Maya Angelou and I used to sit and talk about Dorothy Dandridge's delicate beauty. We kind of wished she had been a bitch and just told people to kiss her beautiful butt. But she never did. She never could."

Nichols also recalled another incident involving Dorothy on the *Porgy and Bess* set. "One day her stand-in was ill. And it being my first movie, I didn't know what a stand-in was. When they asked if anybody wanted to be her stand-in, I said, 'Ooh, I would love to.' When Otto Preminger looked up and saw me as her stand-in, he was furious. 'You're no stand-in. You're a singer,' he said. He told me to stop. I was embarrassed."

Nichols was surprised to suddenly see Dandridge, who "walked over to me and took my hand."

Dandridge told her, "Oh, you must not be my stand-in, Nichelle. You are so beautiful. How can I follow you! I saw you dance. I know you're going to be a big star one day."

Said Nichols, "She did it so gently and so quietly. And I floated.

I loved her from that day on. I could not adopt *any* negative ideas some may have had. The way she said that to me was delicate, beautiful, sensitive, compassionate. This was a lady."

Nichols also noted something else about the attitudes towards Dandridge. "At that time, Dorothy Dandridge's delicate beauty was out of sync with the Black response, Nichols said. "I think because she had very Caucasian features and a delicate body and a delicate demeanor that she was made to feel she was not Black enough by people who were jealous of her, by some people on the picture who were jealous, and by some people just in general who were jealous."

Throughout, Brock Peters saw her confusion and struggle to maintain her composure. Her approach to playing Bess involved a painful and painstaking effort at focus and concentration as she tried getting at the essence of the character's drive and soul. "She was often very unsettled and seemingly a little disoriented until she finally settled down to do what she had to do when working," he recalled. "She didn't always just sail into a scene comfortable and confident. She frequently seemed to be having to get herself right then and there to work. That I was used to seeing."

Peters also understood the larger picture, the nature of Dorothy Dandridge's predicament. "For me, it was clear that she was insecure," he said. "And obviously it wasn't helped by trying to achieve stardom in an industry that had no conscious place for her." He had one basic impression of her. "Unhappy's probably what I always thought she was. And always saw."

Yet once locked into a fantasy, the complicated, contradictory dream world of acting itself, the escape from her own life into her character's, Dandridge was transformed. "When her eyes sparkled in a scene, that really was the only time I can honestly say I could see the life," Peters said. "The rest of the time, I felt she was afraid. She really was just afraid."

As the production continued, other tensions surfaced within this high-powered cast. "These were all competitive careers," said Peters. Nichols remembered, "There were tremendous egos on the set." Sammy Davis, Jr. recalled "hot personality clashes on the set," of "strong stars who wanted things done their way. Pearl Bailey was very outgoing, like me. Sidney Poitier was all inside himself." While the other performers developed a kind of wartime camaraderie and unity in the face of Preminger's tyranny, Dandridge withdrew all the more. She "was simply out on another plane somewhere, and none of us knew where she was heading," said Davis. "She was beautiful, and she was a brilliant Bess, but sometimes it seemed as if she weren't there."

One day she had a run-in with cinematographer Leon Shamroy. He had lost his temper with the cast about some matter pertaining to a shot. But Dandridge became annoyed and upset. She stormed off the set. Sammy Davis went to her dressing room. She was crying.

He tried talking to her. But she refused to go back onto the set until Shamroy apologized. She might have to endure Otto's crap. But she would not take it from Shamroy. Or anybody else.

"Dorothy Dandridge didn't suffer fools or racism easily," said Nichelle Nichols. "If a remark was made accidentally or on purpose, she was not a person to let it go past her. She didn't fight back with Otto Preminger. But she didn't let other people do things. She was a lady who felt people should talk about their problems together, not scream about them."

The production came to a halt. Shamroy would not apologize. Word reached Goldwyn, who summoned Davis to his office.

"What does the girl want from me?" Goldwyn asked. "Shamroy talks like that all the time. But he photographs beautifully. You want me to lose him?"

Sammy explained to Goldwyn that Dorothy was especially "sensitive and hurt easily. She didn't have a broad back like the rest of us."

"You know, whatever I say, he will never apologize," Goldwyn said. "I simply don't understand actresses. Why do they do this to me?"

Dorothy stood her ground. The cast was dismissed for the day.

The next morning Shamroy apologized to all "the ladies" on the set for his behavior the previous day. He had not apologized personally to Dorothy. But she went back to work.

A strange, tense incident later occurred during filming of a tender scene between Dandridge and Poitier. Preminger instructed Dorothy to stroke Poitier's head. But she hesitated. Preminger exploded. Again the set turned quiet, except for murmurs and whispers among the cast and crew. "What was the matter? She couldn't touch a Black man's head?" were the questions Brock Peters recalled hearing. For Dandridge, this had to be an embarrassment. In Hollywood, her reputation for having relationships with White males was already known. Could this simply fuel the notion that she wanted to have nothing to do with Black men? The truth of the matter was that Dandridge no doubt was responding more to Preminger and her uneasiness with the role than to Poitier.

"I think she buckled at the way Otto Preminger wanted her to do it," said Nichelle Nichols. "It was almost like Touch a Nigger's Head For Luck. But Dorothy was very sensitive to Sidney Poitier. Her hesitation was to see if Sidney Poitier wanted her to do that. I think she was concerned about Sidney's responses. She wasn't about to rub this man's head and lose her hand! 'Cause Sidney had great dignity."

On other occasions, blowups erupted between Dorothy and Pearl Bailey. Cast as the chatty, extroverted Maria, Pearl Bailey was a seasoned professional who still believed herself as being every bit as big a star as anyone else on *Porgy and Bess*. Gregarious and extroverted, she was chummy with Preminger and Goldwyn and mingled freely with the cast. Yet even though Dorothy might be distant, people catered to her. Bailey professed to like Dandridge. Perhaps she really did. But the years since *Carmen Jones* did not seem to mute any of Bailey's sense of rivalry with her.

Orin Borsten, by then no longer Dorothy's publicist but now a writer doing a story on the film for a New York paper, recalled the day he interviewed Dorothy and Bailey separately on the set. At one point, Bailey pulled him aside and said, "I should be playing Bess, not Dorothy Dandridge. I can sing. Dorothy Dandridge can't sing. I could have played Carmen Jones, too. I could sing. Dorothy Dandridge can't sing."

Bailey also still had a well-known evil side, a downright mean streak, that was directed at Dorothy whenever possible.

"Pearl raised her [voice] loudly a few times," Brock Peters said. "I think it was a competitive thing. Dorothy may have made some demands about whatever. And Pearl was threatened by it. . . . Pearl seemed to exhibit some difficulty with Dorothy a few times and exploded."

One day Bailey went over to Dorothy to put her arm around her. But Dorothy pushed her away.

Shortly afterwards, Geri Branton received a call at home from Pearl at the studio. "We won't finish this picture if Dorothy keeps this up, if she doesn't get herself together." Bailey told Geri, "She's acting funny." Immediately, Branton drove to the studio. "And I got on the set and she *was acting* funny," said Branton. Dorothy "was like a cowered animal."

Better than anyone else, Geri understood what had happened. "Pearl was two-faced," Geri said. She was well aware of Bailey's moods and jealousies. "Pearl would walk in and try to embrace Dottie and things like that. And Dottie would kind of go off on her, 'Don't touch me!'"

Geri talked to her friend. Soon Dorothy calmed down.

Usually, Dandridge stayed in her dressing room until called to the set. She mingled with almost no one in the cast, except for Joel. He would join her in the dressing room. "Joel was like a father to her. He stood by her," Ivan said.

"Joel kept her together," recalled Nichols. "He went and consoled her. One way or the other, he comforted her. Or he told her to get out there. He'd say, 'They can't do this damn movie without you.' He was the only person who could talk to her like that. She could tell him everything."

But by far the most difficult experience on *Porgy and Bess* came just before filming of the scene in which Brock Peters as Crown rapes Bess. In the film, Bess and Crown have been lovers until he runs away after murdering a longshoreman. Bess—an outcast on Catfish Row—is befriend by the good-hearted Porgy. The two fall in love. But Crown, who still insists that Bess is his gal, catches up with her at the picnic on Kitiwah Island. When she resists his advances, he rapes her. During the afternoon, the scene was rehearsed without problems.

But Preminger said Dandridge called him that night, in a highly agitated state.

"Otto, you must recast him. I can't stand that man," she reportedly said of Brock Peters.

"Dorothy, are you out of your mind? You're not casting the film, I am. I think Brock Peters will be very good in the part. I know he's not ready yet, but you're not perfect either in everything you're doing."

Preminger recalled, "She got more upset. She kept saying she couldn't work with him." Finally, she became hysterical. "When he puts his hands on me I can't bear it. And—and—and he's so Black!"

The next day Dorothy appeared ready to work. The sequence was shot on location in Stockton. Nothing was mentioned to Preminger about the previous night's conversation. As she was being dressed and made-up, she slowly began her preparations—concentration and breathing exercises—for the scene. But unknown to Dorothy, before the rape scene was shot, Preminger took Brock Peters aside and alerted him not to be upset if she became difficult or behaved strangely. "Now, look, she's having difficulty working with you 'cause she thinks you're not right."

"Well, what's the matter? What am I not doing right?"

"You're fine. It's not a problem. It's her problem."

Preminger indicated the trouble had to do with Peters's color. Peters said a number of other people, including Preminger's assistant and also

Goldwyn, knew of the situation. Preminger reassured Peters that the actor's work was fine. He just must ignore any difficulty she posed.

Peters was geared up for more tension or an outburst. With Preminger, Shamroy, the crew, the lights, and cameras all in place and as he and Dorothy hit their marks, Peters looked for signs of her possible uneasiness in working with him. "But I didn't see anything," he said. "She seemed like she often enough was." Once the cameras rolled, Dandridge handled herself like a professional. Peters said of the scene's filming, "My recollection is that it ran fairly well and fairly quickly. I have no recollection of difficulty from her."

Afterwards Dandridge and Peters sat together on a flight from the location in Stockton back to Los Angeles. "We really had an amicable exchange," he said. He found her "wonderfully warm and friendly and interested." The topic of their discussion was mainly actorish matters: she asked where he had studied, with whom. She expressed an interest in coming to New York and getting together with him, Sidney, and Belafonte. Just hanging out as actors often did. "It was her effort to reach out," he said. The two exchanged telephone numbers. Peters remembered thinking, "Well, gee, I'm getting to know her." He also admitted he wanted to open up to her. Later Peters was on the very select list of guests for her wedding.

Peters wondered about the incident on the set. Or rather Preminger's comments before the filming. But for years, he said nothing about it to anyone. "I ran it through my brain a lot. But as I think about it now, she may have been afraid of the scene, not so much of me. And maybe not terribly happy with what was happening in rehearsal and had to lash out somewhere. And maybe that's what happened." He also believed, "What she did in lashing out was probably because she herself was so frightened and uncomfortable about what was a crucial scene."

Peters also questioned Preminger's motives. Why tell a young actor of possible tension from a costar just before the filming of a tense scene? "If he told me because he wanted me to deliver something in the scene that he needed, I think it was a wasted exercise on his part. I think then he did not have to, if that were his reason. If he thought I was going to be exposed to her real anger and it would affect me, he might have done that. I don't know. But why that? Why not something else just to bolster me up? I've never figured that out. I've thought about the ramifications of this thing."

For Otto Preminger—a tough, manipulative, all-controlling director—he got the scene he wanted out of both Peters and Dandridge.

But perhaps mainly at Dandridge's expense. Stories later circulated about her difficulties in the scenes with Poitier and Peters, both dark African American males. What did not make it into those rumors were the pressures Dandridge was confronted with as well as her fears. Nor the fact that both men were sympathetic to her plight.

During the production, other cast members became angered by Preminger's "treatment of everyone but especially Dorothy," said Nichelle Nichols. "He chewed up actors and spat them out for breakfast." Finally, the cast met and called for a meeting with Preminger.

"The actors ate him alive. He knew he had a mutiny on his hands," said Nichols. "I think we deliberately called the meeting when Dorothy had two days off. We specifically talked to him about his treatment of her. The people on *Porgy and Bess* did not show disrespect to Dorothy. They showed compassion. Perhaps they were impatient that she didn't tell Otto Preminger where to take his Prussian. . . . But we told him to treat Dorothy Dandridge differently. She was our queen. It demeaned *us* to see this man attempt to destroy her every day. Everyone knew they had had a relationship. After the meeting, he was more respectful of us. He was a little more respectful of Dorothy. At least, she was able to get through in a more respectful way."

At the end of each day, Dandridge fled the studio and "disappeared back to my quiet house." Often alone and lonely, she lived nonetheless still like a movieland goddess. She continued to see Jack. But rarely did she want to go out or be seen during any period when she was working on a film. So tense was she that sometimes she was not even "in the mood to be very polite."

On occasion, she socialized with some cast members. Sammy Davis, Jr.'s home was across the street from hers. Sometimes after Poitier and Ivan Dixon visited Davis, they hopped over to Dorothy's. During these times and on others after the completion of *Porgy and Bess*, Dixon found it easier to relate to Dorothy, whom he had not especially liked at first. At the studio, she was too remote and self-absorbed. At home, she was warmer and friendlier. He noted though that her star persona was always in place. "There was no way for her to be anybody but Dorothy Dandridge," he said. "It must have been hard at times. But that is who she was."

He also realized something that Brock Peters felt about her. "Her own personal demons came out of everything the industry was at that time. I mean there's no putting those things aside. Her personal life and her personal demons in terms of the negative things that occurred in her personal life are not really that separate from who she was."

Dixon did not see Jack Denison around Dorothy during this time. But Jack stayed on the case. He pressed for marriage, assuring Dorothy that he wanted to take care of her and ease her burdens. With all the pressures on the set of *Porgy and Bess*, she was at her most vulnerable and perhaps most gullible. One evening, Dorothy invited Diahann Carroll over to the house.

"I found a perfect little doll's house—everything in its place; white sofas and rugs, flowers on the piano, total Hollywood elegance everywhere," said Carroll. Dandridge wanted her to meet Denison. Carroll could not understand why because the two women were not close friends.

But Dorothy told her, "I'm about to marry him and he's White and I thought you could give me some advice." Carroll was surprised. She was then married to Monte Kay, who was White. Yet she said his color meant nothing to her. For Dandridge, though, race was an issue. "I felt sorry for Dorothy—I tried to make her understand that she was marrying a man, a human being, not a color."

On October 10th, Louella Parsons reported in the *Los Angeles Examiner* of talk of a possible marriage between Dandridge and Denison. "I have been going around with Jack for a long time and he is my favorite guy," Dorothy told the columnist, "but we haven't gotten around to discussing marriage." Parsons noticed a diamond ring on Dorothy's engagement finger. "Oh, that's to keep the wolves away," Dorothy told her. "You and Jack will be married some day though?" Parsons queried. "I wouldn't be surprised," Dandridge laughed. "But up to now at least, we have made no plans."

But Jack was smoothly manipulating Dorothy. Having gotten himself out of Vegas, he was shrewdly establishing himself in Los Angeles. He had now taken over the Plymouth House restaurant. Dorothy's contacts had proven invaluable. He had secured the deal he wanted. Sammy Davis had poured money into the restaurant, becoming a prime investor. So too was Dorothy, to the tune of $150,000.

The day after the Parsons column appeared, *The Decks Ran Red*, which already played in some areas, opened in New York to lukewarm reviews. Later Sara Hamilton in the *Los Angeles Examiner* praised Dorothy. "Miss Dandridge is not only a beautiful woman," she wrote, "but a fine actress, outstanding in her scenes of fear and hysteria."

Nevertheless, once Otto saw the picture, he was quick to tell Dandridge—within earshot of others on the set—"You were rotten in that."

Slowly, *Porgy and Bess* was winding up. Preminger battled with Goldwyn, much as Mamoulian had, to let him open the picture up, to use more locations. He argued about a waste of money on the wrong things, including Sharaff's costumes for Dorothy, which he believed much too elegant for the character. "Look, you've got a $2 whore in a $2,000 dress," he said. Goldwyn clashed with Preminger over the way too much of the picture was filmed: long, stationary boom shots that took in the expanse of the set but without enough closeups.

Both men were right. When released, *Porgy and Bess*'s elaborate, beautiful sets were a feast for the eye. But the drama seemed stilted and deadlocked in an artificial world without enough real light, air, and sun. Without realistic grime and grit, too. Only in the picnic sequence shot on location did the drama seem to breathe and fully come alive. The lack of closeups also kept the audience at an emotional distance from the characters and the story. The music remained magnificent. The opening sequence as "Summertime" is heard sung seemingly by Diahann Carroll (but actually by Loulie Jean Norman) had power and sweep. "It Ain't Necessarily So" oozed with the appropriate sexy, decadent juices.

But the underlying concept was dated and stereotyped. Already, Dandridge and Poitier in their respective films, *Island in the Sun* and *The Defiant Ones*, had ushered in new images of African Americans as intelligent, troubled, complicated people confronted with contemporary issues of race and racism. *Porgy and Bess* belonged to an earlier time.

Fortunately, some of the actors had some magical moments. Sammy Davis, Jr.'s Sportin' Life was a sleazy, slinky character who seemed to spring out of urban folklore. But Poitier appeared miscast and ill-at-ease as Porgy.

Through it all, Dorothy Dandridge was a striking, transcendent goddess, seemingly in search of a story and a closeup. As luminous and isolated as Garbo but without a camera that, like Mamoulian's in *Queen Christina*, knows when to come in close to capture that light and despair. Preminger's visual conception prevented the audience from clearly seeing the truth of a character's or, in the case of Dandridge, a performer's pain or loneliness; it weakened her highly unusual interpretation of Bess.

Still, while she believed she had failed to create a ladylike Bess, she was wrong. Far too spiritual and far too unapproachable a presence to be the carnal/sensual Bess we hold in our imaginations, she went beyond type to emerge as a star monument to herself and her own pathos. She is simply Dorothy Dandridge, visually haunting and moving.

At times, her body movements seemed stylized yet beautiful, her body lines themselves pure, direct, defined. In her long skirt with the slit up the side and her wide brimmed black hat, she was a phantom, emerging, it seemed, out of the deepest and most private dreams of the audience.

Like all great stars, she was an aesthetic being unto herself; part real, part myth, touching on a collective vision and experience. Yet each viewer could connect with her in the most personal way and project onto Dandridge his or her own personal hopes, fears, fantasies. In *Carmen Jones*, she was the personification of the in-your-face live wire beauty: bold, brash, independent, sure of herself. As Bess, she was a doomed spirit, slowly moving to the inevitable end. Again, the viewer might not believe in the movie. But one always believed in her.

When the critics viewed the film, that was hardly what they discussed and commented on. Dandridge herself was unaware of her assets and presence. On December 16th when the film wrapped, all she knew was that she had finished it and gotten through a nightmare.

HOPING

"*There* have been a lot of rumors that Dorothy Dandridge is secretly married to Jack Denison, although I have never been able to confirm these reports," Louella Parsons wrote in her column in the *Los Angeles Examiner* on January 8, 1959. "She does have a big financial interest in the Jack Denison restaurant."

For a woman who had valued privacy so highly, Dorothy had become a hot topic of conversation because of her relationship with Jack Denison. Most were quick to say it appeared as if she was being used by this man, especially when talk swirled along the movie colony grapevine about Dorothy's investment in Dension's club.

In an effort to put to rest the marriage rumors, Dorothy spoke to a reporter from *Jet*. "When the time comes, it will be announced," she said, "but I am not now married to anyone." She added that the Parsons comment was "premature." "I haven't seen her story," she said, "but I've been told about it by some of my friends. The answer is, not so."

Within a few weeks though, Denison took it upon himself to speak to the press about their romance. "I knew she was the greatest actress and most beautiful woman in the world when I saw her in *Carmen Jones* in 1954. Then in November of that year she came to the Riviera in Las Vegas, where I was Vice President," he told *Jet* in February. "I was completely smitten when I saw her nightclub act and fell in love instantaneously the first time I talked to her." Actually, he had met her in November 1955 and was never a vice president of the Riviera.

Still, nothing could impede the Denison bluster. He explained that "it took me six months to convince her that I loved her and wasn't just another 'stage door Johnny.' I knew this was the woman I wanted to marry. I was married once when I was 21. But there was no understanding, maybe because the girl wasn't Dorothy."

But his comments didn't stop there. "I don't think of Dorothy as a Negro, but as a woman—a woman I love very much. I only hope if she marries me, her race will accept me. Not that I believe it would make any difference to Dorothy, because she's a wonderful woman, but one of the reasons I bought this club was so that if she ever said yes, we would not have to worry for our security or what other people thought about."

He added, "You see I am a man and I would definitely want her to quit her career if we married. I believe the value she would receive in having a husband and devoted lover would more than compensate for what she would lose by giving up show business."

Contacted by the magazine for her response to Denison's comments, Dandridge simply said, "You know you just can't talk about love like this. I don't want to talk about it because marriage is the logical conclusion of love and I haven't made up my mind about marriage yet."

The magazine commented, "She admitted she would not mind giving up her career to marry the right man, nor would his race be of any importance."

And so began the press coverage of Dorothy and Denison.

So too began Dorothy's attempts to incorporate Denison into her life; to bring him fully into her social circles with Nat and Maria Cole, Geri and Leo Branton, Dorothy and Byron Morrow, and scores of others.

But just about everyone who met Denison, and by now her close friends and associates had all been introduced to him, eyed him suspiciously. Far from being an exciting personality on the social scene, he was considered a Hollywood outsider, who was not deemed husband or boy friend or even escort material for Dorothy. A man like Joel, who in industry circles did not have a great professional status, could nonetheless summon up his charm, his knowledge, his wicked wit to make himself acceptable, even desirable, at social gatherings. Denison had none of these qualities.

"I was shocked when she made that selection," said Herb Jeffries. "I don't know how she got hooked up with the guy. I never really approved. I never told her though. I didn't think he was the kind of man for Dorothy. Nor did I think it would be successful because what the hell could he contribute to her from the standpoint of helping her along? He didn't make that much money. And he was a womanizer."

Harold Jovien's impression was no better. During this time, Jovien and his wife Mildred, part of Dorothy's inner group, saw quite a bit of her socially and often encountered Denison at her home. Having known Denison at the Riviera in Las Vegas, Jovien was aware of his reputation as a sleazy manipulator. Jack had always seemed on the make. On the take too.

"I didn't like him really," recalled Jovien. "A typical maitre d' who was trying to ace you out of a $20 bill. Or a $50 or $100 bill to get the best table in the room and then let you know that you'd be in the gallery unless you took care of him."

For Joel Fluellen, Denison was almost beneath contempt. He bristled at the mere mention of Denison's name. Denison in turn disliked Joel, and, aware that Dorothy might listen to Joel's advice, obviously wanted him out of the way. He also had no use whatsoever for Earl Mills. For his part, Mills spotted Jack's craftiness and never trusted him.

"We knew nothing. No one told us anything about him," said Dorothy Nicholas Morrow, who was unimpressed upon meeting Denison. "I knew nothing even when they were going together, other than the fact that I heard he was supposedly a maitre d' trying to get a partnership in a hotel or whatever. You know these were the kinds of things that were thrown around."

Of his cordiality and gratuitous attempts to please, Morrow thought, "It was the way head waiters and maitre d's are when they greet you. He was that all the time. He was the maitre d' always. That's all I got. I never had any conversation with him. If I did, it's blanked out because I don't remember anything with him."

Maria Cole recalled, "I was never impressed. I never saw much of him. He was very handsome. He was very nice to me. He had charm but the kind you could see through. I don't know how she met him. I never attempted to like or dislike him. I just knew he was wrong for Dorothy. He was there for *who* she was and *what* she was."

Dorothy herself had reservations about Jack, whose flaws and shortcomings she was well aware of. Jack was reckless with money, running up bills which she found herself paying off. For clothes, gadgets, travel, the restaurant. He had almost laughable pretensions and grandiose visions for himself. Convinced he could make a fortune with a drama Hollywood would find irresistible, he set out to write a movie script. Said Geri, "He couldn't read. So I know he couldn't write."

Jack was vain, egotistical, slick, and overbearing. Of course, egotistical and overbearing men were nothing new to Dorothy. But in her past, men with such characteristics always had something to back up the egotism. Never could they be dismissed derisively as chump change, or pathetic, over-eager social climbers. Harold, Phil, and Otto were all accomplished. Their egos were large; but so too were their talents. Known and respected within the competitive walls and corridors of Hollywood, these men were never taken lightly. Yet blindly, Dorothy seemed to think Jack's overbearing hand and grand manner meant something—as if they were the signs of strength that she valued in men. No one took Denison lightly either, but for a far different reason: he was the lover of Dorothy Dandridge. Otherwise no one in Hollywood would have given him the time of day. He might have been appreciated as a maitre d', able to secure a table on a crowded night. But never would he have been considered an appropriate dinner guest.

Movie colony residents had borne witness to this kind of sad spectacle for decades. Usually, it was an aging female star on a career slide who had fallen prey to a handsome young stud. Dorothy, however, although approaching the precarious age of thirty-seven, was not considered an aging star. Nor was she—despite her own torment about her career's inertia—perceived as being on a career skid. Dorothy conferred him with status and relevance. At the same time, she diminished her own.

Dorothy had already seen that Denison could be cruel and sadistic. On one occasion, following a quarrel, he stole personal photographs from her home, burned them, and then mailed the charred fragments in a box with a note. It read, "I will shoot you in your stomach. And you will really be sorry for what you are doing."

Then there was a frightening experience at Denison's apartment in Las Vegas when he had grown angry out over the way the dishes were washed. Suddenly, Jack grabbed a plate and smashed it. Then screaming and raging throughout the apartment, he went to a cabinet where he kept a gun, which he pulled out. He threatened to kill her. Dorothy was terrified. Later when Denison left the apartment to go to his job at the Riviera, a shaken Dorothy called Earl Mills in Los Angeles. She asked him to have a pre-paid airline ticket to Los Angeles waiting for her at the ticket counter at Las Vegas's airport. He followed her instructions.

Dorothy jumped into a cab and raced to the airport, where she flew back to Los Angeles and was met by Mills. One look at her and

Mills knew she was disoriented and frightened. He took her to his home and tried to calm her, but he became alarmed after he had left her alone for a few minutes in his living room while he fetched her a glass of water. He returned to find Dorothy nowhere in sight. Then he saw that Dorothy had stepped onto the sun porch of his house, where she was leaning on a railing that overlooked a steep hill. "I was concerned because she was so distressed. I thought she might try to harm herself," said Mills.

She planned to return to her own home that evening. But when Mills spoke to her therapist John Berman, it was suggested that she be brought to the Berman home. Dorothy stayed with Berman and his wife for several days. "Then she contacted Geri Branton, who came over and got her," said Mills. The incident with the gun in Las Vegas left her emotionally rattled for some time. Still, she had resumed the affair with Denison. No one quite understood what the relationship with Denison was all about. Her friends tolerated the relationship.

Dorothy's other reservation about Denison centered on race. She remained hesitant about making a commitment with a man whose cultural background and attitudes were so different from her own. Unlike such men as Preminger and Lawford who seemed eager to explore cultural differences, Denison appeared too narcissistic to appreciate anyone's experiences other than his own.

In telephone conversations that literally went on for hours, Dorothy talked endlessly about Jack and the relationship. She talked to Geri. To Geri's sister and aunt. To Dorothy Nicholas Morrow. They all saw the importance of Denison in her life but did not particularly like what they saw. Repeatedly, she questioned her former sister-in-law Dorothy Nicholas Morrow about her relationship with her husband Byron, who was White.

Did people stop and stare at them? Were there ever misunderstandings between the couple about racial matters? What about the reactions of their families and friends to the marriage? These were the questions she asked.

"We had long conversations about interracial marriages," said Morrow. "She was obviously questioning the effects of such a marriage, should she wed Jack."

The phone conversations simply expressed Dorothy's maddening search for answers and her unwavering romanticism; her belief that everything could somehow turn out well.

"She wanted life to be just the way she pictured it in the schoolbooks," said Dorothy Morrow. "She wanted to be happy and surrounded by happiness. This was always my feeling of Dorothy. She was such a delightful, beautiful, generous giving soul. But she really only wanted to have life and love around her. And because of her desire to have this, she wasn't always able to reason logically and make the best solutions."

"One of the beautiful things and yet one of the most failing things about dear Dorothy is that she wanted to do right," Dorothy Morrow believed. "She wanted to be everything to everybody. And my impression has always been that she wanted to get everybody's opinion. But many times when you get other people's opinions, you always have to be able to come through with your own decision, based on what you want to do. Not based on what he said or she said or they said. But after having listened to all of them, then to arrive at a conclusion that would be the best for whatever it is you wanted to do. My overall impression has been that there was a certain immaturity in her own finalizing of whatever she was going to do."

"Dorothy was ever hoping," concluded Morrow. "The fact that she got with that Jack with all the things that she'd gone through meant that she was still hoping. She was also hoping for Prince Charming too. Jack physically, facially, fit that mode. She couldn't see through the other things. All the warnings. And everybody warned her."

Around Geri Branton, Jack was always "the perfect gentleman, the Silver Fox." Yet she too saw the manipulative, cruel streak that underlay the well-tended exterior. Still, she held back from expressing too strongly her feelings and doubts about Denison. "I was always very careful. You don't tell a woman about a man she's involved with," Geri said. "You don't do that. But I would let her talk about it. And talk it out. I thought that would help her to make a sensible decision."

Shrewdly, Jack sought to cut Dorothy off from most of her old friends as best he could. He persuaded her to get to know his family—his brother, sister, and mother—who, of course, loved her like a sister or daughter. Many of the Denisons worked at his restaurant, which now, with Dorothy as the future Mrs. Denison, was truly a family affair.

But while she deliberated on the possible marriage and as those in the movie colony gossiped about her situation, Dorothy tried focusing again on the career that had kept her glued all these years. In January, she went to New York to talk to the producers about a possible Broadway show, *Queen of Sheba*. She considered the drama, but ultimately didn't do it.

Then came two film possibilities. One was for *A Moon on Rainbow Shawl*, to be shot in Trinidad. Another was from a company headed by Douglas Fairbanks Jr. Originally to be called *Scent of Danger*, this film would be retitled *Moment of Danger*, and finally released in the States as *Malaga*. It was a tale of two jewel thieves on the run. After a big heist in London, one of the thieves betrays the other and leaves England for Spain, with the jewels, of course. The second man then pursues the first. Joining in his pursuit is the other man's lover, an alienated young woman named Gianna, who has also been betrayed by him. As she and the second man travel to Malaga in search of her former lover, the two find themselves drawn to one another. Dorothy was sought for the female lead. The screenplay by David Osbourne, based on a novel by Donald MacKenzie, never specified the race of the female character. There was no need to do so because it had been written with the assumption that the entire cast would be White.

Already signed for the film was one of England's finest and most distinguished actors, Trevor Howard, who was best known to American audiences for his performance in the classic David Lean-directed, Noel Coward-written tale of repressed love, *Brief Encounter*. Another fine actor, Richard Basehart, who had appeared in Federico Fellini's internationally praised *La Strada*, was also just about signed for the film. Its director would be Hungarian born Laslo Benedek.

Dorothy was no more satisfied with the script for *Malaga* than she was with some of the other films she made. But the cast and director made it seem like a promising production. It would be shot in London and parts of Spain, away from Hollywood's sound stages and away from Hollywood's attitudes and perceptions.

By now, she thought her only hope for consistent film work was in Europe, where producers not only viewed her as a viable star, but considered her for different types of roles. Despite her "fiery" Aiche in *Tamango*, she believed that in Europe she could escape playing what she called "the wantons" like Carmen and Bess—and instead portray heroines like the earthy types of Italian neo-realism—the women who populated the films of such postwar European directors as Rossellini, Fellini, and De Sica. In her openly romantic manner, she told Geri she longed to do a film, without much makeup or elaborate coiffures and costumes, where she could walk barefoot in the mud, agonizing over life's tensions and injustices. *Malaga* struck her as a good way to begin.

On February 20th, Louella Parsons broke the news. "Dorothy Dandridge telephoned me to say au revoir, telling me she is leaving almost any day for England," Parsons wrote in her column. She reported that Dorothy had told her, "The movie *Scent of Danger*, which Douglas Fairbanks Jr., is making, starts April 21, and since I am going by boat, I am leaving a little early to discuss the script and my wardrobe. I am happy Trevor Howard is playing opposite me."

Parsons also reported that Dandridge "returns in June for the *Porgy and Bess* opening in New York, and in August is considering going to Trinidad for *A Moon on a Rainbow Shawl*. Said Miss Dandridge, 'I haven't settled definitely on the Trinidad motion picture, but I'll decide soon.'"

She also had to decide soon about Jack. He continued to pressure her to marry him. His main tactic now was to assure her of a secure future in which she did not have to worry about working or taking care of herself.

Though working on *Island in the Sun* and *Tamango* had kept her out of the clubs, she knew it was only a matter of time before she'd have to return to the saloons. By now, Dorothy viewed them a sign of her failure. She hated the atmosphere. The booze. The cigarette smoke. The sexy image. Still, too, she had to contend with the men looking her over. She had to be friendly with the owners and managers. She had to fight her own fears of the audiences. She had to pack and unpack, rush to make a flight here or there; she had to deal with the effects of the constant motion on her system.

At night, she was wired and unable to sleep without a pill. In the mornings, she was up early but groggy as she set out on the never-ending routine of rehearsals, interviews, and personal appearances. She wanted a change.

Dorothy was also painfully aware that the nightclub scene itself was changing. People did not go to the clubs for the kind of sophisticated entertainment they once had sought. Most stayed home at night plopped in front of their television sets. In the old days, the clubs had power and allure because the studios had insisted that their stars be seen at the big showplaces. Now the studio system itself was dead. Stars could rarely be forced to do anything. Those who ventured out for fun preferred smaller, more intimate gatherings. Major establishments like the Mocambo, Ciro's, and the Cocoanut Grove lost their luster and glamour, and folded or floundered.

Denison, however, assured her she need never worry about such matters again. With his restaurant opened, he was making his way in

Los Angeles. She would be able to wait for the right film roles. He also boasted of having "a twenty percent interest in a Vegas hotel," said Mills.

For a woman who had supported herself—and her family—from the time she was a teenager, the idea of being able to sit back, relax, and let someone else carry the burden, appealed to her. Frankly, she was also tired of being alone.

Finally, Dorothy accepted Jack's marriage proposal. The news didn't surprise some friends. To Geri, it was symptomatic of Dorothy's overall tendency now to make the worst of choices.

"She could intellectualize better than any psychiatrist," said Geri. "And she would talk and spend three hours. She could explain the things that were happening better than anybody and tell you what she was going to do. And it would be a wise and good decision. And she'd turn around and do the opposite. So I have to say she wanted to punish herself. She didn't want to solve her problems. She did not. She was becoming purely masochistic. So she knew what she was getting into."

But Geri was not the only one to question Dorothy's choices. Otto did too. After all the tension on *Porgy and Bess*, after Dorothy's unending resentment and Preminger's unending anger over their breakup, he and Dorothy saw each other again. Preminger remembered that she called and invited him to Denison's restaurant on the Sunset Strip. Perhaps it was a way for Dorothy to show Otto that she no longer cared, that she had found a man—a White one—with the courage to be seen publicly with her and also to ask for her hand in marriage. For Denison, it was a testament to his ego. Here was the world-famous director coming through the doors of *his* restaurant.

Otto, however, didn't care what Denison presumed of his appearance at the restaurant: Denison was too much of a nonentity for Otto to think twice about.

Sitting with Preminger at a table, Dorothy told him all about her relationship with Denison and dramatically confessed, "We're in love."

Otto was not impressed. When she informed him of her plans to marry Denison, he still was not impressed. Instead he looked around and did a quick study of the room: the patrons, the decor, the lighting, the staff, and the man at the helm.

"I knew then there was no way for that restaurant to succeed," he said years later. "To run a restaurant, you have to know a lot of people and keep them coming to your place. He didn't know anybody.

And Dorothy wasn't that kind of outgoing person. I knew it just could not succeed."

Otto then asked Dorothy one crucial question.

"Did you invest money in this restaurant?"

Dorothy's response was indirect. "You know me," she said, casually looking down and refusing to let her eyes meet his. "You know I wouldn't put money into anything," she said.

Otto knew Dorothy was being evasive. He also understood why.

Earl Mills tried to reason with her about the wedding plans. But her decision was made. Now he had to watch still another man take over her life and move him aside. With Preminger, Mills had to respect his talent, power, and position. But Denison was a nothing with absolutely nothing going for him. Mills had received a report from a prominent Los Angeles attorney, who had investigated Denison's background at Mills's behest. Denison had no interest in any hotel in Las Vegas. Nor did he have any other significant assets. Mills approached Dandridge with the information. But she refused to listen. Their discussion became heated. Mills was just jealous, she said angrily. Then Mills backed off, resigning himself to the oncoming marriage.

"Dorothy wanted to be married," he said. "She just had this desire to be a wife."

Now arrangements had to be made. Her schedule within the next few months would be hectic. There was the trip to Europe for *Malaga*. Then the opening of *Porgy and Bess*. Then the wedding. This tightly arranged set of plans energized her, made her feel as if something were happening again in her life and career.

Dorothy flew to New York City on March 24th. Arriving at Idlewild Airport, she stepped off her flight and waved for the reporters. Newspapers carried a photograph of a striking Dorothy, dressed elegantly in pearls and a fur-bordered coat with her hair neatly brushed back. She looked older and more thoughtful, less playful and carefree, than the actress most now remembered as Carmen Jones. Yet age became her, transforming her into a luminous, melancholic, ethereal beauty. Her eyes told a story of their own. Their trace of weariness, their suggestion of sadness, and their wistfulness hinted that she had seen something, had been to a place, that the rest of the world had not been privy to.

Afterwards, the wedding news was announced in Los Angeles. "Just before Dorothy Dandridge sailed on the Queen Mary yesterday for England she and Jack Denison, supper club owner, announced their engagement to marry," Louella Parsons wrote in her March 26th column. Shrewdly, Dorothy had avoided discussing the matter with the press by releasing news of the impending marriage just as she embarked for Europe. *Time* ran a photograph of her at Idlewild Airport in its 'People' section; the magazine noted that she "hoisted the conventional pretty wave for the flashbulbs on the day of a proud revelation: her engagement to Jack Denison, White proprietor of a Hollywood supper club." Other press accounts spoke of the upcoming nuptials of the Negro actress and the White restaurateur.

The next week she appeared with Denison on the cover of *Jet*, which ran the banner, "Will Marriage to Jack Denison Hurt Dandridge's Career?" Part of the article dealt with the choices she would have to make between the responsibilities of a career and those of a wife.

"But, as if she had anticipated the question and mulled it around for quite some time," the magazine reported, "Dorothy told *Jet* the night before leaving for England: 'I don't think there is any connection between a career and marriage. I mean there are many career women who are happily married. If I were married today and had a contract to do this picture I would keep it. No, now don't misunderstand, I know that sounds cold and heartless, but what I'm trying to say is that if a lady doctor had to perform an operation in the morning, she kisses her husband goodbye and goes and performs the operation.'"

The magazine commented, "Possessed of a keen mind, but extremely sensitive about her personal life, Dorothy concluded: 'Anyway I don't believe a woman's career is ever primary if she loves her husband.'"

But while Dorothy limited her comments in an effort to maintain her privacy, Denison appeared eager to talk. "How is marriage going to hurt her career?" he said to *Jet* as he sought to present himself as the well-to-do, in-control, husband-to-be. "I am not going to insist that she give it up because I don't want her to say in a couple of years I made her give it up. She'll probably make a few more pictures, do TV things or whatever she wants. And if they're talking about our marriage being an interracial one, let me say we'll never honeymoon in Little Rock and probably never visit Atlanta. But look at Harry Belafonte and Julie, did it hurt his career? Or Lena Horne and Lennie Hayton, Pearl Bailey and Louis Bellson? Man, it helped some of the parties."

He continued, "For instance, who would have known Julie if she hadn't married Harry. Louis was just a drummer, but marrying Pearl made him a named attraction, and Lennie Hayton is definitely doing better since he married Lena. In fact, for that matter, who would have ever known that such a persona as Jack Denison even existed if it hadn't been for Dorothy Dandridge?" His comments revealed part of his motive for marrying her, more than he probably realized.

"People ask me do I think it will hurt my social standing," Denison said, "and I ask: 'What greater compliment can a woman pay a man than to say I'll marry you.' Any true friends I have, it will make no difference to them, and the same is true of Dorothy's friends."

"They ask if marrying me will hurt Dorothy's career and I tell them no, but if I'm wrong, it still will not make any difference, because I bought this club so that Dorothy will always be able to live in the manner she is accustomed to and we will never be beholden to anybody. But more important, this is love and our marriage is going to be for keeps."

Denison was playing the role of the powerful male provider to the hilt.

꙳

Dandridge arrived in London, bruised and brooding, yes, but still every inch the imperial, privileged, haughty glamorous star as she checked into the exclusive Dorchester Hotel. Accompanying her was a Black female companion/secretary.

Her job was to keep the Dorchester household in order, particularly now when Dorothy was not only carefully analyzing *Malaga*'s screenplay, but was preoccupied with thoughts of her upcoming marriage. Arrangements were made for her to view wedding gowns from Berman of London. Through transatlantic telephone calls, she also had to check other wedding details. Geri had already agreed to be her matron of honor; she would also be attended by Jack's sister. Calls also went back and forth across the ocean between Dorothy and her betrothed, the eager-to-please Denison.

Mainly, Dorothy began preparations for *Malaga*. The clothes would not be like Irene Sharaff's elegant, high-fashion designs for *Porgy and Bess*. Nor would they be like David Ffolkes's sophisticated creations for *Island in the Sun*. Nor would they generate the theatrical heat like those of Nyberg for *Carmen Jones*. They would be plain and unadorned, the type worn by a woman concerned about money and unable to consider fashion. What would distinguish the clothes would be Dorothy's figure and carriage. On her, the plainest garb would be transformed; the dark robe that she would wear in her first scene would look like both a simple gown and an elegant, roomy coat that she could get lost in—that could serve as a buffer from a world of pain. Perhaps the one elegant piece of clothing would be a slip which she would wear with a natural sensuality like a second skin.

In London, Dorothy also conferred with director Laslo Benedek. By now, there was an important casting change. Richard Basehart was replaced by handsome dark-haired leading man Edmund Purdom. Earlier the British-born Purdom had made a splash in Hollywood with appearances in such spectacles as *The Egyptian, The Prodigal,* and *The Student Prince.*

Director Benedek was enthusiastic about working with both Trevor Howard and Dandridge, whom he considered important international stars. "I knew her reputation and I saw *Carmen Jones* and was a great admirer of her," he recalled. "I thought that in terms of the character, she would be perfect." Yet Benedek admitted that the initial idea to cast her was not his but that of the young producer Thomas Clyde.

One day during pre-production, when the film package was being put together, Thomas excitedly informed Benedek, "I talked with Dorothy Dandridge. And she is interested. How do you feel about it?"

Benedek's response was immediate. "I would be delighted, of course," he said.

"When I decided to make this film," said Clyde, "I made up my mind that Dorothy should have the leading role, even though her color is quite unimportant to the plot. Anyone of any race could have played the character she portrays." He wanted to approach the story "without any connection to color, any reference to the fact that she was a Colored girl." Very much aware of the limited roles for "any dark-skinned actress," Clyde believed that in *Malaga*, Dorothy would prove herself "as a fine performer—and not as a symbol of her race."

"I thought this was a daring breakthrough to pair a Colored actress with Trevor Howard," said Benedek. "And we all agreed, 'Well, let's try it.'"

"There was no more question of whether casting her would hurt the picture," Benedek recalled. "The writer, myself, and the producer and all the people around, nobody ever mentioned 'Isn't it—casting her—going to be bad in distribution?' At least not that I remember. Not in my presence."

Despite her eagerness to do the picture, she remained uneasy with the script. During her story discussions with Benedek, she said almost nothing. But in her suite at the Dorchester, she was restless and brooding and often in discussions about the script over the phone with Earl Mills in the States. The fact that her character Gianna, despite the Italian name, was not identified by either race or nationality actually bothered her. Much like Margot in *Island in the Sun*, the character struck her as poorly developed and ill-defined without enough said about background or motivations. She was just simply the girl in love with one of the leads.

In one key scene in a hotel room, Gianna reveals something about her background to the man she is falling in love with. She tells him that her father was sentenced to life in prison for killing a man. "I love him very much. I still do," she says. A few minutes later she speaks in Spanish to the hotel proprietor. When asked where she learned the language, Gianna replies, "At home. I picked it up from the kids next door."

When asked if she does not want to go back home, she answers, "I can't. Oh, I've made such a mess of everything. It's such a mess. I can't go back any place."

These promising moments offered the foundation of a character. But the scene ended without further explanation. Nor was anything developed in later sequences. For Dorothy, it was no different than that moment in *Island in the Sun* when Margot started to speak about her background, then dropped the subject to ask about the gramophone. Why did the scripts stop short of any further exploration of these women she played? Why were the characters' lives left so unexamined?

Had the screenplay portrayed her character as a Spaniard, that would have been fine. Had it depicted her as an Italian, that too would have given dimension to the character. But to say nothing of Gianna's roots and bearings made her hollow at the core. "I don't understand this girl," she lamented to Earl Mills. "What's she about? Where does she come from emotionally?"

Most distressing to Dorothy was the fact that while the scriptwriters believed themselves daring in letting a Black actress play a non-racial role, they were not courageous enough to transcend traditional racial codes. In a key sequence in *Malaga*, Dandridge and Trevor Howard were to be alone for days as they journeyed through the south of Spain. They share a hotel room and find themselves caught up in the moody romantic atmosphere of the Spanish countryside. At one point, she and Howard have a quiet, intimate moment outdoors by a stream. Yet again, as in *Island in the Sun*, despite the attraction, they do not so much as kiss, or even fully acknowledge their mutual attraction.

The movie ended with the couple going their separate ways. He would head off to prison, but she would promise to wait for him. Dorothy came to hate *Malaga*'s evasions, half-truths, and dishonesties. She wondered what she had gotten herself into and how she had ever agreed to do the film. But in truth she knew the answer to the latter question. Plain and simple, of course, she needed the work. According to Earl Mills, *Malaga* became a wholly distressing movie experience for her.

Benedek himself was sensitive. Born in Budapest, Hungary, in 1907, he was a well-educated and fairly reflective man who had first studied drama and psychiatry at the University of Vienna and later studied at the Psycho-Analytic Clinic in Berlin under the then well-known Dr. Carl Abraham. Later he became a cameraman at UFA (Universum Film Aktien Gesellschaft) and then a master film editor. He also served as an editor and assistant producer for producer Joe Pasternak, who was then working in Europe. When Hitler came to power, Benedek went to Vienna, later worked in Paris as an editor and English dialogue director, and, in 1937, emigrated to the United States. In Hollywood, he was signed by MGM as an associate producer for Pasternak, now in the film capital himself.

Later he directed *The Kissing Bandit* with Frank Sinatra. He became best known for his 1951 screen version of Arthur Miller's prize-winning drama *Death of a Salesman* and then in 1954 for the cult film *The Wild One* starring a very young Marlon Brando.

Already having shown himself as a director sensitive to characters with personal feelings of failure and to those mavericks standing outside the system, Benedek saw in *Malaga* an opportunity for an unusual character study of two outsiders. The jewel thief and the "girlfriend" Gianna struggle to keep a grip on themselves and to hold their ground in a system in which they are misfits. Benedek's real problem would be to fully define the fears and goals of these two lonely drifters. Indeed, had he brought race or nationality into their dilemma, just passingly, he might well have found the core essentials for creating truly complicated characters and the common element that binds them.

Aware that the script needed work, Benedek enlisted the help of the well-known, Yale-educated, Academy Award-winning Hollywood writer Donald Ogden Stewart. Stewart had written or co-authored the screenplays of such films as *The Philadelphia Story*, *Tales of*

Manhattan, and *A Woman's Face.* Blacklisted during the McCarthy era, he had been living in London since 1951. Benedek's script discussions with Stewart, however, were not about more definition for Dandridge's character, but a stronger story line and more gripping dialogue.

Benedek rather hoped that Dorothy might be able, through her star persona, to fill in some of the holes in the screenplay's characterization. "When you cast a picture and the script is being written and things are a little unsure, you begin to form an image of what you want," he recalled. "And frankly, I felt we were very lucky to have her because I thought she would bring a lot to the role because we didn't have time to make great changes."

As shooting began at Associated British studios at Elstree, little seemed out of the ordinary. For Benedek, *Malaga*'s most pressing problem was the casting of Edmund Purdom as Dorothy's love interest. "He was nothing," said Benedek. "Nothing as an actor. It was just as if he hadn't been there. He was an absolute zero. My recollection is that I didn't remember that he was in the picture. He was a bad actor. He was a nice guy privately. But he certainly was not an actor. I cast him myself because I wanted somebody weaker than Trevor for reasons of characteristics. It was the wrong choice."

But Benedek enjoyed working with Dorothy, whose discipline impressed him. "I don't believe we ever had to wait for her," he said. "You know how sometimes you're ready and you've rehearsed and you sit and wait for the actress to make it to the set or get in the mood or go to the toilet or something. But I don't recall that she ever held us up. I don't remember during the entire picture having any difficulty. We never looked around and said, "'Now where the hell is she?'"

She also appeared to be in a fine mood. "Sometimes she was laughing and I was making jokes and Trevor was making jokes," he said. On occasion, he spoke to her "about a deeper understanding of a scene." "I sometimes talked to her a little more seriously about the character she was playing and how she would put it across because she needed some technique. Once or twice. And she was wonderful and understood and accepted it and tried to play it that way."

He felt that the only problem was her handling of dialogue. "Her beauty and her appearance were perfect for the role. When it came to dialogue, she needed a lot of help." For Benedek, who came from the school that still prized experience in the theatre, Dorothy suffered because "she didn't have a background in stage acting."

Dandridge and Trevor Howard had no problems working together. Like most of her leading men, he appeared enchanted. "During the shooting at the studio, the relationship was extremely friendly," said Benedek. "Trevor liked her very much."

Early in the production, Howard took Benedek aside to discuss Dorothy. "She's fine," the actor confided to the director. "But she really needs a little help. Do you mind if I say something?"

"No, try it," said Benedek.

Afterwards, said Benedek, "Trevor, who, of course, was more experienced than she, was enormously helpful. Suggesting to her. Cutting pauses. Doing things in a way that an actor can help an actress. But not obviously. Once or twice he said to Dorothy, 'Would you like me to do such and such? Would it help you if I didn't look at you? Do you want me to keep my mouth shut and let you have your pauses?' Simple things in terms of acting. He was very helpful. And she accepted the suggestions as help."

Howard understood and respected her talent. He appeared to have been moved by her and was also willing to let her show her sensitivity. In turn, Dandridge responded to Howard's sensitivity and his unexpected rugged gentleness. Perhaps next to Belafonte, he was the leading man she was most comfortable with. Still, between Howard and Dandridge, "There was absolutely no personal contact outside of the professional rehearsal and so on," said Benedek. "Nothing." Nor was there any personal contact between Dorothy and himself.

Both Benedek and Howard admitted to being puzzled by this gorgeous solitary enigma who turned up promptly every day, never missed her mark on the set, and spent a great deal of her down time off by herself in her dressing room.

Once the interiors were shot in London, the company moved to the Costa del Sol in Spain for exteriors. There Dorothy's mood changed. At first, everything appeared fine. "During the location stuff, she was very amenable," Benedek recalled. "To my recollection, we all had a good time. We didn't have a wild time. We didn't all get drunk together and go singing and dancing together. But we enjoyed each other's company." Benedek and just about everyone else at work on *Malaga*, like most casts and crews shooting on location in a new city or town, bonded quickly. Relationships were formed, sometimes intense, sometimes passionate. Off-hours were spent together, usually talking, drinking, eating, gossiping, or partying. Benedek was surprised that Dorothy rarely participated.

During the day, she sometimes joined the cast and crew for their lunch break. "She was perfectly natural and very easy going and laughing. Just like a professional actress," said Benedek. "And then came the evening and we said goodbye to her. She didn't eat dinner with us." Dorothy simply vanished.

"Dorothy was charming and relaxed. But very distant," he said.

True to her now lifelong habits, which were unknown to Benedek, she kept almost completely to herself. The director could not figure out what, if anything, was wrong. Then he noticed the presence of someone he had not seen before. It was the secretary who had accompanied Dorothy to London and who was with her on location in Spain. To Benedek, the woman appeared to have sprung up out of nowhere. Resentful of the woman, whom he found officious and controlling, he believed that "the reason for the distance" growing between Dorothy and himself "was this middle-aged Black woman who was Dorothy's dresser or companion or friend who came on location and traveled with her. And she, far more than Dorothy Dandridge, objected to all these White men. If anyone asked Dorothy Dandridge to have dinner with us, this woman always stopped it. And very rarely did Dorothy have a drink with us that wasn't during a dinner. There wasn't the kind of feeling that I'd imagine any White star having on location. You know, the joking and being in on all kinds of things."

"I mean after all, we were way far off in the hills. And you know movie companies reduce to their own circle and we had a good time," said Benedek. "But Dorothy was not part of it. Whether Dorothy wanted the isolation, I don't know. My private opinion is that she didn't like it. That she would have wanted more contact with Trevor, with myself, with the cameraman. And we all felt it was because the woman just wouldn't permit it."

Finally, Trevor Howard told Benedek to just let Dorothy do as she wanted. "We discussed it among ourselves and we finally reached a point where we said, 'Well, to hell with it. Don't try any more. Don't make any effort.'"

But there was another matter. In *Malaga*, she was the only person of color in the film unit. On past projects like *Island in the Sun* and even *Sundown* which she had done as a teenager, other Black performers were around with whom she could talk and commiserate in a more personal way, should a problem, particularly one involving race, present itself. If she chose—and often she didn't—she could always say something to Belafonte. Or Poitier. Or Sammy Davis, Jr. Here she was completely isolated and alone, playing a part that troubled her.

Writer Donald Ogden Stewart joined the cast in Spain where he attempted to doctor the script. Just about everyone knew there were serious problems.

For Dorothy, the shoot was difficult for a number of reasons. Aside from her concerns about the script, she also remained in the middle of her marriage plans to Denison, and in the middle of her second thoughts about the union.

Dorothy maintained an outer calm when later interviewed by *Jet* for their cover story about her role in the film. "It is not a picture pointing up anybody's nationality," she said. "The fact that they are using a Negro actress has nothing to do with the script and the point has nothing to do with color. I feel these type roles are contributing to the general evolution of the Negro as an actor or actress."

But the truth was she lost faith in *Malaga* before it was even completed, particularly during the location shoot. "A new writer was put on the picture after the shooting had begun," she said. "When he came to Spain from London, we didn't know what kind of people we would be the next day."

She understood that ironically, the mere *suggestion*—through casting—of an interracial romance could present problems. "There may be certain cities in the South that will not want to play this picture because of this interracial aspect," she explained to *Jet*. "But I don't see what difference it makes to lose those few cities in the South. Curious moviegoers in other cities will counter-balance this loss, I'm sure. Anyway, the producers are figuring this from a dollars and cents angle."

It was precisely this dollars-and-cents angle that may have determined the fact that, in pivotal scenes, Dorothy and Trevor Howard were not permitted to show any signs of romance. At a crucial moment of intimacy in one sequence just when the couple might kiss, the director had shouted "cut." She thought it was wholly dishonest and hypocritical, and later discussed the scene with Trevor Howard, who agreed with her.

Years later Laslo Benedek, upon learning of her reaction for the first time, was surprised that until the day the sequence was shot, she had believed there would be a kiss.

"It really seems impossible to me that I would have let the actors believe that they were going to kiss," said Benedek. "I would have said to the actors beforehand that there would be no kiss on the lips in the scene. I would have had to rehearse it in the positions of the lighting and composition."

In later years, Benedek admitted that the scene was dishonest, even if he could not recall why he shot it as he did. "There is no scene of really physical kissing or embracing or lovemaking of any kind. And that certainly is in my mind, one of the great weaknesses of the story. I mean after all they go out on the road and they are alone in nature under the trees and so on. Why can't they make love there? What is there to prevent it? Now looking back at it, I say that must have been very unnatural. Here is a young woman and a man and they are alone supposedly, and they should certainly embrace and kiss. I certainly was interested in the relationship. But I am stunned that I let it come to such a critical scene and they don't kiss. I agree with the way she felt because I can put myself in her position being a Colored woman and being told, 'You can go this far and not any further.'"

"I carried out some directive," he believed. "Maybe somebody in London said, 'It's okay. But don't let them kiss.' Maybe. I think there was an artificial feeling in us, the makers of the film, that it shouldn't go that far. I remember very vaguely now talking to the writer and saying that we better not go into that. Let's keep away from making a definite characterization that she is an American Negress who is going from one bed to another. This was a touchy subject."

"Apparently, I knew how far they could go. Wrong as it was. And as a director I was part of the wrong and I agree with her reaction. I take the blame. Maybe it was the dangerous situation from an American point of view. I don't remember. And I don't want to defend myself. It was my fault. I was the director and I should have known how far they could go on the screen."

Yet Benedek stressed that he did not recall Dandridge ever voicing her concerns. "I was at first annoyed and then I shrugged my shoulders at the fact that I could never talk with her alone. She and I never had a private conversation where I said, 'Well, what's bothering you? Can I be of some assistance?' I never had that conversation with her. I've had it many times with other actresses. But never, never, never with this girl. And I regret it, of course, because she needed help. Maybe she should have spoken up. I probably, being much older, would have been the person to help her. But I didn't have a chance, and I didn't ask for the chance. We were so rushed. I didn't have the time to ask actors how they felt about the scenes. I loved the photographic possibilities with the shadows and the sunlight and so on. I just hurried on to the next shot and the next shot."

"Yet in myself, I always felt a very warm and protective feeling about her," he recalled, "because I always felt that she needed protection. That she was alone in the world somehow."

The sequences in Spain were shot quickly. Then the cast dispersed. "Everybody went his or her way," Benedek said. "And I don't even remember saying goodbye to Dorothy."

Later when he viewed the finished product, Benedek said he was disappointed with his own work. The characters and story had not been strongly enough developed. But he liked Howard's work.

Dorothy, however, puzzled him as much on screen as she had off. "I liked her performance up to a point. But I always felt there was something missing," he said. "She played the character very well. But I never felt she gave it more than what was required. I was satisfied with what was required and she gave that. But I don't think she created a real character. But I also think that the script didn't give her a chance. It didn't give her enough material on which to build this character."

First released in Europe in 1960, *Malaga* met with mixed reviews and fared tepidly at the box-office. Warner Brothers did not release it in the United States until 1962. "They did not like the picture or spend that much on publicity," Benedek recalled. But the studio said nothing about the racial issue. "Maybe if the picture had been better, Warners's might have made more of the issue that this was a Black actress and a White leading man." Reviewers, however, pointed out the unusual casting, which was generally considered a positive sign. "Dorothy Dandridge plays the girl, first Purdom's, later Howard's," wrote James Powers in *The Hollywood Reporter*. "Nothing is made of the racial aspects of the romances."

Variety's reviewer commented, "It's remarkable that a director of the caliber of Laslo Benedek should become involved in such a disappointing picture as *Malaga*." Called "a sad misfire of a film," *Malaga* failed, the reviewer believed, "because it cannot make up its mind whether it's a study of the relationship of two interesting people or a straightforward crime-chase yarn. Director Benedek seems more interested in the Freud stuff." While the reviewer commented that Dandridge "tries hard but is beaten by the script," he also noted that a couple of scenes rose above the general torpor. "Both of these gainfully employ Howard and Miss Dandridge and involve them in some discussion of their past and future hopes. But they are not enough even for such talented thesps."

Yet other critics, especially in England, were moved by Dandridge's performance and her despairing beauty. British reviewer Jympson Harman wrote that Dandridge "without any colour problem to contend with—she is presumably Italian—acts splendidly in her first real straight part." The reviewer for London's *Daily Mirror* commented that "Miss Dandridge provides some poignant moments."

In London's *Daily Express*, the critic rhapsodized that "you can't have everything; and Miss Dandridge as far as I was concerned, was enough in herself. Yes, this film passes the Thursday Test; and may we see a great deal more of Miss Dandridge." The reviewer for London's *Daily Telegraph wrote*, "Miss Dandridge is pretty enough to get away with anything."

Then in *The Sunday London Express*, Derek Monsey commented: "Through all the incredible dialogue and the incomprehensible happenings which follow, Dorothy Dandridge keeps a finger hold on reality; she acts quite well, she looks superb." Monsey also called her "certainly one of the most disturbingly lovely women on the screen." What Monsey was touching on was the essence of Dorothy's work and persona in *Malaga*: her face now sent out "disturbing" messages of disillusionment and despair.

Malaga ended up having a strange life of its own. In years to come, the film turned up on the lower half of bills at theaters in the big cities, notably New York's Times Square area. There the outsiders and seeming rejects of the culture appeared to find pleasure in this portrait of a loner jewel thief, who becomes emotionally bound to a woman for whom he cannot express his deep feelings. And audiences seemed as intrigued by Dandridge's mysterious and moody Gianna as Benedek was by her off-screen mystery.

In *Malaga*, Dandridge, again adrift in a film without a defined character to play, used her own weariness and isolation to create a stunning portrait. Contrary to what Benedek might have thought, it was precisely her experience in film rather than the stage—the awareness that the camera demands one to *be* and *think* rather than act—that endows the character with a sense of realism. Her Gianna, like Dandridge herself, has been to a place the script cannot identify and has returned bruised and saddened and detached.

Her very look is a moving visual statement unto itself. In the plain clothes, the plain hairstyle—actually, a not very becoming wig—and the seemingly plain makeup, her glamour still emanates from within and only heightens her natural, glowing but doomed beauty and allure. Here audiences saw the glamour of wistful disenchantment. In this respect, *Malaga* truly seems European; in its Old World moodiness and angst. Here Dorothy had arrived at the naturalistic tone she once told Geri she hoped to achieve in films.

Strangely, *Malaga* became Dandridge's most haunting performance. Without the kinetic fire of her Carmen (still her best) and without quite the classy distance of her Bess, she is wholly herself, the line between character and actress blurred. Dandridge's bleak despondency, her warmth, her sweet desire for hope are there.

At times the film's story just seems to stop with long, meandering stretches where not much happens at all. But Benedek wants the camera to record Dandridge in some of her most intensely personal moments: as she sits alone in a cafe where men eye her; as she slips into bed wearing sweetly baggy pajamas; as she lies back on her pillow, talking about herself—a snippet of her past history—hoping to sleep. Why count sheep when there are enough hurts and pains to recall to drift off to oblivion?

In a sequence in which she has gone out for the night to sell her body in order that she and Howard might have money for their survival, she returns the weariest and saddest of heroines. In closeups, Dandridge's eyes and mouth, rather than the dialogue, signal her inner psychological drives. In *Porgy and Bess*, she was denied her closeups. In *Malaga*—in key scenes—they are lavished on her.

The key to *Malaga* became the movie within the movie: the interior documentary of Dandridge's performance that is a study in dreamy despair; an unconscious attempt to communicate on screen the absolute mess that she felt her life was becoming; a moving portrait of a ravishing Dandridge adrift. In the scenes with Trevor Howard, which touched on her diminishing romanticism, her Gianna does not want to feel, yet she cannot help responding to this wounded animal who shows up on her doorstep.

Curiously, her scenes with Edmund Purdom, despite director's Benedek's disdain for the actor, have an edge and give the movie some spark. Purdom possessed a dashing quality and a seemingly carefree but smoothly calculating nonchalance that made him the appropriate handsome, callow lover for Dandridge. In some respects, Dorothy, finding herself without much motivation for Gianna, may well have viewed Purdom's character Peter as a surrogate for Jack Denison.

Here she had to contend with a good-looking man who has never spent a day thinking of anyone other than himself. Here is a man accustomed to taking advantage; to uttering pretty lines and lies; to walking away without any thoughts of looking back or any considerations of what he has left behind. Purdom's very vacuity served to make her weariness seem all the more plausible. In her first scene opposite him—with her eyes glazed over and her face an emotional blank—she is a woman who does not want to feel, as if she's too drained to even rise to real anger. Yet in her smoky voice, smoldering embers of past great fires still linger. Brilliantly, she incorporated her untold and unresolved personal tensions into Gianna's.

It was all the more telling that *Malaga* ended on a note of false hope: her decision, we assume, to wait for Trevor Howard's Johnny until he is out of prison. Yet the audience knows Gianna's fate is sealed: she will remain adrift, awaiting the return of a dream. *Malaga* is quintessential Dandridge; not so much a performance as a statement on a state of mind and a hopeless point of view. In this respect, she is altogether compelling.

After completing *Malaga*, she returned to the States and her wedding. A simple ceremony and a reception had already been planned. Then a honeymoon that would also be work—to New York for the opening of *Porgy and Bess*. Already press releases had been sent out. Louella Parsons had written in her May 8th column, "Word comes from London that the famous Negro actress, Dorothy Dandridge and Jack Dennison [sic] have chosen June 21st [sic] as their wedding date."

Dorothy also had been in negotiations with producer Abby Greshler and Sammy Davis, Jr., to star in a film based on Joey Adams's novel *The Curtain Never Falls*. She had no idea whether or not this project would ever see the light of day. But that she could not fret about. Instead she braced herself for the grueling hours and days ahead.

On June 20th, photographers snapped pictures of Dandridge as she arrived at New York's Idlewild Airport. Simply and elegantly dressed in a suit with pearls and gloves and with her hair brushed back from her forehead, she appeared wan and wistful after the long flight. Hers was hardly the radiant look of a bride to be. Reporters followed her inside the airport terminal as she made a quick phone call to the West Coast before boarding another flight that took her to Los Angeles.

Exhausted, she arrived at her home on Evanview to tackle last minute wedding preparations. She and Denison motored to Santa Monica where they picked up their marriage license before the eager eyes of photographers. But again Dorothy didn't look particularly happy.

Then shortly before 5 p.m. on June 23rd, she entered the St.

Sophia Orthodox Cathedral in Los Angeles. Already gathered were a group of some two hundred old friends and family members. Denison's brother served as his best man. His mother and sister were also present.

Dorothy's guest list looked an attempt to recapture something lost from the past. She had invited her childhood friend Henriella Wilkins, Henriella's sister Morrisontine Boykin, and Etta Jones. By now having divorced Gerald Wilson and remarried, Etta arrived with her husband Billy Mills and her stepdaughter. Etta was surprised by the invitation from Dorothy, particularly in light of the fact that the two had never been close. Also on Dorothy's wedding list were Brock Peters, director Andrew Stone and his wife producer Virginia Stone, and Nat Cole—who like Etta went back to the days of the Dandridge Sisters—and Cole's wife Maria. Of course, a jubilant Ruby attended the ceremony. But Earl Mills was not in attendance. "I wasn't asked to go," he said, aware that Dorothy remained piqued by his outspoken warnings about Denison.

Officiating at the ceremony was the Very Reverend Leonidas C. Contos, dean of the Cathedral. Dorothy walked down the aisle, as the press reported, in a "gown of white mousseline de soie and chantilly lace, designed by Berman of London. The dress was ballerina length, with a V-neckline, three-quarter length pouffe sleeves and a full skirt." A striking figure but not a portrait of high spirits, rather of self-imposed disengagement and resignation, she looked like a woman who had struck some sort of bargain with life. Yet whatever the trade-off, it seemed unbalanced on her side.

She was attended by two women, Jack's sister, Mary Denison, who no doubt was included in the ceremony because of his wishes, and, of course, Geri Pate Nicholas Branton. Geri still believed the marriage was a true mistake but she was resigned to support her closest friend nonetheless.

Though surrounded by many old friends and her mother, as she glanced around the chapel, she knew someone important was missing. She still had been unable to reach Vivian.

The traditional Greek wedding ceremony lasted only one half hour. Afterward Dorothy wanly smiled at the crowd, turned her back, and then threw her bridal bouquet over her shoulder. Catching it was Etta's young stepdaughter, who for years afterwards kept the flowers sealed in a book. The guests smiled, laughed, and chatted, hoping for the best, despite the misgivings many secretly harbored.

Following the ceremony, when Dorothy and Denison posed for

photographers, a smiling Ruby joined them and also joyously posed. She appeared ecstatic. Dorothy also posed with Nat Cole. Ruby excitedly mixed with the crowd and told Etta that she had to rush home and pack because she planned to join the couple on their honeymoon. The couple drove off in a sleek Lincoln Continental to a restaurant for a quiet dinner with the wedding guests. There they were toasted with champagne.

Ebony later described the event as a quiet, dignified one "whose un-Hollywoodlike simplicity overturned half a century of Movieland tradition." But photographs taken that day tell a deeper story. Dorothy looked weary, luminously older, and hauntingly, almost heartbreakingly beautiful. But as the day wore on, her detachment appeared to grow, making her seem almost numbed. While at the restaurant reception, she even fell asleep. Actually, she had been on sedatives all day.

After the reception, she and Denison flew to New York for the premiere of *Porgy and Bess*. She was not looking forward to the event, feeling insecure about her performance. Still, she hoped the picture might turn out well. Mainly, though, she dreaded seeing Otto. When she had invited him to Denison's restaurant, she had hoped it would be a moment of triumph for her. But she realized Preminger had been too perceptive to fall for that. Now with Denison on her arm, Otto might silently scoff at her with his eyes or his smile.

The crowded opening at the Warner Theatre was oldstyle New York/Hollywood glamour and glitz. Cars honked loudly as traffic was tied up for blocks around the theatre. Revolving search lights lit up the sky. The New York press and photographers ran about in pursuit of the arriving celebrities. In attendance were Sammy Davis, Jr., Brock Peters, Samuel and Frances Goldwyn, Mrs. Du Bose Heyward, Marlene Dietrich, Danny Kaye, Ambassador Henry Cabot Lodge, Edward R. Murrow, CBS's Dr. Frank Stanton, Broadway star Mary Martin, and the "Today Show" host Dave Garroway. Poitier didn't attend. At the time, he was appearing on Broadway in *A Raisin in the Sun*.

Dressed in a sleek silk gown with brocaded roses on its skirt and a matching evening coat, Dorothy departed from her limousine with Denison by her side and was about to enter the theatre when a group of excited fans, a mix of Black and White, broke through the police barricades and ran up to ask her for autographs. She complied. But she appeared dazed and disoriented, almost as if she were narcotized. She had indeed taken medication to relax. Amid the fanfare, the lights, the shouts, the whistles, the cameras, the waves, and the cheers from the crowd, her eyes met Otto's. As they posed for the press, she felt as resentful as ever toward him. But their meeting passed without any trauma. Relieved when the evening finally ended, she said, "I couldn't wait to get away."

The next day the film opened for the public on a reserved seat basis at a then, hefty $3.75 a ticket. Goldwyn's and Columbia's publicity machines worked effectively at letting audiences know of the movie's arrival. The reviews, however, were mixed. While the sets of Oliver Smith and the cinematography of Leon Shamroy were praised, many critics found the production lifeless.

"The worst thing about Goldwyn's *Porgy*, though, is its cinematic monotony," wrote *Time*, which also commented that "for some strange, wrong reason—perhaps to give the show an elevated operatic tone—the actors speak in precise, cultivated accents that are miles away from the Negro slums of South Carolina. For that matter Sidney Poitier's Porgy is not the dirty, ragtag beggar of the Heyward script, but a swell-scrubbed young romantic hero who is never seen taking a penny from anybody." *Time*'s objection to the actors speaking without a dialect was, of course, the very thing Dorothy had fought for.

The critic who seemed most enthusiastic about the film was Bosley Crowther of *The New York Times*, who opened his review with praise. "The mills of the gods have ground slowly but they have ground exceeding well in delivering at last a fine film version of the famous folk opera *Porgy and Bess*," he wrote, concluding that "for the most part, this is a stunning, exciting and moving film, packed with human emotions and cheerful and mournful melodies. It bids fair to be as much a classic on the screen as it is on the stage."

But of Dorothy, Crowther commented, "Miss Dandridge is too sinuous and sleek and got up to look too much like Kiki to give a fully satisfying portrayal of Bess. A couple of duets are somewhat static. And the climatic incident in the plot—the desertion of Bess—has been covered in a much too mildly allusive scene."

Other critics concurred with Crowther about Dandridge's performance. "Dorothy Dandridge, who emphasizes the elegance of her bones more than the sins of the flesh," wrote *Time*, "makes something of a nice Nellie out of bad Bess." *Variety* commented that "Miss Dandridge is perhaps too 'refined' in type to be quite convincing as the split-skirt, heroin-shuffling tramp." *The New York Herald Tribune*'s Paul V. Beckley believed that "Dorothy Dandridge's Bess is rather too delicate, a sense of actual refinement somehow showing through the 'light woman' veneer."

For Dorothy, the reviews were devastating yet ironic. All the talk about her refinement and delicacy—which were viewed as negatives for the portrayal—was piercing because she believed these were the very qualities a Black woman should bring to the screen; these very aspects of AfricanAmerican female life had never been explored. One of the few critics to look at her work in a different manner was Arthur Knight of *The Saturday Review*, who—in his cover story on the film——wrote that "Miss Dandridge's tragic eyes and womanly warmth elevate Bess from a conventionally sexy good-bad girl to a forlorn, tormented creature, who sins out of weakness rather viciousness."

In its first weeks, the film fared well at the box-office, despite the fact that—politically charged by the Civil Rights movement—the African American community saw *Porgy and Bess* as a relic of the past.

While in New York, Dandridge was interviewed for a cover stor—her second–in the NewYork *Sunday News*'s *Coloroto* magazine, which commented that her roles in *Malaga* and *Porgy and Bess* were "a strong indication that her stature in the films is a high one and that any full-scale return to night clubbery is unlikely. She has not, in fact, worked in the clubs much at all in the past two years." Dorothy told the publication's reporter, "I've been too busy with movies to do anything else. I guess I'll perform in clubs again but as far as devoting a whole career to it, I don't think I'll ever do that again."

The newlyweds flew from New York to San Francisco where they registered in the bridal suite at the Fairmont Hotel. Having performed sold-out engagements there, Dorothy was treated like a queen by management. But it was not the best of wedding nights.

When she should have relaxed and glowed in the happiness of the new marriage and the opening of a major film, she was confronted with a crisis. Dorothy suddenly learned, said Earl Mills, that Denison "was not what he stated he was. In truth, he was a con artist." Denison was drinking as he explained that he had a terrible problem. By now having been on the move so much—and also battling depression again—she had again relied on tranquilizers to calm herself. But she understood every word he was saying.

Denison poured himself a drink and proceeded to tell her that they must talk. He had a problem.

"He needed her help," said Earl Mills. "He told her that on their wedding night. That he needed financial help. He had a restaurant that was failing. And he had a lot of other negative financial situations. Of course, this was bewildering to her. It created a shocking situation."

Then Denison added that she could save the restaurant if she agreed to perform there.

So upset was he about the state of the restaurant, he told her, that he was ready to jump out the window of the Fairmont. Fully aware now of what she had always known but never admitted to herself, that in essence he was using her, she glanced at him, not taken in by his ploy for sympathy.

"Look, dear heart, jump!" she told him.

Then she walked out of the suite.

When she later returned, she and Jack talked quietly but not long. He soon fell asleep. She, however, remained wide awake, sitting up alone and sipping champagne as she looked out the window onto the city of San Francisco below. Of the honeymoon, she said the note on which they started was a banknote.

Upon her return to Los Angeles, she found herself tired and jittery, unable to sit still. To some people around her, she often appeared to be in a state of perpetual panic. To combat the exhaustion, the nervousness, and the memories of that pathetic honeymoon scene in the bridal suite of the Fairmount, she continued to numb herself with tranquilizers. She came to believe that this was the way she would have to live her life; numbed to the very presence of the man she had married. Yet she still hoped somehow the marriage might work.

Coming to Jack's rescue with money to keep him in business, she refused to dwell on her financial situation, even though she knew that the $75,000 she had earned for *Malaga* would go quickly. Instead she considered, at Denison's prompting, a move from Evanview—the home Otto had bought for her—to a larger place.

On August 19, 1959, after long delays, *Tamango* finally made its American debut. It appeared just at a time when the nation was galvanized by the growing civil rights movement. Two years earlier, Congress had passed the Civil Rights Act of 1957, which was the first federal civil rights legislation since 1875. President Eisenhower had sent federal troops into Little Rock, Arkansas to prevent interference with school integration at Central High School. Old-guard segregationists like Arkansas's Governor Orval Faubus and later Alabama's Governor George Wallace fought to hold back the tide of this social activism. But sit-ins, boycotts, demonstrations, and protests had sprung up throughout the South and eventually led to a dramatic change in American society. Gradually, the strategy of passive resistance would give way in the 1960s to more radical methods of confronting American racism. In many respects, *Tamango* was in tune with the new mood, especially a more militant one within Black America, which may explain why it had such distribution problems in the States. It had opened well in Europe, breaking box-office records in England, Spain, and France, where it had a two year run.

Variety also believed the film had potential:

> This could shape as a potent box-office contender on both local and Yank screens because of its rugged matter, a revolt on a slave ship during the early 19th century. There are some torrid clinches between white star Curt Jurgens and American Negro actress Dorothy Dandridge. But this is not cheapened, and film stacks up as an actioner, with plus hypo factors, that could make for a general play-off in the U.S., with perhaps the South excluded.
>
> . . . . Director John Berry, a Yank, has given this splendid mounting and has overcome some dramatic contrivance via emphasis on a fight for freedom. Though ideologies are kept simple, the final revolt of the slaves and Miss Dandridge's. . . . reversion to her own peoples, offer a stirring climax to the film.

The Black press also commented on *Tamango*, which impressed it more as a tale of protest than interracial love. *Jet* reported, "Intense and provocative, *Tomango*[sic] evinces a variety of reactions. It has been called 'a welcome ally to the Negroes' fight for civil rights. . . an excellent motion picture that should do a good job for present-day civil liberties. . . a real story, good for integration.' Other previewers found the racial issue 'too strong,' felt the film 'too vividly portrays the brutality of the white man. . . radiates hostility and 'would not create any goodwill.' Many regretted it could not be shown to 'all the Faubuses' and in 'all sections of every country.' Without doubt *Tomango* stirs the emotions, grips the attention, and will not be among the quickly-forgotten movies."

The California Sentinel's reviewer Darcy DeMille believed

Tamango aired dirty laundry that best be forgotten. Yet he admitted the film had affected him and told some truths that many whites might not feel comfortable with. "A fellow brother of the Inkspots once said the story could never be filmed," wrote DeMille, "and I hasten to add that it should never have been filmed, not as a maker of money. But on the other hand, I'm glad it has been brought out into the open because it presents a good and wonderful argument AGAINST racial discrimination." He added:

> Whites, the mighty and the weak, the liberals and the segregationists, will not like *Tamango* because what they see in their brother-whites, will make them squirm. The foul deeds carried out by the white "masters" will bring home to them the fact that no man is a true master if he has to force another man to carry out even the simplest of orders. The theme of the story, set back during the days of slave-running from Africa to Havana and other port cities, is especially hard to take at this point in the 20th century. Not that what happens is unbelievable, on the contrary, it stirs painful memories for the old and frightens and angers the younger generation. . . .

> The only thing that could be jotted down in the "debit" side is the beauty and amazing performance turned in by Miss Dandridge. . . . Many may condemn her for playing the "White man's trash" in the movie. I say as an actress, she should feel free to select any part which will enable her to exhibit her particular brand of talent. . . . She reaches her peak as an actress, especially is this visible in the scene where she realizes she belongs with her darker brothers.

Despite all the talk, no major American distributor would touch the film. According to Mills, Harry Cohn at Columbia Pictures screened the film, seemed interested, but then said the interracial love scenes were too explicit for American audiences. He feared the South would rise up in arms. Finally, the Hal Roach Company, not a major distributor, released the film. But rather than opening in New York or Los Angeles where it might have garnered important press coverage, *Tamango*'s American debut was at the Fox Theatre in Detroit. It did well there and was also set for showings in such

Southern cities as San Antonio, Texas, Charlotte, North Carolina, and Columbia, South Carolina. But the distribution remained limited. The film was also closed out of other markets. It was banned for showing in the French African colonies as being too inflammatory, supposedly because of its love scenes but most likely because its political revolt proved scary.

The film did little for Dandridge's reputation. "When she did that one," said Brock Peters, "I knew she was going down." Throughout, she was hampered by a weak script. Cast as a woman whose blood is mixed, she is clearly the doomed mulatto; alienated from the Black world and of course, not really accepted by the White. In the explicit love scenes, Dandridge and Jurgens didn't seem romantic at all but rather an overwrought, passionate pair who are usually at each other's throats.

Yet interestingly, *Tamango*, which seemed more like an oldstyle over-the-top Hollywood adventure tale than a European drama, is not a bad viewing experience at all. Later African American audiences enjoyed it. Far too contemporary an actress for this period piece, Dorothy's voice had the tone of a well-bred young woman of the 1950s, rather than an enslaved woman of the 1800s. Nor was she helped by the fact that her voice is dubbed (by her) in many sequences.

But in some scenes with Jurgens, she exhibited grit and a shrewd control and once again she looked as if acting out a drama of her own. Unlike the rather weak male characters of *Carmen Jones* and *Island in the Sun*, Jurgens's captain was a strong, powerful figure who sought to dominate the woman who was literally his slave. Dandridge appears to relish every scene of conflict with him, and she didn't back off from unleashing her anger at the self-righteous title character Tamango, who cries out that Aiche has betrayed her people. In one scene, she turns the tables on Tamango. Here acting clearly—as with so much of *Carmen Jones*—enabled her speak her mind to a domineering and headstrong male. Her moments of brash assertion and rebellion gave *Tamango* its vitality—and sometimes it's surprising, and almost campy, humor. Black audiences, past and present, tended to cheer when her Aiche finally shows her allegience to her people. When she must make a choice, she joins the other slaves in their dance of death in the lower decks.

Yet also touchingly she seems adrift at times and not quite in the movie, as if her thoughts were somewhere else.

Whatever hopes Dorothy had for *Tamango* quickly faded, and the film soon disappeared. Had it appeared at a time—perhaps ten years later—when popular films of dissent were reaching a large young African American audience, *Tamango*—which is a precursor to the films of the blaxploitation era—might have had far better distribution and been a commercial success.

There wasn't much concrete film work on the horizon now. But as usual, there was talk of some. After the death of Billie Holiday in July 1959, producers planned again to launch a movie version of Holiday's autobiography *Lady Sings the Blues*. Joe Glaser, who now owned the rights to the book, wanted Dorothy to play Holiday. She had hopes that the project would work out. But she had fears it would not. Glaser also was in contact with Preminger to direct the film. Otto too expressed interest. After all the outbursts on *Porgy and Bess*, apparently, he still wanted to work with her again.

Dorothy also heard from director Rouben Mamoulian, who invited her to lunch to discuss a project he had in mind for her. The two decided to meet at Romanoff's, one of the industry's most glittering water holes where producers, directors, stars all dined in sumptuous, glamorous style, as if cameras recorded their every move and gesture. Located on Rodeo Drive, the restaurant was a place to be seen and a place where deals were made.

Dorothy entered looking as glamorous as ever. With *Porgy and Bess* running in theatres, she was still a big name and regarded as a major player. Once she was seated with the courtly, debonair Mamoulian, he turned the subject to the film *Cleopatra*, which Walter Wanger—the producer years ago of *Sundown*—was producing for Twentieth Century Fox. Dorothy's old friend, producer Buddy Adler from *The Harlem Globetrotters* was now the production chief at the studio.

Already a great buzz circulated within the industry about the production. It would be a lavish spectacle with millions to be spent on sets and costumes. A parade of Hollywood's most glamorous stars were being considered for the lead: from those deemed plausible like Joan Collins, Sophia Loren, Audrey Hepburn, Jennifer Jones, and Gina Lollibridgida to the not-so-plausible candidates like Marilyn Monroe, Brigitte Bardot, Kim Novak, and model Suzy Parker. Wanger favored Elizabeth Taylor, but she was locked into a contract at MGM that would block his efforts.

Mamoulian was set to direct the film but it was not yet announced. He believed Dorothy was perfect for the leading role of the Egyptian queen. Stunned and unable to believe what she was hearing, she saw that Mamoulian was dead serious. He knew the studio might see it differently. The two discussed the film and their strategy in approaching Fox.

Dorothy by now knew not to let her hopes get too high. About a year earlier, United Artists had begun production on another big-budgetted spectacle *Solomon and Sheba*, the story of the legendary Biblical king's passion for the dark queen. The role was perfect for Dorothy: dramatic, sensual, glamorous, larger-than-life. Signed to direct was King Vidor, who so many years earlier when directing *Hallelujah*, Vidor had been confident that the day of the African American movieleading lady had to come. Yet almost thirty years after *Hallelujah*, Vidor conceded that industry attitudes had not changed much. Italian actress Gina Lollobrigida was selected to play the dark Sheba opposite Tyrone Power. Dorothy had never even been seriously considered for the role. Now as Mamoulian held the tantalizing prospect of starring her as Cleopatra, a realistic Dorothy couldn't be but so optimistic.

"You won't have the guts to go through with this," she told Mamoulian. "They are going to talk you out of it."

Later Mamoulian was formally announced as *Cleopatra*'s director and Elizabeth Taylor as its star. Dorothy was philosophical about losing the role. Never had she expected the studio to be daring enough to cast her anyway. It was one more in a list of disappointments.

But around this time, Dorothy herself—almost shockingly—made a major career miscalculation, due to Denison.

By August, less than two months after the marriage, Denison's restaurant still floundered. The rescue money Dorothy provided had not gone very far. Jack approached her about additional money for the restaurant—because he believed that all his place needed was a major attraction to draw publicity and crowds—and with the idea of her being that major attraction.

In his campaign to win Dorothy, Denison emphasized that it was *their* restaurant. It would be *their* money. There would be no club owners to placate, no crazy traveling schedule to keep her out of the city. She could do exactly as she pleased. He promised to manage her affairs to insure everything went just as she wanted. He would protect her, defend her, keep all things in order for her.

Surprisingly, she listened and against her better instincts, reluctantly agreed. To those who knew Dorothy, Denison was exploiting her in the coarsest way imaginable and almost everyone who knew her could see that she was aware of it but chose to ignore it. "She got a raw deal on that marriage," director Andrew Stone said.

Childhood friend Avanelle Harris probably best expressed the sentiments of most, particularly in Hollywood's Black community, who knew Dorothy and were shocked by the spectacle of her marriage. Said Harris, "With all the men in the world, why marry a White pimp!"

Jack continued to keep her away from most of her old friends. Not long after the marriage, Earl Mills received a "curt telegram" from Dorothy announcing that his services as her manager were no longer needed. Denison assumed management of her career. Mills found himself dumped and shut out of her life. Dorothy still discussed personal matters with Joel Fluellen, but Joel backed away from any direct confrontation with Denison. "Joel was afraid of Jack," said Geri.

As the news about Dorothy's impending appearance at Denison's restaurant circulated, she tried to look at her dismal domestic situation in a positive light. She was quoted in the *Chicago Defender* as having said a short time earlier, "There is only one consideration that might persuade me to return to the night clubs some day: perhaps, if I could have an intimate little spot of my own, on the Sunset Strip. I don't care much for the big places, and the little places couldn't make it worth my while, unless it happened to be a little place which I owned. And if it were on the Strip, it would be almost within walking distance of my front room. But apart from that, I'd rather stay home with my books and my records. I've had the other type of life."

The truth was, of course, that she hated going back to nightclub work, no matter what the circumstances, and everyone knew it.

On August 26th, *The Hollywood Reporter* carried the official announcement, "Dorothy Dandridge opens a stand Sept. 9 at Jack Denison's."

Herb Dell was hired as her conductor/arranger. He also accompanied her on the piano while Mel Pollard performed on bass and Dick Simoneon on drums. Special lyrics were written by Earl Brent. The act itself was staged by Eddie Rio, whom *The Hollywood Reporter* identified as her new "personal manager."

The day before she opened, she rose early and began the final rehearsals at eight in the morning, hoping to shake off her nervousness. But on opening night, her nerves just about overtook her. Matters were not helped by the fact that the restaurant was so small that there was no space for a dressing room. In a lot behind the restaurant stood a trailer in which Dorothy dressed and made up. The walk, as short as it was, from there to the club's floor was—emotionally—a long one.

Cut off from her old support system, she was painfully aware that she had neither Phil Moore nor Nick Perito there to ease her through her initial performance jitters. Upon her entrance, it was apparent that she was frightened. The vulnerabilities that once added to the excitement of her performances were now so out of hand that there was little joy in watching her.

Yet some reviewers praised her. Columnist Mike Connolly, still a fan, cooed that she was "The Lass with the Loot-Lined Larynx" and "still a ball of fire, everything a musical star should be—airy & winning, explosive and elusive, comic and insinuating for the second half of her opening show at 1 a.m. Thursday."

"Run—don't walk—to see Dorothy Dandridge at what should be a SRO nitery every night of her stand," proclaimed *The Hollywood Reporter*. "Miss Dandridge leaves absolutely nothing to be desired in the way of a topflight performer who could easily hold an audience for twice the time of her 45-minute opening turn Wednesday night and have them begging for more. Added to stunning beauty and an equally stunning figure, Miss Dandridge has developed the most important asset any singer can hope to have—a deep, sincerely felt feeling for her vocals that makes every number, regardless whether it's bouncy or sad, a 'message' that has the audience reading her with rapt attention."

Yet *The Hollywood Reporter* commented on what was most obvious to Dorothy's friends and professional colleagues: that "her voice falters hesitantly on top notes and she occasionally underwent a nervousness that found her teeth sticking to her lower lip."

Louella Parsons, still a Dandridge supporter, attended the performance with songwriter Jimmy McHugh. Afterwards the two posed for pictures with Dorothy. Later the columnist wrote a flattering review but also commented that Dorothy was "obviously nervous."

"They were not her best performances," said Harold Jovien. "She was trying, over-trying, to help the cause. It was a little bit embarrassing for her and for the audience. It was a great imposition that Jack forced upon her. Really. And she, as a wife, wanted to accommodate. But the facilities weren't right. The lights weren't right. The sound wasn't right. She was nervous."

Bobby Short had vivid memories. "I went to see her one night," he said. "Now she had been a big star. She had done some remarkable things. Some great things. And there was Dorothy in this little club, which seated at most eighty-five or a hundred people. Singing. And not remarkably. She didn't have Phil Moore. One thing Phil Moore knew was how to give performers a spark and how to bring out this and that and the other. And Dorothy at this point had only her looks and reputation."

Byron Morrow recalled, "I'll never forget it. She was working and working, using her knowledge of the profession to entertain the people that were there. But I felt there was a problem. It was during that performance that I first felt that there was something *personally* wrong."

Dorothy Nicholas Morrow concurred, "This was what was so sad. She was such a sweetheart. But she was just not at her best. She did not go over well at all. She was not herself that night."

"When she finished," said Byron Morrow, "we had a very difficult time trying to get to see her. We were not pleased."

Jack again kept close friends away from her.

Actor Lennie Bluett remembered that most in the entertainment colony thought her appearance at the club was a mistake. "Nightclubs of that caliber were on their way out in those days," said Bluett. "Denison was behind the times. It was going down the toilet when she bought it with him."

Geri recalled, "She committed the worst sin of all when he bought the restaurant. She sang there. It was a real come down."

In a town where status and perceptions are codes by which careers can be made or shattered, she had made a terrible mistake.

Director Andrew Stone, who never went to the club, but nonetheless heard the stories, recalled, "I shuddered when I learned about it. It struck me as all wrong that she'd be there," said Stone. "This guy owned a little nightclub. And he had her singing there. Well, you know that helped his business, having a big star because what little nightclub could get a big star? None. But some little place has to damage a reputation. You just don't take someone from a Goldwyn musical and put them there. You don't do that to people."

Stone probably best summed up what a devastating miscalculation it was for Dorothy. "Look, it's very hard to find any stars as a draw. Say you're a producer. She didn't get very big money. But she got over $75,000. At that time, that's pretty big. Anyway, you're going to cast her in a picture and you want to cast her as a star to draw people in. And well, you can go down and see her in a crappy little nightclub for a beer. It's going to cause massive damage. I've been in the business too long to know how people react. And if you appear in a club where the average woman gets $75 or $100 a week, and then go and ask for $50,000 to $100,000 for a lead in a picture, it doesn't make sense, does it? I think this guy just took outrageous advantage of her."

Stone concluded, "I was shocked. You just don't do that to a star. That means to people that she's down and out. In other words, people figure she can't get a job. She's through."

Dorothy had ignored Otto's cardinal dictates about the importance of appearances and high movie-star style, and consequently, people stopped coming to see her. Some old friends heard that the performances were so poor that they simply stayed away in order not to have to face her. In the past her dressing rooms had been filled to the brim with fans and friends congratulating her. But now the dressing trailer at the back of the club remained as empty and solemn as the nightclub floor itself. Ultimately, Dorothy failed to draw in the big crowds Denison had predicted. He had effectively led the way to the career demise of the goose he figured would lay the golden egg.

Denison showed no sympathy for her, though. He didn't appear to understand how difficult and painful it was for her to go on nightly aware of her own weak performances, and a near empty house.

One afternoon, Dorothy called an old friend Catherine Ruthenberg and invited her to the club. "Oh, come up to see me," she said. "I'll see to it that you get home."

The evening Ruthenberg saw Dorothy perform, the two talked afterwards, sitting with friends at a table in the club. Dorothy tried putting on a bright face. But any illusions she might have had about her performance were shattered when Jack stopped by the table.

"Dorothy, you weren't sassy enough," he said abruptly.

"What do you mean?" Dorothy asked, embarrassed that he had spoken to her in this way while she sat with friends.

"You could have been sassier," Denison said again. "You should do it another way."

Ruthenberg recalled feeling "sorry for her." "She was distraught," said Ruthenberg.

Shaken, Dorothy hoped nonetheless that no real damage had been done to her film career. *The Hollywood Reporter* announced on September 21st that "Producer Philip A. Waxman, who recently completed *The Gene Krupa Story* for Columbia and who is now working on making a biopic of Billie Holiday from her autobiography *Lady Sings the Blues* has secured a verbal agreement from Dorothy Dandridge to portray the late blues singer in the film. Agent Joe Glaser has the screen rights and also represents Miss Dandridge as he did Miss Holiday."

Scanning *Variety* and the other industry trades, she was aware of changes in the world of Black entertainment. A year earlier, Diahann Carroll had performed at New York's posh Persian Room. Promoted as the glamorous new Colored singing sensation, Carroll's coach was, who else but, Phil Moore. Within a year, Carroll would have a major success on Broadway in the Richard Rodgers musical *No Strings*, in which she played a fashion model involved in an interracial love affair. Much press followed.

Shortly afterwards, Carroll would appear as the love interest of Sidney Poitier in the expatriate jazz melodrama *Paris Blues* with Paul Newman and Joanne Woodward with music by Duke Ellington and an appearance by her old friend Pops, Louis Armstrong. Had the film been made a year or two earlier, Dorothy would have been in its cast. Ironically, some years later Carroll would appear in Preminger's third Black-oriented feature, *Hurry Sundown*.

In Hollywood films, no Black actress had yet matched Dorothy's impact and achievements. None was better known to the public. None was more of a movie-star icon for the African American community. None represented in the same way as Dorothy had a few years earlier the idea of social/political progress. Years would pass before the industry would recognize another Black actress as it had Dorothy. Juanita Moore would earn an Oscar nomination for Best Supporting Actress of 1959 for her performance in the remake of *Imitation of Life*, and Beah Richards would be nominated as Best Supporting Actress of 1967 for *Guess Who's Coming to Dinner*. But not until 1972 with Cicely Tyson in *Sounder* and Diana Ross ironically in *Lady Sings the Blues* would a Black woman in Hollywood ever again receive a Best Actress Academy Award nomination.

Yet Harold Jovien believed that Diahann Carroll's budding stardom affected Dorothy. Never was it a case of professional envy or jealousy. Both Geri Branton and Vivian Dandridge were quick to say that Dorothy believed Carroll had star potential and genuinely liked her. "My sister predicted Diahann's stardom," said Vivian. But Dorothy understood that in an industry that wanted only one Black goddess an era, Carroll was being groomed and perceived as her possible replacement; the new Colored golden dreamgirl who could appeal to audiences Black and White. For herself, Dorothy feared the end might be in sight.

She grew easily rattled and sensitive to criticism. Yet, still, she plugged on. In late October, she made a glamorous appearance at a luncheon at the Beverly Hilton Hotel. There she and Sammy Davis, Jr., were recipients of the Los Angeles Council of Negro Women's "meritorious awards." Although she would not make another major appearance at a club in Hollywood, she was asked to return to the Waldorf Astoria in New York and also to appear at the Palmer House's Empire Room in Chicago. She accepted both engagements. Tentative plans and a press announcement for a proposed London cabaret engagement were made but did not materialize.

Then came a wobbly appearance on *The Ed Sullivan Show* in New York in December. *Variety* considered the entire program that evening, including her performance, a disappointment. "Ed Sullivan, to the woodshed, please, for a workout on you-know-where," was the opening comment in the paper. There followed the observation that here "was a layout where a Dorothy Dandridge, film star and quondam nitery name, submitted to being slotted deuce; and her couple songs (one of them 'What Is This Thing Called Love') are not particularly suited to her pipes or style."

Read by the major players in the industry, the review was not a good sign for Dorothy's future. It seemed to indicate the changing attitudes and perspectives that were forming up about her. Within show business, some stars, long after they have faded, still garner good press, which can bolster perceptions about them and also help keep them employed. Countless careers are maintained in this way. Conversely, some performers, no matter how talented, find themselves out of favor with the press or influential critics. A career that might have endured could be cut short. But the press never really turned against Dorothy with a vengeance. In fact, she still received some glowing reviews on occasion. But clearly she was beginning to be considered as a goddess of yesterday.

Problems mounted at Denison's restaurant. Neither patrons nor money were coming in. Money was in jeopardy in other ways.

Dorothy's investments remained tied up mostly in the oil wells, which the law firm of Jerome Rosenthal and Sam Norton continued to handle. In early 1959, she had received a letter, which informed her that a well was successfully drilled in Lea County, New Mexico. "The geologist estimates a recovery of approximately 300,000 barels of oil from the presently producing zone," the letter stated. But it also informed her, as well as other investors, of the following:

> Accompanying this letter are papers relating to the completion and equipping of that well. Please sign all of these papers. I have set forth a list of these papers containing a brief outline of each below: 1. A lease setting forth the terms of the leasing of the equipment to be used on the first Saunders Well. 2. A schedule showing the times and amounts of quarterly payments on the above equipment lease. For the basic six year term thereof the total rental is $144.828.96 which is payable over twenty-four (24) equal quarterly installments of $4,784.54 each. Pursuant to October 20, 1958, agreement here are the shares of our total. Please sign the original of this letter indicating that you have read and approved it and received a copy thereof.
> Sincerely,
> /s/ Jerome B. Rosenthal.

Dorothy signed the agreement, which simply drained her finances all the more. The other investors—Doris Day, Martin Melcher, Gordon MacRae, and Billy Ekstine—also signed. To some, the oil well deal was beginning to look like a scam. Once being told of a successful drill, the investors, rather than being sent a dividend, had been asked to pour more money into the pot. She was warned about her finances by her accountant, but sought to ignore the accelerating financial problems. She ignored as well her own boredom with her marriage and the tension the union caused her.

Jack's temper was still hot and quick, but often his mood was sullen. He also didn't shrink from blaming Dorothy for their financial difficulties. Nor did he hesitate to exploit her further for his professional gain. Denison persuaded her to speak to other entertainers—her friends—about appearances at the club. He berated her to do more, to help more, to push herself more. Finally, she made phone calls in Denison's behalf. Always she tried sounding upbeat and optimistic. But it was obvious that she needed a favor. "She asked me one day if I'd come in there and work," said Herb Jeffries, who appeared at the club afterwards. "Mel Torme worked there too."

But what with the unending problems at the club and Denison's mood swings, she found it increasingly hard to concentrate. In the past, her work had always enabled her to keep a lid on her personal tensions and demons. But she was beginning to feel more and more off-balance and distracted, as if she had to struggle just to keep her breath and to stay in place.

The new year—1960—did not open on the best of psychological notes. But there were some bright spots. Preparations began for the Waldorf-Astoria Empire Room and, on February 2nd, she learned of her nomination for the Hollywood Foreign Press's Golden Globe Award as Best Actress in A Musical or Comedy for her performance in *Porgy and Bess*. Later her old friend Marilyn Monroe won the award for *Some Like It Hot*. But the attention Dorothy received for the nomination temporarily boosted her spirits.

She left by train for New York on February 3rd to begin her four-week engagement at the Empire Room. But once in New York, she took ill with a viral infection that sent her temperature to 102 degrees. A physician was consulted. He suggested that she delay the opening. But she ignored his advice. She opened to a heavy turnout—and some fine notices—on February 8th. *Variety* praised her as "an exciting and provocative personality sheathed in a haute couture confection of deep rose which showed off an admirable chassis. Her tunes are delivered in a sophisticated manner."

But the paper's reviewer also commented that she "works hard to attain a sexy mood and achieves it. That seems to be the sole drawback in her appearance. She builds up a too-much-of-the-same atmosphere at times. A little variation in another direction would give greater force to her sexy takeoffs, and would give a more rounded impression of Miss Dandridge's full capabilities." *Variety* pointed out that the accompaniment was sometimes "too heavy" and unvaried. Yet the audience loved her.

Still running a fever, Dandridge performed the second night. But she was too ill to perform the third evening. Medication was prescribed, as well as some much needed rest. She took to her bed but within a few nights was back on the club's floor. She also made a successful appearance on *The Ed Sullivan Show* on February 14th. While the West Coast club owners no longer saw her as a major player, she was still a darling of the east coast and other parts of the country.

Jack joined her in New York where, for their public outings, he played the role of the thoughtful, attentive husband. But her friends saw through it all as simply a performance. When Dorothy and Jack visited the home of Nick Perito and his wife Judy, she participated in the ruse, playing the happy, enchanted newlywed. But Perito said, "They just seemed phoney to me."

FOURTEEN

COLLAPSE

$\mathcal{T}$here was movement in Dorothy's career, if not peace in her home life. She returned to Los Angeles in mid-March, signed on for new engagements in Puerto Rico and South America, and by the month's end, flew to New York for another appearance on "The Ed Sullivan Show" on March 27th.

The disharmony in her marriage continued, but her hope for it was evidenced by a codicil she added to her will in April of the spring of 1960. It read: "Whatever house I possess and have an interest in upon my death shall pass to Jack Denison, my husband, subject to encumbrances," the document stated. The house, however, was the only provision she made for Denison.

The other important change had to do with Vivian. Tormented by the belief that her sister might be gone forever, Dorothy's will stated that in the dispersing of her estate, "four persons shall be substituted for my sister Vivian Dandridge and my mother Ruby Dandridge." The four named were Dorothy's godson, Chip Branton, the son of Geri and Leo Branton; Ruby Dandridge; Veada Cleveland, the daughter of Dorothy's secretary Veada Cleveland; and Michael Wallace, Vivian's son. Otherwise her will basically remained the same as when originally written in 1957.

She bought a new home, higher in the hills on Viewsite, and almost directly overlooking the house on Evanview. She spent time and money renovating and redecorating it, to turn the new home into a showplace. First the house was gutted, then done over from top to bottom. "I remember the entrance hall," said Geri. "She spent a fortune on marbleized flooring. It wasn't like tile. But it was marble that

467

was installed like tile. In panels. And beautifully done. I think it was something like $50 for each panel."

Built on three levels, the house had four bedrooms with the master bedroom upstairs and at the back. There was also a huge dressing room for Dorothy, the size of a bedroom itself. A combination bedroom-sitting room faced the front of the house.

"She used to use pink in her living room. But her bedroom was always in white with heavy blackout drapes," Geri recalled. "Always the blackout drapes. So when you pulled them, it would be absolutely pitch black inside She worked it electronically."

"There was a lovely dining room," said Geri. "And off from the kitchen, they had a nice, nice room. Jack used to like to serve caviar and champagne in this little room before going to the dining room."

Above the garage at the front of the house was a patio. "The back end was fabulous," said Geri. While the home on Evanview offered "a medium view of the surrounding territory," from this new home farther up in the hills, Dorothy could see—most magnificently from her bedroom at the back of the house—Los Angeles and the valley below. At night, floodlights on the lawn illuminated the house, giving it a tranquil glow, as if the domestic situation inside was peaceful and harmonious. "She got that house because then she was The Queen. She could look down on everybody else," said a catty Joel Fluellen. She could also look down on her former self as well. Fluellen told friends that she had decided she *had* to be *above* Sammy Davis, who had been her neighbor on Evanview.

Some saw the purchase of the home, at a time when she was beginning to have concerns about money and her career, as a purely self-destructive act. She appeared to be behaving in total disregard of her present circumstances, both playacting and living the role of a hell-bent heroine who didn't care what tomorrow might bring her way.

The home pleased Denison, but it did nothing to alter their marital problems. Dandridge tried to maintain some sense of balance, though, and some connection to her past. Veada Cleveland continued to work for her and became a trusted employee, although most of Dorothy's friends still resented Cleveland's overly protective—some called it controlling—manner. And she invited Joel Fluellen to move in. He had experienced some difficult times over the years, living in hotels and sometimes unattractive apartments. Dorothy and Geri both had helped him pay the rent on a number of occasions. But his career was progressing better and he was now saving his money. When Dorothy heard he was looking for yet another new apartment, she suggested he stay on Viewsite. She believed she was offering him a secure living situation, and herself, an ally in her ongoing domestic crisis.

Fluellen moved in. But the arrangement proved uncomfortable. Fluellen pitched a fit because he had been relegated, so he told friends, to the basement of Dorothy's home. "He resented it deeply. Yes, he lived in the basement. But she had it done over beautifully," said Geri.

When Fluellen continued to gripe about the place at every opportunity, Geri finally told him, "It's not a *basement* basement, is it?"

"No, it isn't," he admitted.

"And it's nicer than any apartment you've ever had."

Fluellen did not respond.

"Joel resented this until the day he died. I was so angry with him," said Geri. "Anybody would have been proud to live in something like that."

The truth of the matter was that Fluellen felt too confined in the home, unable to privately bring in friends or potential lovers. He knew all of Dorothy's private life. But he did not want anyone knowing all of his. "She thought she had done something nice for Joel because he had no family in Los Angeles," said Geri. "It never got through to Dottie the kind of life that he lived in his own apartment. It wouldn't have made any difference to her. But she didn't know that he was just frustrated living there like that. So he acted up on occasions and got very evil with her."

Fluellen was also fearful of Jack's temper. He knew Denison didn't want him anywhere around. He saw firsthand how cruel Jack was to Dorothy, belittling and abusing her every chance he got. When, finally, Fluellen moved out, Dorothy never understood why he left.

Needing money to maintain her lifestyle *and* her husband's, she toured again during the spring and summer of 1960. She had to. She opened on April 16th for a two-week engagement at the Caribe Hilton in San Juan, Puerto Rico. In June, she made her Reno debut at the Riverside, which proved to be a great hit. "Rapport is immediate, and Miss Dandridge is in full command for complete turn—and does it with little apparent effort," *Variety* wrote. "She's all pro with the presentation, and the chassis and looks to match her vocal talents."

She breathed a sigh of relief afterwards. These hadn't been major venues but at least she could still please an audience.

Returning to Los Angeles on July 1st, she began discussions for a new film. Having bought the screen rights to Robert Blees's play *Lady By Day,* she planned to star as an undercover intelligence agent on the

Riviera who fronts as the operator of a dress shop. But the negotiations for studio backing went nowhere.

Within two weeks, she had left for an engagement in Mexico City. Then it was on to performances in South America where she remained a popular star. On July 26th, she opened for two weeks at the Copacabana Palace in Rio. It was still a city that held many memories and much heartache for her. She had not forgotten her Brazilian lover of almost ten years ago. Then within a few days of her arrival in the city, a scary incident. Newspapers reported that she was robbed of some $800 and personal documents. The incident left her shaken.

From Rio, she went to Sao Paulo for a week's engagement. On August 23rd, she returned to her home for some rest. In early September, she was back on the road for performances at the Radisson Hotel's Flame Room in Minneapolis. Even at this late date, Dorothy was the first Black performer to appear at the Flame Room. Apparently, much like those earlier years when she had integrated other clubs, there was an incident on opening night. The audience was kept waiting for her to appear for more than a half hour past curtain time. Once she arrived, she was openly nervous and agitated and later told the press that the delay was caused by a mixup in locating the hotel elevator.

When she returned to Los Angeles, there was talk about film work. A role as a Polynesian in *Confessions of An Opium Eater* was dangled before her. Then came renewed interest in starring her with Nat 'King' Cole in a film version of *Lady Sings the Blues*. Once again much enthusiasm and energy were generated about the Billie Holiday film but nothing happened. None of the studios expressed great interest, although Preminger remained enthusiastic about it for years to come. Neither project would ever materialize.

Peter Lawford was in the midst of enlisting the film colony to support the presidential campaign of his brother-in-law Senator John F. Kennedy, and her spirits lifted when she heard from Lawford. A lifelong Democrat, Dorothy eagerly agreed to lend her support. Like much of the Hollywood community, she was dazzled by the young candidate. Later when it was learned that she was the mother of a retarded child, she was asked to do public service announcements on radio for President Kennedy's Committee on Mental Retardation. Again she agreed to participate. But the radio announcements were a painful ordeal.

Now Lynn seemed so removed from her. Having accepted her daughter's condition, she had lost a part of herself. Yet she resigned herself to the fact that Lynn was in the capable hands of someone else. Helen Calhoun had been caring for the child for almost ten years now. Dorothy had been generous to the woman. Everything was bought that might bring some comfort to Lynn. Calhoun now had taken Lynn out of Los Angeles with Dorothy's consent. But the circumstances were odd. Calhoun had fallen under the spell of a charismatic Black minister, whom she followed to Chicago, then to Kansas. "Helen was in his entourage. She worshiped him," said Geri. "So whenever he would tell her to move, she would pick her things up and leave. She moved around a lot. She rented out the house [that Dottie bought her] and left. She was on the road, so to speak, doing what the Reverend said."

Unknown to Dorothy, Calhoun and the minister both were quick to let his followers know that the little girl in her charge was none other than the daughter of the famous Negro actress Dorothy Dandridge. "The reverend was anxious to keep Lynn because Lynn was sort of an attraction for the church people," said Geri. In essence, Lynn was put on display as an oddity for public scrutiny. And the minister's collection plates.

Dorothy Nicholas Morrow was dismayed to see the way others still used Dorothy. "She wanted to do right," said Morrow. "People knew that. The connivers knew that. The people who dwelt on getting the most out of people for nothing, without doing anything, knew that she was a beautiful, giving person and that they could take advantage of her. That was sad because she was all of those things. I personally don't remember Dorothy ever putting a person down or deliberately doing something against a person."

"No matter how much she had learned or how green she might have been in the beginning, she was still green to the very end," said Morrow. "Just a beautiful, beautiful person who always wanted to believe in people."

But the greatest exploiter still resided in her home. Most of her time in Los Angeles was spent doing little more than arguing with Denison. He was constantly in need of money. He constantly hounded her to get people into the club.

Dorothy's old friend Catherine Ruthenberg visited her one afternoon. While the two sat talking and enjoying their time together, Denison suddenly walked into the room. Annoyed by something Dorothy had done, he said, "You should have done it this way."

Dorothy tried to act as if his comment didn't affect her. But Ruthenberg could see that it had. "She didn't mind criticism," said

Ruthenberg. "But it upset her to have him say it in front of company. That I could tell. I didn't dislike Denison. But he was just so demanding. He just bossed her around. It was demeaning the way he would say things to her."

So rattled was Ruthenberg by Denison's treatment of Dorothy that evening, she told her husband, "I don't think I want to go back there." She didn't.

On another occasion, Dorothy's former publicist Orin Borsten was shocked by a comment Denison made. It was at the funeral of newspaper writer Dick Williams, whose review of Dorothy's performance at the Club Gala had been so important in her early club breakthrough. When Borsten and his wife Laura went over to speak to Dorothy, who was obviously saddened, Denison joined in the conversation and said to the Borstens of Dorothy, "What do ya think of my little *schvartze!*" Dorothy appeared to laugh, perhaps out of nervousness. Borsten wasn't sure if she knew what he had said.

But other times, Dorothy responded directly to his moods and insults. When Denison made racial slurs in the presence of Dorothy and Geri, Dandridge turned to her friend and said, "Well, what can you expect from a headwaiter!" He bristled at being described in such a manner. But "the headwaiter" was the way she frequently referred to him. "Dottie could be like that," recalled Geri. "I mean she didn't just sit around and listen to his nonsense. She'd speak up and cut him down to size."

But Dorothy feared his temper. One evening in the thick of a quarrel, Denison raised his arm and struck her. After the first time he hit her, they made up, and Dorothy dismissed his dark abusive mood as an aberration. But the second time and those times that followed, when Jack viciously and physically abused her, finally awakened her to the fact that Jack was a dangerous and ugly man.

Yet she stayed with him. She numbed herself more and more with alcohol. On occasion, it was vodka. But her drink of preference was champagne.

To remain financially afloat, she had to keep working, but she grew lethargic and unable to concentrate. Now as she approached 40, the age which she dreaded, she wondered how much longer audiences would accept her as a sexy goddess. In the few interviews she did, she was quick to say she preferred acting and to debunk her whole sexy image. She was ambivalent about the image, though, because she knew her livelihood depended on it. She went back into the recording studio to do four songs for Verve Records on February 2, 1961.

But the results were little better than those in early 1959 when she recorded the unreleased album for Norman Granz. Of the four recorded new songs—"Stay with It," "Beautiful Evening," "Smooth Operator," and "Somebody"—only "Somebody" was deemed suitable for release. Aside from Dorothy's personal tensions, Harold Jovien believed, the problem was that she desperately needed better professionals around her to tailor the arrangements and work around her vocal limitations. Had that happened, she still might have had a chance to develop as an important stylist—for she could still basically put a song over with an intelligent understanding of the lyrics. But inside Dandridge now knew that her singing career wouldn't progress much further.

Still, she had to keep working.

"Dorothy Dandridge, somewhat absent from the scene for the past several months makes her return to the spotlight this year with several film roles, television guest shots and exclusive club dates as main items," reported the Black newspaper *The Chicago Defender,* which also wrote that her career was now in "operation revival."

The paper's comments summed up the feelings of many within the African American community. What was happening to its dreamgirl? Why had not more been seen of her lately? Why had the success of *Porgy and Bess* had done nothing for her career?

In mid February, she departed for Chicago for a return performance at the Palmer House's Empire Room. But she appeared distracted and disoriented; her performance, tentative and fearful. Critics commented that it looked as if she literally wanted to stand as far away from the patrons as possible.

Variety said that "despite best efforts the session seemed to just hang there. Save for a couple of offbeat titles, most of her catalog didn't much dent the crowd, and the inescapable reaction was dullish." The reviewer added that "she's literally too removed from the customers by operating almost exclusively from a portable stage flush to bandstand. What seems needed by the star is mobility—a chance to stroll the customer-level floor to tap potential rapport. A chance, in short, for the needed intimacy denied by the room." But intimacy with an audience was the last thing she wanted.

Her Chicago performance marked the beginning of the end of the major appearances. She was finished in Los Angeles clubs. Now she would find the East Coast and Midwest closing their venues to her too.

Little was heard of Dorothy for months as she appeared to retreat

more and more into her own private world. In August, she was scheduled to perform during half-time at a football game between the Los
Angeles Rams and the Washington Redskins. It was a *Los Angeles
Times* Charities game. But the NAACP urged her not to attend. The
civil rights organization argued that while the charity game would
raise funds for a four-year college scholarship for "a Negro lad," the
Redskins discriminated against African Americans by excluding them
totally from their ranks. There were Black players on the Rams team.
Joining the NAACP in protest against such discrimination, Dorothy
notified the charities organization that she was cancelling her appearance.

Afterwards the NAACP publicly praised her commitment in a letter published in the *Los Angeles Sentinel*:

> The Labor and Industry Committee of the Los Angeles
> Branch NAACP salutes you for once again proving that you
> are not only a pretty and highly talented entertainer, but as
> well a dedicated and courageous freedom fighter and all
> around good citizen.
>
> Your support of our protest action against the Jim Crow
> Washington Redskins added immeasurably to the success of
> our efforts.

In need of money and now almost desperate for work, she began
plans for an elaborate new nightclub act, quite different from her past
performances. Now she would be supported by a quartet of male
singers and also two male dancers. Stephen Papich staged the act for
her. Herb Dell again worked on her arrangements. Dorothy also
enlisted designer Jean Poch to create a set of eye-catching costumes,
which she lamented cost her a fortune. Part of her growing problem
now was her great overhead. She was responsible for paying the
bills—for the arrangements, the accompanist, the dancers, the singers,
the director, the costumes, and the travel accommodations—and
found it hard to break even.

In August, the new act, which was called the Dorothy Dandridge
All Star Revue, made its debut at a ten-day engagement in Bakersfield,
California. Audiences were receptive. Then came a booking on the
cruise ship S. S. *Matsonia* as it traveled from Los Angeles to Hawaii.
Jack joined her on the trip.

The performances went well. "Dorothy Dandridge has expanded her act," *Variety* wrote. "Not only is it the biggest act Miss Dandridge ever has had, it is her best and further will make a dent of considerable impact. As expected it is Miss Dandridge's razor-keen phrasing and subtle song-selling which keys the act."

But despite her success, the fact that Dorothy was, as she saw it, *reduced,* to performing on a cruise ship simply signalled an ever-watchful film colony that she was on a serious decline.

For Dorothy, it was all becoming a nightmare. She had to work but she did not *want* to work. The money she earned was not as great as before, yet decent. But she still had to maintain appearances and look as spectacular as ever, and the costs of producing spectaculars left her meager profits.

In October, she accepted a last-minute booking at the Chi Chi Club in Palm Springs. Originally, Kathryn Grayson had been scheduled to perform but had taken ill, bowing out of the engagement the day before her opening. Dorothy stepped in as a replacement with her Dorothy Dandridge All Star Revue. Rushed, nervous, and eager to make the most of it, she was not at her best.

Variety reported that her act "drags" and "never really gets hot" until after its first forty-five minutes. "She does a French number with one of her male sextet called 'Comme Ci, Comme Ça' and it came off *comme ci, comme ça* too." The paper also commented on her appearance. "She opens wearing a gray wig and a white strapless gown that must have been designed when she had a plumper bust line because it stood out inches from the top of her torso."

Some film talk, again from Europe, started with an offer for a role in *Marco Polo*. Some years earlier, producer Raoul Levy had scored a huge international success with *And God Created Woman,* starring a then unknown Brigitte Bardot. Now he had ambitious plans for a $4,000,000 production about Marco Polo that would be shot in Afghanistan, Japan, Nepal, Yugoslavia, India, Russia, Outer Mongolia, and China. Levy was an admirer of Preminger's and had been in discussions with the filmmaker about financing and promotion methods for several years. As he finally began to sign an international cast for *Marco Polo,* Levy contacted Dorothy about playing the role of an East Indian princess. It's likely that Otto had recommended her for the part.

Dorothy grew excited. But negotiations between Levy and Dandridge brought nothing definite or concrete. He was struggling to come up with financing. It began to sound like another aborted project.

Then came an offer from MGM-television for an appearance on the series "Cain's Hundred." Produced by Paul Monash's, "Cain's Hundred" was a weekly hour-long drama that centered on the efforts of Nicholas Cain, a former mob lawyer turned federal government agent, to uncover and prosecute the 100 men controlling organized crime in America. With some episodes filmed in a quasi-documentary style, "Cain's Hundred" often focused on social ills and issues.

Monash was planning an episode titled "Blues for a Junkman," which told the story of a doomed jazz singer named Norma Sherman. After serving a jail term for possession of drugs, Norma struggles to put the pieces of her life back in order. But upon her return to night-club work, she is beset by new problems and hassles. Her club license has been revoked, the series of bookings cancelled. All this and still she has to resist the temptations of drugs. She also tries to patch up her relationship with her estranged husband, a jazz musician. "Blues for a Junkman" was the tale of a comeback from professional and personal horrors.

The idea of a troubled, emotionally rattled woman who survives a descent to hell only to discover a new hell awaiting her appealed to Dorothy. She realized, however, that television at this point was still frowned upon by major film stars and not taken seriously by the critics.

But she saw possibilities for herself. Granted, the Mel Goldberg script for "Blues for A Junk Man" was fairly straightforward television material, but it was nonetheless intelligent and relatively sophisticated. As such, it could provide her with some dramatic moments and give her an opportunity to be seen by a large national audience. To sweeten the deal, MGM also planned to shoot additional scenes—some of which called for partial nudity—for a feature film version titled *The Murder Men* to be released in Europe.

Not lost on Dorothy were the similarities between the heroine of "Blues for a Junkman" and Billie Holiday. Upon meeting her, the episode's director John Peyser actually felt the drama could have been Dandridge's story, too, "because Dorothy at this time was not that stable." In fact, he believed the episode might have been specifically created with Dorothy in mind.

Dorothy liked the idea that the shoot would be short, no longer than two weeks. Ivan Dixon, James Coburn, and Ed Asner were also in the cast. The pay was $3,500 with a duplicate payment once the episode re-aired during summer reruns. Not a movie-star salary, but it would pay a few bills—and keep house-husband Denison happy, too.

The MGM-TV lot was abuzz with excitement upon Dorothy's arrival. Nervous and anxious, she managed, however, to maintain that cool, distant, star-glow exterior.

"She had a presence that was commanding and gorgeous," said "Cain's Hundred" star Mark Richman, later known as Peter Mark Richman. "I thought Dorothy Dandridge was a very rare type of Black woman, certainly in films and television. She was vulnerable, classy, feminine, special, and very sexy, and had great potential. She was also very reserved and kind of shy and laid back."

But it didn't take Richman long to see her self-doubts. He had no knowledge of her troubled marriage. But he saw immediately that "she was a very tense person." Forcing herself to focus on her work, she sequestered herself in her dressing room in a conscientious effort to analyze, examine, and understand her character's motivations and fears. "I spent a lot of time with her rehearsing," said Richman. "She had confidence in being with me. She could just relax. She was happy to work with me in that it gave her a kind of security so that our scenes together were comfortable for her."

Richman respected her discipline. "She was ready to work and she was willing and she was eager and responsible. A genuinely good, nice person," he said. "If you wanted to rehearse more, she was not going to dodge." Their rehearsals paid off. "You can see that in the relationship in the episode," he said. Their scenes together were warm and personal. A genuine friendship appeared to exist.

Dorothy also rehearsed with Ivan Dixon, who played her estranged husband. Having witnessed her humiliation on the set of *Porgy and Bess*, he also saw her tension on the "Blues for a Junkman" set and realized that professionally she had slipped. Yet he believed that "she hadn't come down that much." "As far as Black actors were concerned," he said, "anything we did was important. So for a Black actor to do television after doing film isn't that bad. For a White actor, that's different because once you reach the level of film, you're supposed to stay at that level." Yet Dixon knew that Sidney Poitier, now about to reach the peak years of his career, wouldn't have performed in a television drama at this time.

In the past, Dixon had never found Dorothy friendly, except on those rare occasions when he and Poitier visited her home. Or when he saw her with Joel Fluellen. But on the set of "Blues for a Junkman," she was better.

"If you're going to do an intimate scene on screen, some guys can walk in and do it period and not worry. Other people have to get to know someone if they're going to kiss them and hug them and have it look real. She was of the second type," said Dixon. "I think Dorothy felt she had to get to know me better before she could relate on the screen. So she would invite me into her dressing room."

"We would sit and talk," said Dixon, surprised by the openness of her conversations with him, which continued sometime after the completion of the television episode. He couldn't figure out what the talk was really about—its subtext—or why she chose to talk to him. Deep inside, he still felt she did not especially like him.

But here the usually perceptive Dixon seemed to miss the cue. Ivan Dixon was an extremely sensitive and sincere man. It was precisely Dixon's kindness and decency that Dorothy responded to. He was a man—and in particular a strong African American man—whom she felt she could trust. In the midst of her growing delirium and ever-mounting fears, she realized that he wouldn't hurt or fail her. She was right.

Their conversations, however, did not touch on what preoccupied her most: her disintegrating and violent marriage. Daily, she showed up promptly on the set, was courteous, and prepared for work. But nightly, she returned to a hated home where the unabated criticism, recriminations, and arguments raged on; where she calmed and fortified herself with tranquilizers.

Shortly after shooting began, problems arose between the episode's original director Robert Gist and the production company that led to a blowup. Gist was replaced by John Peyser, who shot most of the episode and also the additional scenes for the European version. Later after a dispute with the Director's Guild, Gist received directorial credit. But it was Peyser's film.

Peyser long remembered his initial impression of Dorothy. "The first time I saw her I thought holy cow! What a gorgeous looking broad. I'm just using the Hollywood expression of that time. But she was somebody you'd like to climb into bed with. She had a look that was so appealing. She was beautifully dressed and sedate and all that but with sex appeal. She had the same kind of feeling or air that Grace Kelly used when she was here. Not Grace Kelly in New York. But Grace Kelly when she came to Hollywood. Dorothy gave you the 'queen' feeling. She was a lady."

But Peyser also observed that Dorothy "was scared to death," nervous and unsure of herself. From her behavior, he was convinced she was on pills or medication.

With its new director in place, "Blues for A Junkman" proceeded with nothing out of the ordinary occurring until one morning when Dorothy had missed her call. She had not arrived at the studio. An attempt was made to reach her. Peyser spoke to Dorothy's agent, who became alarmed and suggested that someone go to her home to check on her.

Like so many others before, Peyser had come to like her and to feel so protective that he did something rare for a director in the middle of a tight shooting schedule. He left the studio to go to her home to see if she was all right.

With his assistant director, he got inside her home. His concerns grew because of the quiet stillness. "She had locked herself in the bathroom," he said. Once she opened the door, he discovered her in a drugged state. "She had taken some pills but not enough to incapacitate her," he recalled. "Something had happened. Some sort of upset." The upset, of course, had been Denison.

Gently, Peyser assured her everything would be fine. "I had a long talk with her," he recalled. "We didn't shoot her scenes the rest of that day. We shot around her."

The next day she returned to the set. "She was all right again," said Peyser. But thereafter, he felt "a sadness about her. I don't think she was ever a happy lady. Ever."

Peyser had not seen Denison at Dorothy's home. But Denison occasionally showed up at the studio to watch Dorothy at work. Few spoke to him, though, or even remembered his presence.

For the duration of the filming, Dandridge remained cooperative and easy to work with. Peter Mark Richman recalled the endearing way she sought reassurance after shooting a scene. "Is that okay?" she would ask sweetly.

Peyser recalled the patient manner in which she endured the lengthy lighting set-ups for a night scene in an alley. In this black-and white-production, Peyser wanted the features and skin tones of Dandridge and Dixon to show and not be swallowed up in the darkness. "You had to make sure they got into the light and still didn't look like they were lit up," said Peyser. "So I remember it was a tough scene to shoot. And it took time."

When the day came to film her partial nude scene for the European version, Peyser closed the set. It was a sequence between Dorothy and Ivan in which her breasts were exposed. Neither Peyser nor Dixon recalled any signs of unease as she did the sequence. But screen nudity was new to American actresses during this period and for a woman as private as Dorothy, particularly with a male crew, she had to have experienced some discomfort, to say the least.

She also performed three songs in the episode. Her rendition of "The Man I Love" and briefly, her old favorite, "Taking A Chance On Love," were smoothly done, with intelligent phrasings and interpretations of the lyrics. Yet on the emotionally charged "I'll Get By," her voice was weak. It was almost as if she did not believe the lyrics: "I'll get by/as long as I have you." Yet, like Billie Holiday during the last years when her voice had lost its purity but the emotional intensity transformed each song into the most personal of stories and dramas—Dandridge's rendition proved effectively unsettling—and appropriate in terms of the character—because of the emotional undertones.

Shortly before the broadcast of "Blues for A Junkman," producer Paul Monash took out a full-page ad, in the form of a letter to Dorothy, in *The Hollywood Reporter*. Superimposed over a photograph of Dorothy singing in the episode, the letter read:

Dear Dorothy:

This is to convey my deepest appreciation to you for your moving and perceptive portrayal of 'Norma Sherman' in the 'Blues for a Junkman' segment of CAIN'S HUN-DRED.

The sense of truth and depth of emotion you brought to this complex role should make you proud indeed.

All of us involved in CAIN'S HUNDRED are pleased that our series provided a stage for your dramatic debut on television. We look forward to a speedy return engagement.

> *Sincerely,*
> *Paul Monash*
> *Executive Producer*
> *Cain's Hundred*

On February 27, 1962, "Blues for A Junkman" aired on NBC at 10 p. m. It opened in an unusual way for television. Before any credits, Dorothy's face—weary, fearful, yet perfect—was seen in closeup. She hums as she sits in a jail cell. A large nurse enters and tells her she is free. Now she can go home. "Then I'm free?" says Dandridge as

Norma Sherman, her voice heavy, smoky, and inviting. Thereafter as the series' dramatic theme music is heard, the episode cuts to Dandridge, wrapped inside a coat, as she leaves the prison. In these few seconds—simply and non-glamorously dressed—she paradoxically presents a portrait of a glamorous, emotionally charged woman, much like the heroine in *Malaga*, who seems utterly alone.

There follows in "Blues for a Junkman" a first-rate performance; a highly unusual one for episodic television because of its dreamy and personal intensity. Wisely, director Peyser played on her fragile and earnest sweetness. As her Norma struggles to re-establish her professional and personal identities, Dandridge measures her moves and nuances. In one melodramatic sequence in which she appears headed back toward drugs, she seems to push. But only here. Otherwise she has incorporated her own fatigued, resigned persona into the character's.

Two sequences stand out. The first occurred when she is told that her club bookings have been cancelled by a man she believed was helping her. Dandridge could be charming no matter what the situation. But here, as in parts of *Malaga*, she fearlessly abandons any concerns she might have had that the audience might find her attitude and anger unattractive. Hers is perfectly modulated anger laced with a sense of despair and futility. Not overly dramatic, her tones and rhythms are direct and real.

In the second, she returns to her apartment to find her husband, who is involved with another woman, packing his clothes.

Surprised to see her, he says, "I'll be out of your way in a minute." He adds, "I heard about them killing your tour. I'm sorry."

At first, she has little to say. Mainly she responds only with her expressive weariness. She walks to a couch and sits. Fatigued and saddened, she rests her head on her arm. She wants to sleep, to escape, to be somewhere else. A man she has loved—and may need—is walking out on her.

"You think it's been easy for me," he says. "Look, you know I'd give you my right arm. You want my right arm?"

"I don't want anything from you," she answers.

"I just couldn't go through it again," he says.

Then the camera moves in for a closeup as she tells him, "Then get out. Get lost. And forget you ever knew me." Here the words and the feeling are those of a woman too drained and exhausted to even feel betrayed; too numbed and despairing to feel anger.

After the two kiss, a closeup captures her mixed emotions. She wants his love. But frankly, she doesn't want the hassles or demands of love. She does not even seem to want to look at him. Director Peyser and his director of photographer William W. Spencer kept the camera in for a tight closeup of her. It's a beautiful shot and a magnificent face. Throughout "Blues for a Junkman," the closeups also reveal the vulnerabilities of Peyser and Spencer: these two men are as entranced by Dorothy Dandridge as just about every other man who met her, including those who abused her.

The Hollywood Reporter wrote that "Blues for a Junkman" was "notable for several reasons, the primary one being the TV bow of Dorothy Dandridge as a dramatic actress, a task which she accomplishes with the ease and facility with which she presents a song." The paper also commented that the episode's script and direction "are mature presentations of the problems created by narcotic addiction and its traffic, but avoiding any touch of sensationalism."

"I felt that Dorothy in retrospect was the classiest Black performer of her time," said Richman, "and that if she had not had her personal demons and had not been so insecure and fearful of the future, and that, if given the opportunity, she had great potential. She could have become the kind of Grand Dame of performers in terms of acting, in terms of singing. There weren't many who had her kind of presence. I can't think of anybody else."

At the same time, the *Marco Polo* project came through. Although the finances remained precarious, producer Levy was set to begin shooting. Already lined up for roles were French heartthrob Alain Delon, Dorothy's old friend Anthony Quinn, and France Nuyen. Dorothy flew to Belgrade to film some sequences, but the production schedule called for her to travel later to Nepal and India for other scenes, no doubt once Levy had secured additional financing.

Dorothy began to consider television as a possible way to continue her acting career. African Americans were still a fairly invisible presence on the weekly prime time series schedule. Programs of the early 1950s like "Amos 'n' Andy" and "Beulah," which had starred talented Black performers in stereotyped roles, had now vanished. But they had not been replaced with anything new—more serious, middle-class African American characterizations. Looking at the prime time weekly network series, one would think African American life and culture in the early 1960s did not exist in any significant way.

Dorothy's friend Nat Cole had broken ground in November, 1956, starring in a weekly musical program for NBC, "The Nat 'King' Cole Show." Critically, the show did well, yet it suffered from poor ratings.

NBC also had to contend with the southern affiliates that refused to carry the show. But Cole believed the real villain was Madison Avenue's advertising agencies which didn't aggressively seek a sponsor for the program.

Cole wanted to do television, in part to get off the road, where he had been performing at clubs for years. He and Dorothy began serious discussions of doing a television series in which they would play husband and wife. They came up with the idea of a sitcom, said Dorothy, about "this small-time pair of married performers and all of the things that happen to them as they climb to success." Another idea was for a series in which Nat would play himself and Dorothy would appear as his stagestruck secretary. Dorothy and Cole pitched the idea. But the networks did not bite. Prime time television didn't undergo a significant change until three years later when Bill Cosby appeared as a serious, college-educated Rhodes Scholar-turned-international undercover agent with Robert Culp on the series "I Spy" and still later in 1968, when Diahann Carroll played a working middle-class widowed single mother on "Julia."

Dorothy said in an interview with *The Los Angeles Times* that, "We Negroes finally convinced the entertainment world not to stereotype us as just maids, porters and so on," she said, "but now too many producers are afraid to use us at all. Rather than do wrong, they do nothing." She also explained that on her recent trip to Europe for *Marco Polo*, she had been asked by Europeans about the lack of African Americans on the small screen. "It's difficult to know quite what to say," Dorothy said. "I'm not sure I really understand it myself, especially all of the business about the advertising agencies and how they control the situation." Interestingly around this time, Ruby was appearing on the television series "Father of the Bride," still playing the familiar comic maid.

Dorothy again voiced her opinion that Black performers should be able to play any type of character. "I've often wondered why it is that Negroes can't play other roles, if they look right for the part," she said. "Whites play Negroes. I'll never forget when MGM had Ava Gardner do Julie in *Show Boat* and the studio had Lena Horne under contract at the time. Ava couldn't understand it either."

But she remained opposed to films that cast African Americans in nontraditional ways without creating some kind of ethnic, cultural, or familial background for them, as had been the case with the otherwise forward, looking *Malaga*.

Dorothy soon left the country again to continue work on *Marco*

Polo in India and Lebanon. But the roster of international stars was not helping producer Raoul Levy attract the money to complete it. Worst, the spectacle was plagued by problems, some shocking. Levy rented some two hundred elephants for a sequence in Nepal. The animals, however, were neither cared for nor fed. Seventy-one of them died of malnutrition. Later *Time* reported that Levy was an "inept administrator, a corrosive buttinsky on the set, a compulsive chiseler and a helpless planner" who had "ruined the careers of two Yugoslav bureaucrats when he conned state funds out of them, welshed on everything from actors' salaries to florists' bills."

In the spring, Dorothy returned to the States. To the press, she tried striking an optimistic note about the film. But her private fears that the movie might not see completion proved partly justified. "Finally finished," *Time* reported, "the film was uneditable." A few years later producer Levy died of a self-inflicted gunshot wound.

Hiding her disappointment and frustration, Dorothy consented to an interview with editor Louie Robinson for a major piece in *Ebony*. The magazine planned to showcase her new home

Dorothy put on her best face. So too did Denison. She posed for a series of photographs taken throughout her house, the most striking of which captured her standing, dressed in a pink peignoir. Another portrait of her sitting alone, beautifully dressed, in her living room, ran on *Ebony's* cover.

Ebony's Robinson sought a personal interview that spanned Dandridge's life and career, the type of scrutiny she had artfully dodged in the past. Even though she had sometimes discussed personal matters, it was one of the prices of her fame that she did never seemed willing to pay: to open up her private life for public consumption. There was still too much pain and too much that she could never reveal about Ruby and Cyril. Or Ruby and Ma-Ma.

Robinson's questions, many of which went back to incidents in the early years of her life, were answered as forthrightly as Dorothy could. She spoke about The Wonder Children days but without expressing any great resentment over a lost childhood.

She discussed some early disappointments. "I suppose you could say that I am basically kind of emotional, and there are some things, such as graduations and your husband being there when your baby is born, that are very important to me," she said. "I missed both of those. My husband wasn't there when my baby was born and I did miss my graduation. And I think the only constructive thing I have done about it is instead of crawling in a hole somewhere or dying on the vine, I use it in my acting, which comes out in an emotional way. If I have a scene to do that's emotional, it's easy for me to grab an emotion, because I already have them there—little hurts."

She also spoke of Cyril, who sometimes in the past had been mistakenly identified in the press as April Dandridge. "But even today, I feel that something has always been missing," she said, "because I never really had a father, even though Mother was both mother and father to me and my sister."

Robinson asked Dorothy about the comparisons with Lena Horne, which may have surprised her at this late date. But she was emphatic as she spoke with a note of finality, as if to be done with such comparisons and questions.

"There is no feud between Lena and I," she told Robinson. "I don't know her too well, but I think she's an absolutely beautiful woman. I don't know why there is this feeling of similarity, because actually we don't look anything alike. We have absolutely no features that are the same. We may be a little bit similar in color. I don't believe, of what I have seen Lena do on television—and I've never seen her in a night club—that I work anything like Lena."

When asked about Horne's performance in a recent television special, Dorothy answered, "She was simply marvelous."

Of her career, she said candidly, "There seems to be more enthusiasm for me in Europe." She discussed her recent return from India on *Marco Polo*.

The one point in the interview which in retrospect she fudged on were her comments about Denison. "I think he's so wonderful," she said. "He's kind of an extra-special human being. I think everybody likes Jack."

She also didn't discuss Vivian's disappearance, which still depressed her.

Her confidante and best friend, she said, was Ruby. "My mother taught me that nothing worthwhile is gained without hardships or determination, and I contribute whatever success I have had to her." Her remarks on Ruby ended with the poignant comment, "I call her everyday." No matter what had happened to Dorothy in the past and no matter what transpired shortly in her life, she clung to her belief in her mother.

When the subject turned to Lynn, now nineteen, she was frank but refused to discuss her daughter at any length. "This is the biggest hurt of my whole life," she said. "Making the adjustment is a hurt too. I suppose this is the most difficult thing to do."

Once the magazine—with Dorothy on the cover and a banner that read "The Private World of Dorothy Dandridge"—was about to hit the newsstands, a story arose that a frantic Dorothy wanted to halt the story's publication. Her concern apparently was not about having revealed too much personal information—she still managed to tell the truth without divulging anything terribly secret—but rather out of concern about ongoing problems with the IRS, which had now been questioning her about past income tax since the mid-1950s. Dorothy feared that the IRS might see the lush photographs of her new home, and apply unwanted pressure for payment of back taxes. This notwithstanding, the *Ebony* article hit the newsstands in June 1962.

The IRS, however, was not her only financial concern. Her money situation was worsening, to the point where she was falling seriously behind in payments for basics: invoices had come in from the pharmacy where her prescriptions were filled; from her laundry; from the utilities companies; from hotels. She had also taken out bank loans, which she had problems meeting payments on.

In need of cash, she agreed to appear in an ad endorsing the product Rice-A-Roni. Under a color photograph of her, the copy read, "DOROTHY DANDRIDGE says, 'Something nice has happened to rice and it's called Rice-A-Roni.'" The ad ran in *Ebony*. Agent Joe Glaser also lent her money. But nothing could keep the hungry wolves from her door, demanding payments of debts.

She found little work back in Los Angeles. But there was an offer for a summer regional theatre production of *West Side Story*. Producer Herb Rogers eagerly pursued Dorothy for the role of Anita, even though this role was not usually played by a Black actress. Negotiations, however, didn't get far because she was hesitant, perhaps because of her fear of live audiences. But Rogers persisted.

"I had lunch with her at her home above Sunset," he recalled, "and I talked her into doing the show."

During the summer, Dorothy was briefly but quietly hospitalized. The cause was exhaustion.

Then on August 5th, Dorothy learned, along with the rest of the nation, that her old friend Marilyn Monroe had died: alone on a Saturday night in her bedroom with a telephone near her hand. The death was attributed to an overdose of barbiturates. The two women had not seen each other much since those early years at the Actors Lab and those afternoons and evenings at Dorothy's apartment on Hilldale where they sat together for private talks and commiserations. But they had run into each other at various openings and social affairs. Each was aware of the other's ups and downs, mainly through Peter Lawford.

"Dottie was still very close to Lawford. He was Marilyn's friend, too," said Geri Branton. "So they probably saw each other through that. I'm sure she had them over for dinner." Having always liked Marilyn, she was now, said Juliette Ball, "devastated" by the actress's death.

Dorothy knew that Monroe's fate—her battles with Twentieth Century Fox over roles, her struggle to move beyond the sexy image that had brought her such extraordinary success, her fear of age, her wrecked romances and marriages—in some crucial respects paralleled her own. Yet if Marilyn, the blonde ideal who had not had to contend with the racial attitudes and bigotry in the industry that plagued Dorothy's career, should find herself washed up at age thirty-six, what lay ahead for her?

Dorothy, depressed and listless, departed for Chicago for the performance in the three-week run of *West Side Story*. "Everybody in the production loved her," said producer Rogers. "Everybody got along with her." But even before the opening, she found the play more demanding than she had imagined.

"This particular show is very hard to do," she told the press, "because the part is very active. We had long, 14-hour-a-day rehearsals for two weeks before the show opened."

The show opened on August 14th at the Music Theatre in the Chicago suburb of Highland Park. Cast as the fiery Anita—the role which, ironically, had won her *King and I* replacement Rita Moreno an Oscar as Best Supporting Actress in 1961—Dorothy was the only name in the production. But frail and anxious, she found it difficult to perform. The stage was small. So too was the orchestra handling the Leonard Bernstein score. In the end, she gave an uninspiring performance.

Her reviews were crushing.

"The star whose name and picture adorned the cover was cast in a subordinate part, an often ominous sign," *The Chicago Daily Tribune*'s critic Thomas Willis wrote. "And as you may have guessed, Dorothy Dandridge's Anita was out of her range and element."

But producer Herb Rogers felt differently. "I didn't have a problem with her performance. She was great in my book. But then she could do no wrong as far as I was concerned," he said. "I've done over 700 Equity productions. I have picked and worked with over 7,000 Equity actors. I put Dorothy at the top of my list of the people I've worked with. But once she performed in *West Side Story*, she suddenly got sick on me."

Her nerves frayed and jarred, and finally overwhelmed by her restlessness and fatigue, Dorothy couldn't complete the run of the production. A few days after the opening, she felt dizzy and light-headed as she walked to the theatre's parking lot. Then her feet suddenly gave out under her. She collapsed. Rogers set up an appointment for her with his physician in the area, Dr. Sidney Black.

"My doctor told me something was wrong with her health. Something terribly wrong," said Rogers. "He told me what she was doing could kill her. But he wouldn't say what the problem was."

Finally, the physician insisted, "She can't continue with the show."

Years later Rogers believed, perhaps admitting it to himself for the first time, that Dorothy had been drinking heavily at the time of *West Side Story* and that the physician, clearly entranced by Dorothy, became protective of her, to the point where he didn't want to reveal her drinking problems. "I saw no signs of alcohol," said Rogers. "But I knew something was wrong emotionally. I don't know for a fact that she was drinking. But I'm sure of it. The doctor didn't want me to know. The doctor just loved her. He just told me she had a serious problem."

"On doctor's recommendations for plenty of rest," *The Hollywood Reporter* reported on August 29, 1962, "Dorothy Dandridge exited *West Side Story*."

Later Dorothy said, "I was just too exhausted to go on."

She returned to Los Angeles in a state of defeat and utter dejection. But she knew she had to rest, remain quiet, and be prepared to go back on the road for a September 26th opening in Houston, Texas. Awaiting her, however, was the wrath of Denison, who showed no sympathy for her condition. By now, the restaurant had failed completely. Having had to close up shop and look for a new venture, his days were spent mostly lounging around the house. Or on the patio sunning himself.

Still quarreling with her about money and the direction of her career, he berated her constantly and brutally. While she was distressed by the paucity of work, Jack was infuriated and criticized her constantly for their worsening financial state. He pressured her to heed his advice in making decisions about her career. It clearly didn't occur to him that, since he couldn't successfully manage his own affairs and depended on her support, he wasn't in any position to give advice. Nothing she did pleased him anyway. His verbal and sometimes physical abuse continued. The only time he registered excitement was if he heard she had found work. Then the solicitous, courtly Jack surfaced.

Still she tried to keep up the appearance that everything in the Dandridge-Denison household was in order. On occasion, she still entertained. One evening, her dinner guests were her co-star from "Blues for a Junkman" Peter Mark Richman and his wife Helen. Dorothy and Denison also were guests at the home of the Richmans.

At Dorothy's home, Jack played the role of the modern, adoring husband, preparing dinner and explaining to Peter the proper way to prepare a salad: rub the bowl with garlic, always break the lettuce. He also chatted with Helen Richman in the kitchen. Dorothy hadn't yet appeared. She was upstairs, dressing and making up, still in the habit of having her guests wait while she prepared to face her audience.

Recalling Dorothy's eventual "entrance," Helen said, "She had the most beautiful carriage. Very graceful. She just carried herself in the most wonderful way." For Helen, Dorothy was just absolutely "charming to look at" and "charming to listen to." "She didn't put on airs," said Helen Richman. "I felt very comfortable with her. I had the feeling she was receptive. She was interested in whatever Peter Mark was talking about. She was interested in other people's views. I found her warm."

Yet Peter Richman saw that even away from a set with cameras and the pressures of filming, Dorothy "was not the most comfortable persona under any circumstances," he said. "I mean she could never just be Dorothy. She was part movie star, part major insecurity."

Richman felt her doubts grew out of her insecurity about her education. "Dorothy, despite all her attributes, always felt that she was lacking in many areas," he said.

Denison appeared to be "extremely solicitous" of his wife, said Helen Richman, eager to tend to her needs. It was a calculated act, of course. Both Peter and Helen Richman, however, were aware that Denison was not the man for Dorothy.

"He was certainly very nice," said Richman. "But I never could figure out their relationship. It seemed that he was opportunistic. She was a movie star. He's a White guy. He was a restaurant guy. She was gorgeous. I think it was a coup for him to have her. It never struck me as being a close relationship. It always seemed to be like a separation between their public attitude and what would happen when you close the door."

Richman recalled Denison's behavior on another evening. "We had this lovely dinner at my home. My housekeeper was serving dinner and white wine. So I opened the wine and I poured the wine and I tasted it and let him taste it. But before I opened the bottle, he was talking to me and he inadvertently picked up the bottle and couldn't help but look at the label. He held it in his hand and looked and put it down again. And he went on with the conversation. Now not many people do that at dinner unless you're a maitre d'."

Dorothy's former lover Gerald Mayer, who hadn't seen her in years, also questioned the relationship. When Dorothy invited friends of his—a married couple who lived across the street from her—to a gathering, they mentioned Mayer. She asked them to extend an invitation to him to the party.

Dorothy appeared happy to see him, but "seemed a little forced. A little like she was trying to be charming. When I had known her, she was just so natural," Mayer said. The two didn't have much of an opportunity to talk that day. But he believed he understood the reason for her tension. It was Denison, whom Mayer, meeting for the first time, "did not much like."

"He was almost a cliché of a slick smooth maitre d' who would smile a lot and would say complimentary meaningless things," said Mayer. "There was something really not likeable about him despite his being good-looking. It was startling to me that Dorothy was with him. I can really understand Preminger. He was an exciting, important man with great talent. I can understand Phil Moore. I can understand Lawford. But Denison didn't make any sense to me. My guess is that it never made much sense to anybody."

Mayer also surmised that "the marriage was going badly and they may have even had a fight that day. And she was trying to make the best of it. But I really do remember that it was not the Dorothy I remembered. Not unpleasant certainly because that would not be possible with her. But there was a forced quality."

Mayer stayed a half hour, then left.

Among the other guests at social gatherings at her home on Viewsite were Harold and Mildred Jovien. By now, Harold Jovien had left MCA and gone into business for himself. Mildred Jovien operated a very successful travel agency that booked airline reservations and other travel accommodations for various entertainers, including Dorothy.

Seeing Dorothy's jitteriness on such evenings, Jovien realized

Denison was the cause of some of the tension. He also knew there were financial problems. Ever on the lookout for a quick buck, Denison, having learned of Jovien's success with some stock options, tried persuading Jovien to sell the stock to him.

"He kept hitting me. 'Why don't you sell that stock.' 'It'll probably go down now. It can't go up any further.' And 'We'll be partners' and so forth." As diplomatically as possible, Jovien backed off from the discussions. There was no way he planned to sell Denison stock or ever to become his partner.

Other times, Denison pulled Jovien aside, usually outside on the terrace of Dorothy's home, to make a pitch for a loan. "He said he was in bad straits. And he needed money. He asked for $50,000," said Jovien. "I didn't mention anything to Dorothy about it because it was just not going to happen. So why agitate a family relationship?"

Jovien became concerned, however, about another financial matter pertaining to Dorothy. Although unaware of the specifics of her investments, he knew that the office of lawyer Jerome Rosenthal handled her money. Rosenthal, who had invested heavily in the oil wells and continued to pump Dorothy for more money to be invested, also controlled the financial affairs of such stars as Kirk Douglas and Doris Day. Responsible not only for investing money but paying the bills for these celebrity clients, Rosenthal's office had not paid Mildred Jovien's travel agency for Dorothy's travel expenses. Calls had been made, but nothing happened.

Jovien was hesitant but spoke to Dorothy about the matter, hoping to alert her of possible problems at the Rosenthal office. Soon afterward, said Jovien, the bills were paid. But he felt uneasy about Dorothy's financial security. Jovien also knew Dorothy's career was now headed for serious trouble. Having set up the record deals with Verve, he was aware the material remained unreleased. But Jovien could only say so much. Jack was calling the shots.

Repeatedly, ugly outbursts erupted about Dorothy's failings, often, to Dorothy's embarrassment, in the presence of her secretary Veada Cleveland. She was the cause of all their problems. Jack would Say She had no talent. Trying to placate him, Dorothy found that money usually worked best. But her earnings and savings had dwindled. Still unresolved were the ongoing problems with the IRS.

The financial matters wearied, depressed, and panicked her. Having always prided herself on paying her bills promptly and on being economical, she had discovered that as her stardom grew, so too did the intricacies of her financial affairs. Feeling compelled to leave such matters in other hands, she remained a romantic in a world of her own, not paying enough attention to pertinent business details. Like many artists, she had not astutely managed the people she had hired to manage the money. She had trusted the wrong people. Increasingly nervous and anxious, she needed more medication to sleep at night and to function during the day.

After her years of work, drive, ambition, and accomplishment, to end up in a domestic atmosphere as depressing as that of her mother's home on Fortuna Street made her feel worse. By now, she had determined to get away from Denison. But she remained frightened and confused. The abuse continued.

Byron Morrow remembered well the morning he received an early urgent phone call from Dorothy, sounding urgent and agitated. Could he come over immediately, she asked.

Morrow rushed into his car and drove to Dorothy's home. But upon arriving at Viewsite, Morrow was greeted by Jack who, apparently waiting for him, came out of the house. Everything was all right, Denison explained. It had just been a misunderstanding, merely a husband-and-wife spat. Dorothy was a little upset. But it was nothing serious. Morrow was unsure what to do. People were not supposed to interfere in the lives of married couples. He ended up leaving Viewsite without seeing Dorothy.

"I never felt right about it," said Morrow.

The relentless, debilitating arguments and scenes with Jack escalated. Every minute with him was hell. Finally, when she could endure no more of his tirades and outbursts, when she could foot no more of his debts and incessant demands for cash, when she felt she was in a battle to maintain her sanity and recover her emotional equilibrium, Dorothy told Denison to get out of the house and out of her life. She wanted a divorce. But he laughed and refused to take her seriously. Instead he just turned uglier.

Through the years of the marriage, most of Dorothy's friends were unaware of Denison's sadism. Later when more detail of the beatings came to light, many were angered with Joel Fluellen, who said nothing about the extent of the abuse that he had witnessed during the time he lived on Viewsite.

"He could have said something to us," said Geri. "He could have let me know. It's awfully hard if you have a friend to go and say, 'Are you hurting that much?'" Even Earl Mills, whose relations with Dorothy were now cut off completely, later was infuriated that

Fluellen had not tried to contact him about the state of affairs in Dorothy's home. "I never would have permitted her to have been abused," said Mills.

Others wondered precisely how much Ruby knew. And why she hadn't intervened. Dorothy had spoken to her mother of some matters and certainly of Denison's temper. Years later when Vivian Dandridge resurfaced and sought to re-establish a relationship with Ruby, she spoke to her mother about Denison. Had she only known what was happening with Dorothy, Vivian said, she would have tried to reach her sister.

Vivian was surprised, however, to hear her mother say, "Oh, Jack wasn't so bad."

"Mother, what do you mean?" Vivian asked. "He nearly beat Dorothy to death. You know that."

But Ruby was adamant in saying that Denison had done some nice things for Dorothy; that Vivian had not known the man at all. At that point, Vivian Dandridge knew a real reconciliation with her mother could never come about. Ruby remained as blind to Denison's cruelty and sadism as she had to Ma-Ma's.

Vivian questioned Dorothy's acceptance of the abuse. "Sometimes I wonder why she took it all. But then I remember that when we were growing up she got so many spankings," said Vivian. "I wondered, once I started studying psychology and learned that when girls are abused, either by their father or someone close who gives them a lot of spankings, that they associate it with love.

"I wonder if that was the case with Dottie, if those early spankings somehow threw her off, because I don't know why she would have taken any kind of abuse from anybody, not physically. But I wasn't around then. I was out of the country. I've thought about all this for so long. It was as if maybe Dorothy expected punishment."

Dorothy herself once said that she had set out on a path to wreck her career because it was not the career she wanted. Marrying Denison was part of the wreckage, part of a self-destruction package.

On the one hand, her loathing of her own failures had set her on a course of self-debasement. On the other, something propelled her forward in an attempt to save herself. "She couldn't take any more. He was haranguing and fussing all the time and screaming arguments," said Geri. Finally, she told Denison to get his belongings *and* himself out of her house. The marriage was over.

But a vindictive and angry Denison still refused to budge. Then he committed a series of purely vicious acts. He took her jewelry to a local pawnshop where he sold it for quick cash. Afterwards he returned home and just about threw the pawn tickets in her face.

One day in a rage, he stormed through the house, opening her linen closets, throwing expensive bed and table linens to the floor, and then cutting some with scissors or ripping and tearing others with his hands. Then he tore through the cabinets that held her dinnerware and silver.

"He took her beautiful Wedgwood china, her gorgeous Irish crystal, and just broke it," said Geri. Sometimes he smashed certain pieces so that a set would be incomplete. Unable to smash and demolish her silverware, he simply took pieces out of the house, sometimes forks, sometimes knives, again so serving sets would be incomplete, and threw them away. He did just about any and everything he could to hurt and disorient her.

Depressed, she nevertheless attempted to focus on rehearsals for a forthcoming appearance at the Chi Chi club in Palm Springs in the fall of 1962. She also contacted an attorney, Robert S. Butts, who had handled her divorce from Harold. Now she asked him to draw up separation and divorce papers from Denison.

Once Denison became aware that he was losing her, he began quarreling with her in a particularly ugly way. He ended up brutally and viciously striking Dorothy. Crying and pleading with him to stop, she ran through the house. Stories later circulated throughout Hollywood that Denison had become so violent that Dorothy, trembling and half out of her mind, ran screaming from the house out onto her driveway totally naked.

Eight days later her complaint for a divorce was executed. Somehow in the midst of this horrific domestic situation, she managed to work, agreeing to appear on the television game show "Your First Impression." A few years earlier, a game show would have been beneath her. But now, desperate for money, she had to take whatever she could find. She also opened for her eight-day engagement at the Chi Chi club in Palm Springs. She informed her lawyers that Denison must be out of the house by the time she returned from Palm Springs.

She sought the divorce from Denison on the grounds of "extreme cruelty." She charged that he wrongfully "inflicted upon her grievous mental suffering." Stating that he had struck her on numerous occasions, she called for a restraining order on Denison to keep him away from her.

The papers stated clearly the case of the plaintiff (Dorothy) against the defendant (Denison):

> The defendant has a violent temper and has on occasion inflicted physical violence upon plaintiff, the last occasion being on October 23, 1962. Plaintiff is fearful of defendant and believes that unless defendant is restrained he will again inflict physical violence upon her.

She requested that the court order Denison "to pay the debts and obligations of the parties and also to pay plaintiff's counsel fees and court costs." She wanted to be "restored to the name of Dorothy Dandridge" upon the divorce.

The papers also stated that Denison still resided at Dorothy's home on Viewsite Drive, "which premises are the sole and separate property of plaintiff and title to which is held in the name of plaintiff alone; that plaintiff is unable to live in said premises while defendant remains thereat and desires the defendant be ordered to remove from said premises forthwith, that plaintiff have the exclusive use and occupancy of said premises and that defendant be restrained and enjoined from harassing, molesting or interfering with plaintiff in any manner.

On November 9th, the Superior Court in Los Angeles ordered Denison to be out of the house on Viewsite by November 12th. He told the press he would not fight the divorce.

"I love her too much," he said, adopting the posture of the wounded devoted husband, who was a victim of circumstances and financial pressures. "I wasn't doing too well here," he said of his life in Hollywood. "I feel I love my wife as much as that first day I met her, if not more. And I'm hoping in the very near future we can work it out. I made enough money to sustain two average people very well. After all the average family can live on seven, eight, or nine hundred dollars month. But our living standard was in the $2,000 a month bracket. I couldn't make enough here to tell my wife she didn't have to work. The old man has got to be a breadwinner in a marriage." He added that he and Dorothy were "still very close." He really believed he could win her back.

Afterwards, he pleaded with Herb Jeffries to speak to Dorothy in his behalf. "He knew that she and I had a very close friendship," said Jeffries. "And there came a time when he was calling me almost every night, trying to get me to talk to her for him."

"Just tell her I'm not going to touch her," Denison told Jeffries. "I won't get physical. I've done some ridiculous things. Just tell her I want to see her. I want to sit down and talk to her."

Denison called so frequently that Jeffries finally spoke to Dorothy about him.

Her response was direct. "I don't want to see him," she said. "I don't want to have anything to do with him ever again because he beat me. He struck me. I'm afraid of him."

Jeffries realized that she was terrified of Denison for another reason as well. Recalled Jeffries, "I don't know if this is the case or not. But when a person works in Vegas as long as he did, you have a tendency to feel that person may have some underworld connections. You get a little bit frightened. You're afraid that this person may be able to get somebody to do some harm to you. So you get a double panic."

"Did you talk to her?" Denison asked Jeffries.

"Yes, I talked to her," Jeffries said.

"What did she say?"

He answered honestly that Dorothy wanted nothing more to do with Denison.

Jack spoke to others.

In the meantime though, Denison, ever the crafty survivor, was reported to being drawing up plans to open a new nightclub back on his old turf Las Vegas. If Dorothy's ship should sink, he had no intention of being around.

On November 9th, the day the court ordered Denison out of her home, Dorothy turned forty.

Attempting to maintain some semblance of privacy, she answered questions from the press as discreetly as possible. When asked if there was a hope for a reconciliation, she answered plaintively, "Whenever you file, you don't think so," and added, "We did try to work it out. But when you can't work it out, then it is better to get a divorce before it gets unpleasant."

In mid-December, she appeared in Los Angeles's Superior Court, accompanied by her attorney and her secretary Veada Cleveland. Looking tired, with puffy eyes and face, she testified before Judge Burnett Wolfson. Denison had not approved of the way she handled her career, she said. Despite the fact that she had a business manager, he wanted to take charge of her affairs.

"He has a temper and he wanted to be a part of everything," she told Judge Wolfson. "He would shout and throw things and told me if I didn't listen to him, I would never be successful." Then she touchingly added, "And I do have to be successful."

She explained, "I haven't worked very much because of this hassle going on, but now with the divorce, I think I can get my career together, which I couldn't have done previously."

Veada Cleveland, who testified as a corroborating witness in Dorothy's defense, made the understatement of the day by saying that Dandridge's home life had been "very unpleasant." But she confirmed that Dorothy had been unable to fulfill engagements because of the tension and pressures caused by Denison.

"I think it very cruel when a person such as Miss Dandridge is told she has no talent, as her husband did," said Cleveland.

That same day an episode of the television game show "Your First Impression" aired with Dorothy as a celebrity guest star.

On December 20th, an interlocutory judgment in the divorce case was entered. The divorce would be final a year later. Denison was ordered to pay—"and to hold plaintiff free from liability"—$6,000 to the Budget Finance Corporation; $5,000 due to Joe Glaser; $3,600 due to the Beverly Loan Company. The court ordered him to pay Dorothy's counsel $750 and also $50 for court costs. Denison never appeared to answer the complaints.

Her second marriage had lasted three years, four months, and one day.

Dorothy could breathe a sigh of relief. But she was too emotionally rattled and upset to relax. Her marriage to Denison had cost her almost three crucial years of her career. Hoping some national exposure might help, she flew East on Christmas Day, 1962, for a December 26th appearance on "The Tonight Show," starring Johnny Carson, and broadcast from New York.

But the big club bookings, like the big clubs themselves, which had sustained her all those years, had dried up. The Mocambo closed. Las Vegas still drew large crowds, but within only a few years, she had lost her base there and was no longer considered a major name on that circuit. At those clubs where she did secure bookings, she still had enormous overhead: for gowns, for accompaniment, for travel.

With no reserve savings to support herself—Denison had gone through it all—she was deeply in debt. She worried. She had fallen behind on mortgage payments on her home. She also had problems making payments for Lynn's care. Now almost every dime had to be accounted for.

Except for her accountant, she didn't feel comfortable discussing her finances with anyone, not even Geri. Still proud and accustomed to taking care of herself and no doubt feeling her financial problems were but another sign of failure, she didn't seek help from anyone else either. Whatever she discussed with Ruby appeared not to be taken seriously by her mother. The one person Dorothy might have confided in about her financial fears—and confiding in someone was crucial for her sanity—was Vivian.

At night, engulfed in her fears, her mind raced. She could sleep only with pills. Her sense of self-preservation always led her to thoughts of the career. Just maybe something would turn up that would salvage it.

Had not a cruel fate stepped in, she might have survived. But then the worst imaginable scenario came into play.

In near rapid succession, she learned first from her accountant that the IRS demanded payment of back taxes, both state and federal, to the amount of $8,500, a large sum in 1962.

She also learned that the oil wells she had placed such faith in, which she had been assured repeatedly would provide her with lifetime security, had turned up dry. There would be no gushers for her or any of the other Hollywood stars who had invested. In truth, they all had lost a huge sum of money. For a number of major stars, this would be a devastating blow. Worst, many also had problems with the IRS.

Among those hit were singer Gordon MacRae and his wife Sheila, who found themselves contacted for back taxes by the IRS. "The case grew out of an Indian lands deal that involved not only Gordo [Gordon] and me but a long list of Hollywood names: John Wayne, Kirk Douglas, Doris Day, Dorothy Dandridge, Billy Eckstine, and others less famous," she said.

"In the complicated transaction, the land in question belonged to the Indians and was being acquired by us for future development under a federal program designed to let private entrepreneurs exploit mineral rights. For those who took part in such a deal there were inherent tax benefits. The law required principals to visit the land at least once, a clause that, unfortunately, Gordon did not fulfill. The result was an IRS review of our entire financial structure and a suit against him and me for taxes, not just for those growing out of the land deal, but for those due from other properties. Among those were oil wells on which I believed taxes had been paid. They hadn't been."

Also hit hard were Kirk Douglas and Doris Day. Some years earlier, Douglas discovered that Sam Norton and Jerome Rosenthal had squandered his money in questionable investments. For years, said Douglas, "I was getting letters from Sam about my oil investments: 'Oil continues to flow like liquor at a fireman's ball.'"

But when Douglas had an audit done of his financial affairs, he was shocked to learn that he had no money in the bank and that he owed a huge sum to the IRS. "The solid investments I thought I had, including the oil wells, were dummy corporations that received a percentage of every investment. All the corporations were owned by Sam Norton. The list went on and on. This was in addition to the 10 percent that Rosenthal and Norton took off the top for being my lawyers, and the 10 percent that Sam got personally for being my agent. There had been a lot of money; I had worked steadily and we lived modestly." But, Douglas concluded, "I was penniless and in debt." Douglas immediately took action and fired Rosenthal. He had lost much. But he had saved himself by forcing Norton to repay him for some losses.

Douglas tried warning others, including Doris Day's husband Marty Melcher. But Melcher, who managed Day's career and handled her financial affairs, did nothing about Rosenthal. In the end, Day, through Rosenthal's oil and hotel ventures, lost almost everything. It would take her years to financially re-establish herself. But she would not even get to court with her lawsuit against Rosenthal until 1974, "after five long years of investigation and preparation (not to mention enormous legal fees)," she said.

Said Kirk Douglas, "On July 14, 1987, after nineteen years, she finally succeeded in having him disbarred, and won a judgment of $22 million. He's still protesting his innocence; she's still waiting to collect. Unfortunately, everybody in Hollywood has stories like these. You learn the hard way that the old joke is no joke: 'How do people in Hollywood say, "Fuck you?" "Trust me."

But "by far the worst Rosenthal-related incident," said Doris Day, "involved beautiful actress Dorothy Dandridge." Completely shocked by the turn of events and in a state of panic, Dorothy did not know what to do or to whom to speak. Neither her accountants nor agents could do anything to help her recoup her lost earnings. She admitted she lost at least $150,000 on "bad investments." Dorothy "discovered that she was penniless," said Doris Day. Worst, added Day, Dorothy "had no money to sue." Now every time the phone rang or whenever the mail arrived, Dorothy trembled and panicked. Her life had become a steady stream of phone calls and letters from her creditors.

Unable to cope with the reality of her situation, she tried to live as if it did not exist and retreated into a private world of fantasy. Five lawsuits were brought against her from collection firms, credit services, and banks. With her mortgage payments so seriously behind, the mortgage company finally notified her it was foreclosing on her home on Viewsite. Her $65,000 home was mortgaged to four creditors for $57,000.

"She told me she was being foreclosed six hours before it happened!" said Branton. Dorothy had simply called and said, "I'm going to court this morning because they're going to foreclose on me."

Geri immediately went over to Dorothy's home. If Dorothy had let her know earlier, she felt she could have helped her save the home.

"That was the first I heard she was in jeopardy like that," said Branton. "I did not know. But I was in real estate. I could have had the house re-financed. The other thing was that Jack pawned all her jewelry. She never gave me those tickets. I could have gotten all that out. But I could do nothing six hours before. She was already going downtown."

Dorothy lost the home. But she was given some time to move out. Finally, her lawyers advised her that she would have to file for bankruptcy. There was no other choice.

Aside from the financial catastrophe, Geri was troubled by Dorothy's state of mind. Dorothy did not appear to have done anything to save herself.

"She could have told Preminger. He wasn't that angry with her," said Branton. "By then, he had accepted Jack and that whole relationship. He would have, for business reasons, paid the mortgage to get the house. But the thing is, she wouldn't even help me to help her. Real estate in those days was something I understood well. I was investing in second trustees and I had some knowledge. And my husband Leo could have pulled her out right away. What would have prevented our not doing something about the foreclosure? It never should have happened. Now I don't know enough about the bankruptcy. But it wouldn't have been necessary if the house had been sold. Look, if the house had been sold, she would have had all the equity in the house. And she could have lived a couple years off of that. She could have gotten a smaller house. And there would have been no problem. What I would have done is had her sell the house and take her equity and at that time, she could have gotten eight units and if she had gotten eight units, she could have lived off of that."

"She spent time talking about her relationship with Jack. And she didn't spend time talking about what she should have talked about," Geri said, "But I have to accept the fact that she wanted to fail. She wanted to punish herself. She was a masochist. And she just wanted to do it. But she certainly had other outlets."

On the day the movers came to take her possessions out of Viewsite, she was completely disoriented. Crying and completely overwhelmed by the events, she spent much of the day drinking champagne.

"She just couldn't cope with any of it. Who could have?" said Geri, who along with Joel Fluellen stayed at the house with Dorothy throughout the day."

Because Dorothy couldn't afford the $1,500 moving bill, Geri and her husband paid the expenses. A smaller but comfortable home was found for her on Norman Place, actually, a home too large for one person. Geri paid the first month's security and then the monthly rent on the home. The lawyers prepared the bankruptcy papers.

In late March, she filed the bankruptcy petition. Her debts were listed at $127,994.80, of which, of course, some $8,500 was for back taxes. Her assets totaled $5,000, which were in her home at Viewsite from which she had already moved. "The old home," reported the *Hollywood Citizen News* on April 1st, "is exempt under the California homestead law, preventing possession by creditors."

Her debts included an unpaid $4,000 bank loan and almost $9,000 to Associated Booking. Listed in all were 77 creditors from Vancouver, British Columbia, to Midland, Texas, among them Saks Fifth Avenue of New York and Beverly Hills (she owed $1,033.39), the Brantly Drilling Company of Midland (she owed $551.26), as well as hotels, travel agencies, doctors, a French laundry, a pharmacy, utility companies, and even the supermarket where she had charged food for years. In her petition, Dorothy stated that in the past two years she had earned $100,000. But she was not working now. She was also involved in eight different lawsuits.

Through it all, she still hoped to avoid word of her problems leaking to the press. Her bankruptcy petition was filed under her married name Dorothy Denison. But the press caught wind of the suit and the story was carried on wire services throughout the country. Besieged for interviews or some comment, she went into seclusion and refused to speak to reporters.

"Miss Dandridge has no statement to make," her press representative John Strauss of Cleary, Strauss, Irwin, and Goodman told the press, "and we are advising her to make none."

"Even under ordinary circumstances, Dorothy can be as secretive as a Cape Canaveral missile launch site about her private affairs," a sympathetic *Jet* reported. "And she is too much of an actress to give away on the outside what is going on inside." The publication also sought to put her plight into perspective for its Black readership. "Despite her great beauty and a talent that once brought her an Academy Award nomination, Miss Dandridge has in recent years been forced to accept movie jobs abroad, confining her U.S. exposure to night clubs and a TV performance or two. It was as if Hollywood conferred upon her the honor of stardom, then walked away leaving her with honor alone. She has not lost her beauty, her talent or her pride."

Less than a month after filing for bankruptcy, Dorothy was scheduled to appear on April 24th in downtown Los Angeles at the federal bankruptcy court. Having been caught off-guard by Dandridge's first petition, the press now awaited her arrival for her first public appearance since the news had broken. As she entered the court, reporters and photographers rushed up to ask her questions and to snap pictures.

Dressed simply in a dark dress with pearls and her hair brushed backed, she wore dark glasses, saying she had injured her eye in a fall. Embarrassed, she said little else. For Dorothy, the public humiliation was almost too great to bear. The United Press International photo of her standing in her dark glasses outside the bankruptcy courtroom appeared in newspapers throughout the country.

Following the hearing on April 24th, Dandridge drove to Geri's home. Slowly, she walked inside. She couldn't stop crying. "She stayed here very late," said Geri. "And then she went back to the house."

For Black America, it was a devastating sight: its dreamgirl who seemed so bright and forward looking was now down on her luck and in the worst imaginable circumstances. Perhaps no star's decline since that of Billie Holiday so affected the African American community. To think that the woman who had been so splendidly in control of herself in *Carmen Jones*, a symbol of an independent, self-assured woman, had so lost control and should have to endure such a public display of her sorrow was almost unfathomable.

"It upset and saddened me so much," said actress Nichelle Nichols, "after having seen that beautiful spread in *Ebony*, with her home and her taste. To see all of that falling apart. That was sad for me. And for this woman's memory to be diminished in what can be a vile industry. She deserved better. She was such a lady. Not like some others. She was just first class. I just hated seeing it happen to her."

Olga James recalled, "It was sad that there was no suitable Black partner for her. That she had been exploited by this White man. I really felt awful about that. It was sad that there was no protective partnership for her in life and that she didn't get the kind of treatment and protection that her talent deserved."

Maria Cole recalled, "It makes me ill to think of what happened. She didn't deserve to have those things happen to her. She was too nice, too sweet, too naive. She was probably very proud. You didn't think of her as anything but a lovely, sweet, beautiful woman who had a tragic life. It became tragic because of the failure of her career, which never should have happened. She let people step over her. In this business you have to be tough. No one was around to help. I think what ruined her was Jack."

Bobby Short remembered his feelings upon hearing the news. "It's nothing new in show business. One of the most predictably danger-ous positions one can be in is the position that women performers fall into. It's not a happy life for most of them. Women who depend on their looks and their talent to get ahead. And women who wish to have a so-called normal life along with the career. It's very difficult for them. Dorothy's story could have been anybody's story. We Blacks took it very personally that she was bankrupt. I, however, just thought how sad for *Dorothy*. I just felt sad for her because she was fragile and rather special. Not mean enough to have seen through a Jack Denison or anyone else who was around."

A few months later, *Ebony*, which had celebrated her on its cover in June 1962, ran her on the cover again in July 1963: this time with boxers Joe Louis and Sugar Ray Robinson, and singer Sarah Vaughan. Its headline: "Why the Stars Go Broke."

"This was a disgrace that tore her apart," said Earl Mills. "She never, after that, was the same person."

But then came the final tragic twist.

In the midst of the bankruptcy proceedings, Dorothy heard from Helen Calhoun. "When the world was falling in on me," Dorothy later said, "the woman who had been looking after Lynn from the age of nine to nineteen returned her to me. I was in arrears two months in support of Lynn, after ten years without missing a week."

Calhoun planned to send Lynn by train from Kansas to Los

Angeles. Dorothy would have to meet her at the train station.

"The woman sent her [word] the day after Dottie was in bankruptcy court," recalled Geri. "She said she loved Lynn and all that. But we would have to make arrangements for her care." "Dottie was in a bad way then," said Geri.

Aware that her friend couldn't cope with the situation, Geri said she'd go to the train station to meet Lynn, who was due to arrive at three in the morning.

Upon entering the train station in the chilly, dark early hours, there stood Lynn standing with a suitcase full of her belongings. She was nineteen, but had no knowledge of where she was nor where she was going. "She didn't know us," said Geri. "I just took Lynn, brought her to the house, and took care of her."

Later Geri took Lynn to Dorothy, who looked at her daughter and broke into tears. The very thing she had worked so hard for all these years, that very thing—the care of Lynn—that had motivated her, had sustained her, had somehow given her hope and a reason to push herself, had now, like everything else, fallen to pieces.

Friends who were around Dorothy these days witnessed that she was unable to sit still or to allow herself a quiet moment to contemplate her situation. Manically scurrying about her new home, she cried incessantly. Lynn did not help matters any. She pounded loudly on the piano, just as she had done as a child. The sounds nearly drove Dorothy crazy.

Charlotte Sullivan remembered that Dorothy stared at her daughter, tears in her eyes, and said, "I don't care what anyone tells me. She must know I'm her mother. She has to know that."

To Geri and other friends, it was obvious that Lynn could not remain with Dorothy. Everyone knew Dorothy was in no emotional state to handle her daughter. Harold's mother, Viola Nicholas, stepped in and took care of Lynn for a time. But Lynn demanded constant attention and was still "a twenty-four-hour watch," which proved too much for the older woman.

Stepping in again to help, Geri Branton contacted a lawyer and had papers filed to have Lynn placed in a state institution. First though, Lynn had to be confirmed as a danger to herself and others. This would necessitate Dorothy having to attend a courtroom hearing.

Viola Nicholas and a physician who could explain Lynn's condition accompanied Dorothy to the hearing. Trembling and sometimes gasping to breathe, Dorothy listened to the facts of the case. But she found it hard to sit still or concentrate. At one point, she had to leave the courtroom for water. Her legs buckled and she nearly collapsed.

She was afraid that should the press hear of her presence in the courtroom, she would be subjected to news reporters, cameras, and questions. But, she managed to get through the rest of the day without any incidents. The judge declared Lynn a ward of the state. She was to be placed in the state institution Camarillo for care and treatment for the rest of her life.

Shortly afterwards, Geri, accompanied by her sister Rose and Rose's husband Dr. J. Kennedy Lightfoot, gathered Lynn's few belongings and placed them in Geri's car for the long drive to Camarillo. Dorothy did not go.

"It was the best thing," said Geri. "Lynn received fine care there."

For a romantic woman in search of meaning in life, a talented woman who believed there might be a place for her in the scheme of things if she worked hard enough, the world must have seemed an unbearably alien and cruel. Fate had marked her for so long now: as a little girl in a home where the love between her parents had ended; as a child on the road with her only sister; as a teenager with breasts bound by a woman who shared a bed with her mother; as the daughter who always sought that mother's love and approval; as the young wife of a husband who had no time for her; as the young mother who could only blame herself for the condition of her beautiful brain-damaged child; as the reluctant nightclub goddess who hated the stares and comments of the men in the clubs; as the film actress who had hit a stone wall with too many aborted projects and too few developed characters. Always she feared the hand of fate and the notion of destiny. Yet, she fought it. And now fate had resurfaced to inform her that it had won again and with her help, her complicity, which indeed was what the marriage to Denison represented to her. Now she stayed within the doors of her rented home on Norman Place. In the days, weeks, and months ahead, her thoughts always returned to Lynn. Her little girl was now a teenager but just as helpless and defenseless as the day she was born. She had failed in the most serious way. She could never forgive herself.

FIFTEEN

Lonely Days,
Long Nights,
Last Rites

"*N*ot to worry," she often said during those peak years when she sat with her back ramrod straight, her head held haughtily high, and her chin arched up. How long had it been since she uttered those words?

Now her days were spent in unending worry and anxiety, her mind racing. She found that a mix of vodka and champagne temporarily relieved the anxieties, blotting out memories of the recent turn of events.

She drank heavily, and, like so many others who did the same, struggled to keep it a secret, especially from Ruby who had already begun to suspect a problem. Friends of Dorothy's such as Joel Fluellen knew well that her drinking was out of hand. Geri Branton understood there was a problem but admitted that Dorothy was good, for a time, at covering it up.

Aside from the alcohol, Dorothy lived on a steady diet of medications; all prescribed by a physician who appeared too eager to pump her up or ease her down with pills, Because her body metabolism had changed, she discovered herself retaining more water, which made her feel all the more lethargic and on occasion look heavier and puffy; she took water pills in hopes of losing the weight; other pills, to help her function or to forget.

"That collapse of fortune left me as bewildered a human being as you could find," she said. "Not knowing which way to turn or how to recoup, desiring death more than anything else, I took pills. Pills to pep myself up, pills to slow myself down. I took Benzedrine, a dangerous item if you overuse it. I took Dexamil and Dexedrine, appetite deterrents. I took thyroid pills and digitalis."

Usually, whether alone or talking on the phone with friends, she questioned everything about her life: what, if anything, she had achieved; what she had done wrong; constantly, examining, dissecting, and sometimes retracing and reliving her past. When her head was clear, she tried charting her future. But it was when she drank that she felt any confidence or optimism. Difficult as it might be, she had to get out, to see people, to face the world again.

In May 1963, she joined Dick Gregory, Sammy Davis, Jr., Paul Newman, Joanne Woodward, and Rita Moreno at a large rally for Martin Luther King, Jr., who had become a hero for Dorothy, at Los Angeles's Wrigley Field. Over 50,000 people attended. "This is the largest and most enthusiastic civil rights rally in the history of this nation," King told the crowd that day.

Dorothy seemed spacey but eager to participate in the activities, which formally marked Hollywood's entry into the struggle for civil rights. Ironically, during the proceedings, she was seated next to Rita Moreno, who had replaced her in that film that now seemed so many years away, *The King and I.*

Dorothy's appearance at the rally was noted by the FBI, which still considered King as well as the band of celebrities joining him as possible subversives who had to be observed carefully. Word of Dorothy's presence that day was one of the items in the FBI's files.

Still often alone and lonely, she remained adrift. After the collapse of her marriage, but perhaps to her own surprise, she had began seeing the screenwriter Abby Mann.

Born and reared in Philadelphia, Mann was probably best known for his Oscar-winning screenplay of 1961 *Judgment at Nuremberg.* Directed by Stanley Kramer, this dramatization of the postwar Nazi crime trials at Nuremberg boasted an all-star cast that included Spencer Tracy, Montgomery Clift, Judy Garland, Marlene Dietrich, and Burt Lancaster. Later he wrote the screenplays for *The Condemned of Altona, A Child Is Waiting,* and *Ship of Fools.*

Flush from his recent success, Mann felt, upon meeting Dorothy, that a dream had come true. He had first seen her in the pages of *Life* at the time of the release of *Bright Road.* "I remember looking at this beautiful woman," he said. "I don't even think I saw the movie. But I was taken by her beauty." Later he saw *Carmen Jones* and was impressed. "She had always been one of the most beautiful women in the world to me," he said. "So I sought her out."

Dorothy didn't realize at first that a romance might be in the offing. Instead she seemed relieved to find some type of an acknowledgment from someone in the industry that she still mattered. But for career-driven Mann, dating her struck him as one more sign of his newfound success.

"People would come over to me," he recalled of their evenings together. "I was so proud to take her out." But the "image I had of her as Carmen Jones was not as I found her," he said. "When I met her, she was a tremulous, sad, nice, intelligent, quiet, and at times a terribly bitter person."

Signs of her discontent surfaced the evening he squired her to a Directors Guild screening of A Child Is Waiting, which he had recently scripted. Directed by John Cassavetes and starring Burt Lancaster and Judy Garland, A Child Is Waiting was an early screen attempt to deal frankly with mental retardation. It told the story of a teacher trying to reach a mentally disabled young girl.

Not satisfied with the film himself but wanting it to succeed, Mann was openly nervous about the audience's response. At the end of the screening, Ingo Preminger, his agent, congratulated Mann, who afterwards anxiously turned to Dorothy and asked, "Do you think it really went over well? Do you think Ingo really liked it?"

"I don't know," she answered softly. "There was something in his eyes." Then she gently tried to bolster Mann's spirits.

"She was very philosophical," he recalled. "To show you the kind of person she was, how astute she was, with so much dignity and grace, after A Child Is Waiting was shown, you see, she was so kind and didn't want to me to know that Ingo didn't like it. She didn't want to tell me that it didn't go over all that great. But she would do it in a very guarded fashion."

What later struck Mann though was the fact that Dorothy, having entered the theatre without knowing anything about the film, had been caught off guard. Viewing A Child Is Waiting, especially at this troubled time in her life, was an emotionally wrenching experience that brought up painful memories. Only later did she tell Abby about Lynn.

"It was a little strange," said Mann, "because she must have thought that one of the reasons I took her to see the film was because of her daughter. But I hadn't known that. She seemed disturbed."

Other times, Abby found Dorothy in a more relaxed mood. Among his fondest memories were quiet afternoons the two spent together either seeing movies or reading.

"That was nice," recalled Mann. "Talking about the theater. Sometimes even talking to her on the phone late at night about things.

About life and what it meant and how fleeting things were."

Some afternoons the two read Shakespeare together "when I would be very tired of work," he said, "and she'd come over and we'd just lie in bed together. She liked Shakespeare. So did I. So we'd take different roles. And we'd read the plays. She loved to read plays. We'd do *Romeo and Juliet*. We'd talk about the line after Juliet died, and Romeo says, 'Then I defy you stars!' That was Dorothy's favorite line in Shakespeare. So we'd sit and read and talk about how modern Shakespeare was."

The Shakespearean character that most fascinated Dorothy was Lady MacBeth, that ambitious heroine whose guilt ultimately destroys her and drives her insane; the woman who cannot forget her deeds.

"Why don't you appear in it somewhere?" he asked her. "Do it. Try it. Go to New York. Your name probably means something there."

"No. I don't think it would," Dorothy told him.

Dorothy and Mann often discussed the industry and their pasts. Both admired the African American actress Mildred Smith, who Abby had lived with in London. Smith had appeared in *No Way Out* in 1950. But her career had never lived up to its promise, a fact not lost on Dorothy. She and Mann also often talked about the way Hollywood treated Black women.

"This is a terrifically racist town. I mean it was particularly then," said Mann. "For Black women, it was just terrible. I was shocked because in New York, it wasn't that way. But when I'd have Black women at parties, it was new to California. So you'd see quite attractive girls. It would almost be that they had to sleep around. Not even for parts or anything. But just to be a part of the social milieu. And it was quite ugly. And some of them were such nice people underneath it all. But in those days it was anticipated that no matter how attractive the girl was, if she was Black, she was available. It was so omnipresent. I saw it again and again and again. And it was really disturbing to me."

"Dorothy was a big star. So they didn't see her that way. But I imagined what Dorothy had come through. She said she had to fight for her own turf and her own dignity. People looked at her that way at first and I could see it."

Dorothy, of course, knew that her relationship with Phil Moore had her helped to navigate her way through those rough waters. She didn't discuss Moore with Abby but did reminisce about Harold and Otto. To Mann, Dorothy appeared to regret the way her first marriage had ended, questioning if she had given the marriage enough of a chance.

Her feelings about Otto were mixed, part resentment, part awe. "It was a very important relationship to her," Mann said, "and she was disturbed by it and said that he was cruel to her. And yet she had kind of an affection for him because he had been so important to her career."

⁓

Sometimes Dorothy didn't care about the career, preferring to forget everything. Other times she cared deeply and became all the more depressed. A return to work was essential, she knew. Maybe there was a way to climb back, she hoped. Yet trying to regain her footing was painful.

Abby Mann recalled an evening that he spent with Dorothy at her home. Nothing seemed out of the ordinary. But then suddenly, unexpectedly, Dorothy started to cry. When he asked her what was wrong, she answered simply, "No, I don't really want to talk about it." Mann believed it had to do with her career, that something she had hoped might work out had fallen through. "She was frightened like a child," he recalled.

She worried about her looks. But Mann recalled that she "looked very good."

"I never remember her looking bad," said Mann. "She was aging a little. But not much really. There was fear in her face though. There was a sense of being lost. Of not quite understanding what was happening and being uncertain suddenly. It had nothing to do with color. But there was a double whammy in that not only was she sliding but that she fell in a certain category. So there was that double thing that bothered her. Her dignity meant a great deal to her. She had a great deal of pride. And she didn't want to lose that pride and so that was really frightening to her."

Mann recalled, "Dorothy definitely felt that she had crested. Even as young as she was, she definitely felt that the best days were behind her really."

For a spell, their relationship went well. But Mann's very success reminded her all the more of her failures. He recalled a poignant time when he received "a $50,000 bonus for a little rewrite" on a film. "So I was going to splurge and rent this home at the beach in Santa Monica from Peter Lawford."

Excitedly, he told Dorothy that "Peter Lawford and Kennedy used to go swimming there, and Marilyn Monroe, and so forth. I was going on and on about it."

But she was quiet for a moment, then told him, "On this day, you're going to move out there, and I've lost my home and am moving. You're going there and I'm going here."

Recalled Mann, "So here she was moving to a little place and here I was gushing off like an idiot about going off to Santa Monica."

Her home on Norman Place "was not tasteless or anything," said Mann. "It just seemed that she didn't have enough money for furniture. I was really kind of shocked. Not that it was a slum or anything. But next to where she was living, it was really kind of sad."

For a while when Mann rented a home designed by Frank Lloyd Wright, he invited Dorothy to stay in the guest house on the property. Sometimes she spent weekends there, just to get away from her depressing place on Norman Place.

Often moved by her, sensing her feelings of being alone and adrift, Mann was reminded "oddly enough of Dietrich," he said. "Sounds strange, doesn't it? But Dietrich was a very lonely woman. She would call me up and say, 'What do you think about Kennedy?' Dietrich would love things [like books, which she wanted to talk about]."

Dorothy would also call and want to "talk to me about intellectual things. She felt terribly alone and cut off. It was like somebody terribly lost, and being Black was very much a part of it because at that time she did not know if there was a place for her. When she was a star, [they] made a place for her. And now there was not a niche for her. She was no longer that. She had lost that. And therefore she was frightened of becoming just another commodity in town. That was a big part of it. I really didn't pay as much attention to her as I should. And I'm sorry now. I was seeing a lot of people at the time. She was a fragile person [who] was hurt. A fragile person [who] lost her way."

In July, 1963, Dorothy traveled to Chicago where she attended the NAACP's convention and was a presenter at an NAACP Women's Auxiliary awards ceremony citing African American women for their civic contributions, and then went on to Cleveland to appear as a guest co-host on the syndicated television program "The Mike Douglas Show." Comedian Dick Gregory also appeared. Arriving in Cleveland, she agreed to an interview with the city's African American newspaper *The Call and Post*. Its reporter Allen Howard graciously didn't refer to Dandridge's recent bankruptcy and divorce in the interview. Dorothy appeared eager though to comment on the wave of militancy of a new generation of African Americans.

"Let's face it," she said. "It's the younger people who are opening up more avenues for the Negroes. It's their pressure and unwillingness to be satisfied with the status quo that is causing the changes."

At the taping of the Douglas program, the studio audience's eyes were glued to Dorothy as she calmly took her place on a petal-shaped chair. Her appearance proved to be highly emotional as she talked to another guest, Dr. Gunnar Dwybad, then the executive director of the National Association for Mentally Retarded Children and special consultant to President Kennedy's Committee on Mental Retardation. He discussed the condition of the President's sister Rosemary Kennedy, who had been institutionalized for years, for mental retardation. But the studio audience wasn't affected by Dwybad's comments as it was by Dorothy's.

In the "glare of 50,000 watts of light, and with the unblinking eyes of video cameras," she looked straight ahead and spoke of her recent problems and also, most tellingly and touchingly, spoke about Lynn, the first and only time she ever did so on television.

She began with a simple statement to the audience. "So many of you probably think that the life of show business people is all fun and glitter," she said. "But we are human beings, too. What happens to us is very much the same as what happens to you." From there, she discussed that time in the 1940s when she first learned of Lynn's condition and of the pain that followed.

"I never really thought I could give my daughter up to an institution. I guess the longest period of time that I have ever been away from her was about six months. Actually, she has no conception of time. She doesn't know how long I've been away. She doesn't even know that I'm her mother. She only knows that she likes me and I like her, and she feels warmth and that I'm a nice person."

She explained that Lynn "can't ever be adjusted to society. She would never be able to cope with society." Then she added the words that must have pained her most deeply, "So I recently had her committed to Camarillo State Hospital near Los Angeles. I've just gone through a bankruptcy and I can't afford to keep her with Mrs. Calhoun any longer."

"And I guess I've grown up to realize that she should be places where she can be best cared for by people who understand her problem.

The older she gets, the more difficult it is for people at home to handle her because of the state my daughter is in. There are different degrees. Some people have mental retardation that is not quite as severe as my daughter's."

The television audience sat stunned and silent as she spoke, obviously moved by her sincerity, as were no doubt the millions watching their television sets at home. Mike Douglas asked her if she ever thought of having another child. "Oh, yes," she answered sweetly. Yet she knew that would never happen. Dorothy's candor was partly her attempt to change attitudes about the retarded and to work toward programs that would help such children and adults; and partly an attempt, so it seemed, to fully come to terms with Lynn's condition. After Dorothy spoke, the studio audience and the television crew stood and applauded her.

"It was one of the great moments in television drama," *Jet* wrote. "The best thing that Miss Dandridge had ever done for an audience. But for her it was not a performance. It was something she had finally made up her mind to do. It was something that might help someone else who is carrying the same burden she has carried so many years." The magazine added, "Seldom if ever, has a star discussed a crushing personal problem with such frankness and intelligence."

Jet also reported, "Westinghouse Broadcasting Company officials were so impressed by Miss Dandridge's sincerity that videotapes of the Cleveland show will be shown on Westinghouse outlets in Boston, Baltimore, and Pittsburgh. Later it may be shown in San Francisco and other cities where there are outlets for the Westinghouse establishments."

She also did public service announcements in Cleveland about mental retardation for the President's Committee on Mental Retardation. *Jet* later ran her comments in its Words of the Week section:

> There's a mistaken belief that there's very little that can
> be done to help retarded children. Actually, a great deal can
> be done. But only if we see to it that the
> needs of these children are met. They need recreation,
> education and job training. But above all, they need loving
> care and understanding of the people around them.

For Dorothy, something had come full circle that afternoon on "The Mike Douglas Show."

Dorothy seemed ready to tie up loose ends with her father Cyril, whom she had agreed to see. With his second wife Thelma, Cyril Dandridge visited his famous daughter at her hotel. Less tense than at other times, the two made amends. For Cyril, the occasion had to be bittersweet and fraught with pain. With Vivian, he had already begun to establish a relationship. Now his younger daughter, taken from him at birth, the girl he had never really had the chance to know and to show his love for, was in the midst of her own deep troubles, which Cyril, like everyone else, had read about in the national press.

But as much as Cyril loved her, he knew there was nothing he could do to help her. Almost before Cyril's very eyes, Dorothy was retreating into a private world from which there could be no return. Yet he was grateful for the reunion; the opportunity to spend a little time with her, which perhaps was a sign of more settled days ahead for them. But in truth, Cyril Dandridge would never see his daughter again.

Upon her return to Los Angeles, Dorothy fell again into a despairing mood. Word came that Phil Moore's mother Jimmy had died. Jimmy had gotten to know Dorothy well and seemed to adore her. Dorothy in turn had liked Jimmy. The death meant a part of Dorothy's youth had now vanished.

On the day of Jimmy Moore's funeral, Bobby Short stood among the mourners at Moore's home. He remembered Dorothy's arrival. This was not the glittering, sexy glamor goddess of the clubs. Instead she looked weak and withdrawn.

"Dorothy was very thin," said Short. "And very nervous. Wearing a white suit." Saying little, Dorothy "seemed awfully fluttery and nervous."

As the mourners viewed the body lying in state, Dorothy slowly, nervously, walked toward the casket. Short stood near Dorothy, who looked at the body of Jimmy Moore and spoke in a surprising way.

"Don't look like Jimmy," Dorothy said.

Short recalled, "Well, it wasn't like Dorothy at all to say 'It don't look like Jimmy.' That was a gut reaction. It just came out. Many of us do that. It's something inherent. Someone once made some wonderfully high-flung statement about people who, no matter how high they fly...I'm not talking about Dorothy here...but no matter what, there comes a moment when they become themselves. I suppose under great stress, great grief, great whatever, that you become the person you were when you were first starting out in life. Dorothy was very upset about Phil's mother's death."

That day, Moore and Dorothy didn't talk much. But Bobby Short felt the two had come to terms with any past disagreements.

Dandridge's affair with Abby Mann continued. But her drinking caused problems. About to begin work with director Stanley Kramer on *Ship of Fools*, Mann took Dorothy to the premiere of Kramer's all-star comedy *It's A Mad Mad Mad Mad World*. Afterwards Abby confided that he didn't like the picture. Later at a gathering, Dorothy suddenly turned to Kramer and said, "You know Abby doesn't think the picture is very good. He doesn't think it's very funny."

Mann couldn't believe his ears. He quickly told Kramer that he had liked the film. Kramer took Dorothy's comments in good humor. But Mann became angry with her.

"We had a bit of a spat," he said. "She was a little loaded."

Dorothy, upset and remorseful, called Mann several times to apologize, usually "at night when she had been drinking and she was lonely. She was forlorn about it," he recalled.

"I guess I shouldn't have said it," Dorothy told Mann.

"No, you shouldn't have," he responded.

But the incident passed and soon the two saw each other again, usually attending social affairs to which Abby had been invited. His circle included some of the industry's great glittering figures, stars and filmmakers such as Marlene Dietrich, Stanley Kramer, and Spencer Tracy. But the evenings could be painful for Dorothy. In the past at such gatherings, she had felt herself just as glamorous, just as glittering, just as successful as those she socialized with. But all that was behind her. Now she felt herself too much an observer, too much an unwanted, unnoticed object.

"She wouldn't say much," recalled Mann. "She would watch people. She was at a party and here were all these people. Frank Capra. There was John Gielgud, Vivian Leigh, Henry Fonda. But she was very much by herself. There was such a caste system at that time. It was just such a square town. Here was somebody terribly alone. Sliding. She would smile and so forth, but she felt out of place. Yet, she enjoyed a laugh as much as anybody would. But it was as though she were fragile and no longer felt secure."

Yet sometimes, Dorothy talked to Dietrich and Vivien Leigh. She considered Marlene Dietrich vain, distant, and terribly filled with herself, yet at other times, surprisingly warm and sympathetic. Dietrich may have remembered seeing Dorothy as a teenager in *Jump for Joy*. Or more recently at the opening of *Porgy and Bess*. Vivien Leigh, now in her early 50s, was about to start work on *Ship of Fools*, which would be her last film. A manic depressant with an array of her own insecurities and uncertainties, Leigh, perhaps aware that she and Dorothy were fragile kindred spirits, "was very fond of Dorothy," said Mann. Later after the Dandridge/Mann affair had ended, Leigh frequently asked Abby, "Where that's little dark girl? I liked her."

Dandridge and Abby were together on the day of President John F. Kennedy's assassination. For Dorothy, the morning started off depressingly. Her friends Geri Branton and Maria Cole planned to visit Lynn at Camarillo. But Dorothy wasn't up to the trip. Seeing Lynn had become too painful. As Maria Cole and Branton left Cole's home for the drive, her sister Charlotte heard the news of the assassination and ran from the house shouting to them, hoping to catch them. But the two didn't hear her.

Abby sat in his study working on a draft of *Ship of Fools* when a telephone call from a friend informed him, "The President's been shot." Mann's anger rose as he heard more details on television. He called Dorothy. "Politically, she was quite liberal," said Mann. "But not really intellectually left. I would talk to her a lot about politics. She loved Kennedy."

Stunned by the news, Dorothy and Abby quickly met and ended up having a meal in a Chinese restaurant on Rodeo Drive. A scheduled fashion show took place that day at the restaurant. Both Dorothy and Abby were upset to see a group of fashion models strutting about, casually showing off their dresses. Mann recalled that "Dorothy was very disturbed. It seemed very unreal. People here didn't seem to care. Later it settled in, I guess. But that day it seemed so terribly unreal."

Gradually, Dorothy's affair with Mann fizzled out. But she often called him in the middle of the night, sometimes when he was with other women, frequently when she was drinking. "She would drink, I think, because of the depression," said Mann. "And I think she was getting depressed more and more. Not that she was an alcoholic. She wasn't."

"I don't think of myself very well in this relationship," said Mann. "I was a little thoughtless because I felt she was a little jaded. I felt that she was terribly alone and it worried me that it might happen to me. Because I had just gotten success then. And I know this sounds awful, but it's true. Her being kind of a has-been made me say to myself, 'Jesus, that could happen to me too.' Isn't that horrible? But it's true."

Mann's fear echoed that of so many successful people in Hollywood: their fear of a star on the slide as being a possible contaminant to their own success; a distressing reminder of the fickleness of fame and fortune in Hollywood.

The two remained friends. When Mann was working at Columbia Pictures on *Ship of Fools*, Dorothy sometimes met him for lunch at a nearby restaurant. "I was always happy to see her," he recalled. "But I just had a feeling of terrible tragedy about her."

"Dorothy could jolt you into sensitivity. She was very intuitive about me. She knew things about me. She knew what it was like to be a Jewish kid in East Pittsburgh. She would laugh at the fact that I was seeing other women and whether or not I was having a good time, and she'd say, 'Enjoy it because later on it will be something to remember.' And it was such a statement for such a young, beautiful woman to say. It was odd. One felt she was much older than what she was. One felt that at times it was like Gloria Swanson in *Sunset Boulevard*. There was something terribly tired about her. And yet she was a young, beautiful woman."

"I wanted to help her," Mann said. "But I didn't know how to help her." He spoke to industry people about parts for Dorothy and even wrote a role in his script *Children of Sanchez* for her. But at this point, he said, "They were a little contemptuous, as if that were yesterday's news." Her days now becoming long and lonely, she drank more, and reminisced more too, still on her Proustian quest to understand the past. She kept herself connected in some ways though, seeing old friends like Juliette Ball. Joel Fluellen was around too.

Her loneliness drove her to venture out of the house in new ways where her desperation showed. Near her home on Norman Place was a vacant lot where people—some vagrants—gathered to eat and drank. On some occasions, Dorothy joined them, eating with them and drinking with them too. And, of course, they all knew that in their presence was the movie star Dorothy Dandridge, down on her luck.

Joel Fluellen pitched a fit when he found out what she had been doing. He criticized her conduct, in harsh and frank terms, reminding her that she had a position to maintain. But Dorothy still wandered out to the lot. Secretly, Fluellen became so angry about her behavior that he called Ruby and spoke to her about Dorothy's drinking and the fact that she seemed adrift. Ruby, however, seemed unwilling to cope with or even to acknowledge Dorothy's condition, or to offer any help.

Dorothy herself remained devoted to, but perplexed by her mother, and she brought up the subject of Ruby with Abby one evening.

"I wonder what you would think about her." Dorothy said.

"Well, why don't we go out to dinner or something?" he responded.

But Dorothy "would be shy about that," said Mann. "So I wondered about it. But she talked about her mother as if she were very close to her and that her mother had meant a great deal to her, but I never met her mother."

Dorothy still spoke to Ruby over the telephone every day. She was living comfortably with her companion in an attractive new home. But the other woman, preferred that Dorothy *not* visit or intrude on their lives. Just as with Neva years before, Ruby acquiesced to her lover's wishes.

Regardless, Dorothy visited her mother, usually entering the house and breezing past the woman in haughty movie-star fashion. That, of course, merely angered the woman, who appeared to want some kind of acknowledgment from Dorothy. But Dorothy acted as if the woman didn't exist, questioning why her mother would get so involved with such a woman!

Still, in desperate straits and in need of emotional support and also financial assistance, Dorothy might have been able to cope better had Ruby helped. She and her companion had lucrative real estate holdings. In the end, Geri Branton and her husband Leo paid Dorothy's rent and other bills. But Ruby offered no assistance.

Ruby did discuss Dottie's situation with friends, most frequently Joel Fluellen. Etta Jones also received calls from Ruby, who pumped her for information about Dorothy's comings and goings and asked if Dorothy had become an alcoholic.

"Etta, you know Dottie D.," Ruby said. "She never did drink before."

"Look, Mrs. Dandridge," Etta responded, "I don't know whether Dorothy drinks nor whether she did in the past or anything else."

"Well, everybody's saying that she drinks too much," Ruby said. "And she's driving that car."

"Well, I don't know anything about it," Etta told her, "because I do not see Dorothy. I don't know what she's doing."

After a short time, Dorothy moved from Norman Place. "The

house was really too large for her," said Geri. "She just didn't need all that space."

An apartment was found for her on the second floor of an elegant Spanish colonial-style building on Fountain Avenue in West Hollywood, owned ironically by Pamela Mason, a woman who had once been a dinner guest at Dorothy's homes. Marilyn Monroe had once stayed there, too, in the apartment of friends, but Marilyn had resided on Fountain Avenue on the way up, not down.

Stars on the skid in Hollywood had often ended up in uninviting, sometimes horrifying places: grim, dirty, dark. And for Dorothy who had known the splendors of the Hollywood Hills, the apartment on Fountain must have seemed small and yet another reminder of her decline. Once after visiting her there, Preminger, who could only compare it with past glories, referred to the place as a basement flat. But that wasn't the case at all.

The truth was that Dorothy found herself in an artfully designed building with a romantic aura and a semblance, now partly due to her presence, of true tragic grandeur. It sat above and away from the street on a delicate mound. The grounds were lush with trees and foliage and well landscaped and tended. Arched entrances led to the various units. Tenants on the ground level could gaze out large picture windows, and at night the building was beautifully lit with floodlights.

With its decent-sized living room, a bedroom, a kitchen, a small extra bedroom/study, and a modest-sized bathroom, the apartment on Fountain Avenue must have offered Dorothy some sense of balance and tranquility as well as some space and mobility. Domestic help was hired to keep the house in order for her.

She was a mysterious, solitary spectral figure who drew the curiosity of fellow tenants, who watched her as she came and went. Even now, alone, lonely, and frightened, she still had what Helen Richman had called "a beautiful carriage" and "a charming manner." Even now, Dorothy Dandridge was a woman whom people, even those unsure of who she was, enjoyed observing and fantasizing about. Her fall from grace oddly had made her all the more a haunting and romantic figure.

Still struggling to return to work for both her welfare and her sanity, Dorothy had contacted her former manager Earl Mills. The two met, and he agreed to manage her again. Unwavering in his conviction that she could climb back up to the top, Mills was nonetheless aware that it would be an uphill battle. It had been only four years since she basked in the spotlight. Four years away from the limelight can be a lifetime. Hollywood forgets quickly. People still knew who she was. But she was no longer a viable commodity. Former publicist Orin Borsten, then working on an episode of the television series *The Eleventh Hour*, recalled recommending her for the lead dramatic role. "They turned her down," he said. "They said, 'No, she's passé. She's dead.'"

If there was any hope of a career comeback, she would have to go on calls like any struggling newcomer. Or take whatever bookings at clubs or on television came her away.

During 1964, some work came in. "I chased a will-o'-the-wisp called Comeback," Dorothy said. "It was no comeback: it was jobs, jobs, travel, travel, till being in airplanes wearied me." She traveled to Europe for appearances in London, Venice, Lisbon and Venice. "But my performances were unstable," she said. "I was moving around in a neurotic haze, having spasms before or after singing, sneaking in drinks, taking pills to dehydrate myself."

In March, she appeared on television on the game show "You Don't Say." As scattered club dates came in, Dorothy braced herself. But the familiar fears and doubts returned. With expenses to be paid to arrangers, designers, back-up musicians, she still struggled to simply break even on engagements. Her hassles with the IRS had not ended either. Every incoming penny, she said, had to go to them.

"Finally, when friends, physicians, and lawyers managed to convey to them that I was sick and broke beyond repair," she said, "they put my case in the dead file. Dead file. How true."

Upon hearing of being booked back into Las Vegas at the Flamingo, she felt more relieved than excited in finally having a chance to work at a major club on the Strip. When she learned that newcomer Nancy Wilson was set to appear at the Flamingo's main room and that she instead was relegated to play the lounge at the casino, her disastrous fall on the club circuit was never more apparent. But she had to swallow her pride and accept the engagement.

She began the familiar preparations of selecting gowns and working on musical arrangements. Hired to back her up was a group of musicians that included her old friend pianist Eddie Beale.

Dorothy wondered if she had the stamina to endure the engagement's demands. She also wondered about Denison, who had returned to Las Vegas. For a time, he had continued his attempts for a reconciliation. But once news of her bankruptcy had hit the press, Denison backed off. There was nothing more she could do for him.

Instead Denison maneuvered himself back into business in Las Vegas, opening a restaurant called the Copper Cart. Not a large place, but one that turned a profit.

The thought of being in the same city with Denison made Dorothy jittery. Out of nervousness and her near-desperate need for emotional support, she invited her childhood friend Henriella Dunn to accompany her to Las Vegas. Old friends like Juliette Ball were also invited to attend the opening.

Juliette Ball arrived in Las Vegas with her husband and her sister. Before the performance, they went to Denison's Copper Cart for dinner. Ever the attentive maitre d', he greeted them enthusiastically. Ball informed him that they were in town for Dorothy's opening at the Flamingo, which he knew about. Ball asked if he planned to attend. He said no. Then she asked if he planned to send Dorothy roses.

"No, you send them," he responded.

"He was a real heel," Ball said.

Ball visited Dorothy in her hotel room at the Flamingo before the performance. Then downstairs as she awaited Dorothy's arrival on stage, as she watched the musicians setting up, as she looked around the lounge with its loud flow of people moving in and out, Ball felt very sad. "Because coming from the major room, the lounge was a downer," said Ball. "Only when you play the big room are you in demand. You know that must have hurt. My heart went out to Dottie," said Ball.

But with her chin arched up, Dorothy set out to give the crowd a show. "She was pretty good," said Ball. "She was still gorgeous and sexy. And she tried to perform as if she were back at the Mocambo."

Musician Beale agreed that she could still put a song across and that she had the skills of a stylist. "There is a big difference between singing performers and performing singers. She wasn't a great singer, but she was a good performer. From song to song, her job was to create moods. Each song became a kind of stage play." Good as the performances were, they still weren't great.

"She sang with a jazz group, and you can't expect seven men to play a 15-piece arrangement and make it sound like a 15-piece arrangement," said Beale. "Besides, the lounge can't create the same atmosphere as could be done with Nancy Wilson in the big room. Dorothy had to suffer by comparison."

Afterwards, Dorothy returned to her hotel room depressed and exhausted. Yet she summoned up enough of the old hauteur and glacial cool to greet those friends who came to congratulate her.

"She was an actress to the bitter end," said Juliette Ball. "She never said anything about the evening. About having to play the lounge. Her pride wouldn't let her. She played her part to the hilt like she did when she performed at the big rooms. But you knew in your heart that she couldn't feel very good about it."

She later said she drank heavily during the day and ended up drunk in the evenings as she performed at the Flamingo. She believed the audience knew it, too. The Flamingo management certainly did and threatened to fire her after the third night, but the owner of the Flamingo was an old friend who remembered her from the peak years. Sympathetic to her plight, he interceded with his management people. She finished the engagement.

Producer Herb Rogers, who two years earlier had cast Dorothy in the Highland Park, Illinois, production of *West Side Story*, wanted her to play Julie in a production of *Show Boat*, starring Kathryn Grayson. The musical would inaugurate the Hyatt Music Theatre in Burlingame, California, near San Francisco. Hyatt Hotel owner Don Pritzer had built a sparkling facility with a theatre-in-the-round, then a new type of theatre construction.

Despite Dorothy's previous health problems, Rogers courted her, convinced she could bring a new dimension or perspective to the role. "The role of Julie was usually done by a dark White woman," said Rogers. "There's no reason to do it that way." Agent Ben Pearson recalled, "We finally convinced a fellow in Monterey, California, that the part could be played by a Colored girl as well as White because the part is indeed that of a mulatto. It took a doin'."

Said Rogers, "I felt Dorothy, if anybody, was right for that role, but she had a certain apprehensiveness about playing the part. I had to talk her into it."

She flew into the San Francisco airport where she was met by Rogers. "She was about 41 then, but she looked like she was twenty-one," said Rogers. "Nobody looked better than that woman. Just fabulous."

Rehearsals went well and quickly. "Dorothy was liked and loved by everyone. She had no problems personality-wise," said Rogers. She especially liked Kathryn Grayson, whom she had always respected.

"Dorothy was so talented. A fine actress," said Grayson. "I hadn't met her before *Show Boat*. There are people you meet who you've heard about and you love them immediately. That's how I felt about her. There are other people—many of them—who you meet who you don't love at all. I liked her all the way through the run. She was easy to work with. Everyone loved her. She was a beautiful woman to look at. And inside was beautiful, too. Just a little sad."

The role of Julie, a woman whose life spirals in a downward cycle of despair and degradation once it is revealed she has Negro blood, also affected Dorothy. She was playing a woman whose life and career are destroyed by American racism. Throughout rehearsals, it was the idea of performing in theatre-in-the-round that wracked Dorothy with anxieties. The proximity to the audience reminded her too much of the clubs.

The opening was nonetheless a success. Ruby came to Burlingame to see the production, as did Geri and her son Paul. "I thought she was really good in that one," said Branton. Rogers and Kathryn Grayson concurred. Dorothy pulled it off.

Dorothy and Grayson became friendly. Surprised to learn that Grayson, like herself, loved soul food, Dorothy decided they had to find a restaurant in the area that could prepare them a proper soul food dinner.

"I'm from the South," said Grayson. "So I grew up on soul food. Dorothy just couldn't believe it. She laughed. She had been on the road, and we were both tired of the food you get in hotels. But we did go out and have a soul food dinner. I don't know how but we managed. We had mustard greens, fried chicken, cornbread. Everything. It was a splendid evening."

During the production Grayson didn't detect any problems that Dorothy might be having. But she was aware of Dorothy's torment. "We would sit and talk. And we would hold hands when we talked. She was very sweet, very kind, very considerate. But she was hurting inside."

Dorothy confided some of the ugly details of her marriage to Jack. "I don't think he was particularly kind to her. He seemed to make her unhappy with herself, which is a terrible thing to do to someone. He had done hurtful things to her, and said unbelievably mean things to her. That she told me. But she didn't want sympathy. That was not why she told me anything."

Only "towards the end of the engagement" did Grayson feel Dorothy "was losing her sense of humor." Dorothy didn't say anything to anyone about her discomfort with the theatre. Then her tensions surfaced with a vengeance. Much as had happened during the run of *West Side Story*, one evening she was in "a paralytic state" for hours: she was unable to stand or walk. Producer Rogers called in a physician. Dorothy didn't go on and was replaced by her understudy.

Still, Rogers was puzzled about what was wrong. "She didn't tell me she didn't like theatre-in-the-round. She didn't want to hurt my feelings. It's so intimate with the audience," he said.

"A lot of performers felt that way about theatre-in-the-round," said Herb Rogers's wife Bobbi. "They felt the audience was practically on top of them. It was difficult for other people too."

Her drinking also exacerbated her problems on *Show Boat*. As with *West Side Story*, Rogers saw no concrete evidence of an alcohol problem. Never did he smell alcohol on her breath or see it in her dressing room. But upon learning years later that she had been drinking, he wasn't surprised. It explained many other things about the *West Side Story* disaster.

But Dorothy was not out of *Show Boat* long. "She missed two or three performances. Then she came back and finished the show," said Rogers. "Selflessly, she cared about me. And I cared about her," said Rogers. "She was a good human being. I cared so much about her. She told me some personal things. We had nice chats," he said. "She told me all about her child being in a home, being cared for. She talked about Denison. She also mentioned Poitier and Belafonte. And Preminger. There was so much in her heart. She was just taken advantage of."

Once the show closed, everyone in the production exchanged kisses, addresses, and phone numbers, promising to keep in touch. "I had to go on another tour," said Grayson. "And I meant to get in touch with her. But she changed her number when I returned. So I never talked to her again."

Echoing the feelings of director Laslo Benedek, Rogers recalled, "I only wish I had taken the time to get to know her better. But I didn't. She seemed alone."

Following the engagement, Dorothy, still depressed and sometimes disoriented, spent most of her time secluded in her apartment. Late at night she called friends. Geri. Juliette Ball. Joel Fluellen. Henriella Dunn. Ivan Dixon. Nick Perito. Abby Mann. "She had telephonitis," said Geri. "She was talking to everybody. She talked to her hairdresser. She talked to a lady who worked for her. She was just trying to reach everybody apparently. She just couldn't sleep. So she'd talk to you all hours of the night." The calls were rambling, long, and disturbing to Dorothy's friends.

"She used to call here and sing on the phone to my mother for two or three hours," said Ball. "I could take a shower and come back and she'd still be singing. That was when I knew something was wrong, that she wasn't right."

The first time she called actor Ivan Dixon, he was surprised because he still believed that "Dorothy didn't like me or had no real caring for me as a person. We did a show together and that was about it. I knew it had to be pretty bad for her to be calling me because I was not anybody in her life."

Her calls often came around three in the morning. "It was not so much me talking to her as it was her talking to me. She was the one in need," said Dixon. "There was also that feeling about it that there was just a need for somebody to talk to. She would want to talk for two hours. My wife would wonder like, 'What the heck is she calling you for at this hour of the morning?' It was just weird. I knew that she was going off. We all kind of knew it. I wasn't the only one who knew she was going off. Joel was aware that she was losing it emotionally and psychologically." The topics of her conversation varied.

"I don't think that in her cry, as I would call it, that Dorothy was blaming anybody" for the way her life turned out, Dixon said. "She wasn't saying, 'So-and-so did terrible things to me.' She wasn't doing that. It was like, 'Can I talk to you?' It was like, 'I just want to talk. I'm here alone and there's nobody here.' It was that kind of thing. But she was not attacking people."

Sometimes, Dorothy's calls came two nights in a row. Then Dixon might not hear from her for several weeks. Then again calls would come on three successive nights.

"Her calling gave me a sense of real terrible loneliness and frustration. She said a lot of things that were personal, but I don't even remember what they were. I'd talk to her and listen to her. But I'm one of those people. I'm a listener anyway."

"She was almost at the point of incoherence sometimes," said Dixon. "She was reaching for friends," he said. "Either her friends had given up on her or whatever, that she wasn't able to call them in the middle of the night."

Dixon never refused a call or hung up on her. "I guess I understood it," he said. "I understood that she needed that. And that something was wrong." Dorothy's instincts had served her well. She liked

Ivan Dixon better than he realized. "The only one I spoke to about it was Joel," said Dixon, "and of course, my wife because she was there."

Joel Fluellen would hear from her in particularly strange and troubling ways. Once in the early hours of the morning a panicky Dorothy phoned and asked him to come over immediately. Someone had taken her broiler out of her kitchen. "Dorothy, how could they have taken the broiler away?" he asked.

But crying and nearly hysterical, she pleaded that he come over. When he arrived, the broiler was still on the kitchen stove.

As time went on, when her early morning calls came, Fluellen sometimes talked to her. Other times he didn't.

She also called Nick Perito in New York. She sang tunes to him and asked for suggestions about various music. "We're going to go back and do 'The Sullivan Show,'" she told Perito. "And we're going to do some new arrangements."

"She sounded like she was high," said Perito. "We spoke for almost an hour. And on a previous occasion she had spoken with my wife Judy for almost the same length of time with the same kind of attitude. Very up. Very excited about the future." But he knew she was very unhappy.

Pearl Bailey also heard from her. "In 1964 she used to telephone me at intervals for some months," said Bailey. "I couldn't figure out why, because I didn't think we'd ever become real close—at least not to the point of going to parties or visiting each other's home."

On one occasion years earlier, Dorothy had attended a party at the ranch of Bailey and her husband Louie Bellson. But otherwise, through the years Dorothy "would avoid me in a strange way," said Bailey. The truth was that Dorothy, aware of Bailey's petty jealousies and also remembering the hassles Bailey had caused when they worked together, knew it was best to keep her distance. But now her desperation had taken over.

"Some people were bugged by her," Ivan Dixon recalled. Sometimes they were rude and short with her. Others were critical and cruel. Some, of course, having always been jealous, were happy to see her decline and, while feigning sympathy, relished the fact that the woman who once appeared to have everything now was so openly vulnerable and unhappy.

Geri saw the animosity of some supposed friends of Dorothy. One such woman, who Dorothy had known for years, immediately called Geri after hanging up on Dorothy. "What's wrong with that friend of yours?" she asked. She advised Geri to tell her friend to get herself together.

Geri defended Dorothy and ended the conversation—but not before giving the woman a piece of her mind. "Dorothy was betrayed by the very people she had in the past often tried to help. The very people who had been calling Dorothy to help them find work." Geri preferred that Dorothy not talk to such people. Yet she understood Dorothy's pain. During her calls to Geri, Dorothy's loneliness showed.

"Can I come over and cook dinner for you all?" she would ask.

"I wish I had somebody in the house who would just flush a toilet every once in awhile. I'm so lonely."

"Dottie, I know people would just love to be with you," Geri said.

Then Dorothy's voice rose in a panic, "I don't want them! I don't want them!"

Sometimes she sang "All of Me," said Geri, "Or she sang 'People who love People.' And she sang probably better than I had ever heard her sing. But she sang it with such feeling. And it implied her loneliness. Her loneliness down through the years."

Often she was enveloped in a dreamy haze that grew into a deep, heavy, impenetrable fog that blinded her to anything that might lie ahead, that permitted her only to look behind, to see what had already transpired and could not be altered.

Like a drowning woman, she appeared to be reliving her life, in search of its meaning or the beauty or the pain of the key moments; studying the missteps; analyzing the disappointments and the failures. Often it still led back to the birth of Lynn.

One night, Dorothy phoned the Camarillo State Institution to check on Lynn, insisting that Lynn should play piano and have dance lessons. She also asked that the hospital not let Lynn overeat. It was important that her weight be kept down. Finally, Dorothy said, the hospital threatened to return Lynn if she caused any further problems or disruptions.

Then her fantasies and disorientation became ever more serious. Concerned about her debts, Dorothy called Geri one day, sounding upbeat.

"Geri, I'm going to be able to pay you everything," Dorothy said. "I'm going to pay off everything. Ford Motor Company just signed me for a commercial and I'm getting $40,000."

"Dottie, you know that makes me happy. But we're not worried about you paying your debts. You'll pay your debts."

"Oh, no, that stays on my mind all the time. I've always taken care of myself since age six. And I just have to continue to take care of myself," Dorothy said.

"When are you going?"

"I'm leaving now."

"Oh, that's wonderful."

Twenty minutes later, Geri's telephone rang again.

"I'm back," Dorothy said on the other end. "And I have the check. I did the commercial."

Sadly, Geri realized that there never had been a commercial; that Dorothy, so desperate now, was whirling in reveries of success and regeneration. Sometimes Dorothy mailed Geri a check to pay off loans. "It was no good," said Geri. "But it was a check."

In desperate straits for money and work, Dorothy signed a $10,000 contract to write her autobiography for publisher Bernard Geis. Her comments were expected to be explicit and uncensored. Of particular interest was her affair with Otto. Having guarded her privacy as closely as Garbo and having even found interviews painful because of personal questions, she was now in a position where her very survival depended on revealing the intimate details of her life. Writer Earl Conrad, who had co-authored Errol Flynn's tell-all autobiography *My Wicked, Wicked Ways*, was signed to assist her.

Believing that Dorothy was being exploited all over again, Geri warned her, "Dottie, you can't do this." But Dorothy refused to listen.

"We had such a severe disagreement. That was one of the few serious disagreements we ever had," said Geri. "She went to my husband Leo's office with Earl" to discuss the contract. "Leo threw them out of the office. He couldn't dream of her doing anything like this."

While working on the autobiography, Dorothy remained in a terrible state. Still drinking too much and taking medication, which frequently left her disoriented, her occasional comments about sex, which she hadn't discussed in the past were totally out of character for her. Other times, said Geri, she "told a whole bunch of stuff that wasn't true because she wanted to get that book published. And it was just wrong. Just wrong."

Once Dorothy "did make the error of making tapes" of her supposed experiences, said Geri, she found herself viciously victimized. Geri said the co-writer, Conrad "was a dreadful, dreadful man."

Stories spread that copies of the tapes were sold at Hollywood parties. Party guests huddled about to hear the sexy details, often bursting into laughter or making crude remarks. Geri recalled, "Somebody who went, said they walked out. They were so disgusted." Even at that, Earl Mills, who favored the autobiography, recalled that Conrad didn't work much with Dorothy. Later it appeared as if he simply added stories of his own. Much of the material in the posthumously published autobiography, titled appropriately enough, *Everything and Nothing*, would be a mishmash of fact and fantasy.

Time periods were shifted about. In some instances, one movie experience, *Tamango*, was mistaken for another, *Malaga*. Nick Perito was mistakenly identified as the accompanist in South America with Dorothy, rather than Morty Jacobs. Accounts of her marriage to Harold, while sometimes striking a true note, also seemed the fabrication of the writer. Years later Nicholas was appalled and angered by some of the misleading information on him. The aspect of *Everything and Nothing* with a near ring of truth was the tone and mood in some passages of a desperate, frightened woman. Some of her comments on the tensions of her early childhood years on the road and the dilemmas facing Black women in White America also struck a poignant and truthful note. Occasionally, she also appeared to touch truthfully on her relationships with Preminger and Belafonte, though without enough elaboration. Otherwise the book served to distort, even cheapen and trash her, for a later generation.

"This Conrad book was vicious," said Geri. "But she was out of her head."

During this time, she struck almost everyone who knew her as being all the more hopelessly lost. Sometimes she wandered alone through her neighborhood. She stopped at various small restaurants where she might have a cup of coffee and sit silently. Then she might ask to speak to the chef. Surprisingly, people were patient with her. Her beauty still gave her certain privileges. But as she spoke, her confusion showed. Usually, she was able to persuade the restaurants to give her food to take home.

Other times Dorothy maintained her old façade. She and Juliette Ball sometimes went out for dinner together. Always Ball drove. "Dottie wasn't driving then," Ball recalled. "I had to pick her up all the time." Other times they went to designer showcase presentations. Many times they just sat in the apartment on Fountain Avenue.

"She would reminisce about past times," said Ball, "about the days when Marilyn used to come up to her place on Hilldale and talk and cry about her boyfriends. The days when Ava used to go up to Hilldale and cry too." Ball added, "Dottie didn't seem depressed because she put up a hell of a front. I knew it was a front, though, because her furniture in the living room had disintegrated. And Dottie was such a perfectionist that she would have never tolerated that in the past."

With Herb Jeffries, who also visited her on Fountain Avenue, Dandridge was more open. "It was so shocking that someone of that early age of her life would just black-out, would never have a chance to finish what she wanted to do."

On rare occasions when she went out, she could be an embarrassment for those around her. One evening she showed up at a local jazz joint. At first she sat listening intently to the jazz musicians performing, several of whom she knew, including the headliner. Her head bopped. Her feet tapped. Then she rose from her seat and went to the bandstand. She had decided to perform a number with them.

The entire audience, by now aware that it was Dorothy Dandridge who was behaving so strangely, felt uneasy. "The band did not want to be bothered," said an observer. Some patrons were quietly groaning. But Dorothy, clearly "out of it," joined the band and performed a song. Afterwards the bandleader managed to get her offstage. But word spread of similar incidents.

"She was just going around to clubs and asking friends to let her get on the bandstand and sing a couple of numbers," said Ivan Dixon. "This last period of her life was a terrible time. Terrible to watch. I mean it was almost, in a sense, how can I say it?—almost groveling. It was sad. Something was happening with her mind. But no one seemed able to do anything."

Then there were the nights when, either out of need or loneliness or despair, she drifted into the arms of men. While appearing at the few club engagements that were booked, she was still pursued by men. Often drinking and always depressed, she admitted that while in Toronto for an engagement her morale was so low "that I no longer cared what I did. I threw myself away on a few men, thinking I might as well have an orgasm as there isn't much else. But I didn't succeed. It was an escape or a lapse alien to my real self, and it served only to deepen my self-loathing. If you acquire enough of that, you can hasten an exit off any stage."

Stories also sprang up of her dalliance with a handsome young bisexual bartender who had once worked at a posh New York supper club. There he had seen her at her height, surrounded by the likes of Preminger, MCA founder Jules Stein, and any number of other powerful and wealthy men who fawned and fought over her. Having had long fantasized about her, he ran into her at a party in Los Angeles where he had recently moved. She appeared not even to know where she was. But soon the two became lovers. No one who heard the story could quite accept or believe it. But the tale took wings and became part of the oncoming dramatic tragedy that so many were hearing about.

In February, 1965, Dorothy was shaken upon learning that Nat Cole had died of cancer at age 45. Too much seemed to be slipping away. Some of Hollywood's biggest names—Sammy Davis, Jr., Frank Sinatra, Jack Benny, George Burns, and Peter Lawford—attended the funeral. Although in terrible emotional shape, Dorothy had also planned to attend. But she became all the more upset and disturbed because a friend had advised her not to go to the funeral; that she was not in stable enough emotional shape to be with people grieving over a loss. Finally, though, later in the day, she had another friend drive her to the Cole home in Hancock Park where friends and family had gathered. Entering the house, she was as frail and frightened, as jittery and disoriented, as she had been at the funeral of Phil Moore's mother.

"She looked very sad, confused, and lost," Maria Cole remembered. "She was dressed all in black."

Geri Branton understood why Dorothy had been advised not to attend to the Cole funeral. "She was just out of it," said Branton, "Saying things. Maria was so upset herself that she didn't realize that Dottie was in a bad way."

Not long afterwards, Dorothy heard from Harold and Fayard, who had returned to the States. Their lives had undergone great changes in the past ten years. While living in Paris, Harold had married a French woman, Elyanne Patronne, who bore him a son, Meli. The marriage ended in divorce. Fayard also remarried a woman, Vicky Barron, with whom he and Harold performed. After having worked apart as a duo for several years, the brothers were working together again and preparing for an engagement at the Thunderbird in Las Vegas. She invited them over for a visit.

Neither was prepared for what he saw. Familiar with her problems, having read the newspaper accounts of the divorce and bankruptcy, Harold and Fayard nonetheless remembered her as Dottie, the sweet-tempered teenager; the young bride and mother; the girl whose heart never mended after learning of Lynn's condition. Their only other image of her was as the glamorous international star of *Carmen Jones*.

Upon entering her apartment on Fountain Avenue, they found a wistful, sad-eyed woman, who looked older and a little heavier. She was still a beauty. "But she didn't have that flair that came out when things were going good for her," Harold remembered. Eager to make them comfortable, but clearly out of sorts, her loneliness and nervousness were unmistakable. She "had been drinking a little bit," said Harold, which surprised him because "I never knew her as a drinker." She offered them drinks, as well. Fayard felt she was also on some type of medication. She talked incessantly.

"She was thinking about her career. What was happening," said Harold. "She talked about her manager and all that stuff. I remember that she was disturbed about her situation. That I could see."

Hoping to boost her spirits, they invited her to Vegas during the engagement at the Thunderbird starting in mid-March through late May. "I want you to come up," said Harold softly. He promised to send her tickets.

Not long afterwards, friends detected a serious breach in Dorothy's relationship with Joel Fluellen. "Dorothy had weaned Joel from her," Juliette Ball recalled. "Something had happened. She was not as close to him."

The truth was that Dorothy felt betrayed by him. Fluellen spoke to Ruby often about Dorothy, harshly urging her to face the facts about her daughter. Dorothy, said Fluellen, was an alcoholic.

Though long aware of Dorothy's drinking, Ruby was taken aback by Fluellen's frankness. Joel had finally confirmed what Ruby feared. When her companion heard the news, she appeared happy to have ammunition to fire against Dorothy. She urged Ruby to cut Dorothy off altogether.

Finally, Ruby confronted Dorothy. Was it true what Joel had said, that she was an alcoholic? There followed a painful and embarrassing conversation with Ruby that climaxed with Ruby, in a torrent of criticism, completely losing her temper and shouting that Dorothy had to do something to piece her life together.

Afterwards Dorothy, upset and crying, warned Geri about Fluellen's hypocrisy. "Watch out for Joel," she said. "Joel is not a true friend. Joel is a very mean person. He talks about you. And he talks about me. And what he did, I can never forgive. I'll go to my grave not forgiving him."

"What is that?" Geri asked.

"He told my mother that I was an alcoholic. I don't think that's right. He never discussed it with me. And yet he told my mother. And my mother is screaming and all upset."

At that point, Dorothy broke off her relationship with Joel. In later years Fluellen never wanted to admit to anyone that Dorothy, at the end, had felt betrayed by him. "He just did not want to own up to it," said Geri. "But she was through with Joel."

Dorothy, however, tried to patch up the dispute with Ruby.

"When Dottie went up to her mother's, they practically put her out and didn't help her at all," said Branton. "Ruby Jean's companion didn't want Dottie around. That hurt her."

For Geri, Ruby's behavior was heartless and inexcusable. Here was the daughter who for years had sent money home to her mother, who spoke with her mother daily, who showered her mother with gifts, who still sought her mother's love and approval; here was that daughter at a time when she needed some sign of sympathy or sensitivity from her mother, at a time when such sympathy might have helped her regain her footing. Instead she found herself once more rejected by her mother. "Ruby failed Dottie," said Geri. "She failed her completely. She failed her every single time."

"But Dottie continued her relationship with her mother," said Branton. "She had a thing about her mother like you can't believe. She still loved her mother."

During this time, Dorothy was also visited by Otto, who was both saddened and angered by her living conditions. "The last time I saw her, she was almost penniless," he said.

Had Dorothy but asked, Otto no doubt would have helped her. Though he could be mean and foul-tempered, Preminger was also generous and had a sentimental streak he didn't like to show, yet which could be tapped.

"He was bitter," said Geri, "but he cared." Dorothy, however, still resentful, wanted nothing from Otto.

Then Dorothy took ill.

"She seemed totally out of it," said Geri, alarmed that Dorothy might never recover and be her old self. "She'd sometimes get so nervous. She couldn't reason. She was just out of sorts."

When Geri spoke to a new psychiatrist that Dorothy was seeing, he told her point blank, "Well, I can't do anything for her. She can't pay me."

Finally, she was hospitalized. Said Earl Mills, "She had an acute anemic condition, was deeply angry, bitter, hostile, over-sensitive, drinking heavily. She was constantly at the doctor's." *Ebony* reported that Dorothy's hospitalization was "for rest and treatment of an acute anemic condition and her mental attitude was not brightened by a laboratory technician's premature—and later found erroneous—revelation that medical tests indicated she was possibly suffering from leukemia." But the primary reason for Dandridge's hospitalization was her severe depression, which led to an almost complete emotional breakdown.

Another psychiatrist had insisted that she be checked into the hospital for rest, observation, and rehabilitation. During this time, Geri believed, the antidepressant drug Tofranil was prescribed for her.

"It acted like the drug Prozac," said Geri, "and it appeared to help her regain some semblance of normalcy. She was really on a high. Very easy to reason with. And she wasn't climbing the wall."

Leaving the hospital, Dorothy resolved to put herself on a new regime to regain her health and her peace of mind. Still unhappy with the slight weight gain and the retention of water, she returned to an exercise schedule, although it remained difficult for her to focus. Fortifying herself with iron pills and vitamins, she also daily took prescribed medications, including the Tofranil.

"I persuaded Dorothy to leave the doctor," said Mills, "who was too eager to give her a pill for everything and after finding out how bad her health was, we both went to Rancho La Puerta, a marvelous health ranch in Mexico. At the ranch she ate organic food, exercised daily and slept long peaceful hours."

Still devoted, Mills spoke to her every day and was often at her apartment. Close to Ruby, he said he'd been asked by her to stay at times at Dorothy's apartment to make sure everything was all right.

"He was very good about going over there to see about her comfort," said Geri. "Earl played a significant [part] in that what she planned for herself, he would carry it through. He was good about that. That cannot be denied."

But Dorothy's friends vehemently denied other comments that Mills later made about his relationship with Dandridge, namely that while with her at the health farm Rancho La Puerta, "We became lovers." Though Dandridge herself admitted to other casual flings, those close to her argued that she never would have become involved in a sexual/romantic relationship with Mills. It was the one story about her most tragic years that those closest to her became angriest about. Most were aware of his dogged devotion to her and also of his desire for her. Most were aware too of Dorothy: the type of men she was drawn to; the attitude she always had about Mills. Nick Perito said, "When Earl said that he and Dorothy became lovers, I have to look at that with a grain of salt because I don't think that this in fact was ever true."

Geri concurred, "I must be very adamant and say that's not true [that Earl became Dorothy's lover]." She added that Dorothy considered him a wimp. "He adored her. He absolutely worshiped her. Angel Face [was what he called her]. But it was disgusting. Have you ever had a love affair where somebody worships you—and will do anything for you but you can't stand them? He was just obsessed with her. And he saw the relationship as he wanted to see it. That was his fantasy. And believe me, it was a fantasy."

In later years when Vivian Dandridge resurfaced, she became infuriated by the stories of a sexual liaison between Mills and Dorothy. "I wasn't there with my sister at the end," said Vivian. "I know she had many problems. But my sister never, no matter how upset and confused she might have been, could have had anything to do with him in that way. No way. Never."

Juliette Ball echoed the same sentiments. So, too, did Phil Moore. Mills's comment drew such heated responses because many felt it was one more form of exploitation of Dandridge.

Some work came in. In April, she flew to Puerto Rico for an engagement at the Carnival Room of the Sheraton Hotel. The reception was good. Mills believed Dorothy might be able to pull herself back up. Later she performed in Tokyo and also travelled to Mexico where she performed in a one-hour television special. She talked to Phil Moore about working together again.

Those who saw her during this period were always moved and later haunted by the vision of this lovely but lost specter, who still had the power to suggest poetic grandeur. Arriving at airports, she could strike one of two poses. Either she moved quickly with the head lowered and wrapped in a scarf so as not to be seen. Or she held the head high with eyes glazed in an effort to recapture the hauteur of the glory days. Yet she needed medication to function. Without the Tofranil, she couldn't maintain her equilibrium, although it may have made her look puffy at times.

Her great difficulty was the auditions: the idea of having to prove herself all over again drained her. Pearl Bailey recalled the day she ran into Dorothy at an audition for a film.

Both Bailey and Dorothy were up for the same role and had a wardrobe fitting together for a screen test. "The next day we had the test," said Bailey. But Dorothy was still confused and disoriented. "She held my face in her hands and she said, 'If I don't get the part, I hope you do.'"

Struggling to be optimistic, Dorothy told Bailey of "visions of great pictures she was to make." But she couldn't sustain the optimistic delusion for long before the cracks showed.

Later Bailey sent Dorothy mustard seeds with a message. "These are positive. Spread them around. And don't be sad."

"This was truly a girl of simple tastes, who was put on that pedestal our business is famous for," said Bailey. "Instead of telling her some of the things that were not quite right, telling her when she was famous and strong enough to get knocked down, some waited—until it was too late."

Aware of Bailey's past treatment of Dorothy, Geri wondered if it were guilt on Bailey's part that led her to send the mustard seeds. Or if it were perhaps something else, the actions of a woman relieved that Dorothy was no longer a rival.

Nichelle Nichols also recalled the day she interviewed for the role of a nun who would be the sidekick to the star Debbie Reynolds in the movie *The Singing Nun*. Other young Black actresses of this new era were being interviewed also. "Cicely Tyson was considered for the role," said Nichols. "So was Leslie Uggams." And Pearl Bailey, whom, said Nichols, the studio and the star favored.

Upon her arrival for the reading at MGM, Nichols had just parked her car and was heading for the building when she heard a voice call out to her.

"Nichelle. Nichelle."

She turned. Behind her was a car with a man in the driver's seat. On the passenger side was a woman who had rolled down the window and was calling her.

"Nichelle. It's Dorothy. Hi, darling," she said in that soft, smoky voice.

Nichols almost didn't recognize Dorothy at first. "She did not look well," said Nichols. Her face was puffy and bloated. Learning that Dorothy had gone in on the same call for the role of the sidekick nun, Nichols was "surprised and shocked." But coming out of Dorothy "was such a sweetness."

"Oh, Nichelle, darling. Good luck in there," Dorothy told her. "I hope you get it."

Dorothy kissed her lightly. Then she waved and the car took off.

"My saddest memory was seeing her at MGM Studios that day," said Nichols. "That was the saddest. To think she was auditioning for this role after all she had had."

Once Harold and Fayard opened at the Thunderbird in Las Vegas, Harold was true to his word. "I called her and invited her up," he said. Fayard, however, recalled that it was Dorothy who phoned Harold. Nicholas sent her airline tickets and made arrangements for her to stay at a hotel. The trip to Vegas—to see Harold—perhaps marked her final struggle to come to terms with the past; maybe even to rework it. Neither she nor Harold were in love with one another. Yet Harold meant something to her; he represented a period in her life when she still had hoped; he also remained the one man she had let herself love completely and at first unconditionally.

Upon her arrival in Vegas, she still turned heads. "We met her at the airport," said Fayard. "And she came in and she looked so beautiful." Harold and Fayard were both pleased that she still was a knockout because it meant she hadn't lost interest in herself, hadn't given up.

But despite that outer gloss, Dorothy was still not herself, still seemed withdrawn, languid, listless, unable to focus. It wasn't alcohol that caused the detachment. "She didn't drink much then," said Harold. "No. In fact, she didn't even want to go out to a nightclub, you know, to have a drink or something."

Instead she still relied on medication to coast her through a day, to keep her upright with all the pieces in place. "She was taking a lot of those pills, I think to calm herself down or something like that," said Fayard. "They were mild. They weren't a strong type of thing." When he asked what the pills were for, she told him that she "was taking these pills that the doctor gave her a prescription for."

But Fayard found it hard to keep a conversation with her. When she wasn't nervous, she appeared preoccupied. Or numbed. Or spaced. "She would start talking to us about something and then all of a sudden, she wouldn't finish what she was saying to us and go talk about something else," Fayard recalled.

"She looked like she would go into a trance or something. She'd be talking and all of a sudden, she'd sit down and just sit and stare. So I'd look at her and see what was happening with her and then she'd come back. But I didn't say anything to her. Cause I said, well, maybe she has something on her mind. And then that's when I knew, maybe it was those pills that she was taking that caused the different moods. I tried to keep her jolly and happy. If I saw that she was going off or something, I'd say, 'Come on, Dottie, let's go here and see so and so.' And she'd snap out of it and get back into her old self."

"But I knew something was wrong because she never did act that way when I knew her earlier," said Fayard. "When we first met her, she was full of life and wanted to have a good time. But the last time I saw her, she was depressed or something. She wasn't really herself, the Dorothy Dandridge that I knew years before. But I didn't say anything to her. And my brother didn't say anything to her either. We just knew that something was wrong."

During her time in Vegas, she showed little interest in socializing, preferring instead to stay closeted in her hotel room.

At Harold's urging, she attended a performance of the group The Treniers in the Thunderbird lounge. The crowded, smoky room, with the sounds of slot machines ringing in the background, of people talking and laughing, was the familiar club atmosphere that now summoned up memories of past triumphs and current failures. Sitting in the audience, she did not want to be noticed, observed, or scrutinized. She didn't want to be Dorothy Dandridge. Instead she longed to remain in privacy, to get away from the noise, the people, the activity.

From the stage The Treniers introduced Fayard and Harold in the audience. "Stand up, brothers," they said. Harold and Fayard stood and took a bow. Then, aware that Dorothy was at the table with the brothers, the Treniers announced, "We want to introduce you to a beautiful little girl. She's sitting out there with the Nicholas Brothers. Dorothy Dandridge!" Uncomfortable and self-conscious, Dorothy stood and smiled.

"Later The Treniers came over to our table," said Fayard. "She talked to them. Everything was fine. She didn't withdraw into another world. As long as there were a lot of people talking, she was fine. She had the public personality at that time."

But once the social amenities were over, she was eager to leave the club and return to the safety of her hotel room. She remained self-conscious and restless; as if she believed herself the subject of gossip and speculation about her emotional and financial state; the object of prying, judgmental eyes.

Finally, she informed Harold that she was going back to her room. But there was something she wanted to talk about, she said. Reluctantly, he accompanied her to do her room where the two talked a bit. She seemed to have a great deal on her mind but wasn't able to express it. Troubled by her behavior, Harold urged her to socialize more. But Dorothy remained adamant about keeping to herself.

"She just wanted to stay in the hotel," said Nicholas. "And I was trying to get her out and see if I could get that life back into her because she was becoming a loner."

"No, I don't want to go out," she told Harold. "I don't feel like it."

"Well, what's the matter? Why don't you want to go out?" he asked. "People want to see you. They want to look at you."

"Oh, no, I don't...."

He realized she was despondent but continued to press her about getting out more. Then to his surprise, the discussion became heated and escalated. Before either realized it, the conversation had turned heavy and serious, full of recriminations.

"We got into a big thing," Harold remembered.

He told her, "Come on. Go out. And get off of it. Get yourself together."

Then, unable to control herself, Dorothy started crying. The argument must have struck her as being like so many others that had occurred so many years earlier. Just when she wanted somehow to alter something from the past, maybe in her current state of mind, to somehow redress what she perceived as her wrongs and mistakes, somehow, as she had told Abby Mann, to make up for not having given the marriage or Harold enough of a chance. But she found herself locked in the same old battle, the same predicament, the same frustrations. Hoping perhaps to come to terms with Harold, she didn't want them to go through life still misunderstanding each other. But that didn't happen.

Harold left her alone in the room that night.

Later Fayard said, "I think she didn't want to go out 'cause she wanted to spend more time with him. That's why she didn't want to go out. I don't think it was because she didn't like people. I think she did like people. But she wanted to spend more time with him and didn't want to go out. But he wanted to get out. In her way, I think, she still loved him. But she could never forget the things that he did. I don't think she would ever forget that. She still loved him. I think so."

The next day, Dorothy and Fayard sat in a restaurant, waiting for Harold. Not yet having given up, she wanted to try to talk to him again. It was her last attempt to reach him and thus reach herself.

Briefly, Harold joined Dorothy and Fayard. Then, recalled Fayard, Harold said, "Well, I got to leave you guys now. I got to go play some golf. I have an appointment to play some golf."

Dorothy looked at him and asked, "Why are you leaving us? What's the matter?" She reminded him, "I came here to see you."

"Well, I have this appointment and I got to go," Fayard remembered Harold saying. "I'll see you a little later."

Harold then departed, leaving Dorothy alone with Fayard.

Distressed she turned to Fayard and angrily said, "I don't like this. I came here especially to see him. And he's running off playing golf."

"Well, you and I," Fayard told her gently, "we'll find something to do."

He tried to cheer her up. "But it didn't help. It didn't help," he remembered.

Dorothy decided to leave the restaurant and return to her hotel. He took her back.

"I'll see you a little later," he said.

When he thought she might have calmed down, he called her.

"Well, how are things?" he asked.

"I still don't feel good. He shouldn't treat me like that."

"Well, what are you going to do?"

She said, "I'm going back to Los Angeles."

"No, don't go back. Wait until he comes."

"No, I'm going back," she said. "I've got my ticket."

Realizing she was determined to leave Vegas, Fayard offered to take her to the airport. "I'm gonna take you there," he said.

"No, I've got a taxi. I'm gone."

And she left Vegas alone.

On her flight out of Vegas to Los Angeles, she saw Marlene Dietrich. On this day, the sometimes frank, sometimes snobbish Dietrich was warmer. The two women talked. Dorothy even discussed some of her problems. Loving to play mother hen, Dietrich offered advice. Yet perhaps in her drug-induced state, Dorothy was fascinated not by Dietrich's conversation but by her face. The actress looked as if she'd had had so many facelifts that her skin had become a tight, immobile mask that Dorothy couldn't stop staring at.

Later that day in Las Vegas, Fayard informed Harold, "Dottie's gone."

"Why did she leave?" Harold asked.

"You know why she left. You know exactly why she left."

"What did I do?" Harold asked.

"What did you do? You left her there with me and you went off playing golf. She came here especially to see you."

Years later Fayard commented that Harold "wasn't really a bad man. But he just had this love for golf and it seems as though that was his first love." But the argument in Vegas proved to be one of the great regrets of Harold's life. "We were mad at each other. And the next day, she left. Without letting me know, actually. She left and went on back to L. A. And when I heard about her again, she was gone. The most important and horrible thing was that I never got a chance to apologize to her, you know, for being angry and talking to her the way I did. That kind of tore me up."

Neither Fayard nor Harold ever saw Dorothy again.

Back in Los Angeles, her anger hadn't abated. She talked to Geri about the way Harold had treated her. The trip had been a complete fiasco. Quickly, she slipped back into her reclusiveness, seldom venturing out, mostly, still talking on the phone into the early morning hours.

Then, oddly, unexpectedly, came the prospect of new engagements. There would be a booking at a club in Albuquerque, New Mexico, the first of three engagements that Mills had set up in small clubs in the Southwest. Mills had also been contacted by an Englishman named York Noble, who was living in Mexico and wanted Dorothy for a film he planned to produce. A trip to Mexico was hastily scheduled for Dorothy and Mills to discuss the project.

Bent on engineering a comeback for Dorothy, Joe Glaser also secured a booking for her at the New York club Basin Street East. It formerly had been La Vie En Rose, which, of course, she had saved from bankruptcy years before. Now perhaps the club could save her. The engagement was set to begin on September 10th.

As she threw herself into rehearsals and an exercise regime, and took pains to stay focused, Watts—in August 1965—went up in flames in one of the worst civil disorders in the history of America. The nation was in the midst of the growing Black Power movement with calls for Black nationalism and cultural separatism. For Dorothy, the flames of Watts must have seemed like a surreal occurrence.

But on she went. Dorothy contacted her former accompanist Morty Jacobs, whom she hoped to persuade to accompany her at the Albuquerque engagement. In New York for the funeral of his father, Jacobs was surprised to hear from her. "I don't know how she got hold of me," he recalled. But she was insistent that he work with her again. Overcome with grief, he suggested they speak another time. But Dorothy wouldn't be put off.

"I need you badly," she told him.

"There's no way, honey," he tried to explain.

"You must," she said.

"Sweetheart, I can't. If there's such a thing as impossible in the world."

"Oh, Morty, please."

"Sweetheart, my father died. I'm here. We're taking my mother up to my brother's home in Stamford."

But Dottie persisted, "You can't go. You've got to come with us."

"No, honey, I'm not going to do it. I can't go."

"You don't know what you're doing to me," she told him.

Finally, he pleaded with her, "Look, honey, please, *please* let me off the hook. I can't insult the family, my mother, and the whole idea of the memory of my dad. I can't."

Finally, Dorothy said, "Okay." Then she hung up.

Another accompanist was found.

Feeling stronger and looking fit, she performed well at the Paddock Supper Club in Albuquerque. She had "received the most enthusiastic audience reaction of her entire career" with "standing ovations after each show," *Ebony* later reported. The audience may simply have been thrilled at seeing Dorothy Dandridge back on her feet again. Yet it was a promising start. Having regained some of her powers of concentration, she had not let her doubts overcome her. But then came a blow. A fire broke out at the club in Albuquerque. The engagement was cut short.

Dorothy returned to Los Angeles. She began preparations for the Basin Street East engagement. Again new arrangements had to be developed. New York also required an eye-catching wardrobe. And an eye-catching figure. Neither the press nor the critics would settle for anything less than a Dorothy Dandridge who was a knockout beauty. In some ways, it was the same old story. It might not matter so much what she sang as how she looked. But to be in the best shape for the engagement, which clearly could mark a real career comeback, she worked out at a nearby gym.

She also spoke to Jacobs's wife Madeline, discussing her plans for new engagements and her trip to Mexico, and no doubt still hoping to persuade Morty to return as her accompanist. "We were to have lunch together when she got back," said Madeline.

Some of her former optimism seemed to return. Yet she remained too much the fatalist to have any lasting, long-range visions or hopes about the future. Shortly before Dorothy's trip to Mexico, Herb Jeffries visited her on Fountain Avenue. "She was still beautiful. But you could see the stress," he said. "I saw the sadness." Like the big brother he'd been to her during *Jump for Joy*, Jeffries listened, encouraged her, and tried to make her laugh. About to make a trip, Jeffries promised to talk to her upon his return.

At the end of August, having cut down on the liquor but still relying on the antidepressant Tofranil, Dorothy prepared for Mexico. "But in the last conversation," said Geri Branton, "she didn't mention that at all."

Instead she told her friend, "I'm tired. I'm really tired."

On September 3rd, Dorothy went to the gym to exercise, but she was preoccupied. The day before—September 2nd—had been Lynn's birthday. Her little girl had turned twenty-two. For Dorothy, those were twenty-two lost years that could not be recovered.

"She doesn't even know that I'm her mother," she had conceded to a reporter. "She only knows that she likes me and I like her."

At the gym, while walking down a flight of stairs, she tripped and turned her ankle. Pain shot through her right foot. Returning home that evening, she assumed the pain would pass and continued the last-minute preparations for Mexico. But her foot still ached at the end of the night.

The next day, Dorothy and Earl Mills boarded the flight for Oaxaca, Mexico. Upon her arrival, her spirits lifted. In Latin America, she remained a star.

Most importantly, the movie talks began with Britisher York Noble and Mexican producer Raul Fernandez at the latter's large estate. There she toured the grounds and dined with Fernandez, his daughter Laura, Noble, and their associates. Turning on the charm, she posed with them for photographs. So impressed were Noble and Fernandez that, having originally considered her for one role, they signed her instead for two movies. She would be paid $50,000 for each. Not a top-dollar salary. But not a bad one either, especially considering that she had been paid $75,000 for *Porgy and Bess*. The trip had been a success.

Yet the pain in her foot continued, making her so uncomfortable that it was arranged for her to see a physician, who examined her foot. An x-ray revealed the probability of a tiny bone fracture. She was advised to have the foot set in a cast upon her return to California, scheduled for the next day.

On September 7th, Dorothy departed—seemingly in an upbeat mood—with Mills for Los Angeles. Maybe life did have second acts. Maybe there was a future ahead. Having always felt she had failed and rarely crediting herself with her accomplishments, she could take comfort in the fact that in Mexico she had dazzled them all over again. Maybe Dorothy Dandridge was still Dorothy Dandridge. Yet she no doubt was nagged by questions of what a return to the top meant; how much energy and stamina it required; what it offered; where it led.

Immediately upon her arrival in Los Angeles, Dorothy was driven to the hospital to have her foot examined by her personal physician and an orthopedic specialist. Another x-ray confirmed the tiny bone fracture. Dorothy was told to return to the hospital the next morning to have the break set and the cast put on.

But Dorothy grew anxious about her engagement at Basin Street East. Would this mishap delay the New York trip? Would this injury interfere with her ability to move about during the performance?

Her physician assured her, "You will be able to dance on your feet 24 hours after the cast is on." Mills drove her back to the apartment on Fountain Avenue. He promised to pick her up bright and early— at 7:30 a.m.—for the appointment with the doctor. In her apartment, Dorothy opened trunks and suitcases, gathered personal items, leafed through photographs, all in preparation for the trip East. That next day she was also scheduled to meet at two o'clock with her dress-maker, Gladys Williams, who was to deliver gowns for the Basin Street East engagement. Another woman was also to come by to help pack her wardrobe for the trip.

Before turning in, she began her nightly ritual of telephone calls. Her mood turned nostalgic and sad again. The familiar depression was creeping back. Dorothy also placed a call to the person she talked to daily: her mother Ruby. Pearl Bailey, who was in Las Vegas, said her housekeeper informed her that Dorothy had called. Dorothy talked to Juliette Ball and asked to speak to Juliette's mother.

"She talked at length to my mother," said Ball. "And she sang to her."

Around 7:15 on the morning of September 8th, Earl Mills received a call from Dorothy, who said she had been up late, preparing for the trip east and talking on the phone. Too tired to go to the hospital so early, she wanted to sleep some more.

"Could you arrange a later appointment for the cast?" she asked Mills.

Mills said he would contact the hospital.

A half hour later, at 7:45 a.m., Mills called Dorothy back to let her know the appointment was now set for 9 a.m. But Dorothy asked, "Can you make it later than that?"

Mills called the hospital again. A 10 o'clock appointment was scheduled.

When he called Dorothy back to tell her of the new time, she sounded relieved.

"You know how I am," she told him. "I'll just sleep for a bit and I'll be all right."

But she didn't go to sleep right away. Alone in her apartment, sur-rounded by trunks, suitcases, make-up kits, and clothes to be packed, as well as pictures, scrapbooks, and mementos of the past, she knew the next few days were crucial if order were to come back into her life.

It was now September, the start of the fall season in the entertainment industry; the new nightclub lineups, the new film releas-es, the new theatre productions, the new television season. For enter-tainers, September marked a time of rejuvenation, renewal, and new hopes.

But for Dorothy, September also brought back other memories of past times of promise and optimism. September 1938 was when she had opened as a teenager at the Cotton Club with Vivi and Etta; when she had met the fabulous Nicholas Brothers and immediately developed a crush on Harold. September 1942 was when she and Harold had married. September 1943 was when Lynn was born.

Dorothy made another phone call—to her mother Ruby. Maybe Ruby could assure her that everything would work out.

She swallowed some Tofranils, knowing she couldn't afford for the depression to creep back and incapacitate her at a crucial time. Not now in September, the start of a new season. A second chance. Another try.

Later Mills phoned her again, but there was no answer. At noon, Mills tried once again. But still the phone rang.

"I thought she might be asleep or in the shower," said Mills. "But I went to the apartment anyway."

There, Mills rang the bell. But there was no answer. He knocked on the door. There was no response. He could hear nothing inside. Then he pulled from his pocket the key he had to her place.

"I opened the door but it was chained," he recalled.

He shut the door and left for a couple of hours. Remembering that Gladys Williams was due to be at the apartment at two o'clock with Dorothy's gowns, he went back to the apartment around that time.

The door remained chained. Now Mills feared something was seriously wrong. He went to his car and pulled a tire iron from his trunk. He returned to the apartment and used the tire iron to break the chain.

Inside everything was still and quiet, but eerily so. As he walked through the living room, he called out, "Angel Face." But he got no response. Then he approached the bathroom.

There Dorothy lay on the floor. She was nude except for a blue scarf on her head. Apparently, she had bathed and powdered herself. He couldn't imagine why she was lying there. "Angel Face?" he cried out, kneeling down beside her.

"I touched her foot," said Mills. "She didn't move. I called her name. She didn't respond. When I touched her cold face, I knew she was dead."

Mills rushed in the other room and phoned Dorothy's physician. An ambulance was called. So, too, were the police. Once they arrived, they pronounced Dorothy dead. Mills was stunned.

He called Ruby, who he asked to come to Fountain Avenue immediately. He also tried to contact Geri, but she wasn't at home. Soon reporters and photographers showed up on Fountain Avenue. Mills requested that Dorothy's body not be photographed. They complied. Only as the sheriff's deputies carried the remains from the apartment in a body bag on a stretcher did the cameras snap.

Geri was sitting in a store owned by a friend when the press broke the story. "I heard it on the radio," she recalled. "The police had been calling. But I didn't come home. I just went right over to Dottie's apartment." By then, Dorothy's body had been taken to the coroner's. Geri sadly remembered Dorothy's recent conversations about death and her wishes for her funeral. "About six months before she died, she mailed me a note and then she left all kinds of instructions in her apartment," said Geri. "I went there to get the notes and bring them back."

The next day *The Los Angeles Times* ran a headline above its banner: *Dorothy Dandridge Found Dead*. Newspapers around the country carried articles on her death, which was called mysterious. The cause was unknown. For the African American press, which had covered her as its dream goddess for more than two decades now, the news was a front-page story. For Black America, it seemed unfathomable. Everyone had hoped there would be a happy ending for Dorothy Dandridge.

The Hollywood Reporter's "Rambling Reporter" section, which had chronicled Dorothy's comings and goings over the years, ran a brief, warm comment:

> Yeats might have written it for tragic Dorothy Dandridge: "But is there any comfort to be found? Man is in love and loves what vanishes, what more is there to say?....Rest in Peace, Dorothy.

"Haunted by her memory, director Laslo Benedek said, "I felt very sorry because I was very fond of her and I felt I missed a chance to get close to her. That my relationship was a very cold one and I felt terribly sorry that I didn't make something of the chance that I knew this wonderful woman. I always felt that there is much more to her than what I got in the short time I had to work with her."

Orin Borsten recalled the Dorothy of the past, saying, "A woman like this, her great strength is in preserving herself day by day. That's what she did. She preserved herself everyday. All these things were troubling her. Her child and the background she'd come from. Being Black and being a woman and being in a White world and to always be reminded she was an outsider."

Black actor Mel Bryant remembered that he was so shocked and upset by the news that he drove over to Fountain Avenue. "I went up to the door where they had that police line. I just wanted to make sure," he said. "You know how you just don't want to believe something. I think I cried all the way up there. I loved Dottie for all her talent. Not for what she was or what she could acquire. I just loved her *period*. For what she had done to raise the esteem of Black people in the movies. I went up there and stood in front of that door."

A woman in the building saw him and asked, "Can I help you with something?"

"I was just making sure," he said.

"It's true," she told him.

Bryant recalled, "I got back in my car and went home. I was just out of it for three or four days."

Olga James remembered that she would sometimes drive by Fountain Avenue, always thinking of Dorothy. "I just had to. I was haunted by her death. I don't think she even realized what she meant to so many of us."

A note she had left with Mills sparked more controversy about her death. In a hand-written envelope marked "To Whomever Discovers Me After Death—Important," the hand-written note inside read:

> In case of my death—to whomever discovers it—Don't remove anything I have on—scarf, gown or underwear—Cremate me right away—If I have anything money, furniture, give to my mother Ruby Dandridge—She will know what to do
> —Dorothy Dandridge

Another hand-written note had been mailed six months earlier to Geri Branton, whom Dorothy had told during a recent telephone conversation, "Whatever happens now, Geri, I know you'll understand."

Geri Pate Nicholas Branton embarked on the last act of friendship. She began arrangements for Dorothy's funeral.

Aside from the note sent to Geri, Dorothy left notes scattered throughout her apartment, concerning how her death should be handled. The body was to be embalmed and set in a casket at Los Angeles's premier African American funeral parlor Angelus Funeral Home. Later a memorial and cremation would be performed at Forest Lawn in Glendale. A small group of close friends were invited. Geri also requested that Abby Mann write something about Dorothy. Peter

Lawford, who appeared completely shaken and stunned by the news, was asked to speak, too.

But there were problems with the funeral plans. The Los Angeles coroner's office insisted an autopsy be performed to determine the exact cause of the death. That meant a slight delay in the readiness of the body for the funeral services and then the cremation.

Then, too, Ruby opposed the cremation, no matter what Dorothy had requested.

"Ruby was such a phoney Christian who said you weren't supposed to burn people," Geri recalled. "But I could not let Ruby interfere," said Geri. "Dottie spoke often of cremation. Dottie's wishes had to be observed in this matter. Ruby tried to raise hell. So I gave her the note Dottie had mailed me to me."

Joel Fluellen made an effort to arrange the service and to deliver the eulogy. But Geri wouldn't give in to his power play.

Geri, aware of Dorothy's feelings of having been betrayed, told him, "She would not have wanted it, Joel. She was not speaking to you." Fluellen then turned nasty. But Geri wouldn't budge.

Again following Dorothy's instructions, Geri had Dorothy's body dressed in an expensive cream-colored lace Juel Parke gown with a matching scarf. It was just the type of gown Otto had liked seeing her wear.

"She also told me not to uncover her head whatever I did," said Geri. "I wanted to see that that was done. And she did not want the coffin open. I saw to all of that. She wanted to be cremated immediately."

Later, though, Geri heard that some mourners had managed to sneak into the Angelus Funeral Home earlier in the day to view the body.

Following the body's preparation at Angelus, the memorial service was held inside the Little Church of the Flowers at Forest Lawn. Her body lay in state in a sealed polished walnut coffin under a grass-green nut blanket that was adorned by tiny roses and white satin ribbons. The pallbearers included Byron Morrow, Joel Fluellen, Harold Jovien, J. Kennedy Lightfoot, Leo Branton, Ben Irwin, Terry Hunt, Peter Lawford, and the man who could always make her laugh, comic Slappy White. Among the honorary pallbearers not in attendance were Pearl Bailey, Ivan Dixon, James Mason, Curt Jurgens, Sidney Poitier, and Sammy Davis, Jr.

Puffy-eyed and fighting back his tears, Peter Lawford was so emotionally overcome that at the last minute he told Geri he just couldn't speak. He cried throughout.

Geri sat stoically with her husband Leo. Abby Mann's eulogy was not read. Instead Leo Branton spoke at the brief fifteen-minute services:

"Dorothy believed in God, but she believed that He could be worshiped without a third party. She did not want a eulogy because she felt it was only words. She wanted you to remember her as she was. If you have any respect for Dorothy's life on this earth, you will spend the next five minutes in meditation and reflection."

Among the mourners were Dorothy Nicholas Morrow, Etta Jones Mills, Maria Cole, comedienne Judy Canova, musician Eddie Beale, Morty Jacobs and his wife Madeline, and other early friends of Dorothy. Earl Mills sat near Ruby. So too did her companion. Fayard Nicholas attended and, of course, Harold.

"Harold was sad about it. You could see it in Harold's face," said Fayard. "He wouldn't talk much. Just silent. But you would never see him crying or anything like. He held everything inside. He wouldn't let it come out. But I knew he really felt bad. I could see it. After being with him so long, I knew him. He took it hard."

Others made less charitable comments about Harold. Regardless of his youthful indiscretions, he said he had always loved her. Harold kissed a white rose and gently laid it on the casket.

During the service, a grief-stricken Ruby broke into tears and heavy sobs. Afterwards she had to be escorted from the chapel.

Most were relieved that Jack Denison didn't attend. But others realized that some of those whom Dorothy cared about so much at some point or another were absent. Otto didn't attend. Nor did Phil Moore. Of course, Lynn, in the state institution Camarillo, had no awareness of the fact that her mother had died.

And Dottie's beloved Vivi, who had traveled on the road with her, who for so long had been the dearest person in the world to her, who Dorothy always believed understood her because they had shared so much together, and whose disappearance grieved her to the very end, was absent too. When Vivian learned of her sister's death, she said it was too painful to return.

"I grieved. In my own way. In my privacy," said Vivian. "And for a long, long time I felt very guilty. But Dottie knew I loved her. I know she knew that. She was not the real reason I had left."

Many years passed before Vivian would set foot in Los Angeles again; many years before she would face Ruby.

Cyril Dandridge flew to Los Angeles for the services. But he arrived late. Ruby had given him the wrong date. Most saw it as her final act of cruelty to the man whose daughters had been taken from him.

On September 10th, United Press International reported that the autopsy attributed Dorothy's death to an embolism: a blood clot caused by the tiny fracture in her right foot. "Dorothy Dandridge died because bone marrow particles had entered her blood stream and reached her brain and lungs" was the official word. But doubts lingered about the cause of Dandridge's death.

In November, at a press conference in Los Angeles, L.A. County Chief Medical Examiner Dr. Theodore Curphey told reporters that the earlier analysis "was due to a lack of a complete study and pressure from news media." A new conclusion about the cause of death had been reached. It was drawn from a toxilogical analysis by the Armed Forces Institute of Pathology.

"Dorothy Dandridge died as a result of an overdose of drugs used to treat psychiatric depression." An acute ingestion of Tofranil, the anti-depressant, had killed her. The coroner's office said it "would not attempt to determine whether the death was an accident or a suicide."

Earl Mills also entered Dorothy's handwritten note into court as her last will and testament. But the note was found invalid because it was not dated and failed to qualify as probate, ruled Superior Court Commissioner Victor Donatelli. He divided Dorothy's estate between her mother Ruby and her 22-year-old daughter Lynn. As it turned out, Dorothy had left only $4,000 worth of furniture. She had $2.14 in her bank account. There was, however, an insurance policy, which eventually went to Ruby and Lynn.

But discussions and controversy continued about the cause of Dorothy's death. Finally, the Los Angeles County Coroner's office enlisted a three-man team of psychiatric consultants to conduct a psychological autopsy. Headed by the Beverly Hills psychiatrist Dr. Earl Woods, the psychiatrists interviewed Dorothy's friends and business associates to determine her emotional state of the time prior to her death. Their final ruling was that Dorothy's death had been a "probable accident."

Earl Mills said that at the time of her death, Dorothy had been very happy. It had to be an accidental overdose.

But Geri Branton felt differently.

Dorothy had been trying to kill herself for a long time," said Geri.

"I know it was a suicide. She had talked of it many times." She also recalled Dorothy's words during that last phone conversation; when she had said she knew Geri would understand and that she was tired. "I've had that happen to me three times. I always listen to that when people—from their *gut*—say 'I'm tired.' It's a different thing than 'I'm tired' or 'I need some sleep.' No. It's 'I'm tired of trying. I'm tired of going on. I give up.' And that happened with Dottie and also my friends Carole Landis and Inger Stevens."

Later Ruby told Geri Branton, "We're going to write this book, and when I make money, I'm going to give you back all the money you spent on Dottie 'cause I should have helped her."

"That's not necessary," Geri told her.

Then Ruby sent Branton some books of Dorothy's.

"Please accept these books because Dottie would say you're the only person who can read them. Please."

"I didn't touch the books for a long time," Geri Branton recalled. "But when I did, I found slipped between the volumes a little tissue paper. I opened it. Inside were gorgeous, gorgeous Brazilian jewels. Big ones. Aqua-marine and all colors. Gorgeous. Dottie had talked about the jewels. The tin heir in Argentina had given them to her. And she told me she had some from Brazil. And she wanted them to make a fancy turban. She never said anything else about them."

"I thought, 'Oh, what a delightful thing.' It was two weeks until Mother's Day," Geri said. "I wrapped the jewels very nicely, put them in a little box, and on Mother's Day, I took them to Ruby Jean. Ruby Jean didn't even know the worth of them. She didn't have any appreciation."

But Ruby's eyes widened. She looked at Geri and said, "If you've got any more, send them to me."

Geri was taken aback. "I have absolutely never been so hurt," said Geri. "I walked out of that house. She came over to my house constantly. But I never talked to her again. I wouldn't. I couldn't. If a person places that value on your character, what is the relationship? She called. She sent people over. She did everything. When I'm through, I'm through. I never even told her why. I could have hurt her in so many ways. I could have told her what she had done to Dottie. I never talked to her again."

The later years were not kind to Ruby. Suffering from old age and the onset of Alzheimer's disease, she was placed in a Los Angeles nursing home and then left penniless and deserted by her second lover who walked off with all Ruby's money. Visitors recalled that she had photographs of Dorothy throughout her room. As time went on, Ruby grew mean and nasty. Given to tantrums, she ranted, and cried loudly. She died in 1987.

Cyril Dandridge died in Cleveland in 1989.

Otto Preminger, also suffering from Alzheimer's disease, died in New York in 1986.

Phil Moore died in 1987. Among the items found in his belongings were the cufflinks Dorothy had given him with her note that read, "These are for when we get married."

Jack Denison, upon his return to Las Vegas, married a wealthy woman and lived comfortably. But reports came from some who later saw him that Denison sometimes was given to crying fits. Often he grew upset whenever he talked about Dorothy to anyone who had known her. He later died in Las Vegas.

Joel Fluellen grieved long and hard for Dandridge. Never willing to discuss their final rupture, he sought to keep Dorothy's name alive. He liked using her expression "Not to worry" and sometimes held his head arched high as she had done. In essence, said Geri Branton, Joel sought to become Dorothy. In 1984, his efforts led to the installation of a star in Dorothy's name on the Hollywood Walk of Fame. Later overcome by old age, illness, and blindness, Joel Fluellen pointed a gun to his head and committed suicide at the age of 81 in 1990.

Vivian Dandridge returned to Los Angeles in the 1970s. She hoped with the passage of time to re-establish her relationship with her mother. But Ruby was distant. When Ruby died, she mostly left the little she had to Earl Mills. Vivian was given nothing. In her last years, Vivian lived in Seattle under the name Marina Rozell. She suffered a massive stroke and died in 1991.

Harold Nicholas resides in Manhatten.

Fayard Nicholas lives in Los Angeles.

Geri Branton also resides in Los Angeles.

Harolyn Suzanne Nicholas remains in a California state institution.

And so within the walls of a romantic Spanish-style apartment in West Hollywood, it had come to a close: Dorothy Dandridge's journey to define herself. In the end, she may have believed she had failed, as she felt so often throughout her life. But a generation of African Americans always remembered her accomplishments and her extraordinary presence on the cultural landscape. She had boldly cleared a path for the dramatic Black film actress, and with her death, there was a void in American popular films. Later generations rediscovered her, and she eventually influenced a new era of Black actresses and actors working in the movies, who understood her struggles and valued her achievements. She had done far more than she had ever realized.

In the spring of 1995, Geri Branton awoke from a dream she had about Dorothy, who looked relaxed. "Oh, Geri," Dorothy said sweetly to her friend, "I'd surprise you now. You see, I don't have anything to cry about any more."

Acknowledgments

$\mathcal{T}$he generosity and help of many people made this book possible. I'm not even sure where to begin to express my gratitude.

Foremost I want to thank all the friends and associates of Dorothy Dandridge who consented to be interviewed as I tracked down the facts of Dorothy Dandridge's life. I became friends with many of them, and they've added much to my life.

To begin, I cannot thank Geri Branton enough, a truly remarkable woman who tirelessly and frankly answered all my questions about Dorothy, often sitting for hours in front of my tape recorder. Throughout, she was encouraging, and her insights and intelligence have added greatly to this book. Dorothy was very fortunate to have Geri as her best friend.

Also helpful were Harold Nicholas and Fayard Nicholas, whom I knew socially before beginning work on this book. Harold openly and courageously talked to me about the good times and bad in his marriage to Dorothy. As the years moved on, their youthful passion for one another died, but he felt they always had a love for each other. When he spoke of their problems and of her sensitive nature and most tellingly, of their last time together in Las Vegas, he was warmly reflective and remorseful, with tears welling his eyes. After so many years, he was still moved by memories of her.

Fayard Nicholas proved especially helpful because of his razor-sharp memory. While Harold had forgotten many details of the past, Fayard could recall an event of fifty years ago as if it had occurred yesterday. Throughout a series of interviews, he was jocular and in good spirits.

Dorothy Nicholas Morrow, the sister of Harold and Fayard, was a true surprise. Though she protested that she wasn't sure if she had much to say of importance, my initial interview with her went well. But it wasn't until later when I read a transcript of the interview that I realized *how well* it had gone. Dorothy Nicholas Morrow had a great ability to succinctly sum up an event, a personality, an impression. Throughout the interviews her husband, actor Byron Morrow, was by her side. He, too, took me by surprise because I hadn't realized that he had even known Dandridge. Byron had fine observations and some beautifully detailed recollections.

Harold Jovien, Dorothy's coordinating agent at the Music Corporation of America, was also helpful and encouraging. Not only did he thoughtfully recount some of Dorothy's horrible experiences while performing in Las Vegas, but he also informed me of her recordings, and even provided me with a tape of the material for one of her unreleased record albums. I greatly appreciated his good humor and he was excellent in describing the inner-workings of a big Hollywood agency like MCA. Jovien also introduced me to former agency head, Berle Adams, who provided additional information on Dorothy's MCA years and was also very helpful.

Etta Jones Mills helped me piece together Dorothy's years as a child performer. Her memory proved remarkable. She vividly recalled events and experiences of some sixty-odd years ago. Her humor, warmth, and frankness always made me feel at home around her.

Juliette Ball also was of great assistance in my quest to learn more about Dorothy's early years. Her observations on Ruby Dandridge were direct and honest. She also provided some telling comments on Dorothy's final years.

My dear friend Jeanne Moutoussamy-Ashe put me in touch with Vera Jackson, a pioneering professional Black female photographer, who had first photographed Dandridge in the early 1940s. Jackson was wonderful in giving her impressions of Dorothy, the young wife and mother. She very graciously showed me her portfolio of rare Dandridge photographs, magnificent records of the young woman and shared her impressions of Ruby Dandridge.

Dorothy Hughes McConnell also very graciously opened her home to me and shared her memories of Dorothy.

Herb Jeffries warmly recounted stories about Dorothy, the young woman, and then Dorothy shortly before her death. Bobby Short was perfect in setting the stage for the Dorothy/Phil Moore relationship. Writer/director Abby Mann thoughtfully discussed his relationship with Dorothy and I was also touched by his interest in my work.

My interviews with Dorothy's directors and co-workers were quite fruitful and enlightening. *Bright Road* director Gerald Mayer was thoughtful and reflective as he reminisced about both his professional and personal relationships with her. The *Harlem Globetrotters* director Phil Brown was feisty and energetic as he discussed the making of the film—and the studio's attitude about this low-budget Black picture. He also described the atmosphere in Hollywood during the years of blacklisting. Brown put me in contact with the film's writer Alfred Palca, who was spirited and proud of having worked on this unusual Black film so many years ago. *The Decks Ran Red* director Andrew Stone was crisp and pragmatic as he recalled the making of his film. His anger was apparent as he discussed Dorothy's disastrous second marriage.

Malaga director Laslo Benedek appeared genuinely troubled to hear of Dorothy's feelings about his film's compromises. His impressions of her isolation and her efforts to create a character out of flimsy material were very perceptive and moving. Not long after my interview, Benedek died, and I'm all the more grateful for the time he took to share so much with me.

"Blues for a Junkman" director John Peyser and star Peter Mark Richman provided pertinent details about Dorothy on the set—and off. Peter Mark's wife Helen Richman also shared her recollections.

Also helpful were the Bryants: Clora, Mel, and Joyce. My friend Sally Placksin, who had written about jazz trumpeter Clora Bryant in her book *American Women In Jazz,* set up an introduction. Clora provided wonderful observations on Dorothy and Vivian in the early 1950s. She also put me in touch with her brother, actor Mel Bryant, who recounted engrossing stories about Black Hollywood in the 1940s and 1950s. I was also surprised to learn that Clora and Mel were cousins of Joyce Bryant, whom I had interviewed for my series *Brown Sugar.* But I had lost track of Joyce until Clora put me in touch with her again. As always, Joyce Bryant was a terrific woman to interview.

Others who helped round out Dorothy's early years—-and in some cases, her later ones too-—included actor Lennie Bluett, who had been friendly with Vivian Dandridge and knew the entire Dandridge family; Avanelle Harris, who had first met Vivian and Dorothy as little girls; Catherine Ruthenberg, who first met Dorothy in the 1930s and occasionally saw Dorothy in her later years;

Among those who proved helpful in reconstructing the filming of *Carmen Jones* were Olga James, Brock Peters, Joe Adams, and Herb Ross. James, who played the role of Cindy Lou, described—in vivid detail—Dorothy's determination to give a fine performance. She was also especially sensitive to Dorothy's place as a woman in the industry. It was a pleasure and something of a surprise to talk to director Herb Ross. With Ross's hectic schedule, I wasn't sure we'd ever get to actually do the interview. But once I had Ross on the telephone, he was candid and refreshing as he reminisced about the various personalities on *Carmen Jones.* Brock Peters, a fine actor and a show business veteran of many years, provided observant comments on Dorothy.

Among the others who helped me reconstruct Dorothy's experiences on *Porgy and Bess* was that fine actor Ivan Dixon, who also commented on the filming of "Blues for A Junkman." Ivan's feelings about Dorothy seemed mixed. Yet he discussed her with the utmost respect and sensitivity. I've always felt that she valued Ivan far more than he realized. Nichelle Nichols also gave a fine, energetic interview, perceptively commenting on Dorothy's delicacy and sweetness. Adele Addison was hard to catch up with, but once we met for an early morning interview, she provided a striking account of her meeting with Dorothy.

Very late in the writing of this book, I finally located Dorothy's former publicist Orin Borsten, who thoughtfully discussed Dorothy during the heady years of her fame. His wife Laura Borsten also gave me insights into Dorothy's feelings during this period.

Others who provided personal insights on Dorothy (and in some cases, pertinent comments on Hollywood in the 1940s and 1950s) included Maria Cole; the great hair stylist Sydney Guilaroff; Eddie Bracken; Charlotte Sullivan; Gerald Wilson; Leonard Feather Bernie Hamilton; Stuart Whitman; Nick Stewart; and Zelda Wynn. Kathryn Grayson also warmly recounted the production of *Show Boat,* in which she and Dorothy starred in the 1960s. The show's producer Herb Rogers discussed Dorothy's talent and, very tenderly, her problems during the production. His former wife Bobbi Rogers was also of great assistance.

Nick Perito was terrific in helping me reconstruct part of Dorothy's nightclub tour schedule. So, too, were Marty Paich and especially Morty Jacobs and his wife Madeline Jacobs.

My gratitude is also extended to the late Vivian Dandridge, Otto Preminger, and Phil Moore, all of whom I interviewed years before I started work on this book. Earl Mills did not grant me a new interview for this book, but I want to thank him for answering all the questions I needed verification on—and for providing new information. In some cases, I have used his comments from my PBS series *Brown Sugar*. The same is true of Phil Moore and in some cases, Vivian Dandridge. I was also fortunate to talk to Phil Moore's widow Jeanne Moore Pisano, who warmly shared her memories of both Moore and Vivian Dandridge.

Aside from those interviewed, there are many others to thank.

Most helpful was my researcher and good friend Phil Bertelsen. Having a skilled researcher is always a blessing. But I felt twice blessed in having an imaginative one. He literally got me inside Dorothy's homes, which I'd never thought possible. It was an eerie, haunting experience to walk through the apartment on Fountain Avenue where she died.

On the West Coast, Jerry Silverhardt of Silverhardt Entertainment was always an excellent source to check on and locate entertainment figures. He helped me track down Dorothy's pianist Nick Perito, and for that I am of course extremely grateful. Bart Gallagher and Rick Leslie at Silverhardt Entertainment were also helpful and encouraging.

On the East Coast, my good friend Bruce Goldstein of Film Forum proved helpful. Because Bruce has an encyclopedic knowledge of films and film history, it was good to check certain facts with him, especially those pertaining to the Nicholas Brothers. It was Bruce who originally introduced me to The Nicholas Brothers.

Rigmor Newman very graciously arranged my interview with Harold Nicholas. It was wonderful to discuss my research with her and also to hear her opinions on various matters.

My good friend, the psychiatrist, Harry Ford very patiently helped me understand some of the medical procedures pertaining to Dorothy's daughter Lynn. My sister Jeanne Bogle Charleston also was extremely helpful in explaining other medical procedures.

I also want to thank: Ned Comstock at the University of Southern California's Cinema/TV Library; Lisa Jackson, Samuel Gill, and other staff members at the Margaret Herrick Library of the Academy of Motion Picture Arts and Sciences; Brigitte Kueppers at The Arts Library, Special Collections at UCLA; the staff at the Schomburg Center for Research in Black Culture, New York Public Library with special thanks to Gail Henderson; the staff at the Billy Rose Theater Collection at the Lincoln Center Library for the Performing Arts New York Public Library; Ann Sindelar at the Case Western Reserve Historical Society in Cleveland; the staff at the Louis B. Mayer Library at the American Film Institute in Los Angeles; the late film collector and professor, William K. Everson; Letty Meinold of the Las Vegas Museum and Historical Society; Karen Cooper of Film Forum; Howard Mandelbaum of Photofest; Kent Jones of Scorsese Films; Tony Gittens, my teaching assistant at New York University's Tisch School of the Arts; Josslyn Luckett, who was a true Dorothy aficionado; also Dr. Mary Schmidt Campbell, the dean of Tisch, and Janet Neipris, the chair of Tisch's Department of Dramatic Writing and also my colleague at Tisch; the writer Vernable Herndon, who has been a friend since my kid days in the office of Otto Preminger; Joana Blankson, Lesley Ann Brown, Kim Mallet, Phyllis Lodge, Kathy McKinley, and Willie Perdomo; Audrey Smith Bey in the Afro-American Studies Program at the University of Pennsylvania, and my former Penn students Charles Adams, Michael Gerber, Garfield Johnson, Awura-Adzua Backman, Cheryl Williams, Tracey Gatewood, Asia Slowe, Erica Freeman, Hayley Thomas, and Vincent Roth.

My gratitude is also extended to Anthony Quinn, Elia Kazan, James Coburn, the late Pamela Mason and Pierre Salinger.

Encouraging throughout was my dear friend Debra Martin Chase of Houston Productions as well as Kim Lombard Harrell and Steve Lapcuk. Thanks to Houston Productions, I was able to purchase a collection of rare Dorothy Dandridge material. Naturally, I'd like to express my gratitude to Whitney Houston for her help as well.

My thanks also are extended to Amy Schiffman, Nicole David, and Ron Nolte of the William Morris Agency; and also to the staff of *Essence*, in particular Susan Taylor, Diane Weathers, Pam Johnson, Audrey Edwards, and Yvette Russell.

And, of course, it's always a pleasure to remember those friends and dear ones who were of very special assistance along the way: Jeanne Moutoussamy-Ashe, Joerg Klebe, Anna Deavere Smith, Janet Bogle Schenck, Mariskia Bogle, Robert Bogle, Jr., Mark Mosley, Mechelle Mosley Palmer, Pele Charleston, Lori Stimpson, Ayana Charleston, Hassan Charleston, Bettina Glasgow Batchleor, Ronald Mason, Cheryll Greene, Carol Scott Leonard, Barbara January Nicholas, Sally Placksin, dear Marian Etoile Watson, Evander Lomke, Jeff Conrad, Elisabeth Dyssegaard, Linda Tarrant-Reid, Bob Silverstein, Kathe Sandler, Alan Sukoernig, Hiroko Hatanaka, Emery Wimbish, H. Alfred Farrell, Martin Radburd, Robert Katz, Daniel Beer, Doug Rossini, Ann Marie Cunningham, Susan Peterson, and Tracy Sherrod.

Finally, during the writing of this biography, my editor Malaika Adero read the drafts of the manuscript with the utmost care and attention. She sensitively gave me important suggestions for changes. I appreciate greatly her patience and insights. Others affiliated with Amistad who were helpful were Sandy Head, Gilbert D. Fletcher, Chuck Harris, Francis Harris, Syble Dummitt, Yvonne Honigsberg, and, of course, Kay Radtke and Debbie Mills.

My agent Marie Brown has been reassuring and perceptive throughout. During some very difficult times, she maintained her calm. She also gave me excellent suggestions for the manuscript. She's quite simply the best!

Last but not least, I wish to thank my publisher Charles Harris, who was committed to this book from the very beginning. At a time when other publishers felt there was no interest in Dorothy Dandridge or didn't know who she was or arrogantly didn't care to know anything about her, Charles believed in the book and stuck with it through many adversities and obstacles.

BOOK NOTES

$\mathcal{U}$nless otherwise noted below, all quotations are from interviews (or in rare cases, conversations) conducted by the author. In some instances, friends and associates of Dorothy Dandridge provided the comments attributed to her. Dates for periodicals are given only if they do not already appear in the text itself. Throughout, the discussions of early Black Hollywood are drawn from the author's publications: *Toms, Coons, Mulattoes, Mammies, and Bucks: An Interpretive History of Blacks in American Films*; *Brown Sugar: Eighty Years of America's Black Female Superstars*; and *Blacks in American Films and Television: An Illustrated Encyclopedia*. Also consulted was material from the author's personal collection on Black Hollywood, which is composed of the author's past taped interviews (of such figures as Fredi Washington, Clarence Muse, Mantan Moreland, director King Vidor, and many others), reviews and articles, stills, and other memorabilia of African American actors and filmmakers. Some background information on various Hollywood personalities has also been drawn from Ephraim Katz's *Film Encyclopedia*. Dorothy Dandridge's posthumously published memoir *Everything and Nothing* was also used for background information on her life. Because some information in the book, apparently incomplete at the time of her death and published five years later, was called into question by Dorothy's friends and associates, the author sought to verify incidents and comments with Dandridge's sister Vivian Dandridge as well as with Dandridge's close friends and associates and her manager Earl Mills. Occasionally, the author referred to Earl Mills's biography *Dorothy Dandridge: A Portrait in Black*, but with great caution. Vivian Dandridge, Geri Branton, Phil Moore, and many of Dorothy Dandridge's friends and associates were disturbed and in some cases, infuriated by Mills's book, which they felt had distorted Dorothy's life and was not always accurate. Some quotations and information were also drawn from the transcripts of the videotaped interviews for the author's PBS series *Brown Sugar: Eighty Years of America's Black Female Superstars*, based on his book of the same title.

Material from the Margaret Herrick Library at the Academy of Motion Picture Arts and Sciences has been designated "AMPAS." Material from the author's personal collection on Dorothy Dandridge—composed of either original or copies of letters, cables, contracts, telegrams, film stills, posters, and other memorabilia—has been designated "DBDDC."

Chapter 1: Cleveland

Sections of this chapter were drawn from the author's interviews and conversations with Vera Jackson, Dorothy Hughes McConnell, Vivian Dandridge, Geri Branton, Juliette Ball, Mel Bryant, Avanelle Harris, Lennie Bluett, Jeanne Moore Pisano, Bobby Short, and others. Some of the information on the marriage and divorce of Cyril and Ruby Dandridge was drawn from the couple's divorce records in the Cuyahoga County Court House records, Cleveland, Ohio. Information on early Cleveland, including background on the Shiloh Baptist Church's history, was drawn from the books *Black Americans in Cleveland* and *A Ghetto Takes Shape: Black Cleveland*. Wichita and Cleveland's street directories were used to verify the various residences of George Butler, Cyril Dandridge, Florence Dandridge, and Ruby Butler Dandridge. The birth dates of Ruby Butler Dandridge and Cyril Dandridge were found on their marriage license in Cleveland. The year given for Ruby was 1899, although her marker at Forest Lawn states that she was born in 1900. The birth dates for Vivian and Dorothy Dandridge were verified by their birth certificates in Cleveland. Dorothy Dandridge's recollections of her childhood in *Everything and Nothing* were checked, usually with Vivian Dandridge's comments on that time. In *Everything and Nothing*, Auntie Ma-Ma's real name is incorrectly given as Eloise Matthews. Vivian Dandridge—as well as others who knew Ma-Ma--stated emphatically that her name was Geneva Williams. Also consulted were articles in such publications as *Ebony*, the *New York Post*, the Urban League periodical *Opportunity*, and others, as well as various biographical releases on Dorothy Dandridge from Twentieth Century Fox and Dandridge's various publicists.

1. p. 5 vainly running the streets: Kenneth L. Kusmer, *A Ghetto Takes Shape: Black Cleveland*(Urbana: University of Illinois Press, 1976).

2. p. 5 the White neighborhoods: *Ibid.*

3. p. 11 Vivian and I were: Louie Robinson, "The Private World of Dorothy Dandridge," *Ebony*, June 1962.

4. p. 11 Vivian and I began: Dorothy Dandridge and Earl Conrad, *Everything and Nothing: The Dorothy Dandridge Tragedy* (New York: Abelard-Schuman, 1970).

5. p. 14 I'll do it for: *Ibid.*

6. p. 14 You ain't going to: *Ibid.*

7. p. 16 A proxy parent: *Ibid.*

8. p. 17 Auntie Ma-Ma presided over: *Ibid.*

9. p. 19 were chiefly for the: *Ibid.*

10. p. 20 Having that organization as: *Ibid.*

11. p. 21 several hundred dollars a: *Ibid.*

12. p. 21 After the show: Louie Robinson, "The World of Dorothy Dandridge," *Ebony*, June 1962.

13. p. 21 Even now when I: *Ibid.*

14. p. 22 many years later: *Ibid.*

15. p. 34 I remember sleeping four: *Ibid.*

16. p. 34 hot sun/hot rains/cities of heat: Dandridge and Conrad, *Everything and Nothing: The Dorothy Dandridge Tragedy*.

17. p. 22 I usually had a: *Ibid.*

18. p. 22 disappearing into snow, of: *Ibid.*

19. p. 24 No one is all: *Ibid.*

20. p. 25 hysterical about money for: *Ibid.*

21. p. 25 sacks of potatoes and: *Ibid*

22. p. 25 Don't leave none: *Ibid*

23. p. 28 I'll get the money: *Ibid*

2: A Hollywood Girlhood

Sections of this chapter were drawn from the author's interviews and conversations with Vivian Dandridge, Geri Branton, Phil Moore, Clarence Muse, Avanelle Harris, Etta Jones Mills, Lennie Bluett, Mel Bryant, Jeannie Moore Pisano, Juliette Ball, Fredi Washington, and others. Los Angeles street directories were also used to verify some of the residences of Ruby Dandridge and her children.

Population statistics for African-Americans in Los Angeles during the first half-century come from *Black Los Angeles: The Maturing of the Ghetto, 1940-1950*. Other sources for information on early Black Los Angeles included *The Negro In Los Angeles, A Dissertation*.

Among the periodicals consulted for additional background material on early Black Hollywood were *Ebony*, the Urban League publication *Opportunity*, *The New York Times*, the *New York Mirror*, and *Variety*. Also consulted were the books *Lillian Gish: The Movies, Mr. Griffith, and Me; From Harlem to Hollywood; Gone Hollywood*; and *Inside Oscar: The Unofficial History of the Academy Awards*.

Some information on Madame Sul Te Wan was drawn from *Black Women in America: An Historical Encyclopedia*.

Information pertaining to the divorce of Cyril and Ruby Dandridge was obtained from the Cuyahoga County Court House Records, Cleveland Ohio. Information on the audition for *A Day at the Races* was found in the *Pittsburgh Courier*, February 20, 1937.

1. p. 33 She was devoted to: Lillian Gish and Ann Pinchot, *Lillian Gish: The Movies, Mr. Griffith, and Me* (Englewood Cliffs: Prentice-Hall, Inc. 1969).
2. p. 35 Go back East, Mrs.: Dorothy Dandridge and Earl Conrad, *Everything and Nothing: The Dorothy Dandridge Tragedy* (New York: Abelard-Schuman, 1970).
3. p. 45 nothing of much note: *It Can't Last Forever* review, *Variety*, July 30, 1937.

Chapter 3: The Dandridge Sisters

Parts of this chapter were drawn from the author's interviews and conversations with Vivian Dandridge, Etta Jones Mills, Geri Branton, Harold Nicholas, Fayard Nicholas, Juliette Ball, Gerald Wilson, Leonard Feather, Bobby Short, Joe Adams, Fredi Washington, and others. Some additional background material on the Cotton Club was found in *Lena*; *The Encyclopedia of New York City*; and *The Cotton Club*. Additional Leonard Feather comments are from his book *The Jazz Years: Eyewitness to an Era*. Additional background information on the Nicholas Brothers was compiled from conversations with Bruce Goldstein and Rigmor Newman as well as the books *Jazz Dance* and *Biographies of Selected Leaders in Tap Dance* and articles in *The New York Times* and *The New Yorker*. Additional information was drawn from articles in such publications as *Variety*, *Ebony*, and *The New York Times*.

1. p. 45 My mother had not: Dorothy Dandridge and Earl Conrad, *Everything and Nothing: The Dorothy Dandridge Tragedy* (New York: Abelard-Schuman, 1970).
2. p. 66 I knew him when: Louie Robinson, "The World of Dorothy Dandridge," *Ebony*, June 1962,
3. p. 66 But it was a very: *Ibid*.
4. p. 66 was missing because I: *Ibid*.
5. p. 67 Dandridge Sisters, harmonizers: "Harris Band, Dandridge Sisters

Click In London," *Variety*, June 27, 1939.

6. p. 68 "I caught the Dandridge: Leonard Feather, *The Jazz Years: Earwitness to an Era.* (New York: De Capo Press, 1987).

7. p. 69 She wasn't even Jewish: *Ibid.*

8. p. 69 Somehow she was permitted: *Ibid.*

9. p. 69 We were high more: *Ibid.*

10. p. 69 She beat me till: Dandridge and Conrad, *Everything and Nothing: The Dorothy Dandridge Tragedy.*

11. p. 70 across the face, the: Ibid,

12. p. 73 a hodge-podge of Shakespearian: Brooks Atkinson, "Swinging Shakespeare's 'Dream' With Benny Goodman, Louis Armstrong and Maxine Sullivan," *The New York Times*, November 30, 1939.

13. p. 73 a worthwhile evening's entertainment: December 15, 1939, unnamed publication in the clippings files on *Swingin' the Dream* at the Library for the Performing Arts at Lincoln Center, NYPL.

14. p. 73 One of the costliest: undated and unnamed publication in the clippings files on *Swingin' the Dream* at the Library of Performing Arts at Lincoln Center, NYPL.

15. p. 76 Dandridge Sisters trio: Review, *Variety*, April 17, 1940.

16. p. 76 Dandridge Sisters are a neat: Review, *Variety*, May 15, 1940.

Chapter 4: Career, Courtship, and Marriage

Parts of this chapter are drawn from the author's interviews and conversations with Geri Branton, Harold Nicholas, Fayard Nicholas, Dorothy Nicholas Morrow, Byron Morrow, Vera Jackson, Avanelle Harris, Etta Jones Mills, Maggie Hathaway, Dorothy Hughes McConnell, Herb Jeffries and others. *Hollywood Goes to War* and *From Harlem to Hollywood* were among the books consulted for some additional background information on the era. Some additional information on the Nicholas Brothers was drawn from *To Be or Not to Bop.* Among the sources consulted for information on Million Dollar Pictures were *Lena* and *Amateur Night at the Apollo: Ralph Cooper Presents Five Decades of Great Entertainment.* Additional information was drawn from such books as *Music Is My Mistress* and *Self-Portrait, Gene Tierney,* as well as such publications as *The California Eagle, The New York Sun,* the *New York Post, The New York Daily News, Billboard,* and *Variety.* Also consulted were various clippings files at the New York Public Library for the Performing Arts at Lincoln Center. Information on the marriage of Vivian Dandridge and Jack Montgomery was drawn from the couple's wedding license and divorce papers.

1. p. 79 a young Negro girl: Robert Andrews, "Meet the People," *Colliers*, March 22, 1941.

2. p. 82 Making the picture was: Lena Horne and Richard Schickel, *Lena* (Garden City: Doubleday & Company, Inc., 1965).

3. p. 83 Just about the biggest: "Behind the Scenes With Harry," *The California Eagle*, October 3, 1940.

4. p. 84 I just finished: "Behind the Scenes With Harry," *The California Eagle*, October 10, 1940.

5. p. 84 After a decent interval: Archer Winston, *Four Shall Die* review, *New York Post*, December 13, 1941.

6. p. 87 The dusky Nicholas Brothers: John Rosenfield, "Sonja Henie On Ice Figuratively Speaking, *Dallas Morning News*, September 13, 1941.

7. p. 87 Chattanoga Choo Choo [number]: "The New Movies," *New York Sun*, September 6, 1941.

8. p. 87 the Nicholas Brothers and: Kate Cameron, "Sun Valley Shares Honors With Henrie," *The New York Daily News*, September 6, 1941.

9. p. 88 attempt to correct the: Duke Ellington, *Music Is My Mistress* (Garden City: Doubleday & Company, Inc., 1973).

10. p. 88 Ivie Anderson was billed as "Ivy Anderson" in *Jump for Joy*.

11. p. 89 I thought it remarkable: Gene Tierney and Mickey Herskowitz, *Self-Portrait, Gene Tierney.* (Wyden Books, 1978).

13. p. 90 Scheduled to be hit: "Mayan to 'Jump for Joy' Tonight," *The California Eagle*, July 10, 1941.

14. p. 91 The audience itself was: Duke Ellington, *Music Is My Mistress.*

15. p. 91 Dorothy Dandridge and Marie: Sam Abbott, *Billboard*, undated review in the *Swingin' the Dream* clippings file at the Library of Performing Arts at Lincoln Center, NYPL.

16. p. 92 Don't know whether she: John Kinloch, "'Jump for Joy' Is Sensational Eve in Theater," *The California Eagle*, July 17, 1941.

17. p. 92 Doubling in Paramount's *Bahama*: "Behind the Scenes With Harry," *California Eagle*, August 14, 1941.

18. p. 94 the Negro as a: Gregory D. Black and Clayton R. Koppes, *Hollywood Goes To Was: How Politics, Profits and Propaganda Shaped World War II Movies* (Berkeley: University of California Press, 1987).

19. p. 96 She sent a note: Lena Horne, PBS series *Brown Sugar: Eighty Years of America's Black Female Superstars.*

20. p. 96 an extremely gracious, intelligent: Horne and Schickel, *Lena.*

21. p. 97 She explained how difficult: *Ibid.*

22. p. 97 I have a family: Lena Horne, the PBS series *Brown Sugar: Eighty Years of America's Black Female Superstars.*

23. p. 97 You've got two babies: *Ibid.*

24. p. 97 Miss McDaniel's act of: Horne and Schickel, *Lena.*

Chapter 5: Lynn

Parts of this chapter were drawn from the author's interviews and conversations with Geri Branton, Harold Nicholas, Fayard Nicholas, Vivian Dandridge, Herb Jeffries, Bobby Short, Vera Jackson, Dorothy Hughes McConnell, Sydney Guilaroff, Phil Moore, Andrew Stone, Byron Morrow, and others. Information regarding the divorces and marriages of Vivian Dandridge was drawn from the Los Angeles County Hall of Records.

Additional background information was drawn from *Lena*; *To Be Or Not To Bop*; *Harold Arlen: Happy With the Blues*; *The World of Entertainment: Hollywood's Greatest Musicals*; *Blacks in the Performing Arts*; *This Life*, as well as articles in such publications as *The California Eagle*, *Jet*, *Ebony*, and *The New York Times*. The story that Dandridge was a contender for the lead in *Pinky* was reported in *Zanuck: The Rise and Fall of Hollywood's Last Tycoon*. But *Pinky*'s director Elia Kazan, when contacted by the author, said he did not recall Dandridge's being considered for the film.

Dorothy Dandridge's account of Lynn's treatment and the final diagnosis of her condition have both been drawn partly from her statements in *Everything and Nothing* and partly from her statements on "The Mike Douglas Show" in 1963, excerpts of which were published in *Jet*. Dorothy told Mike Douglas that a male physician named "Dr. Bailey" had given her the final diagnosis. But in *Everything and Nothing*, she indicated that a female physician had finally made her understand Lynn's condition. Geri Branton confirmed that it was a female physician named Ethel Harrington. Vivian

Dandridge was also helpful in piecing together this chronology.

Also consulted were the Federal Bureau of Investigations's files on Dorothy Dandridge.

1. p. 122 In America, men don't: Ephraim Katz, *The Film Encyclopedia* (New York: HarperPerennial, 1994)

2. p. 125 That spouse was none: Neither Pearl Bailey nor Slappy White appeared eager in later years to acknowledge this marriage.

3. p. 128 that something was wrong: Charles Sanders, "Tragic Story of Dandridge's Retarded Daughter," *Jet*, August 22, 1963.

4. p. 128 don't worry. Einstein didn't: *Ibid.*

5. p. 129 I took her to: *Ibid.*

6. p. 129 Then I had an: *Ibid.*

7. p. 129 odyssey of despair: Dorothy Dandridge and Earl Conrad, *Everything and Nothing: The Dorothy Dandridge Tragedy* (New York: Abelard-Schuman, 1970).

8. p. 131 be certain that there: *Ibid.*

9. p. 136-137 It was requested that the British hostess's name be kept anonymous.

10. p. 143 saw and experienced less: Dandridge and Conrad, *Everything and Nothing: The Dorothy Dandridge Tragedy.*

11 p. 144 Neither Dottie nor Geri: Harold Nicholas neither confirmed nor denied this incident with the white comedian. But he does not recall it occurring. Geri Branton, however, has said on numerous occasions that it did indeed occur.

12. p. 145 I want to know: Sanders, "Tragic Story of Dandridge's Retarded Daughter," *Jet*, August 22, 1963.

13. p. 146 I just sat there: *Ibid*

14. p. 146 Later people told me: *Ibid.*

15. p. 146 Inside I never gave: Dandridge and Conrad, *Everything and Nothing: The Dorothy Dandridge Tragedy.*

16. p. 147 Rightly or wrongly: *Ibid.*

Chapter 6: Career Thrust

Parts of this chapter are drawn from the author's interviews and conversations with Geri Branton, Phil Moore, Dorothy Nicholas Morrow, Byron Morrow, Vivian Dandridge, Bobby Short, Phil Moore, Billy Roy, Phil Brown, Alfred Palca, Juliette Ball, and others. Some additional material on Dorothy's domestic experiences with Phil Moore, including some comments on Marilyn Monroe and Ava Gardner, are drawn from Moore's unpublished memoirs *Things I Forgot to Tell You.* Among the sources for background information on the Actors Lab were dissertation *The History of The Actor's Laboratory, Inc.: 1941-1950* and *Papp: An American Life.* Additional details on the Club Gala and the Los Angeles club scene in the 1940s and early 1950s were obtained from *Bobby Short: The Life and Times of A Saloon Singer.* Other information was drawn from *City of Nets: A Portrait of Hollywood in the Forties; Shadow and Act; The Inquisition in Hollywood: Politics in the Film Community, 1930-1960, Naming Names; A Journal of the Plague Years; Thirty Years of Treason: Excerpts from Hearings before the House Committee on Un-American Activities, 1938-1968; Las Vegas: The Entertainment Capital; King of The Jungle: An Illustrated Reference To "Tarzan" On Screen And Television;* and *Tarzan of The Movies.*

Other sources included articles in *The Hollywood Reporter, The Los Angeles Times, The California Eagle, Ebony, Jet, The Washington Post, The New York Times,* and other publications. Details regarding Dorothy's divorce from Harold Nicholas were obtained from documents found in the Los Angeles County Hall of Records. Some information was also drawn from the Production Code Administration Files, AMPAS.

1. p. 154   We've been swamped with: Jim Heneghan, "Rambling Reporter," *The Hollywood Reporter*, September 9, 1948.
2. p. 155   Out of Character. The: Hedda Hopper column, *The Los Angeles Times*, September 13, 1948.
3. p. 156   Mothers, fathers, kids, and: Frank Eng column, the Los Angeles *Daily News*, September 16, 1948.
4. p. 156   One columnist who attacked: *Ibid.*
5. p. 156   Hedda Hopper Joins Ranks: "Hedda Hopper Bitterly Attacks Actor's Lab on Racial Issues," *The California Eagle*, September 16, 1948,
6. p. 158   I carry two extra: "Black Hollywood Honors Fluellen," *Variety*, February 12, 1990.
7. p. 165   There's a girl here: The Mocambo quotes of Morrison, Dandridge, and Moore are from one of the author's interviews with Phil Moore.
8. p. 166   Judy Garland was always: "Phil Moore Broke Color Line in Pics For Black Tuners," *Variety*, January 8, 1986.
9. p. 169   He looked the way: Dorothy Dandridge and Earl Conrad, *Everything and Nothing: The Dorothy Dandridge Tragedy* (New York: Abelard-Schuman, 1970).
10. p. 169   From Phil I was: *Ibid.*
11. p. 170   adjuncts to hotels: *Ibid*
12. p. 177   I thought, 'I just': Charles Sanders, "Tragic Story of Dandridge's Retarded Daughter," *Jet*, August 22, 1963.
13. p. 177   So I moved all: *Ibid*
14. p. 179   with only a small: Phil Moore, *Things I Forgot To Tell You* (unpublished, 1986).
15. p. 179   Man, she was 'acting': *Ibid.*
16. p. 180   had a habit, which: *Ibid.*
17. p. 180   We couldn't imagine these: *Ibid.*
18. p. 180   Between the time with: *Ibid.*
19. p. 183   Care must be exercised: Letter, Production Code Adminstration Files, AMPAS.
20. p. 184   Virginia Huston has only: *Tarzan's Peril* review, *Variety*, March 21, 1951.
21. p. 188   Commercial possibilities are obvious: Ibid.
22. p. 188   Brown plays the role: Ibid.
23. p. 191   A new showbiz career: Review, *Variety*, March 28, 1951.

Chapter 7: Rising

Parts of this chapter have been drawn from the author's interviews and conversations with Geri Branton, Phil Moore, Harold Nicholas, Fayard Nicholas, Harold Jovien, Vivian Dandridge, Clora Bryant, Zelda Wynn, Jeanne Moore Pisano, Earl Mills, Bobby Short, Morty Jacobs, Orin Borsten, Berle Adams, Joyce Bryant, Nick Perito, Dorothy McConnell, and others.   Some information on the Los Angeles club scene was drawn from *Out With the Stars: Hollywood Nightlife In The Golden Era*. Among other sources are *Things I Forgot to Tell You; Lena; The Inquisition in Hollywood: Politics in the Film Community; City of Nets; Red Channels; Jazz Cleopatra: Josephine Baker In Her Time*; and *Dorothy Dandridge: A Portrait In Black*. Among the other sources were articles in such periodicals as *The California Eagle*,

Our World, Ebony, The Cleveland Call and Post, Jet, The Los Angeles Sentinel, the *New York Post, The New York Times, Time, The Daily Worker, Ebony, Look, Cue, Theater Arts*, and *Quick*.

Some information was drawn from the Federal Bureau of Investigations file on Dorothy Dandridge.

Additional information also comes from the author's personal Dorothy Dandridge Collection [DBDDC].

1. p. 193 a cross between a: Jim Heinmann, *Out With the Stars: Hollywood Nightlife in the Golden Era* (New York:Abbeville Press, 1985).
2. p. 193 a medley of soft. *Ibid.*
3. p. 195 first all-Negro TV: "Coast TV Show," *The Los Angeles Sentinel*, June 14, 1951.
4. p. 199 When we were on: Dorothy Dandridge and Earl Conrad, *Everything and Nothing: The Dorothy Dandridge Tragedy* (New York: Abelard-Schuman, 1970).
5. p. 200 Before the engagement ended: Vivian Dandridge spoke of this incident. Earl Mills also wrote of in his book *Dorothy Dandridge: A Portrait in Black*.
6. p. 202 Word came from Lena's: Phil Moore, *Things I Forgot to Tell You* (unpublished, 1986).
7. p. 203 This guy: This Berle Adams quote has been reconstructed from the author's notes and recollections.
8. p. 204 It marks Miss Dandridge's: Review, *The Hollywood Reporter*, November 5, 1951.
9. p. 204 This letter will confirm: Letter, DBDDC.
10. p. 206 Mills recalled that the: Mills refers to this incident in his book *Dorothy Dandridge: A Portrait in Black*. He also confirmed it in a conversation with the author.
11. p. 208 came wriggling out of: "Eye & Ear Specialist," *Time,* February 4, 1952.
12. p. 209 a singing sexation: Earl Wilson column, the *New York Post*, January 22, 1952.
13. p. 209 Dorothy Dandridge is the: "Eye & Ear Specialist," *Time*, February 4, 1952.
14. p. 209 the thing I do: "La Dandridge, Alhambra Star Is 'Pretty Enough,'" *Cleveland Call and Post*, June 7, 1952.
15. p. 214 Dorothy Dandridge Makes Hometown: "Dorothy Dandridge Makes Hometown Hit," *The Cleveland Call and Post*, May 31, 1952.
16. p. 215 Just about everything they've: John E. Fuster, "La Dandridge, Alhambra Star Is 'Pretty Enough,'" *The Cleveland Call and Post*, June 7, 1952.
17. p. 217 fight against any secret: Otto Friedrich, *City of Nets* (New York: Harper & Row Publishers, 1986).
18. p. 218 had come to convince: "Negro Actors Tells FBI Snooper Where To Go," *The Daily Worker*, February 5, 1950.
19. p. 218 Some people, of course: Lena Horne and Richard Schickel, *Lena* (Garden City: Doubleday & Company, Inc., 1965).
20. p. 220-222 A draft of the letter to Nicholas Schenck is in the author's personal collection of Dandridge material. It also appeared in Earl Mills' *Dorothy Dandridge: A Portrait in Black*. Harold Jovien, who drafted the letter, confirmed that this indeed was the one sent to Schenck.

Chapter 8: The Saloons

Parts of this chapter have been drawn from the author's interviews and conversations with Geri Branton, Vivian Dandridge, Nick Perito, Harold Jovien, Gerald Mayer, Morty Jacobs, Earl Mills, Eddie Bracken, and others.

Some background information on Peter Lawford (including two quotes from Lawford's friends about his relationship with Dorothy) has been drawn from *Peter Lawford: The Man Who Kept Secrets*. Some background details on MGM following the war have been drawn from *Heyday: An Autobiography* and *City of Nets*. Among the other sources are articles in *Ebony*, *The Pittsburgh Courier*, *Variety*, the *Las Vegas Review-Journal*, *The New York Times*, *Cue*, the Hollywood *Citizen-News*, the *Los Angeles Daily News*, and *The Saturday Review*.   .

Some details on pertaining to Dorothy and *Bright Road* are derived from the author's personal collection of her contracts and correspondence.

Dorothy identified her Brazilian lover as Juan Alvarez de Costigliana Freyre Vivaldez Martinez in *Everything and Nothing*. Earl Mills book *Dorothy Dandridge: Portrait in Black* identifies him as Christian Marcos.

1. p. 224 He ought to take: Dore Schary, *Heyday: An Autobiography* (Boston: Little, Brown & Company, Inc. 1979).
2. p. 246 It was a story: Howard McClay column, Los Angeles *Daily News*, August 21, 1952.
3. p. 226 It's a current Hollywood: Bob Thomas, "MGM Doing Offbeat Film With An All-Negro Cast," Hollywood *Citizen's News*, August 28, 1952.
4. p. 226 The Negro audience will: *Ibid*.
5. p. 227 she will be readily: "See How They Run," *Ebony*, April 1953.
6. p. 229 He stood against a: Dorothy Dandridge and Earl Conrad, *Everything and Nothing: The Dorothy Dandridge Tragedy* (New York: Abelard-Schuman, 1970).
7. p. 234 a tender and profoundly: "Bright-er Outlook Now," *Cue*, May 2, 1953.
8. p. 234 Negroes are all too: "SR Goes to the Movies," *Saturday Review*, April 25, 1953.
9. p. 234 The most touching and: Bosley Crowther, "The Screen In Review," *The New York Times*, April 29, 1953.
10. p. 236 the vocal hit of: Howard McClay column, the Los Angeles *Daily News*, August 21, 1952.
11. p. 237 She's achieved a more: Review, *Variety*, March 4, 1953.
12. p. 240 I won't stay in: Phyllis Rose, *Jazz Cleopatra: Josephine Baker In Her Time* (Garden City: Doubleday & Company, Inc., New York, 1989).
13. p. 240 One of the top: Review, *Variety*, April 29, 1953.
14. p. 240 While events of atomic: Alan Jarlson, "Here's A Singer Who Lives With Her Song," *Las Vegas Review Journal*, April 26, 1953.
15. p. 241 Let's give it a "Dandridge and Conrad, *Everything and Nothing*.
16. p. 241 I didn't want any: *Ibid*.
17. p. 242 Out of the restaurant: *Ibid*.
18. p. 242 My mother was very: James Spada, *Peter Lawford: The Man Who Kept Secrets* (New York:Bantam Books, 1991).
19. p. 242 I was a halfway: *Ibid*.
20. p. 243 He was very smitten: *Ibid*, quote given by Molly Dunne.
21. p. 245 Peter didn't have the: *Ibid*, quote given by Peter Sabiston.
22. p. 244 Dorothy even fixed chitlins: This story was told by Vivian

Dandridge. It also appears in *Everything and Nothing.*

23. p. 245 Look, I love you: Dorothy repeated to Geri Branton what Peter Lawford had said about their not getting married.

Chapter 9: Making Carmen

Many of the incidents and the dialogue in this chapter were drawn from the author's interviews and conversations with the author: Geri Branton, Otto Preminger, Olga James, Herb Ross, Orin Borsten, Joyce Bryant, Vivian Dandridge, Nick Perito, Juliette Ball, Dorothy Hughes McConnell, Etta Jones Mills, and others. Some biographical information on Otto Preminger was drawn from *Preminger: An Autobiography* as well as from articles in *The New York Times* and other periodicals. Much of the information on Production Code correspondence during the making of *Carmen Jones* was drawn from the Production Code Administration Files, AMPAS. Other information on *Carmen Jones* was drawn from the Twentieth Century Fox Script and Legal Files in the Arts Library, Special Collections at UCLA.

Also consulted were the books *Marilyn Horne: My Life* and *Diahann.*

Some information on Dorothy's therapy sessions was drawn from interviews and conversations with Geri Branton, Vivian Dandridge, Orin Borsten, and Earl Mills as well as correspondence and billing records in the author's personal Dandridge collection. Mills also published a letter from Dorothy to psychologist John Berman in *Dorothy Dandridge: A Portrait in Black.*

1. p. 254 That Dorothy Dandridge came: Review, *Variety*, September 16, 1953.
2. p. 254 The songstress has picked: Review, *The Hollywood Reporter*, September 10, 1953.
3. p. 254 Don't Be Afraid of: "Don't Be Afraid of Sex Appeal," *Ebony*, May 1952.
4. p. 254 The Dandridge doll looked: Mike Connelly, "Rambling Reporter," *The Hollywood Reporter*, September 10, 1953.
5. p. 255 The most exciting woman: "Why Negroes Don't Like Eartha Kitt," *Ebony*, December, 1954.
6. p. 258 What do you want?: Dorothy Foster's comments were provided by Juliette Ball.
7. p. 261 I took one story: Otto Preminger, *Preminger: An Autobiography* (Garden City: Doubleday & Company, Inc, 1977).
8. p. 263 Cry, you little monsters!: Albin Krebs, "Otto Preminger, 80, Dies; Producer and Director," *The New York Times* April 24, 1988.
9. p. 263 I decided not to: Preminger, *Preminger: An Autobiography.*
10. p. 265 Sorry, Otto, this is: *Ibid.*
11. p. 265 I could do anything else: *Ibid.*
12. p. 265 Can I read it?: *Ibid.*
13. p. 265 How is *Carmen Jones*?: *Ibid.*
14. p. 266 the lack of any: Production Code Administration files, AMPAS.
15. p. 266 make certain to omit: *Ibid.*
16. p. 267 I intend to shoot: Twentieth Century Fox Files, UCLA.
17. p.. 267 For this version I: *Ibid.*
18. p. 268 While White indicated that: *Ibid.*
19. p. 269 I guess you want: *Carmen Jones* publicity release.
20. P. 269 I never thought I: Diahann Carroll and Ross Firestone, *Diahann* (Boston: Little, Brown and Company, 1986).
21. p. 271 was seated behind the: *Ibid.*

22. p. 271 Mr. Preminger told me: "On The 'Bright Road' of 'Carmen' and 'Joe,'" *The New York Times*, October 24, 1954.

23. p. 275 I hate the way: Carter Barber, "Harry Belafonte—And the Women In His Life," *Los Angeles Mirror News*, April 16, 1957.

24. p. 275 in larger size type: *Carmen Jones* correspondence in Twentieth Century files, UCLA.

25. p. 277 Because this was to be: Stephen M. Silverman, "That Black 'Carmen,'" *New York Post* , July16, 1986.

26. p. 277 Even though I was: Marilyn Horne with Jane Scovell, *Marilyn Horne: My Life* (New York: Atheneum, 1983).

27. *p.* 277-278 to match the timbre: *Ibid.*

28. p. 278 Later she filmed her scenes: *Ibid.*

29. p. 278 The significant thing about: Stephen M. Silverman, "That Black 'Carmen,'" *New York Post*, July 16, 1986.

30. p. 279 they slicked down my: Carroll and Firestone, *Diahann*.

31. p. 280 She had very few: *Ibid.*

32. p. 280 looks made the other: *Ibid.*

33. p. 286 Dorothy wanted success desperately: *Ibid.*

34. p. 290 He put champagne into: Dorothy Dandridge and Earl Conrad, *Everything and Nothing: The Dorothy Dandridge Tragedy*. Abelard-Schuman,(New York: 1970).

35. p. 291 Nothing?: *Ibid.*

36. p. 292 We were the only: Carroll and Firestone, *Diahann*.

37. p. 292 She had such presence: *Ibid.*

Chapter 10: Stardom

Parts of this chapter were drawn from the author's interviews and/or conversations with Geri Branton, Vivian Dandridge, Orin Borsten, Nichelle Nichols, Earl Mills, and Nick Perito. Some information on Dorothy's nightclub engagements—dates, salaries, etc—is found in the author's personal collection of Dorothy Dandridge material. Information on Vivian Dandridge's financial affairs in 1954 also is from the author's Dorothy Dandridge collection.

Some information on James Baskette's honorary Oscar was drawn from the book *Inside Oscar: The Unofficial History of the Academy Awards*. Also consulted was *Preminger: An Autobiography*. Among the other sources consulted were articles in *The Hollywood Reporter, Ebony, Jet, The California Eagle, Our World, Sepia, Variety, The New York Herald Tribune, Newsweek, Time, The Los Angeles Mirror, The New York Amsterdam News, The Los Angeles Sentinel, The Pittsburgh_Courier, The Chicago Defender, The New York Daily Mirror, Commentary, The Los Angeles Examiner, The New York Journal American, the New York Mirror, The Las Vegas Sun, The New York Daily News, The New York Times,* the *New York Post,* and other publications.

1. p. 296 Dorothy Dandridge has put: "Nitery Notes," *The Hollywood Reporter*, August 27, 1954.

2. p. 298 Hollywood's Newest Love Team: "Hollywood's Newest Love Team," *Jet*, September 30,1954.

3. p. 298 Family of Talent: "Family of Talent," *Sepia*, September 1954.

4. p. 300 Not in a month of: "Selznick's 'Lamp' Discovers America In $1,000,000 Fusion of Talents," *Variety*, October 27, 1954.

5. p. 302 The name Carmen will: *Carmen Jones* advertisement, DBDDC.

6. p. 303 Crowded with fiery music: *Carmen Jones* advertisement, *Variety*, November 17, 1954..

7. p. 303 comes close to the: Archer Winston, Review, *The New York Post*, October 29, 1954.

8. p. 303 an incomparably seductive performance: Otis Guernsey, Review, *The New York Herald Tribune*, October 29, 1954.

9. p. 304 an incandescent Carmen, devilishly: "New Films," *Newsweek*, October 25, 1954.

10. p. 304 The rattle of the: "The New Pictures," *Time*, November 1, 1954.

11. p. 304 there never has been: "Dorothy Dandridge May Get Academy Award Nomination," *The Los Angeles Sentinel*, November 25, 1954.

12. p. 304 Dorothy Dandridge in *Carmen*: "Rambling Reporter," *The Hollywood Reporter*, November 2, 1954.

13. p. 304 It's a terrific picture!: *Carmen Jones* advertisement, *Variety*, November 17, 1954.

14. P. 305 Dear Miss Hopper: Letter, Hedda Hopper Collection, AMPAS.

15. p. 305 *Carmen Jones* is simply: Alvin "Chick" Webb, "Footlights and Sidelights," *Amsterdam News*, November 6, 1954.

16. p. 305 exciting dramatic scenes, good: Hazel Lamarre, "Applause," *The Los Angeles Sentinel*, November 4, 1954.

17. p. 305 I am so prejudiced: George F. Brown, "No Cover Charge," *The Pittsburgh Courier*, October 30, 1954.

18. p 305 Negro speech is parodied: James Baldwin, "Life Straight in De Eye," *Commentary*, January 1955.

19. p. 306 the depth of the hero's: Bosley Crowther, "Negroes In Film," *The New York Times*, October 3, 1954.

20. p. 306 The exciting movie of: Geri Nicholas, "Show Business," *The California Eagle*, November 4, 1954.

21. p. 306 I guess I get: Letter, DBDDC.

22. p. 307 Like the 'Queen Mother': "Dot's Mom Ruby Rules Roast At Pix Premiere," *The Chicago Defender*, November 13, 1954.

23. p. 308 If *Carmen* succeeds in: "On the 'Bright Road' of 'Carmen' and 'Joe,'" *The New York Times*, October 24, 1954.

23. p. 308 Before you can get: Nancy Seely, "The Road Ahead for 'Carmen,'" *New York Post*, November 7, 1954.

24. p. 309 was injured at birth: Sidney Fields, "Only Human," *New York Daily Mirror*, October 29, 1954.

25. p. 310 *Carmen Jones* was among: Otto Preminger, *Preminger: An Autobiography* (Garden City: Doubleday & Company, Inc., 1977).

26. p. 319 volunteered to direct Dorothy: Louella Parsons column, *The Los Angeles Examiner*, February 23, 1955.

27. p. 319 that Negroes should play: Mason Wiley and Damien Bona, *Inside Oscar: The Unofficial Story of the Academy Awards* (New York: Ballantine Books, 1986).

28. p. 320 "swelled with pride at: Dorothy Dandridge's public response nomination, DBDDC.

29. p. 320 CONGRATULATIONS ON YOUR WONDERFUL: Lawford telegram, *Ibid*.

30. p. 322 This was one press: Ralph Pearl, "Vegas Daze and Nites," *The Las Vegas Sun*, February 23, 1955.

31. p. 323 How Good Are Dorothy: "How Good Are Dorothy Dandridge's Chances For An Oscar," *Jet*, March 10, 1955.

32. p. 324 *Ebony*'s feature on Dorothy's Oscar nomination appeared in the July 1955. issue.

33. p. 326 Miss Dandridge heard such: Gene Knight, "A Triumph for Dorothy," *New York Journal American*, April 14, 1955.
34. p. 327 This room has echoed: Review, Frank Quinn, "Waldorf Empire Room Gives Dorothy Dandridge Big Hand," *The New York Mirror*, April 13, 1955.
35. p. 327 Miss Dandridge will wind: Review, *Variety*, April 13, 1955.
36. p. 327 shy, half-frightened manner: Knight, "a Triumph for Dorothy," *New Journal American*, April 14, 1955.
37. p. 327 Two for the Show: "Music," *Time*, May 2, 1955.
38. p. 327 Charlie Morrison, who gave: Ed Sullivan, "Little Old New York," *The New York Daily News*, April 14, 1955.
39. p. 329 Dorothy Dandridge has all: "'Carmen Jones' Creates Box Office Heat in Singapore," *The Hollywood Reporter*, March 23, 1955.
40. p. 331 throng of thousands: "Royalty and Fame Filled Cannes, but it was Dorothy Dandridge's Triumph," *Our World*, August 1955.
41. p. 332 Dorothy Dandridge, here for: Jack Harrison, "U.S. Success at Cannes Seen As Aid in Future Festivals," *The Hollywood Reporter*, May 13, 1955.
42. p. 332 Dorothy Dandridge, getting a: "People," *Jet*, May 26, 1955.
43. p. 337 Whereas, since you were: Letter, DBDDC.
44. p. 337 You are hereby notified: *Ibid.*
45. p. 339 I want to play: From interview with Orin Borsten.

Chapter 11: Peaking

Parts of this chapter were drawn the author's interviews and conversations Orin Borsten, Geri Branton, Vivian Dandridge, Morty Jacobs, Byron Morrow, Earl Mills, Harold Nicholas, Marty Paich, Nick Perito and Otto Preminger. Additional information (including some details on Dandridge's income tax status) comes from the author's personal collection of Dorothy Dandridge material.   Some information was drawn from the Charles Feldman Papers at the American Film Institute, the Production Code Administration Files, and the Los Angeles County Hall of Records. Also consulted were *Joan Collins: Past Imperfect, An Autobiography*; *Don't Say Yes Until I Finish Talking*; and *Zanuck: The Rise and Fall of Hollywood's Last Tycoon.*

Among the other sources were articles in *Jet, The Los Angeles Examiner, The Hollywood Reporter, Ebony, Confidential, The New York Times,* the *New York Post, The New Republic, Time, Variety,* and other publications.

1. p. 344 To endeavor in my: "New Year's Resolutions of Famous People," *Jet*, February 16, 1956.
2. p. 345 Surprising that Dorothy Dandridge: Louella Parsons column, *The Los Angeles Examiner*, April2, 1956.
3. p. 349 Don't pick me up: Geri Branton reported that Dorothy had repeated to her the details of the conversation with Joel Fluellen.
4. p. 350 Well, I need some: Geri Branton reported this comment and those that follow about Dorothy and Kurt Frings, Dorothy and the film producer, and Dorothy and Sukarno.
5. p. 355 Artistically, I started going: Dorothy Dandridge and Earl Conrad, *Everything and Nothing* (New York: Abelard-Schuman, 1970).
6. p. 356 In "Kings Go Forth": Letter, DBDDC.
7. p. 356 Dorothy is said to be: Louella Parsons column, *The Los Angeles Examiner*, October 18, 1956.
8. p. 356 it has some strong: Letter, Charles Feldman Papers Collection in

the American Film Institute's Louis B. Mayer Library.

9. p. 357   will be treated with: Letter, Production Code Administration files, AMPAS.

10. p. 358   In my opinion the: *Ibid.*

11. p 360   They were not telling: All Dandridge quotes pertaining to her feelings about *Island In The Sun* are from letters, DBDDC.

12. p. 361   My dear Dorothy: *Ibid.*

13. p. 362   *Island in the Sun* is: Joan Collins, *Joan Collins: Past Imperfect, An Autobiography,* (New York: Simon & Schuster, 1978).

14. p. 362   You've had nothing until: *Ibid.*

15. p. 363   Harry Belafonte split from: "Rambling Reporter," *The Hollywood Reporter,* November 21, 1956.

16. p. 364   He's so silly: A comment made by Dorothy to Geri Branton.

17. p. 364   We were very good: Lynn Norment, "Harry Belafonte: The Legend Roars Back With New Movie and Old Fire," *Ebony,* September, 1996

18. p. 365   I don't know how: Letter, DBDDC.

19. p. 366   GO AHEAD WITH LADY: Ibid.

20. P. 366   Miss Dandridge is quite: Ibid.

21. p. 367   In this one scene: Louie Robinson, "Torrid New Love Story Stars Interracial Love Code Debate," *Jet,* December 13, 1956.

22. p. 367   John Justin and I: *Ibid.*

23. p. 368   John and I had: *Ibid.*

24. p. 368   We do embrace in: *Ibid.*

25. p. 368   In this movie, where: "ISLAND IN THE SUN, Dandridge, Belafonte Star In Romantic Interracial Film," *Ebony,* July 1957.

26. p. 368   At least I have: *Ibid.*

27. p. 368   There is no scene that: *Ibid.*

28. p. 373   I'm Not Afraid of: Letter, DBDDC.

29. p. 373   The pages of *Confidential*: Joan Collins, *Joan Collins: Past Imperfect, An Autobiography.*

30. p. 373   What Dorothy Dandridge Did: "What Dorothy Dandridge Did," *Confidential,* May 1957.

31. p. 378   Otto was ugly. Truly: Dorothy Dandridge and Earl Conrad, *Everything and Nothing: The Dorothy Dandridge Tragedy.* (New York: Abelard-Schuman, 1970).

32. p 378   my Thunderbird automobile and: Information pertaining to Dorothy's "Last Will and Testament" was found in the Los Angeles County Hall of Records.

33. p. 379   here is the script: Information in this section regarding *Tamango* script approval, DBDDC.

34. p. 382   Dorothy Dandridge is causing: "People," *Jet,* August 1, 1957.

35. p. 383   THIS IS TO LET: Telegram from Vivian Dandridge, DBDDC.

36. p. 383   Sorry just received your: Ibid.

37. p. 383   it raises some Black-: Bosley Crowther, "Color or Class," *The New York Times,* April 23, 1957.

38. p. 383   Toying with its theme: "The New Movies," *Time,* June 24, 1957.

39. p. 385   one would like to: Philip Roth, "*Movies:* 'I Am Black But O My Soul. . .,'" *The New Republic,* July 29, 1957.

40. p. 386   is anything but happy: "Racial Romance In 'Sun' Upsets The Neighbors," *Variety,* June 5,1957.

41. p. 386   They've given me the: Mel Gussow, *Don't Say Yes Until I Finish*

Talking: A Biography of Darryl F. Zanuck (Garden City: Doubleday & Co., 1971).

42. p. 387   is doing very good: "South Wavering on 'Island in the Sun'? L'Ville Clicks Despite Race Angles," *Variety*, June 19, 1957.

43. p. 387   I never liked *Island*: Gussow, *Don't Say Yes Until I Finish Talking: A Biography of Darryl F. Zanuck*.

44. p. 388   I would not have: "Seek To Put More Stars on Stand," *New York Post*, September 4, 1957.

Chapter 12: Making Porgy

Parts of this chapter have been drawn from the author's interviews and conversations with Otto Preminger, Brock Peters, Ivan Dixon, Andrew Stone, Adele Addison, Orin Borsten, Geri Branton, Andrew Stone, Juliette Ball, and others. Among the sources for background information were *The Life and Times of Porgy and Bess: The Story of An American Classic*; *This Life, Diahann*; *Preminger: An Autobiography, Mamoulian, Goldwyn: A Biography*; and *Hollywood in a Suitcase*

Also consulted were the Production Code Administration Files. Other sources included articles in *Life, The New York Times, The Hollywood Reporter, Cue, Variety, Daily Variety, The New York Mirror, The Los Angeles Examiner, Jet, The New York Times, The New York Mirror*, and other publications.

1. p. 395   There was no way: Dorothy Dandridge and Earl Conrad, *Everything and Nothing: The Dorothy Dandridge Tragedy* (New York: Abelard-Schuman, 1970).

2. p. 397   "I didn't want to: Diahann Carrolll and Ross Firestone (Boston: Little, Brown & Co., 1986).

3. p. 398   Him! That monkey!: A. Scott Berg, *Goldwyn: A Biography* (New York: Alfred A. Knopf,New York,.1980)

4. p. 398   Mr. Davis, you are: *Ibid.*

5. p. 398   I want that boy: Sidney Poitier, *This Life* (New York: Alfred A. Knopf, 1980).

6. P. 398   In my judgment, *Porgy*: *Ibid.*

7. p. 398   This is one of: *Ibid.*

8. p. 399   To this day, I: *Ibid.*

9. p. 399   the harsh, terrorized lies: Dandridge and Conrad, *Everything and Nothing: The Dorothy Dandridge Tragedy*.

10. p. 399   Actually, the film should: *Ibid.*

11. p. 399   Don't do it, it: *Ibid.*

12. p. 399   I'm going to think: *Ibid.*

13. p. 400   every actress wants to: "'Porgy and Bess' Director Tells How He lured Poitier and Dandridge," *Jet*, January 23, 1958.

14. p. 400   you wouldn't play *Oklahoma*: *Ibid.*

15. p. 400   The whole point of: *Ibid.*

16. p. 400   Do it. It'll make: Dandridge and Conrad, *Everything and Nothing: The Dorothy Dandridge Tragedy*.

17. p. 400   Look I have spoken: *Ibid.*

18. p. 40l   Why do you always: *Ibid.*

19. p. 401   a limit to the: *Ibid.*

20. p. 403   I ceased to have: *Ibid.*

21. p. 403   I turned violent: *Ibid.*

22. p. 407   A beautiful Negro woman: "Mrs. Sam Goldwyn Finds Negro Beauty Alluring," *Jet*, November 5, 1959.

23. p. 407 I had never known: *Ibid.*
24. p. 408   in view of the: Production Code Administration Files, AMPAS.
25. p. 408   No body, no voice: Berg, *Goldwyn: A Biography.*
26. p. 411   And God's Will Be: Loudon Wainwright, "The One-Man Gang Is In Action Again," *Life,* February 16, 1959.
27. p. 411   like a race horse: Sheilah Graham column, *The New YorkMirror,* September 14, 1958.
28. p. 411   hands unsympathetic to my: "Racial Bias Thrown into 'Porgy' Fight; Stars Backing Preminger," *Daily Variety,* August 7, 1959.
29. p. 412   It may always come: Sheilah Graham column, *The New York Mirror,* September 14, 1958.
30. p. 414   Otto Preminger jumped on: Poitier, *This Life.*
31. p. 414   What's the matter with: *Ibid.*
32. p. 414   visibly shaken: *Ibid.*
33. p. 414   No, no, no—what's: *Ibid.*
34. p. 414   Dorothy Dandridge fell apart: *Ibid.*
35. p. 414   unable to summon up: *Ibid.*
36. p. 414   now heaped upon me: Dandridge and Conrad, *Everything and Nothing: The Dorothy Dandridge Tragedy.*
37. p. 416   hot personality clashes on: Sammy Davis Jr. *Hollywood In A Suitcase.*
38. p. 417   was simply out on: *Ibid.*
39. p. 417   What does this girl: *Ibid.*
40. p. 417   sensitive and hurt easily: *Ibid.*
41. p. 417   You know, whatever I: *Ibid.*
42. p. 419   Otto, you must recast: Otto Preminger, *Preminger: An Autobiography.* (Garden City: Doubleday & Co., Inc. 1977 The entire exchange that follows between Preminger and Dandridge was told to me by Preminger. I've used the quotes that appeared in his autobiography.
43. p. 420   Now, look, she's having: the conversation between Peters and Preminger is drawn from the author's interview with Brock Peters.
44. p. 422   I found a perfect: Carroll and Firestone, *Diahann.*
45. p. 422   I'm about to marry: *Ibid.*
46. p. 422   I felt sorry for: *Ibid.*
47. p. 422   I have been going: Louella Parsons column, *The Los Angeles Examiner,* October 10, 1958.
48. p. 423   Miss Dandridge is not: Sara Hamilton, "'Decks Ran Red' Good Suspense Film," *The Los Angeles Examiner,* October 30, 1958.
49. p. 423   Look, you've got a: Berg, *Goldwyn: A Biography.*

Chapter 13: Hoping

Parts of this chapter have been drawn from the author's interviews and conversations with Laslo Benedek, Geri Branton, Otto Preminger, Harold Jovien, Dorothy Nicholas Morrow, Byron Morrow, Vivian Dandridge, Andrew Stone, Maria Cole, Lennie Bluett, Bobby Short, Herb Jeffries, Earl Mills, Catherine Ruthenberg, and others. Also consulted were *Elizabeth: The Life And Career of Elizabeth Taylor; The Film Encyclopedia; Preminger: An Autobiography,* and articles in *Jet, The Los Angeles Examiner, The Daily Sketch, The Hollywood Reporter, The Daily Mirror, The Sunday Express, The Daily Telegraph, The New York Herald Tribune, The Saturday Review, Variety, Time, The New York Times, The*

New York Sunday News, The Los Angeles Sentinel, The Chicago Defender, The Los Angeles Examiner, and other publications.

1. p. 425   When the time comes: "Dandridge Denies Marriage to White cafe Owner," *Jet*, January 22, 1959.
2. p. 425   I knew she was: "Dot Dandridge's 'Favorite Guy' Tells of His Love for Actress," *Jet*, February 26, 1959.
3. p. 431   Dorothy Dandridge telephoned me: Louella Parsons column, *The Los Angeles Examiner*, February 20, 1959.
4. p. 434   Did you invest money: Otto Preminger, *Preminger: An Autobiography* (Doubleday & Co., Inc., 1977).
5. p. 434   You know me: Ibid.
6. p. 434   Just before Dorothy Dandridge: Louella Parsons column, *The Los Angeles Examiner*, March 26, 1959.
7. p. 435   hoisted the conventional pretty: *Time*, April 6, 1959.
8. p. 435   Will Marriage to Jack: "Will Marriage Hurt Dandridge's Career?," *Jet*, April 9, 1959.
9. p. 437   made up my: *Daily Sketch*, January 20, 1960.
10. p. 443   It is not a picture: "Dandridge Makes Toughest Movie of Her Career," *Jet*, July 23, 1959.
11. p. 445   Dorothy Dandridge plays the: James Power, *Malaga* review, *The Hollywood Reporter*, February 16, 1962.
12. p. 445   It's remarkable that a: *Malaga* review, *Variety*, February 3, 1960.
13. p. 446   Miss Dandridge provides some: Dick Richards, "At the Pictures," *Daily Mirror* (London), January 29, 1960.
14. p. 446   you can't have everything: John Braine, "This is my test about going to pictures," *Daily Express* (London), January 29, 1960.
15. p. 446   Miss Dandridge is pretty: Campbell Dixon, "Crime that Carries Conviction," *Daily Telegraph* (London), January 30, 1960.
16. p. 446   Through all the incredible: Derek Monsey, "Derek Monsey at the new shows," *Sunday Express* (London), January 31, 1960.
17. p. 451   I couldn't wait to: Dorothy Dandridge and Earl Conrad, *Everything and Nothing: The Dorothy Dandridge Tragedy* (New York: Abelard-Schuman, 1970).
18. p. 451   The worst thing about: "The New Pictures," *Time*, July 6, 1959.
19. p. 451   The mills of the: "Sidney Poitier and Dorothy Dandridge Portray denizens of Catfish Row," *The New York Times*, June 25, 1959.
20. p. 451   Dorothy Dandridge, who emphasizes: "The New Pictures," *Time*, July 6, 1959.
21. p. 451   Miss Dandridge is perhaps: *Porgy and Bess* review, *Variety*, July 1, 1959.
22. p. 451   Dorothy Dandridge's Bess is: Paul V. Beckley, *Porgy and Bess* review, *The New York Herald Tribune*, June 25, 1959.
23. p. 452   Miss Dandridge's tragic eyes: Arthur Knight, "SR Goes to the Movies," *The Saturday Review*, July 4, 1959.
24. p. 452   a strong indication that: Don Nelson, "No Dashes for Dot," *Coloroto Magazine*, *New York Sunday News*, June 7, 1959.
25. p. 453   Look, dear heart, jump!: Dandridge and Conrad, *Everything And Nothing: The Dorothy Dandridge Tragedy*.
26. p. 454   This could shape as: *Tamango* review, *Variety*, February 12, 1958.
27. p. 454   Intense and provocative, *Tomango* [sic]: "Movie of the Week," *Jet*, August 27, 1959.

28. p. 455 A fellow brother of: Darcy DeMille, "*Tomango* [sic] Shouldn't Have Been Made," *The Los Angeles Sentinel*, October 8, 1959.

29. p. 458 You won't have the: Louie Robinson, "Dorothy Dandridge: Hollywood's Tragic Enigma," *Ebony*, March 1966.

30. p. 459 There is only one: "Dot Dandridge Stars in Own Club," *The Chicago Defender*, August 8, 1959.

31. p. 459 Dorothy Dandridge opens a: "Dot Dandridge to Play Her Husband's Nitery," *The Hollywood Reporter*, August 26, 1959.

32. p. 460 The Lass with the: Mike Connelly, "Rambling Reporter," *The Hollywood Reporter*, September 11, 1959.

33. p. 460 Run—don't walk—to: Hank Grant, Review, *The Hollywood Reporter*, September 11, 1959.

34. p. 460 obviously nervous: Louella Parsons column, *The Los Angeles Examiner*, September 12, 1959.

35. p. 464 Ed Sullivan, to the: "Ed Sullivan Show," *Variety*, December 16, 1959.

36. p 465 The geologist estimates a: Letter, DBDDC.

37. p. 466 an exciting and provocative: Review, *Variety*, February 10, 1960.

Chapter 14: Collapse

Parts of this chapter were drawn from the author's interviews and conversations with Geri Branton, John Peyser, Peter Mark Richman, Helen Richman, Herb Rogers, Harold Jovien, Maria Cole, Vivian Dandridge, Ivan Dixon, Olga James, Herb Jeffries, Gerald Mayer, Earl Mills, Dorothy Nicholas Morrow, Nichelle Nichols, Catherine Ruthenberg, Bobby Short, and others.

Some information on Dandridge's divorce from Denison was found in the Los Angles County Hall of Records. Also consulted were *The Ragman's Son; Hollywood's Mother of the Year: Sheila MacRae's Own Story; Doris Day: Her Own Story* and articles in *The Los Angeles Examiner*, *The Los Angeles Times*, *The Chicago Defender*, *Variety*, *The Chicago Daily Tribune*, *The Los Angeles Sentinel*, *Ebony*, *Jet*, *The Hollywood Citizen-News*, and other publications.

1. p. 468 Whatever house I possess: Information here and following pertaining to details of Dorothy Dandridge's will were found in the Los Angeles county Hall of Records.

2. p. 474 Dorothy Dandridge, somewhat absent: "1961 May Be the Year For Dorothy Dandridge," *The Chicago Defender*, February 18, 1961.

3. p. 474 despite best efforts the: Review, *Variety*, February 22, 1961.

4. p. 475 The Labor and Industry: "Rams-Giants Rookies May Steal Spotlight," *The Los Angeles Sentinel*, August 17, 1961.

5. p. 476 Dorothy Dandridge has expanded: "Dorothy Dandridge Revue," *Variety*, September 13, 1961.

6. p. 476 She does a French: Review, *Variety*, October 11, 1961.

7. p. 481 Dear Dorothy: Letter, *The Hollywood Reporter*, February 19, 1962.

8. p. 483 notable for several reasons: Vance King, "Blues For A Junkman," *The Hollywood Reporter*, March 1, 1962.

9. p. 484 We Negroes finally convinced: Hal Humphrey, "Wanted: A Brave Sponsor for Cole and Dandridge," *The Los Angeles Times*, February 14, 1962.

10. p. 485 An inept administrator, a: "Producers," *Time*, January 13, 1967.

11. p. 485 "I suppose you could: All quotes with Louie Robinson are from

the "The World of Dorothy Dandridge," *Ebony*, June 1962.

12. p. 488   The star whose name: Thomas Willis, "Alert 'West Side Story' Warms Music Theater," *The Chicago Daily Tribune*, August 15, 1962.

13. p. 489   I was just too: "Ailing Dot Bows Out After Chicago Debut," *Jet*, September 6, 1962.

14. p. 495   inflicted upon her grievous: Dorothy Dandridge and Jack Denison divorce records in Los Angeles County Hall of Records. Other information pertaining to the divorce is found in the records.

15. p 496   I wasn't doing too: "Dot Dandridge Sues for Divorce in Los Angeles," *Jet*, November 22, 1962.

16. p. 497   Whenever you file: *Ibid.*

17. p. 498   He has a temper: "Divorce Granted to Sultry Singer," Hollywood *Citizen-News*, December 18,1962.

18. p. 499   "The case grew out: Sheila MacRae and Paul H. Jeffries, *Hollywood Mother of The Year: Sheila MacRae's Own Story*. (New York: Birch Lane Press, 1992).

19. p. 500   "I was getting letters: Kirk Douglas, *The Ragman's Son* (New York: Simon & Schuster, Inc.,1988)

20. p. 500   On July 14, 1987: *Ibid.*

21. p. 500   by far the worst: A. E. Hotchner, *Doris Day: Her Own Story* (New York: William Morrow & Co., Inc., 1975).

22. p. 500   discovered that she was: *Ibid.*

23. p. 502   The old home: "Entertainer Claims She Is Broke," *Hollywood Citizen-News*, April 1, 1963.

24. p. 503   Miss Dandridge has no: "Why Dorothy Dandridge Is Broke," *Jet*, April 18, 1963.

25. p. 503   Even under ordinary circumstances: *Ibid.*

26. p. 503   When the world was: *Everything And Nothing: The Dorothy Dandridge Tragedy* (New York: Abelard-Schuman, 1970).

Chapter 15: Lonely Days, Long Nights, Last Rites

Parts of this chapter were drawn from the author's interviews and conversations with Geri Branton, Abby Mann, Kathryn Grayson, Juliette Ball, Harold Nicholas, Fayard Nicholas, Herb Rogers, Orin Borsten, Mel Bryant, Maria Cole, Vivian Dandridge, Ivan Dixon, Morty Jacobs, Madeline Jacobs, Olga James, Herb Jeffries, Etta Jones Mills, Earl Mills, Nichelle Nichols, Nick Perito, Bobbi Rogers, and others.

Information was also drawn from *The Raw Pearl*; *Preminger: An Autobiography*; and articles in *Ebony, Jet, The Los Angeles Sentinel, The Cleveland Call and Post, The Hollywood Reporter*, the *New York Post, The New York Times, The Washington Post*, and other publications.

1. p. 507   "That collapse of fortune: Dorothy Dandridge and Earl Conrad, *Everything And Nothing: The Dorothy Dandridge Tragedy* (New York: Abelard-Schuman, 1970).

2. p. 508   This is the largest: Louie Robinson, "50,000 Jam L.A. Ball Park For Biggest Rights Rally,"*Jet*, June 13, 1963.

3. p. 513   Let's face it: Allen Howard, "Dazzling Dot On Local TV," *The Cleveland Call Post*, July 27, 1963.

4. p. 513   the glare of 50,000: Charles Sanders, "Tragic Story of Dandridge's Retarded Daughter," *Jet*, August 22, 1963.

5. p. 513   So many of you: *Ibid.*

6. p. 514   It was one of: *Ibid.*

7. p. 514 There's the mistaken belief: "Words of the Week," *Jet*, January 7, 1965.
8. p. 521 I chased a will-o'-the-wisp: Dandridge and Conrad, *Everything And Nothing: The Dorothy Dandridge Tragedy*.
9. p. 521 Finally, when friends, physicians: *Ibid*.
10. p. 522 There is a big: Louie Robinson, "Dorothy Dandridge: Hollywood's Tragic Enigma," *Ebony*, March 1966.
11. p. 524 paralytic state: Dandridge and Conrad, *Everything And Nothing: The Dorothy Dandridge Tragedy*.
12. p. 527 In 1964 she used: Pearl Bailey, *The Raw Pearl* (New York: Harcourt, Brace & Wold, Inc.,1968).
13. p. 527 would avoid me in: *Ibid*.
14. p. 528 One night, Dorothy phoned: Dorothy commented on this incident in *Everything And Nothing: The Dorothy Dandridge Tragedy*.
15. p. 532 The last time I: Otto Preminger, *Preminger: An Autobiography* (Garden City: Doubleday & Company, Inc, 1977).
16. p. 533 for rest and treatment: Louie Robinson, "Dorothy Dandridge: Hollywood's Tragic Enigma," *Ebony*, March 1966.
17. p. 537 The next day we: Bailey, *The Raw Pearl*.
18. p. 543 received the most enthusiastic: Louie Robinson, "Dorothy Dandridge: Hollywood's Tragic Enigma," *Ebony*, March 1966.
19. p. 544 She doesn't even know: Charles Sanders, "Tragic Story of Dandridge's Retarded Daughter," *Jet*, August 22, 1963.
20. p. 545 You will be able: Louie Robinson, "Dorothy Dandridge: Hollywood's Tragic Enigma," *Ebony*, March 1966.
21. p. 548 Yeats might have written: *The Hollywood Reporter* September 9, 1965.
22. p. 549 In case of my: *New York Post*, October 11, 1965.
23. p. 550 Dorothy believed in God: Louie Robinson, "Peter Lawford Too Overcome To Speak at Dot Dandridge Rites," *Jet*, September 30, 1965.
24. p. 552 was due to a: "Dorothy Dandridge Died of Pill Dosage, Coroner Now Says," *The New York Times*, November 18, 1965.

BIBLIOGRAPHY

A selected listing of the books consulted for this work follows. Not included here are the numerous magazines, newspapers, publicity releases, and other material already cited in either the text or the notes of this book.

Alpert, Hollis. *The Life and Times of Porgy and Bess: The Story of an American Classic.* New York: Alfred A. Knopf, 1990.

American Business Consultants. *Red Channels: The Report of Communist Influence In Radio and Television.* New York: Counterattack, 1950.

Bailey, Pearl. *The Raw Pearl.* New York: Harcourt, Brace & World, 1968.

Baker, Jean-Claude, and Chris Chase. *Josephine: The Hungry Heart.* New York: Random House, 1993.

Bass, Charlotta A. *Forty Years: Memoirs From The Pages of A Newspaper.* Los Angeles: self-published, 1960.

Berg, A. Scott. *Goldwyn: A Biography.* New York: Knopf, 1980.

Black, Gregory D., and Clayton R. Koppes. *Hollywood Goes To War: How Politics, Profits and Propaganda Shaped World War II Movies.* Berkeley: University of California Press, 1987.

Bogle, Donald. *Blacks In American Films and Television: An Illustrated Encyclopedia.* New York: Fireside, 1989.

Bogle, Donald. *Brown Sugar: Eighty Years of America's Black Female Superstars.* New York: Da Capo Press, 1990.

Bogle, Donald. *Toms, Coons, Mulattoes, Mammies, and Bucks: An Interpretive History of Blacks in American Films,* Third Edition. New York: Continuum Publishing, 1994.

Bond, J. Max. *The Negro In Los Angeles: A Dissertation.* Los Angeles:

University. of Southern California, 1936.

Carroll, Diahann, with Ross Firestone. *Diahann*. Boston: Little, Brown & Co., 1986.

Ceplair, Larry, and Steven Englund. *The Inquisition In Hollywood: Politics in the Film Community, 1930-1960.* Garden City: Anchor Press/Doubleday & Company, Inc., 1980.

Collins, Joan. *Joan Collins: Past Imperfect, An Autobiography.* New York. Simon & Schuster, 1978.

Collins, Keith. *Black Los Angeles: The Maturing of the Ghetto, 1940-1950.* Saratoga: Century Twenty One Publishing, 1980.

Cooper, Ralph with Steve Dougherty. *Amateur Night At The Apollo: Ralph Cooper Presents Five Decades of Great Entertainment.* New York: Harper Collins, 1990.

Dandridge, Dorothy and Earl Conrad. *Everything And Nothing: The Dorothy Dandridge Tragedy.* New York: Abelard-Schuman, 1970.

Davis, Russell H.. *Black Americans In Cleveland.* Washington D.C.: Associated Publishers, 1972.

Davis Jr., Sammy. *Hollywood in a Suitcase.* New York: William Morrow & Co., 1980.

Day, Doris, with A. E. Hotchner. *Doris Day: Her Own Story.* New York: William Morrow & Co., 1975.

Douglas, Kirk. *The Ragman's Son.* New York: Simon & Schuster, 1988.

Ellington, Edward Kennedy. *Music Is My Mistress.* Garden City: Doubleday & Company, Inc., 1973.

Epstein, Helen. *Joe Papp: An American Life.* Boston: Little, Brown Company., 1994.

Essoe, Gabe. *Tarzan of The Movies.* New York: Citadel Press, 1968.

Fordin, Hugh. *The World of Entertainment: Hollywood's Greatest Musicals.* Garden City: Doubleday & Company, Inc., 1975.

Friedrich, Otto. *City of Nets: A Portrait of Hollywood in the 1940's.* New York: Harper & Row, 1987.

Fury, David. *Kings of The Jungle: An Illustrated Reference To "Tarzan" on Screen and Television.* Jefferson: McFarland & Co., 1994.

Gillespie, Dizzy, with Al Fraser. *To Be or Not to Bop.* Garden City: Doubleday & Company, Inc., 1979.

Gussow, Mel. *Don't Say Yes Until I Finish: A Biography of Darryl F. Zanuck.* Garden City: Doubleday & Company, Inc., 1971

Haskins, Jim. *The Cotton Club.* New York: Random House, 1977.

Hajdu, David. *Lush Life: A Biography of Billy Strayhorn.* New York: Farrar Straus Giroux, 1996.

Heimann, Jim. *Out with the Stars: Hollywood Nightlife in the Golden Era.* New York: Abbeville Press, 1985.

Hine, Darlene Clark, ed. *Black Women In America: An Historical Encyclopedia.* New York: Clarkson Publishing Inc., 1993.

Horne, Lena, and Richard Schickel. *Lena.* Garden City: Doubleday & Company Inc., 1965.

Horne, Marilyn, with Jane Scovell. *Marilyn Horne: My Life.* New York: Atheneum, 1983.

Houseman, John. *Run Through.* New York: Simon & Schuster, 1972.

Jablonski, Edward. *Harold Arlen: Happy with the Blues.* Garden City: Doubleday & Company, Inc., 1961.

Jackson, Carlton. *Hattie: The Life of Hattie McDaniel.* Lanham: Madison Books, 1990.

James Spada. *Peter Lawford: The Man Who Kept Secrets.* New York: Bantam Books, 1991.

Katz, Ephraim. *The Film Encyclopedia.* New York: Harper Perennial, 1994.

Katz, William Loren. *The Black West.* Garden City: Doubleday and Company, Inc., 1971.

Knepp, Donn. *Las Vegas: The Entertainment Capital.* Menlo Park: Lane, 1987.

Kusmer, Kenneth L.. *A Ghetto Takes Shape: Black Cleveland: 1870-1930.* Urbana: University of Illinois Press, 1976.

Mapp, Edward. *Blacks In The Performing Arts.* Metuchen: The Scarecrow Press, 1978.

MacRae, Sheila, with Paul H. Jeffries. *Hollywood Mother of the Year: Sheila MacRae's Own Story.* New York: Birch Lane Press, 1992.

Mills, Earl. *Dorothy Dandridge: A Portrait in Black.* Los Angeles: Holloway House, 1970.

Milne, Tom. *Mamoulian.* Bloomington: Indiana University Press, 1969.

Moore, Phil. *Things I Forgot To Tell You.* Unpublished, 1986.

Mosley, Leonard. *Zanuck: The Rise and Fall of Hollywood's Last Tycoon.* Boston: Little, Brown and Company, 1984.

Navasky, Victor. *Naming Names.* New York: The Viking Press, 1980.

Poitier, Sidney. *This Life.* New York: Alfred A. Knopf, 1980.

Preminger, Otto. *Preminger: An Autobiography.* Garden City: Doubleday & Company, Inc., 1977.

Ray, Ollie M. *Biographies of Selected Leaders in Tap Dance.* A Dissertation: University of Utah, 1976.

Placksin, Sally. *American Women In Jazz.* New York: Wideview Books, 1982.

Reed, Tom. *The Black Music History of Los Angeles: Its Roots.* Los Angeles: Black Accent, 1992.

Rose, Phyllis. *Jazz Cleopatra: Josephine Baker in Her Time.* New York: Doubleday and Company, Inc. 1989.

Salvi, Delia Nora. *The History of The Actor's Laboratory, Inc.: 1941-1950.* Ann Arbor: University Microfilms International, 1970.

Schary, Dore. *Heyday: An Autobiography.* Boston: Little, Brown and Company, 1979.

Sheppard, Dick. *Elizabeth: The Life And Career of Elizabeth Taylor.* Garden City: Doubleday & Company, Inc., 1974.

Short, Bobby, with Robert Mackintosh. *The Life and Times of A Saloon Singer.* New York: Clarkson N. Potter, 1995.

Spoto, Donald. *Marilyn Monroe.* New York: Harper Collins, 1993.

Stearns, Marshall and Jean. *Jazz Dance.* New York: Schirmer, 1968.

Tierney, Gene, with Mickey Herskowitz. *Self-Portrait, Gene Tierney.* unspecified: Wyden Books, 1978.

Tyler, Bruce M. *From Harlem to Hollywood: The Struggle for Racial and Cultural Democracy 1920-1943.* New York: Garland, 1992.

Vidor, King. *A Tree Is a Tree.* New York: Harcourt, Brace & Company, 1952.

Wiley, Mason, and Damien Bona. *Inside Oscar: The Unofficial History of the Academy Awards.* New York: Ballantine Books, 1986.

THE FILMS OF
DOROTHY DANDRIDGE

The Big Broadcast of 1936 (1935)
Directed by Norman Taurog. Screenplay by Walter DeLeon, Francis Martin, and Ralph Spence. Produced by Benjamin Glazer. Cast: DD with Vivian Dandridge and Etta Jones in an unbilled Dandridge Sisters appearance; The Nicholas Brothers, Bill 'Bojangles' Robinson, George Burns and Gracie Allen, Jack Oakie, Wendy Barrie, Akim Tamiroff, Charles Correll and Freeman Gosden (as Amos 'n' Andy), and Benny Baker. Paramount.

A Day at the Races (1937)
Directed and produced by Sam Wood. Screenplay by Robert Pirosh, George Seaton, and George Oppenheimer. Original story by Robert Pirosh and George Seaton. Director of Photography: Joseph Ruttenberg. Musical numbers staged by Dave Gould. Cast: DD with Vivian Dandridge and Etta Jones in an unbilled Dandridge Sisters appearance; Ivie Anderson and the Crinoline Choir; The Marx Brothers, Maureen O'Sullivan, Margaret Dumont, Leonard Ceeley, Frankie Darro, and—an extra—Carole Landis. MGM.

It Can't Last Forever (1937)
Directed by Hamilton MacFadden. Screenplay by Lee Loeb and Harold Buchman. Produced by Harry L. Decker. Director of Photography: Allen G. Siegler. Cast: DD with Vivian Dandridge and Etta Jones in a Dandridge Sisters appearance in a musical sequence with Eugene Jackson and Charles Bennett; Ralph Bellamy, Betty Furness, and Robert Armstrong. Columbia Pictures.

Going Places (1939)
Directed by Ray Enright. Screenplay by Sig Hersig, Jerry Wald, and Maurice Leo. Based on the play *The Hottentot* by Victor Manes and William Collier, Sr. Director of Photography: Arthur I. Todd. Cast: DD with Vivian Dandridge and Etta Jones in a Dandridge Sisters appearance in a musical sequence with Louis Armstrong and Maxine Sullivan; also Dick Powell, Anita Louise, Allen Jenkins, R Jonald Reagan, Larry Williams, Minna Gombell, Joyce Compton, and Robert Warwick. Warner Bros.

Irene (1940)
Directed and produced by Herbert Wilcox. Screenplay by Alice Duer Miller.

Based on the musical comedy by Josephy McCarthy and Harry Tierney. Director of Photography: Russell Metty. Cast: DD with Vivian and Etta Jones in an unbilled Dandridge Sisters appearance; Anna Neagle, Ray Milland, Arthur Treacher, Billie Burke, Roland Young, Isabel Jewell, and, in the Black musical sequence, Hattie Noel. RKO.

Four Shall Die (1941)
(a.k.a *Condemned Men)* Directed by Leo Popkin. Screenplay by Ed Dewey. Produced by Clifford Sanforth. Cast: DD as Helen Fielding, Mantan Moreland, Neil Pete Webster, Jesse Lee Brooks, Jack Carter, and Reginald Fenderson. Million Dollar Pictures.

Sun Valley Serenade (1941)
Directed by H. Bruce Humberstone. Screenplay by Robert Ellis and Helen Logan. Story by Art Arthur and Robert Harari. Produced by Milton Sperling. Director of Photography: Edward Cronjager. Cast: DD in "specialty" musical sequence with the Nicholas Brothers; also Sonja Henie, John Payne, Milton Berle, Joan Davis, Lynn Bari, Glenn Miller and his orchestra. Twentieth Century Fox.

Lady from Louisiana (1941)
Directed and associate produced by Bernard Vorhaus. Screenplay by Vera Caspary, Michael Hogan, and Guy Endore. Story by Edward James and Francis Faragoh. Director of Photography: Jack Marta. Cast: DD as Felice, John Wayne, Ona Munson, Ray Middleton, Henry Stephenson, and Helen Westley. Republic Pictures.

Sundown (1941)
Directed by Henry Hathaway. Screenplay by Barre Lyndon. Adaptation by Charles G. Booth. Produced by Walter Wanger. Director of Photography: Charles Lang. With special photography by Ray O. Binger. Cast: DD as Kipsang's Bride, Gene Tierney, Bruce Cabot, George Sanders, Jester Hairston, Kenny Washington, Woodrow Strode, Jeni LeGon, Emmett Smith, Prince MOdupe, Hassan Said, Wesley Gale, Blue Washington, Harry Carey, Joseph Calleia, Reginald Gardiner, and Sir Cedric Hardwicke. United Artists.

Bahama Passage (1941)
Directed and produced by Edward Griffin. Screenplay by Virginia Van Upp. Based on a story by Nelson Hayes. Director of Photography: Leo Tover and Allen Davey. Cast: DD as Thalia, Sterling Hayden, Madeleine Carroll, Leo G. Carroll, Flora Robson, Leigh Whipper, Jeni LeGon, and Cecil Kellaway. Paramount Pictures.

Drums of the Congo (1942)
Directed by Christy Cabanne. Screenplay by Paul Huston and Roy Chanslor. Produced by Universal. Cast: DD as Malimi, Ernest Whitman, Jesse Lee Brooks, Turhan Bey, Stuart Erwin, Ona Munson, Napoleon Simpson, and Jules Bledsoe. Universal Pictures.

Lucky Jordan (1942)
Directed by Frank Tuttle. Screenplay by Darrell Ware and Karl Tunberg. Based on a story by Charles Leonard. Produced by Fred Kohlmar. Director of

Photography: John Seitz. Cast: DD in an unbilled appearance as a maid, Alan Ladd, Helen Walker, Marie McDjonald, Sheldon Leonard, and Lloyd Corrigan. Paramount.

Hit Parade of 1943 (1943)
Directed by Albert S. Rogell. Screenplay by Frank Gill Jr. with additional dialogue by Frances Hyland. Produced by Albert J. Cohen. Director of Photography: Jack Marta. Choreography by Nick Castle. Cast: DD in musical sequence with the Count Basie Orchestra; John Carroll, Susan Hayward, Gail Patrick, Eve Arden, Ray McKinley Band, and Jack Williams, the Harlem Sandman. Republic Pictures.

Since You Went Away (1944)
Directed by John Cromwell. Screenplay by David O. Selznick. Based on the novel of the same title by Margaret Buell Wilder. Produced by David O. Selznick. Director of Photography: Stanley Cortez and Lee Garmes. Cast: DD in a very brief unbilled appearance (without dialogue) as a young wife and mother in a train station seeing her G.I. husband off to war; Claudette Colbert, Hattie McDaniel, Jennifer Jones; Shirley Temple, Joseph Cotton, Monty Woolley, Agnes Moorehead, and Robert Walker. United Artists.

Atlantic City (1944)
Directed by Ray McCary. Written by Doris Gilbert and Frank Gill, Jr., and George Carleton Brown. Based on a story by Arthor Caesar. Director of Photography: Musical numbers staged by Seymour Felix. Cast: DD in a musical sequence with Louis Armstrong and his orchestra; also Buck and Bubbles, Constance Moore, Brad Taylor, Charley Grapewin, Jerry Colonna, Adele Mara, Belle Baker, Joe Frisco, and Paul Whiteman and his orchestra. Republic Pictures.

Pillow to Post (1945)
Directed by Vincent Sherman. Screenplay by Charles Hoffman. Based on the stage play by Rose Simon Kohn. Cast: DD in a musical sequence with Louis Armstrong and his orchestra; also Ida Lupino, Willie Best, Sydney Greenstreet, William Prince, Stuart Erwin, Ruth Donnelly, and Paul Harvey. Warner Bros.

Tarzan's Peril (1951)
Directed by Byron Haskin with additional African footage by Phil Brandon. Screenplay by Samuel Newman and Francis Swann. Based on characters created by Edgar Rice Burroughs. Produced by Sol Lesser. Director of Photography: Karl Struss and Jack Whitehead. Cast: DD as Melmendi; Lex Barker, Frederick O'Neal, George MacReady. Bob Davis, Alan Napier, Virginia Huston, and DouglasFowley. RKO

The Harlem Globetrotters (1951)
Dircted by Phil Brown. Screenplay by Alfred Palca. Produced by. Director of Photography: Philip Tannura. Cast: DD as Ann Carpenter; William Brown, Thomas Gomez, William Walker, Angela Clark, and the Harlem Globetrotters. Columbia Pictures.

Bright Road (1953)
Directed by Gerald Mayer. Screenplay by Emmett Lavary. Based on the story "See How They Run" by Mary Elizabeth Vroman. Produced by Sol Baer

Fielding. Director of Photography: Alfred Gilks. Cast: DD as Jane Richards; Harry Belafonte, Philip Hepburn, Barbara Ann Sanders, Maidie Norman, William Walker, Jeni LeGon, Robert Horton, Vivian Dandridge, Patti Marie Ellis, Joy Jackson, Carolyn Ann Jackson, Fred Moultrie, James Moultrie, and Renee Beard. MGM.

Remains to Be Seen (1953)

Directed by Don Weis. Screenplay by Sidney Sheldon. Based on the play by Howard Lindsay and Russel Crouse. Produced by Arthur Hornblow Jr. Director of Photography: Robert Planck. Cast: DD in a musical sequence; June Allyson, Van Johnson, Angela Lansbury, Louis Calhern, and John Beal. MGM.

Carmen Jones (1954)

Directed and produced by Otto Preminger. Screenplay by Harry Kleiner. Based upon the stage book and lyrics of Oscar Hammerstein II, the opera by Georges Bizet, and the original story by Prosper Merimee. Music direction: Herschel Burke Gilbert. Director of Photography: Sam Leavitt. Choreography by Herb Ross. Cast: DD as Carmen Jones; Harry Belafonte, Pearl Bailey, Olga James, Joe Adams, Brock Peters, Roy Glenn, Diahann Carroll, Nick Stewart, Madame Sul Te Wan, Mauri Lynn, DeForrest Covan, June Eckstine, Sandy Lewis, and Bernie Hamilton. With Max Roach, Carmen de Lavallade, Alvin Ailey, Archie Savage and James Truitt in roadhouse dance sequence. Carmen's vocals by Marilyn Horne. Joe's vocals by Le Vern Hutcherson. Husky's vocals by Marvin Hayes.

Island in the Sun (1957)

Directed by Robert Rossen. Screenplay by Alfred Hayes. Based on the novel by Alex Waugh. Produced by Darryl F. Zanuck. Director of Photography: F.A. Young. Cast: DD as Margot Seaton; Harry Belafonte, James Mason, Joan Fontaine, Joan Collins, John Justin, Michael Rennie, Stephen Boyd, Diana Wynyard, Patricia Owens, John Williams, and Basil Sydney. 20th Century Fox.

The Decks Ran Red (1958)

Directed and Screenplay by Andrew Stone. Produced by Virginia and Andrew Stone. Director of Photography: Meredith M. Nicholson. Cast: DD as Mahia; James Mason, Broderick Crawford, Stuart Whitman, Joel Fluellen, Jack Kruschen and Katharine Bard. MGM.

Tamango (1958)

Directed by John Berry. Adapted by John Berry, Lee Gold, Tamara Hovey, and Georges Neveux. Dialogue by Georges Neveux. Based on the novelette by Prosper Merimee. Director of Photography: Edmund Sechan. Cast: DD as Aiche; Curt Jurgens, Alex Cressan, Jean Servais, Roger Hanin, and Guy Mairesse. Hal Roach Release.

Porgy and Bess (1959)

Directed by Otto Preminger. Screenplay by Richard Nash. Produced by Samuel L. Goldwyn. Based on the stage operetta by George Gershwin, which was based on the novel *Porgy* by Du Bose Heywood. Director of Photography: Leon Shamroy. Musical director: Andre Previn. Choreography by Hermes Pan. Cast: DD as Bess; Sidney Poitier, Sammy Davis, Jr., Pearl Bailey, Brock Peters, Diahann Carroll, Ruth Attaway, Joel Fluellen, Clarence Muse, Roy Glenn, Helen

Thigpen, William Walker, Claude Akins, Ivan Dixon, Earl Jackson, Moses LaMarr, and Everdinne Wilson. With Nichelle Nichols and Maya Angelou. Bess's vocals by Adele Addison. Porgy's vocals by Robert McFerrin. Clara's vocals by Loulie Jean Norman. Columbia Pictures.

Malaga (1960)
Directed by Laslo Benedeck. Screenplay by David Osborn and Donald Ogden Stewart. Produced by Clyde Thomas. Based on the novel by Donald MacKenzie. Director of Photography: Desmond Dickinson. Cast: DD as Gianna; Trevor Howard, Edmund Purdom, Michael Hordern, Helen Goss, and Paul Stassino. Warner Bros.

Marco Polo (Uncompleted)
Directed by Christian Jacque. Produced by Raoul Levy.
Cast: DD, Anthony Quinn, Alain Delon, and France Nuyen.

Soundies and Short Films (between 1938 and 1947)

Soundies
Swing For Your Supper
Yes Indeed
Cow Cow Boogie
Birdland Fantasy
Zoot Suit
Jungle Jig
Easy Street
Congo Clambake
Paper Doll
Lazybones

Short Films:
Snow Gets In Your Eyes
I Don't Want To Cry Any More
Basin Street Blues
Flamingo

Compilation Film
Ebony Parade

Television Film
"Blues for a Junkman"
(Also filmed as a European feature titled *The Murder Men*)

INDEX

DD = Dorothy Dandridge.

A

Abbott, Sam, 91
Abraham, Dr. Carl, 439
Academy Awards, 378, 463
DD as first African-American nominee for Best Actress, xxv-xxvi, 311, 317, 319-321, 323-324
DD as first African-American female presenter, 324
Academy of Motion Picture Arts and Sciences, 319
Actors Lab (Los Angeles), 135, 152-157, 160-161, 162, 178, 185-186, 218, 219-220, 222, 391, 487
Actors Laboratory -- see Actors Lab (Los Angeles)
Actors Laboratory Theatre (Los Angeles), 218
Actors Studio (New York City), 135
Adams, Berle, 195, 203-204, 205, 306
Adams, Joe, 60, 268, 275, 278, 284-286, 303
Addison, Adele, 409-410
Adler, Buddy, 186-188, 343
Adventures of Robinson Crusoe, The, 319
Advise and Consent, 262
Affectionately Yours, 34
African American community, attitudes towards treatment in motion pictures, 12, 24-28, 30, 32-34, 39, 47-48, 265, 278, 292-293, 295, 304, 311-313, 317, 319-320, 324, 357-358, 423, 456-457, 463, 478
see also Black Hollywood; "Negro Problem" movies; race movies; racial stereotypes in entertainment
African American militancy, 513, 543
Ailey, Alvin, 269, 281
Algiers Hotel (Miami Beach), 206

Alhambra Tavern (Cleveland), 213, 215
Ali Baba Goes to Town, 54
All the King's Men, 357
All-Colored Vaudeville Show, A, 59
Allen, Gracie, 41
Allen, Steve, 303
Allison, May, 32
Allyson, June, 236, 241
Alvin Hotel (New York City), 335
Alvin Theatre (New York City), 274
Amato, Giuseppe, 345, 356
Ames, Jim (Jimmy), 170, 176
Amos 'n' Andy (radio series), 41, 118, 225
"Amos 'n' Andy" (television series), 75, 118, 483
Amsterdam News -- *see New York Amsterdam News*
Anatomy of a Murder, 262
And God Created Woman, 382, 476
Anderson, Eddie 'Rochester,' 34, 102, 114, 311
Anderson, Ernest, 95
Anderson, Ivie, 45, 46, 88, 90
Anderson, Judith, 300
Andrews, Robert, 79
Andrews Sisters, 63, 166
Angelou, Maya, 412, 415
Angelus Funeral Home (Los Angeles), 549-550
Ankles Aweigh, 335
Anna and the King of Siam, 330
Anna Lucasta, 268
apartheid, 137, 330
Apollo Theatre (New York City), 73, 82, 84, 114, 127
Aramanda and Lita, 45
Archerd, Amy, 323
Arlen, Harold, 125, 329, 339
Armstrong, Henry, 166
Armstrong, Louis, 26, 31, 35, 46, 48-49, 51, 58, 59, 67, 72, 73, 77, 105, 120-121, 123, 167, 311, 359, 403, 463
Arnaz, Desi, 170, 193

Around the World in Eighty Days, 382
Arrivederci (film project), 407
Asner, Ed, 477
Associated Press, 322
Astaire, Fred, 86, 396
Atkinson, Brooks, 73
Atlanta, Georgia, 48
Atlantic City, 105, 121
Ayers, Lemuel, 125

B

Babes in Arms, 59
Bacall, Lauren, 300
Bad and the Beautiful, The, 224
Bahama Passage, 87, 92, 98-99, 411
Bailey, Bill, 72, 73
Bailey, Pearl, 72, 103, 124, 125, 140, 171, 239, 243, 254, 275, 277, 285, 306, 307, 406,
 412, 415-416
DD and, 126, 283-284, 303, 418-419, 527, 537, 546, 550
Baker, Josephine, 26, 59, 67, 140, 159, 202, 206, 240, 254, 330, 389
Balanchine, George, 59
Baldwin, James, 305-306
Ball, Juliette, xxi, 16, 17, 36, 51, 52, 154, 179, 185, 402, 488, 518, 522-523, 525, 530, 533, 536, 546, 551
Ball, Lucille, 32, 167, 193
Baltimore Afro-American, 320
Bankhead, Tallulah, 60, 262
Barber of Seville, The (film project), 310, 339
Bardot, Brigitte, 457, 476
Barker, Lex, 182, 184
Barron, Vicky, marries Fayard Nicholas, 532
Basehart, Richard, 431, 437
Basie, Count, 31, 105, 167, 311
Basin Street Blues, 124
Basin Street East (New York City), 542-545
Baskette, James, 319
Bass, Charlotta, 95, 133
Battle, Lucy, 93
Baum, Martin, 398
Beale, Eddie, 124, 521-522, 551
Beavers, Jessie Mae (Brown), 114, 120
Beavers, Louise, 33, 94, 158, 159, 311
Beck, Edward. 125
Beckley, Paul V., 451
Beery, Wallace, 45
Belafonte, Harry, xvi, 225, 227, 232, 235-236, 310, 311, 313, 357, 360, 362, 368, 384,
 386, 398-399, 420, 435, 441-442
in *Carmen Jones*, 268, 275, 277, 278, 280, 282, 285, 286, 298
relationship with DD, 229-230, 282-283, 363-364, 376, 525, 530
Belafonte, Julie Robinson, 364, 435
Belafonte, Marguerite, 230

Bellamy, Ralph, 45
Belle of the Nineties, 33, 225
Bellson, Louis, 243, 527
Ben Carter's Pickaninny Choir, 40, 54
Benchley, Robert, 27
Benedek, Laslo, 437, 439-447, 525, 548
Benjamin, Robert, 262, 265, 310
Bennett, Charles, 45
Benny, Jack, 34, 397
Berg, Billy, 115
Bergman, Ingrid, 96, 377
Berlandina, Jane, 193
Berle, Milton, 86, 140
Berlin International Film Festival, 329
Berman, John, 259, 345, 355
Bernstein, Leonard, 409, 488
Berry, John, 379, 381, 454
Berry Brothers, The, 56, 75
Best, Willie, 33
Best Years of Our Lives, The, 397
Beulah (radio series), 118
"Beulah" (television series), 118, 228, 483
Bevard, H., 346
Beverly-Hilton Hotel (Los Angeles), 405, 464
Big Broadcast of 1936, 41-42, 47, 59
Billboard, 91
Biltmore Hotel (Lake Tahoe), 335-336
Biltmore Hotel (Los Angeles), 240
Bingo, The (Las Vegas), 170-176, 211, 237, 388
Bingo Long Traveling All-Stars and Motor Kings, 159
Birdland Fantasy, 93
Birth of a Nation, The, 12, 32
Bizet, Georges, 263-264, 277, 304, 330
Black, Dr. Sidney, 489
Black and Tan, 26
Black actors, opportunities for, 135-136, 216-217
Black Hollywood, xx, 24-28, 30, 31-34, 39, 42, 47-49, 83-84, 93, 94, 100, 107, 114, 116, 117, 135-136, 265, 313-314, 412, 463
newer generation, 311-312
older generation, 311-312
see also Motion pictures, African Americans in; "Negro problem" movies; race movies; racial stereotypes in entertainment
Black Moon, 33
Black Network, 59
Blackbirds of 1936, 59
Blackboard Jungle, 218, 334
blackface, in motion pictures, 12
Blake, Eubie, 59
blacklisting, 135, 155, 157, 185-186, 381, 439
DD escapes, 217-223
in Hollywood, 217-218
Blackwell, Jim, 33
Bledsoe, Ralph, 117
Blees, Robert, 470-471
Blood and Sand, 408

Blue Angel, The (film project), 329, 338
"Blues for a Junkman" (episode of "Cain's Hundred"), 477-483
see also Murder Men, The
Blues Opera, 329, 339
Bluett, Lennie, 39-40, 47, 49, 53, 102, 461
B'nai B'rith Brotherhood Week, 221
Bogart, Humphrey, 96, 319
Boite Lord Hotel (Sao Paulo), 247
Bonjour Tristesse, 413
Bontemps, Arna, 125
Borsten, Orin, 195, 255-256, 272-273, 283, 332-333, 336-337, 339, 363-364, 381, 418, 473, 521, 548
Bowery to Broadway, 39
Boyd, Stephen, 357
Boykin, Morrisontine, 449
Boys Quartet, 40
Bracken, Eddie, 240, 241
Brand, Phoebe, 153
Brando, Marlon, 298, 319, 334, 397, 439
Brandon, Phil, 182
Branton, Chip -- see Branton, Paul
Branton, Geraldine Pate Nicholas (Geri), xxiii, 6, 15, 16, 18, 51, 57, 65, 71, 80, 99-100,
113, 115-117, 154, 160, 186, 219, 233, 241, 243, 244, 246, 251, 254, 255, 257-258, 286-287, 297, 338, 339-340, 342, 347-353, 364, 381, 390, 403-406, 408, 418-419, 430, 433, 436, 446, 449, 459, 461, 463, 468-470, 472, 488, 493-495, 505, 547-548, 552-554
friendship with DD, 105, 106-108, 109-110, 111-112, 118-119, 120, 124, 125-127, 129, 130, 133-134, 136-137, 139, 147-148, 164, 172, 178, 228-229, 236-237, 314, 322, 328, 370, 374-376, 378, 388, 401-402, 426, 429, 499, 501-503, 517, 519, 524, 525, 527-529, 533-535, 537, 542, 549-550, 555
marriage to Fayard Nicholas, 104, 105, 124, 125, 133, 141-142, 306, 322
marriage to Leo Branton, 322, 501
Branton, Leo, 322, 372, 374-376, 383, 388, 426, 468, 501, 519, 529, 550
Branton, Paul (Chip), 322, 468, 524
Brave Bulls, The, 187
Breen, Joseph L., 266-267
Breen, Robert, 183, 329
Breen office -- see Production Code Administration
Brennan, Walter, 300
Brent, Earl, 459
Brice, Fanny, 59
Bricktop, 389
Brief Encounter, 431
Bright Road (formerly See How They Run), 216, 219, 224-234, 251, 256, 260, 265, 269, 281, 298, 508
Britt, May, 339
Broadway Bill, 35
Bronze Buckaroo, 91
Bronze Venus, 82

see also Duke Is Tops, The
Brooklyn Dodgers, 153
Brooks, Louise, xvii
Brooks, Richard, 218
Brother's (Los Angeles), 115-116
Brown, Bill, 185, 187-188
Brown, Clarence, 163
Brown, George F., 305
Brown, Norman, 69
Brown, Phil, 153, 185-186, 187
Brown, Troy, 73
Brown Derby (Los Angeles), 341
Brown Sugar, xxi
Brown v. Board of Education, 312
Bryant, Clora, 195-197
Bryant, Joyce, 195, 198, 206, 208, 209, 239, 255, 269, 270, 274, 299
Bryant, Marie, 42, 88, 91, 120
Bryant, Mel, 4, 47-48, 548-549
Brynner, Yul, 333
Buck and Bubbles, 58
Burns, George, 41, 397, 532
Burroughs, Edgar Rice, 182
Burton, Richard, 245
Bus Stop, DD seeks role in, 339
Butler, Charles, 33, 41
Butler, (Rev.) George (Frank) (DD's maternal grandfather), 2-3
Butler, Lauretta, 37
Butler, Nellie Simmons (DD's maternal grandmother), 2-3
Butts, Robert, 176, 495
Butts and Grosenbaugh, 176

C

Cabin in the Sky, 41, 96, 102, 122, 159, 202, 269, 278
Cabot, Bruce, 88
Café It (Los Angeles), 85
Café de Paris (London), 197-200, 326
Café Gala (Los Angeles) -- see Club Gala (Los Angeles)
Caine Mutiny, The, 319
"Cain's Hundred" (television series), 477-482
Calhoun, Helen, 177, 472, 504-505, 513
California Eagle, The, 83, 90, 92, 95, 114, 120, 133-134, 156-157, 182, 195, 222, 306
California Sentinel, 454-455
California Franchise Tax Board, 365
Callas, Maria, 382
Calloway, Cab, 55, 56, 58, 59, 63, 77, 115, 311, 397-398
Cannes International Film Festival, 310-311, 330-332, 382
Canova, Judy, 551
Cansino, Marguerita -- see Hayworth, Rita
Cantor, Eddie, 59
Capital Theatre (New York), 99
Capra, Frank, 516
Caribe Hilton (Puerto Rico), 470

Carlton Hotel (Cannes), 331
Carlyle, Russ, 214
Carmen (Bizet opera), 263, 330
Carmen (Merimée novel), 263, 381
Carmen Jones (film), xv, xvii, xx, xxi, xxv-xxvi, 33, 60, 126, 252, 329, 339, 340, 352, 387, 390, 400, 418, 425, 436, 437, 503, 508
  African American community's reaction to, 267-268, 293, 311-312, 324
  Cannes International Film Festival, 330-332
  casting of, 268-275
  censorship of script, 266-267
  critical success of, 293, 334
  DD as Carmen, 278, 293-295, 317-318, 31, 333, 345, 424, 532
  DD prepares for filming, 279-280
  DD wins role of Carmen, 269-274
  filming of, 278-286, 292
  financial success of, 310, 334
  financing of, 265-266
  operatic singers used in, 277-278
  premiere of, 298, 302-306
  Preminger director of, 260-295, 412
  promotion and publicity, 296, 302-303, 386
  rehearsals for, 276-278
  release of, 300-303
  reviews of, 303-307
  roots -- see *Carmen* (Bizet opera); *Carmen* (Merimée novel); *Carmen Jones* (play)
  script of, 265-267
  sexuality of Carmen, 267, 273-274, 293-295, 302
  significance of, 278, 293-295, 304-306, 317-318, 334
Carmen Jones (play), 263-264, 268
Carmichael, Hoagy, 93
Carnival Room, Sheraton Hotel (Puerto Rico), 536
Carnovsky, Morris, 153
Carousel, The (Pittsburgh), 237
see also Heller, Jackie; Jackie Heller Club
Carpenter, Thelma, 335
Carroll, Diahann, 167, 268, 269, 271, 275, 279, 280-281, 283, 284, 286, 289, 292-293, 303, 311, 406, 412, 413, 422, 423, 463-464, 484
Carroll, Leo G., 98
Carroll, Madeleine, 98-99
Carson, Johnny, 498
Carter, Ben, 33, 39-40, 41, 45, 54, 88
Carter, Juanelda, 92
Casablanca, 96
Cassavetes, John, 509
Cassini, Oleg, 169
Castle, Nick, 86, 88, 92, 104, 110
Catholic Youth Organization, 221
Cavalaro, Tito, 214
"Cavalcade of Stars" (television show), 210
Centennial Summer, 262
Central Casting, 41
Central Park (New York City), 62
Century Theatre (New York City), xxv, xxvi,

323-324
Cerebral Palsy organization, 221
Chaplin, Charles, 345
Chaplin Jr., Charles, 153
Charell, Erik, 72
Charioteers, The, 115
Charlie Chan (film series), 83
Chase Hotel (St. Louis), 211-213, 246-247, 273-274, 336
Chekhov, Michael, 152
Chesnutt, Charles W., 12
Chez Paree (Chicago), 347
Chi Chi Club (Palm Springs), 476, 495
Chicago, Illinois, 24, 26
Chicago Daily Tribune, 488
Chicago Defender, The, 95, 185, 459, 474
"Chicks and the Fiddle, The" (television show), 195-197
Child Is Waiting, A, 508-509
Children of Sanchez, 518
CinemaScope, 264, 305, 357
Ciro's (Los Angeles), 99, 193, 432
Ciro's (Miami Beach), 206-207, 322
Citizen-News (Hollywood), 226, 502
Civil Rights Act of 1957, 452
civil rights movement, xxvi, 134, 152, 211, 396, 452, 453
Clampett, Bob, 102
Claridge Hotel (London), 367
Clarke and Costello, 11
Cleary, Strauss, Irwin, and Goodman, 403
Cleopatra, 457-458
Cleveland, Ohio, 24, 65
  birthplace of DD, 1, 8, 211
  Black churches in, 13-14
  Black community in, 4-6, 12, 13
  Music Hall, 213-214
Cleveland, Veada (DD's secretary), 369-370, 401, 407, 468-469, 492, 497-498
Cleveland, Veada (daughter of DD's secretary), 468
Cleveland Call and Post, The, 213, 214, 215, 512-513
Cleveland *Gazette*, 5
Clift, Montgomery, 508
Club Alabam (Los Angeles), 31, 115
Club Apex (Los Angeles), 31
Club Congo (Los Angeles), 31
Club des Champs-Élysées (Paris), 138
Club Gala (Los Angeles), 189-192, 197, 198, 304, 473
Clyde, Thomas, 437
Coal Black and the Sebben Dwarfs, 102-103
Coburn, James, 477
Cocoanut Grove (Los Angeles), 59, 99, 193, 341, 365-366, 432
Code Office -- *see* Production Code Office
Cohn, Harry, 186, 189, 396, 455
Colbert, Claudette, 34, 332
Cole, Maria, 198, 237, 314, 353, 426, 449, 504, 517, 532, 551
Cole, Nadine, 115

Cole, Nat 'King,' 42, 43, 114-115, 166, 172, 198, 237, 239, 307, 311, 396, 400, 426, 449, 471, 483, 532
proposed television series with DD, 484
Cole, Natalie, 198
"Colgate Comedy Hour" (television show), 203
Colliers magazine, 79
Collins, Joan, 357, 362, 364, 373, 384, 457
Columbia Pictures, 32, 45, 122, 166, 185, 186, 187, 189, 396, 451, 455, 518
Commentary magazine, 305-306
Committee on Mental Retardation, 471, 513-514
El Commodore Hotel (Havana), 345
Communist Party, 222
Communist Party Political Association, 222
Como, Perry, 167, 274
Condemned Men, The, 83
see also *Four Shall Die*
Condemned of Altona, 508
Confessions of an Opium Eater, 471
Confidential magazine, 373-375, 378, 383, 388-389
Congo Clambake, 93
Connolly, Mike, 323, 460
Conrad, Earl, 529-530
Contos, Very Rev. Leonidas C., 449
Converse, Roger, 46
Conway, Nellie -- see Sul-Te-Wan, Madame
Cooper, Gary, 159, 244, 313, 369
Cooper, Ralph, 82, 84
Cooper, Rocky (Mrs. Gary), 244, 313, 369
Copa Club (Miami), 206
Copacabana nightclub (New York City), 327
Copacabana Palace nightclub (Rio de Janeiro), 247, 340, 471
Corregidor, 118
Correll, Charles, 41
see also *Amos 'n' Andy*
Corwin, Norman, 221
Cosby, Bill, 484
Cosmopolitan magazine, 312
Costa del Sol (Spain), 441
Cotten, Joseph, 300
Cotton Club (Culver City), 78
Cotton Club (New York City), 26, 53, 54, 55-56, 58, 59, 60, 63-65, 66, 72, 77, 102, 135, 172, 214, 234, 546
Cotton Club (film project), 181
Council for the Improvement of Negro Theatre Arts, 396
Counterattack magazine, 217
Country Girl, The, 319, 324
Covans studio (Los Angeles), 38
Covington, Floyd C., 27-28
Cow Cow Boogie, 93
Cowan, Lester, 366, 389
Coward, Noel, 197, 431
Cowles, Fleur, 313
Cowron, Fletcher, 313

Crain, Jeanne, 164
Crawford, Broderick, 405
Crawford, Joan, 34, 45, 122, 288, 401
Cressan, Alex, 381
Crinoline Choir, 46
Cronyn, Hume, 153
Crosby, Bing, 41, 85, 319
"crossover," 55, 167
Crowther, Bosley, 234, 306, 451
Cry the Beloved Country, 334
Cue magazine, 209, 211, 234
Cullen, Countee, 125
Culp, Robert, 484
Curphey, Dr. Theodore, 552
Curtis, Tony, 356

D

Daily Legal News (Cleveland), 44
Daily Variety, 323
Daily Worker, The, 218, 220
Dali, Salvador, 193
Dallas Morning News, 87
Dancer, Earl, 95
Dancer from Brazil, The, 85
Dandridge, Cyril (father), 1, 5-6, 16, 24, 52, 290
death, 554
divorce from Ruby Dandridge, 10-12, 19, 31, 43-44
marriage to Ruby Jean Butler, 7-10, 291
marriage to Thelma Rudd Frazier, 214, 515
relationship with DD, 11-12, 16, 44-45, 65-66, 80, 291, 361, 485, 514-515, 551
relationship with Vivian Dandridge, 11-12, 16, 44-45, 65-66, 291, 515
Dandridge, Dorothy Jean (Dottie, Dottie Jean, or Miss D)
Academy Award nomination and, xxv-xxvi, 311, 317, 319-321, 323-324
Academy Award presenter, 324
acting technique of, 152, 153, 310, 446
advertising appearance, 487
African American cultural figure, xv-xvi, xvii, 123, 301-302, 311, 312, 324, 503-504, 554
alcoholic beverages, use of, 473, 507, 516, 518, 523, 525, 529, 533-535
ambivalence about career, 43, 362-363, 390-391, 400-401, 402-403, 476, 494, 521
ambitions of, 50, 76-78, 151, 165, 168-169, 251-252, 446
appearance of, 56, 57, 91-92, 104, 109, 114, 120-123, 139, 186, 196, 323-324, 370, 371, 387-388, 407, 434, 457, 476, 511, 520, 532-533, 536
as mother, 110-113, 128-132, 133, 138, 142, 145-146, 177, 178, 251, 295, 309-310, 360, 377, 485, 504-506
autobiography of, 529-530
aversion to interviews, 21, 308-309, 485
bankruptcy of, 502-504, 512, 521

birth of, 1, 8

blacklisting and, 217-223

Cannes International Film Festival appearances, 330-332, 382

chairmanship of National Urban League, 313

childhood of, 11-12, 14, 15-16, 494

claustrophobia of, 22, 31

compared to Grace Kelly, 479

compared to Lena Horne, 116, 122-123, 124, 175, 181, 201-203, 204, 209, 254, 259, 284, 305, 486

cooking skill of, 105, 244

cover of *Life* (1954), xxiii, 301-302, 321

daughter, *see* Nicholas, Harolyn Suzanne (Lynn)

death of, xvi, 547-549

cause of, 552

demeanor of, 64-65, 152, 167, 314

depressions of, 142-143, 164, 249-250, 259, 334, 354-355, 401, 403-404, 412, 535, 546

design and decorating skill of, 104-105, 113

divorce from Harold Nicholas, 147-148, 162, 176-177, 178, 200, 495

divorce from Jack Denison, 495-498, 512, 521-522

dramatic training of, 135, 136, 152-153, 277, 446

early performances of, 14-15, 17-22, 27-28, 35, 36, 42, 45-46, 59, 62, 67-68

education of, 36-37, 42-43, 53, 55

family relationships of, 49-50

with Cyril Dandridge, 10-12, 44-45, 65-66, 80, 102, 132-133, 214-215, 291, 261, 485, 486, 514-515, 551

with Harolyn Suzanne Nicholas (Lynn), 112, 125-127, 128-132, 133, 145-148, 160, 165, 168, 176-177, 178, 189, 227, 241, 251, 295, 309-310, 360, 371-372, 377, 378-379, 402, 471-472, 485, 486, 498, 504-506, 509, 513-514, 517, 528, 532, 546

with Neva Williams, 16-19, 46-47, 49-51, 56-57, 69-71, 76, 80-82, 102, 105, 107-108, 132-133, 147, 172, 257-258, 291-292, 485

with Ruby Dandridge, 14, 17, 19, 20, 22-23, 49-50, 51-52, 53, 80-82, 102, 104, 105, 107-108, 111, 132-133, 140, 147, 228, 232, 258-259, 280, 291, 319, 371-372, 382, 449, 485, 486, 518-519, 533-534, 546-547, 549-553

with Vivian Dandridge, 11-12, 14-24, 35-38, 48, 49, 64, 69, 76, 111-112, 116-118, 123, 140, 147, 196, 225, 227-228, 232, 279-280, 283, 289-290, 302, 311, 314-316, 319, 323-324, 325, 326, 327-329, 334-335, 340, 350, 369, 378-379, 382-383, 402, 449, 468, 486, 499, 536, 546, 551

fantasy life of, 22-23, 53, 143, 403

film appearances of, xv-xvii, 2, 34, 41-42, 45-47, 59, 82-87, 88-89, 92-94, 97-99, 105, 120-121, 123, 124, 182-188, 224-234, 236, 269-295, 332-333, 336-338, 399-401, 406, 412-424, 436-448

see also specific film titles

finances of, 169-170, 292, 365-366, 371-372, 381, 453, 464-465, 473, 477, 487, 492-493, 498-501, 502-504, 529, 545

friendships of,

with Billie Holiday, 119, 389

with Geri Branton, 105, 106-108, 109-110, 111-112, 118-119, 120, 124, 125, 127, 129-130, 133-134, 136-137, 139, 147-148, 164, 172, 178, 228-229, 236-237, 314, 322, 328, 370, 374-376, 378, 388, 401-402, 426, 429, 499, 501-503, 517, 519, 524, 525, 527-529, 533-535, 542, 549-550

with Harry Belafonte, 229-230, 282-283, 363-364, 399

with Herb Jeffries, 91, 105, 122, 123, 124, 497, 530-531, 544

with Joel Fluellen, 105, 158-162, 169, 320, 349-350, 369-371, 390, 401, 403, 406, 419, 426-427, 458, 469-470, 478, 493-494, 502, 518, 519, 525-527, 533-534, 550

with Louis Armstrong, 121, 359, 463

with Marilyn Monroe, 178-179, 180, 488, 530

funeral of, 379, 549-551

generosity of, 109-110

Golden Globe nomination and, 317

happiness, comments on, 309

health problems of, 31, 106, 216, 466-467, 523-525, 535, 544-546

Hollywood Walk of Fame, star on, 554

insecurities of, 168, 201, 203, 209, 251, 275-276, 300, 353, 400-401, 406, 413-415, 464, 479, 480, 494, 511

interracial dance with Anthony Quinn, 154-157

interracial relationships and, 375-377, 417-418

interview with *Ebony* magazine, 485-487, 504

last will of, 378-379, 468, 553

leaves Dandridge Sisters trio, 76-78

libel suits, 372, 374-376, 378, 383, 388

marriage, article on, 373

marriage to Harold Nicholas, xx, xxv, 104-106, 110, 111-112, 113, 114, 123-124, 127-128, 130, 131-132, 140-142, 147-148, 160, 165, 176-177, 231, 243, 259, 295, 297, 309, 350, 365, 485, 510-511, 530, 540, 546

marriage to Jack Denison, xviii, xxi, xxii, 434-436, 443, 447, 448-453, 458-462, 465-475, 479, 480, 486, 489-495, 502, 504, 506, 521-522, 524, 525

nightclub career, xxv-xxvi, 18-19, 53, 54-57, 63-64, 135, 142, 162, 165, 168, 170, 176, 181-182, 188-192, 194, 203, 205-209, 211-213, 219, 233-234, 236, 237-242, 246-248, 253-257, 259-260, 269, 273-274, 295-296, 307-308, 318-319, 321-328, 332, 341-

343, 344-346, 365-366, 368, 388-389, 412-
413, 432, 458-462, 464, 470-471, 474, 475-
476, 498, 521-523, 536, 542-544
see also specific nightclubs
nontraditional film casting of, 334
performance fears of, 190, 208-209, 251,
275-276, 300, 413-415, 459-460, 479-480,
524-525
persona of, 23, 98-99, 146-147, 259, 281,
314, 370-371, 375, 404
personality of, 68-69, 77-78, 146-147, 314,
370-371
politics of, 134-135, 156-158, 344, 390,
471, 517
popularity of, 312-313
pregnancy with Lynn, 111-112
prescription drugs, use of, 323, 341, 363,
391, 432, 453, 479, 507, 529, 533, 535,
536, 538-539, 541, 544, 547
privacy, desire for, 23-24, 31, 64-65, 259-
260, 280, 314, 442, 529
psychological decline of, 528-532, 538-540
psychology of, 53, 142-143, 146-147, 314,
361, 433, 466
racism, perceptions of, 48, 164, 176, 211-
213, 241, 250-251, 309, 344, 359-360,
375-376, 399, 417, 473
radio appearances of, 118, 471
reading habits of, 108-109, 509-510
recordings of, 403, 404, 473-474
refusal to be stereotyped, 40, 153-154, 483-
484
religious beliefs of, 550-551
reviews of film performances, 85, 87, 97,
184, 188, 234, 236, 301, 303-307, 329,
330, 383-387, 422-423, 445-446, 451-452,
453-457
reviews of nightclub performances, 176,
191-192, 202, 208-209, 215, 237, 240, 245,
254, 326-327, 460, 466, 470, 474, 476, 543
reviews of television performances, 204,
464, 483, 514
reviews of theatrical performances, 91-92,
202, 488
"rivalry" with Lena Horne, 202-203, 486
romantic relationships of, 308-309
with Abby Mann, 508-512, 516-519, 549
with Curt Jurgens, 382, 387, 389, 391, 403
with Fredric March, 347-348
with Gerald Mayer, 230-235, 243, 491
with Harold Nicholas, 61-62, 66-67, 73-74,
76, 80-82, 85, 99, 100, 101-102, 546
with Harry Belafonte, 229-230, 282-283,
363-364, 376, 525, 530
with Jack Denison, 376, 382, 402, 412-413,
422, 425-430, 447, 504
with James Mason, 364
with Otto Preminger, xviii-xix, xx, xxiii,
169, 274, 276, 280, 286-287, 288, 290, 296-
297, 302, 303, 325, 328-329, 331-332, 333,
338, 339-340, 341-343, 347, 350, 355-356,
367, 371, 377-378, 384, 413, 433-434, 450,
453, 491, 510-511, 525, 529, 530, 531, 550
with Peter Lawford, 241-246, 247, 259, 295,
384, 491, 549-550
with Phil Moore, 147, 165-169, 175, 177-
181, 186, 189-192, 194, 195, 198
201, 203-204, 210-211, 216, 232, 243, 289-
290, 295, 297, 350, 491, 510, 516
self-absorption of, 109, 314-315
sex appeal of, 167, 253-256, 325, 375
sexuality of, 167, 169, 253-256, 353
singing talent of, 76, 123, 168, 200-201, 277
skin color of, 18, 35, 63, 109, 122-123, 196,
227
song repertoire of, 64, 142, 162, 167, 168,
190, 199, 240, 296, 325-327, 464, 476
"A-Tisket A-Tasket," 63
"All God's Chillun Got Rhythm," 46
"All of Me," 528
"Baby, Don't You Cry," 121
"Back Home to Joe," 325
"Beautiful Evening," 474
"Blow Out the Candle," 208, 240
"Brother," 115-116
"Brown-Skinned Gal in the Calico Gown,"
90
"Chattanooga Choo-Choo," 86-87
"Cindy with the Two Left Feet," 90
"Comme Ci, Comme Ça," 476
"Cymbal Sockin' Sam," 90
"Good For Nothing Joe," 327
"Groovin'," 121
"Harlem on My Mind," 190
"Harlem on Parade," 121
"Harlem Yodel," 46
"Hickory Stick," 90
"I Ain't Gonna Study War No More," 76
"I Got Rhythm," 325
"If Life Were All Peaches and Cream," 90
"I'll Get By," 481
"It Was Just One of Those Things," 240
"Julie," 378
"Jumpin' Jive," 76
"Just One of Those Things," 327
"Love Isn't Born, It's Made," 208
"Madly in Love," 63
"Man I Love, The," 481
"Minnie the Moocher Is Dead," 76
"Mutiny in the Nursery," 46
"My Heart Belongs to Daddy," 359
"Never Mind the Noise in the Market," 327
"Red Wagon," 76
"Ridin' High," 326
"Smooth Operator," 474
"Somebody," 474
"South American Way," 76
"Stay With It," 474
"Swing Low, Sweet Chariot," 63
"Taking a Chance on Love," 236, 240, 481
"Talk Some Sweet Talk to Me," 208
"Talk Sweet Talk," 240
"What Is This Thing Called Love?", 240,
464

"Whatcha Say," 121
"When," 76
"Woman's Prerogative, A," 190
"You Ain't Nowhere," 76
"You Do Something to Me," 359
"You'd Be So Easy to Love," 327
social activities of, 114, 133-134, 313-314
soundies, appearances in, 92-94
see also specific soundie titles
star quality of, 152, 281, 295, 314, 370-371, 404, 462, 520
style of, xv-xvi, xvii, xxv-xxvi, 146-147, 314, 370-371, 520
suicide attempts of, 143, 249-250, 552-554
tax problems of, 365, 487, 492, 499-500, 521
television appearances of, 203-204, 210, 296, 303, 324, 468, 477-484, 495, 521
proposed series with Nat 'King' Cole, 484
theatrical appearances of, 79-80, 87-88, 120, 487, 523-524
Tuptim, role of, in The King and I, 330, 332-333, 336-338, 341, 343, 355, 488, 508
working habits of, 90, 94, 247, 281-282
see also Dandridge Sisters; The Wonder Children; films (under separate titles)
Dandridge, Florence Locke (DD's paternal grandmother), 5, 6, 43-44, 228
Dandridge, Henry (DD's paternal grandfather), 5
Dandridge, Ruby Jean Butler (DD's mother), xx, xxii, xxv, 63, 159, 214
acting career of, 27-28 , 34-35, 40-41, 52-53, 102, 118, 140, 280, 298-299, 484
caretaker for Lynn, 131, 153, 177
death of, xxii, 553
divorce from Cyril Dandridge, 10-12, 19, 24, 31, 44-45, 291
early life of, 2-5,
leaves husband, 1-2, 7-8, 291
marriage to Cyril Dandridge, 7-10, 65-66, 291, 551
relationship with DD, 14, 17, 19, 20, 51-52, 53, 80-81, 98, 102, 104, 105, 106, 107, 108, 111-112, 132-134, 140, 147, 151, 173, 211, 228, 232, 258-259, 272-273, 280, 291, 306-307, 371-372, 382, 449, 468, 486, 494, 518-519, 524, 533-534, 546-547, 549-553
relationship with Neva Williams, 15-16, 24, 27-28, 29-32, 49-51, 73, 107-108, 257, 291, 494, 519
relationship with Vivian Dandridge, xxii, 20, 51-52, 53, 80, 108, 232, 258-259, 291, 335, 382, 402, 494, 554
stage mother, 14-17, 34-35, 39-40, 41, 43, 45, 46, 48-49, 51, 52, 80, 88-90, 98, 100, 118, 272-273
Dandridge, Thelma Rudd Frazier (DD's stepmother), 214
Dandridge, Vivian Alferetta (Vivi) (DD's sister), xix-xxii, xxiii, xxv, 1, 43, 48-49, 62, 68, 100, 109, 114, 136, 161, 165, 172, 173, 214, 245, 256, 270, 274, 303, 311, 314, 323, 376, 463-464,
birth of, 7
childhood of, 7-12, 14-16, 214
death of, xxii, 554
divorce from Jack Montgomery, 103
divorce from Ralph Bledsoe, 117
early performances, 17-22, 35, 36, 37, 38, 42, 45, 46, 47, 54, 59, 62, 63, 76-78
education of, 36-37, 42-43, 53, 55, 153
film career of, 42, 45, 46, 47, 59, 102-103, 118, 225
gives birth to Michael Wallace, 117
marriage to Gustav Friedrich, 382-383
marriage to Jack Montgomery, 103, 105, 117
marriage to Ralph Bledsoe, 117
nightclub career of, 196, 298-299
personal life of, 103-104
relationship with Babe Wallace, 117
relationship with Cyril Dandridge, 11-12, 16, 44-45, 515
relationship with DD, 11-12, 14-24, 38, 48, 49, 50, 64, 69, 76-77, 104, 105, 110, 116-118, 123, 140, 147, 151, 161, 196, 211, 225, 227-228, 270-273, 279-280, 289-290, 302, 311, 314-316, 323-324, 327-329, 334-335, 340, 369, 378, 402, 449, 468, 486, 494, 499, 536, 551
relationship with Harolyn Suzanne Nicholas (Lynn), 133
relationship with Leonard Feather, 69, 71, 73
relationship with Neva Williams, 16-19, 49, 50, 56-57, 81, 102, 103, 108, 211
relationship with Ruby Dandridge, xxii, 20, 50, 51-52, 80, 103, 108, 211, 258-259, 335, 402, 494, 554
son -- see Wallace, Michael
theatrical career of, 335
see also Dandridge Sisters; The Wonder Children
Dandridge Sisters, xx, xxi, 38, 40, 41-43, 45, 53, 63-64, 67, 71, 73, 74, 75, 76-78, 82, 88, 114, 165, 172, 214, 449
Daniels, Billy, 303
Darnell, Linda, 262, 330
Darro, Frankie, 85
Dassin, Jules, 343, 346
Davis, Bette, 95, 397, 401
Davis, Bob, 162, 183, 311
Davis, Joan, 86
Davis Jr., Sammy, 105, 144, 171, 172, 174-175, 239, 242, 279, 303, 325, 339, 344, 369-370, 373, 397-398, 402, 412, 416-417, 420, 421-422, 423, 442, 448, 450, 464, 469, 508, 532, 550
Day, Doris, 331, 372, 465, 492, 499-500
Day at the Races, A, 44, 45-46, 47, 90
de Havilland, Olivia, 331
de Lange, Eddie, 72
de Lavallade, Carmen, 269

de Marco, Sally, 206
de Marco, Tony, 206
de Mille, Agnes, 72
de Mille, Cecil, 397
de Mille, Darcy, 454-455
de Sica, Vittorio, 431
de Wilde, Brandon, 300
Dean, James, xvii
Death of a Salesman, 439
Deauville Club (Santa Monica), 313
Decks Ran Red, The, 227, 390, 403, 405-406, 422-423
Dee, Ruby, 188, 311, 400
Defiant Ones, The, 334, 398-399, 423
Dell, Herb, 459, 475
Delon, Alain, 483
Delta Rhythm Boys, The, 115, 171
Demetrius and the Gladiators, 254
Denison, Jack (DD's second husband), 341-343, 355, 425-430, 551, 554
divorce from DD, 495-498, 512, 521-522
marriage to DD, xviii, xxi, xxii, 434-436, 443, 448-453, 458-462, 465-475, 479-480, 486, 489-495, 502, 504, 506, 521-522, 524
physical abuse of DD, 473, 479, 489-490, 493-495, 524
relationship with DD, 366-367, 376, 402, 412-413, 422, 425-430, 437, 504
Denison, Mary, 449
DePaul University, 99
Desert Rock (Nevada), 241
Devil's General, The, 382
Dewey, Ed, 83
Dietrich, Marlene, 34, 91, 122, 193, 197, 329, 380, 401, 408, 450, 508, 512, 516-517, 541-542
Directors Guild of America, 411, 479, 509
Disney, Walt, 72
Dixie Jubilee Choir, 26-27
Dixon, Ivan, 159, 406, 410, 411, 413, 415, 421-422, 423, 477-479, 480, 525-527, 550
Dolan, Jim, 189
Doll's House, The, 152
Donatelli, Commissioner Victor, 552
Dorchester Hotel (London), 436, 437
Dorothy Dandridge All-Star Revue, 476
Dorothy Dandridge Revue, 475-476
Douglas, Helen Gahagan, 160
Douglas, Kirk, 372, 493, 499-500
Douglas, Mike, 512-514
see also "Mike Douglas Show" (television program)
Down Argentine Way, 59, 74
Drums of the Congo, 97, 105
DuBois, W. E. B., 31
Duke Is Tops, The, 82, 166
see also Bronze Venus
Dunbar, Paul Laurence, 14, 16
Dunbar Hotel (Los Angeles), 115, 158-159
Dunham, Katherine, 254, 269
Dunn, Henriella, 36, 525, 551
Dunne, Irene, 330

Dunne, Molly, 243
Durant, Jack, 67
Durante, Jimmy, 171, 209
Dwybad, Dr. Gunnar, 513

E

East of Eden, 331
Easter Parade, 242
Easy Street, 93
Easy to Take, 42
Ebony magazine, xv, 184-185, 202, 209-210, 227, 234, 238, 255, 274, 299, 308, 316, 324, 450, 485-487, 504, 543
Eckstine, Billy, 114, 124, 167, 232, 372, 465, 499
Eckstine, June, 114, 124, 232, 237, 314
"Ed Sullivan Show, The" (television show), 204, 464, 466, 468, 527
Eden Roc (France), 380, 382
Edwards, James, xv, 163, 218, 274, 311
Egyptian, The, 437
Eisenhower, Dwight David, 300, 453
El Rancho Vegas (Las Vegas), 171, 174-175, 189, 256, 341
Opera House, 256
Eldridge, Florence (Mrs. Fredric March), 348
"Eleventh Hour, The" (television series), 521
Elizabeth II, Queen of Great Britain, 383
Ellington, Edward Kennedy 'Duke,', 26, 31, 55, 58, 87-88, 90, 91, 92, 140, 311, 344, 370, 463
Ellis, Evelyn, 395
Ellison, Ralph, 163
Elma Warren's Nut House (London), 68
Embrace, 269
Emperor Jones, The, 59
Empire Room, Palmer House (Chicago), 347, 464, 474
Empire Room, Waldorf-Astoria Hotel (New York City), 307-308, 322, 324-328, 330-331, 332, 335, 383, 464, 466
Eng, Frank, 156
Esquire magazine, 299
Evans, Lois, 32
Evans, Lula Bolden, 32
Evers, Medgar, 312
Everything and Nothing (Dandridge and Conrad), 529-530
Exodus, 262-263
Exuberanza, 154

F

Factor, Max, 273
Fairbanks Jr., Douglas, 431, 432
Fairmont Hotel (San Francisco) -- *see* Venetian Room, Fairmont Hotel (San Francisco)
Falkenburg, Jinx, 303

Farina -- *see* Hoskins, Allen
Farouk, King of Egypt, 139
"Father of the Bride" (television series), 118, 484
Father Was a Bachelor, 118
Faubus, Governor Orval, 453
Faulkner, William, 163
Feather, Leonard, 68-69, 73, 103
Federal Bureau of Investigation (FBI), 134-135
Federal Theatre Project Negro unit (Los Angeles), 35, 40
Feldman, Charlie, 245
Fellini, Federico, 320-321, 431
Ferguson, Frank, 337
Fernandez, Raul, 545
Fetchit, Stepin, 27, 33, 42
Ffolkes, David, 357, 436
Fielding, Sol Baer, 225, 226
Fields, Sidney, 310
Fields, W. C., 34
Filho, President Joao Cafe, 340
Film Daily, 317
Finian's Rainbow, 225
Fisher, Eddie, 300
Fisk University, 15, 74
Fitzgerald, Ella, 194, 256, 400
Five Rhythmatics, 40
Flame Room, Radisson Hotel (Minneapolis), 471
Flamingo (*Flamingo Isle*), 124
Flamingo Hotel (Las Vegas), 171, 341, 521-523
Fletcher, Dusty 'Open the Door Richard,' 75
Floyd Ray orchestra, 85
Fluellen, Joel, 105, 157-162, 169, 244, 314, 320, 349-350, 369-371, 390, 401, 403, 406, 419, 426-427, 459, 469-470, 478, 493-494, 502, 518, 519, 533-534, 550, 554
Flynn, Errol, 529
Foch, Nina, 324,
Fonda, Henry, 34, 193, 288, 516
Fontaine, Joan, 357, 362, 368, 384, 385-386
Fontainebleu Hotel (Miami), 322-323, 346-347
Ford, Glenn, 32, 368
Ford, John, 33
Forever Amber, 262
Foster, Elizabeth, 269, 274
Four Shall Die, 77, 82-85, 93-94, 121, 303
see also Condemned Men, The
Fox Pictures, 6
see also Twentieth Century Fox
Fox Theatre (Detroit), 455
Foxx, Redd, 115
Frazier, Thelma Rudd, 214
Freeman, Bea, 135
Freeman, Ernie, 205, 206
Friedrich, Gustav, 383
Friendly Persuasion, 159
Frings, Ketti, 350
Frings, Kurt, 350-351

Fuentes, Reuben, 336
Furness, Betty, 45

G

Gabin, Jean, 193
Gable, Clark, 34, 45-46, 47, 193, 298
Garbo, Greta, 12, 45, 122, 382, 408, 423, 529
Gardner, Ava, 97, 122, 134, 164, 167, 179, 180, 227, 373, 401, 484, 530
Garfield, John, 88, 156
Garland, Judy, 32, 128, 166, 193, 242, 319, 369-370, 397, 508, 509
Garroway, Dave, 450
Garson, Greer, 32
Gaslight, 152
Gazette, Cleveland -- *see* Cleveland *Gazette*
Gearhard, Karl, 140
Geis, Bernard, 529
Gene Autry Show (radio show), 118
Gene Krupa Story, The, 463
General Artists Corporation (GAC), 205
Gernreich, Rudi, 169
Gershwin, George, 389, 395
Gershwin, Ira, 395, 398,
Gershwin, Lee, 398
Gibson, Truman, 358-359
Gielgud, John, 516
Gilbert, Herschel Burke, 268, 275
Gilbert, John, 12
Gillespie, Dizzy, 124
Gilpin Players, 12
Girard, Roland, 346, 379
Gish, Lillian, 33
Gist, Robert, 479
Givenchy, Hubert de, 340
Glaser, Joe, 49, 53, 67, 72, 73, 119, 457, 463, 487, 542
Gleason, Jackie, 210
Glenn, Roy, 277
Globo, O (Brazilian newspaper), 340
Gobel, George, 300
God Sends Sunday (Bontemps), 125
God's Step Children, 135
Going Places, 46-47, 51, 67, 186
Golden Boy, 408
Golden Globe awards
    DD nominated for Best Actress (*Carmen Jones*), 317
    DD nominated for Best Actress (*Porgy and Bess*), 466
Goldwyn, Frances, 313, 407, 450
Goldwyn, Samuel (Sam), 109, 313, 395-399, 401, 406-411, 412, 417, 418, 423, 450, 451, 461
Gone With the Wind, 33, 39, 47, 48, 95, 164, 296, 319
Good News, 242
Goodman, Benny, 72, 73
Gordon, Freddie, 120
Gordon, Mack, 86

Gosden, Freeman, 41
see also Amos 'n' Andy
Grable, Betty, 115, 164, 254
Grace, Princess of Monaco, 382
see also Kelly, Grace
Graham, Sheilah, 311, 323, 332, 412
Granger, Farley, 344, 375
Grant, Allan, 299
Grant, Cary, 193
Granz, Norman, 403, 474
Grapes of Wrath, The, 386
Grayson, Kathryn, 523-524
Great American Broadcast, 59
Great Gildersleeve, 225
Great White Hope, The, 159
Green, Eddie, 39
Green, John P., 10, 44
Green Pastures, 27, 41, 158, 225
Gregory, Dick, 508, 512
Greshler, Abby, 448
Grey, Joel, 254
Grey, Virginia, 46
Griffith, D. W., 12, 32-33, 268
Griffith, Edward, 98
Group Theatre (New York), 152, 153
Guernsey, Otis, 303, 316
Guess Who's Coming to Dinner, 334, 463
Guilaroff, Sydney, 121-122, 227

H

Hairston, Jester, 89
Hal Roach Company, 455-456
Hall, Adelaide, 26, 58
Hall, Juanita, 303
Hall-Johnson Choir, 41
Hallelujah, 26-27, 33, 59, 135, 217, 298, 397, 458
Halsman, Philippe, 299
Hamilton, Bernie, 159
Hamilton, Sara, 423
Hammerstein II, Oscar, 263-264, 267, 277, 303, 330
Handy, W. C., 400
Happy Landing, 54
Harlem (New York City), 54, 56, 62
Harlem Globetrotters, 185, 186
Harlem Globetrotters, The, 185-186, 217, 225, 235, 343
Harlem Rides the Range, 91
Harlow, Jean, 34, 45
Harman, Jympson, 445-446
Harrington, Dr. Ethel, 145-146
Harris, Avanelle, 4, 37, 51, 88, 90, 91, 92, 93, 458
Harris, Jack, 67
Harris, Nat, 207
Harris, Theresa, 94
Harrison, Rex, 330
Haskins, Byron, 183, 184
Hathaway, Henry, 88-89
Hathaway, Maggie, 85

Hawks, Howard, 33
Hawn, Goldie, 167
Hayden, Sterling, 98
Hayes, Alfred, 343
Hayes, Helen, 300
Hayes, Marvin, 277
Haynes, Daniel, 26
Hayton, Lennie, 243, 303, 376, 435
Hayworth, Rita, 32, 86, 115, 122, 254, 396, 408
Heart Campaign, 221
Hearts in Dixie, 26, 27, 33, 35, 40
Hefner, Hugh, 180
Heller, Jackie, 237
see also Carousel, The; Jackie Heller Club
Henaghan, Jim ("Rambling Reporter"), 154-155, 157, 222
Henie, Sonja, 86
Hep magazine, 372, 378
Hepburn, Audrey, xxvi, 209, 319, 334, 350, 457
Hepburn, Katharine, 34, 298, 401
Hepburn, Philip, 225
Hepsations 1945, 124
Heralds of Swing, 69
Hernandez, E.K., Productions, 42
Hernandez, Juano, 72, 224, 400
Heyward, Du Bose, 395, 450, 451
"Hickory Stick," 90
Hill, Lorenzo, 62
Hill, Ruby, 125
Hit Parade of 1943, 105
Hit the Deck, 118
Hitchcock, Alfred, 262
Hitler's Children, 225
Holden, William, 245, 324
Hole in the Head, A, 118
Holiday, Billie, xvii, 31, 119, 159, 194, 254, 366, 389, 457, 463, 477, 481, 503
Hollywood Arts, Sciences, and Professions Council, 218-220, 221
Hollywood Democratic Committee, 134, 156, 218-219
Hollywood Foreign Correspondents Association, 316-317, 466
see also Golden Globe awards
Hollywood Independent Citizens Committee of Arts, Sciences, and Professions, 134
Hollywood Reporter, The, 154-155, 157, 204, 222, 254, 273, 274, 278, 292, 296, 304, 323, 329, 332, 336, 363, 389, 445, 459-460, 462-463, 481, 483, 548
Hollywood Theatre Alliance, 79
Hollywood Walk of Fame, DD's star on, 554
Home in Oklahoma, 118
Home of the Brave, 162-163, 218
homosexuality, in Hollywood, 159-160
Hope, Bob, 59, 323
Hopper, Hedda, 155-157, 220, 222, 231, 245, 304-305, 310, 311, 319-320, 323
"Horn and Hardart Kiddie Hour, The," 58

Horne, Lena, 56, 82, 91, 96-97, 102, 121, 124, 166, 167, 171, 172, 184, 194, 217-218, 243, 298, 299, 303, 311, 376, 401, 435, 484 compared to DD, 116, 122-123, 160, 167, 175, 181, 201-203, 209, 254, 259, 284, 305, 486 "rivalry" with DD, 202-203, 486
Horne, Marilyn (or Marilynn), 277-278
Horton, Lester, 269
Horton, Robert, 235
Hoskins, Allen, 13
Hotel du Cap D'Antibes (France), 380
Hotel Theresa (New York City), 303
House Committee on Un-American Activities, 154, 217, 218
House of Flowers, 284
Howard, Allen, 512
Howard, Gertrude, 33
Howard, Jane, 245
Howard, Trevor, 431, 432, 437, 438, 440-448
Howard Theatre (Washington, D.C.), 73
Howard University, 151
Huckleberry Finn, 35
Hue magazine, 185
see also Sepia magazine
Hughes, Genevieve, 9, 213-214, 215
Hughes, Langston, 5, 30, 31, 35, 88, 91, 109
Humberstone, H. Bruce, 86
Hunt, Terry, 550
Hurok, Sol, 321
Hurry Sundown, 463
Huston, John, 95
Huston, Virginia, 183, 184
Hutcherson, Le Vern, 277
Hutton, Barbara, 193
Hyatt Hotel (Burlingame, California), 523
Hyatt Music Theatre (Burlingame, California), 523

I

"I Spy" (television series), 484
S.S. *Ile de France*, 71
Imitation of Life (1934 film), 135, 158
Imitation of Life (1959 film), 152-153, 159, 463
Impelliterri, Mayor Vincent, 209
In Old Chicago, 33
"In the Morning" (Dunbar), 14
In This Our Life, 95
Indrisano, Johnny, 278
Infamy -- see The Decks Ran Red
Inge, William, 339
Ingram, Clifford, 33
Ingram, Rex, 33, 125
Inn of the Sixth Happiness, The, 382
Internal Revenue Service (IRS), 365, 487, 492, 499-500, 521
interracial love scenes in films, 343, 357, 367-368, 386-387, 405, 443-444
interracial marriages, 243, 429
interracial relationships, 243-245, 290, 375

Intruder in the Dust, 162-163, 224
Irene, 74
Irwin, Ben, 550
Island in the Sun, 279, 343, 345, 346, 355-357, 381, 384-387, 405-406, 423, 432, 436, 438, 442
filming of, 360-368
script of, 361-362, 383
It Can't Last Forever, 45, 47

J

Jackie Heller Club (Pittsburgh), 216, 219
see also Carousel, The; Heller, Jackie
Jackie Robinson Story, The, 159, 188
Jackson, Eugene, 40, 45
Jackson, Fay M., 95
Jackson, Freddie, 40
Jackson, Jigsaw, 56
Jackson, Mahalia, 400
Jackson, Vera, 120
Jackson Brothers, The, 45
Jackson, Rev. J. S., 7
Jackson, Vera, 3
Jacobs, Madeline, 250-251, 544, 551
Jacobs, Morty, 200-201, 247-251, 318, 348, 530, 543, 544, 551
Jamaica, 401
James, Olga, 273-274, 275, 277, 279, 280-282, 283-284, 285-286, 303, 390, 504, 549
Jarlson, Alan, 240-241
Jarvis, Al, 221
Jason, Will, 186
Jazz Singer, The, 25
Jeffries, Herb, 88, 89, 91, 105, 122-123, 124, 162, 167, 244, 342, 344, 369-370, 373, 426-427, 466, 497, 530-531, 544
Jessel, George, 181
Jessyee, Eva, 26
Jet magazine, 185, 202, 216, 298, 323, 332, 338, 344, 382, 425-426, 436-437, 443, 454, 503, 514
Jim Crow laws, 22, 172-176, 241
see also segregation
Johnson, George, 13
Johnson, John H., 185
Johnson, Ken, 69
Johnson, Noble, 13, 33
Johnson, Mae, 56
Johnson, Van, 236, 241, 331
Jolson, Al, 20, 24, 396
Jones, Etta, xii, 37, 41, 42-43, 45-46, 47, 51, 53, 54, 57, 60, 62, 63, 66, 68, 69, 71, 73-74, 76, 77, 78, 104, 117, 136, 165, 172, 402, 449-450, 519, 546, 551
Jones, Jennifer (Mrs. David O. Selznick), 370, 407, 457
Jones, Paul, 38, 104
Jones, Shirley, 359
"Jonesy" (nanny for Lynn), 113-114, 126, 133
Jovien, Harold, xxii, 205, 219-220, 223,

238-239, 241, 403, 404, 427, 460, 463, 474, 491-492, 550
Jovien, Mildred, 205, 219-220, 241, 427, 491, 492
Judy Canova Show (radio), 118
Juel Park (Beverly Hills boutique), 340, 349, 550
"Julia" (television series), 484
Jump for Joy, 87-88, 89-92, 168, 216, 280, 517, 544
Junior Miss, 118
Jungle Jig, 92-93
Jurgens, Curt, 381, 454, 456, 550
relationship with DD, 382, 387, 389, 391, 403
Justin, John, 357, 367-368, 384-385

K

Kahn, Nick, 254
Karloff, Boris, 83
Karamu House (Cleveland), 12
Kay, Monte, 422
Kaye, Danny, 327, 450
Kazan, Elia, 163, 356-357, 397
Kelly, Gene, 128, 331, 332
Kelly, Grace, xxvi, 319, 324, 331, 334, 479
see also Grace, Princess of Monaco
Kelly, Nick, 207
Kennedy, Jacqueline, 382
Kennedy, President John F., 471, 512
assassination of, 517
Kennedy, Ambassador Joseph P., 380-381
Kennedy, Rose, 381
Kennedy, Rosemary, 513
Kerr, Deborah, 333
Kid Millions, 59
King and I, The (film), 330, 387
DD and role of Tuptim, 330, 332-333, 336-338, 341, 343, 355, 488, 508
King and I, The (musical), 330
King Jr., Rev. Martin Luther, 312, 508
King Cole Trio, 85, 114-115
Kings Go Forth, 356
Kinloch, John, 92
Kiss Me Kate, 269
Kissing Bandit, The, 439
Kit Carson Club (Las Vegas), 341
Kitt, Eartha, 255, 299, 327, 373, 375, 400
Kleiner, Harry, 265-266
Knight, Arthur, 452
Knight, Gene, 327
Kramer, Stanley, 163, 331, 398-399, 508, 516
Krim, Arthur, 262, 265, 310
Ku Klux Klan, 206
Kuller, Sid, 88

L

La Strada, 431
La Vie en Rose (New York City), 207-210,

216, 229, 269, 271, 326, 542
Ladies of Washington, 118
Ladies Home Journal magazine, 216, 225-226
Lady By Day (play and film project), 470-471
Lady from Louisiana, 85, 97-98
Lady Sings the Blues (Holiday autobiography), 366, 457, 463
Lady Sings the Blues (film project), 366, 378, 389, 457, 463, 471
Lady Sings the Blues (1972 film), 463
Ladd, Alan, 97
Lafayette Players, 35
Lake Tahoe (California-Nevada), 181-182, 219-220, 373-374, 388-389
Lamarr, Hedy, 193, 254
Lamarre, Hazel, 305
Lancaster, Burt, 508, 509
Lanchester, Elsa, 22
Landis, Carole, 115, 139-140, 553
Lane, Lovie, 124
Larry Potter's Supper Club (Los Angeles), 181
Las Vegas, Nevada, 170-176, 237-241
Las Vegas Review-Journal, 240-241
Las Vegas Sun, 322
Last Frontier Hotel (Las Vegas), 237, 240-241, 269, 321-322
swimming pool incident, 238-239
Last Parade, The, 35
Latin Casino (Philadelphia), 345
Laura, xxiii-xxiv, 411
Lavery, Emmett, 225-226
Law of Nature, The, 13
Lawford, Lady, 242, 245
Lawford, Peter, 273, 369, 371, 429, 471, 488, 511-512, 532
relationship with DD, 241-246, 247, 256, 259, 320, 344, 491, 549-550
Lawford, Sir Sydney, 242
Lazybones, 93
Le Gon, Jenni, 89, 167, 225
Lean, David, 431
Learning Tree, The, 159
Leavitt, Sam, 268
Lee, Canada, 218
Lee, Johnny ('Calhoun'), 75
Lee, Peggy, 256
Legion of Decency (Roman Catholic), 262
Leigh, Vivian, 516-517
Leslie, Lew, 27, 59
Lesser, Sol, 182, 183
Levene, Sam, 153
Levette, Harry, 307
Levy, Raoul, 476, 483, 484-485
Lewis, Jerry, 203, 209
Libel!, 261
Liberace, 219, 373
Life magazine, 189, 200-201, 202, 211, 238, 301-302, 312, 321, 508
Lightfoot, J. Kennedy, 550

"Light's Diamond Jubilee" (television program), 296, 300-301
Lilies of the Field, 334
Lincoln Motion Picture Company, 13
Lincoln Theatre (Los Angeles), 31, 84, 114
Little Church of the Flowers (Glendale), 550
Little Colonel, The, 41, 42
Littlest Rebel, The, 42
Lloyd, Harold, 13, 58
Lodge, Ambassador Henry Cabot, 450
Lollobridgida, Gina, 457, 458
Loren, Sophia, 457
Lowe Jr., Arthur, 375
Loew's, Inc., 221-222
Loews State Theatre (New York), 99
Logan, Ella, 254
Lombard, Carole, 193
London Casino (London), 136
London Daily Express, 446
Sunday London Express, 446
London Daily Mirror, 446
London Daily Telegraph, 446
"London Town," 301
Look magazine, 202, 209, 238, 312, 313
Loper, Don, 170, 236
Lord Jeff, 242
Los Angeles Council of Negro Women, 464
Los Angeles Daily News, 156, 203, 236
Los Angeles Examiner, 181, 319, 401, 422, 423, 425
Los Angeles Mirror, 191, 304
Los Angeles Rams, 475
Los Angeles Sentinel, 305, 311, 475
Los Angeles Times, The, 155, 245, 475, 484, 548
Lost Boundaries, 162-163
Louis, Joe, 60, 373, 504
Louise, Anita, 46, 186
Love and Hisses, 54
L'Overture, Toussaint, 83
Lowe, James B., 13, 33
Loy, Myrna, 397
Lucas, Sam, 13, 33
Lucky Jordan, 97, 98
Lucy Gallant, 159
Lunceford, Jimmie, 58, 73, 74-75, 403
Lunceford band, 58, 73, 74-76, 77
Lunick, Olga, 194
Lux Radio Theatre (radio series), 118

M

Mabley, Jackie 'Moms,' 72
MacKenzie, Donald, 431
MacMahon, Aline, 153
MacNamara, Maggie, 288, 413
MacRae, Gordon, 219, 254, 359, 372, 465, 499
MacRae, Sheila, 499-500
Macready, George, 183
Mad Miss Manton, The, 34
Magnificent Obsession, 319

Magnificent Yankee, The, 225
Maid of Salem, The, 33
Malaga, 227, 431, 432, 434, 436-445, 452, 481, 484, 530
Malden, Karl, 324
Mamoulian, Rouben, 125, 395, 397, 399-400, 408-412, 423, 457-458
Man With the Golden Arm, The, 262, 297, 343
Mankiewicz, Joseph L., 397
Mann, Abby, 525, 540
eulogy of DD, 550-551
relationship with DD, 508-512, 516-519, 549
March, Fredric, 347-348, 350, 369, 397
Marco Polo (film project), 476, 483, 484-485, 486
Margaret, Princess, 345, 383
Margin for Error (play), 261
Margin for Error (film), 261
Markham, Dewey "Pigmeat," 58
Marshall, Thurgood, 312
Marshall, William, 254
Martin, Dean, 203, 209, 242
Martin, Mary, 450
Martin, Tony, 209
Martin and Lewis, 209
Martin and Lewis show -- see "Colgate Comedy Hour"
Marty, 331
Marx, Chico, 44, 46
Marx, Groucho, 44, 46
Marx, Harpo, 44, 45-46
Marx Brothers, 44, 45-46
see also Marx, Chico; Marx, Groucho; Marx, Harpo
Maryland, 33, 39
Mason, James, 159, 319, 357, 364, 369, 384, 405-406, 550
relationship with DD, 364
Mason, Pamela, 364, 369, 406, 520
Mastin, Will, 174
S.S. Matsonia, 475
Mayan Theatre (Los Angeles), 91, 120
Mayer, Gerald, 225, 226-227, 238
relationship with DD, 230-235, 243-244, 491
Mayer, Louis B., 32, 122, 193, 224, 225, 230
MCA -- see Music Corporation of America (MCA)
McCarthy, Frank, 266, 358
McCarthy, Senator Joseph, 217
McClay, Howard, 236
McConnell, Dorothy Hughes, 3, 6, 7, 9, 107, 118, 213-214, 215
McConnell, Woodrow, 215-216
McCrary, Tex, 303
McDaniel, Hattie, 34, 48, 94, 95, 96-97, 114, 159, 164, 311, 319, 324
McFerrin, Robert, 408, 409
McGuire, Dorothy, 72
McHugh, Jimmy, 460

McKinney, Nina Mae, 27, 31, 59, 97, 135, 158, 298, 401
McQueen, Butterfly, 33, 72, 94
McRae, Carmen, 194
Meet the People, 77-78, 79-80, 82, 134, 151, 153, 216
Melcher, Martin, 372, 465, 500
Mercer, Johnny, 125
Merimée, Prosper, 263, 381
Merman, Ethel, 41
Metro-Goldwyn-Mayer (MGM), 20, 26, 32, 45, 46, 82, 96, 97, 102, 121, 122, 128, 135, 136, 166, 179, 216-217, 218-219, 222-225, 230, 235, 313, 439, 457, 484, 537
MGM -- *see* Metro-Goldwyn-Mayer
MGM-Television, 477-478
Michaux, Oscar, 13, 135
Midnight Shadow, 67
Midsummer Night's Dream, A (Shakespeare), 72
Mighty Joe Young, 159
"Mike Douglas Show" (television program), 512-514
Milland, Ray, 74
Millender, Lucky, 58
Miller, Arthur, 439
Miller, Glenn, 86-87
Miller, Glenn, Orchestra, 86-87
Miller and Lee, 120
Million Dollar Productions, 82-85
Mills, Billy, 449
Mills, Earl, 195, 200, 204, 205, 206, 211, 219, 230, 233, 237, 238, 240, 250, 257, 259, 270, 271-272, 276, 278, 279, 286-287, 316, 318, 319, 324, 328, 336-337, 338, 341, 342, 344-346, 355, 361, 364-366, 368, 379-380, 383, 427, 432-434, 438, 449, 452-453, 455, 459, 493-494, 520, 529-530, 535-536, 542, 544-546, 547, 551, 552, 554
Mills, Etta Jones -- *see* Jones, Etta
Mills, Florence, 26, 67
Mills Brothers, 69, 93, 171
Mingus, Charlie, 167
Minnelli, Vincente, 128
miscegenation -- *see* interracial relationships
Mitchell, Helen, 37
Mitchell, Nettle, 37
Mitchum, Robert, 263, 288
mixed-race issue, 122-123
Mocambo (Los Angeles), 165, 170, 192-194, 197, 198, 216, 236, 253-254, 256, 260, 326, 327, 432, 498, 522
Modern Screen magazine, 185, 312
Moment of Danger -- *see Malaga*
Monash, Paul, 477, 481
Monroe, Marilyn, xvi, xxvi, 122, 153, 167, 178-179, 180, 242, 255, 263, 288, 299, 330, 333, 339, 353-354, 373, 401, 413, 466, 487-488, 512, 520, 530
Monsey, Derek, 446
Montgomery, Jack, 103, 104

Moon Is Blue, The (film), 262, 263, 265, 266, 288
Moon Is Blue, The (play), 262
Moon on Rainbow Shawl, A (film project), 431, 432
Moore, George, 166
Moore, Jimmy, 166, 515-516, 532
Moore, Juanita, 93, 152-153, 463
Moore, Phil, xxii, 31, 43, 45, 46, 53, 54-55, 76, 77, 103, 170-172, 179, 183, 202-203, 206-208, 209, 210-211, 255, 256, 388, 428, 532, 536, 551, 554
relationship with DD, 147, 165-169, 175, 177-181, 186, 189-192, 194, 197-201, 204-205, 216, 232, 243, 289-290, 297, 327, 344, 460-461, 491, 516
Moore, Tim ('Kingfish'), 75
Morehouse College, 83
Moreno, Rita, 338, 488, 508
Moreland, Mantan, 33, 39, 42, 83, 85, 311
Morrison, Charlie, 165, 167, 192-194, 253, 327
Morrison, Ernest Frederic (Sunshine Sammy), 12-13, 33, 85
Morrow, Byron, 134, 161-162, 191, 370, 390, 426, 429, 461, 493, 550
Morrow, Dorothy Nicholas, 80, 109, 145, 162, 178, 191, 316, 370, 426, 427, 429-430, 461, 472, 551
see also Nicholas, Dorothy
Moscow Art Theatre, 395
Moscowitz, Joseph, 265-266, 310
Moseley, Lilian, 32
Moses, Ethel, 135
Moses, Lucia Lynn, 135
Motion Picture Association, 267
Motion Picture magazine, 185, 312
Motion picture studios, 263
see also individual studios
Motion pictures, African Americans in, 12, 24-28, 30, 32-34, 39, 47-48, 265, 278, 292-293, 295, 304, 311-313, 317, 319-320, 324, 357-358, 367-368, 423
see also Black Hollywood; "Negro Problem" movies; race movies; racial stereotypes in entertainment
Movietone News, 302
Mrs. Miniver, 242
Munson, Ona, 85, 98
Murder Men, The, 477, 480
see also "Blues for a Junkman" (episode of "Cain's Hundred")
Murrow, Edward R., 450
Muse, Clarence, 27, 33, 35-36, 52, 412
Music Corporation of America (MCA), 195, 203, 205, 210, 211, 219, 223, 238-239, 240, 257, 270, 306, 308, 326, 403, 531
Music Hall (Cleveland), 213
Music Theatre (Highland Park, Illinois), 488
My Favorite Blond, 166
"My Friend Irma" (television series), 189
My Wicked, Wicked Ways (Flynn and

Conrad), 529
My Wild Irish Rose, 118

N

Napier, Alan, 183
Nash, N. Richard, 406, 408
Nash Studio (Los Angeles), 38
Nashville, Tennessee, 19-23, 29
"Nat 'King' Cole Show," 483-484
National Association for Mentally Retarded Children, 513
National Association for the Advancement of Colored People (NAACP), 94-95, 96, 116, 156,
221, 246, 268, 290, 376, 379, 397, 512
Los Angeles branch, 475
St. Louis chapter, 246-247
West Coast branch, 411
Women's Auxiliary, 512
National Baptist Convention (Nashville), 20-21, 30
National Negro Congress, 219, 221
National Negro Network, 303
National Urban League, 27, 156, 303, 313, 368, 376, 378-379, 404-405
NBC television network, 481, 483
Neagle, Anna, 74
Negri, Pola, 12
Negro Actors Guild, 135
Negro Art Guild, 158
"Negro Problem" movies, 163, 188, 265
see also race movies
Nevada Biltmore (Las Vegas), 171
New Faces of 1952, 255
New York Amsterdam News, 95, 185, 305
New York Daily Mirror, 309-310, 327
New York Daily News, 87, 327
Sunday News Coloroto, 316, 452
New York Herald Tribune, 303, 316, 451
New York Journal American, 326-327
New York Post, 84-85, 209, 303, 308
New York Sun, 87
New York Times, The, 73, 234, 306, 308, 330-331, 451
Newman, Paul, 288, 463, 508
Newman, Samuel, 184
Newsweek, 304
Nicholas, Dorothy, 58, 151, 161, 162
see also Morrow, Dorothy Nicholas
Nicholas, Fayard (Big Mo) (DD's brother-in-law), xxii, 56, 58-60, 61, 62, 73-74, 79, 86, 87, 90, 91, 95, 99, 100, 106-107, 110-111, 119, 124-125, 128, 130, 131-132, 133, 136-137, 139-140, 148, 172, 200, 256-257, 399-400, 533, 538-542
marriage to Geri Pate, 104, 105, 127, 141-142, 306, 322
marriage to Vicky Barron, 532
see also Nicholas Brothers
Nicholas, Geri -- *see* Branton, Geraldine Pate Nicholas (Geri)

Nicholas, Harold (Little Mo) (DD's first husband), xxii, 57, 58-62, 79, 86, 87, 95, 100, 119, 125, 134, 136, 138-139, 143, 151, 256-257, 283, 387, 399-400, 428, 505, 533, 538-539, 541-542
as father, 110-112, 130, 176, 292
divorce from DD, 147-148, 162, 176-177, 181, 200, 292
marriage to DD, xx, xxv, 104-106, 110, 123-124, 127-128, 130, 131-132, 160, 172, 221, 243, 259, 309, 365, 530, 540, 546
marriage to Elyanne Patronne, 532
relationship with DD, 61-62, 66-67, 73-74, 76, 80-82, 85, 99, 101-102, 376, 546
see also Nicholas Brothers
Nicholas, Harolyn Suzanne (Lynn) (DD's daughter), xx, xxv, 111-112, 113, 126, 168, 170,
173, 176, 177, 181, 189, 517, 546, 552-554
developmental disability, 120, 127, 128-132, 133, 138, 140, 145-146, 147-148, 160, 165, 227, 241, 309-310, 360, 377, 402, 471-472, 486, 498, 504-506, 509, 513-514, 528, 532
institutionalization, 505-506
Nicholas, Meli, 532
Nicholas, Paul, 178
Nicholas, Tony, 114, 120, 126-127, 128, 178
Nicholas, Ulysses, 58, 59
Nicholas, Viola, 58, 59, 80, 95, 100-101, 104, 177, 505
Nicholas Brothers, xxv, 41, 42, 48, 56-61, 66-67, 73, 77, 86-87, 99-100, 101, 110, 115, 119, 124-125, 127, 128, 136, 138, 140, 144, 160, 172, 256-257, 399-400, 539, 546
see also Nicholas, Fayard; Nicholas, Harold
Nichols, Nichelle, 312, 412, 413, 415-416, 417, 418, 421, 503-504, 537-538
Nicholson, Meredith, 406
Nicodemus -- *see* Stewart, Nick 'Nicodemus'
Nina, 345, 356
Niven, David, 245, 300
No Strings, 463
No Way Out, 188, 334, 510
Noble, York, 541, 545
Noel, Hattie, 39, 74
Norfolk Journal and Guide, 185
Norman, Loulie Jean, 423
Norman, Maidie, 182, 225, 311
Norton, Sam, 372, 464-465, 500
Novak, Kim, 300, 334, 373, 457
Novarro, Ramon, 12
Nuyen, France, 483
Nyberg, Mary Ann, 279, 436

O

O'Brien, Virginia, 79
O'Casey, Sean, 400
O'Hara, Maureen, 254, 373, 388
O'Herlihy, Dan, 319

O'Neal, Frederick, 183
Oakwood College, 255
Oberon, Merle, 397
Office of War Information Motion Picture Bureau, 95
Olivier, Laurence, 397
On the Waterfront, 319
On With the Show, 26
Onassis, Aristotle Socrates, 382
One Mile From Heaven, 135
Oppenheimer, J. Robert, 247-248
Opportunity magazine, 27
Orchestra Wives, 59
Orenstein, Oskir, 340
Orpheum Theatre (Los Angeles), 85, 99
Osbourne, David, 431
Oscars -- see Academy Awards; Academy of Motion Picture Arts and Sciences
Our Gang (film series), 13, 40
Our World magazine, 185, 202, 210, 308, 331
Outward Bound, 261
Owens, Patricia, 357, 362

P

Pace, Judy, 159
Paddock Supper Club (Albuquerque), 543
Paich, Marty, 344-346
Palace Theatre (New York), 99
Palacio Theatre (Rio de Janeiro), 340
Palca, Alfred, 185-186
Palladium Theatre (London), 67, 140
Palm Beach Story, The, 166
Palmer House (Chicago) -- see Empire Room, Palmer House (Chicago)
Pantages Theatre (Los Angeles), 323
Paper Doll, 93
Papich, Stephen, 475
Papirofsky, Joseph (Joe Papp), 152, 156
Paramount Pictures, 41, 92, 166
Paramount Theatre (Los Angeles), 99
Paramount Theatre (New York City), 75, 99
Paris Blues, 463
Paris Match, 329
Park Lane Hotel (Denver), 318
Parker, Charlie, 124
Parker, Suzy, 457
Parks, Gordon, 159
Parks, Rosa, 312
Parsons, Louella, 155, 181, 311, 312, 319, 329, 345, 401, 425, 431-432, 434-435, 448, 460
Pasternak, Joe, 88, 439
Patch of Blue, A, 334
Pate, Eloise, 117-118
Pate, Geraldine -- see Branton, Geraldine Pate Nicholas
Patronne, Elyanne, marries Harold Nicholas, 532
Patterson, Floyd, 373
Patterson and Jackson, 124

Payne, John, 86
Pearl, Ralph, 322
Pennies from Heaven, 268
People's Voice, The, 135
Perito, Judy, 467, 527
Perito, Nick, 109, 210-213, 214-215, 219, 228, 236, 237-238, 247, 256, 259, 274, 296, 318-319, 320, 322, 325-326, 335-336, 353-354, 371, 375, 460, 467, 525, 527, 530, 536
"Perry Como Show, The," 240, 274
Persian Room (New York City), 463
Peter Pan, 225
Peters, Anne, 54
Peters, Brock (Broc), 268, 275, 277, 280, 282, 284-285, 290, 406, 412, 413, 416-421, 449, 450, 456
Peters, Jean, 334
Peters, Mattie, 33, 54
Peters, Virginia, 54
Peters Sisters, 54, 68
Petry, Ann, 378
Peyser, John, 477, 479-483
Phil Moore Four, The, 166
Philadelphia, Pennsylvania, 26
Philadelphia Story, The, 439
The Philadelphia Tribune, xv, 185
Philip, Duke of Edinburgh, 345-346
Philipe, Gerard, 346
Photoplay magazine, 185, 312-313
Pie Pie Blackbird, 59
Pied Piper, The, 261
Pillow to Post, 121, 123
Pinky, 162-164, 317, 319, 386-387
Pirate, The, 128, 136
Pisano, Jeanne Moore, 43, 51, 52
Pittsburgh Courier, The, 45, 95, 185, 221, 303, 305, 320
Plantation Club (Los Angeles), 31, 115
Playboy magazine, 180
Poch, Jean, 475
Poitier, Sidney, 147, 158, 218, 269, 311, 333-334, 376, 398-401, 406, 412, 413-418, 420-421, 423, 442, 450, 451, 463, 478, 525, 550
Polk, Oscar, 39, 72, 73
Pollard, Mel, 459
Poor Old Bill, 242
Popkin, Harry, 82
Popkin, Leo, 82-83
Porgy (Heyward novel), 395
Porgy and Bess (film), 125-126, 147, 280, 313, 432-434, 447, 448, 450-452, 457, 474, 478, 517, 545
DD cast as Bess, 399-401
DD's performance, 409
filming of, 395-424
Porgy and Bess (Gershwin operetta), 305, 306, 309, 389, 395
Black attitudes toward, 396-397
Porter, Cole, 193, 359
Pot, Pan, and Skillet, 88
Powell, Adam Clayton, 135

Powell, Dick, 46
Power, Tyrone, 375, 458
Preminger, Ingo, 260, 261, 270, 509
Preminger, Josefa, 260, 261
Preminger, Marc, 260, 261
Preminger, Mary Gardner, 289, 297, 364
Preminger, Otto Ludwig, xviii-xix, xx, xxvi, 305, 306, 310, 389, 406, 428, 462, 471, 476, 520, 551
charges of racism against, 411-412
death of, 554
directing career of, 260-263, 287-289, 367, 457, 463
directs *Carmen Jones*, xxvi, 260-295
directs *Laura*, xxiii-xxiv, 261, 411
directs *Porgy and Bess*, 395, 411-424, 457
relationship with DD, xviii-xix, xx, 169, 274, 276, 280, 286-287, 288-290, 296-297, 302, 303, 317-319, 320-321, 323, 325-326, 327, 328-329, 331-332, 333, 338, 339-340, 341-343, 344, 347, 350, 355-356, 364, 367, 371, 375, 376-378, 400, 413, 433-434, 450, 453, 491, 500, 525, 529, 530, 531, 550
Previn, Andre, 407
Price, Leontyne, 408
Prince George Hotel (Toronto), 205
Princess Tam-Tam, 330
Pritzer, Don, 523
Prodigal, The, 437
Production Code Administration -- *see* Production Code office
Production Code office, 164, 183-184, 262, 266-268, 298, 357-358, 381, 405, 408
Progressive Citizens of America, 221
Progressive Worker, The, 220
Proser, Monte, 207-209
Purdom, Edmund, 437, 445, 447

Q

Queen Christina, 408, 423
Queen of Sheba (Broadway project), 430
Queens of Swing, The, 195
Quick magazine, 210
Quinn, Anthony, 153, 154-157, 373, 483
Quinn, Frank, 327

R

race movies, 13, 82-85, 135-136, 235, 265
see also Black Hollywood, "Negro Problem" movies
racial stereotypes in entertainment, 88, 92-93, 94-96, 98, 122-123, 153-154, 358-359, 367-368,
396, 483-484
racism, xviii, 12, 144, 153-154, 163, 238, 250-251, 375, 385-387
African American women as objects of, 375-376
Radio City Center Theatre (New York City), 72-73

Radisson Hotel (Minneapolis) -- *see* Flame Room, Radisson Hotel (Minneapolis)
Raft, George, 115
Rainier, Prince of Monaco, 382
Rainmaker, The, 406
Raisin in the Sun, A, 450
Rancho La Puerta (Mexico), 535
Randolph, Lillian, 225
Ray, Johnny, 303
Rayettes, 85
RCA Victor, 166, 298
Reagan, Ronald, 158, 217
Realization of a Negro's Ambition, The, 13
Rebecca of Sunnybrook Farm, 54
Red Ball Express, 334
Red Channels magazine, 217-218
Red Cross, 221
Reed, George, 33
Reed, Leonard, 120
Regal Theatre (Chicago), 73, 99
Reinhardt, Max, 260
Remains to Be Seen, 236
Remarque, Erich Maria, 380
Rennie, Michael, 357, 364, 375
Republic Picture Studios, 85, 105
Reynolds, Debbie, 537
Richards, Beah, 463
Richman, Helen, 490, 520
Richman, (Peter) Mark, 478, 480, 483, 490-491
Richmond, June, 77
Rififi, 343
Rio, Eddie, 459
Riot in Cell Block 11, 159
Ritter, Thelma, 323
River of No Return, The, 263, 265
Riverside (Reno), 470
Riviera Hotel (Las Vegas), 338, 341-342, 425
Rivoli Theatre (New York City), 302-303
RKO Pictures, 74, 166, 182, 277, 278
Roach, Hal, 13
Roach, Max, 269
Robbins, Harold, 378
Robe, The, 264
Robeson, Paul, 33, 59, 134, 135, 155, 218-219, 330
Robinson, Bill 'Bojangles,' 41-42, 55, 59, 67, 72, 77, 115, 125, 126, 135, 171, 298, 311
Robinson, Elaine (Sue), 115, 125
Robinson, Jackie, xv, xxvi, 153, 211, 301, 312, 344, 373
Robinson, Julie, 283
see also Belafonte, Julie Robinson
Robinson, Louie, 485
Robinson, Mamie, 237
Robinson, 'Sugar Chile,' 214
Robinson, Sugar Ray, 237, 344, 373, 504
Robson, Flora, 98
Robson, Mark, 163
Rodgers, Richard, 330, 463
Roger Williams University, 19

Rogers, Bobbi, 525
Rogers, Ginger, 86
Rogers, Herb, 487-489, 523-525
Rogers, J. A., 95
Rogers, Timmie, 254
Romanoff's (Beverly Hills), 457
Romeo and Juliet (Shakespeare), 510
Rooney, Mickey, 45, 88
Rose, Billy, 264, 269, 303, 304
Rose Maternity Hospital (Los Angeles), 112
Rosenfeld, John, 87
Rosenthal, Jerome, 372, 380, 464-465, 499-501
Rosenthal and Norton, 372, 464-465, 500-501
Ross, Diana, 463
Ross, Frank, 356
Ross, Herbert, 268, 269, 278, 281, 284, 286
Rossellini, Roberto, 377, 431
Rossen, Robert, 187, 357, 361, 364-365, 367, 381
Roth, Philip, 386
Roxy Theatre (New York City), 99
Roy, William, 171, 172-176, 388
Royal, Evelyn, 195
Royal, Marshall, 195
Rozell, Marina -- *see* Dandridge, Vivian
Run Silent, Run Deep, 159
Running Wild, 26
Russell, Florence, 277
Russell, Rosalind, 122
Ruthenberg, Catherine, 462, 472-473

S

Sabiston, Peter, 245
Sabrina, 319
Sahatis Stateline Casino (California-Nevada), 219
Saint, Eve Marie, 324
Saint Joan, 367, 413
St. Louis, Missouri, 26
Black community, 246-247
St. Louis Blues, 26, 400
St. Louis Woman, 125, 283, 399-400
St. Sophia Orthodox Cathedral (Los Angeles), 448-450
Salome (Wilde), 321, 339
Sanders, Barbara Ann, 225
Sanders, George, 359
Sanders of the River, 135
Sands Hotel Casino (Las Vegas), 256
Sans Souci (Havana), 344-345
Sans Souci Hotel (Miami), 269
Santa Maria Hotel (Grenada), 360
Saperstein, Abe, 185, 303
Saturday Review magazine, 234, 452
Savage, Archie, 269
Savoy Hotel (London), 343, 344-345, 370
Saxer, Walter, 407
Scar of Shame, 135
Scarlet Sister Mary, 310

Scent of Danger -- *see Malaga*
Schary, Dore, 216, 224-226, 313
Schenck, Joseph, 260-261
Schenck, Nicholas, 221-222
Schnee, Charles, 224-225
Schulman, Max, 300
Schwab's Drugstore (Hollywood), 152, 154
Scott, Hazel, 96, 97, 217
Scott, Mabel, 120
Screen Actors Guild (SAG), 156-158, 217, 226
Seberg, Jean, 288, 367, 413
"See How They Run" (Vroman), 216
See How They Run -- *see Bright Road*
segregation, 22, 47, 115, 171-174, 206, 211-213, 238-239, 241, 250-251, 471
see also Jim Crow laws
Segure, Roger, 54-55, 76
Seldes, Gilbert, 72
Selznick, David O., 105, 296, 300, 301, 324
Sepia magazine, 185, 298-299, 372-373
see also Hue magazine
Sepia Tones, 195
Seroity, Jean, 133
Servais, Jean, 381
Seven Brides for Seven Brothers, 319
sex symbols, Black women as, 255-256, 311-313, 510-511
"Shadow and the Act, The" (Ellison), 163
Shamroy, Leon, 406-407, 417, 420, 451
Sharaff, Irene, 407, 413, 423, 436
Shaw, Irwin, 300
Shearer, Norma, 32, 45
Sheffield, Maceo, 95
Shiloh Baptist Church (Cleveland), 13-14
Ship of Fools, 508, 516-518
Short, Bobby, 4, 56, 114, 116, 126, 164-165, 167, 169, 189-192, 197-198, 236, 460-461, 504, 515-516
Short Cut, 343, 345, 346
Show Boat (motion picture), 33, 97, 164, 179, 317, 484
Show Boat (musical), 523-525
Shuffle Along, 26, 166,
Siegel, Benjamin 'Bugsy,' 171
Silver, Arthur, 45, 82, 162
Silvera, Frank, 317
Simms, Hilda, 299
Simoneon, Dick, 459
Simpson, Sloane, 326
Sinatra, Frank, 118, 167, 242, 356, 397, 439, 532
Since You Went Away, 105
Singing Nun, The, 537
Sloane, Paul, 26
Smith, Bessie, 26
Smith, Mildred Joanne, 188, 311, 510
Smith, Muriel, 269
Smith, Oliver, 407, 451
Smith, Wonderful, 88, 324
Smuts, Jan, 136-137
Snow Get in Your Eyes, 46

Snowden, Carolynne, 13, 33
Sokolsky, George, 218
Solomon and Sheba, 458
Some Like It Hot, 466
Song of Songs, 408
Song of the South, 319-320
"Songs for Sale" (television show), 210
Sothern, Ann, 32, 167
soul food, 105, 175, 215, 244, 318, 350-351, 524
Sounder, 463
soundies, 92-93
South Pacific, 269
Spiegel, Sam, 326
Spingarn medal (NAACP), 246
Spivey, Victoria, 26
Squaw Man, The, 397
Stalag 17, 261
Standard (Philadelphia theatre), 58
Stanislavski, Konstantin, 152
Stanton, Dr. Frank, 450
Stanwyck, Barbara, 408
Star Is Born, A, 319
Star Trek, 412
State Lake Theatre (Chicago), 76
Stead, Michael, 225
Steel Magnolias, 268
Steele, Nancy, 308-309
Stein, Jules, 326, 531
Stevens, George, 33
Stevens, Inger, 553
Steinbeck, John, 300
Stern, Der, 329
Stewart, Donald Ogden, 439, 442-443
Stewart, James, 288
Stewart, Nick 'Nicodemus,' 72, 73, 118, 268
Stone, Andrew, 144, 390, 403, 405, 406, 449, 459, 461-462
Stone, Virginia, 403, 406, 449
Stoopnocracy, 59
Storch, Larry, 206
Storm, Tempestt (Herb Jeffries's wife), 369
Stormy Weather, 96, 103, 110, 117, 122, 136, 144, 269, 278, 298, 306
Strand Theatre (New York City), 67
Strauss, John, 503
Strayhorn, Billy, 88
Street, The, 378
Strip (Las Vegas), 170, 172-173, 256
Strode, Woody, 89
Student Prince, The, 437
Sturges, Preston, 33-34
Sukarno (President of Indonesia), 352
Sul-Te-Wan, Madame (Nellie Conway), 32-33, 268-269, 311
Sullivan, Charlotte, 314, 505
Sullivan, Ed, 210, 307, 327, 464
see also "Ed Sullivan Show, The"; "Toast of the Town"
Sullivan, Maxine, 46, 72, 77
Sun Valley Serenade, 85-87, 100, 163, 303
Sundown, 87, 88-89, 97, 98, 442, 457

Sunset Boulevard, 518
Sunshine Sammy -- *see* Morrison, Ernest Frederic
Supremes, The, 167
Swann, Francis, 184
Swanson, Gloria, 518
Sweet 'n' Hot, 120
Swig, Benjamin, 233
Swing for Your Supper, 93
Swingin' the Dream, 72-73

T

Taft-Hartley bill, 221
Tahoe Village Club (Lake Tahoe), 181-182
Tales of Manhattan, 439
Tales of Manhattan, 41
Tall Target, 188
Tamango, 346, 356, 366, 378, 379-387, 389, 403, 431, 432, 453-457, 530
Tan, 185
Tap Roots, 118
Tarzan and the Jungle Goddess -- *see Tarzan's Peril*
Tarzan's Peril, 182-185, 188
Taurog, Norman, 300
Taylor, Elizabeth (Liz), xxvi, 122, 242, 288, 299, 304, 333, 334, 350, 382, 401, 457, 458
Taylor, Laurette, 261
Taylor, Libby, 39, 225
Temple, Shirley, 41, 42
Tenney, John, 154
Tenney Committee, 154
Terry, Daniel, 181-182, 388-389
Thalberg, Irving, 135
Tharpe, Sister Rosetta, 56, 77
Theatre Arts magazine, 209
They Got Me Covered, 261
This Gun For Hire, 166
Thomas, Bob, 226
Thomas, Michel, 381
Three Coins in the Fountain, 319
Three Little Girls in Blue, 118
Thunderbird Hotel (Las Vegas), 538
Tierney, Gene, 88-89
Timmie and Freddie, 56
Time magazine, 202, 208, 209, 211, 304, 327, 383, 384, 435, 451, 485
Tin Pan Alley, 39, 59
Tish, 118
"Toast of the Town" (television show), 210, 240, 307, 325
"Today Show" (television series), 450
Todd, Mike, 331, 382
Tonight at Hoagy's (radio show), 118
"Tonight Show" (television program), 498
Tormé, Mel, 466
Toussaint, Pierre (fictional character), 83
Tower Theatre (Kansas City, Mo.), 76
Town Casino (Buffalo, N.Y.), 205
Towne Casino (Cleveland), 237
Tracy, Spencer, 298, 508, 516

Travilla, 170
Treasure Island, 183
Treniers, The, 539
Triton Hotel (Rochester, N.Y.), 205
Trocadero (Los Angeles), 193
Trooper of Troop K, 13
Truitt, James, 269
Tucker, Sophie, 209
Turner, Big Joe, 88
Turner, Lana, 32, 115, 193, 242, 298
Turning Point, The, 268
Twentieth Century Fox, 39, 74, 85, 86, 94, 99, 110, 122, 136, 163, 181, 260, 261, 263, 264, 265, 277, 292-293, 301, 317, 321, 329, 330, 333-334, 336-338, 341, 343, 345, 365, 366, 387-388, 457, 488
see also Fox Pictures
Two-Gun Man from Harlem, 91
Tyson, Cicely, 463, 537

U

UFA (Universum Film Aktien Gesellschaft), 439
Uggams, Leslie, 167, 537
Uncle Tom's Cabin (film versions), 13
Uncle Tom's Cabin pantomime in *The King and I*, 333
Under Two Flags, 332
Under Two Flags (film project), 338, 339
Under Your Spell, 261
United Artists, 265, 458
United Press International, 503, 551-552

V

Valentino, Rudolph, 12
Van Heusen, Jimmy, 72
Variety, 45, 63, 67, 76, 97, 184, 188, 204, 234, 240, 254, 300, 327, 387, 445, 451, 454, 464, 466, 470, 474, 476
Variety School for Handicapped Children, 241
Vaughan, Sarah, 194, 344, 504
Venetian Room, Fairmont Hotel (San Francisco), 233, 296, 452-453
Verve Records, 403, 404, 473-474
Vidor, King, 26, 135, 217, 300, 397, 458
Viva Zapata, 334
Von Sternberg, Josef, 33
Voorhees, Don, 72
Vroman, Mary Elizabeth, 216, 225-226

W

Waldorf-Astoria Hotel (New York City) -- *see* Empire Room, Waldorf-Astoria Hotel
Wallace, Babe, 117
Wallace, Governor George, 453
Wallace, Michael (son of Vivian Dandridge), 117, 258, 335, 368

Wanger, Walter, 88, 94, 457
War of the Worlds, 183
Warner, Barbara, 326
Warner, Jack, 217, 382
Warner Brothers, 24, 121, 217, 382, 445
Warner Theatre (New York City), 450
Warren, Harry, 86
Warwick Hotel (New York City), 302
Washington, Dinah, 167, 194
Washington, Fredi, 26, 33, 59, 97, 135, 217, 401
Washington, Hazel, 122
Washington, Kenny, 89
Washington, Mildred, 27, 33
Washington Senators, 475
Waters, Ethel, 26, 55, 90, 102, 126, 164, 167, 171, 202, 311, 319, 401
Waugh, Alec, 343, 345
Waxman, Philip A., 462-463
Way Down South, 30, 35
Wayne, John, 85, 288, 499
Webster, Neil, 83
Weinberger, Andrew D., 372
Well, The, 182
Welles, Orson, 255, 366,
Wellman, William, 300
Wells, Bob, 325, 327
Werker, Alfred, 163
West, Mae, 33, 34, 135, 167, 373
West Side Story (Chicago stage production), 487-489, 523, 524-525
Whale, James, 33
Where the Sidewalk Ends, 262
Whipper, Leigh, 98, 411-412
Whirlpool, 262
White, Paul, 88, 93
White, Slappy, 75, 115, 125-126, 254, 311, 550
White, Walter, 94, 96, 116, 246-247, 267-268
White Cliffs of Dover, The, 242
White Zombie, 35
Whithead, Jack, 184
Whitman, Stuart, 405
Wichita, Kansas, 1-4, 29
Black community, 2
Wild One, The, 439
Wilde, Oscar, 321
Wilder, Billy, 261
Wiley College, 83
Wilkins, Dave, 69
Wilkins, Henrietta, 449
Will Mastin Trio, 175, 325
William Morris Agency, 124, 127, 136
Williams, Dick, 191, 304, 473
Williams, Esther, 331
Williams, Geneva (Neva or Auntie Ma-Ma), 41, 159
caretaker for Lynn, 133, 151, 177
chaperon, 54, 56-57, 61-63, 67, 73-74, 75, 172
drama coach, 17-19, 36, 37

dramatic talents of, 15, 46-47
education of, 15
marriage of, 15
relationship with DD, 16-19, 46-47, 49-51, 56-57, 69-71, 80-82, 100, 102, 104, 105, 107-108, 132-133, 147, 211, 257-258, 485
relationship with Ruby Dandridge, 15-16, 24, 27-28, 29-32, 49-51, 53, 73, 107-108, 257-258, 290-292, 494, 519
relationship with Vivian Dandridge, 16-19, 46-47, 51, 81, 102, 103, 211
Williams, Gladys, 545, 547
Williams, Paul, 246
Williams, Spencer, 13
Willis, Thomas, 488
Willkie, Wendell, 94
Wilson, Dooley, 96
Wilson, Earl, 209, 364
Wilson, Frank, 395
Wilson, Gerald, 74-75, 76, 77, 449
Wilson, Marie, 189
Wilson, Nancy, 521-522
Winchell, Walter, 303
Winston, Archer, 84-85, 303
Wolfson, Judge Burnett, 497
Woman's Face, A, 439
Women, The, 33
Women's Civic League (Cleveland), 213
The Wonder Children, xx, xxv, 19-22, 24-25, 36, 38, 62-63, 172, 485
The Wonder Kids -- *see* The Wonder Children
Wood, Natalie, 356
Woodward, Joanne, 463, 508

Works Progress Administration (WPA), 40-41
see also Federal Theatre Project
Wright, Frank Lloyd, 512
Wuthering Heights, 397
Wyler, William, 397
Wyman, Jane, 159, 319
Wynn, Keenan, 245
Wynn, Zelda, 169, 198-199

Y

Yarbo, Lillian, 94
Yes Indeed, 93
Yordan, Philip, 269
"You Don't Say" (television game show), 521
Young, F. A., 357
Young, Felix, 193
Young, Loretta, 236
"Your First Impression" (television game show), 495, 498

Z

Zanuck, Darryl F., 86, 94, 163, 260, 261-262, 265-267, 293, 317-318, 321, 329-330, 334, 336-338, 339, 343, 355, 356-358, 361-362, 367-368, 380-381, 382, 383, 386-387
Zapata, Emiliano, 334
Zephyrs, The, 75
Ziegfeld Follies of 1936, 59, 140
Zoot Suit, A, 93
Zou Zou, 330

CREDITS

1. Philippe Halsman

2. Archive Photos

3. Vera Jackson

4. - 7 The author

8 - 9. Harold Nicholas

10. Vera Jackson

11. Geri Branton

12. The author

13 - 14 Vera Jackson

15. Photofest

16. Harold Nicholas

17 - 18. Geri Branton

19. Dorothy Nicholas Morrow

20. Geri Branton

21. Vera Jackson

22. Photofest

23. - 28. The author

29. Dorothy Hughes McConnell

30 - 31. The author

32. Archive Photos

33. Philippe Halsman photo

45.-37. The author

38. Archive Photos

39. The Academy of Motion Picture Arts and Sciences

40. Archive Photos

41. Archive Photos

42. The author

43. Philippe Halsman

44. The author

45. Geri Branton

46 - 47. Photofest

48 - 51. The author

52. Library of Congress

53. The Academy of Motion Pictures, Arts and Sciences

54 - 55. The author

56. Photofest

57 - 58. The author

59. Library of Congress

60 - 61. The author

ABOUT THE AUTHOR

*D*onald Bogle, one of the foremost authorities on African Americans in films, is the author of three prize winning books. His book *Toms, Coons, Mulattoes, Mammies, and Bucks: An Interpretive History of Blacks in American Films* is considered a classic study of African American movie images. He adapted his book *Brown Sugar: Eighty Years of America's Black Female Superstars* into a four-part documentary series for PBS. Mr. Bogle wrote and executive-produced the series and headed the production's film research team. He is also the author of *Blacks in American Films and Television: An Illustrated Encyclopedia*. His articles have appeared in *Essence, Film Comment, Spin, Ebony, Freedomways*, and other publications. He lectures at universities and museums around the country, and teaches at the University of Pennsylvania and New York University's Tisch School of the Arts. He divides his time between New York and Los Angeles.